# CLYMER®

# *HONDA*

## *FOURTRAX FOREMAN 400 • 1995-2001*

*The world's finest publisher of mechanical how-to manuals*

# PRIMEDIA
Business Magazines & Media

*P.O. Box 12901, Overland Park, Kansas 66282-2901*

Copyright ©2002 PRIMEDIA Business Magazines & Media Inc.

FIRST EDITION
First Printing July, 1999

SECOND EDITION
First Printing September, 2002

Printed in U.S.A.

CLYMER and colophon are registered trademarks of PRIMEDIA Business Magazines & Media Inc.

ISBN: 0-89287-834-7

Library of Congress: 2002111127

*TECHNICAL PHOTOGRAPHY: Ron Wright, with assistance by Clawson Motorsports, Fresno, California.*

*TECHNICAL ILLUSTRATIONS: Steve Amos.*

*WIRING DIAGRAMS: Robert Caldwell.*

*TOOLS AND EQUIPMENT: K & L Supply Co. at www.klsupply.com.*

*COVER: Mark Clifford Photography, Los Angeles, California. TRX400 provided by Dick Allen's Yamaha-Honda-Sea-Doo, Newhall, California.*

# CONTENTS

# QUICK REFERENCE DATA

## ATV INFORMATION

MODEL:_____ YEAR:_____

VIN NUMBER:_____

ENGINE SERIAL NUMBER:_____

CARBURETOR SERIAL NUMBER OR I.D. MARK:_____

## TIRE INFLATION PRESSURE

|  | Front and rear tires psi (kPa) |
| --- | --- |
| Normal pressure | 3.6 (24.8) |
| Minimum pressure | 3.2 (22) |
| Maximum pressure | 4.0 (27.6) |

## RECOMMENDED LUBRICANTS AND FUEL

| | |
| --- | --- |
| Engine oil | |
| Grade | API SF or SG |
| Viscosity | SAE 10W-40 * |
| Differential oil | |
| Front and rear gearcase | Hypoid gear oil SAE 80 |
| Air filter | Foam air filter oil |
| Brake fluid | DOT 3 or DOT 4 |
| Steering and suspension lubricant | Multipurpose grease |
| Fuel | Octane rating of 86 or higher |

* See text for additional information.

## MAINTENANCE TORQUE SPECIFICATIONS

| | ft.-lb | N•m | in.-lb |
| --- | --- | --- | --- |
| Clutch adjusting screw locknut | 22 | — | 16 |
| Engine oil drain bolt | 25 | — | 18 |
| Engine oil filter cover mounting bolts | 10 | 88 | — |
| Rear differential gearcase | | | |
| Drain plug | 12 | 106 | — |
| Oil check plug | 12 | 106 | — |
| Oil fill cap | 12 | 106 | — |
| Front differential gearcase | | | |
| Oil fill cap | 12 | 106 | — |
| Drain plug | 12 | 106 | — |
| Spark plug | 18 | — | 13 |
| Tie rod locknut | 55 | — | 41 |
| Timing hole cap | 10 | 88 | — |
| Valve adjuster locknut | 17 | — | 12 |
| Wheel nuts (front and rear) | 65 | — | 48 |

**Table 10  TUNE-UP SPECIFICATIONS**

| | |
|---|---|
| Engine compression* | |
|    Decompressor affected | |
| 5.5-8.5 kg/cm2 (78-121 psi) | |
|    Decompressor not affected | |
| 12.4-14.5 kg/cm2 (178-206 psi) | |
|   Engine idle speed | |
| 1400   100 rpm | |
|   Ignition timing | |
|     F mark | |
| 10   BTDC at 1400 rpm | |
|     Full advance | |
| 30   BTDC at 4500 rpm | |
|   Spark plugs | |
|     Standard | |
| NGK DPR7EA-9 or Denso X22EPR-U9 | |
|     Colder plug (for riding below 5 C/41 F) | NGK DPR6EA-9 or Denso X20EPR-U9 |
| Hotter plug for extended high speed riding | NGK DPR8EA-9 or Denso X24EPR-U9 |
|   Spark plug gap | |
| 0.8-0.9 mm (0.03-0.04 in.) | |
|    Idle speed | 1300-1500 rpm |
|    Valve clearance | |
|     Intake and exhaust | 0.15 mm (0.006) |

* Refer to the text for information on the different engine compression specifications.

**Table 5 REPLACEMENT BULBS**

| | Voltage-wattage |
|---|---|
| Headlight | 12V-25W |
| Assist headlight | 12V-45W |
| Neutral indicator | 12V-1.7W |
| Oil light indicator | 12V-1.7W |
| Reverse indicator | 12V-1.7W |
| Taillight | 12V-5W |

# CHAPTER ONE

# GENERAL INFORMATION

This detailed, comprehensive manual covers the Honda TRX400FW ATVs from 1995-on. The expert text provides complete information on maintenance, tune-up, repair and overhaul. Hundreds of photos and drawings guide you through every step. This book includes all you will need to know to keep your Honda running right.

A shop manual is a reference. You want to find information fast. As in all Clymer books, this one is designed with you in mind. All chapters are thumb tabbed. Important items are extensively indexed at the rear of the book. All procedures, tables, photos and illustrations in this manual are designed for the reader who may be working on the vehicle or using this manual for the first time. The most frequently used specifications and capacities are summarized in the *Quick Reference Data* pages at this front of this book.

Keep this book handy in your tool box or tow vehicle. It will help you better understand how your vehicle runs, lower repair costs and generally improve your satisfaction with the vehicle.

**Table 1** lists model coverage with engine and frame serial numbers.

**Table 2** lists general vehicle dimensions.

**Table 3** lists vehicle weight.

**Table 4** lists decimal and metric equivalents.

**Table 5** lists general torque specifications,

**Table 6** lists conversion tables.

**Table 7** lists technical abbreviations.

**Table 8** lists metric tap drill sizes.

**Tables 1-8** are at the end of this chapter.

## MANUAL ORGANIZATION

All dimensions and capacities are expressed in metric and U.S. standard units of measure.

This chapter provides general information and discusses equipment and tools useful both for preventive maintenance and troubleshooting.

Chapter Two provides methods and suggestions for quick and accurate diagnosis and repair of problems. Troubleshooting procedures discuss typical symptoms and logical methods to isolate the cause of the problem.

Chapter Three explains all periodic lubrication and routine maintenance necessary to keep the Honda running well. Chapter Three also includes the recommended tune-up procedures, eliminating the need to constantly consult other chapters on the various assemblies.

Subsequent chapters describe specific systems such as the engine, clutch, transmission, fuel, exhaust, suspension and brakes. Each chapter provides disassembly, repair and assembly procedures in simple step-by-step form.

The text indicates procedures that are impractical for the home mechanic. Usually, it is faster and less expensive to take such repairs to a dealership or competent repair shop. Specifications concerning a particular system are included at the end of the respective chapter.

Some of the procedures in this manual specify special tools. In most cases, the tool is illustrated either in use or alone. Well-equipped mechanics may find they can substitute a similar tool or fabricate a suitable equivalent.

## NOTES, CAUTIONS AND WARNINGS

The terms NOTE, CAUTION and WARNING have specific meanings in this manual. A NOTE provides additional information to make a step or procedure easier or clearer. Disregarding a NOTE could cause inconvenience, but would not cause equipment damage or personal injury.

A CAUTION emphasizes areas where equipment damage could result. Disregarding a CAUTION could cause permanent mechanical damage; however, personal injury is unlikely.

A WARNING emphasizes areas where personal injury or even death could result from negligence. Mechanical damage may also occur. WARNINGS *are to be taken seriously*. In some cases, serious injury or death has resulted from disregarding similar warnings.

## SAFETY FIRST

Professional mechanics can work for years and never sustain a serious injury. If you observe a few rules of common sense and safety, you can enjoy many safe hours servicing your machine. If you ignore these rules, you may injure yourself or someone working nearby, or damage the equipment.

1. *Never* use gasoline or any type of low flash point solvent to clean parts.

> *NOTE*
> *Flash point is the lowest temperature at which the vapor from a combustible liquid will ignite in air. A low flash point solvent will ignite at a lower temperature than a high flash point solvent.*

2. *Never* smoke or use a torch in the vicinity of flammable liquids or materials.

3. If welding or brazing is required on the machine, remove the fuel tank, carburetor, and rear shock to a safe distance, at least 50 ft. (15 m) away.

4. Use the proper sized wrenches to avoid damage to fasteners and injury to yourself.

5. When loosening a tight or stuck nut, be guided by what would happen if the wrench slips.

6. When replacing a fastener, make sure to use one with the same measurements and strength as the old one. Incorrect or mismatched fasteners can result in damage to the vehicle and possible personal injury. Avoid fastener kits filled with inexpensive and poorly made nuts, bolts, washers and cotter pins. Refer to *Fasteners* in this chapter for additional information.

7. Keep all hand and power tools in good condition. Wipe grease and oil off of tools after using them. They are difficult to hold and can cause injury. Replace or repair worn or damaged tools.

8. Keep the work area clean and uncluttered.

9. Wear safety goggles during all operations involving drilling, grinding, the use of a cold chisel, using chemicals, cleaning parts, when using compressed air or *anytime* you feel unsure about the safety of your eyes.

10. Wear the correct type of clothes for the job. Tie long hair up or cover it with a cap so that it cannot accidentally fall out where it could be quickly grabbed by a piece of moving equipment or tool.

11. Keep an approved fire extinguisher nearby. Be sure it is rated for gasoline (Class B) and electrical (Class C) fires.

12. When drying bearings or other rotating parts with compressed air, never allow the air jet to rotate the bearing or part. The air jet is capable of rotating them at speeds far in excess of those for which they were designed. The bearing or rotating part is very likely to disintegrate and cause serious injury and damage. To prevent bearing damage when using compressed air, hold the inner bearing race by hand.

> *WARNING*
> *The improper use of compressed air is very dangerous. Using compressed air to dust off your clothes, equipment or workbench can cause flying particles to be blown into your eyes or skin. Never direct or blow compressed air into your skin or through any body opening (in-*

*cluding cuts) as this can cause severe injury or death. Compressed air should be used carefully; never allow children to use or play with compressed air.*

13. Never work on the upper part of the machine while someone is working underneath it.

14. Never carry sharp tools in your pockets.

15. There is always a right and wrong way to use tools. Learn to use them the right way.

16. Do not start and run the vehicle in a closed area. The exhaust gases contain carbon monoxide, a colorless, tasteless, poisonous gas. Carbon monoxide levels build quickly in a small closed area and can cause unconsciousness and death in a short time.

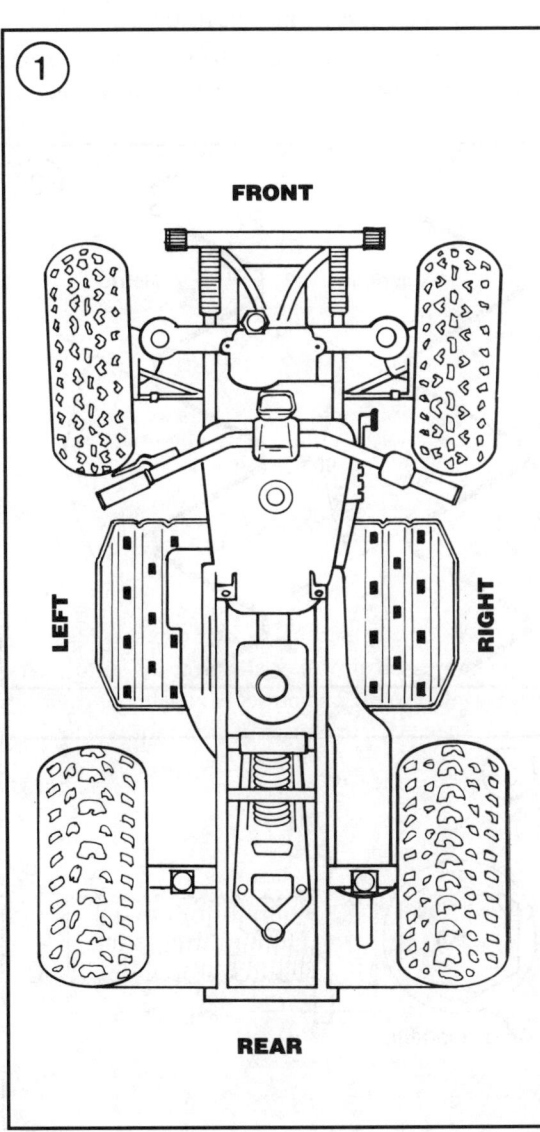

When it is necessary to start and run the vehicle during a service procedure, always do so outside, or in a service area equipped with a ventilating system.

## SERVICE HINTS

Most of the service procedures covered are straightforward and can be performed by anyone reasonably handy with tools. However, consider your capabilities carefully before attempting any operation involving major disassembly.

Take your time and do the job right. Do not forget that a newly rebuilt engine must be broken-in the same way as a new one. Refer to *Engine Break-In* in Chapter Five.

1. Front, as used in this manual, refers to the front of the vehicle; the front of any component is the end closest to the front of the vehicle. The left- and right-hand sides refer to the position of the parts as viewed by a rider sitting on the seat facing forward. For example, the throttle control is on the right-hand side. These rules are simple, yet confusion can cause a major inconvenience during service. See **Figure 1**.

2. Secure the vehicle in a safe manner and apply the parking brake when servicing the engine, clutch or suspension component.

3. Tag all similar internal parts for location and mark all mating parts for position. Record shim number, thickness and alignment when removed. Identify and store small parts in plastic sandwich bags. Seal and label them with masking tape.

4. Place parts from a specific area of the engine (cylinder head, cylinder, clutch, shift mechanism) into plastic boxes to keep them separated.

5. Label all electrical wiring and connectors before disconnecting them. Again, do not rely on memory alone.

6. Protect finished surfaces from physical damage or corrosion. Keep gasoline and brake fluid off painted surfaces.

7. Use penetrating oil on frozen or tight bolts, then strike the bolt head a few times with a hammer and punch (use a screwdriver on screws). Avoid the use of heat where possible, as it can warp, melt or affect the temper of parts. Heat also ruins finishes, especially paints and plastics.

8. Unless specified in the procedure, parts should not require unusual force during disassembly or assembly. If a part is difficult to remove or install, find out why before continuing.

9. To prevent small objects and abrasive dust from falling into the engine, cover all openings after exposing them.

10. Read each procedure completely while looking at the actual parts before starting a job. Make sure you thoroughly understand the procedural steps and then follow the procedure, step by step.

11. Recommendations are occasionally made to refer service or maintenance to a Honda dealer or a specialist in a particular field. In these cases, the work will be done more quickly and economically than if you performed the job yourself.

12. In procedural steps, the term replace means to discard a defective part and replace with a new or exchange unit. Overhaul means to remove, disassemble, inspect and replace part as are required to major systems or parts.

13. Some operations require the use of a hydraulic press. If you do not own or know how to operate a press, it is wiser to have these operations performed by a shop equipped for such work, rather than to try to do the job yourself with makeshift equipment that may damage your machine.

14. Repairs go much faster and easier if your machine is clean before you begin work. There are many special cleaners on the market, like Bel-Ray Degreaser, for washing the engine and related parts. Follow the manufacturer's directions on the container for the best results. Clean all oily or greasy parts with cleaning solvent as you remove them.

> *WARNING*
> *Never use gasoline as a cleaning agent. It presents an extreme fire hazard. Be sure to work in a well-ventilated area when using cleaning solvent. Keep a fire extinguisher, rated for gasoline fires, handy in any case.*

> *CAUTION*
> *If you use a car wash to clean your vehicle, do not direct the high pressure water hose at steering bearings, carburetor hoses, suspension components, wheel bearings or electrical components. High-pressure water will flush grease out of the bearings, damage the seals and enter electrical components.*

15. Much of the labor charge at a dealership is for the time involved during the removal, disassembly, assembly, and reinstallation of other parts to reach

the defective part. It is frequently possible to perform the preliminary operations yourself, then take the defective unit to the dealership for repair at considerable savings.

16. When special tools are required, arrange to get them before you start. It is frustrating and time-consuming to get partly into a job and then be unable to complete it.

17. Make diagrams (or take a Polaroid picture) wherever similar-appearing parts are found. For instance, crankcase bolts are often not the same length. You may think you can remember where everything came from, but mistakes are costly. There is also the possibility that you may be sidetracked and not return to work for days or weeks in which time the carefully laid out parts may be disturbed.

18. When assembling parts, be sure all shims and washers are installed exactly as they came out.

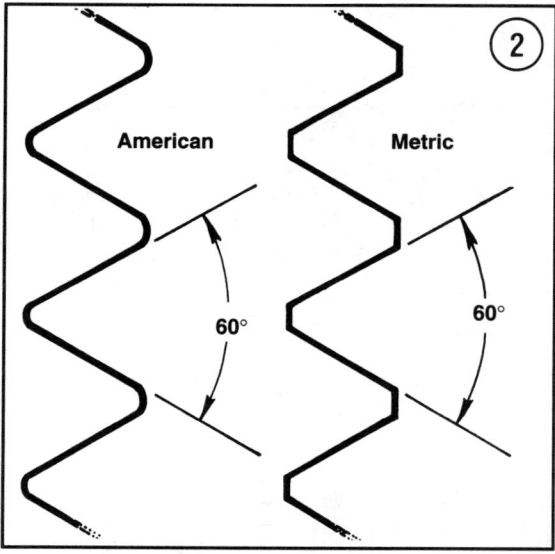

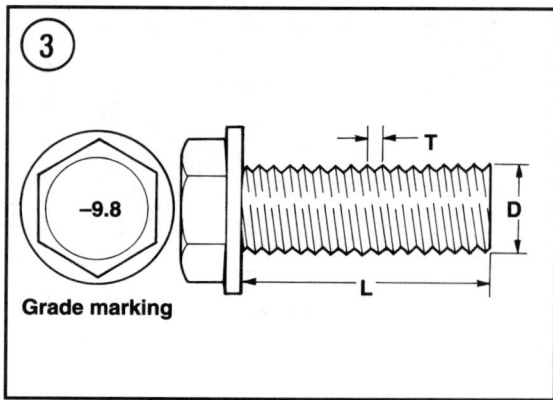

19. Whenever a rotating part butts against a stationary part, look for a shim or washer. Use new gaskets if there is any doubt about the condition of the old ones. A thin coat of oil on non-pressure type gaskets may help them seal more effectively.

20. Use cold heavy grease to hold small parts in place if they tend to fall out during assembly. However, keep grease and oil away from electrical and brake components.

## TORQUE SPECIFICATIONS

The materials used in the manufacture of your Honda may be subjected to uneven stresses if the fasteners used to hold the sub-assemblies are not installed and tightened correctly. Improper bolt tightening can cause cylinder head warpage, crankcase leaks, premature bearing and seal failure and suspension failure. An accurate torque wrench (described in this chapter) should be used together with the torque specifications listed at the end of most chapters.

Torque specifications throughout this manual are given in Newton-meters (N•m) and foot-pounds (ft.-lb.).

Existing torque wrenches calibrated in meter kilograms can be used by performing a simple conversion. All you have to do is move the decimal point one place to the right; for example, 3.5 mkg = 35 N•m. This conversion is accurate enough for mechanical work even though the exact mathematical conversion is 3.5 mkg = 34.3 N•m.

Refer to **Table 5** for standard torque specifications for various size screws, bolts and nuts not listed in the respective chapter tables. To use the table, first determine the size of the bolt or nut with a vernier caliper.

## FASTENERS

The materials and designs of the various fasteners used on your Honda are not arrived at by chance or accident. Fastener design determines the type of tool required to work the fastener. Fastener material is carefully selected to decrease the possibility of physical failure and ease assembly and maintenance.

Nuts, bolts and screws are manufactured in a wide range of thread patterns. To join two fasteners, the diameter and thread size of both parts must be the same.

The best way to tell if two fastener threads match is to turn the nut on the bolt (or the bolt into the threaded hole in a piece of equipment) with fingers only. Be sure both pieces are clean. When excessive force is required, check the thread condition on each fastener. If the thread condition is good but the fasteners jam, the threads sizes are different. When necessary, use a thread pitch gauge to determine thread pitch. Honda motorcycles and ATV's are manufactured with ISO (International Organization for Standardization) metric fasteners. The threads are cut differently than American fasteners (**Figure 2**).

Most threads are cut so that the fastener must be turned clockwise to tighten it. These are called right-hand threads. Some fasteners have left-hand threads; they must be turned counterclockwise to be tightened. Left-hand threads are used in locations where normal rotation of the equipment could loosen a right-hand threaded fastener.

### ISO Metric Screw Threads
### (Bolts, Nuts and Screws)

ISO (International Organization for Standardization) metric threads come in three standard thread sizes: coarse, fine and constant pitch. The ISO coarse pitch is used for almost all common fastener applications. The fine pitch thread is used on certain precision tools and instruments. The constant pitch thread is used mainly on machine parts and not for fasteners. The constant pitch thread, however, is used on all metric thread spark plugs.

Metric fasteners are classified by length (L, **Figure 3**), diameter (D) and distance between thread crests (T). A typical bolt might be identified by the numbers 8-1.25x130, which indicates that the bolt has a diameter of 8 mm, the distance between thread crests is 1.25 mm, and the bolt length is 130 mm.

> *CAUTION*
> *Do not install screws or bolts with a lower strength classification than installed originally by the manufacturer. Doing so may cause engine or equipment failure and possible injury.*

### Machine Screws

There are many different types of machine screws. **Figure 4** shows a number of screw heads requiring different types of turning tools. Heads are also designed to protrude above the metal (round) or slightly recessed in the metal (flat). See **Figure 5**.

## Nuts

Nuts are manufactured in a variety of types and sizes. Most are hexagonal (six-sided) and fit on bolts, screws and studs with the same diameter and pitch. **Figure 6** shows several types of nuts. The common nut is generally used with a lockwasher. Self-locking nuts have a nylon insert which prevents the nut from loosening; no lockwasher is required. Wing nuts are designed for fast removal by hand and are used for convenience in non-critical locations.

To indicate the size of a metric nut, manufacturers specify the diameter of the opening and the thread pitch. This is similar to bolt specifications, but without the length dimension. The measurement across two flats on the nut indicates the proper wrench size to be used.

## Self-Locking Fasteners

Several types of bolts, screws and nuts incorporate a system that develops an interference between the bolt, screw, nut or tapped hole threads. Interference is achieved in various ways: by distorting threads, coating threads with dry adhesive or nylon, distort-

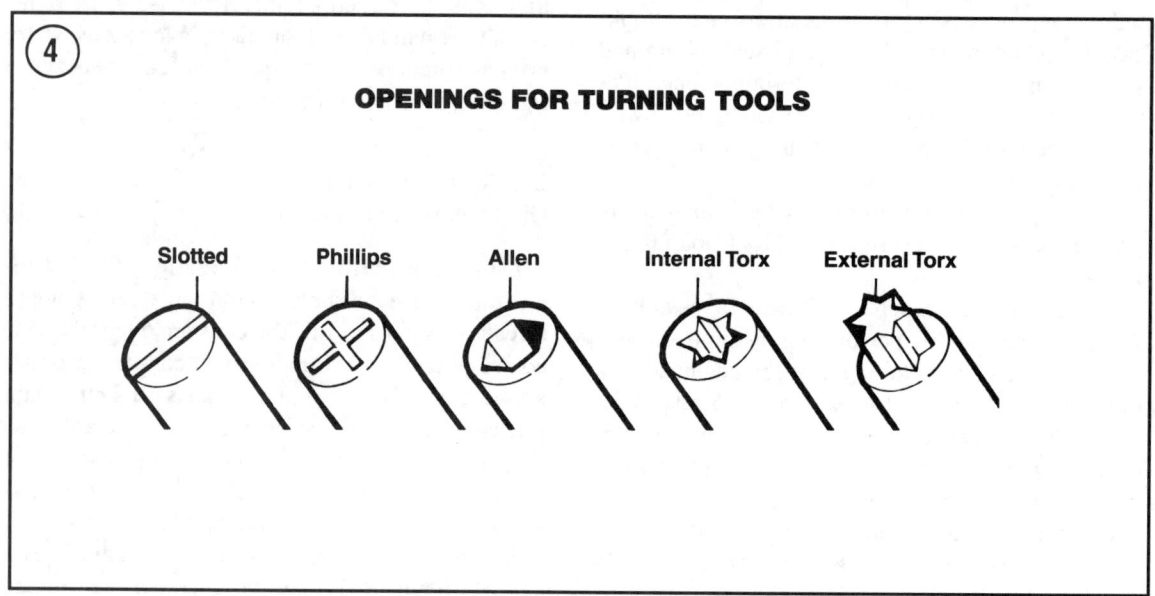

**(4)**

**OPENINGS FOR TURNING TOOLS**

Slotted     Phillips     Allen     Internal Torx     External Torx

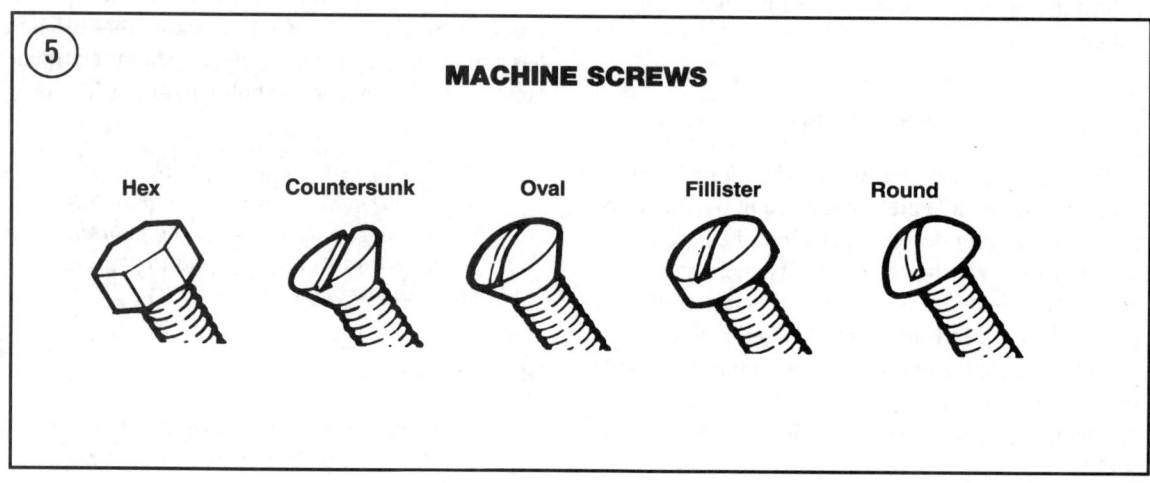

**(5)**

**MACHINE SCREWS**

Hex     Countersunk     Oval     Fillister     Round

ing the top of an all-metal nut, using a nylon insert in the center or at the top of a nut.

Self-locking fasteners offer greater holding strength and better vibration resistance. Some self-locking fasteners can be reused if in good condition. Others, like the nylon insert nut, form an initial locking condition when the nut is first installed. The nylon forms closely to the bolt thread pattern, thus reducing any tendency for the nut to loosen. For greatest safety, discard previously used self-locking fasteners and install new ones during reassembly.

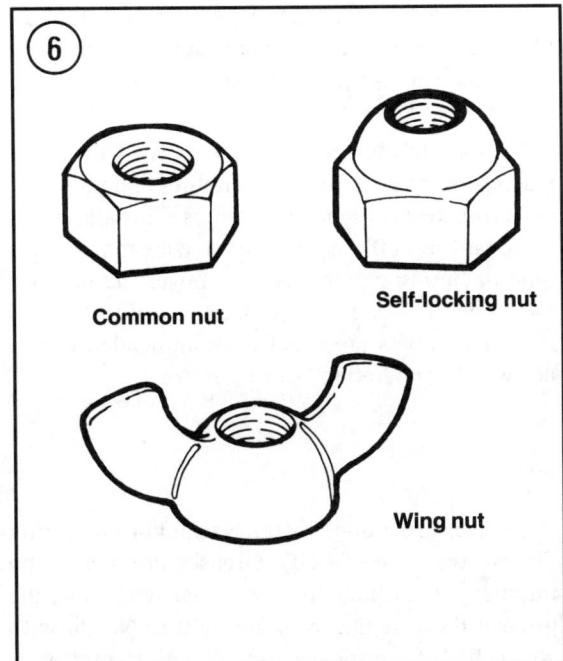

Common nut

Self-locking nut

Wing nut

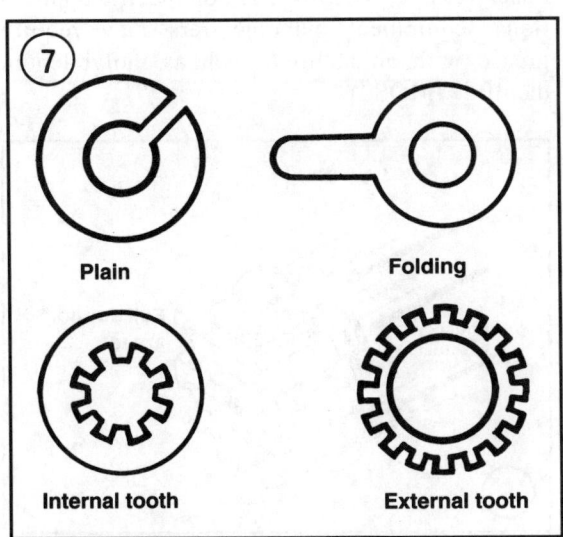

Plain

Folding

Internal tooth

External tooth

### Washers

There are two basic types of washers: flat washers and lockwashers. Flat washers are simple discs with a hole to fit a screw or bolt. Lockwashers are designed to prevent a fastener from working loose due to vibration, expansion and contraction. **Figure 7** shows several types of washers. Washers can be used in the following functions:

    a.  As spacers.

    b.  To prevent galling or damage of the equipment by the fastener.

    c.  To help distribute fastener load during torquing.

    d.  As seals.

Note that flat washers are often used between a lockwasher and a fastener to provide a smooth bearing surface. This allows the fastener to be turned easily with a tool.

> *NOTE*
> *As much care should be given to the selection and purchase of washers as to bolts, nuts and other fasteners. Beware of washers made of thin and weak materials. These will deform and crush the first time they are used in a high torque application.*

### Cotter Pins

Cotter pins (**Figure 8**) are used to secure special kinds of fasteners. The threaded stud, bolt or axle

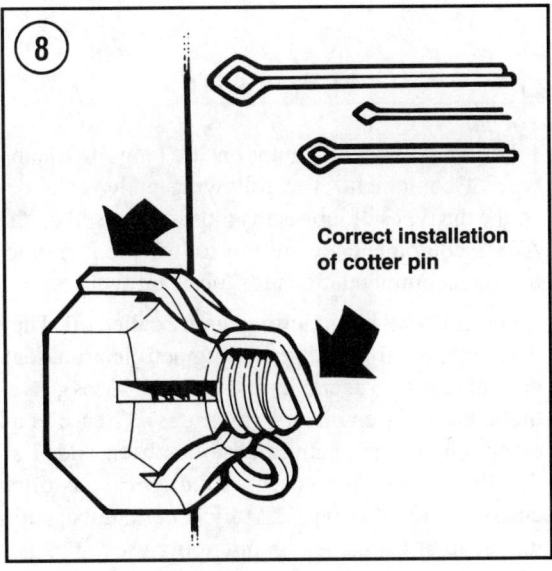

Correct installation of cotter pin

must have a hole in it; the nut or nut lock piece has castellations around which the cotter pin ends wrap. Do not reuse cotter pins.

## Circlips

Circlips can be internal or external design. They are used to retain items on shafts (external type) or within tubes (internal type). In some applications, circlips of varying thickness' are used to control the end play of assemblies. These are often called selective circlips. Circlips should be replaced during installation, as removal weakens and deforms them.

Two basic styles of circlips are available: machined and stamped circlips. Machined circlips (**Figure 9**) can be installed in either direction (shaft or housing) because both faces are machined, thus creating two sharp edges. Stamped circlips (**Figure 10**) are manufactured with one sharp edge and one rounded edge. When installing stamped circlips in a thrust situation (transmission shafts, fork tubes, etc.), the sharp edge must face away from the part producing the thrust. When installing circlips, observe the following:

a. Compress or expand circlips only enough to install them.

b. After the circlip is installed, make sure it is completely seated in its groove.

c. Transmission circlips become worn with use. For this reason, always use new circlips during transmission assembly.

## LUBRICANTS

Periodic lubrication helps ensure long life for any type of equipment. The following paragraphs describe the types of lubricants most often used on the ATV's equipment. Be sure to follow the manufacturer's recommendations for lubricant types.

Generally all liquid lubricants are called oil. They may be mineral-based (including petroleum bases), natural-based (vegetable and animal bases), synthetic-based or emulsions (mixtures). Grease is an oil to which a thickening base has been added so that the end product is semi-solid. Grease is often classified by the type of thickener added; lithium-soap based grease is commonly used.

## Engine Oil

Motorcycle and ATV oil is graded by the American Petroleum Institute (API) and the Society of Automotive Engineers (SAE) in several categories. Oil containers display these ratings on the top or label. API oil grade is indicated by letters; oils for gasoline engines are identified by an S. Honda models described in this manual require SG graded oil.

Viscosity is an indication of the oil's thickness. The SAE uses numbers to indicate viscosity; thin oils have low numbers while thick oils have high numbers. A W after the number indicates that the viscosity testing was performed at low temperature to simulate cold-weather operation. Engine oils fall into the 5 to 50 range.

Multigrade oils (for example 10W-40) are less viscous (thinner) at low temperatures and more viscous (thicker) at high temperatures. This allows the oil to perform efficiently across a wide range of engine operating conditions. The lower the number, the easier the engine will start in cold climates. Higher numbers are usually recommended during hot weather operation.

## Grease

Greases are graded by the National Lubricating Grease Institute (NLGI). Greases are graded by number according to the consistency of the grease; these range from No. 000 to No. 6, with No. 6 being the most solid. A typical multipurpose grease is NLGI No. 2. For specific applications, equipment manufacturers may require grease with an additive such as molybdenum disulfide (MOS2).

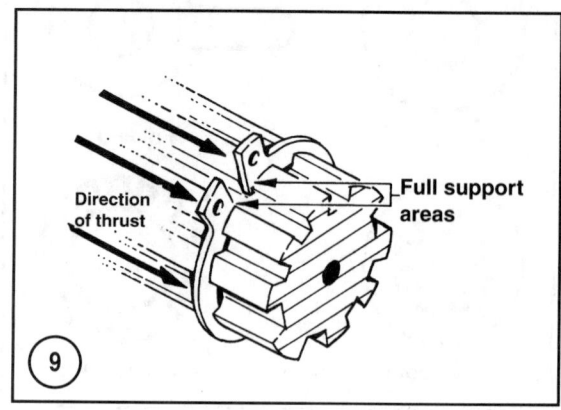

Direction of thrust

Full support areas

9

## SEALANT, CEMENTS AND CLEANERS

### Sealants and Adhesives

Many mating surfaces of an engine require a gasket or seal between them to prevent fluids and gases from passing through the joint. At times, the gasket or seal is installed as is. However, some times a sealer is applied to enhance the sealing capability of the gasket or seal. Note, however, that a sealing compound may be added to the gasket or seal during manufacturing and adding a sealant may cause premature failure of the gasket or seal.

*NOTE*
*If a new gasket leaks, check the two mating surfaces for warpage, old gasket residue or cracks. Also check to see if the new gasket was properly installed and if the assembly was tightened correctly.*

### RTV Sealants

One of the most common sealants is RTV (room temperature vulcanizing) sealant. This sealant hardens (cures) at room temperature over a period of several hours, which allows sufficient time to reposition parts if necessary without damaging the gaskets.

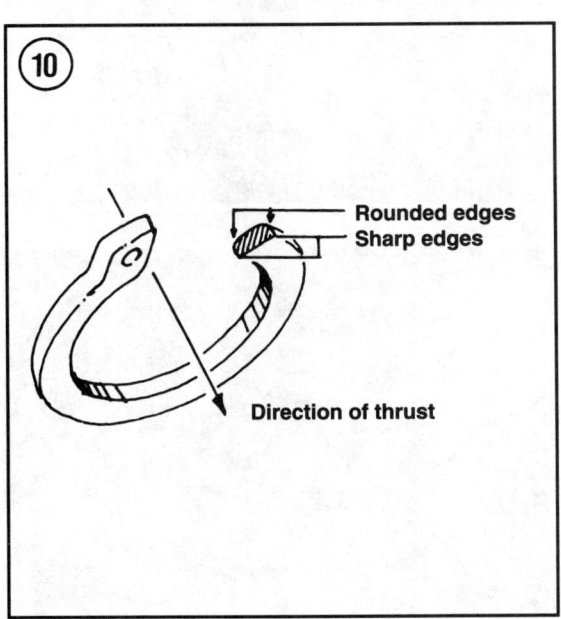

RTV sealant is available in different strengths. For example, while many RTV compounds offer excellent chemical resistance where oil and water is prevalent, but most RTV compounds offers poor chemical resistance to gasoline. Always follow the manufacturer's recommendations when purchasing and using a particular compound.

### Cements and Adhesives

A variety of cements and adhesives are available to suit the materials to be sealed, and to some extent, the personal preference of the mechanic. Automotive parts stores offer a wide selection of cements and adhesives. Some points to consider when selecting cements or adhesives: the type of material being sealed (metal, rubber or plastic), the type of fluid contacting the seal (gasoline, oil or water) and whether the seal is permanent or must be broken periodically, in which case a pliable sealant is desirable. Unless you are experienced in the selection of cements and adhesives, follow the recommendation if the text specifies a particular sealant.

### Cleaners and Solvents

Cleaners and solvents are helpful in removing oil, grease and other residue when maintaining and overhauling your vehicle. Before purchasing cleaners and solvents, consider how they will be used and disposed of, particularly if they are not water soluble. Local ordinances may require special procedures for the disposal of certain cleaners and solvents.

*WARNING*
*Some cleaners and solvents are harmful and may be flammable. Follow any safety precautions noted on the container or in the manufacturer's literature. Use petroleum-resistant gloves to protect hands and arms from the harmful effect of cleaners and solvents.*

A number of cleaners and solvents are available for servicing your Honda. Cleaners designed for ignition contact cleaning are excellent for removing light oil from a part without leaving a residue. Some degreasers will wash off with water. Ease the removal of stubborn gaskets with an aerosol gasket remover.

One of the more powerful cleaning solutions is carburetor cleaner. It is designed to dissolve the varnish that may build up in carburetor jets and orifices. A good carburetor cleaner is usually expensive and requires special disposal. Carefully read directions before purchase; do not immerse non-metallic parts in a carburetor cleaner.

### Gasket Remover

Stubborn gaskets can take a long time to remove. Consequently, there is the added problem of secondary damage occurring to the gasket mating surfaces from the incorrect use of gasket scraping tools. To remove stubborn gaskets, use a spray gasket remover. Spray gasket remover can be purchased through automotive parts houses. Follow the manufacturer's directions for use.

### THREADLOCKING COMPOUND

A threadlocking compound is a fluid applied to fastener threads. After tightening the fastener, the fluid dries to a solid filler between the mating threads, thereby locking the threads in position and preventing loosening due to vibration. They are also used on threaded parts to help seal against leaks.

Before applying a thread locking compound, clean the contacting threads with an aerosol electrical contact cleaner. Use only as much threadlocking compound as necessary, depending on the size of the fastener. Excess fluid can work its way into adjoining parts.

Threadlocking compound is available in different strengths, so make sure to follow the manufacturer's recommendations when using their particular compound. Two manufacturers of threadlocking compound are ThreeBond of America and the Loctite Corporation. The following threadlocking compounds are recommended for many threadlock requirements described in this manual:

    a. ThreeBond 1342: low strength, frequent repair for small screws and bolts.

    b. ThreeBond 1360: medium strength, high temperature.

    c. ThreeBond 1333B: medium strength, bearing and stud lock.

    d. ThreeBond 1303: high strength, frequent repair.

    e. Loctite 242: low strength, frequent repair.

    f. Loctite 271: high strength, frequent repair.

There are other quality threadlocking brands available.

### SERIAL NUMBERS

Honda makes frequent changes during a model year, some minor, some relatively major. When you order parts, always order by frame and engine numbers. The frame serial number is stamped on the front of the frame (**Figure 11**). The engine number is stamped on a raised pad on the rear crankcase (**Figure 12**). The carburetor serial number is stamped on the carburetor body above the float bowl.

Write the numbers down and carry them with you to the dealership when ordering parts. Compare the new parts with the old parts before buying them. If they are not alike, have the parts manager explain the difference to you. **Table 1** lists engine and frame serial numbers for the Honda models covered in this manual.

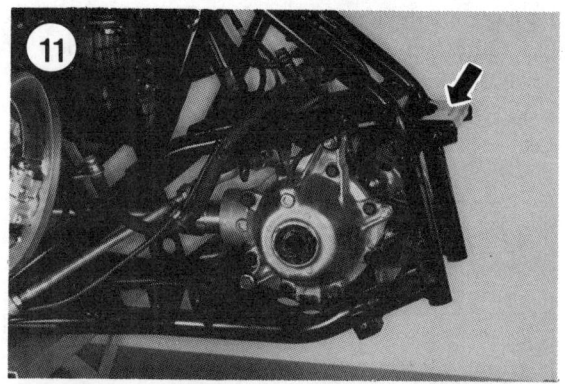

## WARNING LABELS

A number of warning are attached to your Honda. These labels contain information that is important to your safety when operating, transporting and storing your vehicle. Refer to your Owner's Manual for a description and location of each label. If a label is missing, order a replacement label from a Honda dealership.

## BASIC HAND TOOLS

Many of the procedures in this manual can be carried out with simple hand tools and test equipment familiar to the average home mechanic. Keep your tools clean and in a tool box. Keep them organized with related tools stored together. After using a tool, wipe off dirt and grease with a clean cloth and return the tool to its correct place.

Top quality tools are essential. They are also more economical in the long run. If you are now starting to build your tool collection, avoid the advertised specials featured at some parts houses, discount stores and chain drug stores. These are usually poor grade tools that are poorly made and sold cheaply.

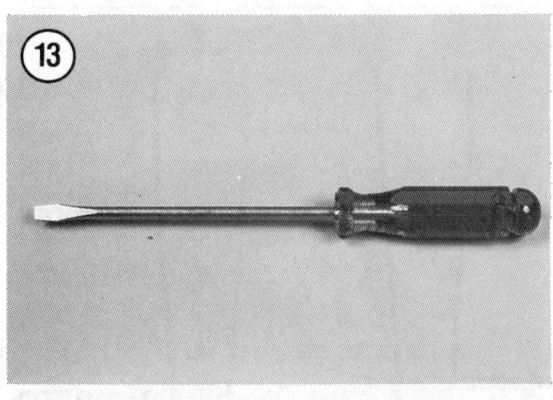

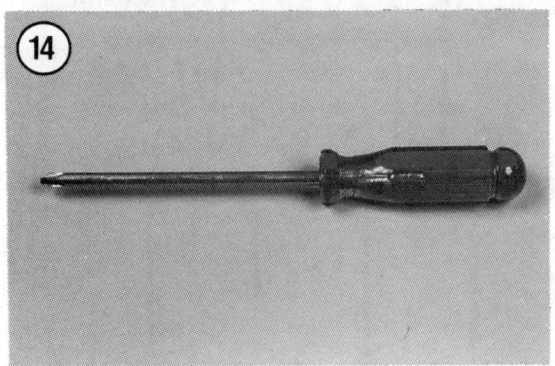

They are usually made of inferior material, and are thick, heavy and clumsy. Their rough finish makes them difficult to clean and they usually do not last very long. After using these tools, you will probably find out that the wrenches do not fit the heads of bolts and nuts correctly and damage the fastener.

Quality tools are made of alloy steel and are heat treated for greater strength. They are lighter and better balanced than cheap ones. Their surface is smooth, making them a pleasure to work with and easy to clean. The initial cost of good quality tools may be more but they are cheaper in the long run. Do not try to buy everything in all sizes in the beginning; buy a few at a time until you have the necessary tools.

### Screwdrivers

The screwdriver is a very basic tool, but if used improperly, it will do more damage than good. The slot on a screw has a definite dimension and shape. A screwdriver must be selected to conform with that shape. Use a small screwdriver for small screws and a large one for large screws; otherwise, the screw head will be damaged.

Two basic types of screwdriver are required: slotted (flat-blade) screwdrivers (**Figure 13**) and Phillips screwdrivers (**Figure 14**).

Screwdrivers are available in sets which often include an assortment of common and Phillips blades. If you buy them individually, buy at least the following:

    a. Slotted screwdriver—5/16 × 6 in. blade.
    b. Slotted screwdriver—3/8 × 12 in. blade.
    c. Phillips screwdriver—size 2 tip, 6 in. blade.
    d. Phillips screwdriver—size 3 tip, 6 and 10 in. blades.

Use screwdrivers only for driving screws. Never use a screwdriver for prying or chiseling metal. Do not try to remove a Phillips or Allen head screw with a common screwdriver (unless the screw has a combination head that will accept either type); you can damage the head so that even the proper tool will be unable to remove it. Keep screwdrivers in the proper condition and they will last longer and perform

better. Always keep the tip of a common screwdriver in good condition. **Figure 15** shows how to grind the tip to the proper shape if it becomes damaged. Note the symmetrical sides of the tip.

## Pliers

Pliers come in a wide range of types and sizes. Pliers are useful for cutting, bending and crimping. Do not use them to cut hardened objects or turn bolts or nuts. **Figure 16** shows several pliers useful in ATV and motorcycle repair, each designed for a specialized function. Combination (slip-joint) pliers are general purpose pliers used mainly for gripping and for bending. Needlenose pliers are used to hold or bend small objects. Adjustable joint pliers can be adjusted quickly to hold various sizes of objects; the jaws remain parallel to grip around objects such as pipe or tubing. There are many more types of pliers.

## Locking Pliers

Locking pliers (**Figure 17**) are used to hold objects very tightly like a vise. But avoid using them unless necessary since their sharp jaws will permanently scar any objects which are held. Locking pliers are available in many types for more specific tasks.

## Circlip Pliers

Circlip pliers (**Figure 18**) are made for removing and installing circlips. External pliers (spreading or expanding) are used to remove circlips that fit on the outside of a shaft or similar part. Internal circlips are located inside a tube, gear or housing and require pliers that squeeze the ends of the circlip together so that the circlip can be removed.

> *WARNING*
> *Circlips can fly off and cause eye injury. Always wear safety goggles when removing and installing circlips.*

## Box-end, Open-end and Combination Wrenches

Box-end and open-end wrenches (**Figure 19**) are available in sets or separately in a variety of sizes. The number stamped on open and box-end wrenches refers to the distance between two parallel flats of nut or bolt head. Combination wrenches have a box-end wrench on one end and an open-end wrench

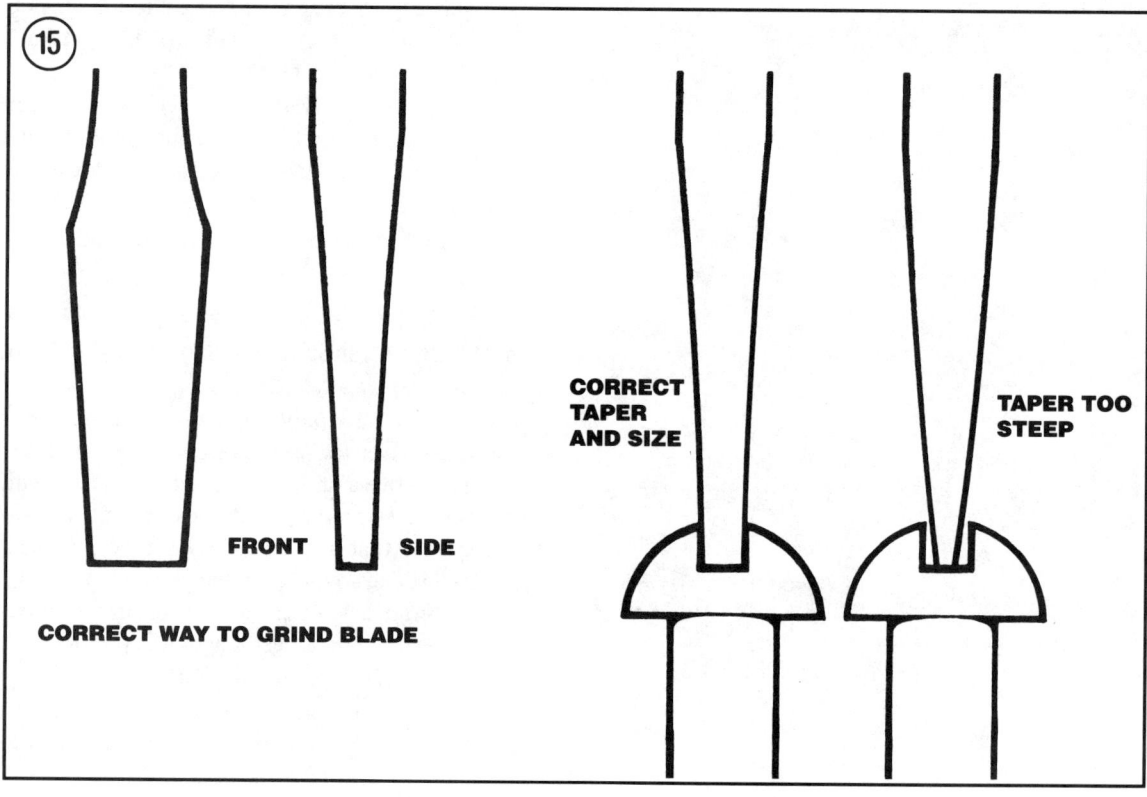

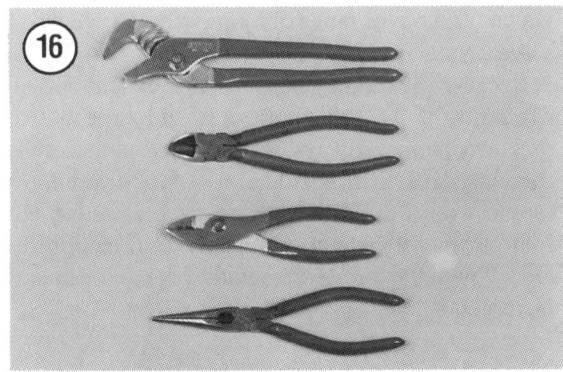

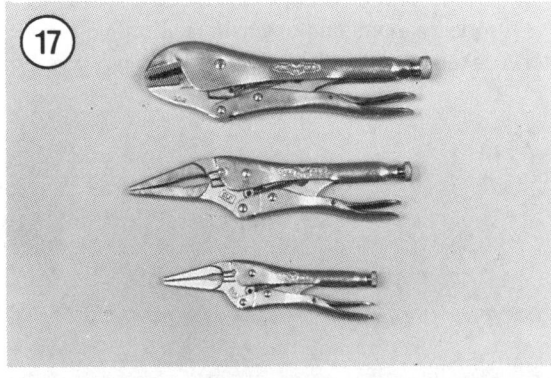

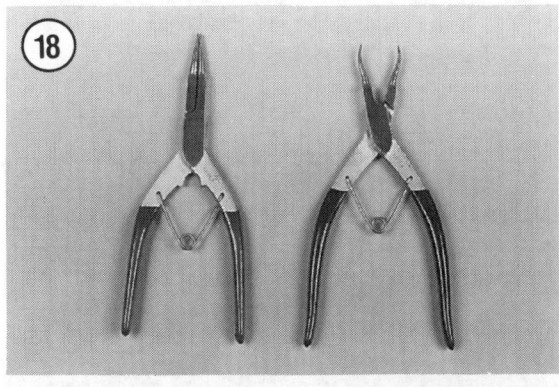

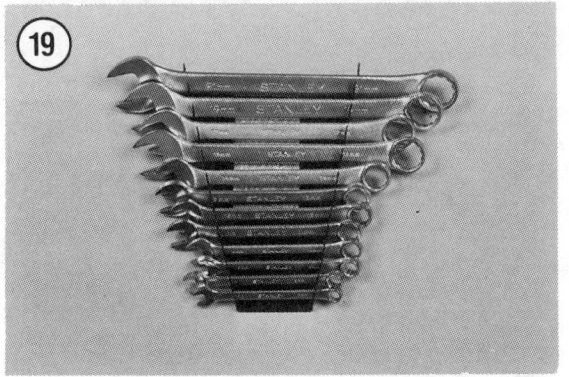

of the same size on the other end. The wrench size is stamped near the center of combination wrenches.

Open-end wrenches are speedy and work best in areas with limited overhead access. Their wide flat jaws make them unsuitable for situations where the bolt or nut is sunken in a well or close to the edge of a casting. These wrenches only grip on two flats of a fastener so if either the fastener head or the wrench jaws are worn, the wrench may slip off.

Box-end wrenches require clear overhead access to the fastener but can work well in situations where the fastener head is close to another part. They grip on all six edges of a fastener for a very secure grip. Box-end wrenches may be either 6-point or 12-point. The 6-point gives superior holding power and durability but requires a greater swinging radius. The 12-point works better in situations where there is only a small amount of room to turn the wrench.

No matter what style of wrench you choose, proper use is important to prevent personal injury. When using any wrench, get in the habit of pulling the wrench toward you. This reduces the risk of injuring your hand if the wrench should slip. If you have to push the wrench away from you to loosen or tighten a fastener, open and push with the palm of your hand. This technique gets your fingers and knuckles out of the way should the wrench slip. Before using a wrench, always consider what could happen if the wrench slips or if the fastener breaks.

**Adjustable Wrenches**

An adjustable wrench (sometimes called crescent wrench) can be adjusted to fit nearly any nut or bolt head which has clear access around its entire perimeter. Adjustable wrenches (**Figure 20**) are best used as a backup wrench to keep a large nut or bolt from

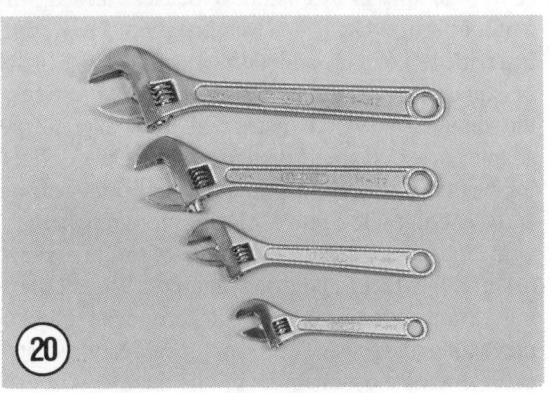

turning while the other end is being loosened or tightened with a proper wrench.

Adjustable wrenches have only two gripping surfaces where one is adjustable. This design makes adjustable wrenches directional in how they should be used. The solid jaw must be the one transmitting the force. Applying directional force against the adjustable surface may cause the wrench to slip and round-off the fastener head.

Adjustable wrenches come in all sizes. Purchasing one in the 6 to 8 in. range and one in the 12 to 14 in. range is recommended for general use.

### Socket Wrenches

This type is undoubtedly the fastest, safest and most convenient to use. Sockets which attach to a ratchet handle (**Figure 21**) are available with 6-point or 12-point openings and 1/4, 3/8, 1/2 and 3/4 in. drives. The drive size indicates the size of the square hole which mates with the ratchet handle.

### Impact Driver

This tool makes removal of fasteners easy and eliminates damage to bolts and screw slots. Impact drivers and interchangeable bits (**Figure 22**) are available at most large hardware, motorcycle or auto parts stores. Do not buy a cheap one as it will not work as well and require more force than a moderately priced one. Impact sockets can be used with a hand impact driver. Do not use regular hand sockets as they may shatter during impact use.

### Torque Wrench

A torque wrench is used with a socket, torque adapter or similar extension to measure how tightly a nut, bolt or other fastener is installed. They come in a wide price range and with either a 1/4, 3/8 or 1/2 in. square drive. The drive size indicates the size of the square drive which mates with the socket, torque adapter or extension. Popular types are the deflecting beam (A, **Figure 23**), the dial indicator and the audible click (B, **Figure 23**) torque wrenches. As with any series of tools, each type of torque wrench has its advantages and disadvantages. When choosing a torque wrench, consider its torque range, accuracy rating and price. The torque specifications listed at the end of most chapters in this manual will give

you an idea on the range of torque wrench needed to service your Honda.

Because the torque wrench is a precision tool, do not throw it in with other tools and expect it to remain accurate. Always store a torque wrench in its carrying case or in a padded tool box drawer. All torque wrenches require periodic recalibration. To find out more about this, read the information included with the torque wrench or write to the manufacturer.

### Torque Wrench Adapters

Torque adapters and extensions allow you to extend or reduce the reach of your torque wrench. For

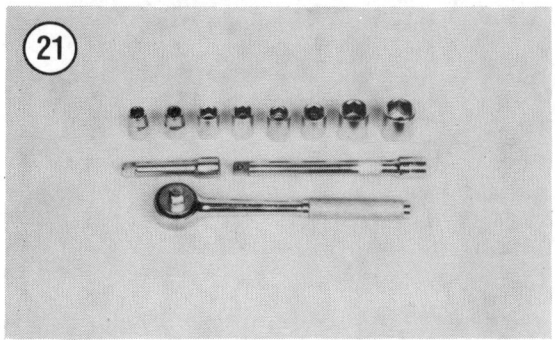

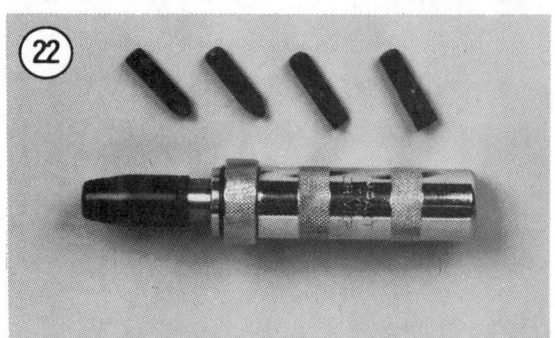

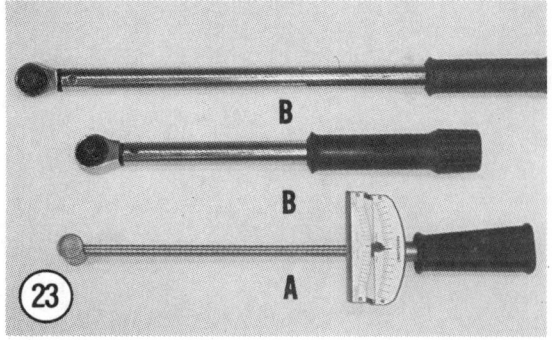

example, the torque adapter wrench shown in **Figure 24** can be used to extend the length of the torque wrench to tighten fasteners that cannot be reached with a torque wrench and socket. When a torque adapter is used to lengthen or shorten the torque wrench (**Figure 24**), the torque reading on the torque wrench will not be the same amount of torque that is applied to the fastener. Before using a torque adapter in this way, it is necessary to recalibrate the listed torque specification to compensate for the effect of the added torque adapter length. When a torque adapter is set at a right angle on the torque wrench, recalibration is not required (see information and figure below).

To recalculate a torque reading when using a torque adapter, it is first necessary to know the lever length of the torque wrench, the length of the adapter from the center of square drive to the center of the

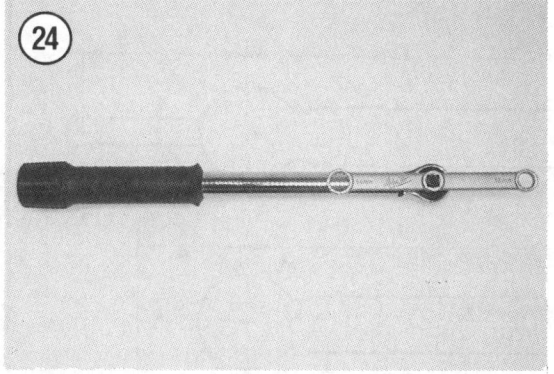

nut or bolt, and the actual amount of torque desired at the nut or bolt (**Figure 25**). The formula can be expressed as:

$$TW = \frac{TA \times L}{L + A}$$

TW = This is the torque setting or dial reading to set on the torque wrench when tightening the fastener.

TA = Actual torque setting. This is the torque specification listed in the service manual and will be the actual amount of torque applied to the fastener.

A = This is the length of the adapter from the centerline of the square drive (at the torque wrench) to the centerline of the nut or bolt. If the torque adapter extends straight from the end of the torque wrench (**Figure 26**), the center line of the torque adapter and torque wrench are the same.

However, when the center lines of the torque adapter and torque wrench do not line up, the distance must be measured as shown in **Figure 26**. Also note in **Figure 26** that when the torque adapter is set at a right-angle to the torque wrench, no calculation is needed (the lever length of the torque wrench did not change).

L = This the lever length of your torque wrench. This specification is usually listed in the instruction manual that came with your torque wrench, or you can determine its length by measuring the distance

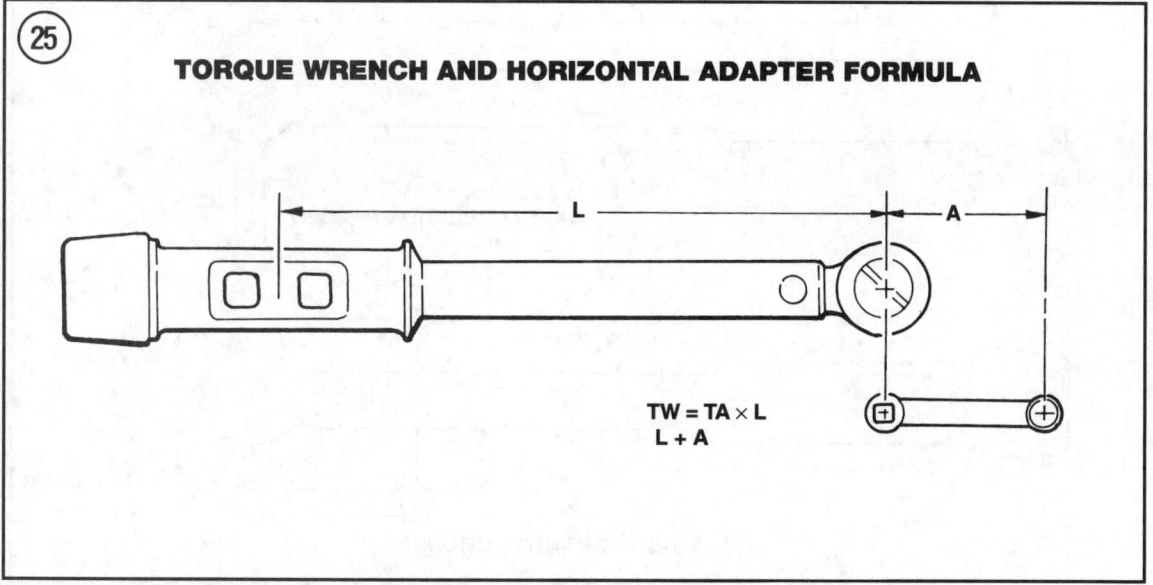

**TORQUE WRENCH AND HORIZONTAL ADAPTER FORMULA**

$$TW = \frac{TA \times L}{L + A}$$

from the center of the square drive on the torque wrench to the center of the torque wrench handle (**Figure 25**).

Example:

TA = 20 ft.-lb.

A = 3 in.

L = 14 in.

TW = 20 × 14 = 280 16.5 ft.-lb.

14 + 3 = 17

In this example, the recalculated torque value of 16.5 ft.-lb. is the amount of torque to set on the torque wrench. When using a dial or beam-type torque wrench, torque would be applied until the pointer aligns with the 16.5 ft.-lb. dial reading. When using a click type torque wrench, the micrometer dial would be pre-set to 16.5 ft.-lb. In all cases, even though the torque wrench dial or pre-set reading was 16.5 ft.-lb., the fastener would actually be tightened to 20 ft.-lb.

### Support Jacks

A support jack is necessary when supporting the ATV with its wheels off the ground. This is neces-

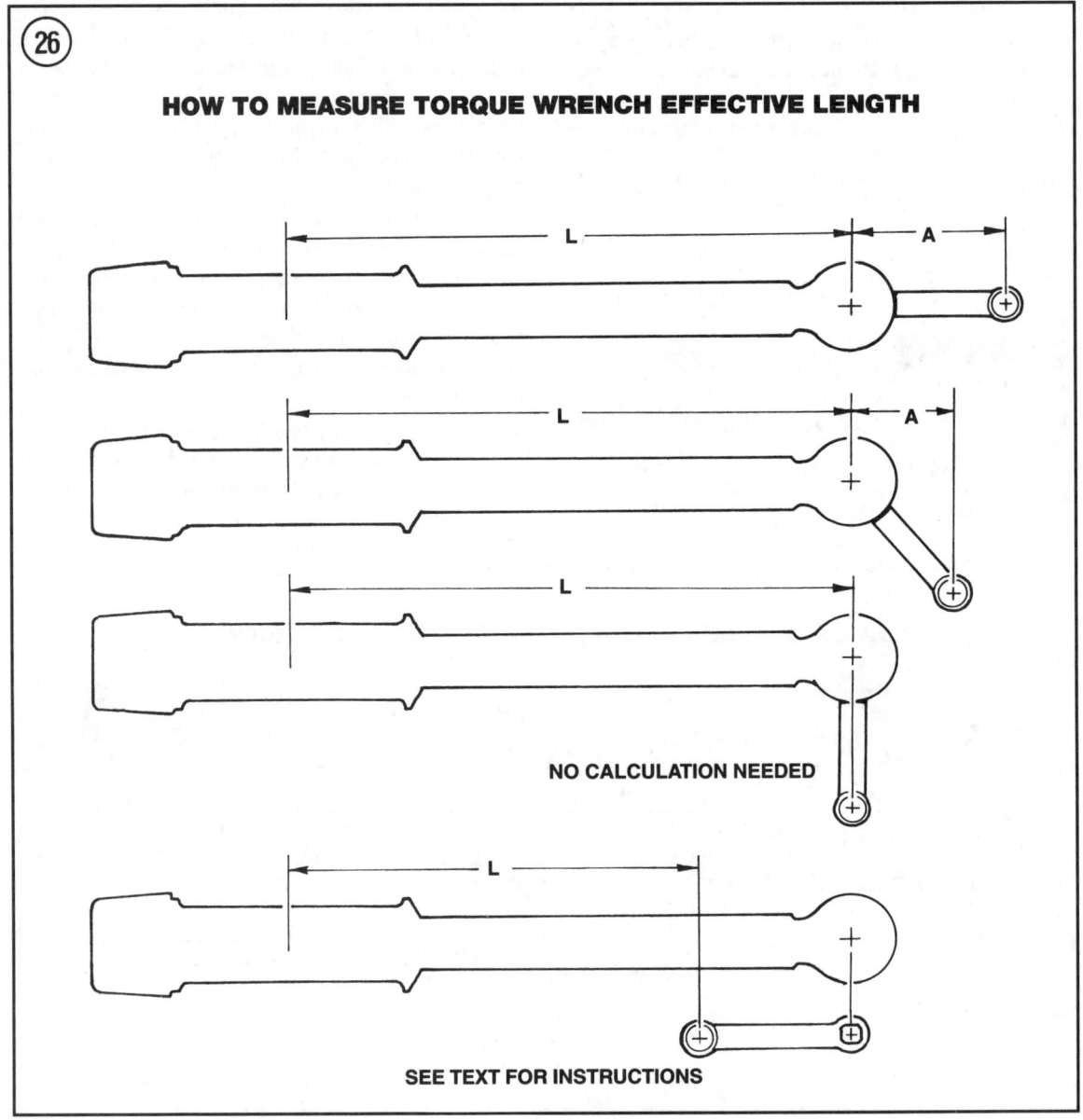

**HOW TO MEASURE TORQUE WRENCH EFFECTIVE LENGTH**

**NO CALCULATION NEEDED**

**SEE TEXT FOR INSTRUCTIONS**

1

sary during many steering, brake and suspension service procedures. The K&L MC450 Center Stand (part No. 37-9882 [**Figure 27**]) is an adjustable scissors-type jack that can be ordered through Honda dealerships. It is suitable for all of the service procedures described in this manual. A standard floor jack may also be used. However, when using a floor jack, supplement its use with safety stands and/or wood blocks in the event the jack slips or looses pressure.

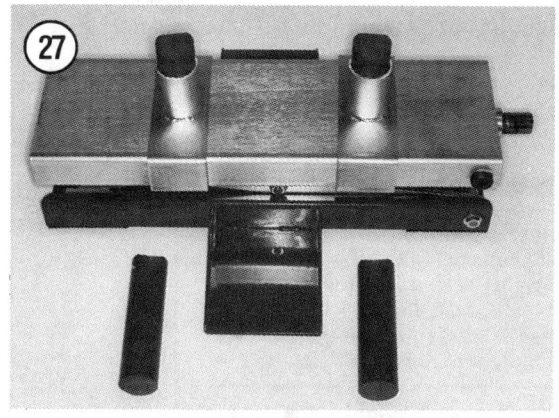

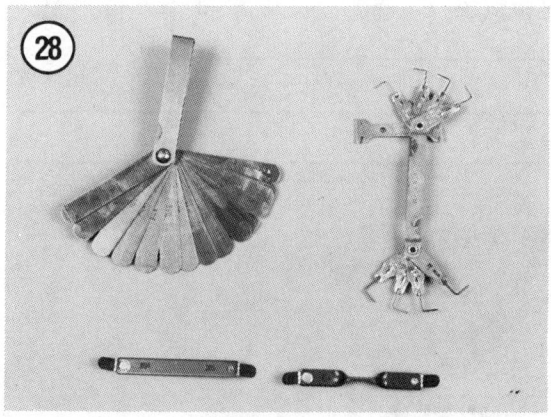

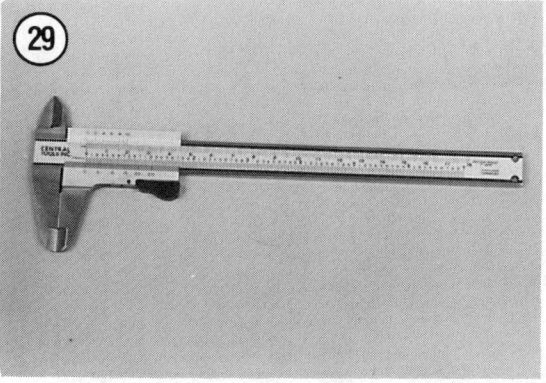

## PRECISION MEASURING TOOLS

Measurement is an important part of motorcycle service. When performing many of the service procedures in this manual, you will be required to make a number of measurements. These include basic checks such as engine compression and spark plug gap. As you expand your shop work into engine disassembly and service, measurements will be required to determine piston and cylinder bore measurements, crankshaft runout and so on. When making these measurements, the degree of accuracy dictates which tool is required. Precision measuring tools are expensive. If this is your first experience at engine service, it may be worthwhile to have the checks and measurements made at a dealership. However, as your skills and enthusiasm for doing your own service work increase, you may want to purchase some of these specialized tools. The following is a description of the measuring tools used in this manual.

### Feeler Gauge

Feeler gauges are available in sets of various sizes and types (**Figure 28**). The gauge is made of either a piece of a flat or round hardened steel of a specified thickness. Round gauges are used to measure spark plug gap. Flat gauges are used for most other measurements.

### Vernier Caliper, Dial Caliper and Digital Electronic Caliper

These tools (**Figure 29**, typical) read inside, outside and depth measurements. Although a caliper is not as precise as a micrometer, they allow reasonable precision, typically to within 0.025 mm (0.001 in.). Common uses are when measuring spring length, the thickness of clutch plates, shims and thrust washers, brake lining thickness and bearing bore depth. The caliper jaws must be kept clean and free of burrs to obtain accurate measurements. There are several types of vernier calipers available. The standard vernier caliper has a graduated scale on the handle (**Figure 29**) in which the measurements must be calculated. The dial indicator caliper is equipped with a small dial and needle that indicates the measurement reading. The digital electronic caliper uses an LCD display tot show the measurement reading.

Because some calipers require calibration, always refer to the manufacturer's instructions when using a new or unfamiliar caliper.

### Outside Micrometers

An outside micrometer is a precision tool used to accurately measure parts using the decimal divisions of the inch or meter (**Figure 30**). While there are many types and styles of micrometers, this section will describe steps on how to use the outside mi-crometer. The outside micrometer is the most common type of micrometer used when servicing a motorcycle or ATV. It is useful in accurately measuring the outside diameter, length and thickness of parts. These include the piston, piston pin, crankshaft, piston rings and shims. The outside micrometer is also used to measure the dimension taken by a small hole gauge or a telescoping gauge described later in this section.

Other types of micrometers include the depth micrometer and screw thread micrometer. **Figure 31**

## DECIMAL PLACE VALUES*

| | |
|---|---|
| 0.1 | Indicates 1/10 (one tenth of an inch or millimeter) |
| 0.01 | Indicates 1/100 (one one-hundredth of an inch or millimeter) |
| 0.001 | Indicates 1/1,000 (one one-thousandth of an inch or millimeter) |

**\* This chart represents the values of figures placed to the right of the decimal point. Use it when reading decimals from one-tenth to one one-thousandth of an inch or millimeter. It is not a conversion chart (for example: 0.001 in. is not equal to 0.001 mm.).**

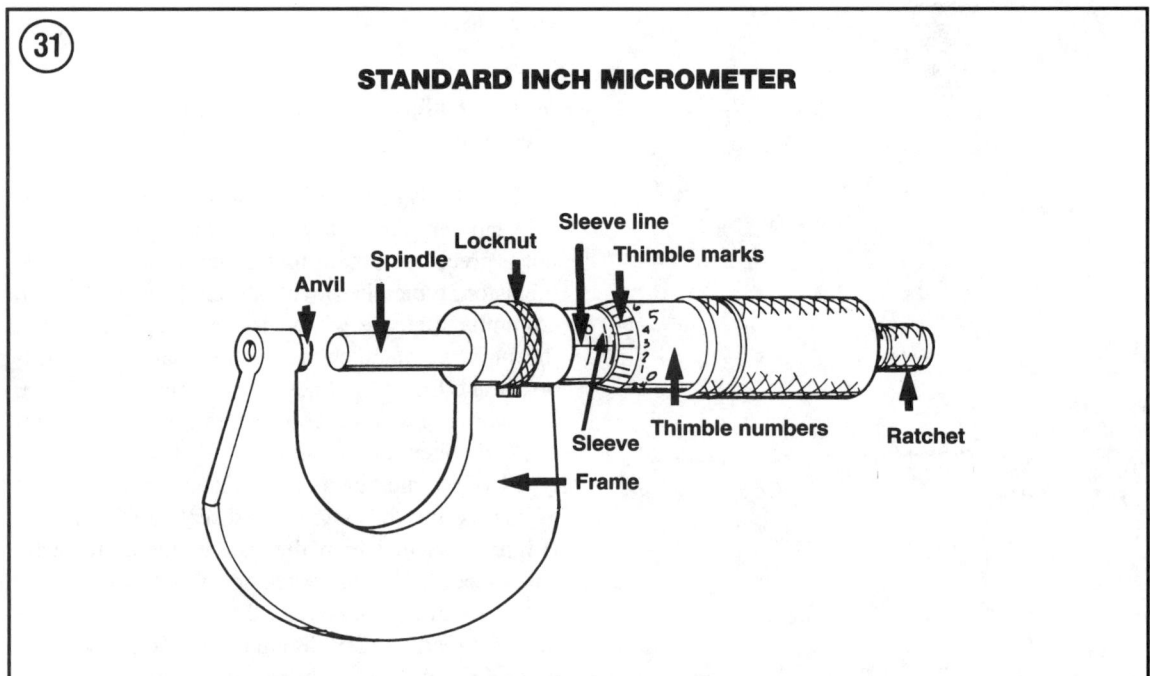

## STANDARD INCH MICROMETER

illustrates the various parts of an outside micrometer with its part names and markings identified.

## Micrometer Range

A micrometer's size indicates the minimum and maximum size it can measure. The usual sizes are: 0-1 in. (0-25 mm), 1-2 in. (25-50 mm), 2-3 in. (50-75 mm) and 3-4 in. (75-100 mm). These micrometers use fixed anvils.

Some micrometers use the same frame with interchangeable anvils of different lengths. This allows the installation of the correct length anvil for a particular job. For example, a 0-4 in. interchangeable micrometer is equipped with four different length anvils. While purchasing one micrometer to cover a range from 0-4 or 0-6 inches is less expensive, its overall frame size makes it less convenient to use.

## How to Read a Micrometer

When reading a micrometer, numbers are taken from different scales and then added together. The following sections describe how to read the standard inch micrometer, the vernier inch micrometer, the standard metric micrometer and the metric vernier micrometer.

### Standard inch micrometer

The standard inch type micrometer is accurate to one-thousandth of an inch (0.001 in.). The heart of the micrometer is its spindle screw with 40 threads per inch. Every turn of the thimble moves the spindle 1/40 of an inch or 0.025 in. (to change 1/40 of an inch to a decimal: 1/40 = 0.025 in.).

Before you learn how to read a micrometer, study the markings and part names in **Figure 31**. Turn the micrometer's thimble until its zero mark aligns with the zero mark on the sleeve line. Now turn the thimble counterclockwise and align the next thimble mark with the sleeve line. The micrometer now reads 0.001 in. (one one-thousandth) of an inch. Thus, each thimble mark is equal to 0.001 in. Every fifth thimble mark is numbered to help with reading: 0, 5, 10, 15 and 20.

Reset the micrometer so the thimble and sleeve line zero marks align. Then turn the thimble counterclockwise one complete revolution and align the thimble zero mark with the first line in the sleeve line. The micrometer now reads 0.025 in. (twenty-five thousandths) of an inch. Thus, each sleeve line represents 0.025 in.

Now turn the thimble counterclockwise while counting the sleeve line marks. Every fourth mark on the sleeve line is marked with a number ranging from 1 through 9. Manufacturers usually mark the last mark on the sleeve with a 0. This indicates that you have reached the end of the micrometer's measuring range. Each sleeve number represents 0.100 in. For example, the number 1 represents 0.100 in. and the number 9 represents 0.900 in.

When reading a standard inch micrometer, take the following three measurements described and add them together. The first two readings are taken from the sleeve. The last reading is taken from the thimble. The sum of the three readings give you the measurement in thousandths of an inch (0.001 in.).

To read a standard inch micrometer, perform the following steps while referring to the example in **Figure 32**.

1. Read the sleeve line to find the largest number visible—each sleeve number mark equals 0.100 in.

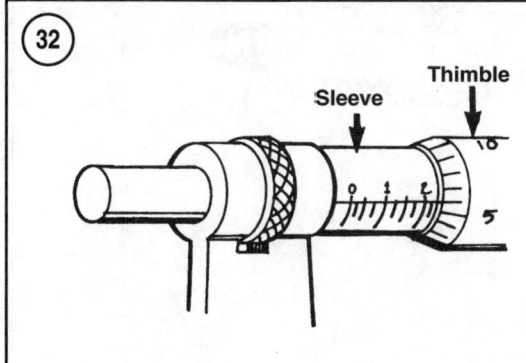

**32**

Sleeve    Thimble

| 1. Largest number visible on the sleeve line | 0.200 in. |
| 2. Number on sleeve marks visible between the numbered sleeve mark and the thimble edge | 0.025 in. |
| 3. Thimble mark that aligns with sleeve line | 0.006 in. |
| Total reading | 0.231 in. |

2. Count the number of sleeve marks visible between the numbered sleeve mark and the thimble edge—each sleeve mark equals 0.025 in. If there are no visible sleeve marks, continue with Step 3.

3. Read the thimble mark that aligns with the sleeve line—each thimble mark equals 0.001 in.

*NOTE*
*If a thimble mark does not align exactly with the sleeve line but falls between 2 lines, estimate the fraction of decimal amount between the lines. For a more accurate reading, use a vernier inch micrometer.*

4. Add the micrometer readings in Steps 1-3 to obtain the actual measurement.

### Vernier inch micrometer

A vernier inch micrometer can accurately measure in ten-thousandths of an inch (0.0001 in.) increments. While it has the same markings as a standard micrometer, a vernier scale scribed on the sleeve (**Figure 33**) makes it unique. The vernier scale consists of eleven equally spaced lines marked 1-9 with a 0 on each end. These lines run parallel on the top of the sleeve where each line is equal to 0.0001 in. Thus, the vernier scale divides a thousandth of an inch (0.001 in.) into ten-thousandths of an inch (0.0001 in.).

To read a vernier inch micrometer, perform the following steps while referring to the example in **Figure 34**.

1. Read the micrometer in the same was as on the standard inch micrometer. This is the initial reading.

2. If a thimble mark aligns exactly with the sleeve line, reading the vernier scale is not necessary. If a thimble mark does not align exactly with the sleeve line, read the vernier scale in Step 3.

3. Read the vernier scale to find which vernier mark aligns with one thimble mark. The number of that vernier mark is the number of ten-thousandths of an inch to add to the initial reading taken in Step 1. See Step 4 in **Figure 34**.

### Metric micrometer

The metric micrometer is very similar to the standard inch type. The differences are the graduations on the thimble and sleeve as shown in **Figure 35**.

The standard metric micrometer can accurately measure to one one-hundredth of a millimeter (0.01 mm). On the metric micrometer, the spindle screw is ground with a thread pitch of one-half millimeter (0.5 mm). Thus, every turn of the thimble will move the spindle 0.5 mm.

The sleeve line is graduated in millimeters and half millimeters. The marks on the upper side of the sleeve line are equal to 1.00 mm. Every fifth mark above the sleeve line is marked with a number. The actual numbers will depend on the size of the micrometer. For example, on a 0-25 mm micrometer, the sleeve marks are numbered 0, 5, 10, 15, 20 and 25. On a 25-50 mm micrometer, the sleeve marks are numbered 25, 30, 35, 40, 45 and 50. This numbering sequence continues with larger micrometers (50-75

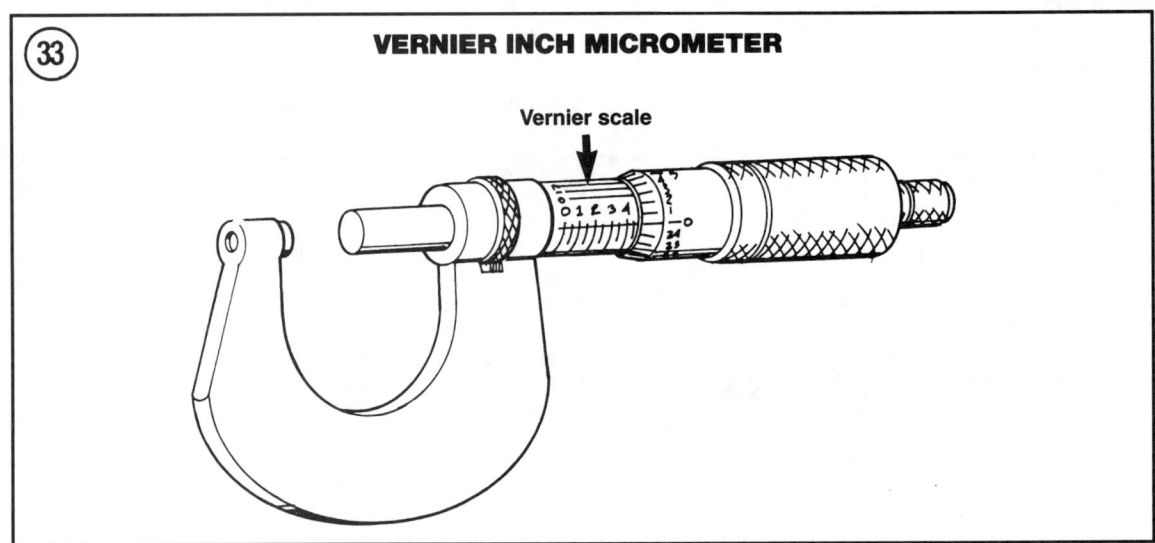

**VERNIER INCH MICROMETER**

Vernier scale

**34**

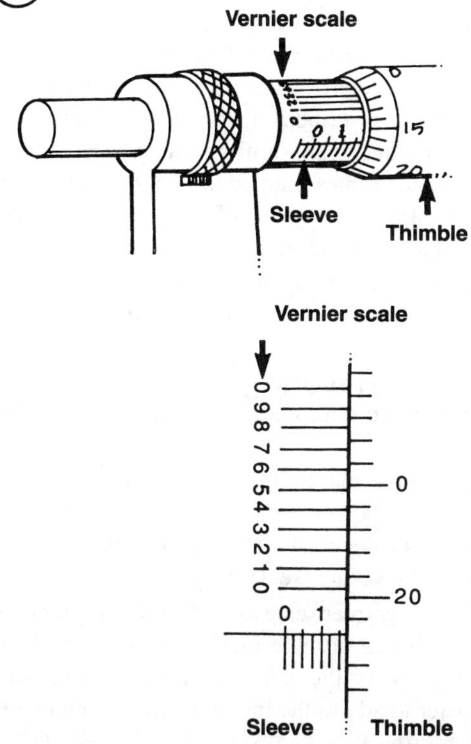

Vernier scale

Sleeve          Thimble

Vernier scale

Sleeve    Thimble

1. Largest number visible on
   sleeve line                                   0.100 in.
2. Number of sleeve marks visible
   between the numbered sleeve
   mark and the thimble edge                     0.050 in.
3. Thimble is between 0.018 and 0.019
   inches on the sleeve line                     0.018 in.
4. Vernier line coinciding with
   line thimble line                             0.0003 in.
                            Total reading         0.1683 in.

**35**

## STANDARD METRIC MICROMETER

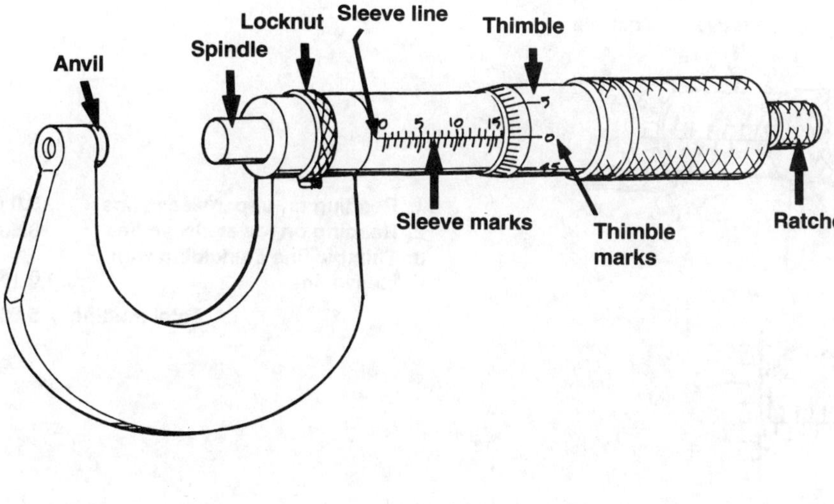

Anvil     Spindle     Locknut   Sleeve line   Thimble

Sleeve marks      Thimble       Ratchet
                  marks

and 75-100). Each mark on the lower side of the sleeve line is equal to 0.50 mm.

The thimble scale is divided into 50 graduations: one graduation is equal to 0.01 mm. Every fifth thimble graduation is numbered to help with reading from 0-45. The thimble edge is used to indicate which sleeve markings to read.

To read a metric micrometer, add the number of millimeters and half-millimeters on the sleeve line to the number of one one-hundredth millimeters on the thimble. To do so, perform the following steps while referring to the example in **Figure 36**.

1. Take the first reading by counting the number of marks visible on the upper sleeve line. Record the reading.

2. Look below the sleeve line to see if a lower mark is visible directly past the upper line mark. If so, add 0.50 to the first reading.

3. Now read the thimble mark that aligns with the sleeve line. Record this reading.

*NOTE*
*If a thimble mark does not align exactly with the sleeve line but falls between 2 lines, estimate the decimal amount between the lines. For a more accurate reading, use a metric vernier micrometer.*

4. Add the micrometer readings in Steps 1-3 to obtain the actual measurement.

### Metric vernier micrometers

A metric vernier micrometer is accurate to two thousandths of a millimeter (0.002 mm). While it has the same markings as a standard metric micrometer, a vernier scale scribed on the sleeve (**Figure 37**) makes it unique. The vernier scale consists of five equally spaced lines marked 0, 2, 4, 6 and 8. These lines run parallel on the top of the sleeve where each line is equal to 0.002 mm.

To read a metric vernier micrometer, perform the following steps while referring to the example in **Figure 38**:

1. Read the micrometer in the same way as the metric standard micrometer. This is the initial reading.

2. If a thimble mark aligns exactly with the sleeve line, reading the vernier scale is not necessary. If a thimble mark does not align exactly with the sleeve line, read the vernier scale in Step 3.

3. Read the vernier scale to find which vernier mark aligns with one thimble mark. The number of that vernier mark is the number of thousandths of a millimeter to add to the initial reading taken in Step 1. See **Figure 38**.

### Micrometer Accuracy Check

Before using a micrometer, check its accuracy as follows:

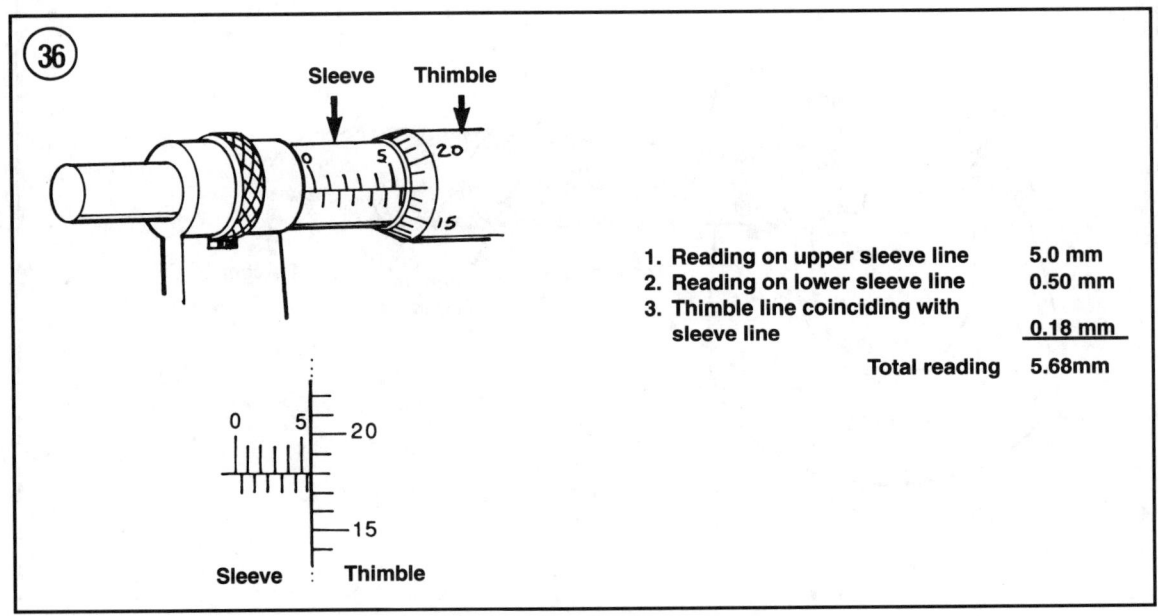

| | |
|---|---|
| 1. Reading on upper sleeve line | 5.0 mm |
| 2. Reading on lower sleeve line | 0.50 mm |
| 3. Thimble line coinciding with sleeve line | 0.18 mm |
| **Total reading** | 5.68mm |

1. Make sure the anvil and spindle faces (**Figure 31**) are clean and dry.

2. To check a 0-1 in. or 0-25 mm micrometer, perform the following:

    a. Turn the thimble until the spindle contacts the anvil. If the micrometer has a ratchet stop, use it to ensure that the proper amount of pressure is applied against the contact surfaces.

    b. Read the micrometer. If the adjustment is correct, the 0 mark on the thimble will align exactly with the 0 mark on the sleeve line. If the

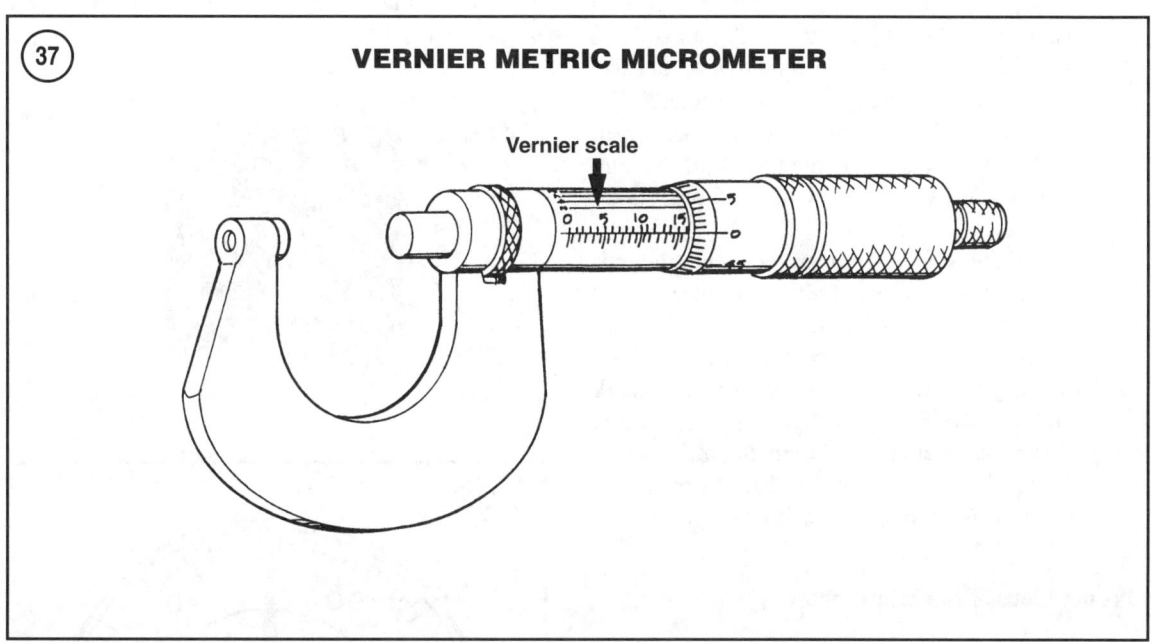

**VERNIER METRIC MICROMETER**

Vernier scale

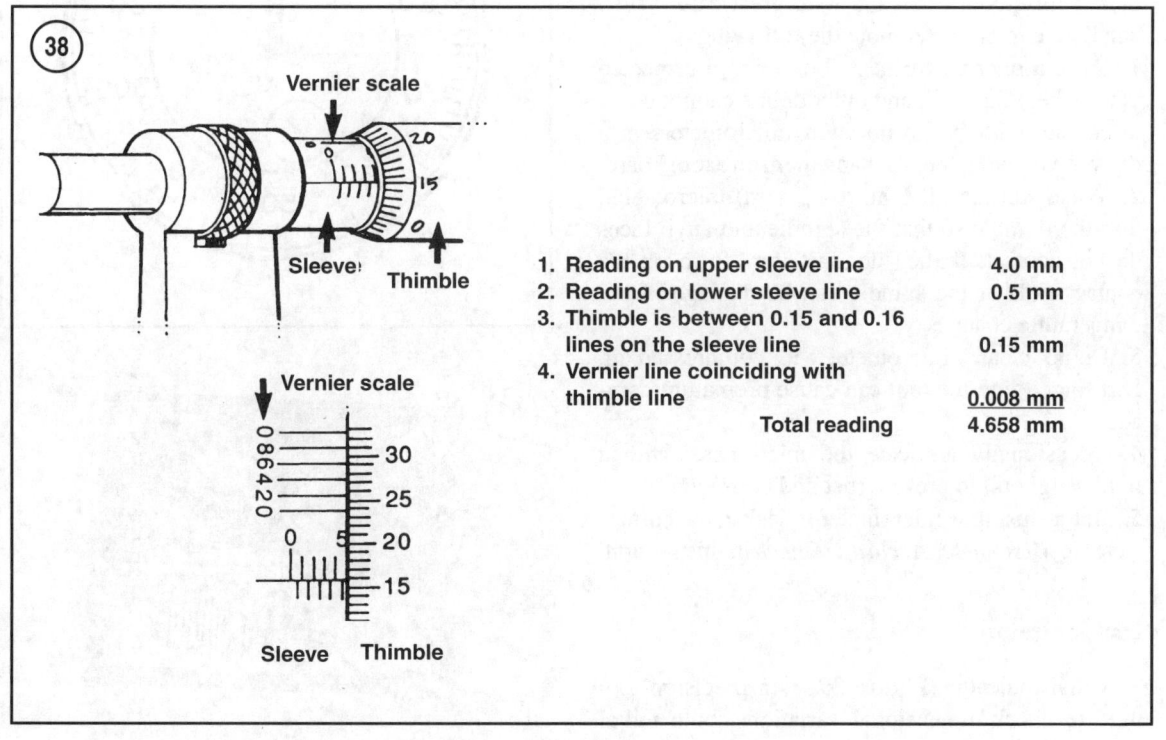

Vernier scale

Sleeve
Thimble

Vernier scale

Sleeve    Thimble

| | |
|---|---|
| 1. Reading on upper sleeve line | 4.0 mm |
| 2. Reading on lower sleeve line | 0.5 mm |
| 3. Thimble is between 0.15 and 0.16 lines on the sleeve line | 0.15 mm |
| 4. Vernier line coinciding with thimble line | 0.008 mm |
| Total reading | 4.658 mm |

the 0 marks do not align, the micrometer is out of adjustment

  c. To adjust the micrometer, follow the manufacturer's instructions given with the micrometer.

3. To check the accuracy of micrometers above the 1 in. or 25 mm size, perform the following:

  a. Manufacturers usually supply a standard gauge with these micrometers. A standard is a steel block, disc or rod ground to an exact size to check the accuracy of the micrometer. For example, a 1-2 in. micrometer is equipped with a 1 inch standard gauge. A 25-50 mm micrometer is equipped with a 25 mm standard gauge.

  b. Place the standard gauge between the micrometer's spindle and anvil and measure its outside diameter or length. Read the micrometer. If the adjustment is correct, the 0 mark on the thimble will align exactly with the 0 mark on the sleeve line. If the 0 marks do not align, the micrometer is out of adjustment.

  c. To adjust the micrometer, follow the manufacturer's instructions given with the micrometer.

**Proper Care of the Micrometer**

The micrometer is a precision instrument and must be used correctly and with great care. When handling a micrometer, note the following:

1. Store a micrometer in its box or in a protected place where dust, oil, and other debris cannot come in contact with it. Do not store micrometers in a drawer with other tools or hang them on a tool board.

2. When storing a 0-1 in. (0-25 mm) micrometer, turn the thimble so that the spindle and anvil faces do not contact. If they do, rust may form on the contact ends or the spindle can be damaged from temperature changes.

3. Do not clean a micrometer with compressed air. Dirt forced into the tool can cause premature damage.

4. Occasionally lubricate the micrometer with a light weight oil to prevent rust and corrosion.

5. Before using a micrometer, check its accuracy. Refer to *Micrometer Accuracy Check* in this section.

**Dial Indicator**

A dial indicator (**Figure 39**) is a precision tool used to check dimensional variations, both radial and axial runout, of machined parts such as transmission shafts and to check crankshaft runout and end play. For motorcycle and ATV service procedures, select a dial indicator with a continuous dial (**Figure 40**). When using a dial indicator, it must be held securely to ensure accurate measuring results. Various mounts are available for specific measuring requirements.

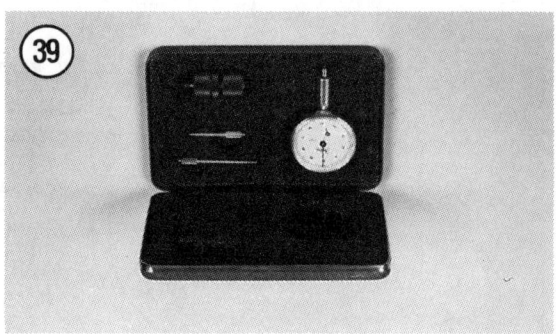

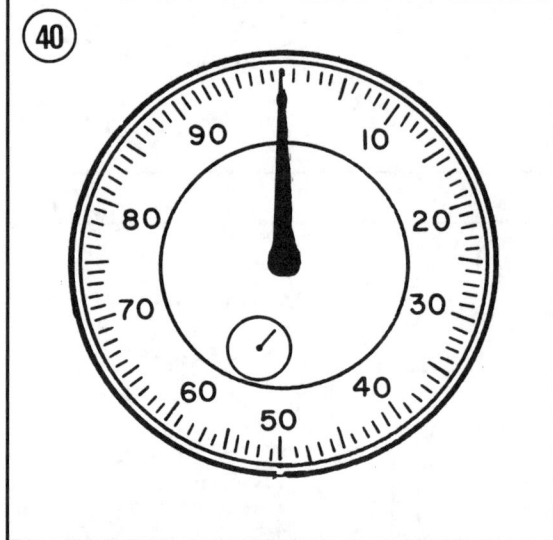

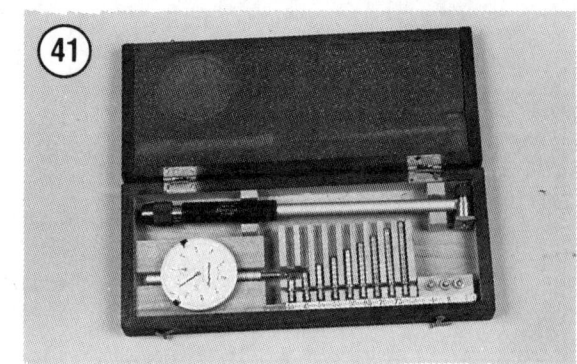

## Cylinder Bore Gauge

The cylinder bore gauge is a very specialized precision tool. The gauge set shown in **Figure 41** is comprised of a dial indicator, handle and a number of different length adapters to adapt the gauge to different bore sizes. The bore gauge is used to make cylinder bore measurements such as bore size, taper and out-of-round. In some cases, an outside micrometer must be used together with the bore gauge to determine bore dimensions.

Select the correct length adapter (A, **Figure 42**) for the size of the bore to be measured. Zero the bore gauge according to its manufacturer's instructions,

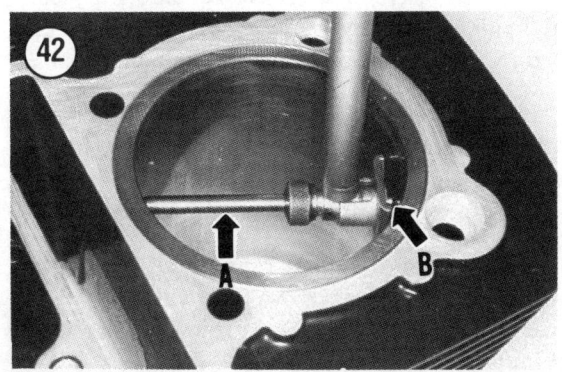

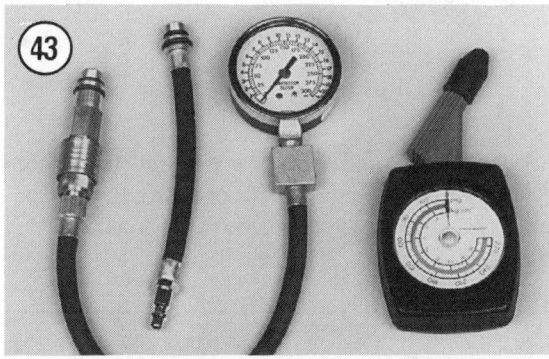

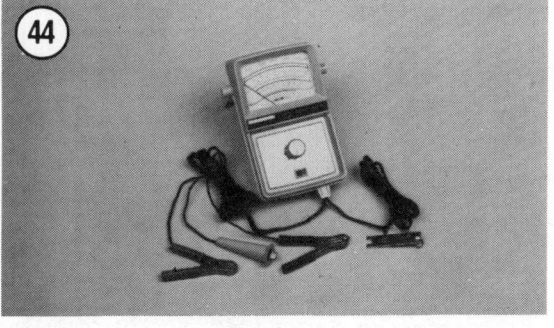

insert the bore gauge into the cylinder and carefully move it around in the bore to make sure it is centered and that the gauge foot (B, **Figure 42**) is sitting correctly on the bore surface. This is necessary in order to obtain a correct reading. When using a bore gauge, follow the manufacturer's instructions.

## Compression Gauge

An engine with low compression cannot be properly tuned and will not develop full power. A compression gauge (**Figure 43**) measures engine compression. The one shown on the left has a flexible stem with an extension that allows you to hold it while operating the starter. Open the throttle all the way when checking engine compression. See Chapter Three.

## Multimeter or VOM

A VOM (Volt and Ohm Meter) is a valuable tool for all electrical system troubleshooting (**Figure 44**). The voltage application is used to indicate the voltage applied or available to various electrical components. The ohmmeter portion of the meter is used to check for continuity, or lack of continuity, and to measure the resistance of a component. Some tests are easily accomplished using meter with a sweeping needle (analog), but other components must be tested using a digital VOM (DVOM).

In some test procedures, the vehicle's manufacturer will instruct you to use their specific test meter due to the internal design of their meter. They will specify that the resistance reading may differ if another type of test meter is used in the test procedure. Such requirements will be noted at the beginning of the electrical test procedure.

### *To measure voltage*

> *NOTE*
> *Make sure the negative (–) or ground surface being used is clean and free of paint and/or grease. If possible, use an unpainted bolt that is attached directly to the frame.*

1. Make sure the meter's battery power source is at full power; if its condition is doubtful, install a new battery(s).

2. Select the meter voltage range to *one scale higher* than the voltage value of the circuit to be tested.

3. Touch the red test probe to the *positive* (+) end and the black test probe to the *negative* (–), or ground, end of the circuit.

4. Read the position of the needle on the VOLTS or VOLTAGE scale of the meter face, or the digital readout, and refer to the specified voltage listed in the test procedure. Refer to the manufacturer's instruction for any special conditions relating to the meter that you are using.

### To calibrate an analog ohmmeter

> *NOTE*
> *Every time an analog ohmmeter is used to measure resistance it must be calibrated in order to obtain a correct measurement. Most digital ohmmeters are not equipped with a zero ohms adjust feature—when turned on they are automatically set at zero (providing the meter's battery is at full power).*

1. Make sure the meter's battery power source is at full power; if its condition is questionable, install a new battery(s).

2. Make sure the test probes are clean and free of corrosion.

3. Touch the two test probes together and observe the meter needle location on the OHMS scale on the meter face. The needle must be on the 0 mark at the end of the scale.

4. If necessary, rotate the ohms adjust knob on the meter in either direction until the needle is directly on the 0 mark on the scale. The meter is now ready for use.

### To measure resistance

1. Calibrate the analog meter as previously described.

2. Disconnect the component from the circuit. If you take a reading with the component connected in the circuit, the resistance reading will be smaller than the correct resistance value of the component.

3. Place the test probe at each end of the component, read the meter and refer to the specified resistance in the test procedure.

### Continuity test

A continuity test determines the integrity of a circuit. Continuity is indicated by a low resistance reading, usually zero ohms, on the meter. No continuity is indicated by an infinity reading. A broken or open circuit has no continuity, while a complete circuit has continuity. A continuity is also useful to check components for a short to ground. A shorted component has a complete circuit (continuity) between the component and ground.

1. Calibrate the analog meter as previously described in this section.

2. Place the test probe at each end of the component, or circuit and read the position of the needle on the OHMS scale of the meter face, or digital readout.

3. If there is *continuity (low resistance)* the meter will indicate a certain amount of resistance. In this test the resistance value is not important—all you want to know is if the circuit is complete or not.

4. If there is *no continuity (infinite resistance)* the meter needle will not move and will stay at the infinity symbol or the digital readout will indicate infinity.

## SPECIAL TOOLS

A few special tools may be required for major service. These are described in the appropriate chapters and are available either from a Honda dealer or other manufacturers as indicated.

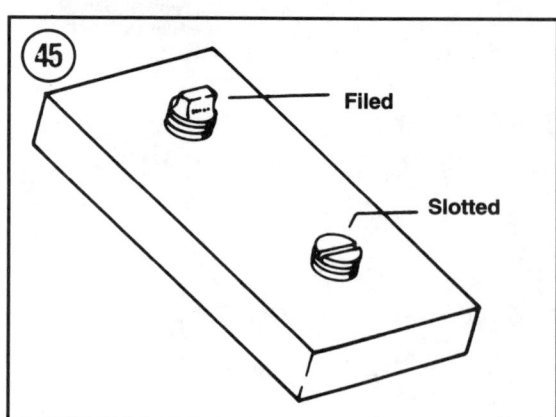

## MECHANIC'S TIPS

### Removing Frozen Nuts and Screws

If a fastener rusts and cannot be removed, several methods may be used to loosen it. First, apply penetrating oil such as Liquid Wrench or WD-40 (available at hardware or auto supply stores). Apply it liberally and let it penetrate for 10-15 minutes. Rap the fastener several times with a small hammer, then try to loosen it with a suitable tool; do not hit or turn it hard enough to cause damage. Reapply the penetrating oil if necessary.

To loosen frozen screws, apply penetrating oil as described, then insert a screwdriver in the slot and rap the top of the screwdriver with a hammer. This may loosen the rust so the screw can be removed in the normal way. If the screw head is too damaged to use this method, grip the head with locking pliers and twist the screw out.

Avoid applying heat unless specifically instructed, as it may melt, warp or remove the temper from parts.

### Removing Broken Screws or Bolts

If the head breaks off a screw or bolt, several methods are available for removing the remaining portion. If a large portion of the fastener projects out, try gripping it with locking pliers. If the projecting portion is too small, file it to fit a wrench or cut a slot in it to fit a screwdriver (**Figure 45**).

If the head breaks off flush, use a screw extractor (**Figure 46**) as follows:

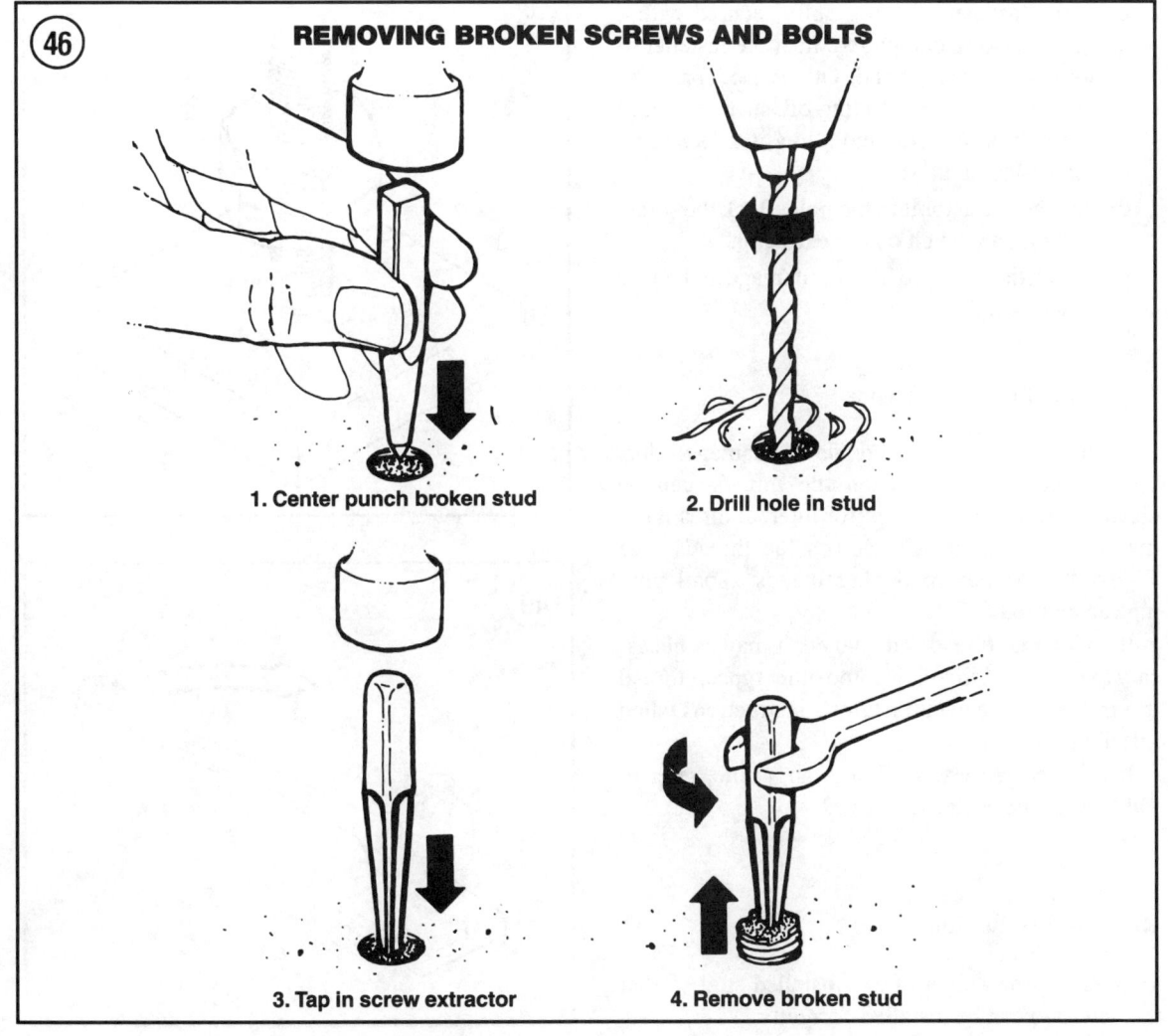

**REMOVING BROKEN SCREWS AND BOLTS**

1. Center punch broken stud

2. Drill hole in stud

3. Tap in screw extractor

4. Remove broken stud

*NOTE*
*In the following step, it is important to drill in the exact center of the broken fastener. This ensures that there will be enough room to install the extractor and that it will be able to grip and lock into the broken fastener correctly. If the hole is drilled off center, the extractor may bite into the threaded hole when installed, further complicating the removal procedure.*

a. Center punch the exact center of the remaining portion of the screw or bolt.

b. Select the correct extractor bit and drill bit for the fastener being removed. Follow the manufacturer's instructions for drill size and hole depth. Then drill a hole into the broken fastener.

c. If the fastener was originally secured with a threadlocking compound, heat the fastener to loosen the sealer bond. Otherwise, spray the fastener with a penetrating oil, such as Liquid Wrench or WD-40, and allow it to penetrate for 10-15 minutes.

d. Tap the extractor into the hole. Back the screw out with a wrench on the extractor.

e. Check the threaded hole for damage and repair if necessary.

**Repairing Stripped Threads**

Occasionally, fastener threads are damaged during service or repair. Often the threads can be cleaned up by running a tap (for internal threads) or die (for external threads) across the threads. See **Figure 47**. To repair spark plug threads, a spark plug tap can be used.

If an internal thread is damaged, it may be necessary to install a Helicoil or some other type of thread insert. Follow the manufacturer's instructions when installing their insert.

If it is necessary to drill and tap a hole, refer to **Table 8** for metric tap drill sizes.

**Studs**
**Removal/Installation**

1. Measure the height of the installed stud so that the new stud can be installed correctly.

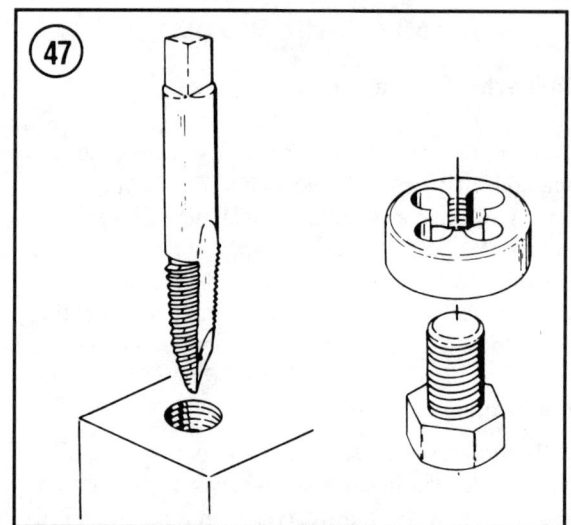

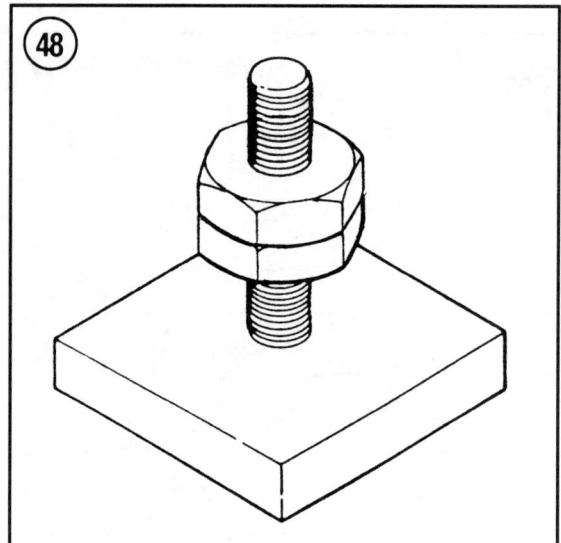

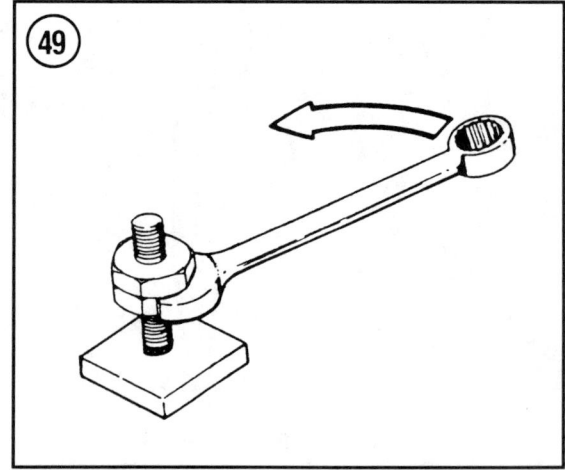

2A. If some threads of a stud are damaged, but some remain, you may be able to removed the stud as follows. If there are no usable threads, remove the stud as described in Step 2B.

    a. Thread two nuts onto the damaged stud (**Figure 48**), then tighten the nuts against each other so that they are locked.

    b. Turn the bottom nut (**Figure 49**) and unscrew the stud.

2B. If the threads on the stud are damaged, remove the stud with a stud remover or with a pair of locking pliers.

3. Clean the threads with solvent or contact cleaner and allow to dry thoroughly.

4. Clean the threaded hole with contact cleaner or solvent and a wire brush. Try to remove as much of the threadlock residue from the hole as possible.

5. Install 2 nuts on the top half of the new stud as in Step 2A. Make sure they are locked securely.

6. Apply a high-strength threadlock to the bottom threads on the new stud.

7. Turn the top nut and thread the new stud in. Install the stud to its correct height position (Step 1) or tighten it to its correct torque specification (see appropriate chapter).

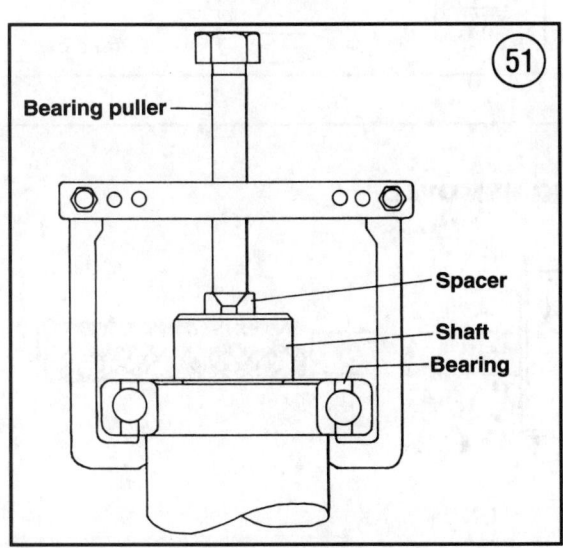

Bearing puller

Spacer
Shaft
Bearing

8. Remove the nuts and repeat for each stud as required.

## BALL BEARING REPLACEMENT

Ball bearings (**Figure 50**) are used throughout the engine and drive assembly to reduce power loss, heat and noise resulting from friction. Because ball bearings are precision made parts, they must be maintained by proper lubrication and maintenance. If a bearing is found to be damaged, it must be replaced immediately. However, when installing a new bearing, be careful to prevent damage to the new bearing.

*NOTE*
*Unless otherwise specified in the service procedure, install bearings with their manufacturer's mark or number facing outward.*

### Bearing Removal

While bearings are normally removed only when damaged, there may be times when it is necessary to remove a bearing that is in good condition. However, improper bearing removal will damage the bearing and maybe the shaft or case half. Note the following when removing bearings.

*WARNING*
*Failure to use proper precautions may result in damaged parts and personal injury.*

1. Before removing the bearings, note the following:

    a. Remove any oil seal(s) that interfere with bearing removal. Refer to *Oil Seals* in this chapter.

    b. When removing more than one bearing, identify the bearings before removing them. Refer to the bearing manufacturer's size code marks on the bearing.

    c. Note and record the direction the bearing marks face for proper installation.

    d. Remove any set plates or bearing retainers before removing the bearings.

2. When using a puller to remove a bearing from a shaft, care must be taken so that the shaft is not damaged. Always place a spacer (**Figure 51**) between the end of the shaft and the puller screw. In

addition, place the puller arms next to the inner bearing race.

3. When using a hammer to remove a bearing from a shaft, do not strike the hammer directly against the shaft. Instead, support the bearing races with wooden blocks (**Figure 52**) and use a brass or aluminum driver between the hammer and shaft.

4. The ideal method of bearing removal is with a hydraulic press. However, certain procedures must be followed or damage may occur to the bearing or equipment. Note the following when using a press:

a. Always make sure the press is of sufficient capacity to remove the bearing. A 10-12 ton press should be adequate to remove the bearings called out in this manual. However, when overhauling the crankshaft, a 20-30 ton press will be required.

b. Always support the inner and outer bearing races with the proper size wood or aluminum spacer (**Figure 53**). If only the outer race is supported, the balls and/or the inner race will be damaged.

c. Always make sure the press ram (**Figure 53**) aligns with the center of the shaft. If the ram is not centered, it may damage the bearing and/or shaft.

d. The moment the shaft is free of the bearing, it will drop to the floor. Secure or hold the shaft to prevent it from falling.

5. Use a blind bearing remover to remove bearings installed in blind holes (**Figure 54**).

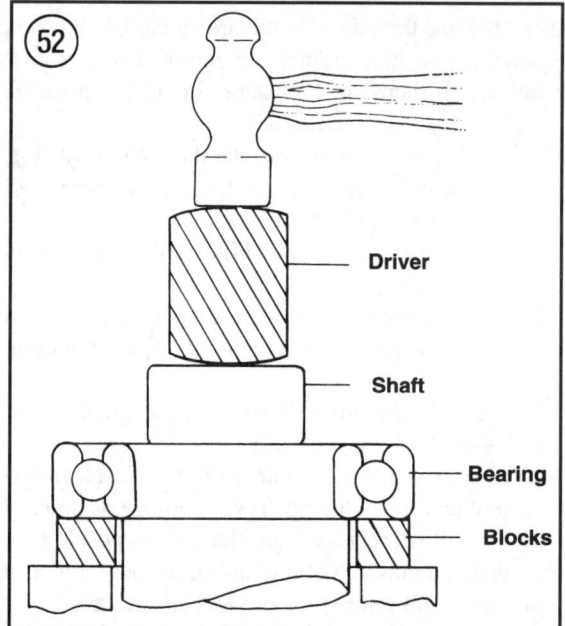

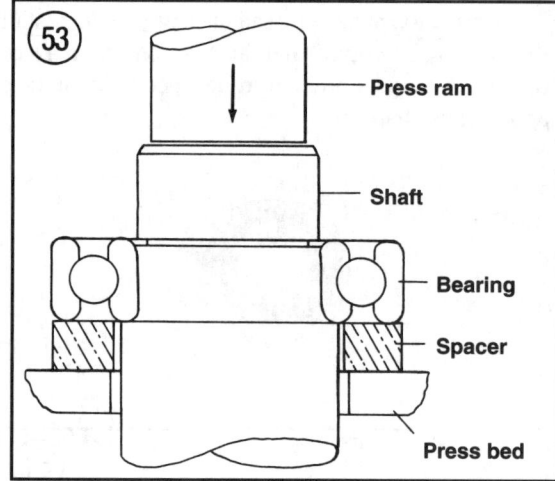

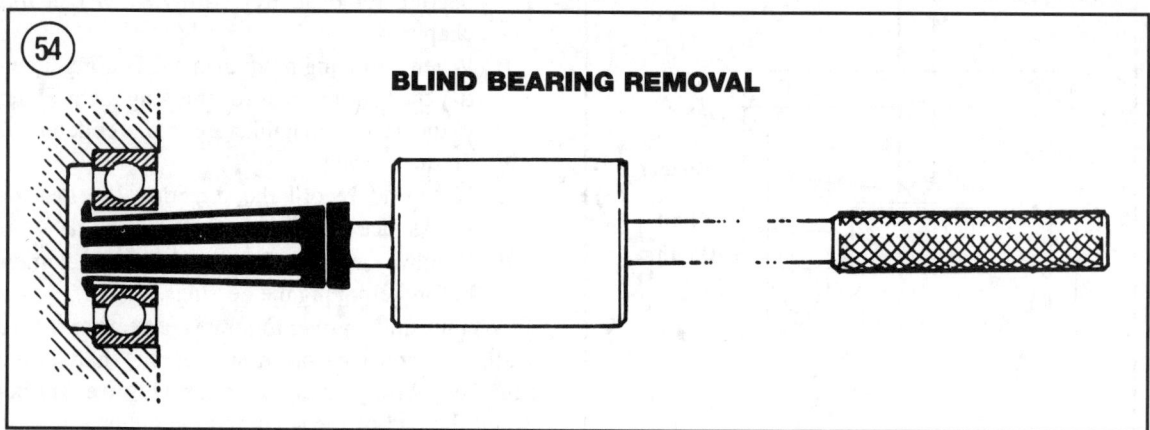

## Bearing Installation

1. Before installing the new bearing(s), perform the following:

   a. Clean and inspect the bearing bore or shaft.

   b. Remove any burrs from the bearing bore or shaft.

   c. Compare the old and new bearings to make sure the correct bearing is being installed.

2. When installing a bearing in a housing, apply pressure to the *outer* bearing race (**Figure 55**). When installing a bearing on a shaft, apply pressure to the *inner* bearing race (**Figure 56**).

3. When installing a bearing as described in Step 2, some type of driver will be required. Never strike the bearing directly with a hammer or the bearing will be damaged. When installing a bearing, use a driver with a diameter that matches the bearing race. See **Figure 55** and **Figure 56**.

4. Step 2 describes how to install a bearing in a case half and over a shaft. However, when installing a bearing over a shaft and into a housing at the same time, a snug fit is required for both outer and inner bearing races. In this situation, a spacer must be installed underneath the driver tool so that pressure is applied evenly across both races. See **Figure 57**. If the outer race is not supported as shown in **Figure 57**, the balls will push against the outer bearing track and damage it.

## Shrink Fit

1. *Installing a bearing over a shaft*: When a tight fit is required, the bearing inside diameter will be smaller than the shaft. In this case, driving the bearing on the shaft may cause bearing damage. Instead, heat the bearing before installation. Note the following:

   a. Secure the shaft so that it is ready for bearing installation.

   b. Clean all residue from the bearing surface of the shaft. Remove burrs with a file or sandpaper.

   c. Fill a suitable pot or beaker with clean mineral oil. Place a thermometer (rated higher than 120° C [248° F]) in the oil. Support the thermometer so that it does not rest on the bottom or side of the pot.

   d. Secure the bearing with a piece of heavy wire bent to hold it in the pot. Hang the bearing in

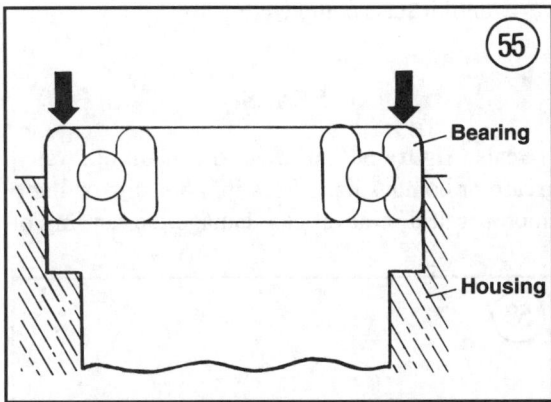

55

Bearing

Housing

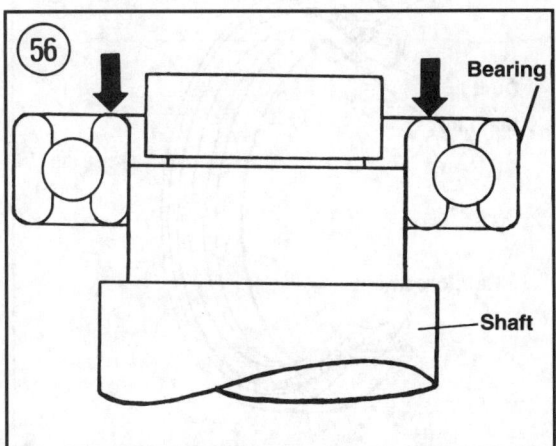

56

Bearing

Shaft

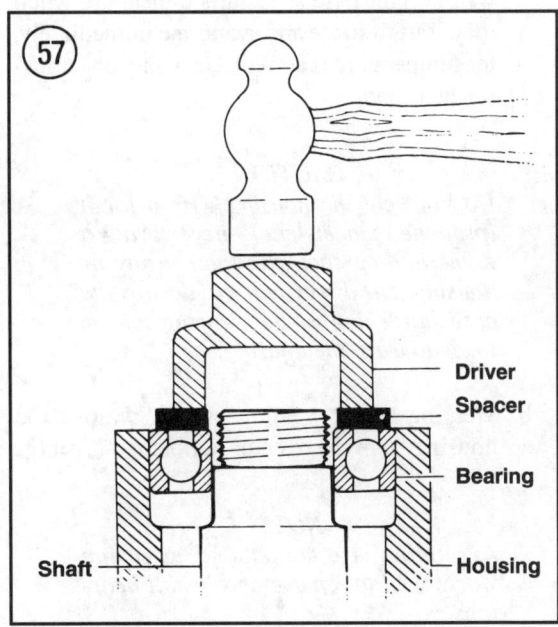

57

Driver

Spacer

Bearing

Shaft

Housing

the pot so that it does not touch the bottom or sides of the pot.

e. Turn the heat on and monitor the thermometer. When the oil temperature rises to approximately 120° C (248 F), remove the bearing from the pot and quickly install it. If necessary, place a socket on the inner bearing race and carefully tap the bearing into place. As the bearing cools, it will tighten on the shaft so you must work quickly when installing it. Make sure the bearing is installed all the way.

2. *Installing a bearing in a housing*: Bearings are generally installed in a housing with a slight interference fit. Driving the bearing into the housing may damage the housing or cause bearing damage. Instead, heat the housing before installing the bearing. Note the following:

*CAUTION*
*Before heating the crankcases in this procedure to remove the bearings, wash the cases thoroughly with detergent and water. Rinse and rewash the cases as required to remove all traces of oil and other chemical deposits.*

a. The housing must be heated to a temperature of about 212° F (100° C) in an oven or on a hot plate. An easy way to check if it is at the proper temperature is to place tiny drops of water on the case as it starts to heat up; when they start to sizzle and evaporate immediately, the temperature is correct. Heat only one housing at a time.

*CAUTION*
*Do not heat the housing with a torch (propane or acetylene)—never bring a flame into contact with the bearing or housing. The direct heat will destroy the case hardening of the bearing and is likely to warp the housing.*

b. Wearing heavy welding gloves, remove the housing from the oven or hot plate—it is hot.

*NOTE*
*A suitable size socket and extension works well to remove and install bearings.*

c. Hold the housing with the bearing side down and tap the bearing out. Repeat for all bearings in the housing.

d. Prior to heating the bearing housing, place the new bearing in a freezer, if possible. Chilling a bearing will slightly reduce its outside diameter while the heated bearing housing assembly is slightly larger due to heat expansion. This will make bearing installation much easier.

*NOTE*
*Always install bearings with their manufacturer's mark or number facing the driver.*

e. While the housing is still hot, install the new bearing(s) into the housing. Install the bearings by hand, if possible. If necessary, lightly tap the bearing(s) into the housing with a driver placed on the outer bearing race (**Figure 55**). Do not install new bearings by driving on the inner bearing race. Install the bearing(s) until it seats completely.

## SEALS

Seals (**Figure 58**) are used to contain oil, water, grease or combustion gasses in a housing or shaft. Improper seal removal can damage the housing or

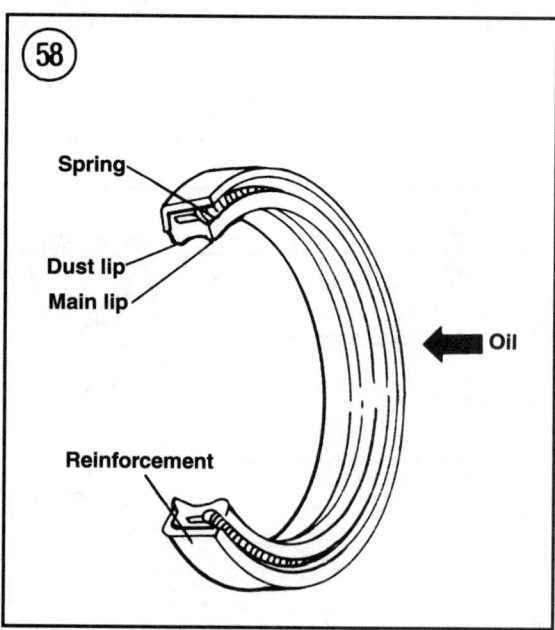

shaft. Improper installation of the seal can damage the seal or cause leakage. Note the following:

1. Prying is generally the easiest and most effective method of removing a seal from a housing. However, always place a rag underneath the pry tool to prevent damage to the housing. See **Figure 59**, typical.

2. Pack the specified grease in the seal lips before installing the seal.

3. While oil seals are usually installed with their manufacturer's numbers or marks facing out, this is not always the case. In situations where a double sided seal is used, record the markings on the side of the seal that faces out. In some instances, the seal may be marked on both sides; for example, OUTSIDE and INSIDE. Look for these marks and install the seal correctly.

4. Oil seals can be installed by hand or may require the use of force. When using force, use a bearing driver on the outer portion of the seal, then drive it squarely into its mounting bore. Never install a seal by hitting it against the top of the seal with a hammer.

**Table 1 ENGINE AND FRAME SERIAL NUMBERS**

| Model | Engine starting serial number | Frame starting serial number |
|---|---|---|
| **1995 TRX400FW** | | |
| Models sold in New Hampshire | TE20E-8000001- | TE203 SA000001- |
| All other models | TE20E-8000001- | TE200 SA000001- |
| **1996 TRX400FW** | | |
| Models sold in New Hampshire | TE20E-8100001- | TE203 TA100001- |
| All other models | TE20E-8100001- | TE200 TA100001- |
| **1997 TRX400FW** | | |
| Models sold in New Hampshire | TE20E-8200001- | TE203 VA200001- |
| All other models | TE20E-8200001- | TE200 VA200001- |
| **1998 TRX400FW** | | |
| Models sold in California | TE20E-8300001- | TE201 WA000001- |
| All other models | TE20E-8300001- | TE200 WA300001- |
| **1999 TRX400FW (All)** | TE20E-8400001- | TE200-XA400001- |
| **2000 TRX400FW (All)** | TE20E-8400001- | TE201-Y4100001- |
| **2001 TRX400FW (All)** | TE20E-8500001- | TE200-14200001- |

**Table 2 GENERAL DIMENSIONS**

| | mm | in. |
|---|---|---|
| Overall width | 1156 | 45.5 |
| Overall length | 1944 | 76.5 |
| Overall height | | |
| 1995-1996 | 1080 | 42.4 |
| 1997-on | 1094 | 43.1 |
| Wheelbase | 1240 | 48.8 |
| Front and rear tread | 850 | 33.5 |
| Seat height | 785 | 30.9 |
| Footpeg height | 307 | 12.1 |
| Ground clearance | 186 | 7.3 |

## Table 3 WEIGHT SPECIFICATIONS

| | | |
|---|---|---|
| Dry weight | | |
| 1995-1996 | 249.5 | 551 |
| 1997-on | 251 | 553 |
| Curb weight | | |
| 1995-1996 | 260 | 574 |
| 1997-on | 262 | 578 |
| Maximum weight capacity | 220 | 485 |

## Table 4 DECIMAL AND METRIC EQUIVALENTS

| Fractions | Decimal in. | Metric mm | Fractions | Decimal in. | Metric mm |
|---|---|---|---|---|---|
| 1/64 | 0.015625 | 0.39688 | 33/64 | 0.515625 | 13.09687 |
| 1/32 | 0.03125 | 0.79375 | 17/32 | 0.53125 | 13.49375 |
| 3/64 | 0.046875 | 1.19062 | 35/64 | 0.546875 | 13.89062 |
| 1/16 | 0.0625 | 1.58750 | 9/16 | 0.5625 | 14.28750 |
| 5/64 | 0.078125 | 1.98437 | 37/64 | 0.578125 | 14.68437 |
| 3/32 | 0.09375 | 2.38125 | 19/32 | 0.59375 | 15.08125 |
| 7/64 | 0.109375 | 2.77812 | 39/64 | 0.609375 | 15.47812 |
| 1/8 | 0.125 | 3.1750 | 5/8 | 0.625 | 15.87500 |
| 9/64 | 0.140625 | 3.57187 | 41/64 | 0.640625 | 16.27187 |
| 5/32 | 0.15625 | 3.96875 | 21/32 | 0.65625 | 16.66875 |
| 11/64 | 0.171875 | 4.36562 | 43/64 | 0.671875 | 17.06562 |
| 3/16 | 0.1875 | 4.76250 | 11/16 | 0.6875 | 17.46250 |
| 13/64 | 0.203125 | 5.15937 | 45/64 | 0.703125 | 17.85937 |
| 7/32 | 0.21875 | 5.55625 | 23/32 | 0.71875 | 18.25625 |
| 15/64 | 0.234375 | 5.95312 | 47/64 | 0.734375 | 18.65312 |
| 1/4 | 0.250 | 6.35000 | 3/4 | 0.750 | 19.05000 |
| 17/64 | 0.265625 | 6.74687 | 49/64 | 0.765625 | 19.44687 |
| 9/32 | 0.28125 | 7.14375 | 25/32 | 0.78125 | 19.84375 |
| 19/64 | 0.296875 | 7.54062 | 51/64 | 0.796875 | 20.24062 |
| 5/16 | 0.3125 | 7.93750 | 13/16 | 0.8125 | 20.63750 |
| 21/64 | 0.328125 | 8.33437 | 53/64 | 0.828125 | 21.03437 |
| 11/32 | 0.34375 | 8.73125 | 27/32 | 0.84375 | 21.43125 |
| 23/64 | 0.359375 | 9.12812 | 55/64 | 0.859375 | 22.82812 |
| 3/8 | 0.375 | 9.52500 | 7/8 | 0.875 | 22.22500 |
| 25/64 | 0.390625 | 9.92187 | 57/64 | 0.890625 | 22.62187 |
| 13/32 | 0.40625 | 10.31875 | 29/32 | 0.90625 | 23.01875 |
| 27/64 | 0.421875 | 10.71562 | 59/64 | 0.921875 | 23.41562 |
| 7/16 | 0.4375 | 11.11250 | 15/16 | 0.9375 | 23.81250 |
| 29/64 | 0.453125 | 11.50937 | 61/64 | 0.953125 | 24.20937 |
| 15/32 | 0.46875 | 11.90625 | 31/32 | 0.96875 | 24.60625 |
| 31/64 | 0.484375 | 12.30312 | 63/64 | 0.984375 | 25.00312 |
| 1/2 | 0.500 | 12.70000 | 1 | 1.00 | 25.40000 |

## Table 5 GENERAL TORQUE SPECIFICATIONS

| Fastener size or type | N·m | in.-lb. | ft.-lb. |
|---|---|---|---|
| 5 mm | 3.4-4.9 | 30-43 | — |
| 6 mm | 5.9-7.8 | 52-69 | — |
| 8 mm | 14-19 | — | 10.0-13.5 |
| 10 mm | 25-39 | — | 19-25 |
| 12 mm | 44-61 | — | 33-45 |
| 14 mm | 73-98 | — | 54-72 |
| 16 mm | 115-155 | — | 83-115 |
| 18 mm | 165-225 | — | 125-165 |
| 20 mm | 225-325 | — | 165-240 |

## Table 6 CONVERSION TABLES

| Multiply | By | To get equivalent of |
|---|---|---|
| **Length** | | |
| Inches | 25.4 | Millimeter |
| Inches | 2.54 | Centimeter |
| Miles | 1.609 | Kilometer |
| Feet | 0.3048 | Meter |
| Millimeter | 0.03937 | Inches |
| Centimeter | 0.3937 | Inches |
| Kilometer | 0.6214 | Mile |
| Meter | 3.281 | Mile |
| **Fluid volume** | | |
| U.S. quarts | 0.9463 | Liters |
| U.S. gallons | 3.785 | Liters |
| U.S. ounces | 29.573529 | Milliliters |
| Imperial gallons | 4.54609 | Liters |
| Imperial quarts | 1.1365 | Liters |
| Liters | 0.2641721 | U.S. gallons |
| Liters | 1.0566882 | U.S. quarts |
| Liters | 33.814023 | U.S. ounces |
| Liters | 0.22 | Imperial gallons |
| Liters | 0.8799 | Imperial quarts |
| Milliliters | 0.033814 | U.S. ounces |
| Milliliters | 1.0 | Cubic centimeters |
| Milliliters | 0.001 | Liters |
| **Torque** | | |
| Foot-pounds | 1.3558 | Newton-meters |
| Foot-pounds | 0.138255 | Meters-kilograms |
| Inch-pounds | 0.11299 | Newton-meters |
| Newton-meters | 0.7375622 | Foot-pounds |
| Newton-meters | 8.8507 | Inch-pounds |
| Meters-kilograms | 7.2330139 | Foot-pounds |
| **Volume** | | |
| Cubic inches | 16.387064 | Cubic centimeters |
| Cubic centimeters | 0.0610237 | Cubic inches |
| **Temperature** | | |
| Fahrenheit | (F − 32) 0.556 | Centigrade |
| Centigrade | (C × 1.8) | Fahrenheit |
| **Weight** | | |
| Ounces | 28.3495 | Grams |
| Pounds | 0.4535924 | Kilograms |
| Grams | 0.035274 | Ounces |
| Kilograms | 2.2046224 | Pounds |
| **Pressure** | | |
| Pounds per square inch | 0.070307 | Kilograms per square centimeter |
| Kilograms per square centimeter | 14.223343 | Pounds per square inch |
| Kilopascals | 0.1450 | Pounds per square inch |
| Pounds per square inch | 6.895 | Kilopascals |
| **Speed** | | |
| Miles per hour | 1.609344 | Kilometers per hour |
| Kilometers per hour | 0.6213712 | Miles per hour |

## Table 7 TECHNICAL ABBREVIATIONS

| | |
|---|---|
| ABDC | After bottom dead center |
| ATDC | After top dead center |
| BBDC | Before bottom dead center |

(continued)

## Table 7 TECHNICAL ABBREVIATIONS (continued)

| | |
|---|---|
| BDC | Bottom dead center |
| BTDC | Before top dead center |
| C | Celsius (Centigrade) |
| cc | Cubic centimeters |
| CDI | Capacitor discharge ignition |
| cu. in. | Cubic inches |
| F | Fahrenheit |
| ft.-lb. | Foot-pounds |
| gal. | Gallons |
| H/A | High altitude |
| hp | Horsepower |
| in. | Inches |
| kg | Kilogram |
| kg/cm2 | Kilograms per square centimeter |
| kgm | Kilogram meters |
| km | Kilometer |
| L | Liter |
| m | Meter |
| MAG | Magneto |
| ml | Milliliter |
| mm | Millimeter |
| N•m | Newton-meters |
| oz. | Ounce |
| psi | Pounds per square inch |
| PTO | Power take off |
| pt. | Pint |
| qt. | Quart |
| rpm | Revolutions per minute |

## Table 8 METRIC TAP DRILL SIZES

| Metric (mm) | Drill size | Decimal equivalent | Nearest fraction |
|---|---|---|---|
| 3 × 0.50 | No. 39 | 0.0995 | 3/32 |
| 3 × 0.60 | 3/32 | 0.0937 | 3/32 |
| 4 × 0.70 | No. 30 | 0.1285 | 1/8 |
| 4 × 0.75 | 1/8 | 0.125 | 1/8 |
| 5 × 0.80 | No. 19 | 0.166 | 11/64 |
| 5 × 0.90 | No. 20 | 0.161 | 5/32 |
| 6 × 1.00 | No. 9 | 0.196 | 13/64 |
| 7 × 1.00 | 16/64 | 0.234 | 15/64 |
| 8 × 1.00 | J | 0.277 | 9/32 |
| 8 × 1.25 | 17/64 | 0.265 | 17/64 |
| 9 × 1.00 | 5/16 | 0.3125 | 5/16 |
| 9 × 1.25 | 5/16 | 0.3125 | 5/16 |
| 10 × 1.25 | 11/32 | 0.3437 | 11/32 |
| 10 × 1.50 | R | 0.339 | 11/32 |
| 11 × 1.50 | 3/8 | 0.375 | 3/8 |
| 12 × 1.50 | 13/32 | 0.406 | 13/32 |
| 12 × 1.75 | 13/32 | 0.406 | 13/32 |

# TROUBLESHOOTING

Diagnosing mechanical and electrical problems is relatively simple if you use orderly procedures and keep a few basic principles in mind. The first step in any troubleshooting procedure is to define the symptoms closely, then localize the problem. Subsequent steps involve testing and analyzing those areas that could cause the symptoms. A haphazard approach may eventually solve the problem, but it can be very costly in wasted time and unnecessary parts replacement.

Proper lubrication, maintenance and periodic tune-up, as described in Chapter Three, will reduce the necessity for troubleshooting. Even with the best of care, however, all vehicles are prone to problems that will require troubleshooting.

Never assume anything. Do not overlook the obvious. If the engine will not start, the engine stop switch or ignition switch may be shorted or damaged. When trying to start the engine, you may have flooded it.

If the engine suddenly quits, what sound did it make? Consider this and check the easiest, most accessible area first. If the engine sounded as if it ran out of fuel, check for fuel in the tank. If there is fuel in the tank, is it reaching the carburetor? If not, the fuel tank vent hose may be plugged, preventing fuel from flowing from the fuel tank to the carburetor.

If nothing obvious turns up during a quick inspection, look a little further. Learning to recognize and describe symptoms will make repairs easier for you or a mechanic at the shop. Describe problems accurately and fully.

Gather as many symptoms as possible to aid in diagnosis. Note whether the engine lost power gradually or all at once, what color smoke came from the exhaust and so on. Remember that the more complicated a machine is, the easier it is to troubleshoot because symptoms point to specific problems.

After defining the vehicle's symptoms, test and analyze areas that could cause the problem. Guessing at the cause of a problem may provide the solution, but it can easily lead to frustration, wasted time and a series of expensive, unnecessary parts replacements.

You do not need expensive equipment or complicated test gear to determine whether repairs can be attempted at home. A few simple checks could save a large repair bill and lost time while the bike sits in a dealership service department. On the other hand, be realistic and do not attempt repairs beyond your abilities. Dealership service departments tend to charge heavily for putting together a disassembled engine that may have been abused. Some will not even take on such a job. Use common sense and do not get in over your head.

## OPERATING REQUIREMENTS

An engine needs three basics to run properly: correct fuel/air mixture, compression and a spark at the right time. If one basic requirement is missing, the engine will not run. Four stroke engine operating principles are described in Chapter Four under *Engine Principles*.

## TROUBLESHOOTING INSTRUMENTS

Chapter One lists the instruments needed for the troubleshooting procedures and provides detailed instruction on their use.

## STARTING THE ENGINE

If your engine refuses to start, frustration can cause you to forget basic starting principles and procedures. The following outline will guide you through the basic starting procedure. In all cases, make sure there is an adequate supply of fuel in the tank.

A rich air/fuel mixture is required when starting a cold engine. To accomplish this, the carburetor is equipped with a choke circuit and primer circuit. Use the choke circuit when the ambient temperature is -15 to 35° C (5 to 95° F). Use the primer circuit when the ambient temperature is below - 15° C (5° F).

The choke circuit is controlled by a choke lever (A, **Figure 1**) mounted on the handlebar. To *open* the choke circuit for starting a cold engine, push the choke lever all the way to the left (ON position). After the engine starts and warms up, push the choke lever all the way to the right (OFF position).

The primer circuit is operated by the primer knob (**Figure 2**) mounted on the carburetor float bowl. To use the primer circuit, push the knob in two or three times before operating the starter button or recoil starter.

*CAUTION*
*When trying to start the engine in the following procedure, Do not operate the*

*starter motor for more than 5 seconds at a time as this can cause the starter to overheat and become damaged. Wait approximately 10 seconds before operating the starter button again. If necessary, use the recoil starter.*

**Starting a Cold Engine**

1. Shift the transmission into NEUTRAL and set the parking brake.
2. Turn the ignition switch to the ON position.
3. Turn the fuel valve to the ON position.
4. Move the choke lever (A, **Figure 1**) to its ON position.

*NOTE*
*If the ambient temperature is below - 15° C (5° F), push the primer knob (**Figure 2**) two or three times before operating the starter button or recoil starter.*

5. With the throttle completely closed, push the starter button or operate the recoil starter.

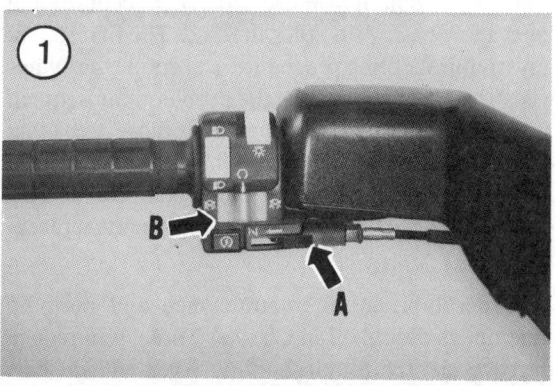

6. When the engine starts, work the throttle slightly to keep it running.

7. Idle the engine for approximately a minute or until the throttle responds cleanly, then move the choke lever to its OFF position.

### Starting a Warm or Hot Engine

1. Shift the transmission into NEUTRAL and set the parking brake.

2. Turn the ignition switch to the ON position.

3. Turn the fuel valve to the ON position.

4. Make sure the choke lever (A, **Figure 1**) is in its OFF position.

5. Open the throttle slightly and push the starter button or operate the recoil starter.

### Starting a Flooded Engine

If the engine is hard to start and there is a strong gasoline smell, the engine is probably flooded. If so, place the choke (A, **Figure 1**) in the OFF position. Then open the throttle all the way and push the starter button or operate the recoil starter until the

engine starts. If the engine is flooded badly, you may have to remove the spark plug and dry off its insulator, or install a new plug. When a flooded engine first starts to run, it will initially cough and run slowly as it burns the excess fuel. Then as this excess fuel is burned, the engine will accelerate quickly. Release the throttle at this point. Because a flooded engine smokes badly when it first starts to run, start the engine outside and in a well-ventilated area with its muffler pointing away from all objects. Do not start a flooded engine in a garage or other closed area.

*NOTE*
*If the engine refuses to start, check the carburetor overflow hose attached to the fitting at the bottom of the float bowl (**Figure 3**). If fuel is running out of the hose, the float valve is stuck open or leaking, allowing the carburetor to overfill. If this problem exists, remove the carburetor and correct the problem as described in Chapter Eight.*

### STARTING DIFFICULTY

If the engine cranks but is difficult to start, or will not start at all, do not drain the battery. Check for obvious problems even before getting out your tools. Go down the following list step by step. Perform each step while remembering the three engine operating requirements described in this chapter.

If the engine still will not start, refer to the appropriate troubleshooting procedure that follows in this chapter.

1. Is the choke lever in the right position? See *Starting the Engine* in this chapter.

2. Is there fuel in the tank? Fill the tank if necessary. Has it been a while since the engine has run? If in doubt, drain the fuel and fill with a fresh tank full. Check for a clogged fuel tank vent tube (**Figure 4**). Remove the tube from the filler cap, then wipe off one end and blow through it. Remove the filler cap and check for a plugged hose nozzle.

*WARNING*
*Do not use an open flame to check in the tank. A serious explosion is certain to result.*

3. Disconnect the fuel line (**Figure 5**) from the carburetor and insert the end of the hose into a clear container. Turn the fuel valve to the ON position and

see if fuel flows freely. If fuel does not flow and there
is a fuel filter installed in the fuel line, remove the
filter and turn the fuel valve on again. If fuel flows,
the filter is clogged and must be replaced. If no fuel
comes out, the fuel valve may be shut off, blocked
by foreign matter, or the fuel cap vent may be
plugged. Reconnect the fuel line to the carburetor
fitting.

4. If you suspect that the cylinder is flooded, or there
is a strong smell of gasoline, open the throttle all the
way and push the starter button or operate the recoil
starter. If the cylinder is severely flooded (fouled or
wet spark plug), remove the spark plug and dry the
base and electrode thoroughly with a soft cloth.
Reinstall the plug and attempt to start the engine. See
*Starting the Engine* in this chapter.

5. Check the carburetor overflow hose on the bottom of the float bowl (**Figure 3**). If fuel is running
from the hose, the float valve is stuck open or leaking. Turn the fuel valve off and tap the carburetor a
few times. Then turn on the fuel valve. If fuel continues to run out of the hose, remove and repair the
carburetor as described in Chapter Eight. Check the
carburetor vent hoses to make sure they are clear.
Check the end of the hoses for contamination.

*NOTE*
*If fuel is reaching the carburetor, the fuel*
*system could still be the problem. The*
*jets (pilot and main) could be plugged*
*or the air filter could be severely re-*
*stricted. However, before removing the*
*carburetor, continue with Step 6 to make*
*sure that the ignition provides an ade-*
*quate spark.*

6. Make sure the engine stop switch (B, **Figure 1**)
is operating correctly. If necessary, test the engine
stop switch as described under *Switches* in Chapter
Nine.

*NOTE*
*If you have installed an aftermarket kill*
*switch, check the switch for proper op-*
*eration. This switch may be faulty.*

7. Is the spark plug high-tension wire and cap (**Figure 6**) on tight. Push it on and slightly rotate it to
clean the electrical connection between the spark
plug and the wire connector. Hold the high-tension
wire and screw the plug cap on tightly.

*NOTE*
*If the engine will still not start, continue*
*with the following.*

8. Perform a spark test as described under *Engine
Fails to Start (Spark Test)* in this chapter. If there is
a strong spark, perform Step 9. If there is no spark
or if the spark is very weak, test the ignition system
as described under *Ignition System* in this chapter.

9. Check cylinder compression as follows:

   a. Turn the engine stop switch (B, **Figure 1**) to
      its OFF position.

   b. Turn the fuel valve off.

   c. Remove the spark plug and ground the spark
      plug shell against the cylinder head.

   d. Put your finger tightly over the spark plug
      hole.

   e. Operate the starter, or have an assistant operate
      the recoil starter. When the piston comes up
      on the compression stroke, pressure in the
      cylinder should force your finger from the
      spark plug hole. If your finger pops off, the
      cylinder probably has sufficient compression
      to start the engine.

*NOTE*
*You may still have a compression problem even though it seems good with the previous test. Check engine compression using a compression gauge as described under Tune-up in Chapter Three.*

**Engine Fails to Start
(Spark Test)**

An engine that refuses to start or is difficult to start is very frustrating. More often than not, the problem is minor and can be found with a simple and logical troubleshooting approach.

Perform the following spark test to determine if the ignition system is producing adequate spark. When checking spark, turn the engine stop switch to RUN and the ignition switch to ON.

*CAUTION*
*Before removing the spark plug in Step 1, clean all dirt and debris away from the plug base. Dirt that falls into the cylinder will cause rapid engine wear.*

1. Disconnect the plug wire and remove the spark plug.

*NOTE*
*A spark tester (**Figure 7**) is a useful tool for checking the ignition system. Insert this tool in the spark plug cap and ground its base against the cylinder head. A number of different spark testers are available through motorcycle and automotive parts stores. The spark tester shown in **Figure 7** is manufactured by Motion Pro.*

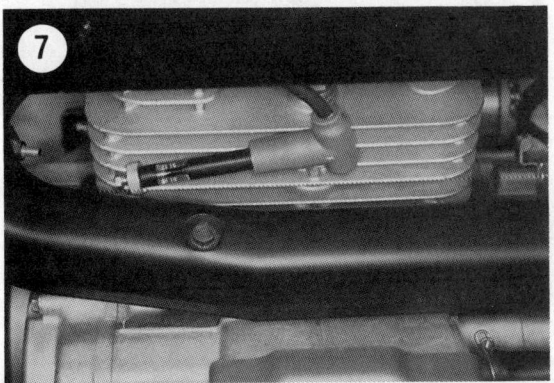

2. If using an adjustable spark tester, set its air gap to 6 mm (0.24 in.).

3. Insert the spark plug (or spark tester) into the plug cap and touch its base against the cylinder head to ground it (**Figure 7**). Position the plug so you can see the electrodes.

*CAUTION*
*Mount the spark plug or spark tester away from the plug hole in the cylinder head so that the spark from the plug or tester cannot ignite the gasoline vapor in the cylinder.*

4. Turn the engine over with the starter button or operate the recoil starter. A fat blue spark should be evident across the spark plug electrodes or spark tester terminals.

*WARNING*
*Do not hold or touch the spark plug (or spark checker), wire or connector when making a spark check. A serious electrical shock may result.*

5. If the spark is good, check for one or more of the following possible malfunctions:
    a. Obstructed fuel line or fuel filter (if used).
    b. Low compression or engine damage.
    c. Flooded engine.

6. If the spark is weak (white or yellow in color) or if there is no spark, check for one or more of the following conditions:
    a. Fouled or wet spark plug. If you get a spark across a spark tester but not across the original spark plug, the plug is fouled. Repeat the spark test with a new spark plug.
    b. Loose or damaged spark plug cap connection. Hold the spark plug wire and turn the spark plug cap to tighten it. Then install the spark plug into the cap and repeat the spark test. If there is still no spark, bypass the plug cap as described in the next step.
    c. Check for a damaged spark plug cap. Hold the spark plug wire and unscrew the spark plug cap (**Figure 6**). Then hold the end of the spark plug wire 6 mm (0.24 in.) from the cylinder head as shown in **Figure 8**. Have an assistant turn the engine over and repeat the spark test. If there is a strong spark, the spark plug cap is faulty. Replace the plug cap and repeat the spark test.

d. Loose or damaged spark plug wire connections (at coil and plug cap).
e. Faulty ignition coil or faulty ignition coil ground wire connection.
f. Faulty ICM unit or stator coil(s).
g. Sheared flywheel key.
h. Loose flywheel nut.
i. Loose electrical connections.
j. Dirty electrical connections.

*NOTE*
*If the engine backfires when you attempt to start it, the ignition timing may be incorrect. Because the ignition timing is not adjustable, incorrect ignition timing is caused by a loose flywheel, sheared flywheel key, loose ignition pulse generator mounting screws or connector, or a damaged or defective ignition system component. Refer to* **Ignition System** *in this chapter.*

### Engine is Difficult to Start

The following section groups the three main engine operating systems with probable causes.

### Electrical System

Honda ignition systems are relatively trouble-free. If an ignition problem occurs, it can usually be traced to a point in the wiring harness, at the connectors or in one of the switches.

1. *Spark plug:*
   a. Fouled spark plug.
   b. Incorrect spark plug gap.
   c. Incorrect spark plug heat range (too cold). See Chapter Three.
   d. Worn or damaged spark plug electrodes.
   e. Damaged spark plug.
   f. Damaged spark plug cap or spark plug wire.

*NOTE*
*Refer to* **Reading Spark Plugs** *in Chapter Three for additional information.*

2. *Ignition coil:*
   a. Loose or damaged ignition coil leads.
   b. Cracked ignition coil body—look for carbon tracks on the ignition coil.
   c. Loose or corroded ground wire.
3. *Switches and wiring:*

a. Dirty or loose fitting terminals.
b. Damaged wires or connectors (**Figure 9**).
c. Damaged ignition switch.
d. Damaged engine stop switch.
4. *Electrical components:*
   a. Damaged ignition pulse generator.
   b. Damaged ICM unit.
   c. Sheared flywheel Woodruff key.

### Fuel System

A contaminated fuel system will cause engine starting and performance related problems. It only takes a small amount of dirt in the fuel valve, fuel line or carburetor to cause a problem.

1. *Air filter:*
   a. Plugged air filter element.
   b. Plugged air filter housing.
   c. Leaking or damaged air filter housing-to-carburetor air boot.
2. *Fuel valve:*
   a. Plugged fuel hose.
   b. Plugged fuel valve filter.
3. *Fuel tank:*
   a. No fuel.
   b. Plugged fuel filter.
   c. Plugged fuel tank breather hose (**Figure 4**).
   d. Contaminated fuel.

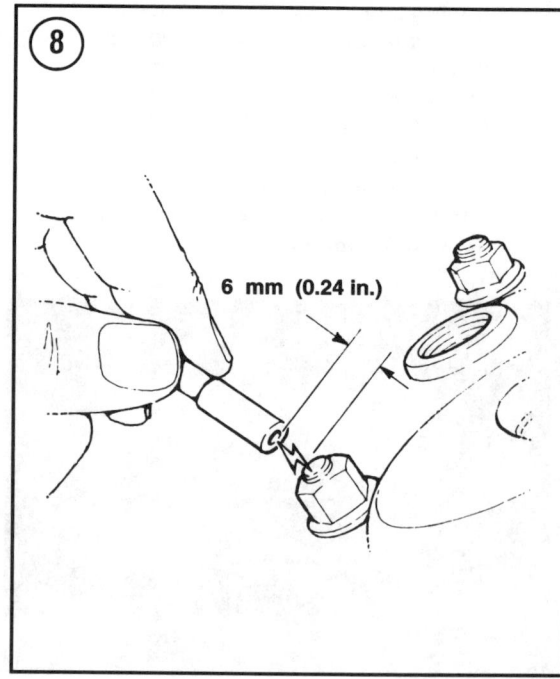

6 mm (0.24 in.)

4. *Carburetor*:
   a. Plugged or damaged choke system.
   b. Plugged main jet.
   c. Plugged pilot jet.
   d. Loose pilot jet or main jet.
   e. Plugged pilot jet air passage.
   f. Incorrect float level.
   g. Leaking or damaged float.
   h. Worn or damaged needle valve.

### Engine Compression

Check engine compression as described in Chapter Three. To obtain a more accurate gauge of engine wear, perform an engine leak down test. Refer to *Engine Leak Down Test* in this chapter.
1. *Cylinder and cylinder head*:
   a. Loose spark plug.
   b. Missing spark plug gasket.
   c. Leaking cylinder head gasket.
   d. Leaking cylinder base gasket.
   e. Worn or seized piston, piston rings and/or cylinder.
   f. Loose cylinder and/or cylinder head fasteners.
   g. Cylinder head incorrectly installed and/or torqued.
   h. Warped cylinder head.
   i. Valve(s) adjusted too tight.
   j. Bent valve.
   k. Worn valve and/or seat.
   l. Worn or damaged valve guide(s).
   m. Damaged compression release cam (mounted on camshaft).

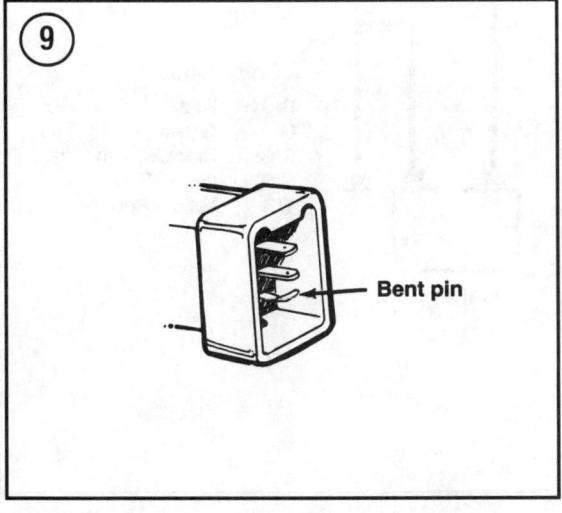

⑨

Bent pin

n. Bent pushrod(s).
o. Damaged cam follower.
2. *Piston and piston rings*:
   a. Worn piston rings.
   b. Damaged piston rings.
   c. Piston seizure or piston damage.
3. *Crankcase and crankshaft*:
   a. Seized connecting rod.
   b. Damaged crankcases.

### POOR IDLE SPEED PERFORMANCE

If the engine starts but off-idle performance is poor (engine hesitates or misfires), check the following:
1. Clogged or damaged air filter element.
2. *Carburetor*:
   a. Plugged pilot jet.
   b. Loose pilot jet.
   c. Damaged choke system.
   d. Incorrect throttle cable adjustment.
   e. Incorrect pilot screw adjustment.
   f. Flooded carburetor (visually check carburetor overflow hose for fuel).
   g. Vacuum piston does not slide smoothly in carburetor bore.
   h. Loose carburetor.
   i. Damaged intake manifold O-ring.
3. *Fuel*:
   a. Water and/or alcohol in fuel.
   b. Old fuel.
4. *Engine*:
   a. Low engine compression.
5. *Electrical system*:
   a. Damaged spark plug.
   b. Damaged ignition coil.
   c. Damaged ignition pulse generator.
   d. Damaged ICM unit.

### POOR MEDIUM AND HIGH SPEED PERFORMANCE

Refer to *Engine is Difficult to Start*, then check the following:
1. *Carburetor*:
   a. Incorrect fuel level.
   b. Incorrect jet needle clip position (if adjustable).
   c. Plugged or loose main jet.
   d. Plugged fuel line.

e.  Plugged fuel valve.

f.  Plugged fuel tank vent tube.

2.  Plugged air filter element.

3.  *Engine:*

a.  Incorrect valve timing.

b.  Weak valve springs.

4.  *Other considerations:*

a.  Overheating.

b.  Clutch slippage.

c.  Brake drag.

d.  Engine oil level too high.

## ELECTRIC STARTING SYSTEM

This section describes troubleshooting procedures for the electric starting system (**Figure 10**). A
fully charged battery, ohmmeter and jumper cables

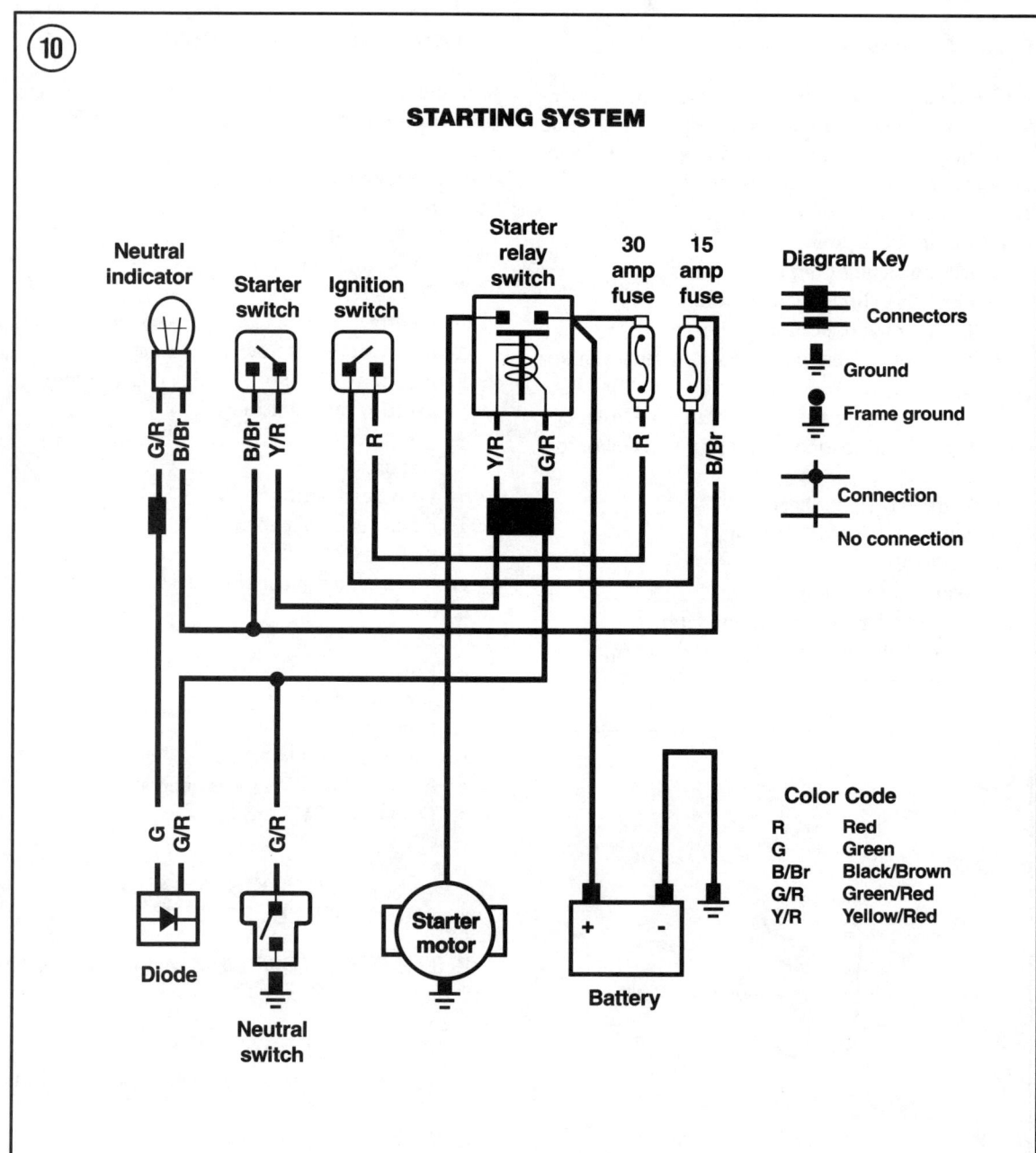

**STARTING SYSTEM**

are required to perform many of these troubleshooting procedures.

## Description

An electric starter motor (**Figure 11**) is used on all models. The starter motor is mounted horizontally at the left side of the engine.

The electric starting system requires a fully charged battery to provide the large amount of current required to operate the starter motor. A charge coil (mounted on the stator plate) and a voltage regulator, connected in circuit with the battery, keeps the battery charged while the engine is running. The battery can also be charged externally.

The starting circuit consists of the battery, starter motor, neutral/reverse switch, neutral indicator, starter relay, ignition switch and engine stop switch.

The starter relay (**Figure 12**) carries the heavy electrical current to the starter motor. Depressing the starter switch allows current to flow through the starter relay coil. The starter relay contacts close and allow current to flow from the battery through the starter relay to the starter motor.

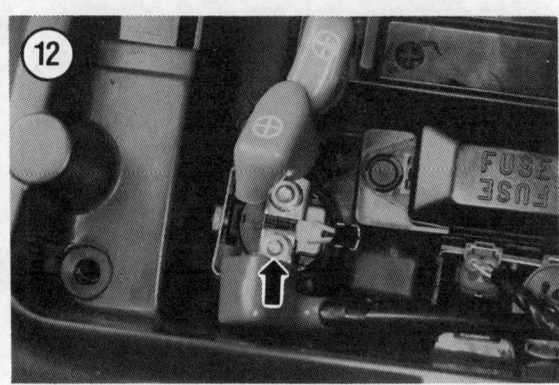

When the ignition switch is turned on and the engine stop switch is in its RUN position, the starter motor can be operated only if the transmission is in NEUTRAL.

> *CAUTION*
> *Do not operate an electric starter motor continuously for more than 5 seconds. Allow the motor to cool for at least 10 seconds between attempts to start the engine.*

## Troubleshooting

Before troubleshooting the starting circuit, make sure that:

a. The battery is fully charged.
b. Battery cables are the proper size and length. Replace cables that are undersize or damaged.
c. All electrical connections are clean and tight.
d. The wiring harness is in good condition, with no worn or frayed insulation or loose harness sockets.
e. The fuel system is filled with an adequate supply of fresh gasoline.

### Starter Troubleshooting

If the starter does not operate, perform the following tests.

When operating the starter switch, turn the engine stop switch to RUN and the ignition switch to ON.

1. Refer to Chapter Fifteen and remove the following components to access the starting circuit in this procedure:
    a. Seat.
    b. Front fender.
2. First check the 30 amp main fuse. Open the fuse holder and pull the fuse out and visually inspect it. If the fuse is blown, replace it as described under *Fuse* in Chapter Nine. If the main fuse is good, reinstall it, then continue with Step 3.
3. Test the battery as described under *Battery* in Chapter Three. Note the following:
    a. If the battery is fully charged, perform Step 3.
    b. If necessary, clean and recharge the battery. If the battery is damaged, replace it.
4. Check for loose, corroded or damaged battery cables. Check at the battery, starter motor, starter relay and all cable-to-frame connections.

5. Turn the ignition switch on. Then push the starter button and listen for a click sound at the starter relay switch (**Figure 12**). Note the following:

   a. If the relay clicked, perform Step 6.

   b. If the relay did not click, go to Step 7.

6. Test the battery as follows:

   a. Park the vehicle on level ground and set the parking brake. Shift the transmission into NEUTRAL.

   b. Remove the fuel tank as described in Chapter Eight.

   c. Disconnect the cable from the starter motor (**Figure 11**).

*WARNING*
*Because a spark will be produced in the following steps, perform this procedure away from gasoline or other volatile liquids. Make sure that there is no spilt gasoline on the Honda or gasoline fumes in the work area.*

   d. Momentarily connect a jumper cable (thick gauge wire) from the positive battery terminal to the starter motor terminal (**Figure 11**). If the starter motor is working properly, it will turn when making the jumper cable connection.

   e. If the starter motor did not turn, remove the starter motor and service it as described in Chapter Nine.

   f. If the starter motor turned, check for a loose or damaged starter motor cable. If the cable is okay, the starter relay (**Figure 12**) is faulty. Replace the starter relay and retest.

7. Check that the neutral indicator light (A, **Figure 13**) comes on when the transmission is in neutral and the ignition switch is turned on. Note the following:

   a. If the neutral indicator light does not work properly, check for a blown bulb. If the bulb is okay, perform Step 8.

   b. If the neutral indicator light works properly, go to Step 9.

8. Test the following items as described in Chapter Nine:

   a. Neutral/reverse switch.

   b. Ignition switch.

   c. Diode.

9. Perform the starter relay switch voltage test as described under *Starter Relay Switch* in Chapter Nine. Note the following:

   a. If the voltmeter shows battery voltage, continue with Step 10.

   b. If there was no voltage reading, check the ignition switch and starter switch as described in Chapter Nine. If both switches are good, check the yellow/red wire continuity between the starter switch and the starter relay switch.

10. Perform the starter relay switch continuity test as described under *Starter Relay Switch* in Chapter Nine. Note the following:

   a. If the meter reading is correct, continue with Step 11.

   b. If the meter reading is incorrect, check for an open circuit in the yellow/red and light green/red wires. Check the wire ends for loose or damaged connectors.

11. If you have not found the starting system problem after performing these steps in order, recheck the wiring system for dirty or loose-fitting terminals or damaged wires; clean and repair as required.

12. Make sure all connectors disconnected during this procedure are free of corrosion and reconnected properly.

**Starter Motor Turns Slowly**

If the starter motor turns slowly and all engine components and systems are normal, perform the following:

1. Test the battery as described in Chapter Three.

2. Check for the following:

   a. Loose or corroded battery terminals.

   b. Loose or corroded battery ground cable.

   c. Loose starter motor cable.

3. Remove, disassemble and bench test the starter as described under *Starter* in Chapter Nine.

4. Check the starter for binding during operation. Disassemble the starter and check the armature shaft for bending or damage. Also, check the starter clutch as described in Chapter Five.

### Starter Motor Turns but the Engine Does Not

If the starter motor turns but the engine does not, perform the following:

1. Check for a damaged starter clutch (Chapter Five).

2. Check for damaged starter reduction gears (Chapter Five).

### CHARGING SYSTEM

The charging system (**Figure 14**) consists of the battery, alternator and a voltage regulator/rectifier. A 30 amp main fuse protects the circuit.

A malfunction in the charging system generally causes the battery to remain undercharged.

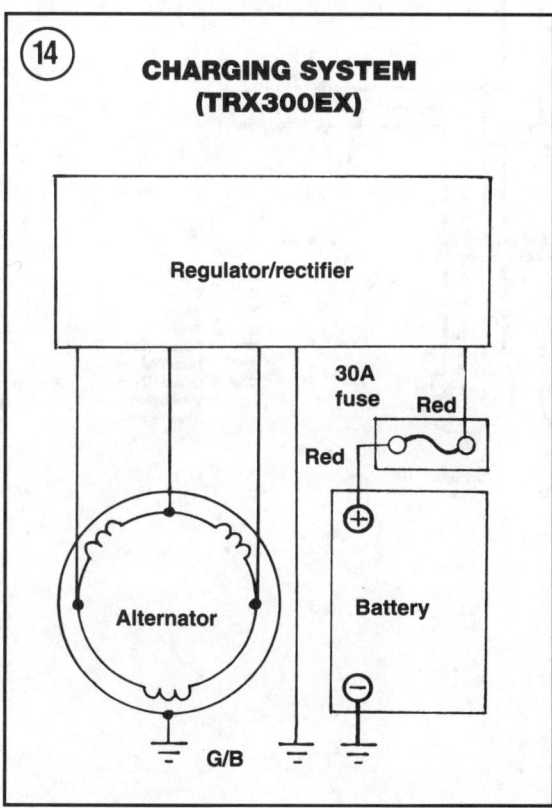

**CHARGING SYSTEM (TRX300EX)**

Regulator/rectifier

30A fuse Red

Red

Battery

Alternator

G/B

### Battery Discharging

1. Check all of the connections (**Figure 14**). Make sure they are tight and free of corrosion.

2. Perform the *Charging System Leakage Test* as described in Chapter Nine. Note the following:
   a. If the current leakage exceeds 0.1mA, perform Step 3.
   b. If the current leakage is 0.1mA or less, perform Step 4.

3. Perform the *Regulator/Rectifier Unit Resistance Test* described in Chapter Nine. Note the following:
   a. If the resistance readings are correct, perform the *Stator Coil Resistance Test* described in Chapter Nine. If the test results are correct, the ignition switch is probably faulty; test the ignition switch as described in Chapter Nine.
   b. If the resistance readings are incorrect, replace the regulator/rectifier unit and retest.

4. Perform the *Charging Voltage Test* in Chapter Nine. Note the following:
   a. If the test readings are correct, perform Step 5.
   b. If the test readings are incorrect, go to Step 6.

5. Test the battery with a battery tester and note the following:

> *NOTE*
> *If you do not have access to a battery tester, remove the battery from your Honda and take it to a dealership for testing.*

   a. If the test readings are correct, check for an open circuit in the wiring harness and for dirty or loose-fitting terminals; clean and repair as required.
   b. If the test readings are incorrect, the battery is faulty or electrical components are overloading the charging system.

6. Perform the battery charging line and ground line tests as described under *Regulator/Rectifier Wiring Harness Test* in Chapter Nine. Note the following:
   a. If the test readings are correct, perform Step 7.
   b. If the test readings are incorrect, check for an open circuit in the wiring harness and for dirty or loose-fitting terminals; clean and repair as required.

7. Perform the charging coil line tests at the regulator/rectifier connector as described under *Regula-*

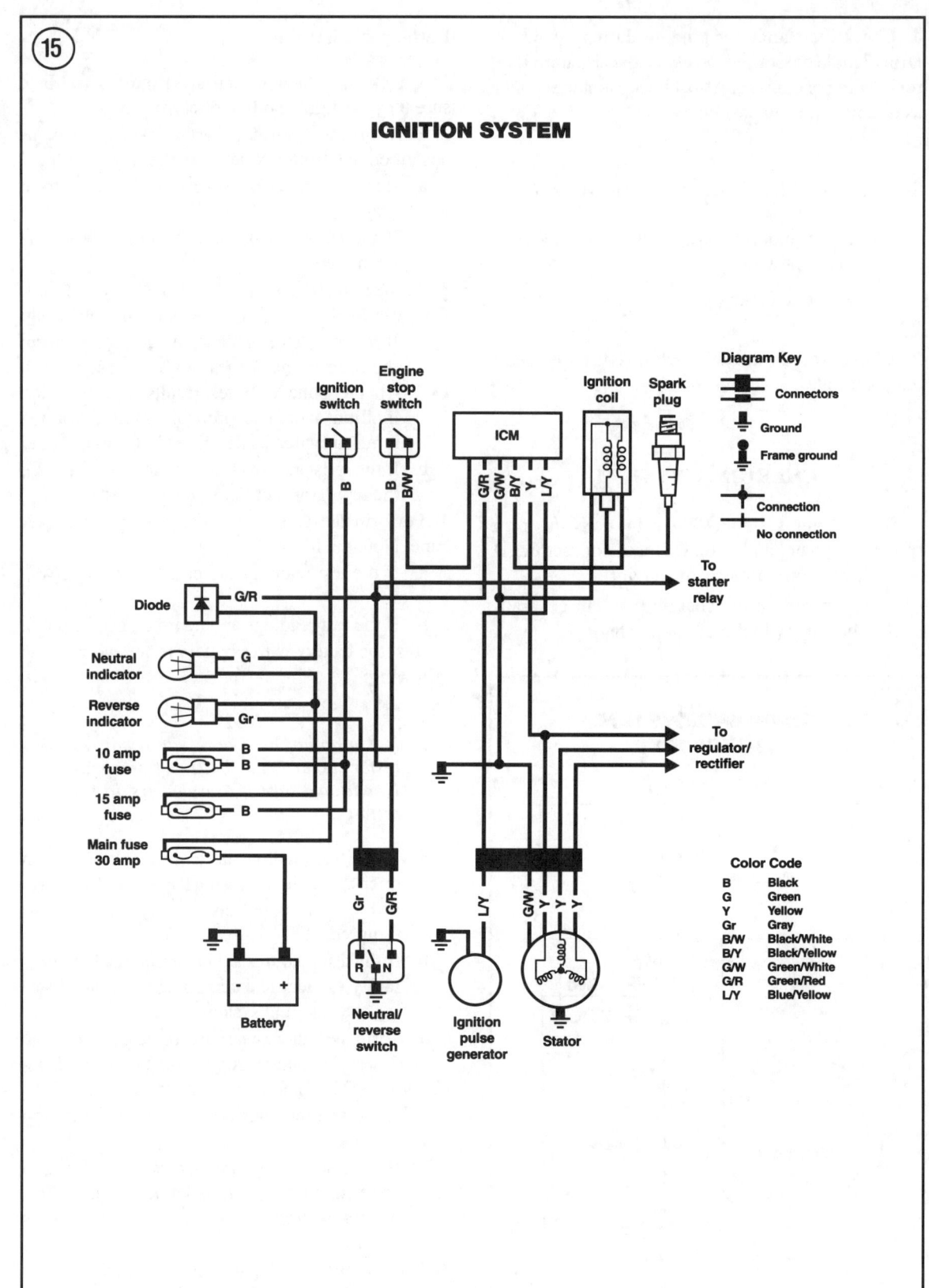

IGNITION SYSTEM

*tor/Rectifier Wiring Harness Test* in Chapter Nine. Note the following:

    a. If the test readings are incorrect, replace the alternator and retest.

    b. If the test readings are correct, replace the regulator/rectifier unit and retest.

### Battery Overcharging

If the battery is overcharging, the regulator/rectifier unit is faulty. Replace the regulator/rectifier unit as described in Chapter Nine.

### IGNITION SYSTEM

All models are equipped with a capacitor discharge ignition (CDI) system (**Figure 15**). This solid state system uses no contact breaker point or other moving parts.

Because of the solid state design, problems with the capacitor discharge system are rare. If a problem occurs, it generally causes a weak spark or no spark at all. An ignition system with a weak spark or no spark is relatively easy to troubleshoot. It is difficult, however, to troubleshoot an ignition system that only malfunctions when the engine is hot or under load.

### Test Notes

Honda recommends the use of the Imrie Diagnostic Tester (Model 625) or the Honda peak voltage adapter (part no. 07HGJ-0020100) with a commercially available digital multimeter with an impedance of 10M ohms/DVC minimum to troubleshoot the ignition system. Because these are not practical tools for the home mechanic, the following troubleshooting section isolates and tests the different ignition system components and wiring that can be performed by the home mechanic. If you cannot locate the problem after performing the troubleshooting procedure, refer further testing to a Honda dealership.

### Troubleshooting

> *NOTE*
> *If the problem is intermittent, perform the tests with the engine cold, then hot. Then compare the test results.*

1. Perform the following ignition spark gap test as follows:

> *NOTE*
> *If you do not have an adjustable spark tester, perform the spark test as described under **Engine Fails to Start (Spark Test)** in this chapter.*

    a. Disconnect the plug wire.

> *NOTE*
> *A spark tester is a useful tool to check the ignition system. **Figure 7** shows the Motion Pro Ignition System Tester. This tool is inserted in the spark plug cap and its base is ground against the cylinder head. The tool's air gap is adjustable, and it allows you to see and hear the spark while testing the intensity of the spark.*

    b. Adjust the spark tester so that its air gap distance is 6 mm (0.24 in.).

    c. Insert the spark tester into the plug cap and touch its base against the cylinder head to ground it (**Figure 7**). Position the tester so you can see its terminals.

> *CAUTION*
> *If you removed the spark plug from the engine, mount the spark tester away from the plug hole in the cylinder head so that the spark from the tester cannot ignite the gasoline vapors in the cylinder.*

    d. Turn the engine over with the starter button or operate the recoil starter. A fat blue spark should be evident across the spark tester terminals.

> *WARNING*
> *Do not hold the spark tester or connector or a serious electrical shock may result.*

    e. If the spark jumps the gap and is dark blue in color, the ignition system is good. If the spark does not jump the gap, hold the spark plug cable and twist the plug cap a few times to tighten it. Then recheck the spark gap. If there is still no spark or if it jumps the gap but is yellow or white in color, continue with Step 2.

f. Remove the spark tester from the spark plug cap.

2. Unscrew the spark plug cap (**Figure 6**) from the ignition coil plug wire and hold the end of the wire 6 mm (0.24 in.) from the cylinder head and away from the spark plug hole as shown in **Figure 8**. Have an assistant turn the engine over for you. A fat blue spark should be evident passing from the end of the wire to the cylinder head. If there is no spark, perform Step 3.

3. Test the ignition coil secondary and primary resistance as described under *Ignition Coil Testing* in Chapter Nine. Note the following:

   a. If the ignition coil is good, perform Step 4.

   b. If the ignition coil fails to pass the tests described in Chapter Nine, the ignition coil is probably faulty. However, before replacing the ignition coil, take it to a dealership and have them test the spark with an ignition coil tester. Replace the ignition coil if faulty and retest the ignition system.

4. Test the engine stop switch as described under *Switches* in Chapter Nine. Note the following:

   a. If the switch is good, perform Step 5.

   b. If the switch fails to pass the test as described in Chapter Nine, the switch is faulty and must be replaced. Replace the switch and retest the ignition system.

5. Test the ignition switch as described under *Switches* in Chapter Nine. Note the following:

   a. If the switch is good, perform Step 6.

   b. If the switch fails to pass the test as described in Chapter Nine, the switch is faulty and must be replaced. Replace the switch and retest the ignition system.

6. Perform the *AC Sensor Line Wiring Test* in Chapter Nine. Note the following:

   a. If both tests are correct, perform Step 7.

   b. If one or both tests are incorrect, check the wiring between each connector tested in the procedure. Repair or replace the damaged wiring or connectors.

7. Perform the *Pulse Generator Resistance Test* in chapter Nine. Note the following:

   a. If the resistance reading is correct, perform Step 8.

   b. If the resistance reading is incorrect, replace the stator coil assembly as described under *Alternator Cover* in Chapter Five.

8. If you have not been able to locate the damaged component, check the ignition system wiring harness and connectors. Check for damaged wires or loose, dirty or damaged connectors. If the wiring and connectors are good, the ICM unit (**Figure 16**) is faulty and must be replaced.

*NOTE*
*The ICM unit cannot be tested effectively using conventional equipment. Because ignition system problems are most often caused by an open or short circuit or poor wiring connections, replace the ICM only if you are certain that all other ignition system components are functioning properly. The ICM is expensive, and once purchased, generally cannot be returned. Therefore, repeat the preceding tests to verify the condition of the ignition system before replacing the ICM.*

9. Install all parts previously removed. Make sure all of the connections are free of corrosion and are reconnected properly.

## LIGHTING  SYSTEM

### Faulty Bulbs

If the headlight or taillight bulb(s) continually burn out, check for one or more of the following conditions:

1. Incorrect bulb type. See Chapter Nine for the correct replacement bulb types for your model.

2. Damaged battery.

3. Damaged rectifier/regulator.

4. Damaged ignition switch and/or light switch.

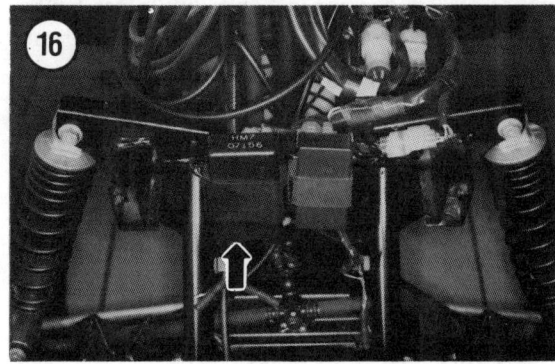

## Headlight Operates Darker than Normal

Check for one or more of the following conditions:

1. Incorrect bulb type. See Chapter Nine for the correct replacement bulbs for your model.

2. Charging system problem.

3. Too many electric accessories added to the wiring harness. If you have added one or more aftermarket electrical accessories to the wiring system, disconnect them one at a time and then start the engine and check the headlight operation. If this is the cause of the problem, contact the aftermarket manufacturer for more information.

4. Incorrect ground connection.

5. Poor main and/or light switch electrical contacts.

## Lighting System Troubleshooting

If the headlight and/or taillight do not work, perform the following test procedures.

1. Check for a blown bulb as described in Step 1 in the following section.

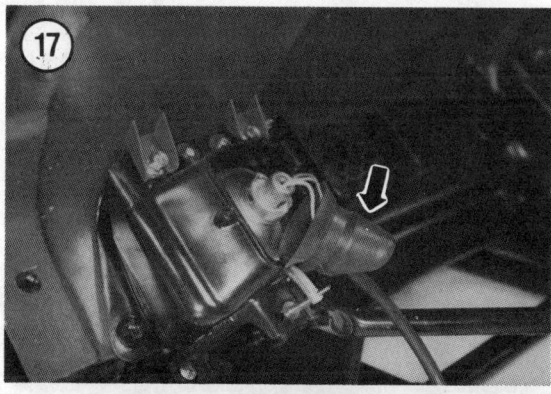

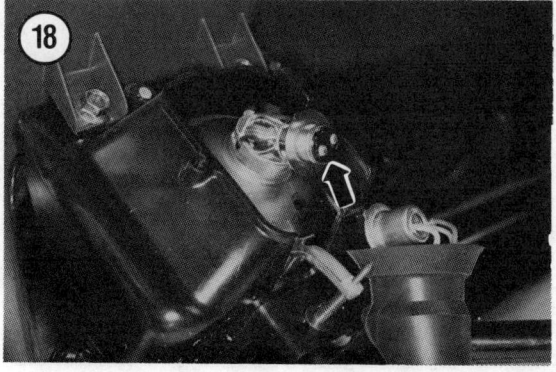

2. Check all of the lighting system connectors and wires for loose or damaged connections.

3. Check the main fuse as described in Chapter Nine. Replace a blown or damaged fuse.

4. Test the battery as described in Chapter Three. Note the following:

   a. If the battery is fully charged, perform Step 5.

   b. If necessary, clean and recharge the battery. If the battery is damaged or will not hold a charge, replace it. If you bought the vehicle used, check the battery to make sure it is the correct one (size and type) for your model. See *Battery* in Chapter Three.

5. Test the ignition switch as described in Chapter Nine. If the ignition switch is good, continue with Step 6.

6. If you have not been able to solve the problem, perform the *Lighting System Check* in the following section.

## Headlight

If the headlights do not come on, perform the following test.

1. Remove the headlight bulb (Chapter Nine) and disconnect the headlight socket wiring harness (**Figure 17**) from the main wiring harness.

   a. Connect an ohmmeter to the bulb terminals (**Figure 18**). The reading should be zero ohms. Replace the bulb if the ohmmeter indicates an open circuit.

   b. Connect an ohmmeter to one of the headlight socket terminals and to its mating electrical connector, then check for continuity. Repeat for the other wires and their terminals. Each reading should indicate continuity. If any reading does not meet specifications, replace the headlight socket if it cannot be repaired.

   c. If both sets of readings were correct, continue with Step 2.

2. Install the headlight bulb into its socket and reconnect the socket back into the wiring harness. Do not install the socket into its headlight housing. The headlight bulb and socket must be connected to the wiring harness when making the following tests.

3. Switch a voltmeter to its 20 volt (DC) scale. In Step 4 and Step 5, connect the voltmeter leads to the headlight socket electrical connectors with the headlight connector connected to the main wiring harness.

4. Connect the voltmeter positive lead (+) to the headlight connector white lead and the voltmeter negative lead (–) to the headlight connector green lead. Turn the ignition switch to its ON position and the dimmer switch to its LO position. Note the voltmeter reading:

a. If the voltmeter reads battery voltage, continue with Step 5.

b. If the voltmeter does not read battery voltage check the wiring harness from the ignition switch to the headlight socket for damage.

5. Turn the ignition switch to its OFF position. Connect the voltmeter positive lead (+) to the headlight connector blue/black lead and the voltmeter negative lead (–) to the headlight connector green lead. Turn the ignition switch to its ON position and the dimmer switch to its HI position. Note the voltmeter reading:

a. If the voltmeter reads battery voltage, continue with Step 6.

b. If the voltmeter does not read battery voltage, check the wiring harness from the ignition switch to the headlight socket for damage.

6. Turn the ignition switch to its OFF position and disconnect the voltmeter leads.

### Assist headlight

If the assist headlight does not come on, perform the following test.

> *NOTE*
> *The assist headlight uses a quartz-halogen bulb. Because traces of oil on this type of bulb will reduce the life of the bulb, do not touch the bulb glass with your fingers. Clean any traces of oil or other chemicals from the bulb with a cloth moistened in isopropyl alcohol or lacquer thinner.*

1. Remove the assist headlight bulb (Chapter Nine) and disconnect the bulb socket two-prong connector (**Figure 19**) from the main wiring harness.

a. Connect an ohmmeter to the bulb terminals. The reading should be zero ohms. Replace the bulb if the ohmmeter reads infinity.

b. Connect an ohmmeter to one assist headlight socket terminal and its mating electrical connector. Repeat for the other wire. Each reading

should be zero ohms. If not, replace the assist headlight socket if it cannot be repaired.

c. If both sets of readings are correct, continue with Step 2.

2. Install the assist headlight bulb into its socket and reconnect the socket into the main wiring harness. Do not reinstall the socket into the assist headlight housing (mounting position). The assist headlight bulb and socket must be connected to the main wiring harness when making the following tests.

3. Switch a voltmeter to its 20 volt scale. In Step 4, connect the voltmeter leads to the assist headlight socket electrical connectors with the assist headlight connector connected to the main wiring harness.

4. Connect the voltmeter positive lead (+) to the assist headlight connector brown lead and the voltmeter negative lead (–) to the assist headlight connector green lead. Turn the ignition switch to its ON position and the dimmer switch to its HI or LO position. Note the voltmeter reading:

a. If the voltmeter reads battery voltage, continue with Step 5.

b. If the voltmeter does not read battery voltage, check the wiring harness from the ignition switch to the assist headlight socket for damage.

5. Turn the ignition switch to its OFF position and disconnect the voltmeter leads. If the voltmeter reads battery volatage in Step 4, the assist headlight wiring circuit is good.

### Taillight

If the taillight does not come on, perform the following test.

1. Remove the taillight bulb (Chapter Nine) and disconnect the taillight socket from the wiring harness.

   a. Connect an ohmmeter to the bulb terminals. The reading should be zero ohms. Replace the bulb if the ohmmeter reads infinity.

   b. Connect an ohmmeter to one taillight (**Figure 20**) socket terminal and to its mating electrical connector to check continuity. Repeat for the other wire. Each reading should be zero ohms. If any reading indicates an open circuit, replace the taillight socket if it cannot be repaired.

2. Install the taillight bulb into its socket and reconnect the socket into the main wiring harness. Do not reinstall the socket into the taillight housing (mounting position). The taillight bulb and socket must be connected to the main wiring harness when making the following tests.

3. Switch a voltmeter to its 20volt scale. In Step 4, connect the voltmeter leads to the taillight socket electrical connectors with the taillight connector connected to the main wiring harness.

4. Connect the voltmeter positive lead (+) to the taillight connector brown lead and the voltmeter negative lead (–) to the taillight connector green lead. Turn the ignition switch to its ON position and note the voltmeter reading:

   a. If the voltmeter reads battery voltage, continue with Step 5.

   b. If the voltmeter does not reads battery voltage, check the wiring harness from the ignition switch to the taillight socket for damage.

5. Turn the ignition switch to its OFF position and disconnect the voltmeter leads. If the voltmeter reads battery voltage in Step 4, the taillight wiring circuit is good.

## OIL TEMPERATURE INDICATOR

The oil temperature indicator circuit (**Figure 21**) is designed to warn you when the engine oil gets too hot. The oil temperature indicator (B, **Figure 13**) should come on when the ignition switch is turned on and then go off in a few seconds. If the indicator does not come on after starting the engine, check for a faulty bulb (Chapter Nine). If the oil temperature indicator does not come on after turning the ignition switch on, or if it does not go off, test the oil temperature circuit as described in the following section.

### Troubleshooting

*Oil temperature indicator does not come on after turning the ignition switch on*

1. Remove the front fender (Chapter Fifteen).
2. Turn the ignition switch on and check for battery voltage at the fan control unit (**Figure 22**) connectors:

   a. If there is battery voltage, perform Step 3.

   b. If there is no battery voltage, check for loose or damaged fan control unit connectors.

3. Disconnect the fan control unit four-prong connector (A, **Figure 22**).

4. Connect the voltmeter positive lead (+) to the fan control unit white/black lead and the voltmeter negative lead (–) to the green lead. Read the voltmeter and note the following:

   a. If the voltmeter reads battery voltage, continue with Step 5.

   b. If the voltmeter does not read battery voltage, check the wiring harness for damage.

5. Connect the voltmeter positive lead (+) to the fan control unit blue/red lead and the voltmeter negative lead (–) to the green lead. Read the voltmeter and note the following:

   a. If the voltmeter reads battery voltage, continue with Step 6.

   b. If the voltmeter does not read battery voltage, check the wiring harness for damage.

6. Turn the ignition switch off.

7. Switch an ohmmeter to the R × 1000 scale. Then disconnect the fan control unit two-prong connector (B, **Figure 22**) and measure the resistance between its blue wire terminal and the green wire terminal on the four-prong connector. The ohmmeter should read 10,000 ohms. Note the following:

*NOTE*
*If the engine is hot, the resistance read-*
*ing will be lower than 10k ohms.*

a. If the reading in incorrect, perform Step 8.

b. If the reading is correct, the fan control unit is faulty and must be replaced (Chapter Nine).

8. Perform the following:

a. Check for an open circuit in the two-prong blue wire between its connector and the oil temperature sensor.

b. Check for loose or damaged connectors.

c. Test the oil thermosensor (Chapter Nine).

9. Install all parts previously removed. Make sure all of the connectors disconnected during this proce-dure are free of corrosion and are reconnected prop-erly.

### *Oil temperature indicator does not go off*

If the oil temperature indicator does not go off after turning the ignition switch on, perform the following:

1. Remove the front fender (Chapter Fifteen).

2. Disconnect the fan control unit two-prong and four-prong connectors (A and B, **Figure 22**).

3. Switch an ohmmeter to the R × 1000 scale. Meas-ure the resistance between its blue wire terminal and the green wire terminal on the four-prong connector.

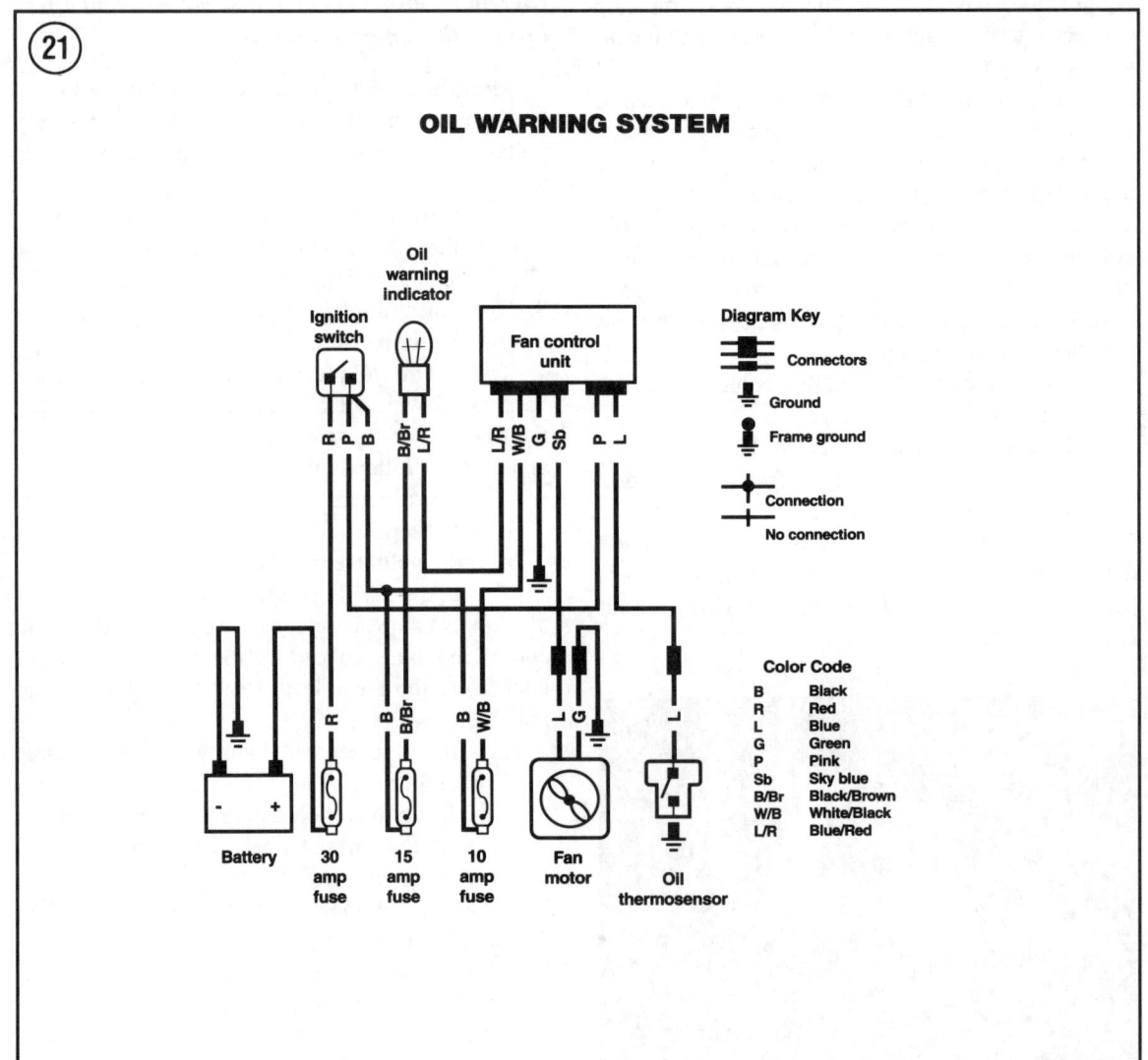

**(21)**

**OIL WARNING SYSTEM**

The ohmmeter should read 10,000 ohms. Note the following:

> *NOTE*
> *If the engine is hot, the resistance reading will be lower than 10,000 ohms.*

a. If the reading is incorrect, perform Step 4.

b. If the reading is correct, perform Step 5.

4. Perform the following:

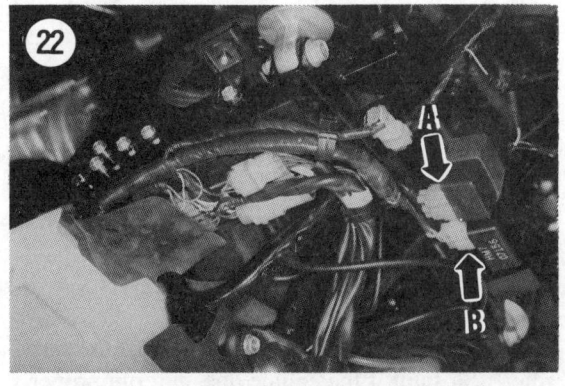

a. Check for an open circuit in the two-prong blue wire between its connector and the oil temperature sensor.

b. Test the oil temperature sensor (Chapter Nine).

5. Switch an ohmmeter to the R× 1 scale and check for continuity between the four-prong connector blue/red and green wire terminals. Note the following:

a. If there is continuity, check for a short in the blue/red wire.

b. If there is no continuity, the fan control unit is faulty and must be replaced (Chapter Nine).

6. Install all previously removed parts. Make sure all of the connectors disconnected during this procedure are free of corrosion and are reconnected properly.

## COMBINATION METER

Refer to **Figure 23** when troubleshooting the combination meter system circuit. The speedometer sensor (**Figure 24**) is mounted on the engine.

**COMBINATION METER CIRCUIT**

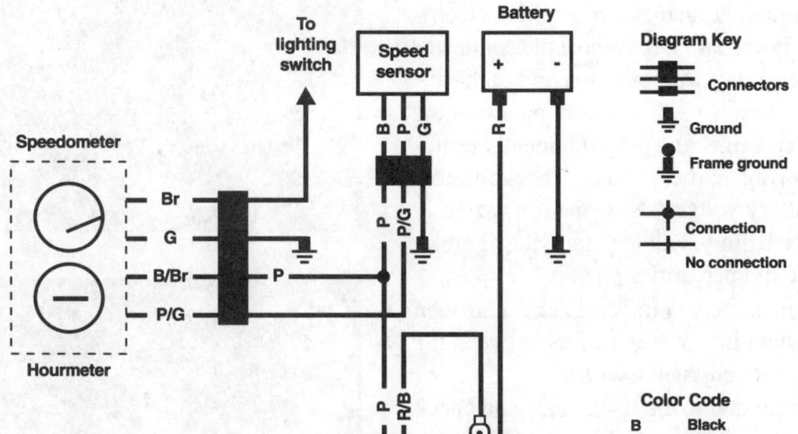

Speedometer

Br

G

B/Br — P

P/G

Hourmeter

To lighting switch

Speed sensor

Battery
+ —

Diagram Key

Connectors

Ground

Frame ground

Connection

No connection

Ignition switch

15 amp fuse

**Color Code**

| B | Black |
|---|-------|
| R | Red |
| G | Green |
| P | Pink |
| Br | Brown |
| RBL | Red/Black |
| P/G | Pink/Green |
| B/Br | Black/Brown |

**Troubleshooting**

*The speedometer works correctly, but the hour meter does not operate*

The hour meter is damaged. Replace the speedometer assembly.

*The speedometer does not work correctly*

1. Before testing the combination meter circuit, perform the following. If all of the following components are okay, continue with Step 2:
    a. Check the fuses as described in Chapter Nine. Check both the main and sub-fuses.
    b. Make sure the battery is fully charged. Test the battery as described in Chapter Three.
    c. Check the connectors (**Figure 23**) for corrosion or damage.
2. Disconnect the sensor three-prong connector (**Figure 25**). Turn the ignition switch on and measure voltage between the pink and green connector terminals (on the wiring harness side). The voltmeter should show battery voltage. Note the following:
    a. If there is battery voltage, perform Step 3.
    b. If there is no battery voltage, check for an open circuit in the pink or green wires between the battery and speedometer sensor.
3. Remove the front fender (Chapter Fifteen).
4. Locate the combination meter four-prong electrical connector (**Figure 26**). Disconnect the connector and check the terminals for corrosion and damage.
5. Turn the ignition switch on and measure the voltage between the pink and green connector terminals (on the wiring harness side). The voltmeter should show battery voltage. Note the following:
    a. If there is battery voltage, turn the ignition switch off and perform Step 6.
    b. If there is no battery voltage, check for an open circuit in the pink or green wires between the battery and speedometer sensor.
6. Switch an ohmmeter to the R × 1 scale and check for continuity between the speedometer and speedometer sensor pink wires. The ohmmeter should read zero ohms. Note the following:
    a. If the reading is correct, perform Step 7.
    b. If the reading is incorrect, check for an open circuit or loosen terminal connection in the pink wire.

7. Remove the speedometer sensor from the engine (Chapter Nine).
8. Reconnect the speedometer sensor connector (**Figure 25**) to the wiring harness.
9. Connect the voltmeter positive lead (+) to the speedometer sensor pink/green terminal and the voltmeter negative lead (−) to the speedometer sensor green lead. Turn the ignition switch to its ON position and slowly turn the speedometer sensor (**Figure 27**) with your finger. The voltmeter should flunctuate between 0 and 5 volts. Note the following:
    a. If the voltmeter reading is correct, and you have not found another problem, the speedometer is faulty.
    b. If the voltmeter reading is incorrect, the speedometer sensor is faulty.
10. Install all of the parts previously removed. Install the speedometer sensor as described in Chapter Nine.

## FUEL SYSTEM

Many riders automatically assume that the carburetor is at fault if the engine does not run properly.

While fuel system problems are not uncommon, carburetor adjustment is seldom the answer. In many cases, adjusting the carburetor only compounds the problem by making the engine run worse.

When troubleshooting the fuel system, start at the fuel tank and work through the system, reserving the carburetor as the final point. Most fuel system problems result from an empty fuel tank, a plugged fuel filter or fuel valve or sour fuel. Fuel system troubleshooting is covered thoroughly under *Engine Is Difficult To Start, Poor Idle Speed Performance and Poor Medium and High Speed Performance* in this chapter.

The carburetor choke can also present problems. A choke stuck open will cause a hard starting problem; one that sticks closed will result in a flooding condition. Check choke operation by moving the choke lever (A, **Figure 1**) by hand. The choke should move freely without binding or sticking in one position. If necessary, remove the choke as described under *Carburetor Disassembly* in Chapter Eight and inspect its plunger and spring for excessive wear or damage.

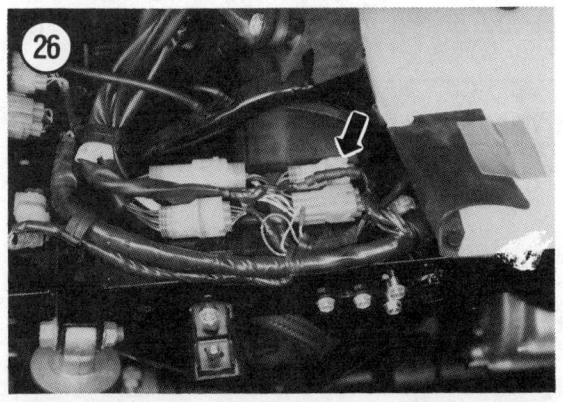

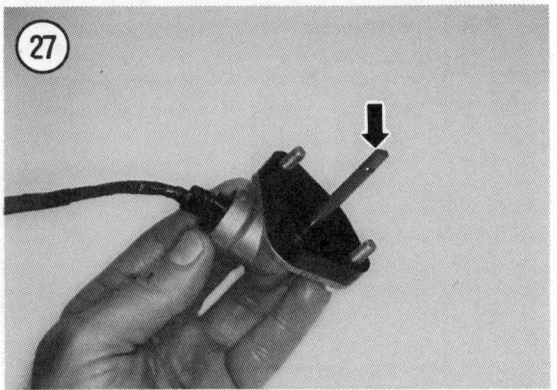

## ENGINE OVERHEATING

Engine overheating is a serious problem because it can quickly cause engine seizure and damage. The following section groups 5 main systems with probable causes that can lead to engine overheating.

1. Ignition system:
   a. Incorrect spark plug gap.
   b. Incorrect spark plug heat range. See Chapter Three.
   c. Faulty ICM unit/incorrect ignition timing.
2. Engine compression system:
   a. Cylinder head gasket leakage.
   b. Heavy carbon buildup in combustion chamber.
3. Fuel system:
   a. Carburetor fuel level too low.
   b. Incorrect carburetor adjustment or jetting.
   c. Loose carburetor boot clamps.
   d. Leaking or damaged carburetor-to-air filter housing air boot.
   e. Incorrect fuel/air mixture.
4. Engine load:
   a. Dragging brake(s).
   b. Damaged drive train components.
   c. Slipping clutch.
   d. Engine oil level too high.
5. Electric cooling system:
   a. Damaged cooling fan.
   b. Plugged or damaged oil cooler.
   c. Restricted oil cooler. Check for any cargo placed in the front of the vehicle which could be restricting the air flow to the oil cooler assembly.

## ENGINE

### Preignition

Preignition is the premature burning of fuel and is caused by hot spots in the combustion chamber. The fuel ignites before spark ignition occurs. Glowing deposits in the combustion chamber, inadequate cooling or an overheated spark plug can all cause preignition. This is first noticed as a power loss but will eventually result in damage to the internal parts of the engine because of higher combustion chamber temperature.

## Detonation

Commonly called spark knock or fuel knock, detonation is the violent explosion of fuel in the combustion chamber instead of the controlled burn that occurs during normal combustion. Severe damage can result. Use of low octane gasoline is a common cause of detonation.

Even when using a high octane gasoline, detonation can still occur. Other causes are over-advanced ignition timing, lean fuel mixture at or near full throttle, inadequate engine cooling, or the excessive accumulation of carbon deposits in the combustion chamber and on the piston crown.

## Power Loss

Several factors can cause a lack of power and speed. Look for a clogged air filter or a fouled or damaged spark plug. A piston or cylinder that is galled, incorrect piston clearance or worn or sticking piston rings may be responsible. Look for loose bolts, defective gaskets or leaking machined mating surfaces on the cylinder head, cylinder or crankcase.

## Piston Seizure

This may be caused by incorrect bore clearance, piston rings with an improper end gap, compression leak, incorrect air fuel mixture, spark plug of the wrong heat range or incorrect ignition timing. Overheating from any cause may result in piston seizure.

## Piston Slap

Piston slap is an audible slapping or rattling noise resulting from excessive piston-to-cylinder clearance. If allowed to continue, piston slap will eventually cause the piston skirt to crack and shatter.

To prevent piston slap, clean the air filter element on a regular schedule. If you hear piston slap, disassemble the engine top end and measure the cylinder bore and piston diameter and check for excessive clearance. Replace parts that exceed wear limits or show damage.

## ENGINE NOISES

1. *Knocking or pinging during acceleration*—Can be caused by using a lower octane fuel than recommended or a poor quality of fuel. Incorrect carbure-

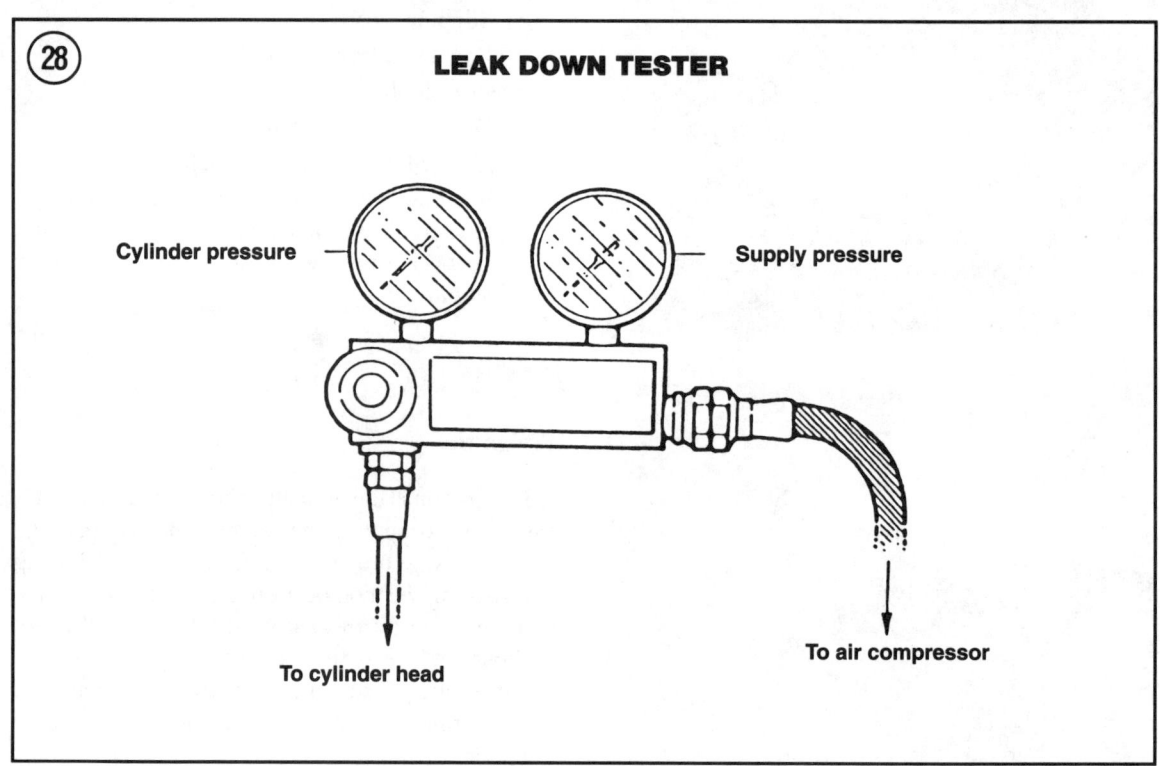

(28) LEAK DOWN TESTER

Cylinder pressure

Supply pressure

To cylinder head

To air compressor

tor jetting or a spark plug that is too hot can also cause pinging. Refer to *Correct Spark Plug Heat Range* in Chapter Three. Check also for excessive carbon buildup in the combustion chamber or a faulty ICM unit.

2. *Slapping or rattling noises at low speed or during acceleration*—Can be caused by excessive piston-to-cylinder wall clearance. Check also for a bent connecting rod or worn piston pin and/or piston pin holes in the piston.

3. *Knocking or rapping while decelerating*—Usually caused by excessive rod bearing clearance.

4. *Persistent knocking and vibration or other noise*—Usually caused by worn main bearings. If the main bearings are good, consider the following:
   a. Loose engine mounts.
   b. Cracked frame.
   c. Leaking cylinder head gasket.
   d. Exhaust pipe leakage at cylinder head.
   e. Stuck piston ring.
   f. Broken piston ring.
   g. Partial engine seizure.
   h. Excessive connecting rod small end bearing clearance.
   i. Excessive connecting rod big end side clearance.
   j. Excessive crankshaft runout.
   k. Worn or damaged primary drive gear.

5. *Rapid on-off squeal*—Compression leak around cylinder head gasket or spark plug.

## CYLINDER LEAKAGE TEST

A cylinder leakage test can determine if an engine problem is caused by leaking valves, a blown head gasket or broken, worn or stuck piston rings. A cylinder leakage test is performed by applying com-

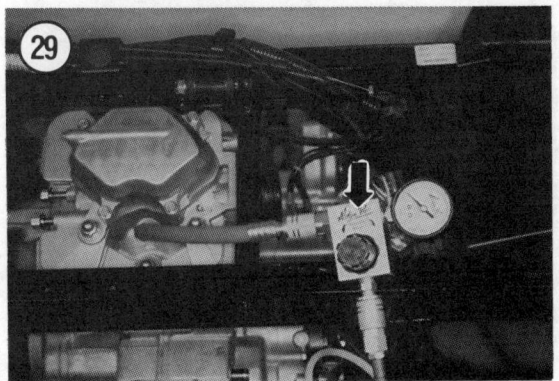

pressed air to the cylinder and then measuring the percent of leakage. A cylinder leakage tester and an air compressor are required to perform this test (**Figure 28**). Follow the tester manufacturer's directions along with the following information when performing a cylinder leakage test.

1. Start and run the engine until it reaches normal operating temperature. Then turn the engine off.

2. Remove the air filter assembly as described in Chapter Three. Open and secure the throttle in the wide-open position.

3. Set the piston to TDC on its compression stroke. See *Valve Clearance Check and Adjustment* in Chapter Three.

4. Remove the spark plug.

*NOTE*
*The engine may turn when air pressure is applied to the cylinder. To prevent this from happening, shift the transmission into fifth gear and set the parking brake.*

5. Install the cylinder leakage tester into the spark plug hole (**Figure 29**).

6. Make a cylinder leakage test following the tester manufacturer's instructions. Listen for air leaking while noting the following:
   a. Air leaking through the exhaust pipe indicates a leaking exhaust valve.
   b. Air leaking through the carburetor indicates a leaking intake valve.
   c. Air leaking through the crankcase breather tube indicates worn piston rings.

7. A cylinder with 10% or more cylinder leakage requires further service.

8. Remove the tester and reinstall the spark plug.

## CLUTCH

All clutch service, except adjustment, requires partial engine disassembly to identify and cure the problem. Refer to Chapter Six.

The TRX400 uses two clutch assemblies: centrifugal (A, **Figure 30**) and change (B, **Figure 31**).

### Clutch Slipping

1. *Clutch wear or damage*:
   a. Incorrect clutch adjustment.
   b. Worn clutch shoe (centrifugal clutch).

c. Loose, weak or damaged clutch spring (change and centrifugal clutch).
d. Worn friction plates (change clutch).
e. Warped steel plates (change clutch).
f. Worn clutch center and/or clutch outer (change clutch).
g. Incorrectly assembled clutch.

2. *Engine oil*:
a. Low oil level.
b. Oil additives.
c. Low viscosity oil.

## Clutch Dragging

1. *Clutch wear or damage:*
a. Incorrect clutch adjustment.
b. Damaged or incorrectly assembled clutch lever assembly.
c. Warped steel plates.
d. Swollen friction plates.
e. Warped pressure plate.
f. Incorrect clutch spring tension.
g. Incorrectly assembled clutch.
h. Loose clutch nut.
i. Incorrect clutch mechanism adjustment (change clutch).

2. *Engine oil:*
a. Oil level too high.
b. High viscosity oil.

## Rough Clutch Operation

1. Damaged clutch outer slots (change clutch).
2. Damaged clutch center splines (change clutch).
3. Incorrect engine idle speed.

## Transmission is Hard to Shift

1. *Clutch wear or damage:*
a. Incorrect clutch adjustment.
b. Damaged clutch lifter mechanism.
2. *Damaged shift drum shifter plate.*

## TRANSMISSION

Transmission symptoms can be difficult to distinguish from clutch symptoms. Be sure that the clutch is not causing the trouble before working on the transmission.

## Difficult Shifting

If the shift shaft does not move smoothly from one gear to the next, check the following.
1. *Shift shaft:*
a. Incorrectly installed shift lever.
b. Stripped shift lever-to-shift shaft splines.
c. Bent sub-gearshift spindle.
d. Damaged sub-gearshift spindle return spring.
e. Damaged gearshift linkage assembly shift shaft where it engages the shift drum.
f. Shift drum positioning lever binding on pivot bolt.

2. *Stopper arm:*
a. Seized or damaged stopper arm roller.
b. Weak or damaged stopper arm spring.
c. Loose stopper arm mounting bolt.
d. Incorrectly assembled stopper arm assembly.

3. *Shift drum and shift forks:*
a. Bent shift fork(s).
b. Damaged shift fork guide pin(s).
c. Seized shift fork (on shaft).
d. Broken shift fork or shift fork shaft.
e. Damaged shift drum groove(s).
f. Damaged shift drum bearing surfaces.

## Gears Pop Out Of Mesh

If the transmission shifts into gear but then slips or pops out, check the following:
1. *Gearshift linkage:*
a. Incorrectly assembled sub-gearshift spindle and gearshift A arm assembly.
b. Stopper arm fails to move or set properly.

2. *Shift drum:*
a. Incorrect thrust play.
b. Worn or damaged shift drum groove(s).

3. Bent shift fork(s).
4. *Transmission:*
   a. Worn or damaged gear dogs.
   b. Excessive gear thrust play.
   c. Worn or damaged transmission shaft circlips or thrust washers.

## Transmission Overshifts

If the transmission overshifts when shifting up or down, check for a weak or broken shift lever return spring or a weak or broken stopper arm and spring assembly.

## Transmission Fails to Shift into Reverse

If the transmission fails to shift into or operate in reverse properly, check the following:
1. Incorrect reverse cable adjustment.
2. Loose or damaged reverse stopper arm.
3. Damaged reverse stopper shaft.

## DRIVE TRAIN TROUBLESHOOTING

Noise is usually the first indication of a drive train problem. It is not always easy to diagnose the trouble by determining the source of the noise and the operating conditions that produce it.

Some clues as to the cause of the trouble may be gained by noting whether the noise is a hum, growl or knock; whether it is produced when the vehicle is accelerating under load or coasting; and whether it is heard when the vehicle is going straight or making a turn.

Drive train service procedures are covered in Chapter Eleven (front) and Chapter Twelve (rear).

> *CAUTION*
> *Improperly diagnosed noises can lead to rapid and excessive drive train wear and damage. If you are not familiar with the operation and repair of the front and rear final drive assembly, refer troubleshooting to a qualified Honda dealership.*

## Oil Inspection

Drain the gearcase oil (Chapter Three) into a clean container. Wipe a small amount of oil on one of your fingers, then rub your finger and thumb together. Check for the presence of metallic particles. Also check the drain bolt for metal particles. While a small amount of particles in the oil is normal, an abnormal amount of debris is an indication of bearing or gear damage.

## Front Differential Troubleshooting

### *Consistent noise while cruising*

   a. Low oil level.
   b. Gear oil contamination.
   c. Chipped or damaged gear teeth.
   d. Worn or damaged ring gear bearing.
   e. Worn or damaged ring gear.
   f. Worn pinion gear or shaft side washers.
   g. Worn or damaged ring gear and drive pinion.
   h. Incorrect ring gear and drive pinion tooth contact.

### *Consistent gear noises during coasting*

   a. Damaged or chipped gears.
   b. Gear oil contamination.
   c. Incorrect ring gear and drive pinion tooth contact.

### *Gear noise during normal operation*

   a. Low oil level.
   b. Gear oil contamination.
   c. Chipped or damaged gear teeth.
   d. Incorrect ring gear and drive pinion tooth contact.

### *Overheating*

   a. Low oil level.
   b. Insufficient ring gear and drive pinion gear backlash.

### *Oil leak*

   a. Oil level too high.
   b. Plugged breathe hole or tube.
   c. Damaged oil seal(s).
   d. Loose cover mounting bolts.
   e. Housing damage.

*Abnormal noises during*
*starting or acceleration*

    a. Worn or damaged clutch spring.
    b. Worn or damaged clutch disc assembly.
    c. Excessive pinion gear backlash.
    d. Worn propeller shaft splines.
    e. Excessive ring gear and drive pinion backlash.
    f. Loose pinion joint nut.

*Abnormal noises when turning*

    a. Worn or damaged clutch spring.
    b. Damaged drive shaft splines.
    c. Worn or damaged clutch disc.
    d. Damaged pinion shaft, pinion or side gear.
    e. Worn or damaged ring gear bearing.

**Rear Differential Troubleshooting**
**Excessive Noise**

    a. Low oil level.
    b. Excessive ring gear and pinion gear backlash.
    c. Worn or damaged drive pinion and splines.
    d. Damaged driven flange and wheel hub.
    e. Worn or damaged driven flange and ring gear shaft.

## HANDLING

Poor handling will reduce overall performance and may cause you to loose control and crash. If you are experiencing poor handling, check the following items:

1. *If the handlebars are hard to turn, check for the following:*
    a. Low tire pressure.
    b. Incorrect throttle cable routing.
    c. Damaged steering shaft bushing and/or bearing.
    d. Bent steering shaft or frame.
    e. Steering shaft nut too tight.
2. *If there is excessive handlebar shake or vibration, check for the following:*
    a. Loose or damaged handlebar clamps.
    b. Incorrect handlebar clamp installation.
    c. Bent or cracked handlebar.
    d. Worn wheel bearing(s).
    e. Excessively worn or damaged tire(s).
    f. Damaged rim(s).

    g. Loose, missing or broken engine mount bolts and mounts.
    h. Cracked frame, especially at the steering head.
    i. Incorrect tire pressure.
    j. Damaged shock absorber damper rod.
    k. Leaking shock absorber damper housing.
    l. Sagged shock spring(s).
    m. Loose or damaged shock mount bolts.
3. *If the rear suspension is too soft, check for the following:*
    a. Damaged shock absorber damper rod.
    b. Leaking shock absorber damper housing.
    c. Sagged shock spring.
    d. Loose or damaged shock mount bolts.
4. *If the rear suspension is too hard, check for the following:*
    a. Rear tire pressure too high.
    b. Incorrect shock absorber adjustment.
    c. Damaged shock absorber damper rod.
    d. Leaking shock absorber damper housing.
    e. Sagged shock spring.
    f. Loose or damaged shock mount bolts.
5. *Frame—check the following:*
    a. Damaged frame.
    b. Cracked or broken engine mount brackets.
6. *Wobbling wheel:*
    a. Loose wheel nuts.
    b. Loose or incorrectly installed wheel hub.
    c. Excessive wheel bearing play.
    d. Loose wheel bearing.
    e. Bent wheel rim.
    f. Bent frame or other suspension component.
7. *If vehicle pulls to one side:*
    a. Incorrect tire pressure.
    b. Incorrect tie rod adjustment.
    c. Bent or loose tie rod.
    d. Incorrect wheel alignment.
    e. Bent frame or other suspension component.

## FRAME NOISE

Noises traced to the frame or suspension are usually caused by loose, worn or damaged parts. Various noises that are related to the frame are listed below:

1. Drum brake noise—A screeching sound during braking is the most common drum brake noise. Some other drum brake associated noises can be caused by:
    a. Glazed brake lining or drum surface.
    b. Excessively worn brake linings drums.

2

c. Warped brake drum.

*2. Front or rear shock absorber noise—Check for the following:*

   a. Loose shock absorber mounting bolts.

   b. Cracked or broken shock spring.

   c. Damaged shock absorber.

*3. Some other frame associated noises can be caused by:*

   a. Cracked or broken frame.

   b. Broken swing arm or shock linkage.

   c. Loose engine mounting bolts.

   d. Damaged steering shaft bearings.

   e. Loose mounting bracket.

## BRAKES

The front and rear brakes are critical to riding performance and safety. Inspect the brakes frequently and repair any problem immediately. When replacing or refilling the front brake fluid, use only DOT 3 or DOT 4 brake fluid from a sealed container. See Chapter Thirteen for additional information on brake fluid selection and drum brake service.

### Front Drum Brake Troubleshooting

If the front drum brakes are not working properly, check for one or more of the following conditions:

   a. Incorrect front brake adjustment.

   b. Air in brake line.

   c. Brake fluid level too low.

   d. Loose brake hose banjo bolts. Brake fluid is leaking out.

   e. Loose or damaged brake hose or line.

   f. Worn or damaged brake drum.

   g. Worn or damaged brake linings.

   h. Oil on brake drum or brake lining surfaces.

   i. Worn or damaged wheel cylinder(s).

   j. Weak or damaged brake return springs.

### Rear Drum Brake Troubleshooting

If the rear drum brake is not working properly, check for one or more of the following conditions:

   a. Incorrect rear brake adjustment.

   b. Incorrect brake cam lever position.

   c. Worn or damaged brake drum.

   d. Worn or damaged brake linings.

   e. Oil on brake drum or brake lining surfaces.

   f. Worn or damaged wheel cylinder(s).

   g. Weak or damaged brake return springs.

### Water Entering the Front Brake Drum(s)

   a. Damaged waterproof seal.

   b. Incorrectly installed waterproof seal.

   c. Loose or unsealed wheel cylinder assembly.

   d. Damaged hub O-ring.

   e. Loose front axle nut.

   f. Damaged brake panel O-ring.

   g. Damaged wheel hub dust seal.

   h. Damaged brake drum dust seal.

   i. Damaged brake drum.

   j. Damaged steering knuckle axle seal.

   k. Loose brake panel mounting bolt(s).

   l. Incorrect breather tube routing.

# CHAPTER THREE

# LUBRICATION, MAINTENANCE AND TUNE-UP

This chapter explains lubrication, maintenance and tune-up procedures required for the Honda models covered in this book.

**Table 1** lists the factory recommended maintenance and lubrication schedule for 1995-1997 models.

**Table 2** lists the factory recommended maintenance and lubrication schedule for 1998-on models.

**Table 3** lists tire inflation specifications.

**Table 4** lists maintenance and tune-up torque specifications.

**Table 5** lists battery capacity.

**Table 6** lists maintenance free battery voltage readings.

**Table 7** lists recommended lubricants and fuel.

**Table 8** lists engine oil capacity.

**Table 9** lists front and rear differential oil capacity.

**Table 10** lists tune-up specifications.

**Tables 1-10** are at the end of this chapter.

## PRE-RIDE CHECK LIST

Perform the following checks before the first ride of the day. All of these checks are described in this chapter. If a component requires service, refer to the appropriate section.

1. Inspect all fuel lines and fittings for leakage.

2. Make sure the fuel tank is full of fresh gasoline.

3. Make sure the engine oil level is correct.

4. Check the throttle operation for proper operation in all steering positions. Open the throttle all the way and release it. The throttle should close quickly with no binding or roughness.

5. Check that the brake levers operate properly with no binding. Replace any broken lever. Check the lever housings for damage.

6. Check the brake fluid level in the front master cylinder reservoir. Add DOT 3 or DOT 4 brake fluid if necessary.

7. Check the parking brake operation and adjust if necessary.

8. Inspect the front and rear suspension. Make sure they have a good solid feel with no looseness. Turn the handlebar from side to side to check steering play. Service the steering assembly if excessive play is noted. Make sure the handlebar cables do not bind.

9. Check the drive shaft boots for damage.

10. Check the front and rear differential oil level. Top off if necessary.

11. Check tire pressure (**Table 3**).

12. Check the exhaust system for looseness or damage.

13. Check for missing or damaged skid plates.

14. Check the tightness of all fasteners, especially engine, steering and suspension mounting hardware.

15. Make sure the headlight and taillight work.

16. Check that all switches work properly.

17. Check the air filter drain tube for contamination.

18. If carrying cargo, check that it is properly secured.

19. Start the engine, then stop it with the engine stop switch. If the engine stop switch does not work properly, test the switch as described under *Switches* in Chapter Nine.

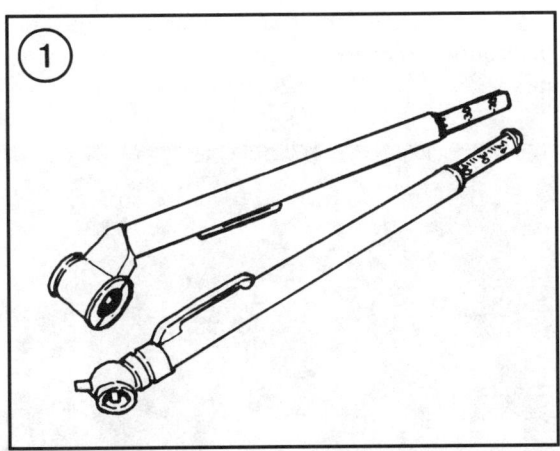

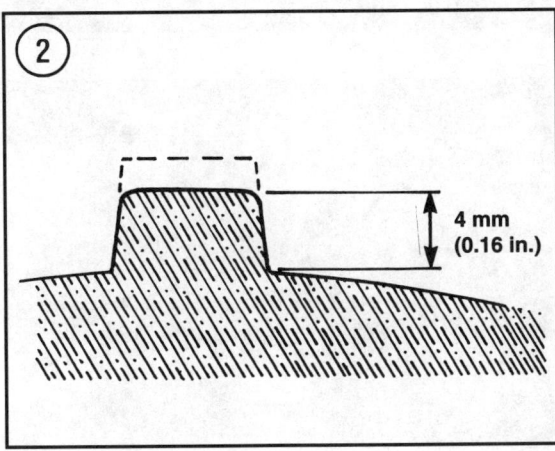

## MAINTENANCE SCHEDULE

**Table 1** and **Table 2** are factory maintenance schedules for the TRX400. Strict adherence to these recommendations will help ensure long service from your vehicle. Perform the services more often when operating the vehicle commercially and in dusty or other harsh conditions.

Most of the services shown in **Table 1** and **Table 2** are described in this chapter. However, some procedures which require more than minor disassembly or adjustment are covered elsewhere in the appropriate chapter and are so indicated.

## TIRES AND WHEELS

### Tire Pressure

Check and adjust tire pressure to maintain the smoothness of the tire, good traction and handling and to get the maximum life from the tire. A simple, accurate gauge (**Figure 1**) can be purchased for a few dollars and should be carried in your tool box. The appropriate tire pressures are listed in **Table 3**. Check tire pressure when the tires are cold.

> *WARNING*
> *Always inflate both tire sets (front and rear) tires to the correct air pressure. If the vehicle is run with unequal air pressures, the vehicle may run toward one side, causing poor handling.*

> *CAUTION*
> *Do not overinflate the stock tires as they can be permanently distorted and damaged.*

### Tire Inspection

The tires take a lot of punishment due to the variety of terrain they are subjected to. Inspect them daily for excessive wear, cuts, abrasions or punctures. If you find a nail or other object in the tire, mark its location with a light crayon before removing it. Service the tire as described in Chapter Ten.

To gauge tire wear, inspect the height of the tread knobs. If the average tread knob height measures 4 mm (0.16 in.) or less (**Figure 2**), replace the tire as described in Chapter Ten.

*WARNING*
*Do not ride your vehicle with damaged*
*or excessively worn tires. Tires in these*
*conditions can cause you to lose con-*
*trol. Replace damaged or severely worn*
*tires immediately.*

## Rim Inspection

Inspect the wheel rims for damage. Rim damage
may be sufficient to cause an air leak or knock it out
of alignment. Improper wheel alignment can cause
vibration and result in an unsafe riding condition.

Make sure the wheel nuts (**Figure 3**) are tightened
securely on each wheel. Tighten the wheel nuts in a
crisscross pattern as specified in **Table 4**.

## BATTERY

Many electrical system troubles can be traced to
battery neglect. Inspect and clean the battery at periodic intervals.

## Battery Application

A maintenance-free battery is used on all models.
This battery is sealed at the time of service and does
not require additional water. Do not try to remove
the sealing caps to add electrolyte or water or the
battery may be damaged.

*NOTE*
*Because a maintenance-free battery re-*
*quires a higher voltage charging sys-*
*tem, do not replace a maintenance-free*
*battery with a standard battery. Always*
*replace the battery with its correct type*
*and designated capacity. Refer to the*
*battery capacity specifications in* **Table**
**5** *when purchasing a new battery.*

## Safety Precautions

When working with batteries, use extreme care to
avoid spilling or splashing the electrolyte. This solution contains sulfuric acid, which can ruin clothing
and cause serious chemical burns. If you spill or
splash the electrolyte on your clothing or skin, immediately neutralize the affected area with a solution
of baking soda and water. Then flush the area with
an abundance of clean water. While the TRX400

uses a sealed battery, it vents gases and electrolyte
can leak through cracks in the battery case.

*WARNING*
*Battery electrolyte is extremely harmful*
*when splashed into your eyes or any*
*open sore. Always wear safety glasses*
*and appropriate work clothes when*
*working with batteries. If the electrolyte*
*gets into your eyes, flush the area thor-*
*oughly with clean water and get prompt*
*medical attention.*

When charging a battery, highly explosive hydro-
gen gas forms in each cell. Some of this gas escapes
through filler cap openings and can form an explosive atmosphere in and around the battery. This
condition can persist for several hours. Sparks, an
open flame or a lighted cigarette can ignite the gas,
causing an internal battery explosion and possible
serious personal injury.

When servicing the battery, note the following
precautions to prevent an explosion or personal injury:

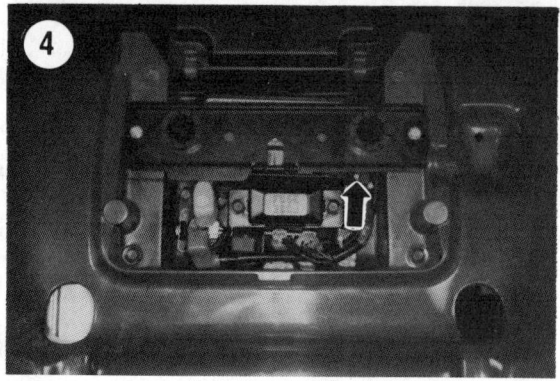

1. Do not smoke or permit any open flame near any battery being charged or near a recently charged battery.

2. Do not disconnect live circuits at battery terminals because a spark usually occurs when a live circuit is broken.

3. Take care when connecting or disconnecting any battery charger. Be sure its power switch is off before making or breaking connections. Poor connections are a common cause of electrical arcs that cause explosions.

4. Keep all children and pets away from charging equipment and batteries.

5. Do not try to open the maintenance free battery.

## Removal/Installation
## Battery

On all models covered in this manual, the negative side is grounded. When removing the battery, disconnect the negative (–) cable first, then the positive (+) cable. This sequence reduces the chance of a tool shorting to ground when disconnecting the "hot" positive cable.

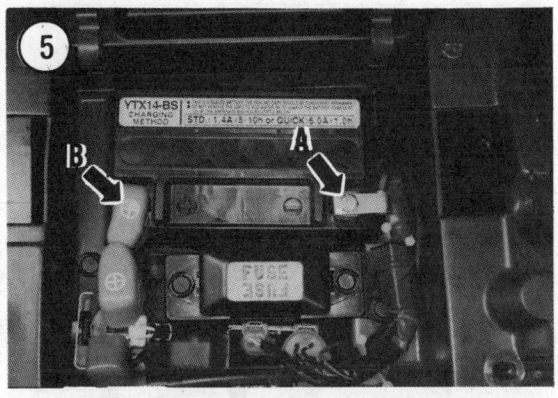

*WARNING*
*When performing the following procedures, protect your eyes, skin and clothing. If electrolyte gets into your eyes, flush your eyes thoroughly with clean water and get prompt medical attention.*

1. Read the information listed under *Service Precautions* in this section, then continue with Step 2.
2. Check that the ignition switch is turned off.
3. Remove the seat (Chapter Fifteen).
4. Remove the bolts and the battery holder bracket (**Figure 4**).
5. Disconnect the negative battery cable (A, **Figure 5**)from the battery .
6. Disconnect the positive battery cable(A, **Figure 5**) from the battery.
7. Remove the battery (**Figure 5**).
8. Service the battery as described in this section.
9. Install the battery into the battery box with its terminals facing in the direction shown in **Figure 5**.
10. Coat the battery terminals (**Figure 6**) with a thin layer of dielectric grease. This will help to retard corrosion and decomposition of the terminals.
11. Attach the positive battery cable (B, **Figure 5**) to the battery.
12. Attach the negative battery cable (A, **Figure 5**) to the battery.
13. Install the battery holder bracket (**Figure 4**) and tighten the mounting bolts securely.
14. Install the seat (Chapter Fifteen).

### Inspection

For a preliminary test, connect a digital voltmeter to the battery negative and positive terminals and measure battery voltage (**Figure 7**). A fully charged battery will read between 13.0-13.2 volts. If the voltmeter reads 12.3 volts or less, the battery is under charged. If necessary, charge the battery as described in this chapter. **Table 6** lists battery state of charge readings for maintenance-free batteries.

### Battery Testing

A bench type battery tester (Honda part No. 07GMJ-0010000 or equivalent) can be used to accurately test the maintenance-free battery. When using a battery tester, follow the manufacturer's instructions and test results. For best results, make sure the tester's cables are in working order and clamp tightly onto the battery terminals.

> *NOTE*
> *A battery tester suitable for testing motorcycle batteries can be ordered through your dealership from K&L Supply Co. in Santa Clara, California.*

## Charging

Always follow the manufacturer's instructions when using a battery charger.

> *CAUTION*
> *Never connect a battery charger to the battery with the battery leads still connected. Always remove the battery from the vehicle before charging it.*

1. Remove the battery as described in this chapter.
2. Connect the positive (+) charger lead to the positive battery terminal and the negative (–) charger lead to the negative battery terminal.

> *CAUTION*
> *Do not exceed the recommended charging amperage rate or charging time on the label attached to the battery (**Figure 6**).*

> *CAUTION*
> *Do not charge the battery with a high rate charger. The high current forced into the battery will overheat the battery and damage the battery plates.*

3. Set the charger to 12 volts. If the charger output is variable, select a low setting. Use the following suggested charging amperage and length of charging time:
   a. Standard charge: 1.4 amps at 5 to 10 hours.
   b. Quick charge: 6.0 amps at 1 hour.
4. Turn the charger on.
5. After charging the battery the specified amount of time, turn the charger off and disconnect the charger leads.
6. Connect a digital voltmeter to the battery terminals (**Figure 7**) and measure battery voltage. A fully charged battery will read 13.0-13.2 volts. See **Table 6**.
7. If the battery voltage remains stable for one hour, the battery is charged.

8. Clean the battery cable connectors, battery terminals and case. Coat the terminals with a thin layer of dielectric grease. This will help to retard corrosion and decomposition of the battery terminals.
9. Reinstall the battery as described in this chapter.

## Battery Cables

To ensure good electrical contact between the battery and the electrical cables, keep the cables clean and free of corrosion.

1. If the electrical cable terminals are badly corroded, disconnect them from the battery as described under *Battery Removal/Installation* in this chapter.
2. Thoroughly clean each connector with a wire brush and then with a water and baking soda solution. Wipe dry with a clean cloth.
3. After cleaning, apply a thin layer of dielectric grease to the battery terminals before reattaching the cables.
4. If disconnected, reconnect the battery cables as described under *Battery Removal/Installation* in this chapter.

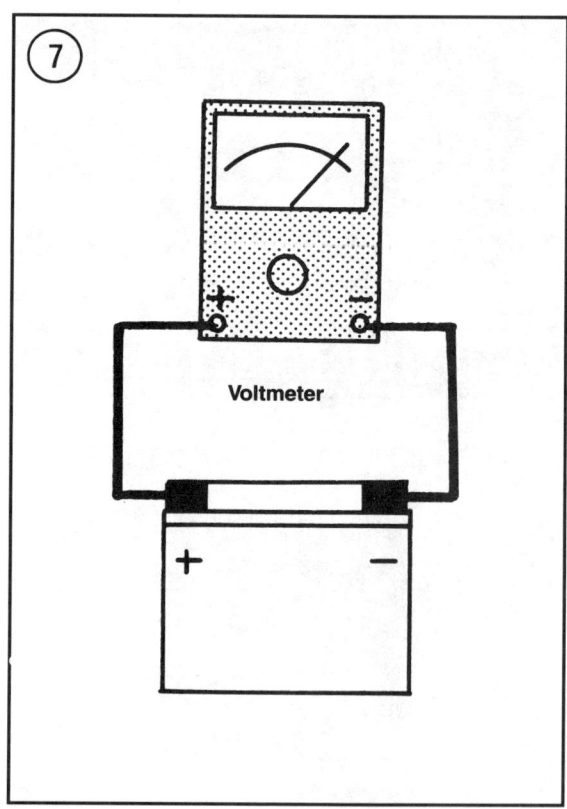

(7)

**Voltmeter**

5. Coat the terminals with a thin layer of dielectric grease. This will help to retard corrosion and decomposition of the battery terminals.

### New Battery Installation

Always replace the sealed battery with another sealed-type battery. Your Honda's charging system is designed to operate with this type of battery in the system.

Before installing a new battery, make sure it is fully charged. Failure to do so will prevent the battery from ever obtaining a complete charge.

> *NOTE*
> ***Recycle your old battery****. When you replace the old battery, turn in the old battery. The lead plates and the plastic case can be recycled. Most motorcycle dealers will accept your old battery in trade when you purchase a new one.* ***Never*** *place an old battery in your household trash since it is illegal, in most states, to place any acid or lead (heavy metal) contents in landfills. There is also the danger of the battery being crushed in the trash truck and spraying acid on the truck or landfill operator.*

### LUBRICANTS

**Engine Oil**

Oil is graded according to its viscosity, which is an indication of how thick it is. The Society of Automotive Engineers (SAE) distinguishes oil viscosity by numbers, called weights. Thick (heavy) oils have higher viscosity numbers than thin (light)

oils. For example, a 5 weight (SAE 5) oil is a light oil while a 90 weight (SAE 90) oil is relatively heavy. The viscosity of the oil has nothing to do with its lubricating properties.

**Grease**

Unless otherwise specified, use water-resistant grease when grease is needed. Water does not wash grease off parts as easily as it washes off oil. In addition, grease maintains its lubricating qualities better than oil over a longer period of time.

### CLEANING SOLVENT

A number of solvents can be used to remove old dirt, grease and oil. See your Honda dealership or a motorcycle or auto parts store.

> *WARNING*
> *Never use gasoline as a cleaning solvent. Gasoline is extremely volatile and contains tremendously destructive potential energy. The slightest spark in the presence of gasoline vapor could cause a fatal explosion.*

### PERIODIC LUBRICATION

Refer to **Table 1** or **Table 2** for lubrication service intervals.

**Engine Oil and Filter**

*Recommended engine oil*

Honda recommends the use of Honda GN4-4-stroke oil or an equivalent 10W-40 engine oil with an API service classification of SG. The quality rating is stamped or printed on the can or label on plastic bottles (**Figure 8**). Try to use the same brand of oil at each oil change. Do not use oils with graphite or molybdenum additives as these can cause clutch slippage and other clutch related problems. Refer to **Figure 9** for the correct oil weight to use under anticipated ambient temperatures (not engine oil temperature).

*Engine oil level check*

Check the engine oil level with the dipstick/oil fill cap mounted on the left side of the engine.

1. Park the vehicle on level ground and set the parking brake.

2. Start the engine and let it run approximately 2-3 minutes.

3. Shut off the engine and let the oil drain into the crankcase for a few minutes.

4. Unscrew and remove the dipstick/oil fill cap (**Figure 10**) and wipe it clean. Reinsert it onto the threads in the hole; do not screw it in (**Figure 11**). Then remove the dipstick and check the oil level.

5. The level is correct when it is between the two dipstick lines (**Figure 12**). If necessary, add the recommended type oil (**Table 7**) to correct the level.

6. Replace the dipstick O-ring (**Figure 12**) if damaged.

7. Install the dipstick/oil fill cap (**Figure 10**) and tighten it securely.

*Engine oil and filter change*

Tables 1 and 2 list the factory recommended oil and filter change intervals. This assumes that you operate the vehicle in moderate climates. If you operate it in dusty conditions, the oil will get dirty more quickly and will require more frequent oil changes.

To change the engine oil and filter you need the following:

a. Drain pan.
b. Funnel.
c. Wrench and sockets
d. 2-3 quarts of oil (**Table 8**).
e. New oil filter.

There are different ways to discard the old oil *safely.* Never drain the oil onto the ground.

*NOTE*
*Some service stations and oil retailers will accept your used oil for recycling. Do not discard oil in your household*

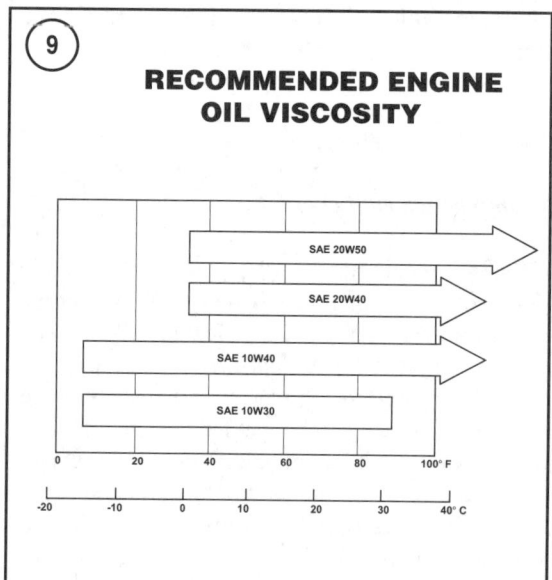

**RECOMMENDED ENGINE OIL VISCOSITY**

SAE 20W50
SAE 20W40
SAE 10W40
SAE 10W30

**3**

*trash or pour it onto the ground. Never add brake fluid or any other type of petroleum-based fluid to any engine oil that you want to recycle. Most oil retailers may not accept the oil if you have combined other fluids with it.*

> *NOTE*
> *Running the engine heats the oil, which enables the oil to flow more freely and carry contaminates and sludge out with it when drained.*

1. Park the vehicle on level ground and apply the parking brake.
2. Start the engine and let it warm to normal operating temperature. Then shut the engine off.
3. Place a clean drain pan underneath the engine.
4. Remove the drain plug (**Figure 13**) located in the bottom of the engine and allow the oil to drain.
5. Remove the dipstick/oil fill cap (**Figure 10**) to help speed up the flow of oil.
6. Allow the oil to drain completely.
7. To replace the oil filter, perform the following:
   a. Remove the engine oil filter cover mounting bolts and cover (**Figure 14**).
   b. Remove and discard the oil filter (A, **Figure 15**).
   c. Remove the spring (**Figure 16**) from the engine.
   d. Remove the O-ring (B, **Figure 15**) from the oil filter cover groove.
   e. Remove the O-ring (C, **Figure 15**) from the engine groove.
   f. Clean the spring and the filter cover in solvent and dry thoroughly.
   g. Replace any cracked or damaged O-ring.
   h. Lubricate each O-ring with engine oil.
   i. Install the O-ring into the engine groove (C, **Figure 15**).
   j. Install the O-ring into the filter cover groove (B, **Figure 15**).
   k. Install the spring (**Figure 16**).

> *CAUTION*
> *Installing the oil filter backwards will restrict oil flow and cause engine damage.*

l. Install the new oil filter with its outside mark (**Figure 17**) facing out. See A, **Figure 15**.

m. Install the engine oil filter cover (**Figure 14**) and tighten its mounting bolts as specified in **Table 4**.

8. Replace the drain plug gasket if damaged or if it was leaking. Then install the drain plug (**Figure 13**) and gasket and tighten as specified in **Table 4**.

9. Insert a funnel into the oil fill hole and fill the engine with the correct weight and quantity oil; see *Recommended Engine Oil* in this section. Refer to **Table 7** for engine oil capacity.

> *NOTE*
> *Honda lists three different engine oil capacities (**Table 8**), each specified for the type of service being performed. Make sure to install the correct oil capacity.*

10. Screw in the dipstick/oil fill cap (A, **Figure 10**) securely.

11. Start the engine and run at idle speed.

12. Turn the engine off and check the drain bolt and oil filter cover for leaks.

13. Check the oil level and adjust if necessary.

> *WARNING*
> *Prolonged contact with used oil may cause skin cancer. Wash your hands with soap and water after handling or coming in contact with motor oil.*

### Oil screen

An oil screen (**Figure 18**) is mounted inside the engine. Because the engine must be disassembled to service the oil screen, servicing it is not part of the engine periodic maintenance schedule. However, service the oil screen when troubleshooting a lubrication system problem or when internal engine damage occurs.

## Front Differential Gearcase

### Recommended gearcase oil

Honda recommends Honda shaft drive oil or an equivalent SAE 80 hypoid gear oil (**Table 7**).

### Oil level check

1. Park the vehicle on a level surface and set the parking brake.

2. Wipe clean the area around the oil fill cap and unscrew the oil fill plug (**Figure 19**).

3. The oil level should be level with the bottom thread of the fill plug hole. If the oil level is low, add hypoid gear oil (**Table 7**) until the level is correct.

4. Inspect the oil fill plug O-ring and replace if damaged.

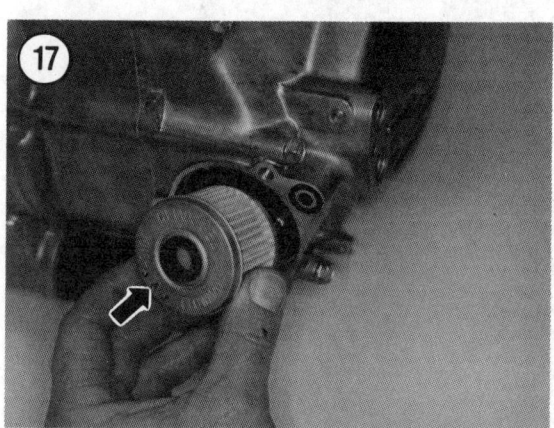

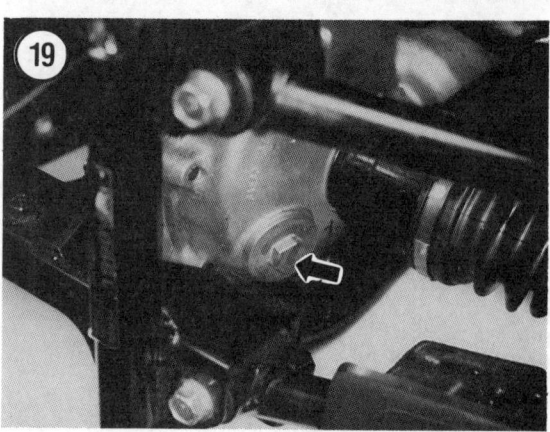

5. Screw on the oil fill cap and tighten as specified in **Table 4**.

## Oil change

The factory recommended oil change interval is listed in **Table 1** and **Table 2**.

To drain the oil you need the following:

a. Drain pan.

b. Funnel.

c. Hypoid gear oil. See **Table 7** (oil type) and **Table 9** (oil quantity).

Discard old oil in the same manner as outlined under *Engine Oil and Filter Change* in this chapter.

> *NOTE*
> *A short ride heats the front differential gearcase oil, which enables the oil to flow more freely and carry more contaminates and sludge when drained.*

1. Ride the vehicle until normal operating temperature is reached, then park the vehicle on a level

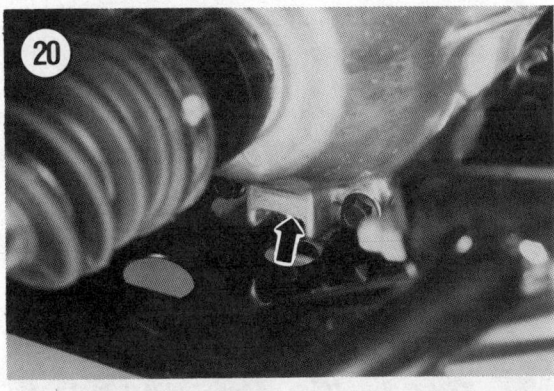

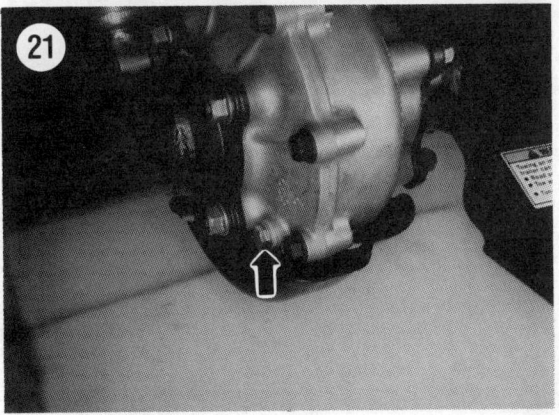

surface and set the parking brake. Turn the engine off.

> *NOTE*
> *Skid plate removal is not necessary for access to drain plug.*

2. Place a drain pan underneath the drain plug (**Figure 20**).

3. Remove the oil fill plug (**Figure 19**).

4. Remove the drain plug (**Figure 20**) and allow the oil to drain.

5. Replace the drain plug gasket if leaking or damaged.

6. Install the drain plug and gasket and tighten as specified in **Table 4**.

7. Insert a funnel into the oil fill plug hole and pour in the recommended type (**Table 7**) and quantity (**Table 9**) of gear oil.

8. Remove the funnel and check the oil level. It should come up to the bottom thread of the fill plug hole. Add additional oil if necessary.

9. Inspect the oil fill plug O-ring and replace if damaged.

10. Install the oil fill plug (**Figure 19**) and tighten as specified in **Table 4**.

11. Test ride the vehicle and check for leaks. After the test ride recheck the oil level and adjust if necessary.

### Rear Differential Gearcase

#### Recommended gearcase oil

Honda recommends Honda shaft drive oil or an equivalent SAE 80 hypoid gear oil (**Table 7**).

#### Oil level check

1. Park the vehicle on a level surface and set the parking brake.

2. Wipe the area around the oil check plug (**Figure 21**) and remove it. Oil should immediately start to flow out of the check hole. If oil flows out of the hole, the oil level is correct. Reinstall the oil check plug and tighten as specified in **Table 4**. If oil did not flow out of the hole, continue with Step 3.

3. Remove the oil fill cap (**Figure 22**) and slowly add hypoid gear oil (**Table 7**) until oil starts to flow out of the check hole. Then reinstall the oil check plug and tighten as specified in **Table 4**.

4. Install the oil fill cap (**Figure 22**) and tighten as specified in **Table 4**.

### Oil change

The factory recommended oil change interval is listed in **Table 1** and **Table 2**.

To drain the oil you need the following:
a. Drain pan.
b. Funnel.
c. Hypoid gear oil. See **Table 7** (oil type) and **Table 9** (oil quantity).

Discard old oil in the same manner as outlined under *Engine Oil and Filter Change* in this chapter.

> *NOTE*
> *A short ride heats the rear gearcase oil, which enables the oil to flow more freely and carry more contaminates and sludge out when drained.*

1. Ride the vehicle until normal operating temperature is reached, then park the vehicle on a level surface and set the parking brake. Turn the engine off.
2. On 1995-1996 models, remove the rear differential skid plate.

> *NOTE*
> *On 1997 and later models, the rear gearcase skid plate is machined with two holes that allow draining the rear differential oil without removing the skid plate.*

3. Place a drain pan underneath the drain plug (**Figure 23**). Unscrew the drain plug and remove it. Allow the oil to drain out.
4. Wipe clean the area around the oil fill cap and unscrew the oil fill cap (**Figure 22**).
5. Inspect the drain plug washer and replace if leaking or damaged.
6. When the oil stops draining, install the drain plug and gasket and tighten as specified in **Table 4**.
7. Insert a funnel into the oil fill cap hole and add the recommended type (**Table 7**) and quantity (**Table 9**) gear oil.
8. Inspect the oil fill cap O-ring and replace if damaged.
9. Install the oil fill cap (**Figure 22**) and tighten as specified in **Table 4**.
10. Test ride the vehicle and check for leaks.

11. On 1995-1996 models, install the rear differential skid plate.

### Control Cable Lubrication

Clean and lubricate the throttle, brake, choke and reverse cables at the intervals indicated in **Table 1** or **Table 2**. In addition, check the cables for kinks, excessive wear, damage or fraying that could cause the cables to fail or stick. Cables are expendable items even under the best conditions.

The most positive method of control cable lubrication involves the use of a cable lubricator and a can of cable lube or a general lubricant. Do not use chain lube as a cable lubricant.

1. Disconnect the cable to be lubricated. Note the following:
a. To service the throttle cable, refer to *Throttle Housing and Cable* in Chapter Eight.
b. To service the brake cables, refer to *Rear Brake Pedal and Cable* and *Rear Brake Lever/Parking Brake Cable* in Chapter Thirteen.
c. To service the choke cable, refer to *Choke Cable Replacement* in Chapter Eight.

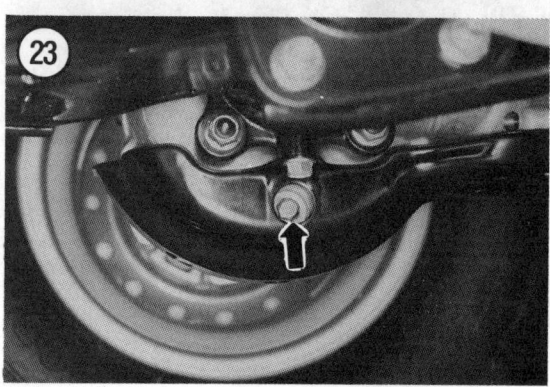

d. To service the reverse cable, refer to *Reverse Selector Cable Replacement* in Chapter Seven.

2. Attach a cable lubricator to the end of the cable following its manufacturer's instructions (**Figure 24**).

3. Inject cable lubricant into the cable until it begins to flow out of the other end of the cable.

> *NOTE*
> *Place a shop cloth at the end of the cable to catch the oil as it runs out.*

4. Disconnect the lubricator.

5. Apply a light coat of grease to the cable ends before reconnecting them. Reconnect the cable and adjust as described in this chapter.

6. Reverse Step 1 to reconnect the cables.

7. After lubricating the throttle cable, operate the throttle lever at the handlebar. It should open and close smoothly with no binding.

8. After lubricating the brake cable(s), check brake operation.

## UNSCHEDULED LUBRICATION

The services listed in this section are not included in **Table 1** and **Table 2** (maintenance and lubrication

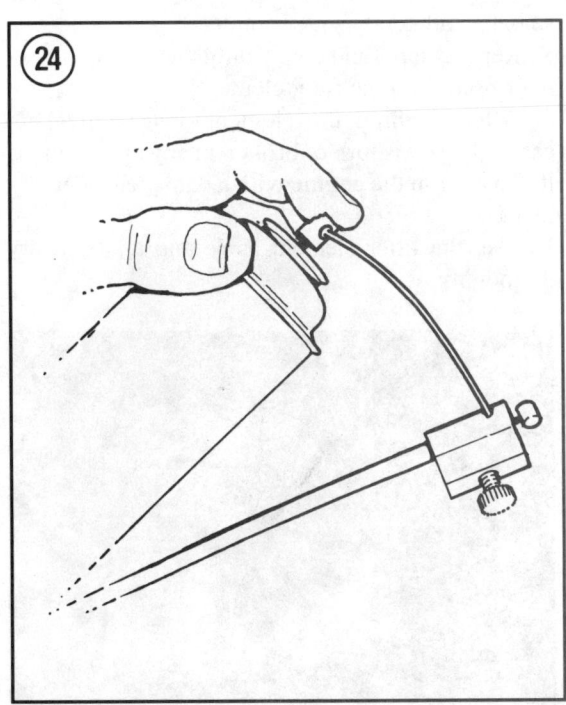

schedule). However, lubricate these items throughout the service year. Lubrication and service intervals depend on vehicle use. Use a water-resistant bearing grease when grease is specified in the following sections.

### Steering Shaft Lubrication

Remove the steering shaft (Chapter Ten) and lubricate the bushing with grease. At the same time, check the lower bearing and seals for damage.

### Front Upper and Lower Arm Lubrication

Remove the upper and lower arm pivot bolts and lubricate the bolts and bushings with grease. Refer to Chapter Ten for service.

### Front Wheel Bearing Seals

Lubricate the front wheel bearing seals with grease. If the front wheel bearings are not sealed, lubricate them also. Refer to Chapter Ten for service.

### Rear Shock Absorber Mounting Bolt Lubrication

Remove the front (Chapter Ten) and rear (Chapter Twelve) shock absorbers and lubricate the mounting bolts with grease.

## PERIODIC MAINTENANCE

Periodic maintenance intervals are listed in **Table 1** and **Table 2**.

### Air Box Drain Tube

Inspect the drain tube (**Figure 25**) mounted on the bottom of the air box. If the hose is filled with water, dirt and other debris, clean and reoil the air filter. Then clean the air box and drain the drain tube at the same time.

### Air Filter

A clogged air filter will decrease the efficiency and life of the engine. Never run the engine without an air filter properly installed. Dust that enters the engine can cause severe engine wear and clog carburetor jets and passages.

Refer to **Figure 26** when servicing the air filter in this section.

### Removal and installation

1. Remove the seat (Chapter Fifteen).

> *NOTE*
> *The rear fender was removed for clarity in the following illustrations. It is not necessary to remove the rear fender for this procedure.*

2. Release the air box cover retaining clips and remove the cover (**Figure 27**).
3. Loosen the air filter hose clamp (A, **Figure 28**) and remove the air filter assembly (**Figure 29**).
4. On 1998 California models, and all later models, remove the dust cover (**Figure 30**).
5. Disassemble, clean and oil the air filter as described in the following procedure.
6. Check the air box and carburetor boot for dirt or other contamination.
7. Wipe the inside of the air box with a clean rag. If you cannot clean the air box with it bolted to the frame, remove and clean the air box (Chapter Eight).
8. On 1998 California models, and all later models, clean the dust cover (**Figure 31**) with compressed air. Then install the dust cover into the air box (**Figure 30**). Check that the dust cover sits flat in the air box (**Figure 30**).
9. Cover the air box opening with a clean shop rag.
10. Inspect all fittings, hoses and connections from the air box to the carburetor.
11. Assemble the air filter as described under *Air Filter Cleaning and Reoiling* in this chapter.
12. Install the air filter into the housing (**Figure 28**), making sure the holder (B, **Figure 28**) seats into the bracket in the back of the housing. Then tighten the air filter hose clamp (A, **Figure 28**) securely.
13. Install the air box cover (**Figure 27**) and secure with the retaining clips.
14. Install the seat (Chapter Fifteen).

### Air filter cleaning and reoiling

Service the air filter element in a well-ventilated area, away from all sparks and flames.

1. Turn the holder (A, **Figure 32**) counterclockwise and remove it.
2. Remove the hose clamp (B, **Figure 32**), then remove the element core from the filter element. See **Figure 33**.

> *WARNING*
> *Do not clean the filter element with gasoline.*

3. Clean the filter element with a filter solvent to remove oil and dirt.
4. Inspect the filter element. Replace if it is torn or broken in any area.
5. Fill a clean pan with liquid detergent and warm water.
6. Submerge the filter element in the cleaning solution and gently work the cleaner into the filter pores. Soak and squeeze (gently) the filter element to clean it.

> *CAUTION*
> *Do not wring or twist the filter element when cleaning it. This could damage the filter pores or tear the filter loose at a seam. This would allow unfiltered air to enter the engine and cause severe and rapid wear.*

7. Rinse the filter element under warm water while soaking and gently squeezing it.
8. Repeat Step 6 and Step 7 until there is no dirt being rinsed from the filter element.
9. After cleaning the element, inspect it again carefully. If it is torn or broken in any area, replace it. Do not run the engine with a damaged filter element.
10. Set the filter element aside and allow to dry thoroughly.

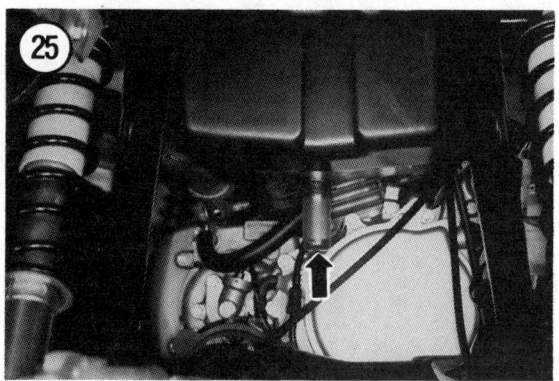

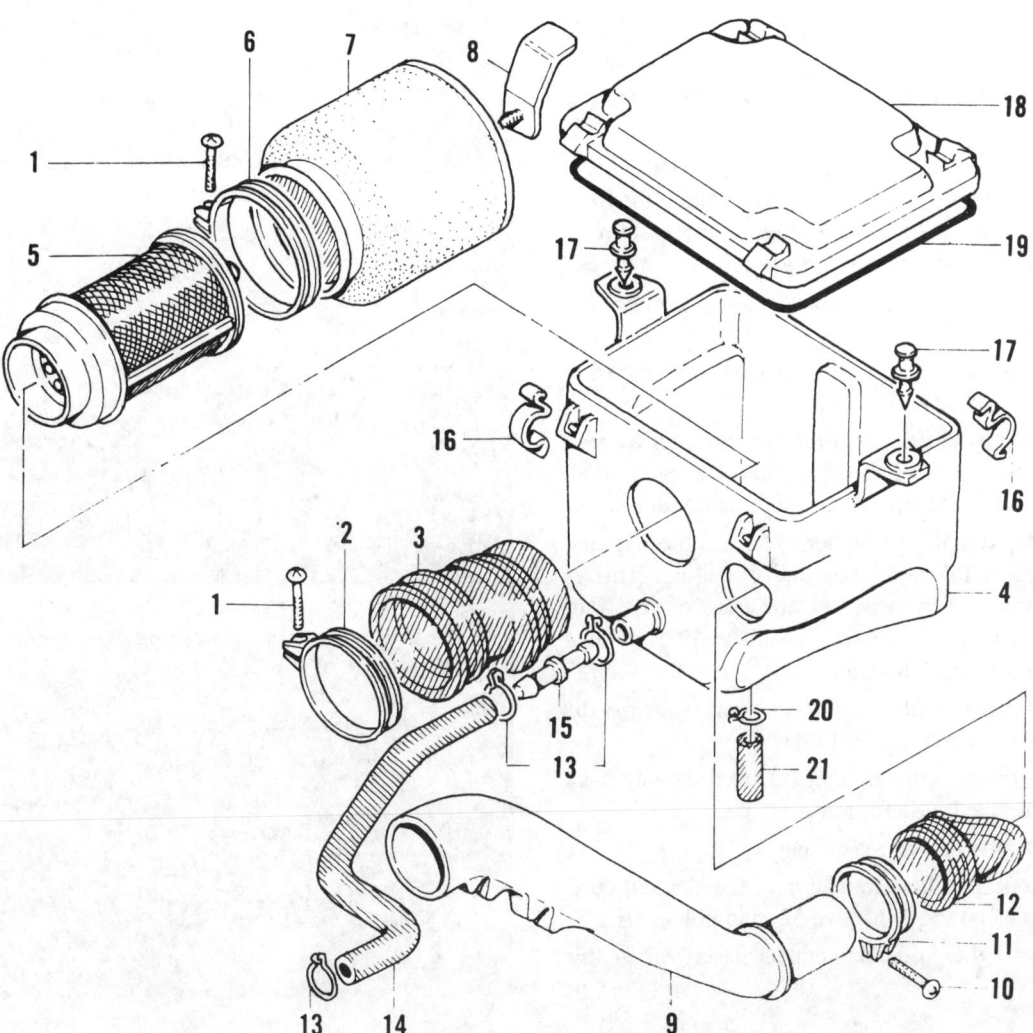

**26**

**AIR BOX ASSEMBLY**

| | | |
|---|---|---|
| 1. Screw | 8. Holder | 15. Hose nozzle |
| 2. Hose clamp | 9. Intake air duct | 16. Retaining clip |
| 3. Intake hose | 10. Screw | 17. Retaining pin |
| 4. Air box | 11. Hose clamp | 18. Cover |
| 5. Element core | 12. Hose | 19. Seal |
| 6. Hose clamp | 13. Clamp | 20. Clamp |
| 7. Filter element | 14. Crankcase breather tube | 21. Drain tube |
| | (1998 California) | |

3

11. Clean and dry the element core. Check the element core for damage and replace if necessary.

*CAUTION*
*Make sure the filter element is completely dry before oiling it.*

12. Properly oiling an air filter element is a messy but important job. Wear a pair of disposable rubber gloves when performing this procedure. Oil the filter as follows:

a. Purchase a box of gallon size storage bags. The bags can be used when cleaning the filter as well as for storing engine and carburetor parts during disassembly service procedures.

b. Place the filter element into a storage bag (**Figure 34**).

c. Pour foam filter oil (**Figure 34**) onto the filter to soak it.

d. Gently squeeze and release the filter to soak filter oil into the filter's pores. Repeat until all of the filter's pores are saturated with oil.

e. Remove the filter element from the bag and check the pores for uneven oiling. This is indicated by light or dark areas on the filter element. If necessary, soak the filter element and squeeze it again.

f. When the filter oiling is even, squeeze the filter element a final time.

g. Pour the leftover filter oil from the bag back into the bottle for reuse.

h. Dispose of the plastic bag.

13. Install the filter element over the element core. Install the clamp (B, **Figure 32**) and holder (A).

14. Install the filter element as described in this chapter.

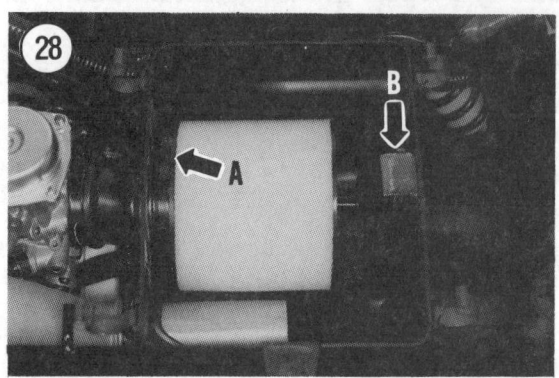

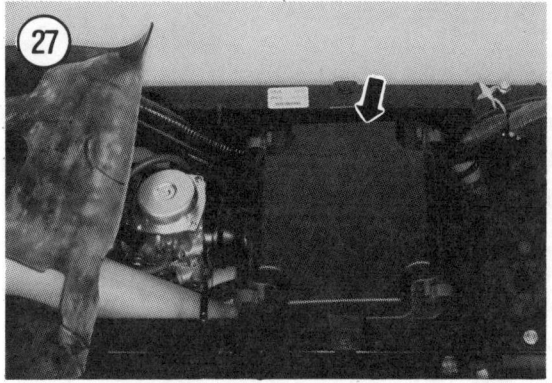

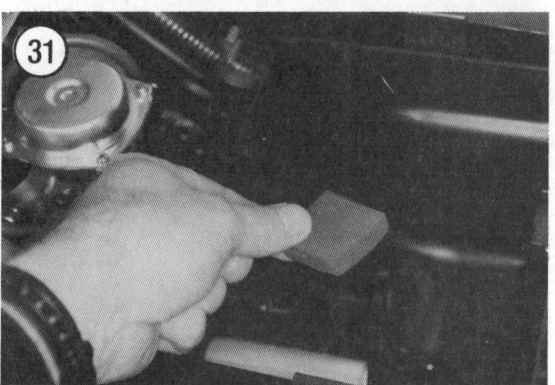

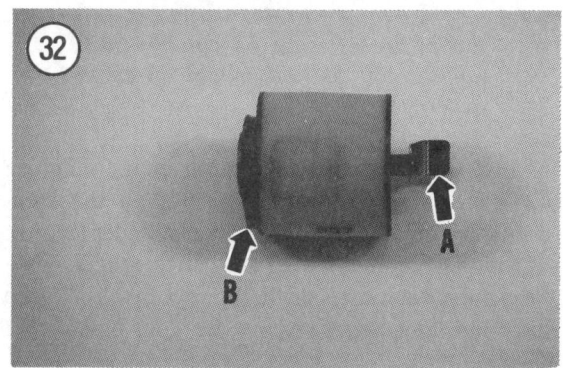

## Fuel Line Inspection

> *WARNING*
> *Some fuel may spill when performing the procedure in this section. Because gasoline is extremely flammable, perform the following procedure away from all open flames (including appliance pilot lights) and sparks. Do not smoke or allow someone who is smoking in the work area. Always work in a well-ventilated area. Wipe up any spills immediately.*

Inspect the fuel line (**Figure 35**) for leaks, cracks, hardness, age deterioration or other damage. Make sure each end of the hose is secured with a hose clamp. Check the carburetor overflow and vent hose ends for contamination.

> *WARNING*
> *A damaged or deteriorated fuel line presents a very dangerous fire hazard to both the rider and machine.*

## Fuel Tank Vent Hose

Check the fuel tank vent hose (**Figure 36**) for proper routing and make sure it is not kinked. Check the end of the hose for contamination.

## Front Brake Lining Check

1. Remove the rubber inspection cap (**Figure 37**) from the front wheel and brake drum.

2. Move the vehicle in either direction until the inspection hole aligns with one of the brake linings.

*NOTE*
*Figure 38 shows a brake shoe with the brake drum removed for clarity. It is not necessary to remove the brake drum for this procedure.*

3. Inspect the lining thickness (**Figure 38**). The standard lining thickness is 4.0 mm (0.16 in.). The service limit is 1.0 mm (0.04 in.). If the lining thickness seems thin or excessively worn, remove the brake drum (Chapter Thirteen) to inspect and measure the lining thickness.

4. Repeat Step 3 for the other three front brake linings.

5. Install the rubber inspection cap (**Figure 37**).

**Rear Brake Lining Check**

Apply the rear brake fully. If the indicator plate (A, **Figure 39**) aligns with the fixed index mark on the brake panel (B, **Figure 39**), replace both rear brake shoes (Chapter Thirteen).

**Front Brake Adjustment**

1. Perform the *Front Brake Lining Check* in this chapter. If the brake lining thickness is within specifications, continue with Step 2.

2. Apply the front brake lever and measure the amount of free play travel until the front brakes start to engage (**Figure 40**). The correct front brake lever free play measurement is 25-30 mm (1-1/4 in.). If the brake linings contact the brake drum too early or too late, continue with Step 3 to adjust the front brakes.

*NOTE*
*Contamination inside the brake drum can cause the brakes to take hold too soon. If you determine there is dirt or other debris inside the drum, remove the brake drum and inspect the drum surface and brake linings as described in Chapter Thirteen.*

3. Support the vehicle with the front wheels off the ground.

4. Remove the rubber plug (**Figure 37**) from one of the brake drums.

5. Turn the wheel to align the hole with one of the brake adjusters (**Figure 41**).

*NOTE*
*Each wheel is equipped with two brake adjusters. It does not matter which adjuster you adjust first.*

6. Insert a slotted screwdriver into the hole (**Figure 42**) and rotate the adjuster (**Figure 55**) in the direction of the arrow cast on the wheel cylinder (**Figure 41**) until the drum is locked and can no longer move. From this position, rotate the adjuster in the opposite direction three clicks. Apply the front brake lever several times.

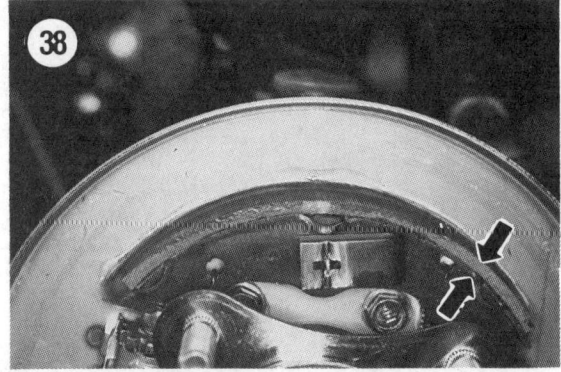

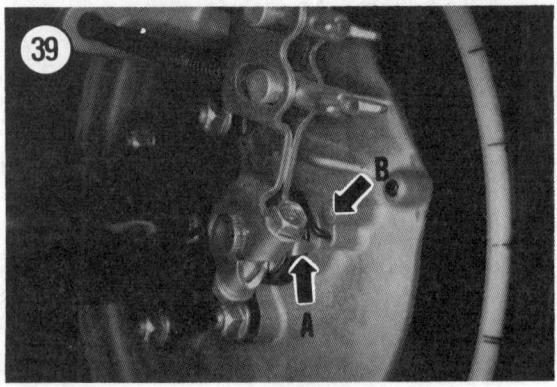

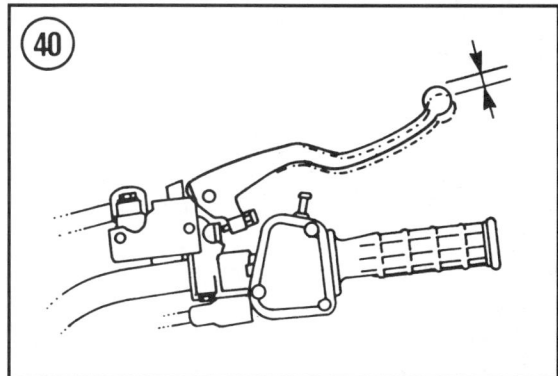

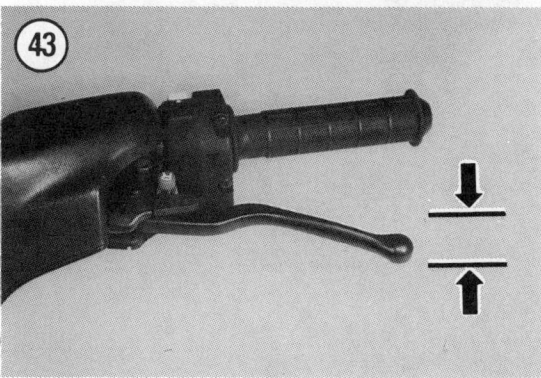

7. Rotate the wheel and check that the brake is not dragging on the drum.

*NOTE*
*A buildup of rust and dirt in the brake drum can cause the brake linings to drag.*

8. Turn the wheel to align the hole with the other brake adjuster and repeat Steps 6 and 7.

9. Repeat Steps 4-8 for the opposite front wheel.

10. After adjusting the brakes on both front wheels, recheck the brake lever free play (Step 2). It should be within specification.

*NOTE*
*If the free play is excessive after adjusting the brakes, there is probably air in the brake line. Bleed the front brakes, (Chapter Thirteen) then recheck the brake lever free play.*

11. Install the rubber plug (**Figure 37**) into each brake drum.

12. Install the front wheels (Chapter Ten).

13. Lower the vehicle so that all four wheels are on the ground.

*WARNING*
*Do not ride the vehicle until the brakes are working properly.*

**Rear Brake Adjustment**

1. Before adjusting the rear brake, check the brake pedal, brake cables and adjusters for loose or damaged connections. Replace or repair any damage before continuing with Step 2.

2. Lubricate the rear brake cables as described in this chapter.

3. Release the parking brake if it is set.

4. Perform the *Rear Brake Lining Check* in this chapter. If the brake lining thickness is within specifications, continue with Step 5.

5. Apply the rear brake lever and measure the amount of free play travel until the rear brake starts to engage (**Figure 43**). The correct rear brake lever free play is 15-20 mm (5/8-3/4 in.). Note the following:

    a. If the brake linings contact the brake drum too early or too late, perform Step 6.

    b. If the free play travel is within specification, go to Step 7.

*NOTE*
*Contamination inside the brake drum can cause the brakes to apply too soon. If you determine there is dirt or other debris inside the drum, remove the brake drum and inspect the drum surface and brake linings as described in Chapter Thirteen.*

6. Turn the *lower* adjusting nut (A, **Figure 44**) in or out to achieve the correct amount of free play.

*NOTE*
*Make sure the cutout relief in the adjust nut is properly seated on the collar.*

7. At the brake pedal, apply the rear brake and check the pedal free play. With the pedal in the at rest position, apply the brake pedal and check the distance it travels until the rear brake is applied (**Figure 45**) The correct brake pedal free play is 15-20 mm (5/8-3/4 in.). If out of adjustment, turn the *upper* adjusting nut (B, **Figure 44**) in or out to achieve the correct amount of free play.

*NOTE*
*Make sure the cutout relief in the adjusting nut is properly seated on the collar.*

8. Support the vehicle with the rear wheels off the ground.
9. Rotate the rear wheels and make sure the brake is not dragging. If the brake is dragging, repeat this procedure until there is no drag.

*NOTE*
*Brake drag can also be caused by dirt and other contamination in the brake drum and on the brake linings. If necessary, remove the brake drum (Chapter Thirteen) and check the brake drum and linings.*

10. Lower the vehicle so that all four wheels are on the ground

**Brake Fluid Level Check**

1. Turn the handlebar so that the master cylinder is level.
2. Check the brake fluid level through the master cylinder inspection window (**Figure 46**). The level should be above the LOWER level line. If necessary, add brake fluid as follows.

*NOTE*
*If the brake fluid is low, check the front brake lining wear as described in this chapter.*

3. Remove the handlebar cover (Chapter Fifteen).
4. Clean any dirt from the cover and master cylinder.
5. Remove the two cover screws, cover ( **Figure 47**) and diaphragm.
6. Add new DOT 3 or DOT 4 brake fluid to raise the brake fluid level.

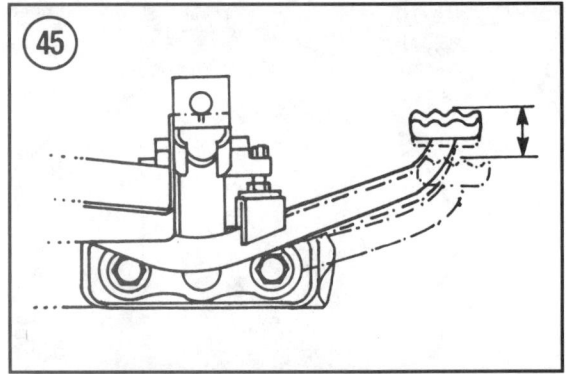

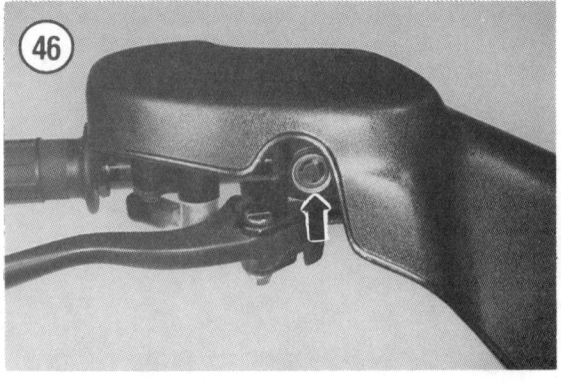

*WARNING*
*Use brake fluid clearly marked DOT 3 or DOT 4. Others may cause brake failure. Do not intermix different brands or types of brake fluid as they may not be compatible. Do not intermix a silicone based (DOT 5) brake fluid as it can cause brake component damage leading to brake system failure.*

*CAUTION*
*Be careful when handling brake fluid. Do not spill it on painted or plastic surfaces as it will destroy the surface. Immediately wash the area with soap and water and thoroughly rinse it off.*

7. Reinstall the diaphragm and cover (**Figure 47**). Install the screws and tighten securely.

8. Install the handlebar cover (Chapter Fifteen).

## Disc Brake Hoses

Inspect the brake hoses for cracks, cuts, bulges, deterioration and leaks. Check the metal brake lines

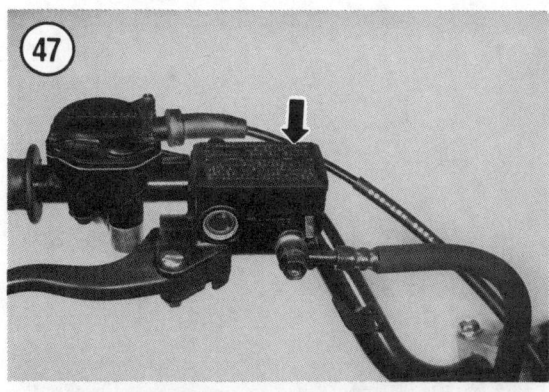

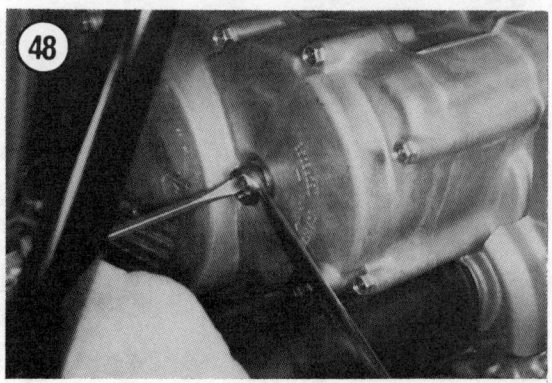

for cracks and leaks. Refer to Chapter Thirteen for service procedures.

## Disc Brake Fluid Change

Every time the master cylinder top cover is removed, a small amount of dirt and moisture can enter the brake fluid. The same thing happens if a leak occurs or if any part of the hydraulic system is loosened or disconnected. Dirt can clog the system and cause wear and brake failure. Water in the brake fluid will cause corrosion inside the hydraulic system, impairing the hydraulic action and reducing the brake's stopping ability.

To maintain peak performance, change the brake fluid every 2 years or whenever rebuilding or replacing the master cylinder or a wheel cylinder. To change brake fluid, follow the brake bleeding procedure in Chapter Thirteen.

*WARNING*
*Use brake fluid clearly marked DOT 3 or DOT 4 only. Others may cause brake failure. Dispose of any used fluid according to local EPA regulations. Never reuse brake fluid. Contaminated brake fluid can cause brake failure.*

## Clutch Adjustment

Adjust the clutch at the intervals specified in **Table 1** or **Table 2**.

This adjustment pertains only to the change (manual) clutch. The centrifugal clutch requires no adjustment. Since there is no clutch cable, the mechanism is the only component that requires adjustment. This adjustment takes up slack due to clutch component wear.

1. Loosen the clutch adjusting screw locknut (**Figure 48**).

2. Turn the adjusting screw (**Figure 48**) counterclockwise until resistance is felt, then stop.

3. From this point, turn the adjusting screw (**Figure 48**) clockwise 1/4 of a turn, then stop.

*NOTE*
*Make sure the adjusting screw does not move when tightening the locknut in Step 4.*

4. Hold the adjusting screw and tighten the locknut (**Figure 48**) as specified in **Table 4**.

5. Test ride the vehicle to make sure the clutch is operating correctly. Readjust if necessary.

*NOTE*
*If the clutch adjustment is difficult, the friction plates may be worn. Remove the clutch cover and inspect the friction plates as described in Chapter Six.*

## Throttle Cable
## Check and Adjustment

1. Before adjusting the throttle cable, operate the throttle lever and make sure it opens and closes properly with the handlebar turned in different positions. If not, check the throttle cable for damage or improper routing. Check the throttle lever for damage. Replace or repair any damage before continuing with Step 2.

2. Lubricate the throttle cable as described in this chapter.

3. Operate the throttle lever and measure the amount of free play travel (**Figure 49**) until the cable play is taken up and the carburetor lever starts to move. The correct throttle lever free play measurement is 3-8 mm (1/8-5/16 in.). If the free play is out of specification, continue with Step 4.

4. At the upper throttle cable adjuster on the handlebar, slide the rubber boot (A, **Figure 50**) off the adjuster and loosen the cable adjuster locknut (B, **Figure 50**). Turn the adjuster (B, **Figure 50**) in or out until the free play is correct. Then hold the adjuster and tighten the locknut securely. Recheck the throttle lever free play while noting the following:
   a. If the proper amount of free play cannot be achieved at the throttle end of the cable, continue with Step 5.
   b. If the free play measurement is correct, slide the rubber boot (A, **Figure 50**) over the adjuster, then go to Step 11.

5. Loosen the upper cable adjuster locknut and loosen the adjuster (B, **Figure 50**) to obtain as much throttle cable free play as possible.

6. Remove the seat (Chapter Fifteen).

7. On 1998-on models, remove the rubber snorkel (**Figure 51**).

8. Slide the rubber boot (A, **Figure 52**) off the lower cable adjuster and loosen the cable adjuster locknut (B, **Figure 52**). Turn the adjuster to remove some of the cable free play, then tighten the locknut (B, **Figure 52**).

9. Repeat Step 4 to adjust the throttle lever free play. If necessary, readjust the lower (B, **Figure 52**) and upper (B, **Figure 50**) cable adjusters until the free play is correct. Then tighten both cable adjuster locknuts securely. Slide the rubber boots over the cable adjusters.

*WARNING*
*Do not turn either adjuster so far out that the adjuster cannot be tightened*

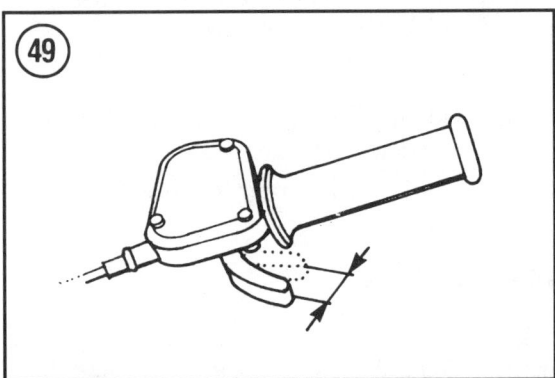

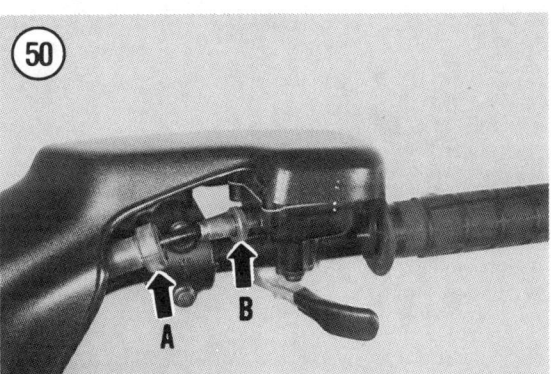

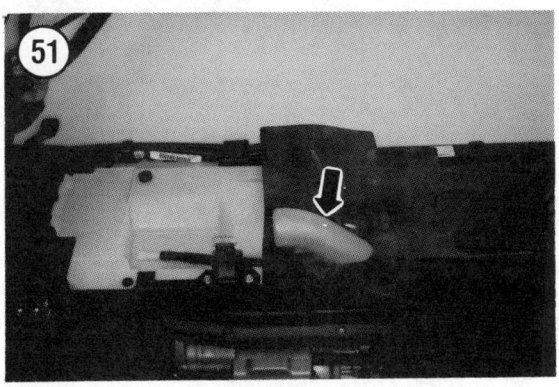

*securely with its locknut. This could allow the throttle to stick open and cause you to lose control of the vehicle.*

10. If the throttle cable cannot be adjusted properly, the cable has stretched excessively and must be replaced as described in Chapter Eight.

11. Make sure the throttle lever moves freely from its fully closed to fully open positions and has 3-5 mm (0.12-0.20 in.) of free play.

12. Apply the parking brake.

13. Start the engine and allow it to idle in NEUTRAL. Turn the handlebar from side to side. If the engine speed increases as the handlebar is being turned, the throttle cable is routed incorrectly or

there is not enough cable free play. Readjust the throttle cable, or if necessary, replace the throttle cable as described in Chapter Eight.

*NOTE*
*A damaged throttle cable will prevent the engine from idling properly.*

14. On 1998-on models, reinstall the rubber snorkel (**Figure 51**).

### Choke Cable Inspection

There is no choke cable adjustment. Inspect the choke cable as described in this procedure

1. Operate the choke lever (**Figure 53**), checking that the lever moves smoothly and the cable is working properly.

2. If necessary, lubricate the choke cable as described in this chapter.

3. Visually inspect the choke cable for cracks or other damage. If necessary, replace the choke cable as described in Chapter Eight.

### Reverse Lock System Check and Adjustment

1. Check the reverse selector cable for loose or damaged cable ends. Check the reverse lever for damage. Repair or replace any damaged parts.

2. If necessary, lubricate the reverse selector cable as described in this chapter.

3. Push the reverse selector knob (**Figure 54**) in while squeezing the rear brake lever, then measure the reverse lever free play (**Figure 54**). The correct amount of free play is 2-4 mm (1/16-5/32 in.).

4. To adjust, loosen the reverse selector cable locknut (A, **Figure 55**) and turn the adjuster (B) in or out to achieve the correct amount of free play. Tighten the locknut and recheck the free play.

5. Start the engine and then shift the transmission into reverse following your normal operating procedures. Check that the transmission shifts into and out of reverse correctly.

### Spark Arrestor

Clean the spark arrestor at the intervals indicated in **Table 1** or **Table 2** or sooner if a considerable amount of slow riding is done.

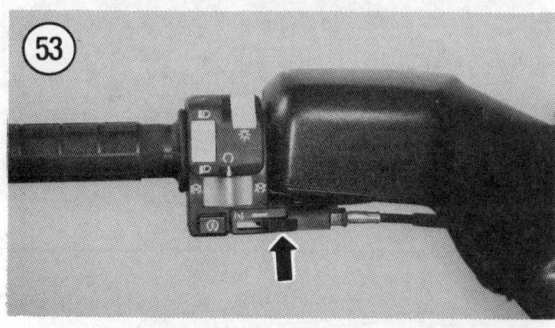

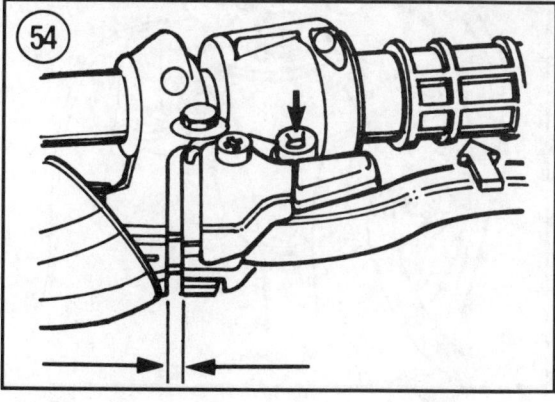

*WARNING*
*To avoid burning your hands, do not perform this cleaning operation when the exhaust system is hot. Work in a well-ventilated area (outside of your garage or work area) that is free of any fire hazards. Be sure to protect your eyes with safety glasses or goggles.*

1. Remove the bolt (**Figure 56**) from the base of the muffler.

2. Wear heavy gloves, such as welding gloves, and block the muffler opening with several shop cloths that are free of all chemicals (**Figure 57**).

3. Have an assistant start the engine. Open and close the throttle several times to blow out accumulated carbon in the tail section of the muffler. Continue until carbon stops coming out of the muffler opening.

4. Turn the engine off and let the muffler cool.

5. Install the bolt (**Figure 56**) and tighten securely.

## Steering Shaft and Front Suspension Inspection

Inspect the steering system and front suspension at the interval indicated in **Table 1** or **Table 2**. If any of the following mentioned front suspension and steering fasteners are loose, refer to Chapter Ten for the correct service procedures and tightening torques.

1. Park the vehicle on level ground and set the parking brake.

2. Visually inspect all components of the steering system. Repair or replace damaged components as described in Chapter Ten.

3. Check the shock absorbers as described in the next section.

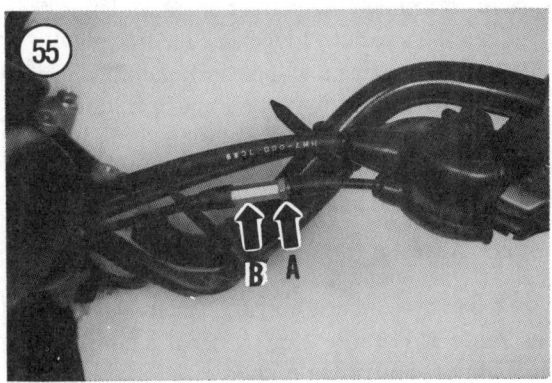

4. Remove the handlebar cover (Chapter Fifteen). Check that the handlebar holder bolts are tight. Reinstall the handlebar cover.

5. Make sure the front axle nuts are tight and that all cotter pins are in place.

6. Check that the cotter pins are in place on all steering components. If any cotter pin is missing, check the nut for looseness. Torque the nut and install a new cotter pin as described in Chapter Ten.

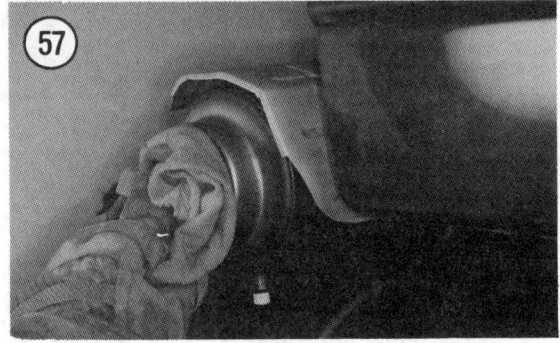

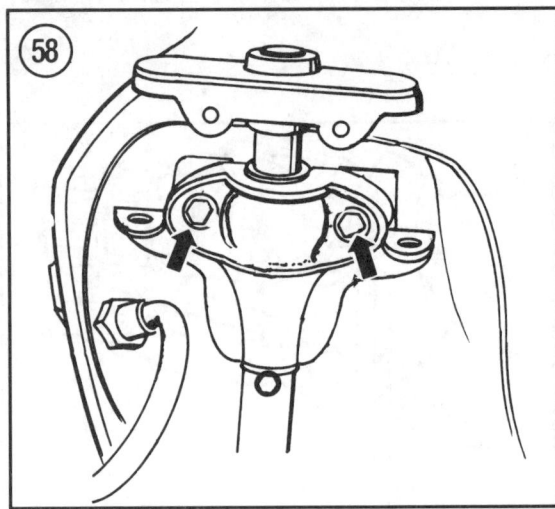

7. Check the steering shaft play as follows:
   a. Support the vehicle with the front wheels off the ground.
   b. To check steering shaft radial play, move the handlebar from side to side (without attempting to move the wheels). If radial play is excessive, the upper steering bushing is probably worn or the bushing holder mounting bolts (**Figure 58**) are loose. Replace the upper bushing or tighten the bushing holder bolts as necessary.
   c. To check steering shaft thrust play, lift up and then push down on the handlebar. If you find

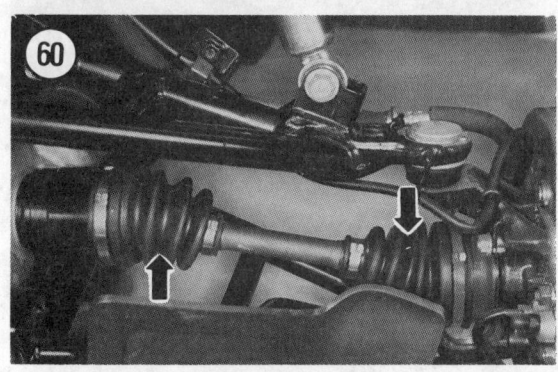

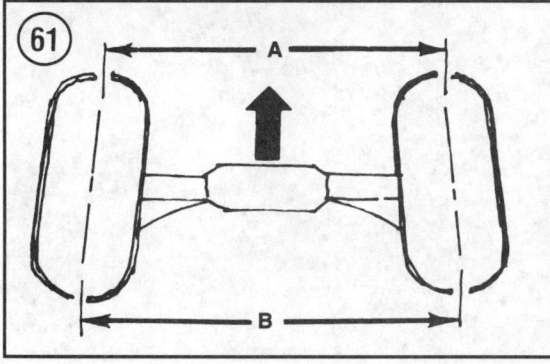

excessive thrust play, check the lower steering shaft nut (**Figure 59**) for looseness. If the nut is tightened properly, check the lower steering shaft bearing for excessive wear or damage.
   d. If necessary, service the steering shaft as described in Chapter Ten.
   e. Lower the vehicle so that all four tires are on the ground.
8. Check the steering knuckle and tie rod ends as follows:
   a. Turn the handlebar quickly from side to side. If there is appreciable looseness between the handlebar and tires, check the tie rod ends for excessive wear or damage.
   b. Service the steering knuckle and tie rods as described in Chapter Ten.

*NOTE*
*If any cotter pins were removed in this section, install new cotter pins during reassembly.*

### Shock Absorber Inspection

1. Check the front and rear shock absorbers for oil leaks, a bent damper rod or other damage.
2. If necessary, replace the shock absorbers as described in Chapter Ten (front) or Chapter Twelve (rear).

### Front Axle Joint Boot Inspection

At the interval specified in **Table 1** or **Table 2**, inspect the front axle joint boots (**Figure 60**) for tearing or other damage. Replace damaged boots as described in Chapter Eleven.

### Toe-In Adjustment

Toe-in is a condition where the front of the tires are closer together than the back (**Figure 61**). Check the toe-in adjustment at the intervals specified in **Table 1** or **Table 2**, after servicing the front suspension or when replacing the tie rods.

Adjust toe-in by changing the length of the tie rods.

1. Inflate all four tires to the recommended pressure specified in **Table 3**.

2. Park the vehicle on level ground and set the parking brake. Then raise and support the front of the vehicle so that both front tires just clear the ground.

3. Turn the handlebar so the wheels are facing the straight-ahead position.

4. Using a tape measure, carefully measure the distance between the center of both front tires as shown in A, **Figure 61**. Mark the tires with a piece of chalk at these points. Record the measurement.

5. Rotate each tire exactly 180° and measure the distance between the center of both front tires at B, **Figure 61**. Record the measurement.

6. Subtract the measurement in Step 4 from Step 5 as shown in **Figure 61**. Toe-in is correct if the difference is 16 mm (0.63 in.). If the toe-in measurement is incorrect, continue with Step 7. If the toe-in is correct, go to Step 10.

7. Loosen the locknut (A, **Figure 62**) at each end of both tie rods.

8. Use a wrench on the flat portion (B, **Figure 62**) of the tie rods and slowly turn both tie rods the same amount until the toe-in measurement is correct.

> *NOTE*
> *Turn both tie rods the same number of turns. This ensures that the tie rod length will remain the same on each side. If you feel that the left- and right-side tie rod lengths are different, refer to* **Tie Rods** *in Chapter Ten.*

> *WARNING*
> *If the tie rods are not adjusted equally, the handlebar will not be centered while traveling straight ahead. This condition may cause you to lose control of the vehicle. If you cannot adjust the toe-in properly, have it adjusted at a Honda dealership or qualified shop.*

9. When the toe-in adjustment is correct, hold each tie rod in place and tighten the locknuts as specified in **Table 4**.

10. Lower the vehicle so that both front wheels are on the ground.

11. Start the engine and make a slow test ride on level ground. Ride in a straight-ahead position while checking that the handlebar does not turn toward the left- or right-side.

### Rear Suspension Check

1. Support the vehicle so that the rear wheels are off the ground.

2. Try to move the rear axle (**Figure 63**) sideways while checking for excessive play at the swing arm bearings.

3. If there is any play, check the swing arm pivot bolts for looseness (Chapter Twelve). If they are tightened properly, the swing arm bearings may require replacement. See Chapter Twelve.

4. Lower the vehicle so that all four tires are on the ground.

### Skid Plates

Check the front, middle and rear skid plates for damage and loose mounting bolts. Repair or replace damaged skid plates. Replace missing or damaged mounting bolts. Tighten the mounting bolts securely.

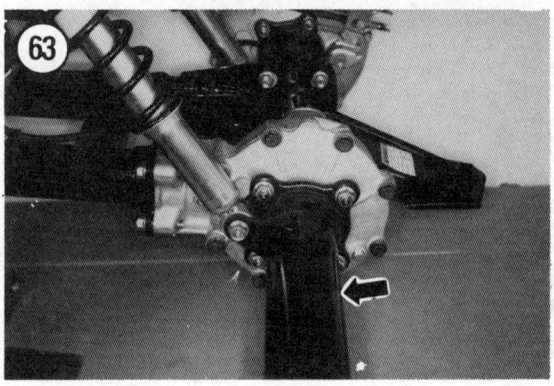

### Nuts, Bolts, and Other Fasteners

Constant vibration can loosen many of the fasteners on the vehicle. Check the tightness of all fasteners, especially those on:
   a. Engine mounting hardware.
   b. Cylinder head bracket bolts.
   c. Engine crankcase covers.
   d. Handlebar.
   e. Gearshift lever.
   f. Brake pedal and lever.
   g. Exhaust system.

   h. Steering and suspension components.

### ENGINE TUNE-UP

The number of definitions of the term tune-up is probably equal to the number of people defining it. For the purposes of this book, a tune-up is general adjustment and maintenance to ensure peak engine performance.

The following paragraphs discuss each phase of a proper tune-up which should be performed in the order given. Unless otherwise specified, the engine should be thoroughly cool before starting any tune-up procedure.

Have the new parts on hand before you begin.

To perform a tune-up on your Honda, you need the following tools and equipment:
   a. 14 mm spark plug wrench.
   b. Socket wrench and assorted sockets.
   c. Phillips head screwdriver.
   d. Spark plug feeler gauge and gap adjusting tool.
   e. Feeler gauge set.
   f. Compression gauge.
   g. Tachometer.
   h. Timing light.

### Camshaft Chain Adjustment

The engine is equipped with an automatic camshaft chain tensioner. No adjustment is required.

### Valve Clearance Check and Adjustment

Check and adjust the valve clearance while the engine is cold (below 35° C [95° F]).

1. Park the vehicle on level ground and set the parking brake.

2. Remove the fuel tank and the engine heat guard (Chapter Eight).

3. Remove the bolts and the cylinder head cover (**Figure 64**) and gasket.

4. Remove the O-ring (A, **Figure 65**).

5. Remove the spark plug. This will make it easier to turn the engine by hand and align the timing marks.

6. Remove the timing hole cap (**Figure 66**).

7. The engine must be set to top dead center (TDC) on its compression stroke when checking and adjusting the valve clearance. Perform the following:

a. Pull the recoil starter handle slowly and align the T mark on the flywheel with the index mark on the rear crankcase cover (**Figure 67**).

b. Now move both rocker arms by hand. When the engine is set at TDC on its compression stroke, both rocker arms will have some side clearance, indicating that the intake and exhaust valves are closed. If the rocker arms are tight (indicating that the valves are open), turn the crankshaft 360° and realign the T mark as described in substep a. The engine should now be set at TDC on its compression stroke.

8. Check the clearance of both the intake valve and exhaust valve by inserting a flat feeler gauge between the rocker arm pad and the valve stem as shown in **Figure 68**. See **Table 10** for the intake and exhaust valve clearances. When the clearance is correct, there will be a slight resistance on the feeler gauge when it is inserted and withdrawn.

9. To correct the valve clearance, perform the following:

a. Loosen the locknut and turn the adjuster (**Figure 69**) in or out until the clearance is correct. There should be a slight resistance felt when the feeler gauge is drawn from between the adjuster and valve tip.

b. Hold the adjuster to prevent it from turning and tighten the locknut securely.

c. Recheck the clearance to make sure the adjuster did not move when the locknut was tightened. If necessary, readjust the valve clearance.

10. Install the spark plug and spark plug cap. Tighten as specified in **Table 4**.

11. Inspect the O-ring for cracks or other damage and replace if necessary.

12. Lubricate the O-ring with oil and install it into the rocker arm holder groove (A, **Figure 65**).

13. Remove all gasket residue from the cylinder head cover and cylinder head gasket surfaces. Replace the cylinder head cover gasket if leaking or damaged.

14. Install the cylinder head cover gasket.

15. Clean the cylinder head cover and oil passages with solvent and compressed air.

16. Install the cylinder head cover (**Figure 64**) and tighten its mounting bolts securely.

17. Install the timing hole cap and O-ring and tighten as specified in **Table 4**.

18. Install the engine heat guard and fuel tank (Chapter Eight).

## Cylinder Compression

A cylinder compression test is one of the quickest ways to check the condition of the rings, head gasket, piston and cylinder. It is a good idea to check compression during each tune-up, and compare it with the reading you get at the next tune-up. This will help you spot any developing problems.

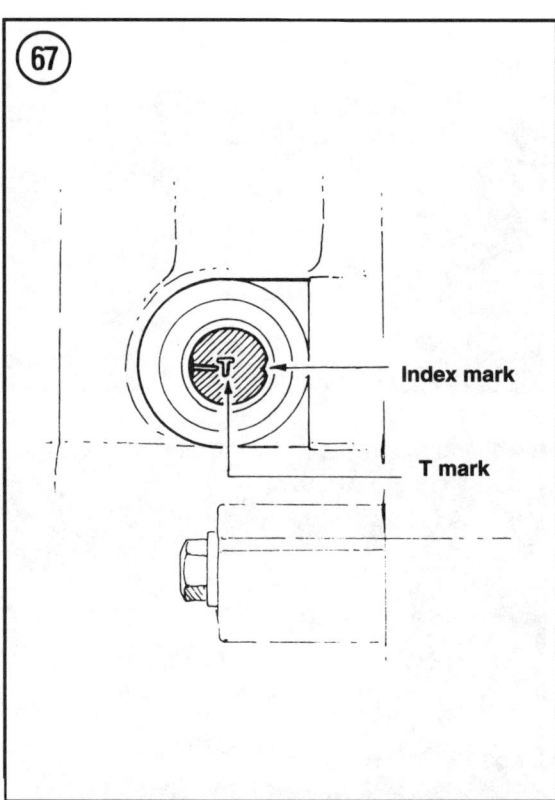

**67**

Index mark

T mark

**68**

1. Warm the engine to normal operating temperature.

2. Remove the fuel tank and heat guard (Chapter Eight).

3. Remove the spark plug. Then insert the plug into the plug cap and ground the plug against the cylinder head (**Figure 70**).

4. Install a compression gauge into the cylinder head spark plug hole. Make sure the gauge is seated properly against the hole.

5. Turn the engine stop switch to OFF.

*NOTE*
*The battery must be fully charged when cranking the engine over with the starter motor or a false compression reading*

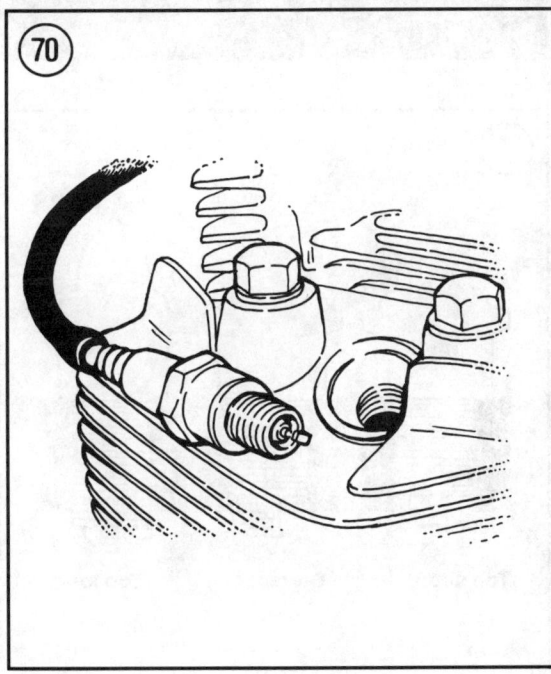

*may be obtained. Because the engine must be turning at least 450 rpm when making the compression test, do not use the recoil starter to turn the engine over.*

6. Hold the throttle wide open and crank the engine with the starter motor for several revolutions until the gauge stabilizes at its highest reading. Record the pressure reading and compare to the decompressor effected compression specification listed in **Table 10**. Press the gauge button to release pressure from the gauge.

*NOTE*
*The TRX400 is equipped with a compression release assembly built into the camshaft. Because this decompressor effects compression readings, Honda lists two different compression pressure readings for the TRX400 engine. These are identified as decompressor affected and decompressor not affected specifications in Table 10.*

7. If the reading is higher than normal, there may be a buildup of carbon deposits in the combustion chamber or on the piston crown. This condition can cause detonation and overheating. Service the piston as described in Chapter Four.

8. If a low reading is obtained, perform the following:

a. Remove the cylinder head cover as described under *Valve Adjustment* in this chapter.

b. Loosen the exhaust valve locknut and turn the adjuster 1 1/2 turns counterclockwise to loosen the exhaust valve adjuster and increase the exhaust valve clearance. Then retighten the locknut.

c. Temporarily install the cylinder head cover and secure it with its mounting bolts.

d. Repeat the compression test (Step 4) and then refer to the decompressor not affected compression specification in **Table 10**.

e. If the compression readings are now correct, the camshaft decompressor may be damaged. If necessary, remove and service the camshaft as described in Chapter Four. Otherwise, allow the engine to cool and then reset the valve clearance as described in this chapter.

f. If the compression readings are still low, perform substep g and then continue with Step 7.

g. Allow the engine to cool, then adjust the valves as described in this chapter.

*NOTE*
*If you adjusted the valve clearance as described in Step 8, start the engine and allow it to reach normal operating temperature before performing Step 9.*

9. Low compression readings indicate a leaking cylinder head gasket, a leaking valve or worn, stuck or broken piston rings. To determine which, pour about a teaspoon of engine oil through the spark plug hole onto the top of the piston. Crank the engine once to clear some of the excess oil, then make another compression test and record the reading. If the compression increases significantly, the valves are good but the rings are worn or damaged. If compression does not increase, the valves or the cylinder head gasket is leaking. A valve could be hanging open or a piece of carbon could be on the valve seat.

*NOTE*
*If you suspect worn, stuck or broken piston rings, disconnect the crankcase breather tube (**Figure 71**) while the engine is running. If there is smoke inside the tube, check for a stuck or damaged piston ring(s).*

10. Remove the compression tester. Install the spark plug and reconnect the spark plug cap.

*NOTE*
*If the compression is low, the engine cannot be tuned to maximum performance.*

11. Install the heat guard and fuel tank (Chapter Eight).

## Correct Spark Plug Heat Range

Spark plugs are available in various heat ranges, hotter or colder than the plugs originally installed at the factory.

Select plugs of the heat range designed for the loads and conditions under which your Honda will operating. Use of the incorrect heat range can cause the plug to foul or overheating and piston damage.

In general, use a hot plug for low speeds and low temperatures. Use a cold plug for high speeds, high engine loads and high temperatures. The plug should operate hot enough to burn off unwanted deposits, but not so hot that it burns itself or causes preignition. A spark plug of the correct heat range will show a light tan color on the insulator after the plug has been in service.

The reach (length) of a plug is also important. A plug that is too short will cause excessive carbon buildup, hard starting and plug fouling. A plug that is too long will cause overheating or may contact the top of the piston. Both conditions will cause engine damage. See **Figure 72**.

**Table 10** lists the standard heat range spark plug.

## Spark Plug Removal

1. Grasp the spark plug lead as near the plug as possible and pull it off the plug. If it is stuck to the plug, twist it slightly to break it loose.

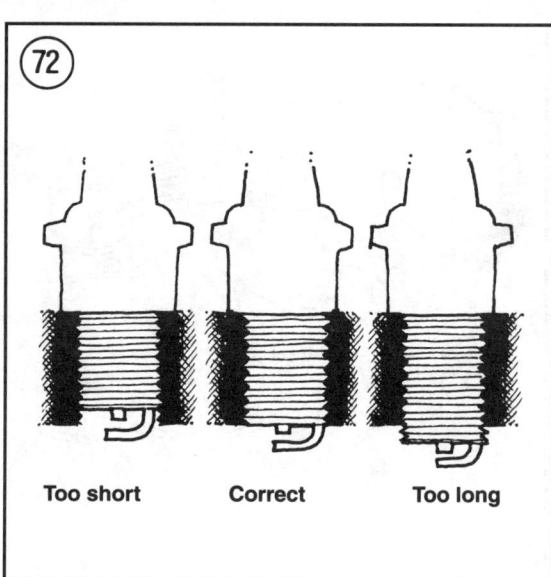

Too short     Correct     Too long

*CAUTION*
*Whenever the spark plug is removed, dirt around it can fall into the plug hole. This can cause expensive engine damage.*

2. Blow away any dirt that has collected around the spark plug.

3. Remove the spark plug (**Figure 73**) with a spark plug socket.

*NOTE*
*If the plug is difficult to remove, apply penetrating oil, like WD-40 or Liquid Wrench, around the base of the plug and let it soak about 10-20 minutes.*

4. Inspect the plug carefully. Look for a broken center porcelain, excessively eroded electrodes and excessive carbon or oil fouling.

**Gapping and Installing the Plug**

Carefully adjust the electrode gap on a new spark plug to ensure a reliable, consistent spark. Use a spark plug gapping tool and a wire feeler gauge.

1. If using the stock spark plug cap, remove the small terminal from the end of the plug (**Figure 74**).

2. Insert a wire feeler gauge between the center and side electrode of the plug (**Figure 75**). The correct gap is listed in **Table 10**. If the gap is correct, you will feel a slight drag as you pull the wire through. If there is no drag, or the gauge will not pass through, bend the side electrode with a gaping tool (**Figure 76**) to set the proper gap.

3. Apply an antiseize compound to the plug threads before installing the spark plug. Do not use engine oil on the plug threads.

*NOTE*
*Antiseize compound can be purchased at most automotive parts stores.*

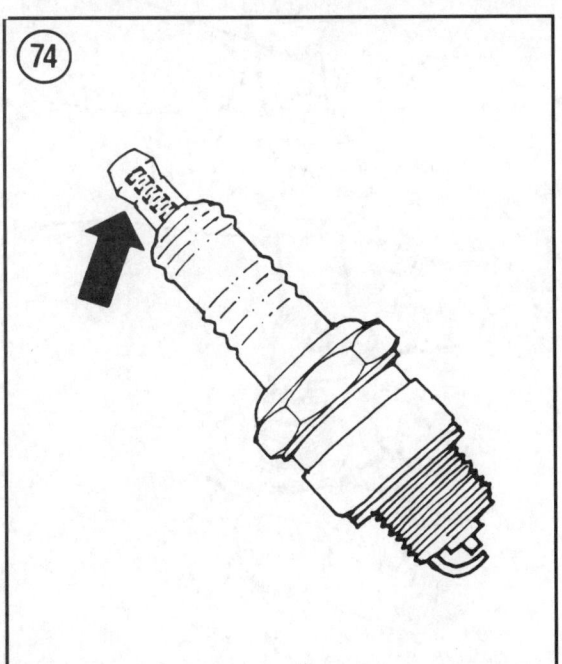

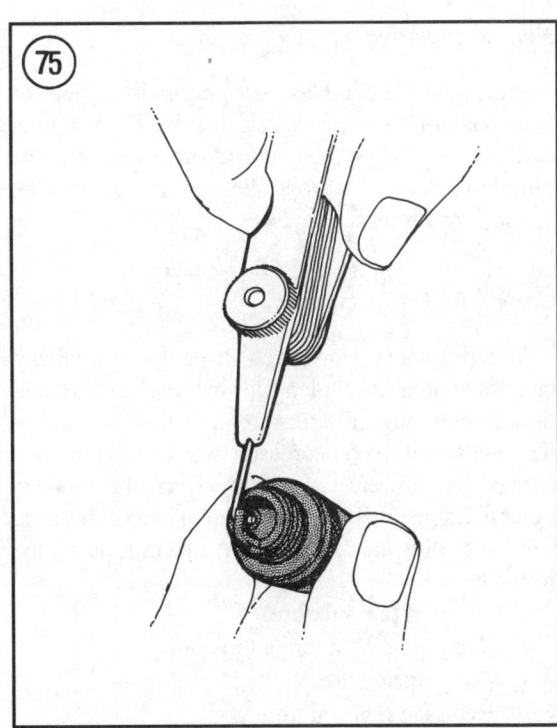

4. Screw the spark plug in by hand until it seats. Very little effort should be required. If force is necessary, the plug may be cross-threaded. Unscrew it and try again.

5. Use a spark plug wrench and tighten the new spark plug as specified in **Table 4**. If you do not have a torque wrench, tighten the plug an additional 1/4 to 1/2 turn after the gasket has made contact with the head. If you are installing a used spark plug, only tighten an additional 1/4 turn.

> *NOTE*
> *Do not overtighten. This will only crush the gasket and destroy its sealing ability.*

### Reading Spark Plugs

Much information about engine and spark plug performance can be determined by careful examination of the spark plug. This information is only valid after performing the following steps.

1. Ride the vehicle at full throttle.

2. Push the engine stop switch to the OFF position before closing the throttle and simultaneously shift to neutral, then coast and brake to a stop.

3. Remove the spark plug and examine it. Compare it to **Figure 77** and note the following:

#### Normal condition

If the plug has a light tan- or gray-colored deposit and no abnormal gap wear or erosion, good engine, carburetion and ignition condition are indicated. The plug in use is of the proper heat range and may be serviced and returned to use.

#### Carbon fouled

Soft, dry, sooty deposits covering the entire firing end of the plug are evidence of incomplete combustion. Even though the firing end of the plug is dry, the plug's insulation decreases. An electrical path is formed that lowers the voltage from the ignition system. Engine misfiring is a sign of carbon fouling. Carbon fouling can be caused by one or more of the following:

  a. Too rich fuel mixture.

  b. Spark plug heat range too cold.

  c. Clogged air filter.

  d. Retarded ignition timing.

  e. Ignition component failure.

  f. Low engine compression.

  g. Prolonged idling.

#### Oil fouled

The tip of an oil fouled plug has a black insulator tip, a damp oily film over the firing end and a carbon layer over the entire nose. The electrodes are not be worn. Common causes for this condition are:

  a. Incorrect carburetor jetting.

  b. Low idle speed or prolonged idling.

  c. Ignition component failure.

  d. Spark plug heat range too cold.

  e. Engine still being broken in.

Oil fouled spark plugs may be cleaned in an emergency, but it is better to replace them. It is important to correct the cause of fouling before the engine is returned to service.

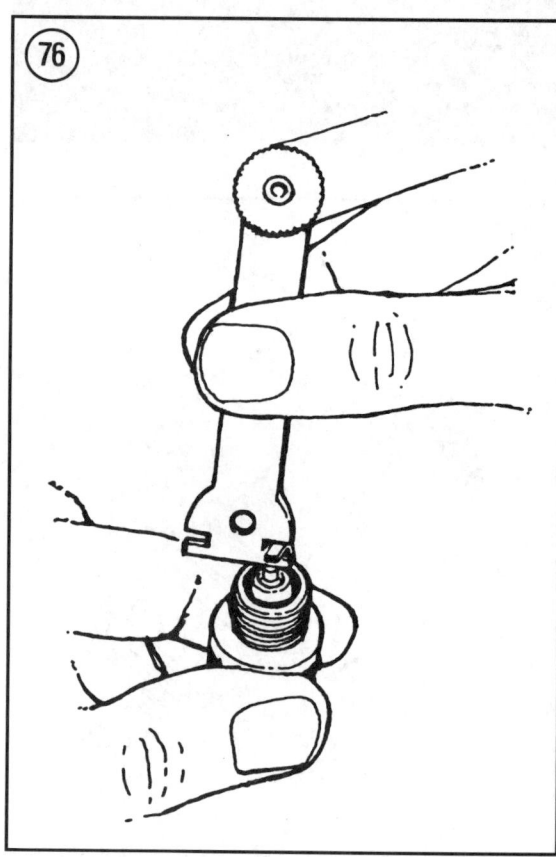

**SPARK PLUG CONDITION**

**NORMAL**

**GAP BRIDGED**

**CARBON FOULED**

**OVERHEATED**

**OIL FOULED**

**SUSTAINED PREIGNITION**

3

### Gap bridging

Plugs with this condition exhibit gaps shorted out by combustion deposits between the electrodes. If this condition is encountered, check for an improper oil type or excessive carbon in the combustion chamber. Be sure to locate and correct the cause of this condition.

### Overheating

Badly worn electrodes and premature gap wear, along with a gray or white blistered porcelain insulator surface are signs of overheating. The most common cause for this condition is using a spark plug of the wrong heat range (too hot). If you have not changed to a hotter spark plug but the plug is overheated, consider the following causes:

    a.  Lean fuel mixture.
    b.  Ignition timing too advanced.
    c.  Engine lubrication system malfunction.
    d.  Engine vacuum leak.
    e.  Improper spark plug installation (too tight).
    f.  No spark plug gasket.

### Worn out

Corrosive gases formed by combustion and high voltage sparks have eroded the electrodes. Spark plugs in this condition require more voltage to fire under hard acceleration. Replace with a new spark plug.

### Preignition

If the electrodes are melted, preignition is almost certainly the cause. Check for carburetor mounting or intake manifold leaks and over advanced ignition timing. It is also possible that a plug of the wrong heat range (too hot) is being used. Find the cause of the preignition before returning the engine into service.

### Ignition Timing

All models are equipped with a capacitor discharge ignition system (CDI). Ignition timing is factory set and is not adjustable. Check the ignition timing to make sure all components within the ignition system are working correctly. If the ignition timing is incorrect, troubleshoot the ignition system as described in Chapter Two. Incorrect ignition timing can cause a drastic loss of engine performance and efficiency. It may also cause overheating.

Before starting this procedure, check all electrical connections related to the ignition system. Make sure all connections are tight and free from corrosion and that all ground connections are clean and tight.

1.  Start the engine and let it warm approximately 2-3 minutes.

2.  Park the vehicle on level ground and apply the parking brake. Shut off the engine.

3.  Remove the timing hole cap and O-ring (**Figure 78**).

4.  Connect a portable tachometer following its manufacturer's instructions.

5.  Connect a timing light following its manufacturer's instructions.

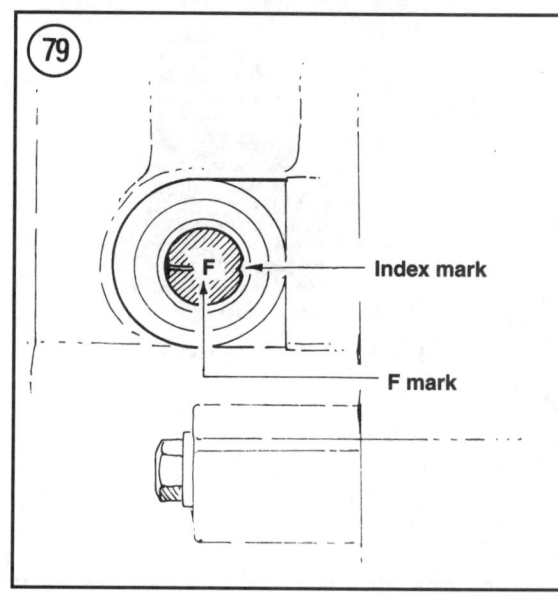

6. Restart the engine and let it run at the idle speed indicated in **Table 10**. Adjust the idle speed if necessary as described in this chapter.

7. Aim the timing light at the timing window (**Figure 78**) and pull the trigger. The F mark on the flywheel should align with the index mark on the rear crankcase cover as shown in **Figure 79**. If the ignition timing is incorrect, troubleshoot the ignition system as described in Chapter Two.

8. Turn the ignition switch off and disconnect the timing light and portable tachometer.

9. Install the timing hole cap and O-ring and tighten as specified in Table 4.

**Pilot Screw Adjustment**

The pilot screw is factory set and does not require adjustment unless the carburetor has been overhauled or a new pilot screw was installed. To adjust the pilot screw under these conditions, refer to *Carburetor Adjustments* in Chapter Eight.

**Idle Speed Adjustment**

1. Start the engine and let it warm up approximately 10 minutes.

2. Park the vehicle on level ground, apply the parking brake and shut off the engine.

3. Connect a portable tachometer to the engine following its manufacturer's instructions.

4. Remove the right lower side cover (Chapter Fifteen).

5. Restart the engine and turn the idle adjust screw (**Figure 80**) to set the idle speed. See **Table 10** for the idle speed specification.

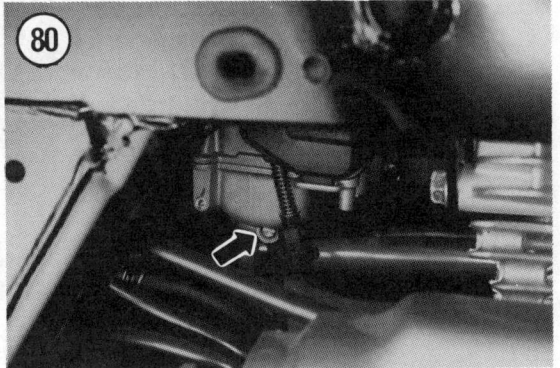

6. Open and close the throttle a couple of times and check for variation in idle speed. Readjust if necessary.

> *WARNING*
> *With the engine idling, move the handlebar from side to side. If idle speed increases during this movement, the throttle cable needs adjusting or may be incorrectly routed through the frame. Correct this problem immediately. Do not ride the vehicle in this unsafe condition.*

7. Turn the engine off and disconnect the portable tachometer.

8. Install the right lower side cover (Chapter Fifteen).

**STORAGE**

Several months of inactivity can cause serious problems and a general deterioration of your Honda. This is especially true in extreme climates. This section describes procedures on how to prepare your Honda for storage.

**Selecting a Storage Area**

The most likely place to store your vehicle is in your home garage or workshop. If you do not have a home garage or suitable building, facilities suitable for long-term vehicle storage are readily available for rent or lease in most areas. When selecting a building, consider the following points.

1. The storage area must be dry. Heating is not necessary, but the building should be well insulated to minimize extreme temperature variation.

2. Buildings with large window areas should be avoided, or such windows should be masked if direct sunlight can fall on the vehicle.

**Preparing Vehicle for Storage**

Careful preparation will minimize deterioration and make it easier to restore the vehicle to service later. Use the following procedure.

1. Wash the vehicle completely. Make certain to remove all dirt in all the hard to reach areas. Completely dry all parts.

2. Run the engine long enough to warm the engine oil. Drain the oil, regardless of the time since the last oil change. Refill with the normal quantity and type of oil as described in this chapter.

3. Drain all gasoline from the fuel tank, fuel hose, and the carburetor. Make sure the fuel tank filler cap is tightened securely and that the vent hose is connected properly.

4. Clean and lubricate the control cables as described in this chapter.

5. Remove the spark plug and add about one tablespoon of engine oil into the cylinder. Then turn the engine over the recoil starter to distribute the oil to the cylinder wall and piston. Reinstall the spark plug and connect the spark plug cap.

6. Tape or tie a plastic bag over the end of the muffler to prevent the entry of moisture.

7. Inflate the tires to the correct pressure and move the vehicle to the storage area. Support the vehicle with all four wheels off the ground.

8. Remove the battery and charge it as described in this chapter. Then store the battery in a safe area away from freezing or excessively warm temperatures. Inspect and charge the battery once a month.

9. Clean the battery terminals, then lubricate them with dielectric grease.

10. If you store the vehicle in a humid or salt-air area, spray all exposed metal surfaces with a light film of oil. Do not spray the seat, tires or any rubber part.

11. Cover the vehicle with a tarp, blanket or heavy plastic drop cloth. Place this cover over the vehicle mainly as a dust coverCdo not wrap it tightly, especially any plastic material, as it may trap moisture and cause rust to form. Leave room for air to circulate around the vehicle.

**Restoring Vehicle to Service**

A vehicle that has been properly prepared and stored in a suitable area requires only light maintenance to service.

1. Before removing the vehicle from the storage area, check air pressure in the tires and inflate the tires to the correct pressure.

2. Remove the plug from the end of the muffler.

3. When the vehicle is brought to the work area, refill the fuel tank with fresh gasoline.

4. Install a fresh spark plug and start the engine.

5. Perform the standard tune-up as described earlier in this chapter.

6. Check the operation of the engine stop switch. Oxidation of the switch contacts during storage may make it inoperative.

7. Check the brakes and throttle controls before riding the vehicle.

---

**Table 1 MAINTENANCE AND LUBRICATION SCHEDULE (1995-1997)**

Initial week of operation or every 30 operating hours
  Inspect throttle operation
  Inspect valve clearance
  Change engine oil and filter
  Check engine idle speed
  Inspect brake system
  Inspect reverse lock system
  Inspect clutch system
  Inspect for loose or missing fasteners
  Inspect tires and wheels
Every 30 operating days or 100 operating hours
  Inspect throttle operation
  Inspect carburetor choke
  Clean and reoil the air filter*
  Drain air filter housing drain tube*
  Inspect spark plug
  Inspect valve clearance
  Change engine oil and filter
  Check engine idle speed

(continued)

**Table 1 MAINTENANCE AND LUBRICATION
SCHEDULE (1995-1997) (continued)**

Every 30 operating days or 100 operating hours (continued)
  Check brake fluid level
  Inspect brake system
  Inspect reverse lock system
  Inspect clutch system
  Inspect for loose or missing fasteners
  Inspect tires and wheels
  Clean spark arrestor
  Inspect front and rear suspension
  Inspect drive shaft boots
  Inspect engine guard and skid plates
Every year
  Inspect fuel line
  Inspect brake shoe wear**
  Inspect steering system
  Inspect steering shaft holder bearings
  Check front differential and final gear case oil level
Every 2 years
  Change front brake fluid
  Change front differential oil
  Change final gear case oil

* Inspect more frequently when operating in wet or muddy conditions or when riding in sand, snow or in dusty areas.

**Table 2  MAINTENANCE AND LUBRICATION SCHEDULE (1998-ON)**

Initial maintenance: 100 miles (150 km) or 20 hours, whichever comes first
  Inspect valve clearance
  Replace engine oil and filter
  Check engine idle speed
  Inspect brake fluid level**
  Inspect brake system
  Inspect reverse lock system
  Inspect clutch system
  Check for loose or missing fasteners
  Inspect wheels and tires
Regular maintenance: 600 miles (1000 km) or 100 hours, whichever comes first
  Clean air filter*
  Drain air filter housing drain tube*
  Inspect spark plug
  Inspect valve clearance
  Replace engine oil and filter
  Check engine idle speed
  Clean spark arrestor
  Inspect drive shaft boots
  Inspect brake system
  Inspect reverse lock system
  Inspect clutch system
  Check for loose or missing fasteners
  Check engine guard and skid plates
  Inspect wheels and tires
  Inspect front and rear suspension
Regular maintenance: 1200 miles (2000 km) or 200 hours, whichever comes first
  Check throttle operation
  Check fuel line
  Check carburetor choke

(continued)

**Table 2 MAINTENANCE AND LUBRICATION
SCHEDULE (1998-ON) (continued)**

Regular maintenance: 1200 miles (2000 km) or 200 hours, whichever comes first (continued)
   Drain air filter housing drain tube**
   Inspect spark plug
   Inspect valve clearance
   Replace engine oil and filter
   Check engine idle speed
   Clean spark arrestor
   Inspect brake fluid level*
   Inspect brake shoe wear*
   Inspect brake system
   Inspect reverse lock system
   Inspect clutch system
   Check for loose or missing fasteners
   Check engine guard and skid plates
   Inspect wheels and tires
   Inspect front and rear suspension
    Check for loose or missing fasteners
   Inspect steering shaft bearing holder
   Inspect steering system
Every 2 years
   Change front differential oil
   Change rear final gear case oil

* Inspect more frequently when operating in wet or muddy conditions or when riding in sand, snow or in dusty areas.

**Table 3 TIRE INFLATION PRESSURE**

| | Front and rear tires psi (kPa) |
| --- | --- |
| Normal pressure | 3.6 (24.8) |
| Minimum pressure | 3.2 (22) |
| Maximum pressure | 4.0 (27.6) |

**Table 4 MAINTENANCE TORQUE SPECIFICATIONS**

| | ft.-lb | N•m | in.-lb |
| --- | --- | --- | --- |
| Clutch adjusting screw locknut | 22 | — | 16 |
| Engine oil drain bolt | 25 | — | 18 |
| Engine oil filter cover mounting bolts | 10 | 88 | — |
| Rear differential gearcase | | | |
|   Drain plug | 12 | 106 | — |
|   Oil check plug | 12 | 106 | — |
|   Oil fill cap | 12 | 106 | — |
| Front differential gearcase | | | |
|   Oil fill cap | 12 | 106 | — |
|   Drain plug | 12 | 106 | — |
| Spark plug | 18 | — | 13 |
| Tie rod locknut | 55 | — | 41 |
| Timing hole cap | 10 | 88 | — |
| Valve adjuster locknut | 17 | — | 12 |
| Wheel nuts (front and rear) | 65 | — | 48 |

**Table 5 BATTERY CAPACITY**

| Battery | |
|---------|--|
| Type | Maintenance free |
| Capacity | 12 volt, 12 amp hour |

**Table 6 MAINTENANCE FREE BATTERY VOLTAGE READINGS**

3

| State of charge | Voltage readings |
|-----------------|------------------|
| 100% | 13.0-13.2 volts |
| 75% | 12.8 volts |
| 50% | 12.5 volts |
| 25% | 12.2 volts |
| 0 % | 12.0 volts or less |

**Table 7  RECOMMENDED LUBRICANTS AND FUEL**

| Engine oil | |
|------------|--|
| Grade | API SG |
| Viscosity | SAE 10W-40 * |
| Differential oil | |
| Front and rear gearcase | Hypoid gear oil SAE 80 |
| Air filter | Foam air filter oil |
| Brake fluid | DOT 3 or DOT 4 |
| Steering and suspension lubricant | Multipurpose grease |
| Fuel | Octane rating of 87 or higher |

* See text for additional information.

**Table 8  ENGINE OIL CAPACITY**

| | Liters | U.S. qt. | Imp |
|--|--------|----------|-----|
| Oil change only | 2.0 | 2.10 | 1.76 |
| Oil and filter change | 2.1 | 2.21 | 1.85 |
| After engine disassembly | 2.7 | 2.84 | 2.38 |

**Table 9  FRONT AND REAR DIFFERENTIAL OIL CAPACITY**

| | ml | U.S. oz. | Imp. oz. |
|--|-----|----------|----------|
| Front differential | | | |
| Oil change | 190 | 6.43 | 6.67 |
| After disassembly | 200 | 6.76 | 7.02 |
| Rear differential | | | |
| Oil change | 90 | 3.04 | 3.16 |
| After disassembly | 100 | 3.38 | 3.51 |

### Table 10  TUNE-UP SPECIFICATIONS

| | |
|---|---|
| Engine compression* | |
| Decompressor affected | 5.5-8.5 kg/cm2 (78-121 psi) |
| Decompressor not affected | 12.4-14.5 kg/cm2 (178-206 psi) |
| Engine idle speed | 1400 ± 100 rpm |
| Ignition timing | |
| F mark | 10° BTDC at 1400 rpm |
| Full advance | 30° BTDC at 4500 rpm |
| Spark plugs | |
| Standard | NGK DPR7EA-9 or Denso X22EPR-U9 |
| Hotter plug (for riding below  5° C/41° F) | NGK DPR6EA-9 or Denso X20EPR-U9 |
| Colder plug for extended high speed riding | NGK DPR8EA-9 or Denso X24EPR-U9 |
| Spark plug gap | 0.8-0.9 mm (0.03-0.04 in.) |
| Idle speed | 1300-1500 rpm |
| Valve clearance | |
| Intake and exhaust | 0.15 mm (0.006) |

* Refer to the text for information on the different engine compression specifications.

# ENGINE  TOP  END

The TRX400FW engine uses an overhead valve pushrod engine. The camshaft is mounted in the crankcase and is driven off the crankshaft by a short cam chain. The camshaft operates followers which move the pushrods against the rocker arms

This chapter provides complete service and overhaul procedures, including information for disassembly, removal, inspection, service and reassembly of the engine top end components. These include the rocker arms, cylinder head, valves, cylinder block, piston, piston rings and camshaft. Exhaust system service is also covered. Before starting any work, read the service hints in Chapter One. You will do a better job with this information fresh in your mind.

**Table 1** lists general engine specifications and **Table 2** lists engine service specifications. **Tables 1-3** are at the end of the chapter.

## ENGINE  PRINCIPLES

**Figure 1** explains basic four-stroke engine operation. Refer to this information when troubleshooting or repairing the engine.

## CLEANLINESS

Repairs go much faster and easier if the engine is clean before you begin work. This is important when servicing the engine's top end. Clean the engine and surrounding area before working on the engine top end.

## EXHAUST  SYSTEM

Refer to **Figure 2** when servicing the exhaust system in this section.

**Removal/Installation**

> *WARNING*
> *Do not remove the exhaust pipe or muffler while they are hot.*

1. Remove the side cover and rear fender (Chapter Fifteen).
2. Loosen the exhaust pipe flange nuts.
3. Remove the muffler as follows:
   a. Loosen the muffler clamp bolts (**Figure 3**).
   b. Remove the muffler mounting bolts (A, **Figure 4**), collars and washers.
   c. Remove the muffler (B, **Figure 4**) and gasket (8, **Figure 2**).
4. Remove the exhaust pipe as follows:
   a. Remove the exhaust pipe mounting nuts (A, **Figure 5**) at the cylinder head.
   b. Remove the exhaust pipe (**Figure 6**) and gasket (3, **Figure 2**).

(1)

## 4-STROKE ENGINE PRINCIPLES

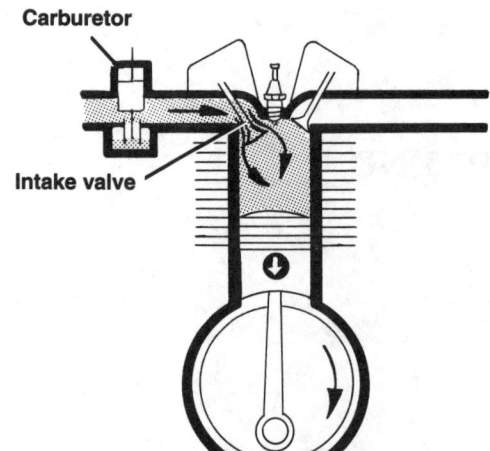

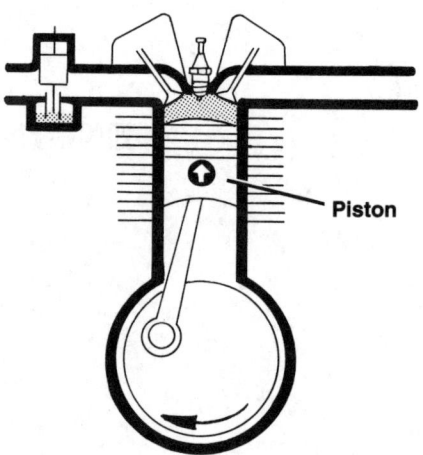

As the piston travels downward, the exhaust valve is closed and the intake valve opens, allowing the new air-fuel mixture from the carburetor to be drawn into the cylinder. When the piston reaches the bottom of its travel (BDC), the intake valve closes and remains closed for the next 1 1/2 revolutions of the crankshaft.

While the crankshaft continues to rotate, the piston moves upward, compressing the air-fuel mixture.

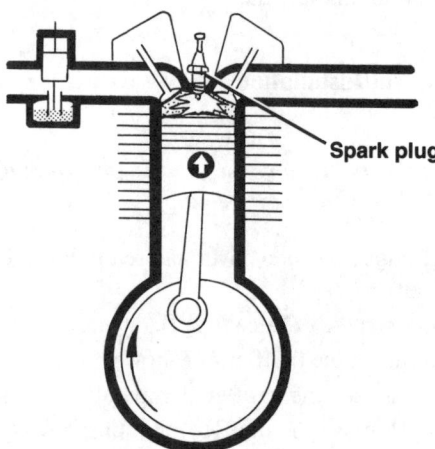

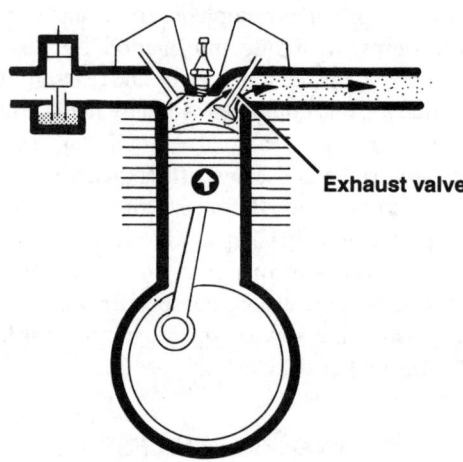

As the piston almost reaches the top of its travel, the spark plug fires, igniting the compressed air-fuel mixture. The piston continues to top dead center (TDC) and is pushed downward by the expanding gases.

When the piston almost reaches BDC, the exhaust valve opens and remains open until the piston is near TDC. The upward travel of the piston forces the exhaust gases out of the cylinder. After the piston has reached TDC, the exhaust valve closes and the cycle starts all over again.

5. Refer to **Figure 2** to replace the heat protectors. Tighten the heat protector mounting bolts as specified in **Table 3**.

6. Install the exhaust pipe and muffler by reversing these removal steps, plus the following:

   a. Install new gaskets (3 and 8, **Figure 2**).

   b. Loosely install all of the exhaust pipe nuts and bolts. Then tighten the exhaust pipe mounting nuts and the muffler mounting bolts in the following order.

   c. Tighten the exhaust pipe mounting nuts (A, **Figure 5**) securely.

   d. Tighten the muffler clamp bolts (**Figure 3**) as specified in **Table 3**.

   e. Tighten the muffler mounting bolts (A, **Figure 4**) as specified in **Table 3**.

   f. Start the engine and check for exhaust leaks.

4

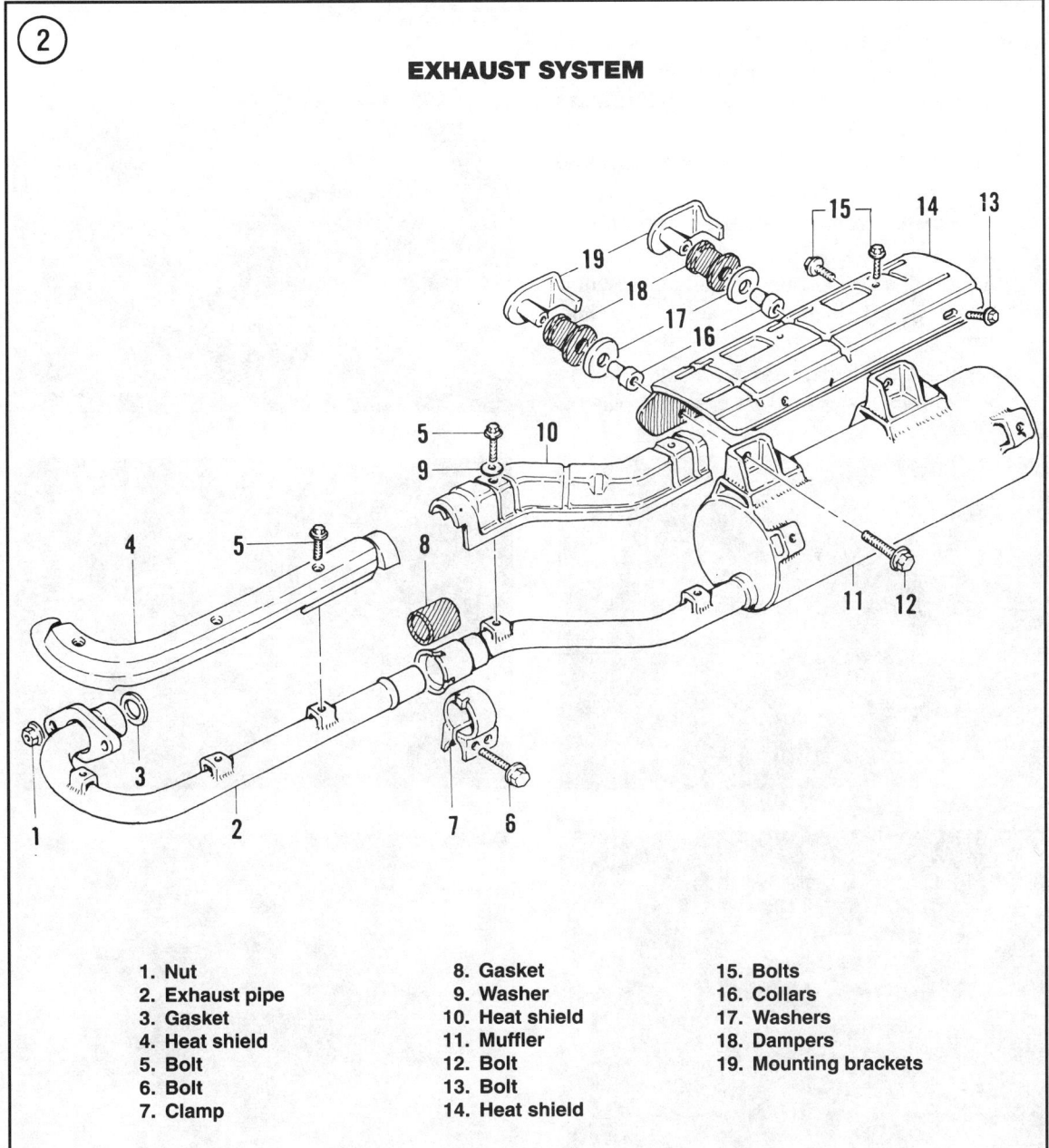

**(2)**

**EXHAUST SYSTEM**

1. Nut
2. Exhaust pipe
3. Gasket
4. Heat shield
5. Bolt
6. Bolt
7. Clamp
8. Gasket
9. Washer
10. Heat shield
11. Muffler
12. Bolt
13. Bolt
14. Heat shield
15. Bolts
16. Collars
17. Washers
18. Dampers
19. Mounting brackets

## CYLINDER HEAD COVER

### Removal/Installation

1. Remove the seat (Chapter Fifteen).

2. Disconnect the negative battery cable from the battery.

3. Remove the fuel tank and heat guard (Chapter Eight).

4. Remove the bolts, cylinder head cover (B, **Figure 5**) and gasket.

5. Remove the O-ring (**Figure 7**).

6. Clean and dry the cylinder head cover. Flush the cylinder head cover oil passages and holes (**Figure 8**) with compressed air.

7. Install the cylinder head cover by reversing these removal steps, plus the following:

    a. Replace the cylinder head cover gasket if leaking or damaged.

    b. Lubricate a new O-ring with oil and install it into the groove in the rocker arm holder (**Figure 7**).

    c. Tighten the cylinder head cover bolts securely in two or three steps and in a crisscross pattern.

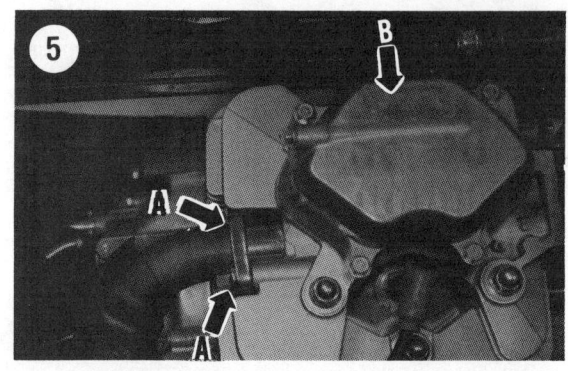

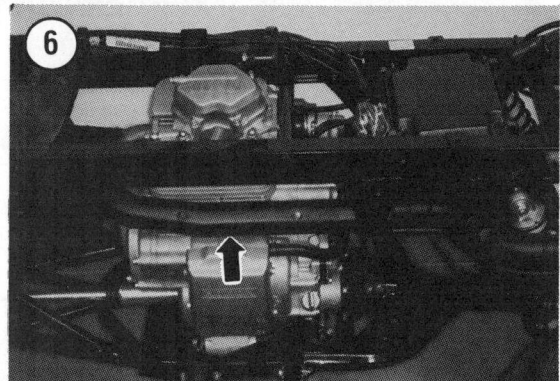

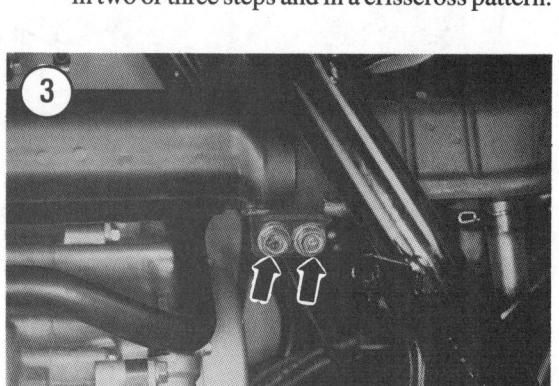

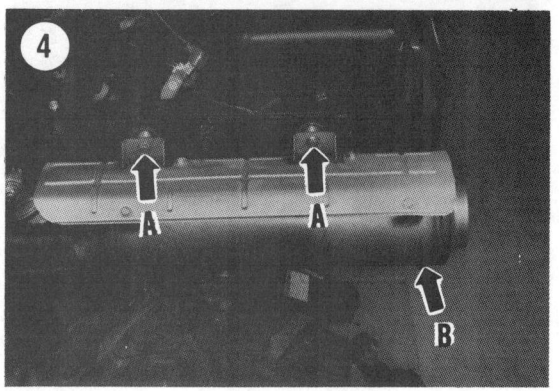

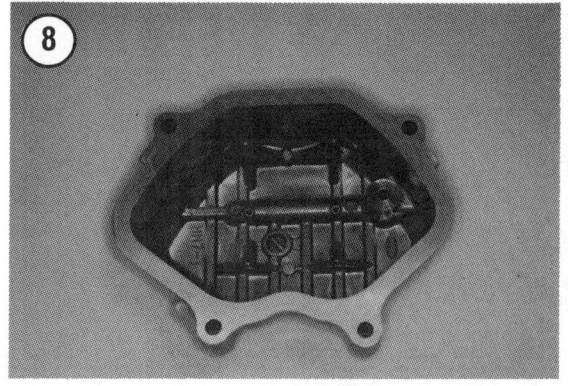

## ROCKER ARMS, PUSHRODS AND CYLINDER HEAD

The rocker arms, pushrods and cylinder head (**Figure 9**) can be removed with the engine mounted in the frame. Some of the following photographs show the engine removed from the frame for clarity.

**Removal**

*NOTE*
*Perform steps 1-6 if the engine is mounted in the frame.*

1. Remove the fuel tank and heat guard (Chapter Eight).

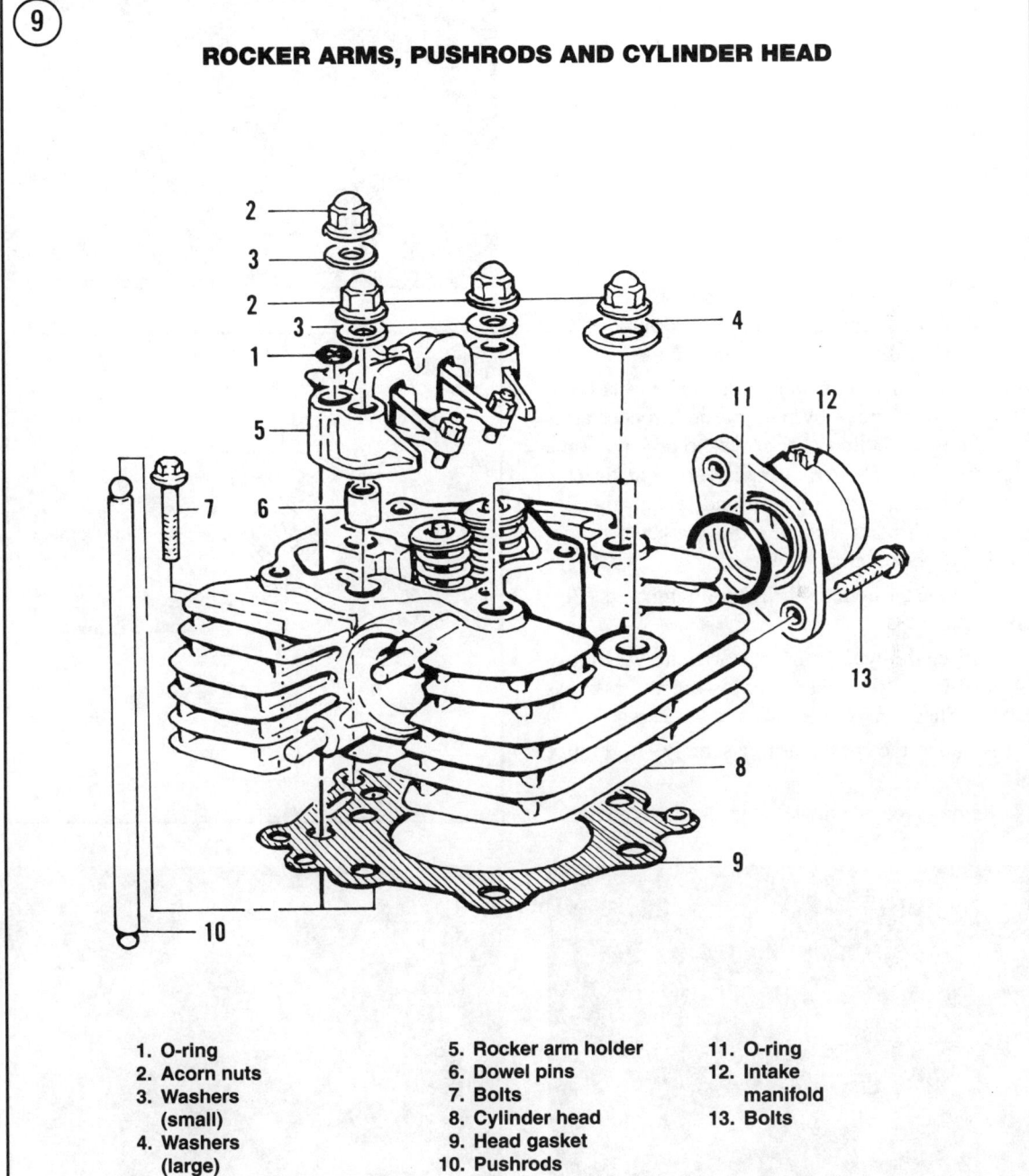

**⑨**

**4**

**ROCKER ARMS, PUSHRODS AND CYLINDER HEAD**

1. O-ring
2. Acorn nuts
3. Washers (small)
4. Washers (large)
5. Rocker arm holder
6. Dowel pins
7. Bolts
8. Cylinder head
9. Head gasket
10. Pushrods
11. O-ring
12. Intake manifold
13. Bolts

2. Remove the exhaust pipe as described in this chapter.

3. Remove the carburetor (Chapter Eight).

4. Remove the bolts and the left fuel tank bracket (A, **Figure 10**).

5. Remove the upper engine hanger bolts, bracket bolts and engine hanger (B, **Figure 10**).

6. Remove the bolts, intake manifold and O-ring (C, **Figure 10**).

7. Remove the cylinder head cover as described in this chapter.

8. Remove the timing hole cap (**Figure 11**) and O-ring.

9. Remove the spark plug and ground it against the cylinder head.

10. Position the engine at TDC on its compression stroke as follows:

    a. Slowly pull the recoil starter and align the flywheel T mark with the index mark on the rear crankcase cover (**Figure 12**).

    b. Check that the piston is at TDC on its compression stroke by moving both rocker arms by hand; both rocker arms should have some free play. If both rocker arms are tight, turn the crankshaft one full turn and realign the flywheel T mark with the index mark. Check that both rocker arms are loose.

11. Remove the cylinder head mounting bolts (**Figure 13**).

12. Loosen the cylinder head acorn nuts (A, **Figure 14**) in two or three steps following a crisscross pattern. Then remove the nuts and washers.

13. Remove the rocker arm assembly (B, **Figure 14**).

14. Remove the two dowel pins (A, **Figure 15**).

*NOTE*
*Identify the two pushrods (**Figure 16**) so that they can be installed in their original position.*

15. Remove the two pushrods (B, **Figure 15**).

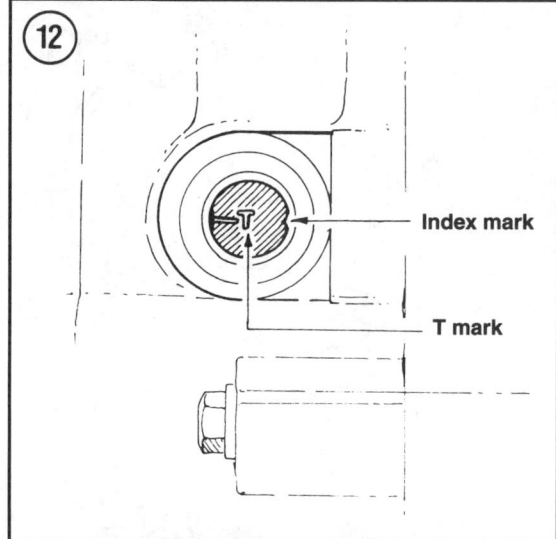

Index mark

T mark

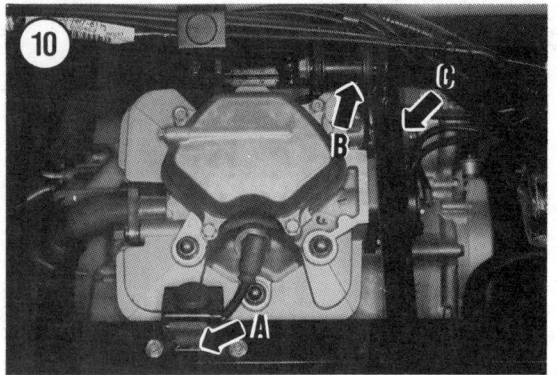

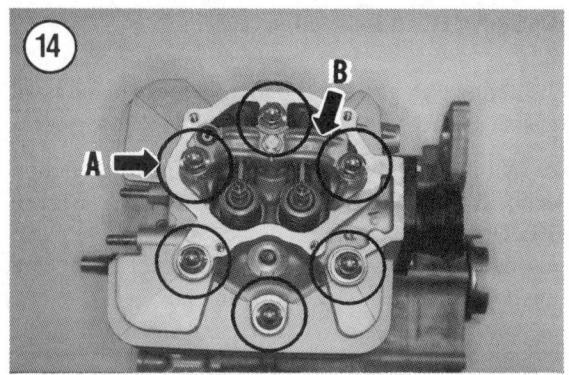

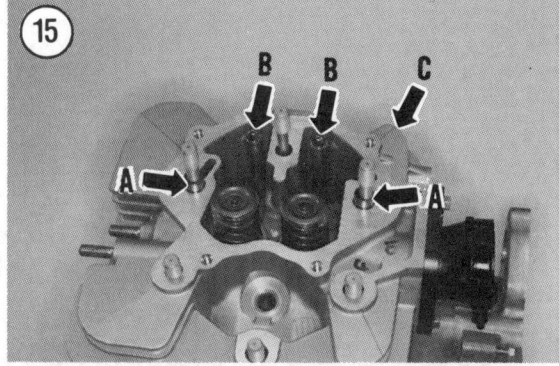

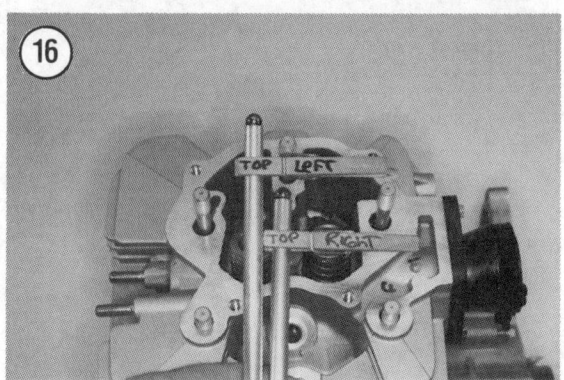

16. Remove the cylinder head (C, **Figure 15**). If the head is stuck, tap the head with a plastic mallet to break it loose.

17. Remove the cylinder head gasket and dowel pins (**Figure 17**).

### Rocker Arm Holder
### Disassembly/Inspection/Reassembly

Refer to **Table 2** when measuring the rocker arm components in this section. Replace worn or damaged parts.

*NOTE*
*Before removing the rocker arms in Step 1, mark the position of both rocker arms so that they can be installed in their original position.*

1. Remove the bolt (A, **Figure 18**), rocker arm shaft (B) and both rocker arms (C).

2. Clean and dry the rocker arm holder assembly. Flush all oil passages with compressed air.

3. Inspect the rocker arm socket where it rides against the pushrod and where the adjuster rides on the valve stem (**Figure 19**). Check for cracks, uneven wear or signs of heat damage.

4. Inspect the valve adjuster pads (**Figure 19**) for flat spots, cracks or other damage. Inspect the locknuts for damage or rounded hex corners.

5. Inspect the rocker arm shaft (**Figure 19**) for scoring, cracks or other damage, and replace if necessary.

6. Measure the rocker arm bore inside diameter (**Figure 19**) with a snap gauge. Measure the snap gauge with a micrometer. If within specification, record the dimension and continue with Step 7.

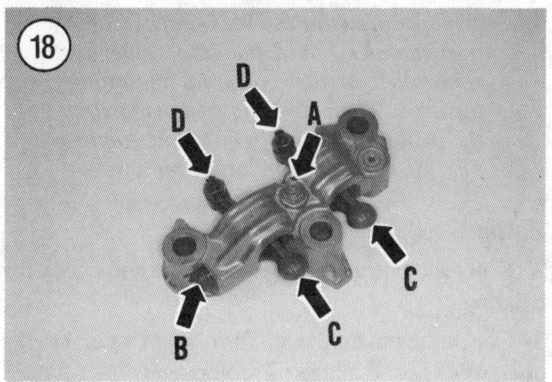

7. Measure the rocker arm shaft outside diameter (**Figure 19**) where both rocker arms ride. If within specification, record the dimension and perform Step 8.

8. Calculate the rocker arm-to-rocker arm shaft clearance as follows:

   a. Subtract the rocker arm shaft outside diameter (Step 7) from the rocker arm bore inside diameter (Step 6) to determine rocker arm-to-shaft clearance.

   b. Replace the rocker arms and/or the rocker arm shaft if the clearance is out of specification.

9. Lubricate the rocker arm bores and rocker arm shaft with engine oil.

> *NOTE*
> *If using the original rocker arms, install them in their original mounting position.*

10. Install the rocker arms (C, **Figure 18**) into the rocker arm holder, then install the rocker arm shaft (B, **Figure 18**) with its screwdriver slot end facing out.

11. Turn the rocker arm shaft to align the hole in the rocker arm shaft with the bolt hole in the rocker arm holder. Install the rocker arm shaft mounting bolt (A, **Figure 18**) and tighten as specified in **Table 3**.

12. Check that both rocker arms pivot smoothly on the rocker arm shaft.

## Pushrod Inspection

Replace the pushrods (10, **Figure 9**) if they show excessive wear or damage.

> *NOTE*
> *While both pushrods are identical (same part number), used pushrods must be reinstalled in their original mounting position. When cleaning and inspecting the pushrods, do not remove the identification marks made during removal.*

1. Clean and dry the pushrods.

2. Roll each pushrod on a flat surface and check for bending.

3. Check the pushrod ends for uneven wear, cracks or signs of heat damage (discoloration).

## Cylinder Head Inspection

1. Remove all gasket residue from the cylinder head gasket surfaces. Do not scratch the gasket surface.

2. Without removing the valves, remove all carbon deposits from the combustion chamber (A, **Figure 20**). Use a fine wire brush dipped in solvent or make a scraper from hardwood. Take care not to damage the head, valves or spark plug threads.

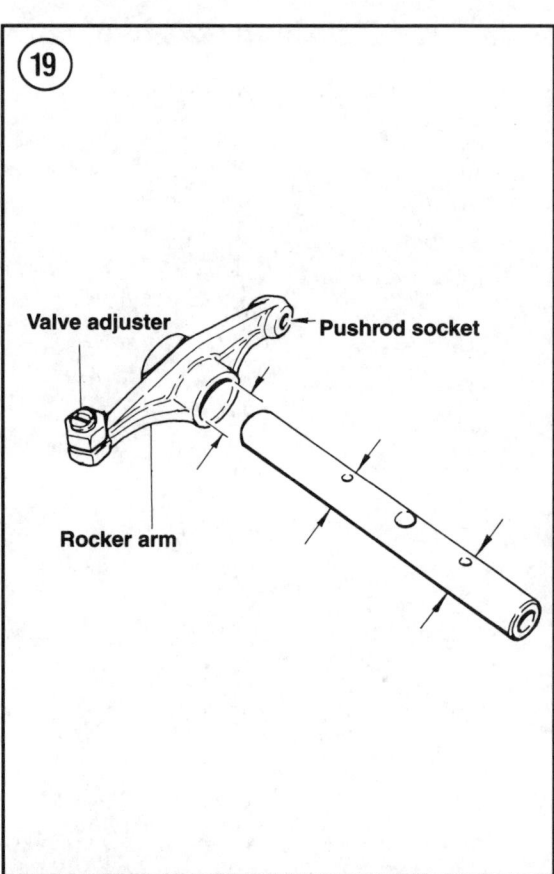

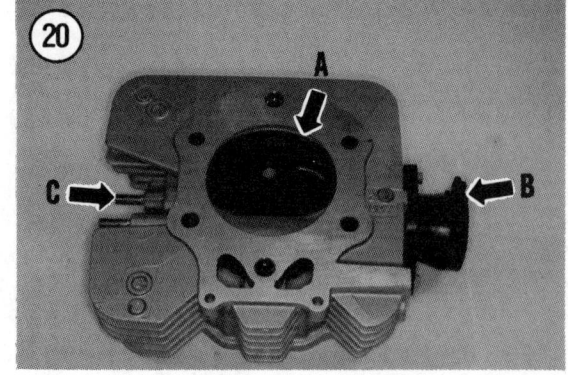

*CAUTION*
*Do not clean the combustion chamber after removing the valves. Otherwise, you may damage the valve seat surfaces and cause poor valve seating.*

3. Examine the spark plug threads in the cylinder head for damage. If damage is minor or if the threads are dirty or clogged with carbon, use a spark plug thread tap to clean the threads following the manufacturer's instructions. If thread damage is excessive, restore the threads with a steel thread insert.

*NOTE*
*When using a tap to clean spark plug threads, coat the tap with an aluminum tap cutting fluid or kerosene.*

*NOTE*
*Aluminum spark plug threads can be damaged by galling, cross-threading and overtightening. To prevent galling, apply an anti-seize compound on the plug threads before installation and do not overtighten.*

4. After cleaning the combustion chamber, valve ports and spark plug thread hole, clean the entire head in solvent.

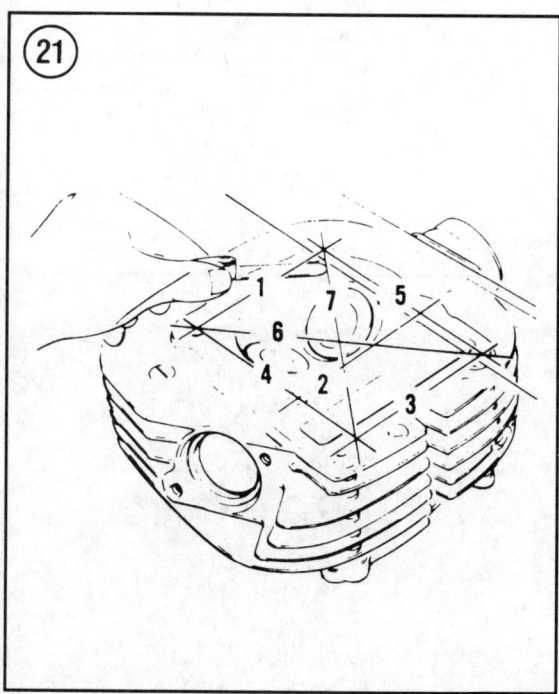

*NOTE*
*If the cylinder head was bead-blasted, clean the head first with solvent, and then with hot soapy water. Residue grit that seats in small crevices and other areas can be hard to dislodge. Also, chase each exposed thread with a tap to remove grit trapped between the threads. Residue grit left in the engine will cause premature piston, ring and bearing wear.*

5. Examine the piston crown. The crown must show no signs of wear or damage. If the crown appears pecked or spongy-looking, also check the spark plug, valves and combustion chamber for aluminum deposits. If these deposits are found, the cylinder is suffering from excessive heat caused by a lean fuel mixture or preignition.

6. Inspect the intake manifold (B, **Figure 20**) for cracks or other damage that would allow unfiltered air to enter the engine. Replace the intake manifold O-ring (11, **Figure 9**) if excessively worn or damaged.

*NOTE*
*If the engine is installed in the frame, do not install the intake manifold until after the cylinder head is installed on the engine.*

7. Check the exhaust pipe studs (C, **Figure 20**) for damage. Replace the studs as described in Chapter One.

8. Check the combustion chamber (A, **Figure 20**) and exhaust port for cracks.

9. Place a straightedge across the gasket surface at several points (**Figure 21**). Measure warpage by inserting a feeler gauge between the straightedge and cylinder head at each location (**Figure 21**). **Table 2** lists the maximum allowable warpage. Warpage or nicks in the cylinder head surface could cause an air leak and overheating. If the cylinder is warped, resurface or replace the cylinder head. Consult with a Honda dealership or a machine shop for this type of work.

10. Check the acorn nuts for thread damage. Discard the washers as new washers must be installed during installation.

11. To service the valves, refer to *Valves and Valve Components* in this chapter.

## Installation

1. Clean the cylinder head and cylinder mating surfaces of all gasket residue.

2. Install the two dowel pins (**Figure 17**) and a new cylinder head gasket. Install the head gasket so that it faces in the direction shown in **Figure 22**.

3. Install the cylinder head (C, **Figure 15**). Make sure to seat the two dowel pins and head gasket against the cylinder head.

4. Lubricate the pushrod ends with engine oil. Then install both pushrods (B, **Figure 15**) by seating them into the center of the cam follower grooves as shown in **Figure 23**.

> *NOTE*
> *When installing the original pushrods, make sure to install them in their original operating position. Refer to your marks (**Figure 16**) made during removal.*

5. Install the two rocker arm holder dowel pins (A, **Figure 15**).

6. Loosen the two valve adjuster locknuts and loosen the adjusters (D, **Figure 18**).

7. If you turned the engine over after removing the pushrods and rocker arm holder, reposition the engine at TDC by slowly pulling the recoil starter and aligning the flywheel T mark with the index mark on the rear crankcase cover (**Figure 12**).

> *CAUTION*
> *The engine must remain at TDC while the pushrods, rocker arm holder and cylinder head nuts are installed and tightened.*

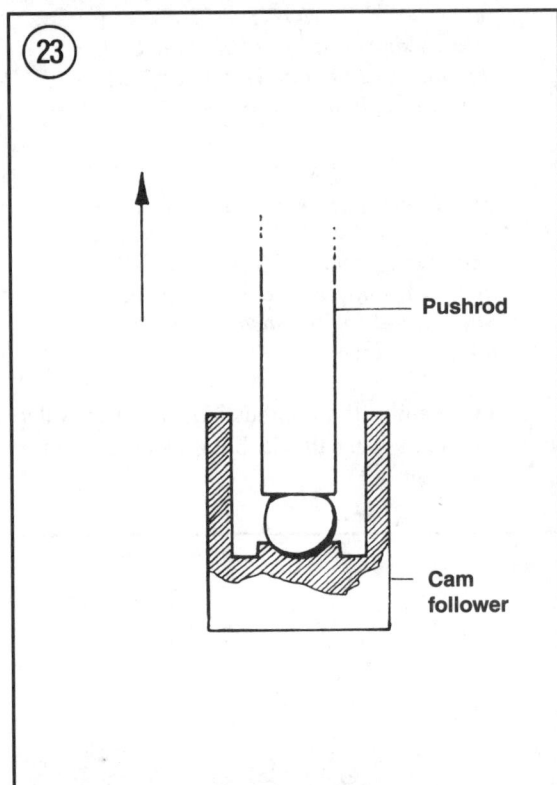

Pushrod

Cam follower

8. Lubricate the rocker arm contact surfaces (**Figure 24**) with engine oil. Install the rocker arm holder (**Figure 25**) over the crankcase studs. Push the rocker arm holder in place while positioning the two rocker arms over the pushrod ends (A, **Figure 26**).

> *NOTE*
> *Two different size washers are used. Install the three smaller washers (A, **Figure 27**) onto the rocker arm holder. Install the three larger washers (B, **Figure 27**) onto the cylinder head.*

9. Install the cylinder head acorn nuts (**Figure 28**) and tighten to the torque specification specified in

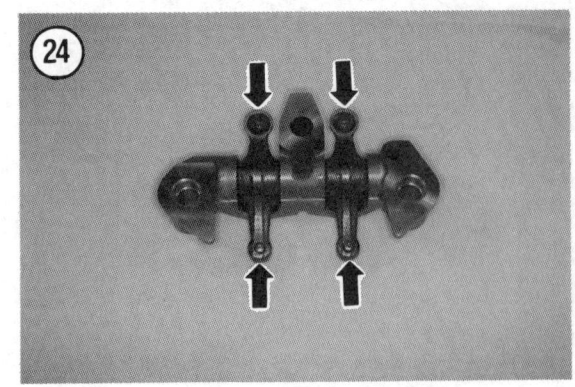

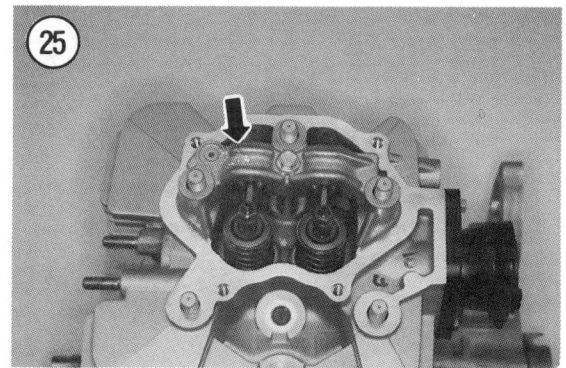

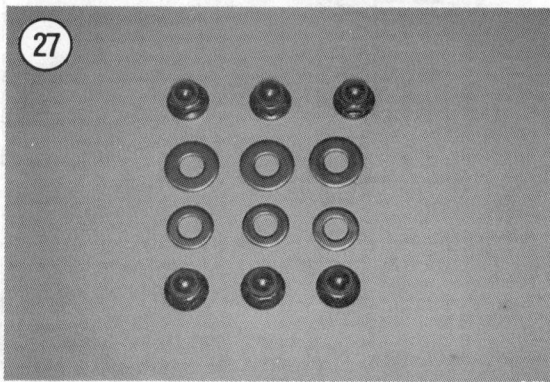

**Table 3**. Tighten in 2-3 steps in the sequence shown in **Figure 28**.

10. Install the two cylinder head 6 mm bolts (B, **Figure 26**) and tighten securely.

11. Adjust the valve clearance. See Chapter Three.

12. Reverse Steps 1-9 of *Removal* in this section to complete installation.

13. Tighten the upper engine hanger bolt and the upper engine hanger bracket bolt as specified in **Table 3**.

## VALVES AND VALVE COMPONENTS

A complete valve job, consisting of reconditioning the valve seats and replacing the valve guides, requires specialized tools and experience. This section describes service procedures on checking the valve components for wear and how to determine what type of service is required. Refer all valve service work requiring grinding and guide replacement to a Honda dealership.

### Special Tools

A valve spring compressor is required to remove and install the valves. This tool compresses the valve springs so that the valve keepers can be released from the valve stem. Do not attempt to remove or install the valves without a valve spring compressor. Because of the limited working area found in the typical ATV and motorcycle cylinder head, most automotive type valve spring compressors will not work. Instead, rent or purchase a valve spring compressor designed for ATV and motorcycle applications.

### Solvent Test

For proper engine operation, the valves must seat tightly against their seats. Any condition that prevents the valves from seating properly can cause valve burning and reduced engine performance. Before removing the valves from the cylinder head, perform the following solvent test to check valve seating.

1. Remove the cylinder head as described in this chapter.

2. Support the cylinder so that the exhaust port faces up (**Figure 29**) and pour solvent or kerosene into the

port. Then check the combustion chamber for fluid leaking past the exhaust valve seat.

3. Repeat Step 2 for the intake port and intake valve and seat.

4. If there is fluid leaking around a valve seat, the valve is not seating properly on its seat. The following conditions can cause poor valve seating:

    a. A bent valve stem.

    b. A worn or damaged valve seat (in cylinder head).

    c. A worn or damaged valve face.

    d. A crack in the combustion chamber.

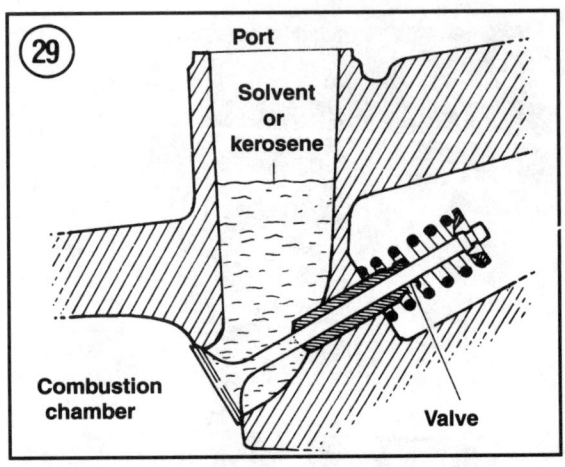

### Removal

A valve spring compressor will be required to remove and install the valves.

Refer to **Figure 30** for this procedure.

1. Remove the cylinder head as described in this chapter.

2. Install a valve spring compressor squarely over the valve spring seat with the other end of tool placed against valve head (**Figure 31**). Position the compressor head so that you can reach and remove the valve keepers in Step 3.

> *NOTE*
> *When compressing the valve springs in Step 3, do not compress them any more than necessary.*

> *WARNING*
> *Wear safety glasses or goggles when performing Step 3.*

3. Tighten the valve spring compressor to remove all tension from the upper spring seat and valve keepers. Then remove the valve keepers (1, **Figure 30**) with pliers or a magnet.

4. Slowly loosen the valve spring compressor and remove it from the head.

5. Remove the valve spring retainer and both valve springs.

> *CAUTION*
> *Remove any burrs from the valve stem groove (**Figure 32**) before removing the valve; otherwise, the valve guide can be damaged as the valve stem passes through it.*

6. Remove the valve from the cylinder head.

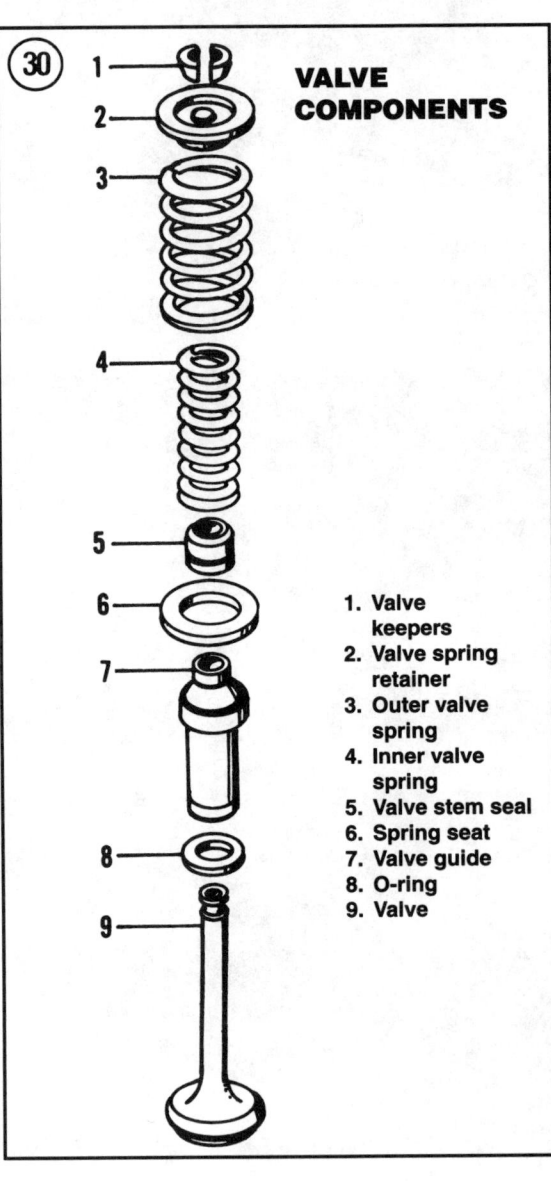

**VALVE COMPONENTS**

1. Valve keepers
2. Valve spring retainer
3. Outer valve spring
4. Inner valve spring
5. Valve stem seal
6. Spring seat
7. Valve guide
8. O-ring
9. Valve

7. Pull the valve stem seal (**Figure 33**) off the valve guide and discard it.

8. Remove the lower spring seat.

*CAUTION*
*Keep all parts of each valve assembly together. Do not mix components from*

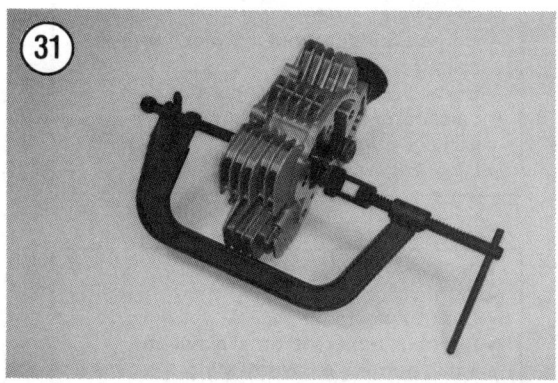

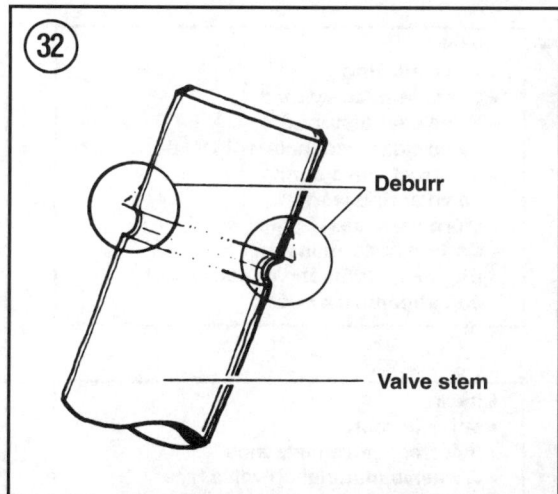

Deburr

Valve stem

*the different valves or excessive wear may result.*

9. Repeat Steps 2-8 to remove the remaining valve.

**Inspection**

When measuring the valve components (**Figure 30**) in this section, compare the actual measurements to the specifications in **Table 2**. Replace parts that are out of specification or show damage as described in this section.

Refer to the troubleshooting chart in **Figure 34** when inspecting and troubleshooting the valves in this section.

1. Clean the valves in solvent. Do not gouge or damage the valve seating surface.

2. Inspect the contact surface (**Figure 35**) of each valve for burning. Minor roughness and pitting can be removed by lapping the valve as described in this chapter. Excessive unevenness in the contact surface is an indication that the valve is not serviceable.

3. Inspect the valve stems for wear and roughness. Measure the valve stem diameter for wear (**Figure 36**).

4. Remove all carbon and varnish from the valve guides with a stiff spiral wire brush before measuring wear.

*NOTE*
*If you do not have the required measuring tools, proceed to Step 7.*

5. Measure each valve guide at its top, center and bottom inside diameter with a small hole gauge. Then measure the small hole gauge with a micrometer to determine the valve guide inside diameter.

6. Subtract the measurement made in Step 3 from the measurement made in Step 5. The difference is the valve stem-to-guide clearance. Replace any guide or valve that is not within tolerance. Refer valve guide replacement to a dealership.

7. If a small hole gauge is not available, insert each valve in its guide. Hold the valve just slightly off its seat and rock it sideways (**Figure 37**). If the valve rocks more than slightly, the guide is probably worn. However, as a final check, take the cylinder head to a dealership and have the valve guides measured.

8. Check the inner and outer valve springs as follows:

    a. Check each valve spring for visual damage.

**34** VALVE TROUBLESHOOTING

| Valve deposits |
|---|

Check:
- Worn valve guide
- Carbon buildup from incorrect engine tuning
- Carbon buildup from incorrect carburetor adjustment
- Dirty or gummed fuel
- Dirty engine oil

| Valve sticking |
|---|

Check:
- Worn valve guide
- Bent valve stem
- Deposits collected on valve stem
- Valve burning or overheating

| Valve burning |
|---|

Check:
- Valve sticking
- Cylinder head warped
- Valve seat distorted
- Valve clearance incorrect
- Incorrect valve spring
- Valve spring worn
- Worn valve seat
- Carbon buildup in engine
- Engine ignition and/or carburetor adjustments incorrect

| Valve seat/face wear |
|---|

Check:
- Valve burning
- Incorrect valve clearance
- Abrasive material on valve face and seat

| Valve damage |
|---|

Check:
- Valve burning
- Incorrectly installed or serviced valve guides
- Incorrect valve clearance
- Incorrect valve, spring seat and retainer assembly
- Detonation caused by incorrect ignition timing and/or carburetor adjustments

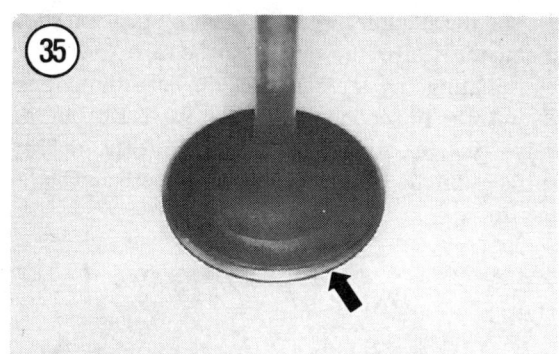

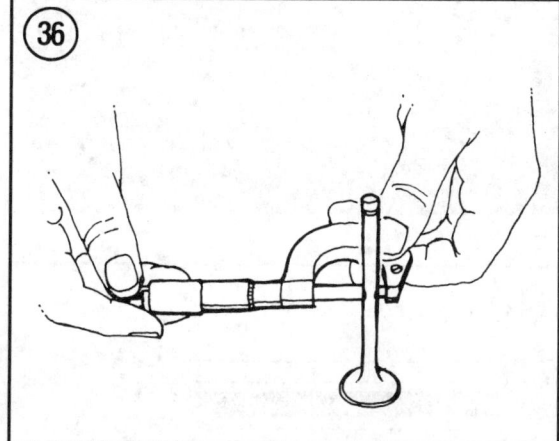

b. Use a square and check each spring for distortion or tilt (**Figure 38**).

c. Measure the valve spring free length with a vernier caliper (**Figure 39**).

d. Replace worn or damaged springs as a set.

9. Check the valve spring seats and valve keepers for cracks or other damage.

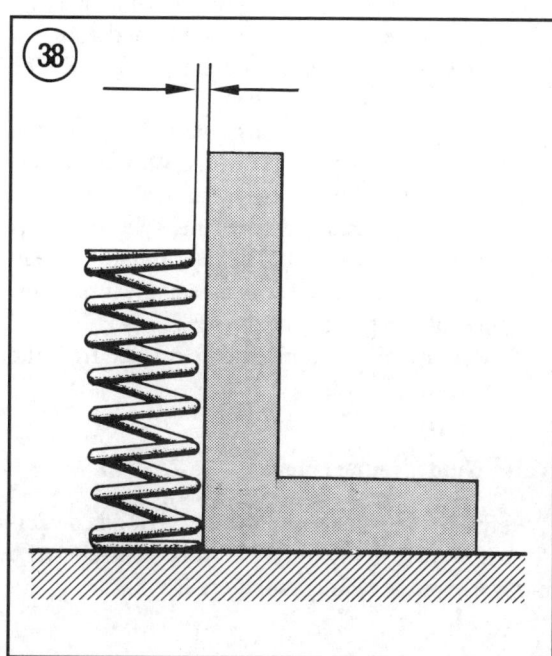

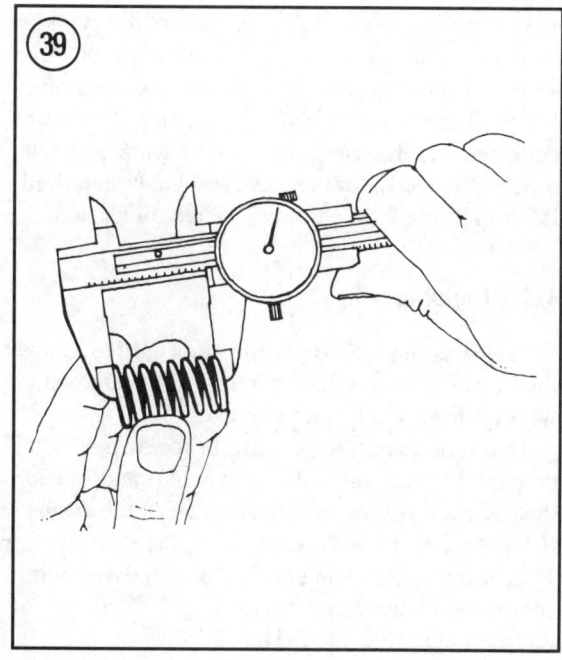

10. Inspect the valve seats (**Figure 40**) for burning, pitting, cracks, excessive wear or other damage. If worn or burned, they may be reconditioned as described in this chapter. Seats and valves in near-perfect condition can be reconditioned by lapping with fine carborundum paste. Check as follows:

a. Clean the valve seat and valve mating areas with contact cleaner.
b. Coat the valve seat with machinist's blue.
c. Install the valve into its guide and rotate it against its seat with a valve lapping tool. See *Valve Lapping* in this chapter.
d. Lift the valve out of the guide and measure the seat width (**Figure 41**) with a vernier caliper.
e. The seat width for intake and exhaust valves should measure within the specifications listed in **Table 2** all the way around the seat. If the seat width exceeds the service limit, have a dealership machine the seats.
f. Remove all machinist's blue residue from the seats and valves.

## Valve Guide Replacement

Refer valve guide replacement to a Honda dealership. If you are going to do the work yourself, a 5.5 mm valve guide reamer is required.

## Valve Seat Reconditioning

The valve seats are an integral part of the cylinder head and cannot be replaced separately. Minor valve seat wear and damage can be repaired by regrinding. Refer this service to a Honda dealership. If you are equipped and experienced to do the work yourself, refer to **Figure 42** for the valve seat angles required. Refer to **Table 2** for valve seat width dimensions.

## Valve Lapping

Valve lapping is a simple operation used to restore the valve seal without machining—if the amount of wear or distortion is not too great.

This procedure should only be performed after determining that the valve seat width and outside diameter are within specifications. See the *Inspection* procedure in this section.

1. Smear a light coating of fine grade valve lapping compound on the valve face seating surface.
2. Insert the valve into the head.

3. Wet the suction cup of the lapping stick and stick it onto the head of the valve. Lap the valve to the seat by spinning the lapping stick in both directions. Every 5 to 10 seconds, rotate the valve 180° in the valve seat. Continue this action until the mating surfaces on the valve and seat are smooth and equal in size.

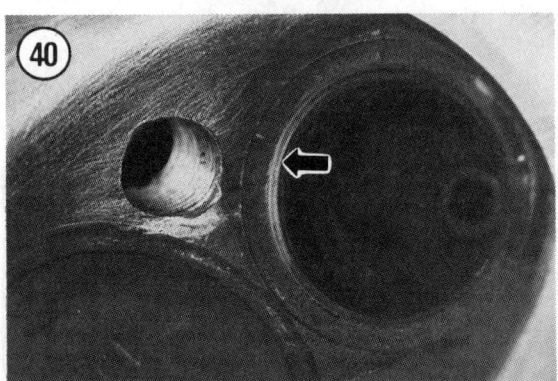

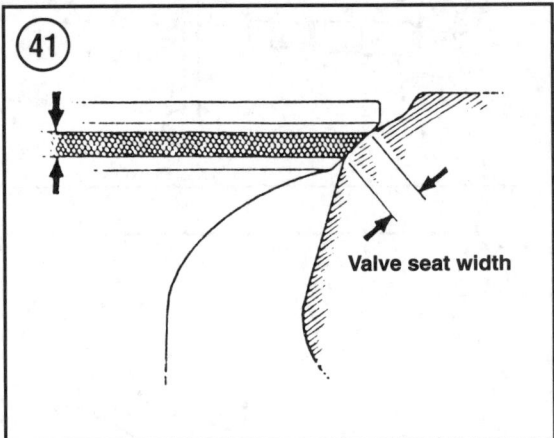

Valve seat width

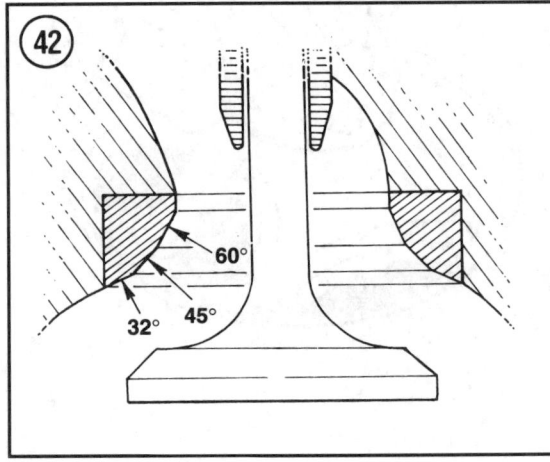

4. Closely examine the valve seat in the cylinder head. It should be smooth and even with a smooth, polished seating ring.

5. Thoroughly clean the valves and cylinder head in solvent and then with hot soapy water to remove all lapping compound. Any compound left on the valves or the cylinder head will contaminate the engine oil and cause excessive wear and damage. After drying

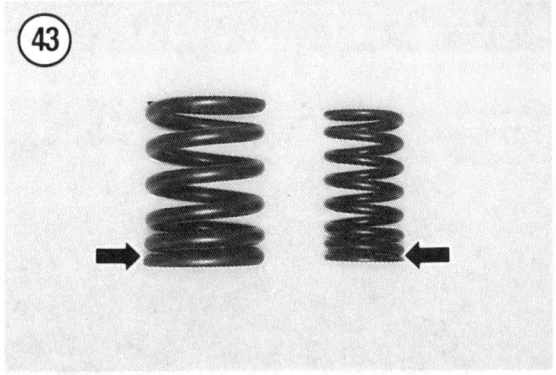

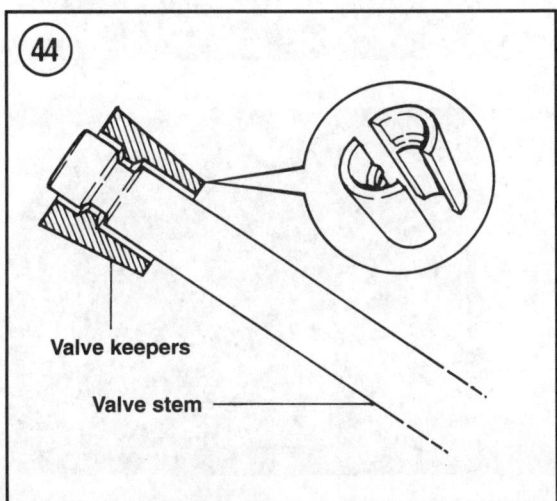

Valve keepers

Valve stem

the cylinder head, lubricate the valve guides with engine oil to prevent rust.

6. After installing the valves into the cylinder, test the valve seat seal as described under *Solvent Test* in this section. If fluid leaks past the seat, remove the valve assembly and repeat the lapping procedure until there is no leakage. When there is no leakage, remove both valve sets and reclean the cylinder head assembly as described in Step 5.

### Valve Installation

1. Clean and dry all parts. If the valve seats were reground or lapped, or the valve guides replaced, thoroughly clean the valves and cylinder head in solvent and then with hot soapy water to remove all lapping and grinding compound. Any abrasive residue left on the valves or in the cylinder head will contaminate the engine oil and cause excessive wear and damage. After drying the cylinder head, lubricate the valve guides with engine oil to prevent rust.

2. Install the spring seat (6, **Figure 30**).

3. Install *new* valve seals as follows:

> *NOTE*
> *New valve seals must be installed whenever the valves are removed.*

   a. Lubricate the inside of each new valve seal with molybdenum disulfide paste.

   b. Install the new valve seal over the valve guide and seat it into place (**Figure 33**).

4. Coat a valve stem with molybdenum disulfide paste and install it into its correct guide.

> *NOTE*
> *Install both valve springs with their end with coils closest together (**Figure 43**) toward the cylinder head.*

5. Install the inner and outer valve springs.

6. Install the valve spring retainer.

> *WARNING*
> *Wear safety glasses or goggles when performing Step 7.*

7. Install the valve spring compressor (**Figure 31**). Push down on the upper valve seat and compress the springs, then install the valve keepers (**Figure 44**). Release tension from the compressor and check that the keepers seat evenly around the end of the valve. Then tap the end of the valve stem (**Figure 45**) with

a soft-faced hammer to ensure that the keepers are properly seated.

8. Repeat Steps 2-7 for the opposite valve.

9. After installing the cylinder head and rocker arm holder onto the engine, adjust the valve clearance. See Chapter Three.

## CYLINDER

The alloy cylinder block has a pressed-in cast iron cylinder liner. Oversize piston and ring sizes are available through Honda dealerships and aftermarket piston suppliers.

The cylinder and piston can be serviced with the engine mounted in the frame. Because of the engine's mounting position in the frame, the following photographs are shown with the engine removed for clarity.

### Removal

1. Remove the pushrods and cylinder head as described in this chapter.

2. Remove the two cylinder mounting bolts (**Figure 46**).

3. Loosen the cylinder by tapping around the perimeter with a rubber or plastic mallet.

4. Pull the cylinder (**Figure 47**) straight up and off the crankcase. Remove and discard the base gasket.

5. Remove the gasket (A, **Figure 48**) and two dowel pins (B, **Figure 48**).

6. If necessary, remove the piston as described under *Piston and Piston Rings* in this chapter.

7. If necessary, remove the cam followers as described under *Camshaft* in this chapter.

8. Cover the crankcase opening to prevent objects from falling into the crankcase.

### Inspection

Refer to **Table 2** when measuring the cylinder block in this section.

1. Remove all gasket residue from the top and bottom cylinder block gasket surfaces.

2. Wash the cylinder block (**Figure 49**) in solvent. Dry with compressed air.

3. Check the dowel pin holes for cracks or other damage.

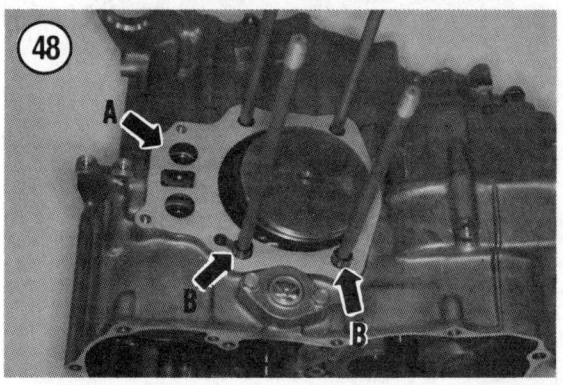

4. Check the two cylinder block studs (**Figure 49**) for looseness or damage. Tighten the old studs or install new studs as described in Chapter One.

5. Check the cylinder block for warpage with a feeler gauge and straightedge as shown in **Figure 50**. Check at several places on the cylinder block and compare to **Table 2**. If out of specification, refer service to a Honda dealership.

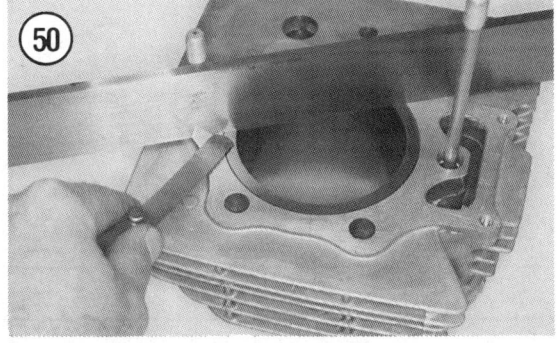

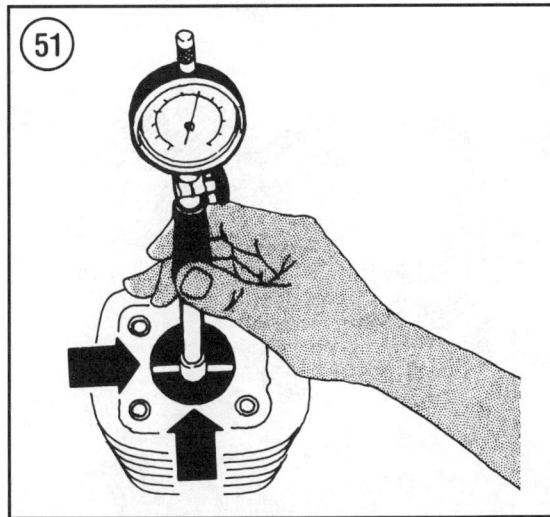

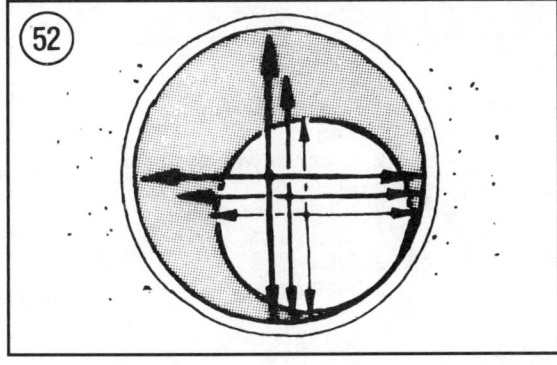

*NOTE*
*Unless you have precision measuring equipment and know how to use it properly, have the cylinder bore measured by a Honda dealership or machine shop.*

6. Measure the cylinder bore with a bore gauge or inside micrometer (**Figure 51**) at the points shown in **Figure 52**. Measure in 3 axes—aligned with the piston pin and at 90° to the pin. Use the maximum bore dimension to determine cylinder wear. Average the other measurements to determine taper and out-of-round. If any dimension is out of specification (**Table 2**), the cylinder must be rebored and a new piston and ring assembly installed. Refer this service to a Honda dealership.

*NOTE*
*To determine piston clearance, refer to*
***Piston and Piston Rings*** *in this chapter.*

7. If the cylinder is not worn past the service limit, check the bore for scratches or gouges. The bore still may require boring and reconditioning.

8. After servicing the cylinder, wash the bore in hot soapy water. This is the only way to clean the cylinder wall of the fine grit material left from the bore or honing job. After washing the cylinder wall, run a clean white cloth through it. The cylinder must be free of all grit and other residue. If the rag is dirty, rewash the cylinder wall again and recheck with the white cloth. Repeat until the cloth comes out clean. When the cylinder is clean, lubricate it with engine oil to prevent the cylinder liner from rusting.

*CAUTION*
*The soap and water described in Step 8 is the only solution that can wash the fine grit residue out of the cylinder crevices. Solvent and kerosene cannot do this. Grit residue left in the cylinder will act like a grinding compound and cause rapid and premature wear to the new rings and cylinder bore surface.*

**Installation**

1. Check that the top and bottom cylinder surfaces are clean of all gasket residue.

2. If removed, install the cam followers as described under *Camshaft* in this chapter.

3. If removed, install the piston and rings as described under *Piston and Piston Rings* in this chapter.

> **CAUTION**
> *Make sure you install and secure the piston pin circlips.*

4. Install the two dowel pins into the crankcase (B, **Figure 48**).
5. Apply a non-hardening liquid gasket sealer to the crankcase mating surfaces shown in **Figure 53**.

> **CAUTION**
> *Do not get any of the sealer on the piston skirt or cam followers. Otherwise, engine damage may result.*

6. Install a new base gasket (A, **Figure 48**). Make sure all holes align.
7. Install a piston holding fixture under the piston.

> **NOTE**
> *You can make a piston holding fixture out of wood as shown in* **Figure 54**.

8. Lubricate the cylinder wall, piston and rings with engine oil.
9. Stagger the piston rings around the piston as shown in **Figure 55**.

> **NOTE**
> *It is easier to install the cylinder over the piston if you first compress the rings with a ring compressor. As the cylinder is installed over the piston, the rings pass into the cylinder compressed and then expand out once they are free of the ring compressor. A hose clamp works well for this. Before using a ring compressor or hose clamp, lubricate its ring*

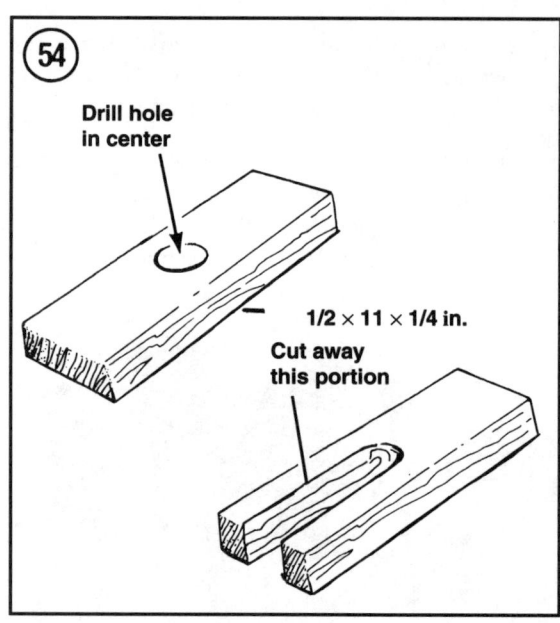

Drill hole
in center

$1/2 \times 11 \times 1/4$ in.

Cut away
this portion

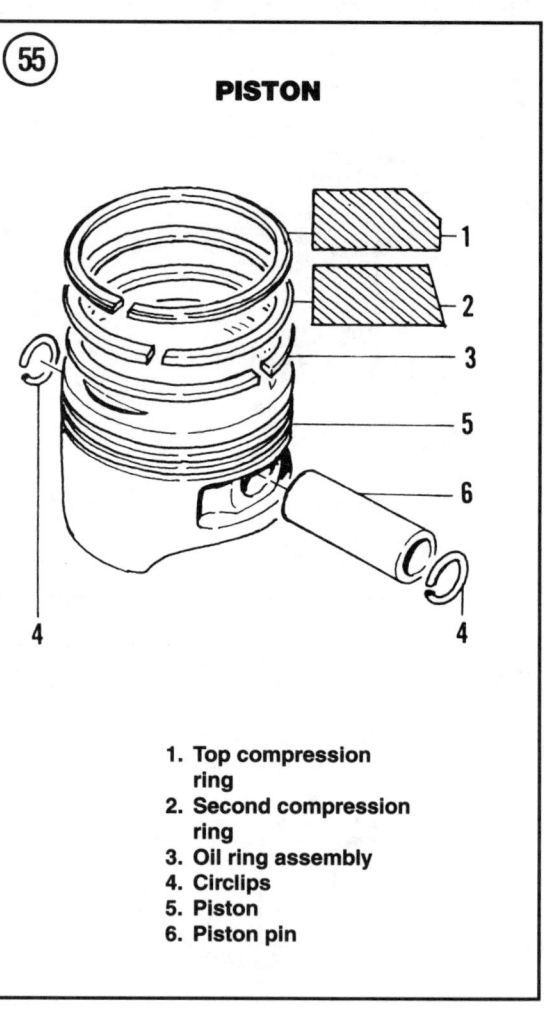

**PISTON**

1. Top compression ring
2. Second compression ring
3. Oil ring assembly
4. Circlips
5. Piston
6. Piston pin

*contact side with engine oil. When using a ring compressor or hose clamp, do not overtighten. The tool should be able to slide freely as the cylinder pushes against it.*

10A. Compress the rings with a ring compressor or appropriate size hose clamp. Then align the cylinder with the piston and carefully slide it down past the rings. When all of the rings are installed in the cylinder, hold the cylinder block and remove the ring compressor or hose clamp.

10B. If you are not using a ring compressor or hose clamp, align the cylinder with the piston and install the cylinder—compress each ring with your fingers as the ring enters the cylinder.

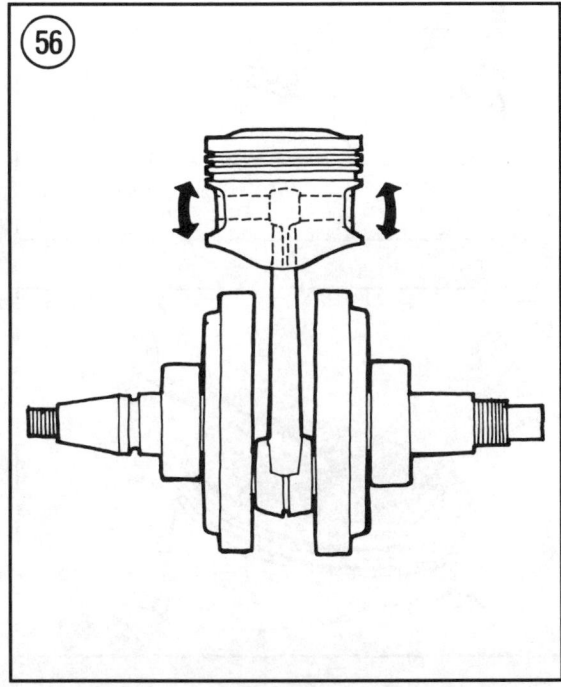

11. Remove the piston holding fixture and slide the cylinder all the way down (**Figure 47**).

12. While holding the cylinder down with one hand, operate the recoil starter. The piston must move up and down in the bore with no binding or roughness.

*NOTE*
*If the piston does not move smoothly, one of the piston rings may have slipped out of its groove when the cylinder was installed. Lift the cylinder and piston up together so that there is space underneath the piston. Install a clean rag underneath the piston to catch any pieces from a broken piston ring, then remove the cylinder.*

13. Install the two cylinder mounting bolts (**Figure 46**) and tighten securely.

14. Install the cylinder head and pushrods as described in this chapter.

## PISTON AND PISTON RINGS

The piston is made of an aluminum alloy. The piston pin is made of steel and is a precision fit in the piston. The piston pin is held in place by a clip at each end.

Refer to **Figure 55** when servicing the piston and rings in the following section.

### Piston
### Removal/Installation

1. Remove the cylinder as described in this chapter.

2. Block off the crankcase below the piston to prevent the piston pin circlips from falling into the crankcase.

3. Before removing the piston, hold the rod and rock the piston (**Figure 56**). Any rocking motion (do not confuse with the normal sliding motion) indicates wear on the piston pin, rod bore, pin bore, or a combination of all three.

*WARNING*
*Wear safety glasses or goggles when removing the circlips in Step 4.*

4. Remove the circlips from the piston pin bore grooves (**Figure 57**).

*NOTE*
*Discard the piston circlips. You must install new circlips during reassembly.*

5. Push the piston pin (A, **Figure 58**) out of the piston by hand. If the pin is tight, use a homemade tool (**Figure 59**) to remove it. Do not drive the piston pin out as the force may damage the piston pin, connecting rod or piston.

6. Lift the piston (B, **Figure 58**) off the connecting rod.

7. Inspect the piston as described in this chapter.

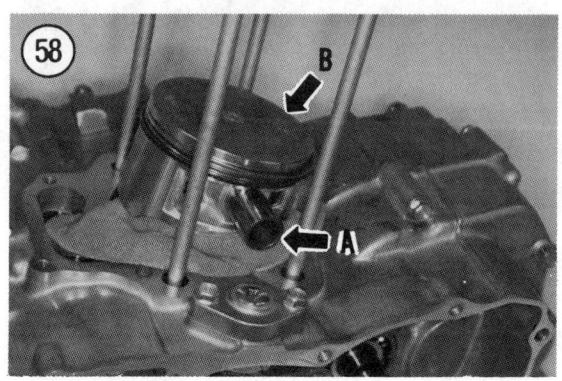

## Piston Inspection

1. Remove the piston rings as described in this chapter.

2. Clean the carbon from the piston crown (**Figure 60**) with a soft scraper. Large carbon accumulations reduce piston cooling and result in detonation and piston damage.

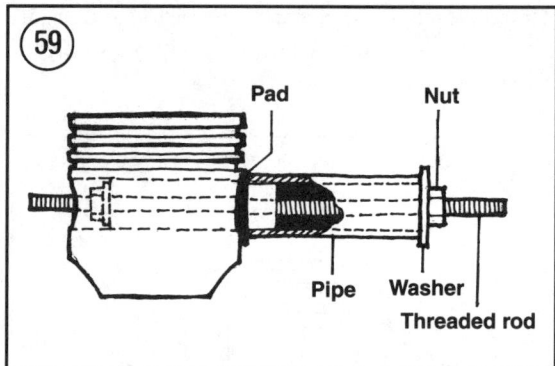

*CAUTION*
*Do not wire brush the piston skirt.*

3. After cleaning the piston, examine the crown. The crown must show no signs of wear or damage. If the crown appears pecked or spongy-looking, also check the spark plug, valves and combustion chamber for aluminum deposits. If these deposits are found, the engine is overheating.

4. Examine each ring groove (**Figure 61**) for burrs, dented edges or other damage. Pay particular attention to the top compression ring groove as it usually wears more than the others. Because the oil rings are bathed in oil, their rings and grooves wear less than compression rings and their grooves. If there is evidence of oil ring groove wear or if the oil ring is tight and difficult to remove, the piston skirt may have collapsed due to excessive heat. Replace the piston.

5. Check the piston oil control holes for carbon or oil sludge buildup. Clean the holes with wire.

6. Check the piston skirt (**Figure 62**) for cracks or other damage. If the piston shows signs of partial seizure (bits of aluminum on the piston skirt), replace the piston.

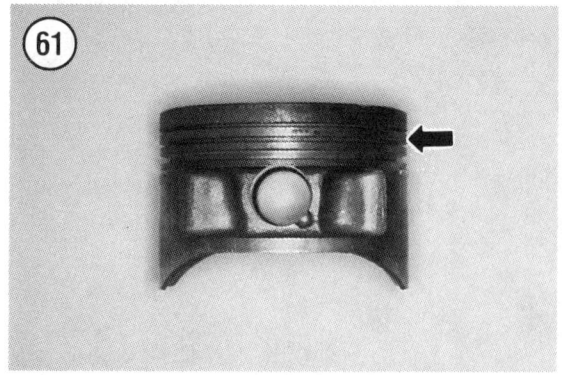

*NOTE*
*If the piston skirt is worn or scuffed unevenly from side-to-side, the connecting rod may be bent or twisted.*

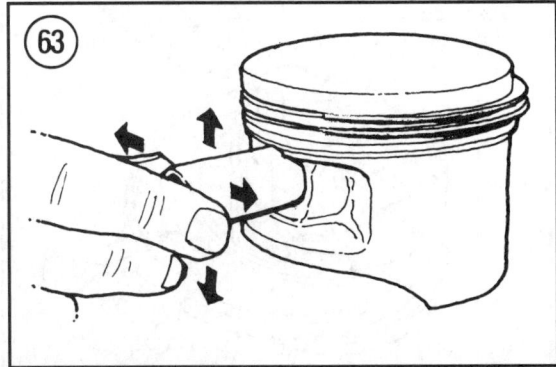

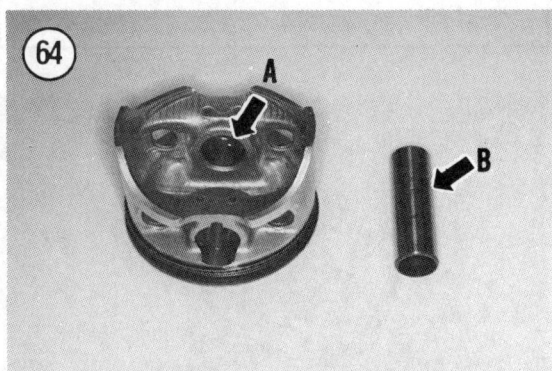

7. Check the piston circlip grooves for wear, cracks or other damage. If a circlip groove is worn, replace the piston.

8. Measure piston-to-cylinder clearance as described under *Piston Clearance* in this chapter.

### Piston Pin Inspection

Refer to **Table 2** when measuring the piston pin components in this section. Replace parts that are out of specification or show damage.

1. Clean and dry the piston pin.

2. Inspect the piston pin for chrome flaking, cracks or signs of heat damage.

3. Lubricate the piston pin and install it in the piston. Slowly rotate the piston pin and check for excessive play as shown in **Figure 63**. Determine piston pin clearance by performing the following steps.

4. Measure the piston pin bore diameter (A, **Figure 64**). If within specification, record the dimension and continue with Step 5.

5. Measure the piston pin outside diameter (B, **Figure 64**). If within specification, record the dimension and continue with Step 6.

6. Subtract the measurement made in Step 5 from the measurement made in Step 4 to determine the piston-to-piston pin clearance. Replace the piston and/or piston pin if the clearance is excessive.

### Connecting Rod
### Small End Inspection

1. Inspect the connecting rod small end (**Figure 65**) for cracks or signs of heat damage.

2. Measure the connecting rod bore diameter with a snap gauge (**Figure 66**). Then measure the snap gauge with a micrometer and check against the dimension in **Table 2**. If the bore wear is excessive, replace the crankshaft assembly. The connecting cannot be replaced separately.

### Piston Clearance

Unless you have precision measuring equipment and know how to use it properly, have this procedure performed by a Honda dealership or machine shop.

1. Make sure the piston and cylinder walls are clean and dry.

2. Measure the cylinder bore with a bore gauge or inside micrometer (**Figure 51**) at the points shown in **Figure 52**. Measure aligned with the piston pin and 90° to the pin. This measurement determines the cylinder bore diameter. Write down the bore diameter measurement.

3. Measure the piston diameter with a micrometer at a right angle to the piston pin bore (**Figure 67**). Measure 6-26 mm (0.2-1.0 in.) from the bottom edge of the piston skirt (**Figure 67**). Write down the piston diameter measurement.

4. Subtract the piston diameter from the largest bore diameter; the difference is piston-to-cylinder clearance. If clearance exceeds the service limit in **Table 2**, the cylinder must be bored and a new piston/ring assembly installed.

### Piston Installation

1. Install the piston rings onto the piston as described in this chapter.

2. Coat the connecting rod bore, piston pin and piston with engine oil.

3. Slide the piston pin into the piston until its end is flush with the piston pin boss as shown in **Figure 68**.

4. Place the piston over the connecting rod so the IN mark (**Figure 69**) on the piston crown faces toward the intake side of the engine.

5. Align the piston pin with the hole in the connecting rod. Push the piston pin (A, **Figure 58**) through the connecting rod and into the other side of the piston and center it in the piston.

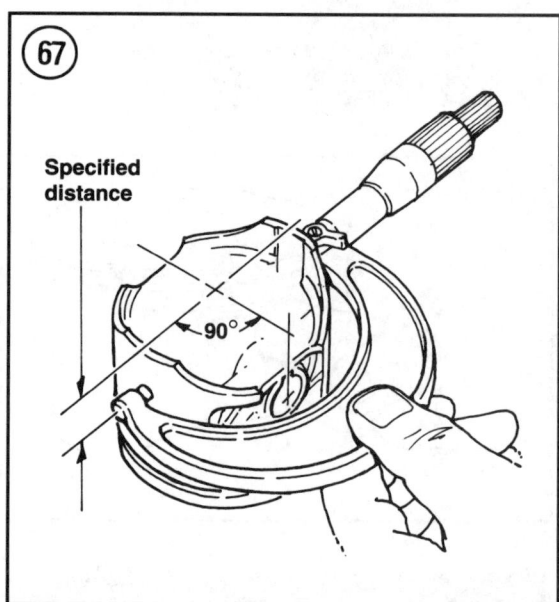

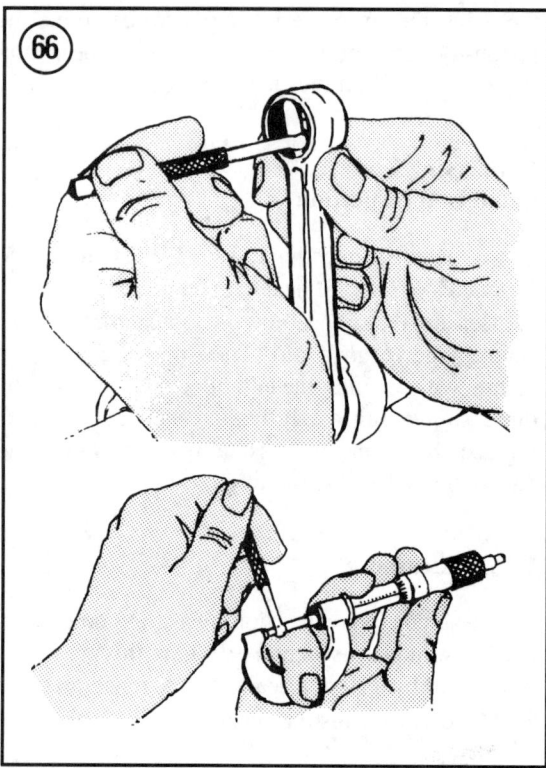

6. Cover the crankcase opening with clean rags.

*WARNING*
*Wear safety glasses or goggles when installing the piston pin circlips in Step 7.*

7. Install *new* piston pin circlips (**Figure 70**) in both ends of the piston pin bore (**Figure 71**). Make sure the circlips seat in the piston clip grooves completely. Turn the circlips so that their end gaps do not align with the cutout in the piston (**Figure 71**).

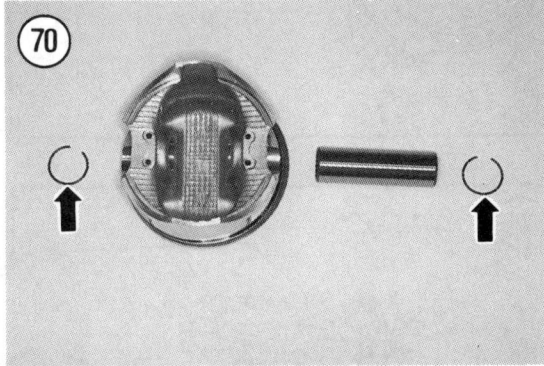

8. Install the cylinder as described in this chapter.

### Piston Ring Inspection and Removal

A three-ring type piston and ring assembly is used (**Figure 72**). The top and second rings are compression rings. The lower ring is an oil control ring assembly (consisting of two ring rails and an expander spacer).

1. Measure the side clearance of each compression ring in its groove with a flat feeler gauge (**Figure 73**) and compare with the specifications in **Table 2**. If the clearance is greater than specified, replace the rings. If the clearance is still excessive with the new rings, replace the piston.

*WARNING*
*The edges of all piston rings are very sharp. Be careful when handling them to avoid cut fingers.*

*NOTE*
*Store the rings in order of removal.*

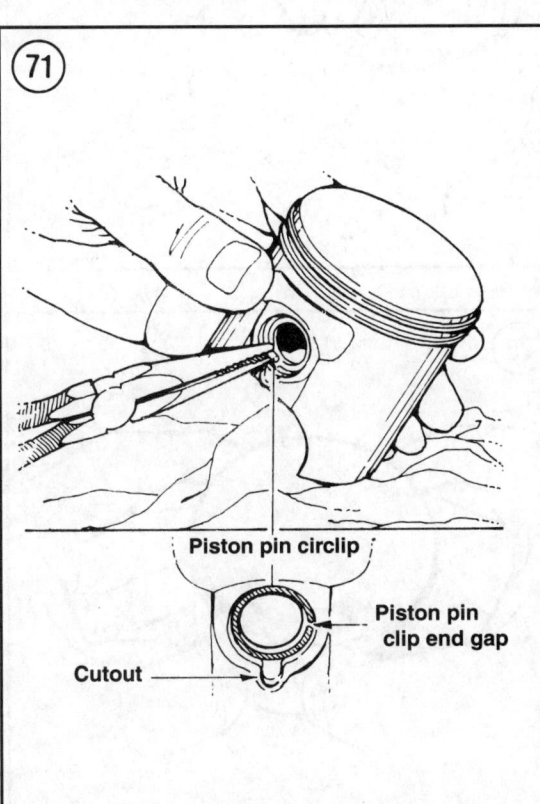

Piston pin circlip

Piston pin clip end gap

Cutout

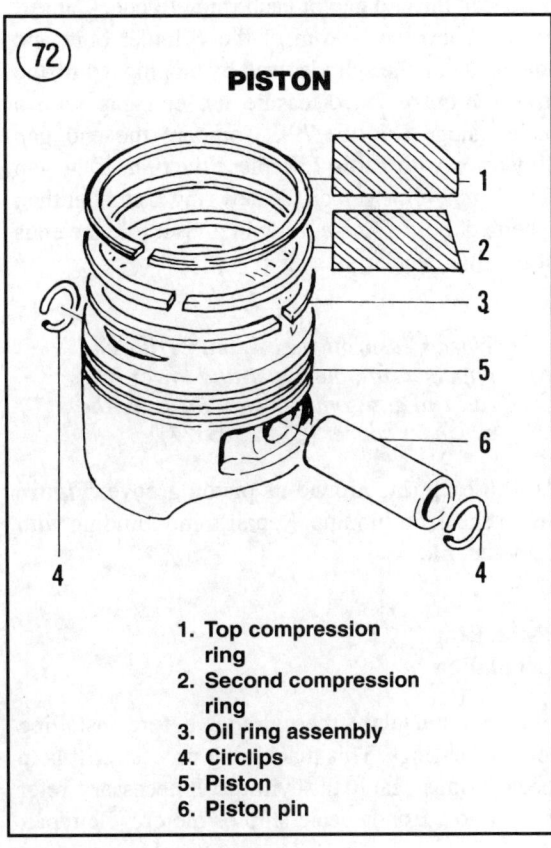

**PISTON**

1. Top compression ring
2. Second compression ring
3. Oil ring assembly
4. Circlips
5. Piston
6. Piston pin

2. Remove the compression rings with a ring expander tool (**Figure 74**) or spread the ring ends with your thumbs and lift the rings out of their grooves and up over the piston (**Figure 75**).

3. Remove the oil ring assembly (**Figure 76**) by first removing the upper (A, **Figure 77**) and then the lower (B, **Figure 77**) ring rails. Then remove the expander spacer (C, **Figure 77**).

> *NOTE*
> *When cleaning the piston ring grooves in Step 4, use the same type of ring that operates in the groove. Using a ring that is dissimilar to the groove will damage the groove.*

4. Using a broken piston ring, remove carbon and oil residue from the piston ring grooves (**Figure 78**).

> *CAUTION*
> *Do not remove aluminum material from the ring grooves as this will increase ring side clearance.*

5. Inspect the ring grooves for burrs, nicks or broken or cracked lands. Replace the piston if necessary.

6. Check the end gap of each ring. To check, insert the ring into the bottom of the cylinder bore and square it with the cylinder wall by tapping it with the piston (**Figure 79**). Measure the end gap with a feeler gauge (**Figure 79**). Compare the end gap dimension with **Table 2**. Replace the rings if the gap is too large. If the gap on the new ring is smaller than specified, hold a fine-cut file in a vise. File the ends of the ring to enlarge the gap.

> *NOTE*
> *When measuring the oil control ring end gap, measure the upper and lower ring rail end gaps only. Do not measure the expander spacer (C, **Figure 77**).*

7. Roll each ring around its piston groove (**Figure 80**) to check for binding. Repair minor binding with a fine-cut file.

## Piston Ring Installation

1. Hone or deglaze the cylinder before installing new piston rings. This machining process will help the new rings seat in the cylinder. If necessary, refer this job to a Honda dealership or motorcycle repair

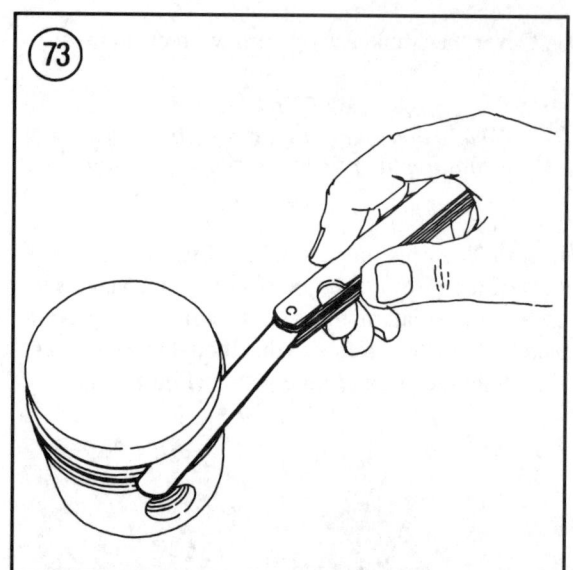

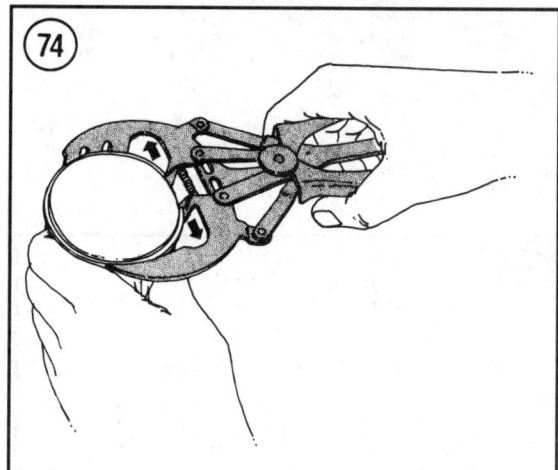

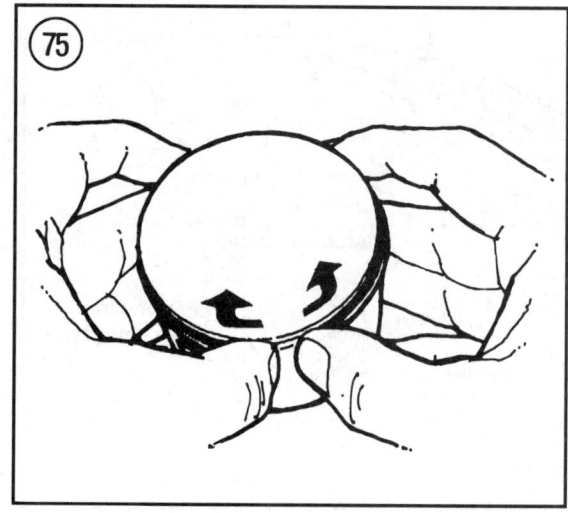

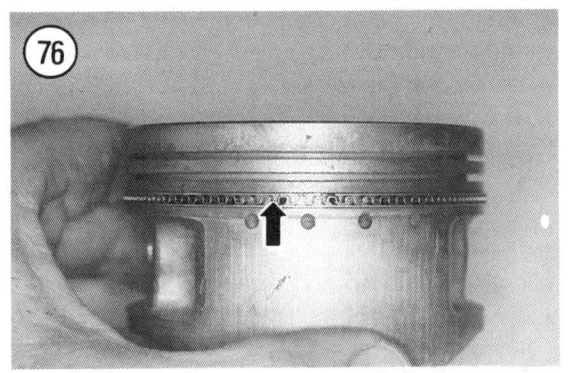

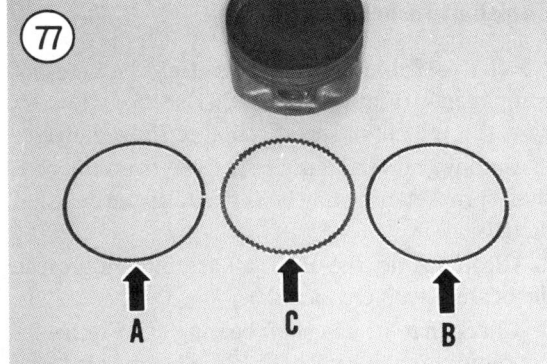

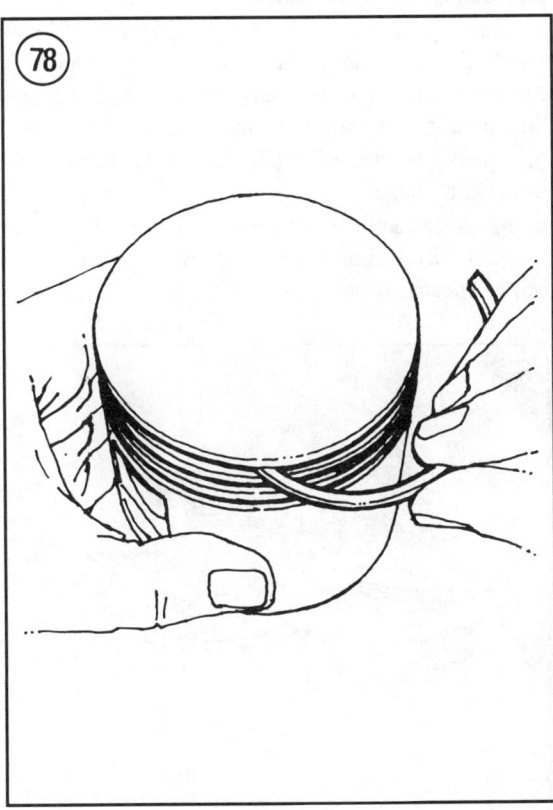

shop. After honing, measure the end gap of each ring and compare to the dimensions in **Table 2**.

2. Clean the piston and rings with hot soapy water, then dry with compressed air.

3. If the cylinder was honed, clean the cylinder as described under *Cylinder Block Inspection* in this chapter.

4. Clean the piston and rings in solvent. Dry with compressed air.

*NOTE*
*The top and second compression rings are different. Refer to **Figure 72** to identify the rings.*

5. Install the piston rings as follows:

*NOTE*
*Install the piston rings—first the bottom, then the middle, then the top ring— by spreading the ring ends with your thumbs or a ring expander tool, then slip the rings over the top of the piston.*

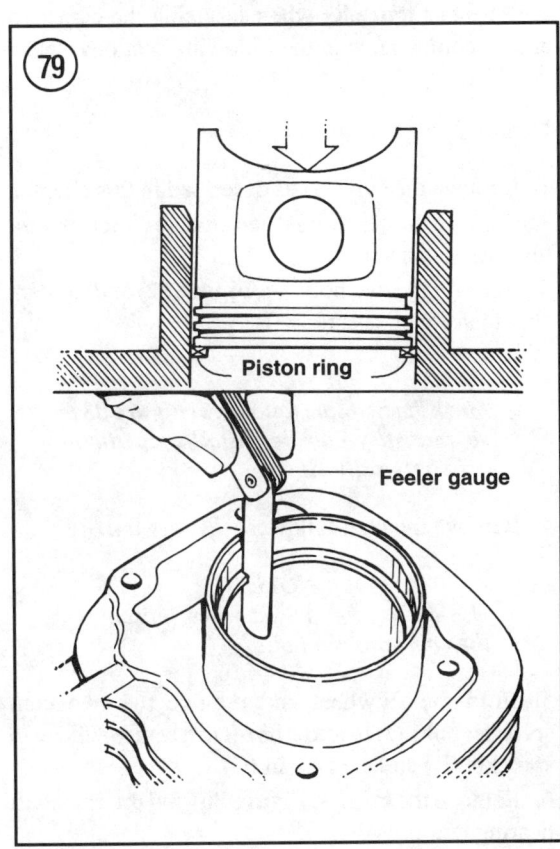

a. Install the oil ring assembly into the bottom ring groove. First install the expander spacer, then the bottom and top ring rails (**Figure 76**).

b. Install the compression rings with their manufacturer's marks facing up.

*NOTE*
*On OEM pistons, the top compression ring is thinner than the second compression ring.*

c. Install the second compression ring.

d. Install the top compression ring.

6. Position the end gaps around the piston as shown in **Figure 72**. Check that the piston rings rotate freely.

## CAMSHAFT

The camshaft and chain tensioner assembly can be removed with the engine mounted in the frame. Because of the engine's position in the frame, the following illustrations show the engine removed for clarity.

Refer to **Figure 81** when servicing the camshaft and its components in the following sections.

### Removal

1. Remove the cylinder as described in this chapter.

2. Remove the centrifugal and change clutch assemblies (Chapter Six).

3. Remove the two bolts (A, **Figure 82**) and the cam chain tensioner assembly (B).

*NOTE*
*Mark the two cam followers (**Figure 83**) so that they can be installed in their original positions.*

4. Remove the cam followers (**Figure 84**).

*NOTE*
*Use a six-point socket when loosening the cam sprocket bolts.*

5. Hold the flywheel and remove the two cam sprocket bolts (A, **Figure 85**). Then remove the cam sprocket (B) and cam chain (C).

6. Remove the bolt (A, **Figure 86**) and the camshaft bearing retainer (B).

7. Align the camshaft timing mark (C, **Figure 86**) with the crankcase index mark (D) and remove the camshaft. See **Figure 87**.

8. If necessary, remove the cam chain slipper (A, **Figure 88**) as follows:

a. Remove the three bolts and the oil pump (B, **Figure 88**). Store the oil pump in a plastic bag until reassembly.

b. Remove the cam chain slipper (A, **Figure 88**).

9. Remove the two bolts and the cam chain tensioner arm (A, **Figure 89**).

### Camshaft Inspection

Refer to **Table 2** when measuring the camshaft components (**Figure 90**) in this section. Replace parts that are out of specification or show damage.

1. Remove all thread sealer residue from the camshaft sprocket mounting bolts and from the camshaft threads.

2. Clean and dry the camshaft assembly. Lubricate the bearing with engine oil.

3. Check that the camshaft bearing (A, **Figure 91**) fits tightly on the camshaft. If the bearing is loose, replace the camshaft assembly.

4. Turn the camshaft bearing (A, **Figure 91**) by hand. The bearing must turn without roughness, catching, binding or excessive play. If the bearing is damaged, replace the camshaft assembly.

5. Check the cam lobes (B, **Figure 91**) for scoring or other damage.

6. Measure each cam lobe height with a micrometer (**Figure 92**). Replace the camshaft if either lobe is out of specification.

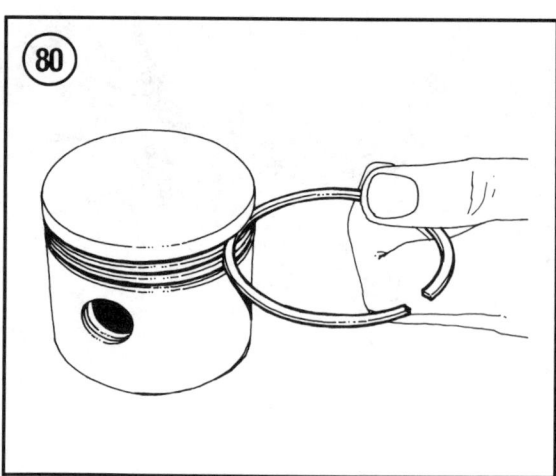

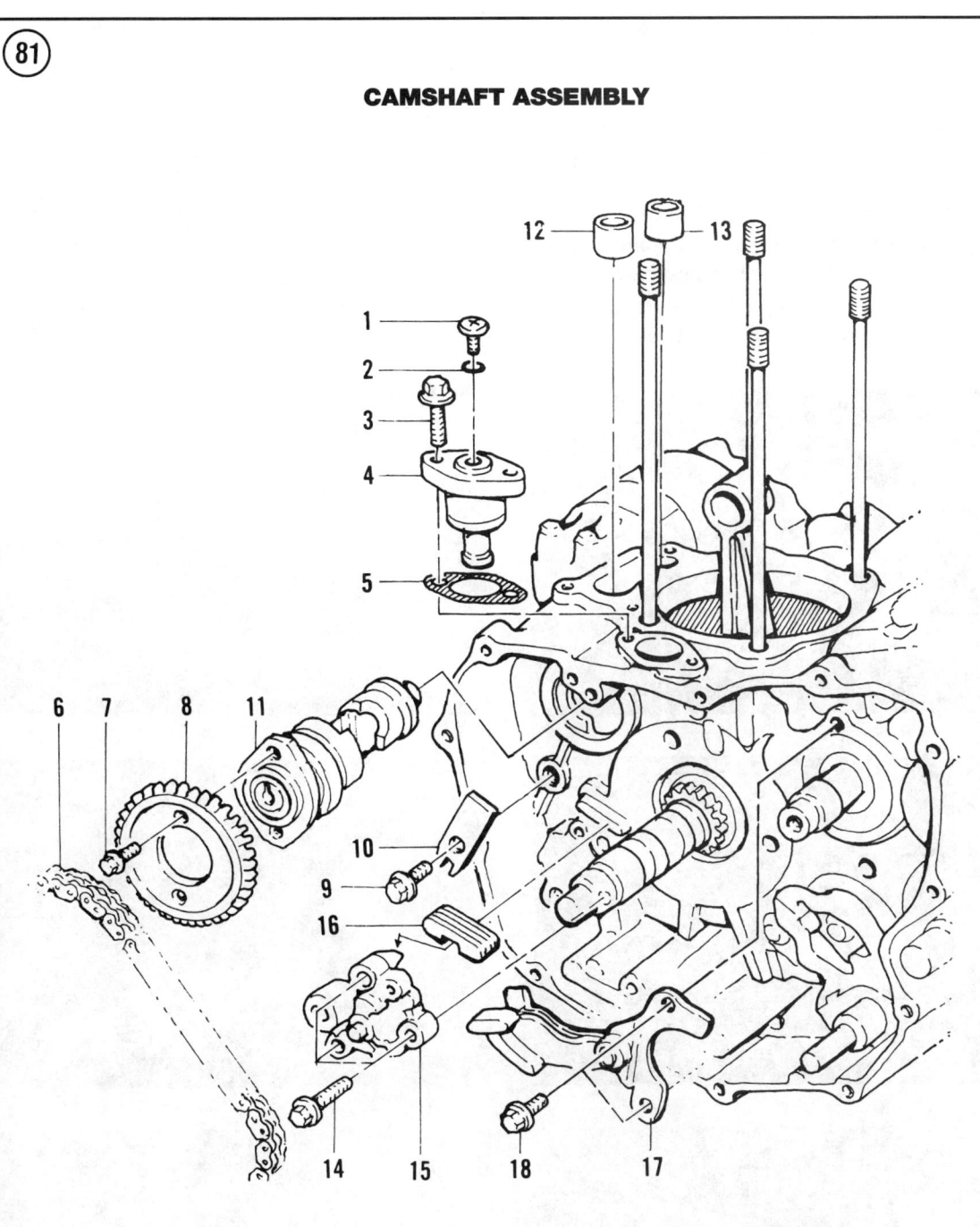

**CAMSHAFT ASSEMBLY**

81

1. Sealing screw
2. O-ring
3. Bolts
4. Cam chain tensioner
5. Gasket
6. Cam chain
7. Bolts
8. Cam sprocket
9. Bolt
10. Bearing retainer
11. Camshaft
12. Cam follower
13. Cam follower
14. Bolts
15. Oil pump
16. Slipper
17. Cam chain tensioner arm
18. Bolts

4

7. Check the decompressor cam operation as follows:

   a. Press on the decompressor cam as shown in **Figure 93**. When doing so, the decompressor cam should move and lock above the exhaust base.

   b. Press on the opposite side of the decompressor cam. When doing so, the decompressor lobe should move below the exhaust base.

8. If the camshaft, bearing or decompressor cam fail to operate properly or are excessively worn, replace

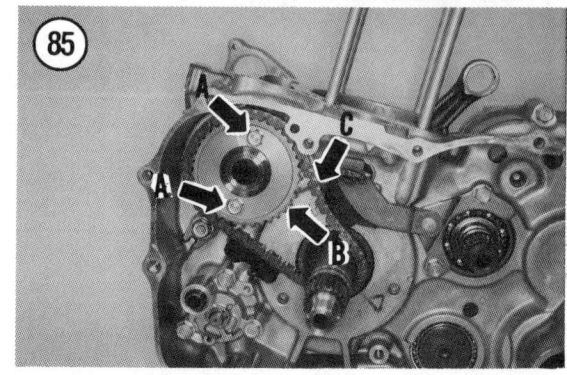

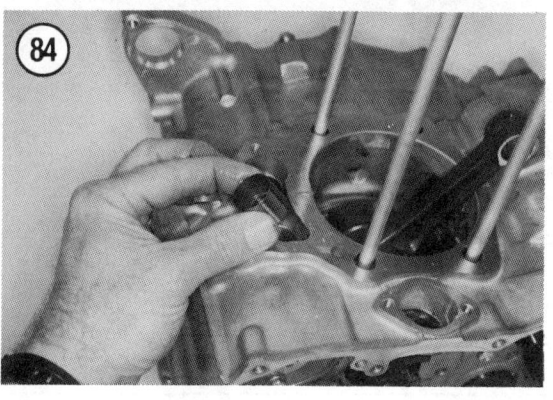

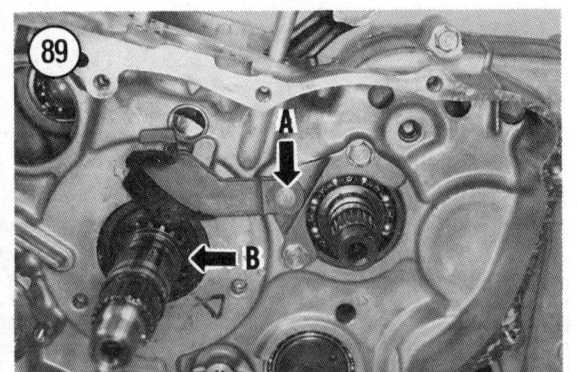

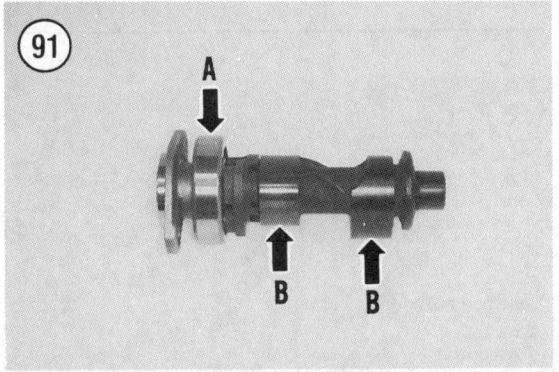

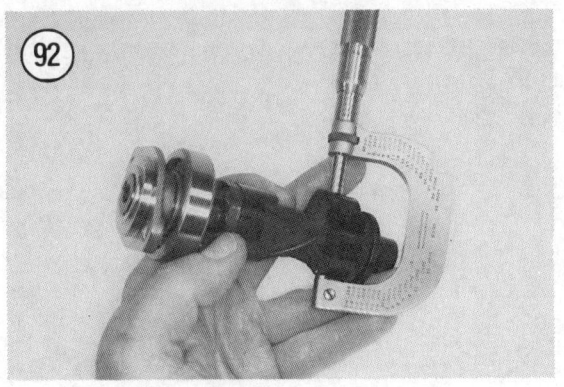

the camshaft assembly. The bearing and decompressor cam are not available separately.

**Cam Follower**
**Inspection**

Refer to **Table 2** when measuring the cam followers and cam follower bores in this section. Replace parts that are out of specification or show damage.

*CAUTION*
*The cam followers must not be interchanged when cleaning them in Step 1. Each cam follower should be installed in its original operating position.*

1. Clean and dry the cam followers.

2. Inspect the cam followers (12 and 13, **Figure 81**) for scoring, cracks or other damage.

3. Inspect the cam follower bores (**Figure 83**) for scoring, severe wear or other damage.

4. Measure the cam follower outside diameter (**Figure 94**). Record the dimension. Replace the cam follower if out of specification.

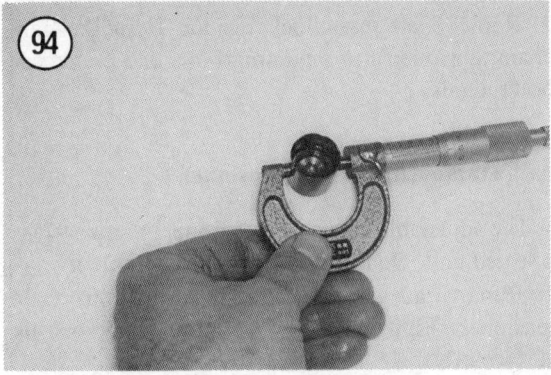

5. Measure the cam follower bore inside diameter (**Figure 95**). Record the dimension. Replace the crankcase half if the bore is out of specification.

*NOTE*
*The front and rear crankcase halves can be replaced separately. See Chapter Five.*

6. If the cam followers and cam follower bore inside diameters are within specifications, determine the cam follower-to-bore clearance as follows:

   a. Subtract the dimension in Step 5 from the dimension in Step 4. The result is cam follower-to-bore operating clearance. Repeat for both cam followers.

   b. If out of specification, replace the cam follower and then remeasure. If the operating clearance is still out of specification, replace the crankcase half.

## Camshaft Chain and Sprocket Inspection

1. Inspect the camshaft sprockets (B, **Figure 89** and **Figure 90**) for broken or chipped teeth. Also, check the teeth for cracks or other damage. If the drive sprocket (B, **Figure 89**) is damaged, replace the crankshaft assembly; see Chapter Five.

2. Inspect the cam chain (**Figure 90**) for severe wear, loose or damaged pins, cracks or other damage. Replace if damaged.

## Cam Chain Tensioner Slipper Surface Inspection

1. Check the cam chain tensioner slipper surfaces (**Figure 96**) for excessive wear or damage. Replace if necessary.

2. Remove all threadlock residue from the cam chain tensioner arm mounting bolts and crankcase bolt threads.

## Adjustable Cam Chain Tensioner

The adjustable cam chain tensioner (**Figure 97**) is a sealed unit. Do not attempt to disassemble it.

1. Remove all gasket residue from the cam chain tensioner (**Figure 97**) and cylinder block mating surfaces.

2. Remove the sealing bolt and O-ring (**Figure 97**) from the tensioner housing. Replace the O-ring if damaged.

3. Check the tensioner rod and housing for damage.

4. Turn the cam chain lifter shaft clockwise with a small screwdriver and release it. The shaft should move with no binding or other noticeable damage.

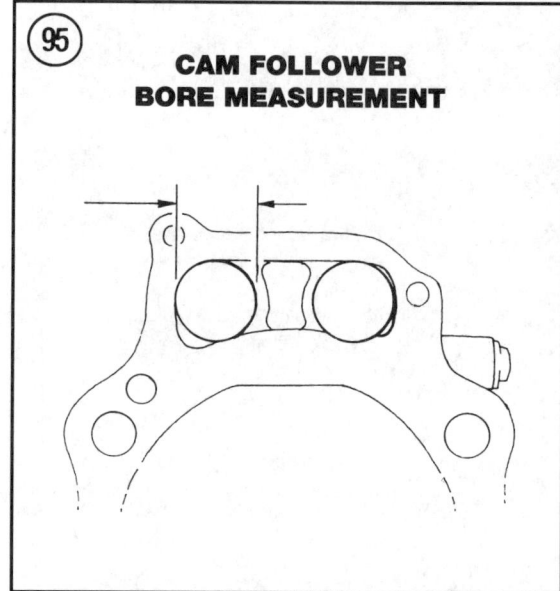

**CAM FOLLOWER BORE MEASUREMENT**

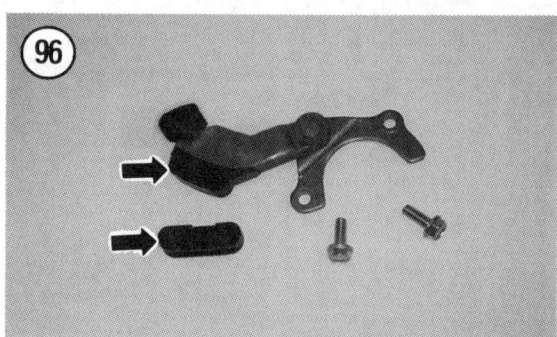

## Camshaft Stopper Plate

Before installing the camshaft, make a stopper plate using a piece of 1 mm (0.040 in.) thick metal shaped in the dimensions shown in **Figure 98**. The stopper plate holds the cam chain tensioner shaft in

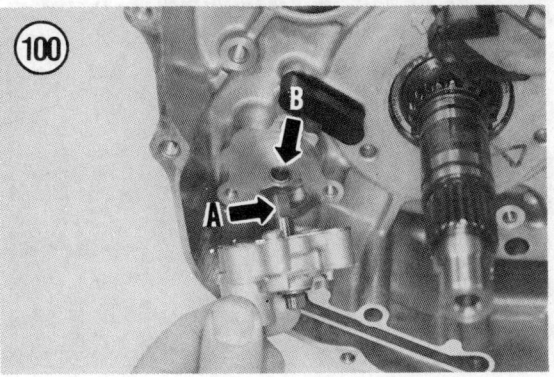

its retracted position when installing the tensioner onto the engine.

## Camshaft Installation

1. Apply a medium strength threadlock onto the two cam chain tensioner arm mounting bolts. Then install the chain tensioner arm (A, **Figure 89**) and tighten its mounting bolts securely.

2. Install the cam chain slipper onto the crankcase boss as shown in **Figure 99**.

3. If removed, install the oil pump as follows:

   a. Align the shoulder on the end of the pump shaft (A, **Figure 100**) with the groove in the end of the balancer shaft (B, **Figure 100**) and install the oil pump. Then align the side plate tab on the oil pump with the cam chain slipper groove.

   b. Install and tighten the oil pump mounting bolts (B, **Figure 88**).

   c. Check pump engagement by turning the crankshaft back and forth. When doing so, the pump shaft (visible on the outside of the pump) should turn.

4. Remove the timing hole cap (A, **Figure 101**) and O-ring.

5. Position the engine at TDC by slowly pulling the recoil starter (B, **Figure 101**) and aligning the flywheel T mark with the index mark on the rear crankcase cover (**Figure 102**).

> *NOTE*
> *The engine must remain at TDC when installing the camshaft, chain and cam sprocket in the following steps.*

6. Lubricate the camshaft lobes and the cam followers with engine oil before installing them in the following steps.

7. Install the camshaft (**Figure 87**) into the crankcase with its cam lobes facing down.

8. Install the bearing retainer by aligning its groove with the crankcase boss as shown in B, **Figure 86**. Apply a medium strength threadlock onto the retainer mounting bolt threads, then install the mounting bolt (A, **Figure 86**) and tighten securely.

9. Align the camshaft timing mark (A, **Figure 103**) with the crankcase index mark (B). Then check that the flywheel T mark is properly aligned with the index mark (**Figure 102**).

10. Install the cam chain over the cam sprocket. The timing mark on the cam sprocket must face out.

11. Install the cam sprocket and cam chain (**Figure 104**). Align the timing mark on the cam sprocket with the crankcase index mark (**Figure 105**).

12. Apply a medium strength threadlock compound to the cam sprocket mounting bolts and install the bolts (**Figure 105**).

13. Confirm that the flywheel T mark aligns with the rear crankcase cover index mark (**Figure 102**) and that the camshaft timing mark aligns with the

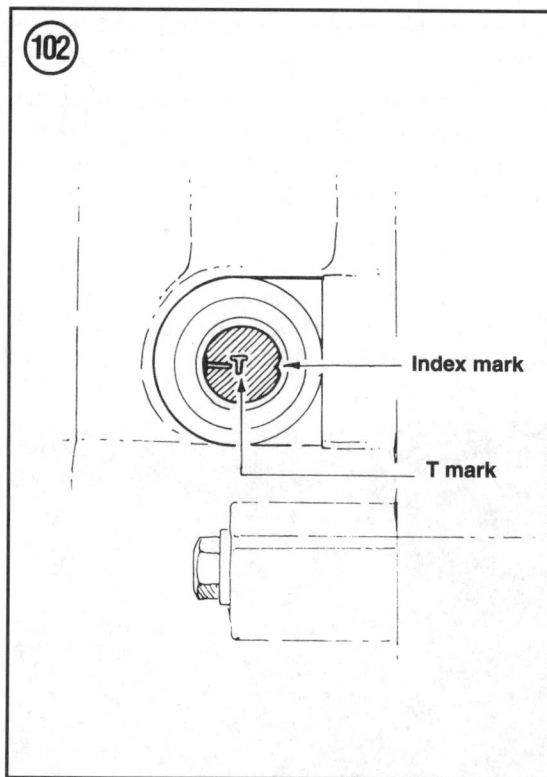

Index mark

T mark

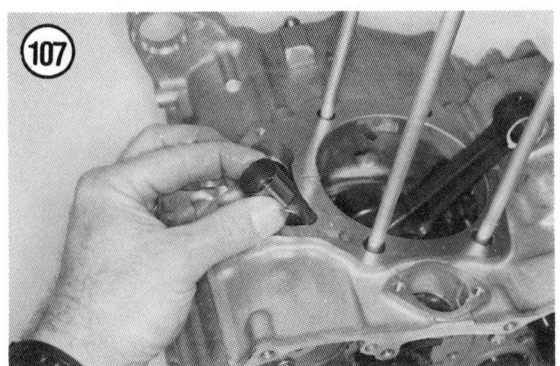

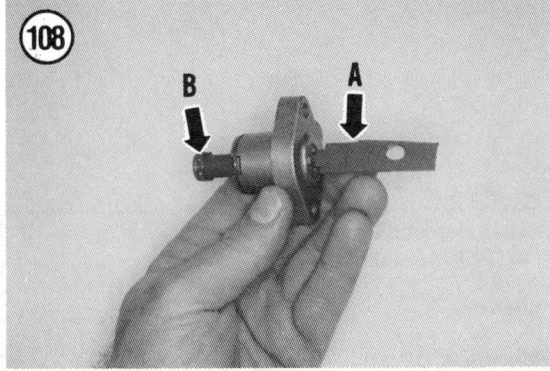

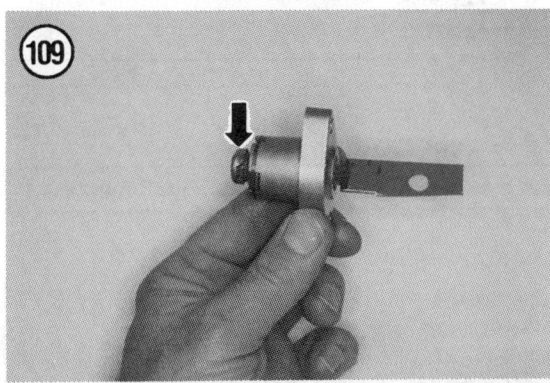

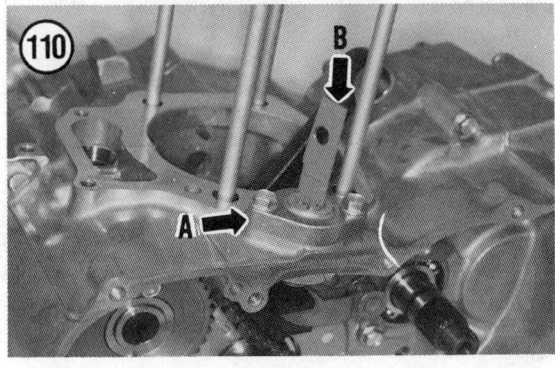

crankcase index mark (**Figure 105**). These timing marks must align as shown. If not, the camshaft timing is incorrect.

14. Tighten both cam sprocket mounting bolts (**Figure 105**) as specified in **Table 3**.

15. Turn the engine over with the recoil starter and realign the flywheel T mark. Check that both sets of timing marks align as described in Step 13.

> *CAUTION*
> *Improper cam timing can cause severe engine damage. Before completing engine assembly, make sure the timing marks align as described in this section.*

16. Lubricate the cam followers with engine oil.

> *CAUTION*
> *The original cam followers must not be interchanged when installing them in Step 17.*

17. Install each cam follower (**Figure 106**) in its original operating position. Refer to your marks made during removal. Install each cam follower with its open side (**Figure 107**) facing up.

18. Install the adjustable cam chain tensioner (**Figure 97**) as follows:

    a. Fabricate a camshaft stopper plate as described in this section.

    b. Remove the sealing screw and O-ring from the end of the camshaft tensioner housing.

    c. Insert the stopper plate (A, **Figure 108**) into the slot in the middle of the tensioner housing and turn it clockwise to retract the tensioner shaft (B, **Figure 108**), then insert the stopper plate between two of the notches in the top of the housing to hold the tensioner shaft (**Figure 109**) in position.

    d. Install a new gasket (**Figure 97**) on the cam chain tensioner.

    e. Install the cam chain tensioner (A, **Figure 110**) onto the engine and tighten its mounting bolts securely.

    f. Remove the stopper plate (B, **Figure 110**) to release the tensioner shaft. Now check that the tensioner shaft pushes against the cam chain tensioner arm as shown in **Figure 111**.

    g. Install the O-ring and sealing screw (**Figure 112**). Tighten the screw securely.

19. Install both clutch assemblies (Chapter Six).

20. Install the cylinder as described in this chapter.

### Table 1 GENERAL ENGINE SPECIFICATIONS

| | |
|---|---|
| Engine | 4-stroke, overhead valve pushrod engine |
| Displacement | 395 cc (24.10 cu.-in) |
| Compression ratio | 8.2:1 |
| Cooling system | Air cooled |
| Valve timing | |
|   Intake valve opens | 10 degrees BTDC |
|   Intake valve closes | 40 degrees ABDC |
|   Exhaust valve opens | 40 degrees BBDC |
|   Exhaust valve closes | 10 degrees ATDC |

### Table 2 ENGINE SERVICE SPECIFICATIONS

| | New mm (in.) | Service limit mm (in.) |
|---|---|---|
| Cylinder head warpage limit | — | 0.10 |
| | — | (0.004) |
| Cam lobe height | | |
|   Intake | 36.423-36.583 | 36.25 |
| | (1.4340-1.4402) | (1.427) |
|   Exhaust | 36.267-36.427 | 36.10 |
| | (1.4278-1.4341) | (1.421) |
| Cam follower outside diameter | 22.467-22.482 | 22.459 |
| | (0.8845-0.8851) | (0.8842) |
| Cam follower bore diameter | 22.510-22.526 | 22.54 |
| | (0.8862-0.0068) | (0.887) |
| Cam follower-to-bore clearance | 0.028-0.059 | 0.07 |
| | (0.0011-0.0023) | (0.003) |
| Rocker arm bore inside diameter | 12.000-12.018 | 12.05 |
| | (0.4724-0.4731) | (0.474) |
| Rocker arm shaft outside diameter | 11.964-11.984 | 11.92 |
| | (0.4710-0.4718) | (0.469) |
| Rocker arm-to-shaft clearance | 0.016-0.054 | 0.08 |
| | (0.0006-0.0021) | (0.003) |
| Valve clearance | 0.15 | — |
| | (0.006) | |
| | (continued) | |

**Table 2 ENGINE SERVICE SPECIFICATIONS (continued)**

| | New | Service limit |
|---|---|---|
| Valve stem diameter | | |
| Intake | 5.475-5.490 | 5.45 |
| | (0.2156-0.2161) | (0.215) |
| Exhaust | 5.455-5.470 | 5.43 |
| | (0.2148-0.2154) | (0.214) |
| Valve guide inside diameter | 5.500-5.512 | 5.525 |
| | (0.2165-0.2170) | (0.2177) |
| Valve stem-to-guide clearance | | |
| Intake | 0.010-0.037 | 0.12 |
| | (0.0004-0.0015) | (0.005) |
| Exhaust | 0.030-0.057 | 0.14 |
| | (0.0012-0.0022) | (0.006) |
| Valve seat width | 1.2 | — |
| | (0.05) | |
| Valve spring free length | | |
| Inner | 36.31 | 35.2 |
| | (1.430) | (1.39) |
| Outer | 41.34 | 40.0 |
| | (1.628) | (1.57) |
| Cylinder bore diameter (standard bore) | 86.000-86.010 | 86.10 |
| | (3.3858-3.3862) | (3.390) |
| Cylinder out of round limit | — | 0.10 |
| | — | (0.004) |
| Cylinder taper limit | — | 0.10 |
| | | (0.004) |
| Cylinder warpage limit | — | 0.10 |
| | | (0.004) |
| Piston diameter (standard piston) | 85.974-85.985 | 85.90 |
| | (3.3848-3.3852) | (3.382) |
| Piston measuring point | see text | — |
| Piston-to-cylinder clearance | 0.015-0.045 | 0.10 |
| | (0.0006-0.0018) | (0.004) |
| Piston pin bore diameter | 19.002-19.008 | 19.08 |
| | (0.7481-0.7483) | (0.751) |
| Piston pin outside diameter | 18.994-19.000 | 18.96 |
| | (0.7478-0.7480) | (0.746) |
| Piston-to-piston pin clearance | 0.002-0.014 | 0.12 |
| | (0.0001-0.0006) | (0.039) |
| Piston ringside clearance | | |
| Top compression ring | 0.03-0.06 | 0.09 |
| | (0.001-0.002) | (0.004) |
| Second compression ring | 0.015-0.045 | 0.09 |
| | (0.0006-0.0018) | (0.004) |
| Piston ring end gap | | |
| Top compression ring | 0.15-0.30 | 0.5 |
| | (0.006-0.012) | (0.02) |
| Second compression ring | 0.30-0.45 | 0.6 |
| | (0.012-0.018) | (0.02) |
| Oil ring (side rails) | 0.20-0.70 | — |
| | (0.008-0.028) | |
| Connecting rod bore inside diameter | 19.020-19.041 | 19.07 |
| | (0.7488-0.7490) | (0.751) |
| Connecting rod-to-piston pin clearance | 0.020-0.047 | 0.10 |
| | (0.0008-0.0019) | (0.004) |

4

### Table  3  ENGINE  TIGHTENING  TORQUES

|  | N·m | in.-lb. | ft.-lb. |
|---|---|---|---|
| Cam chain tensioner lifter sealing bolt | 4 | 35 | — |
| Cam chain tensioner mounting bolt | 12 | 106 | — |
| Cam sprocket mounting bolts | 20 | 15 | — |
| Camshaft bearing retainer bolt | 27 | 20 | — |
| Cylinder head acorn nuts | 40 | — | 29 |
| Exhaust system |  |  |  |
|   Exhaust pipe protector bolts | 20 | — | 15 |
|   Muffler clamp bolts | 23 | — | 17 |
|   Muffler mounting bolts | 20 | — | 15 |
|   Heat guard bolts | 20 | — | 15 |
|   Heat protector bolts | 20 | — | 15 |
| Rocker arm holder flange cap nut | 40 | — | 29 |
| Rocker arm shaft mounting bolt | 7 | 62 | — |
| Upper engine hanger bolt | 55 | 41 | — |
| Upper engine hanger bracket bolt | 33 | 24 | — |

# ENGINE LOWER END

This chapter describes service procedures for the following lower end components:

1. Recoil starter.
2. Alternator cover.
3. Flywheel and starter clutch.
4. Gearshift linkage.
5. Reverse shaft assembly.
6. Oil pump.
7. Relief valve.
8. Oil strainer screen.
9. Crankcase and crankshaft.
10. Transmission shifting check.

Before you begin work, read Chapter One again. You will do a better job with this information fresh in your mind.

Throughout the text there is frequent mention of the front and rear sides of the engine. This refers to the engine as it sits in the vehicle's frame, not as it sits on your workbench. Likewise, the references to the left and right sides of the engine refer to the engine as it is mounted in the frame.

**Table 1** lists general engine specifications and **Table 2** lists oil pump service specifications. **Table 3** lists crankshaft service specifications. **Table 4** lists engine tightening torques. **Tables 1-4** are at the end of this chapter.

## SERVICING ENGINE IN FRAME

You can service many engine components with the engine mounted in the frame. The following compo-

nents can be serviced with the engine mounted in the frame:

1. Cylinder head.
2. Cylinder and piston.
3. Clutch.
4. Recoil starter.
5. Oil pump.
6. Carburetor.
7. Alternator.
8. Oil pump.

## ENGINE

Refer to **Figure 1** when removing and installing the engine in the frame.

### Removal/Installation

1. Park the vehicle on a level surface and set the parking brake.
2. Before disassembling the engine, perform a compression test (Chapter Three) and leak down test (Chapter Two). Record the readings for future use.
3. Remove the seat (Chapter Fifteen).
4. Disconnect the negative battery cable at the battery (Chapter Three).
5. If you are going to disassemble the engine, drain the engine oil (Chapter Three).
6. Remove the fuel tank and heat guard (Chapter Eight).
7. Remove the front fender (Chapter Fifteen).

8. Remove the under mudguard (Chapter Fifteen).

9. Remove the carburetor (Chapter Eight).

10. Remove the exhaust system (Chapter Four).

11. Remove the bolts, collars and right side engine cover (**Figure 2**).

12. Disconnect the oil cooler hoses from the engine as follows:

a. Remove Allen bolt and holder (A, **Figure 3**), then disconnect the two oil hoses (B) from the engine. Cover the hose ends to prevent oil leakage and contamination.

b. Remove the two oil hose O-rings (**Figure 4**).

13. Remove the starter motor (Chapter Nine).

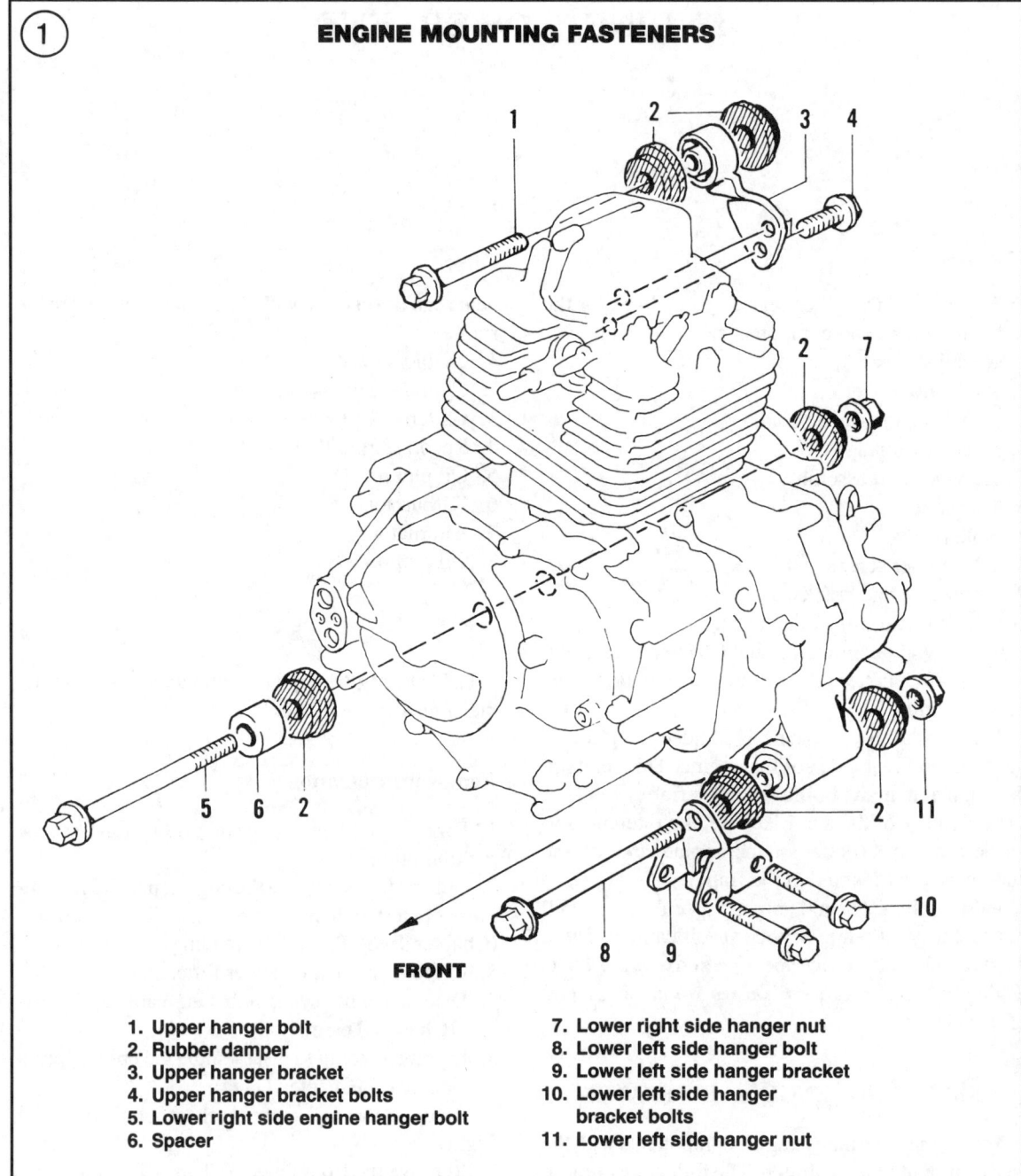

**ENGINE MOUNTING FASTENERS**

**FRONT**

1. Upper hanger bolt
2. Rubber damper
3. Upper hanger bracket
4. Upper hanger bracket bolts
5. Lower right side engine hanger bolt
6. Spacer
7. Lower right side hanger nut
8. Lower left side hanger bolt
9. Lower left side hanger bracket
10. Lower left side hanger bracket bolts
11. Lower left side hanger nut

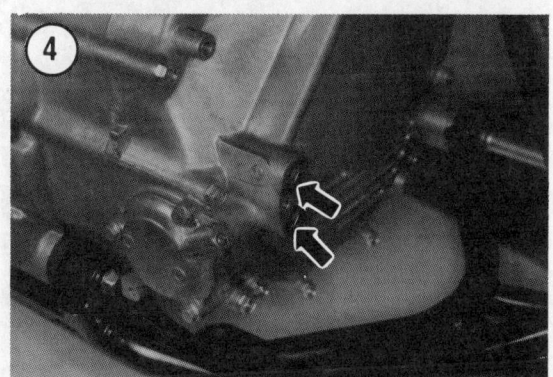

14. Remove the bolt and disconnect the two ground cables (**Figure 5**) at the engine.

15. Disconnect the following electrical connectors:

    a. On 1996 and later models: Speed sensor connector (A, **Figure 6**).

    b. Alternator/pulse generator connector (B, **Figure 6**).

    c. Neutral/reverse switch connector (C, **Figure 6**).

    d. Oil thermosensor connector (D, **Figure 6**).

*NOTE*
*The oil thermosensor connector can also be disconnected at the engine.*

16. Disconnect the reverse control cable (**Figure 7**) from the lever mounted on the engine.

17. Remove the bolts, collars and left side engine cover (A, **Figure 8**).

18. Remove the left footpeg (B, **Figure 8**).

19. Remove the shift pedal (C, **Figure 8**).

20. Remove the front differential mounting bolts and remove the front drive shaft (**Figure 9**) as described in Chapter Eleven.

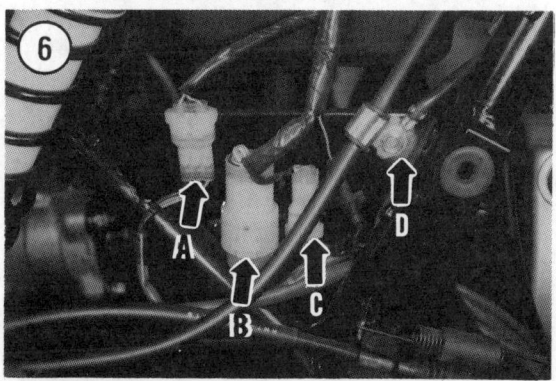

21. Disconnect the crankcase breather tube (A, **Figure 10**) at the engine.

22. Loosen the front swing arm boot clamp (B, **Figure 10**).

23. Remove the engine upper hanger bolt (A, **Figure 11**).

24. Remove the engine upper hanger bracket bolts (A, **Figure 12**), upper hanger bracket (B) and both rubber dampers (B, **Figure 11**).

25. Place a jack (**Figure 13**) underneath the engine and support the engine with just enough tension to remove weight from the lower engine hanger mounting bolts when removing them in the following steps. Place a block of wood between the jack and engine to protect the engine cases.

26. Remove the lower right side engine hanger nut, bolt, spacer and rubber dampers (**Figure 14**).

27. Remove the lower left side engine hanger nut and bolt (A, **Figure 15**) and allow the engine to rest on the jack.

28. Remove the bolts and the lower left side engine hanger bracket (B, **Figure 15**).

> *CAUTION*
> *If you are removing an assembled engine, the following steps will require the aid of a helper to remove the engine from the frame.* ***Table 1*** *lists the approximate weight of the engine.*

29. Move the engine forward to disconnect the universal joint from the rear drive shaft, then remove the engine from the left side of the frame. Support the engine on a workbench.

30. Install the engine in the frame by reversing these steps, plus the following:

    a. Replace damaged engine mount fasteners.

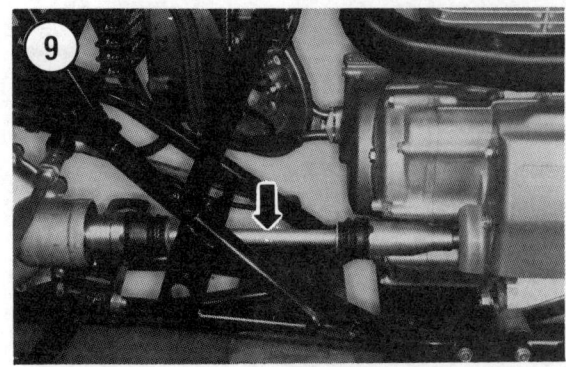

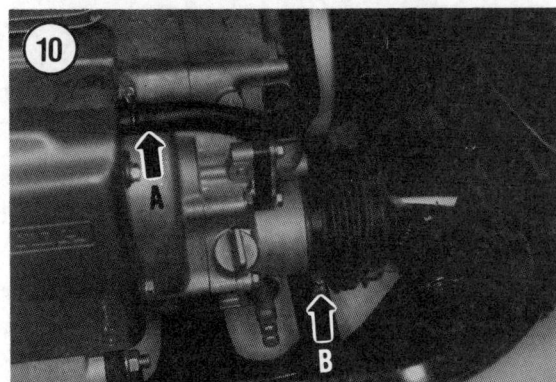

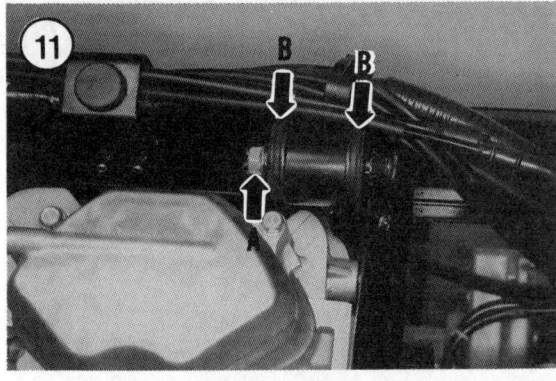

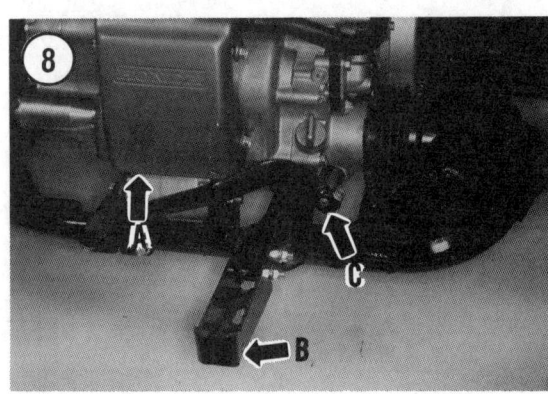

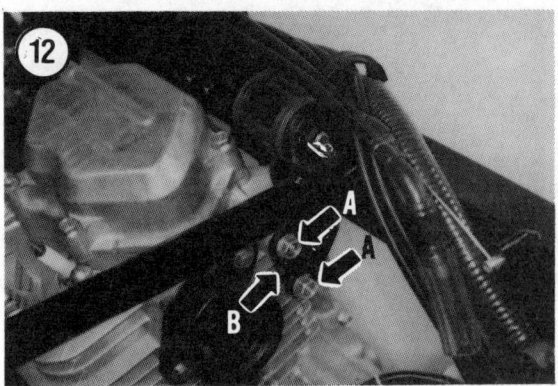

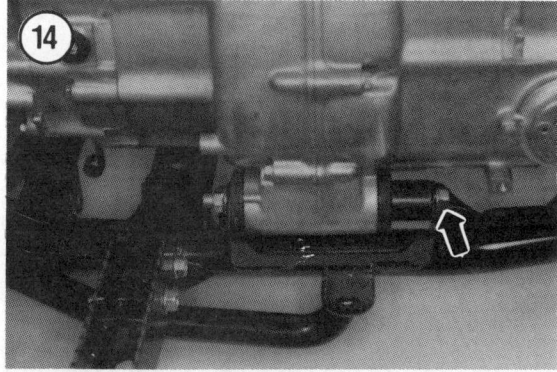

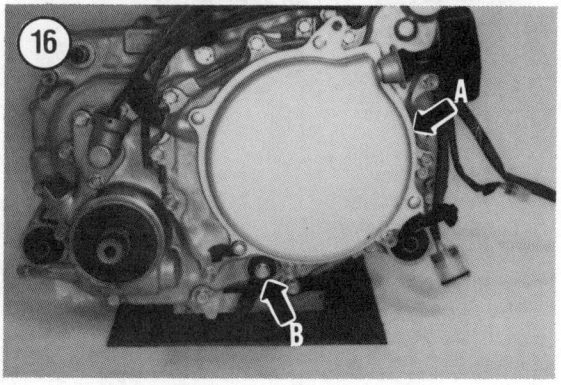

b. Apply an antiseize compound to the shoulders on each engine mount bolt. This will help to prevent rust and corrosion.

c. Lubricate the universal joint, engine and final drive shaft splines with molybdenum disulfide grease.

d. Install the lower engine rubber dampers with their wide side facing the engine (2, **Figure 1**).

e. Install the upper engine rubber dampers with their wide side facing the upper engine hanger bracket (2, **Figure 1**).

f. Tighten the lower left side engine hanger bracket bolts (B, **Figure 15**) as specified in **Table 4**.

g. Tighten the lower left side engine hanger nut (A, **Figure 15**) as specified in **Table 4**.

h. Tighten the lower right side engine hanger nut (**Figure 14**) as specified in **Table 4**.

i. Tighten the upper engine hanger bracket bolts (A, **Figure 12**) as specified in **Table 4**.

j. Tighten the upper engine hanger bolt (A, **Figure 11**) as specified in **Table 4**.

k. Check the electrical connectors for corrosion. Pack the connectors with dielectric grease before reconnecting them.

l. Fill the engine with the recommended type and quantity of oil; refer to Chapter Three.

m. Check the throttle operation (Chapter Three).

n. Check the reverse selector cable adjustment (Chapter Three).

## RECOIL STARTER

The recoil starter can be removed and installed with the engine mounted in the frame. The following procedures are shown with the engine removed for clarity.

### Removal/Installation

1. If the engine is mounted in the frame, remove any wires or cables from the guides mounted on the recoil starter assembly.

2. Remove the bolts and the recoil starter assembly (A, **Figure 16**).

3. Install the recoil starter assembly by reversing these removal steps, plus the following:

a. Install the guide bracket at the point shown in B, **Figure 16**.

b. Tighten the recoil starter assembly mounting bolts securely.

c. Pull the recoil starter handle to check its operation.

**Disassembly**

Refer to **Figure 17** for this procedure.

1. Remove the starter housing as described in this chapter.

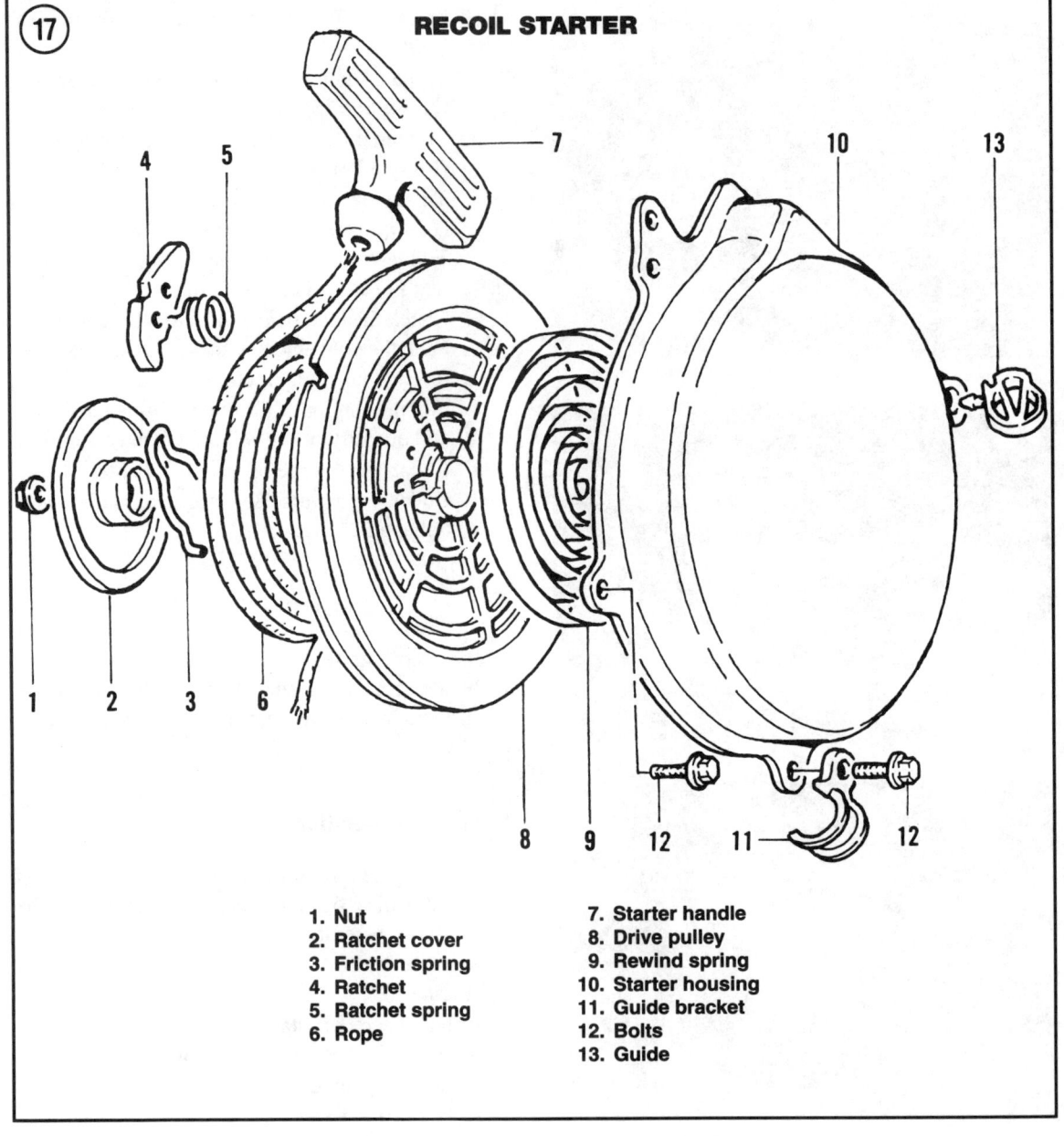

**RECOIL STARTER**

1. Nut
2. Ratchet cover
3. Friction spring
4. Ratchet
5. Ratchet spring
6. Rope
7. Starter handle
8. Drive pulley
9. Rewind spring
10. Starter housing
11. Guide bracket
12. Bolts
13. Guide

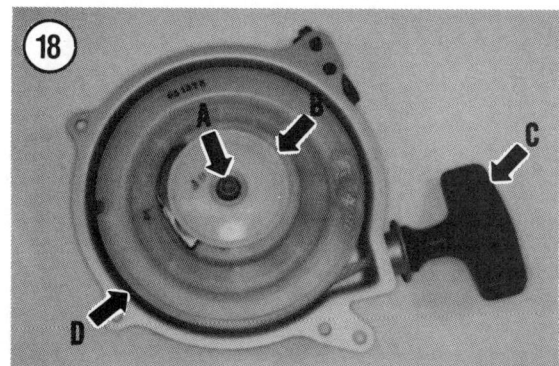

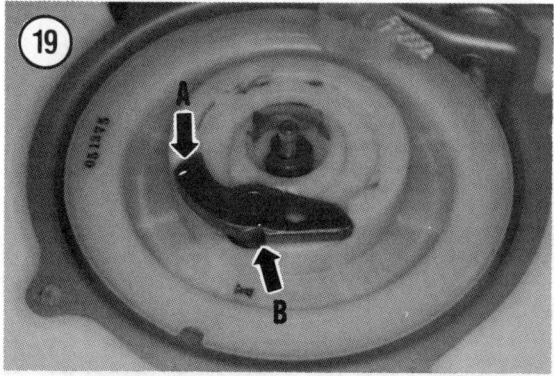

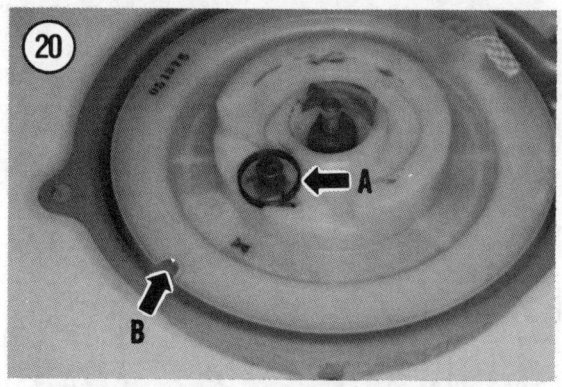

2. Remove the nut (A, **Figure 18**) and ratchet cover (B).

3. Remove the ratchet (A, **Figure 19**) and spring (A, **Figure 20**).

4. Untie the starter rope and remove the starter handle (C, **Figure 18**), then release the starter rope slowly and allow the drive pulley to unwind. Remove the drive pulley (D, **Figure 18**) and starter rope assembly.

5. Remove the starter rope from the drive pulley.

6. If necessary, remove the rewind spring from the housing as follows:

   a. Place the starter housing on the floor with the spring side facing down.

   b. Tap on the top of the housing with a plastic hammer while holding the housing firmly against the floor. The spring should fall out and unwind inside the housing.

**Inspection**

Replace worn or damaged parts as described in this section.

1. Clean and dry all parts. Do not clean the drive pulley, rope and ratchet cover in solvent.

2. Check the starter shaft in the starter housing. Replace the starter housing if the starter shaft is severely worn or damaged.

3. Check the drive pulley for severe wear or damage.

4. Check the ratchet and ratchet spring (**Figure 21**) for damage.

5. Check the rewind spring (**Figure 22**) for cracks or damaged ends.

6. Check the starter rope for tearing, fraying or other damage.

7. Check the ratchet cover and spring for damage.

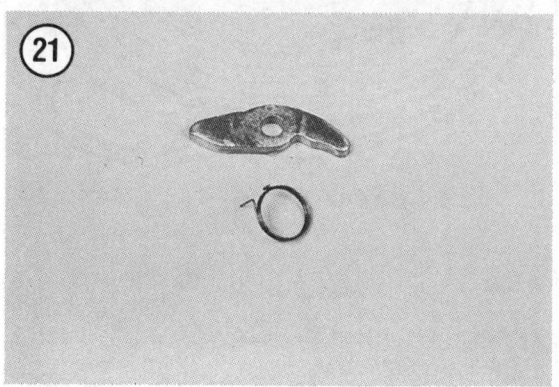

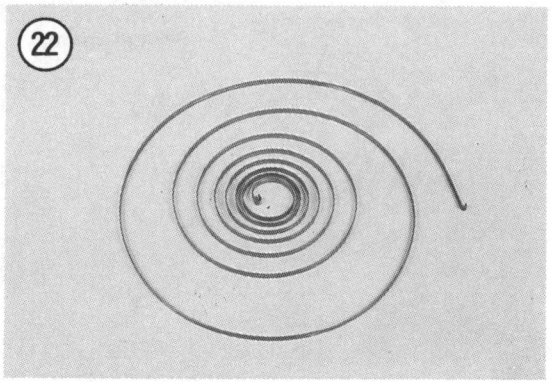

## Assembly

1. If removed, install the rewind spring into the starter housing as follows:

> *WARNING*
> *The rewind spring is put under pressure when installing it in the following steps. Safety glasses and gloves must be worn when installing the rewind spring and assembling the starter assembly.*

  a. Before installing the rewind spring, wipe some grease onto a clean rag, then slide the spring against the rag to lubricate it with grease. Wipe off any excess grease.
  b. Lubricate the starter housing shaft with the same type of grease.
  c. Hook the outer end of the rewind spring onto the spring guide as shown in **Figure 23**.
  d. Wind the rewind spring counterclockwise—working from the outside of the spring—into the starter housing. When you come to the end of the rewind spring, push it down so that it contacts the starter housing shaft (**Figure 23**).
  e. Compare the rewind spring ends with **Figure 23**, then confirm that the spring lies flat in the housing.

2. Before installing the rope, check the rope ends for fraying. Apply heat with a heat gun (**Figure 24**) to tighten up loose or frayed rope ends. Do not overheat.

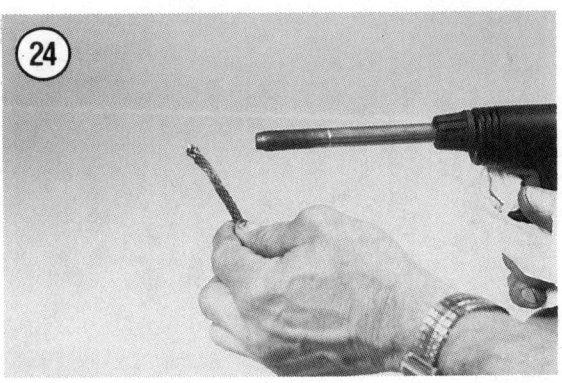

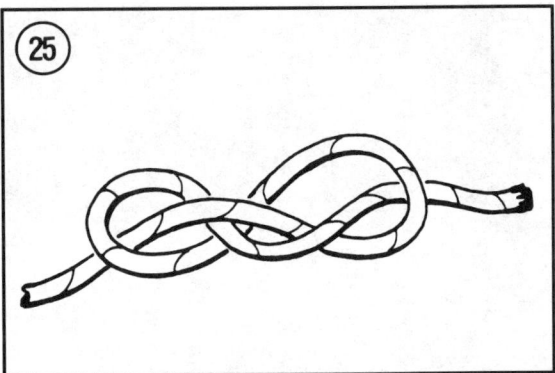

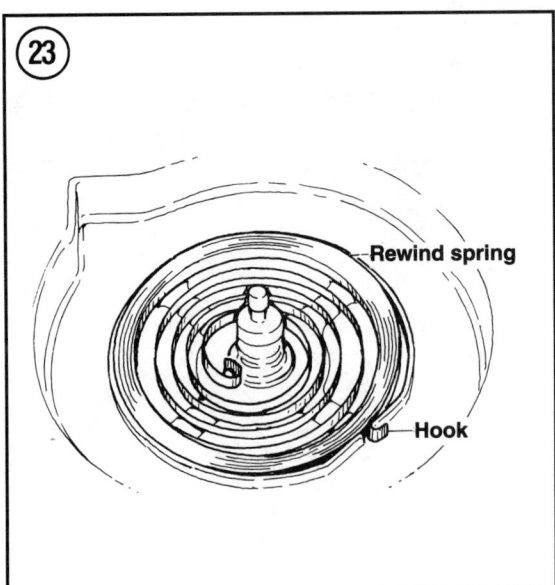

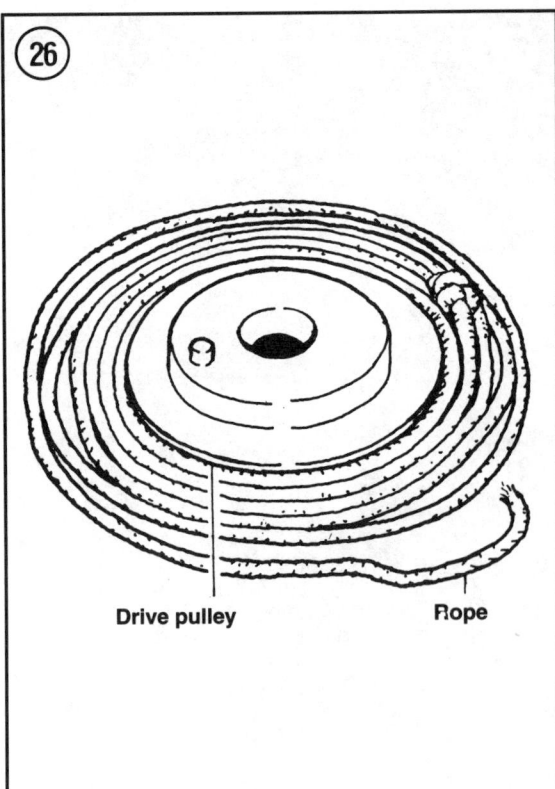

Drive pulley          Rope

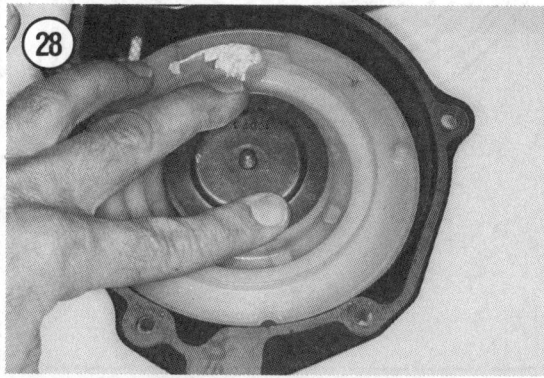

3. To install the rope, perform the following:

    a. Tie a knot in one end of the rope (**Figure 25**).

    b. Insert the rope through the hole in the drive pulley. Pull the rope tight so that the knot enters the raised shoulder on the pulley (**Figure 26**).

    c. With the ratchet side of the drive pulley facing up, wind the rope clockwise around the drive pulley as shown in **Figure 26**.

4. Grease the drive pulley shaft bore.

5. Install the drive pulley into the starter housing as follows:

    a. Align the hook in the bottom of the drive pulley with the end of the rewind spring and install the drive pulley into the housing.

    b. Rotate the drive pulley slightly until it drops into place, indicating that the hook in the drive pulley meshes with the rewind spring end.

6. Extend the rope, then catch the rope in the drive pulley notch (B, **Figure 20**).

7. Rotate the drive pulley 2 1/2 turns clockwise and hold in this position—do not let go of the drive pulley.

8. Feed the rope through the starter housing rope hole and secure it in place with a pair of locking pliers (**Figure 27**). Then slip the rope out of the drive pulley notch.

9. Insert the starter handle over the rope. Tie a knot in the end of the rope.

10. Remove the locking pliers and allow the drive pulley to unwind in the housing while pulling the rope into the housing (**Figure 28**).

11. Grease the ratchet spring and ratchet.

12. Install the end of the ratchet spring into the hole in the drive pulley. See A, **Figure 20**.

13. Install and hook the ratchet against the ratchet spring as shown in B, **Figure 19**.

14. If removed, install the friction spring (A, **Figure 29**) onto the back of the ratchet cover (B).

15. Grease the friction spring and ratchet cover surfaces.

16. Install the ratchet cover (**Figure 30**) by aligning the friction spring with the ratchet as shown in Figure 30.

17. Install and tighten the nut (A, **Figure 18**).

18. Pull the starter handle and confirm that the ratchet extends as shown in **Figure 31**. If the ratchet does not extend, remove the ratchet cover and reassemble the parts.

5

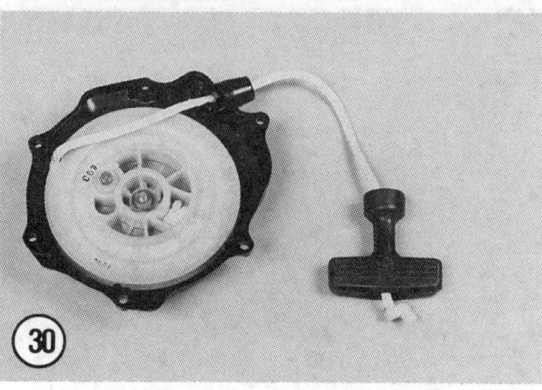

## DRIVEN PULLEY

### Removal/Installation

1. Remove the recoil starter assembly as described in this chapter.

2. Secure the driven pulley with the Honda recoil puller holder (part No. 07SMB-HM70100 [**Figure 32**]) or an equivalent holder.

3. Loosen and remove the driven pulley bolt and O-ring (A, **Figure 33**).

4. Remove the driven pulley (B, **Figure 33**).

5. Inspect the driven pulley for cracks or other damage. Replace if necessary.

6. Inspect the O-ring (A, **Figure 33**) and replace if damaged.

7. Install the driven pulley by reversing these removal steps, plus the following:

    a. Align the shoulder on the end of the driven pulley (**Figure 34**) with the groove in the flywheel, then install the driven pulley.

    b. Lubricate the O-ring with engine oil and install it onto the driven pulley bolt.

    c. Secure the driven pulley with the same tool used during removal.

    d. Install the driven pulley bolt and tighten as specified in **Table 4**.

## ALTERNATOR COVER

The following components are mounted onto the alternator cover:

1. Starter bearing.
2. Stator coil assembly.
3. Ignition pulse generator.
4. Neutral/reverse switch.

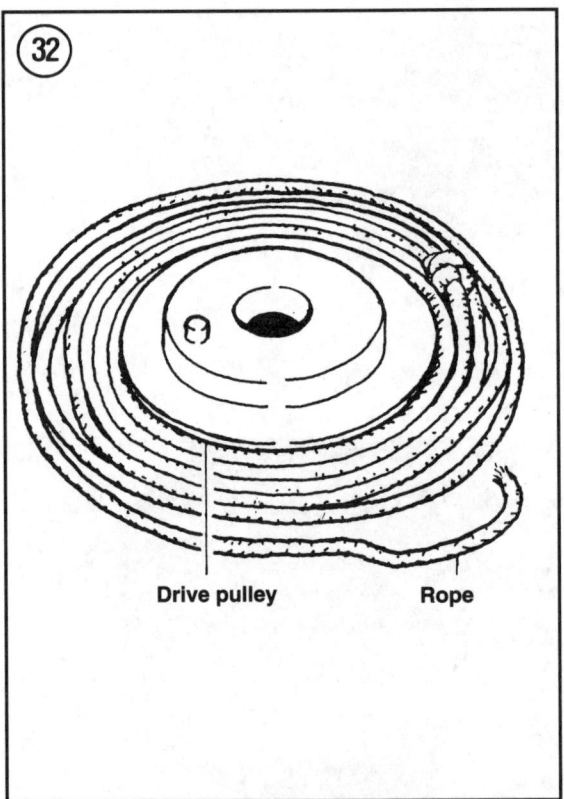

Drive pulley            Rope

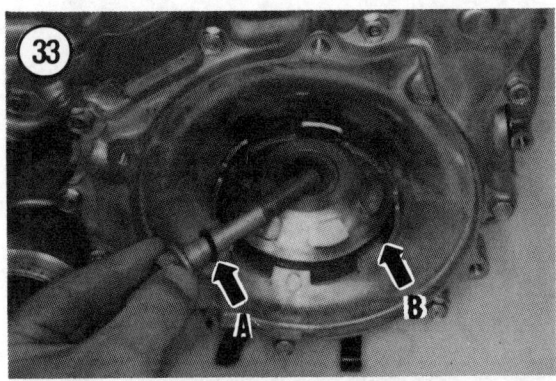

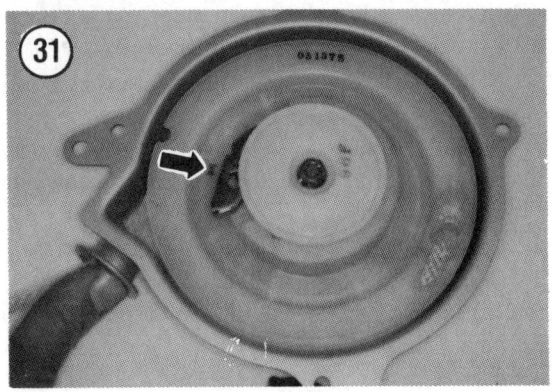

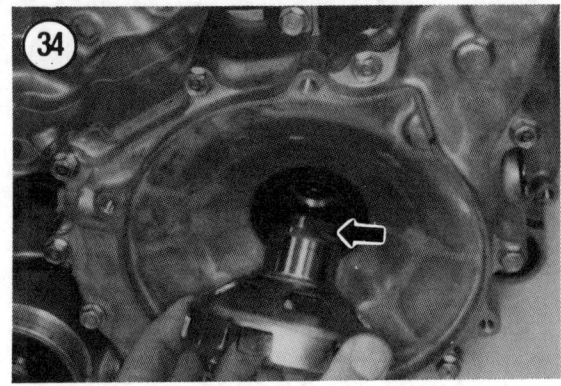

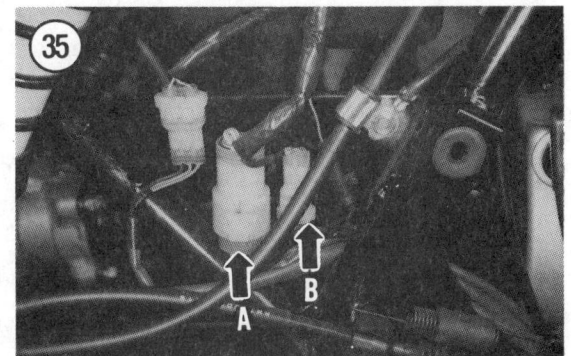

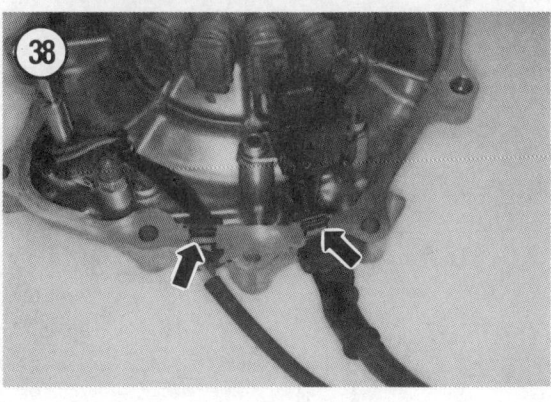

### Removal/Installation

1. Remove the driven pulley as described in this chapter.

2. If the engine is mounted in the frame, perform the following:

   a. Remove the seat (Chapter Fifteen).

   b. Disconnect the negative battery cable (Chapter Three).

   c. Drain the engine oil (Chapter Three).

   d. Remove the fuel tank (Chapter Eight).

   e. Remove the rear fender assembly (Chapter Fifteen).

   f. Disconnect the alternator/pulse generator connector (A, **Figure 35**).

   g. Disconnect the neutral/reverse switch connector (B, **Figure 35**).

*NOTE*
*The starter gears may fall out of the rear crankcase cover when removing the alternator cover in Step 3.*

3. Remove the bolts and the alternator cover (**Figure 36**).

4. Remove the O-ring (A, **Figure 37**) and dowel pins (B).

5. Reinstall the starter gear washer (C, **Figure 37**) if it came off with the alternator cover.

6. Install the alternator cover by reversing these removal steps, plus the following:

   a. If the starter gears fell out, reinstall them as described under *Flywheel and Starter Clutch* in this chapter.

   b. Remove all sealer residue from the alternator cover and rear crankcase cover mating surfaces.

   c. Replace the O-ring (A, **Figure 37**) if leaking or damaged.

   d. Install the O-ring into the rear crankcase cover groove (A, **Figure 37**).

   e. Apply Yamabond No. 4 (or equivalent) onto the two grommets (**Figure 38**) and onto the alternator cover (**Figure 39**).

   f. Shift the transmission into NEUTRAL by aligning the shift drum groove (A, **Figure 40**) with the index mark (B) on the crankcase.

   g. Align the long end of the neutral/reverse switch pin (A, **Figure 41**) with the N mark (B) cast into the top of the switch housing.

5

h. Install and tighten the alternator cover mounting bolts securely.

### Alternator Cover Oil Seal Inspection/Replacement

1. Inspect the alternator cover oil seal (**Figure 42**) for oil leakage, wear or damage.
2. Replace the alternator cover oil seal as follows:
   a. Pry the oil seal out of the cover with a wide-blade screwdriver. Pad the bottom of the screwdriver to prevent it from damaging the alternator cover.
   b. Pack the lips of the new oil seal with grease.
   c. Press in the oil seal with its flat side (**Figure 42**) facing out.

### Starter Bearing Inspection/Replacement

1. Turn the starter bearing inner race (A, **Figure 43**). The bearing should turn without any catching,

roughness or excessive noise. Also check that the bearing's outer race is a tight fit in the alternator cover. If any of these conditions are present, clean the bearing and then recheck its condition. If the bearing's condition did not change, replace the bearing as described in Step 2. If the bearing is a loose fit in the alternator cover, check the bearing bore for cracks or damage.

2. Replace the starter bearing as follows:
   a. Support the alternator cover on the workbench.

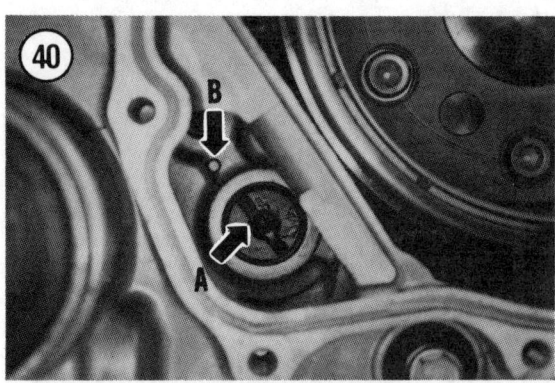

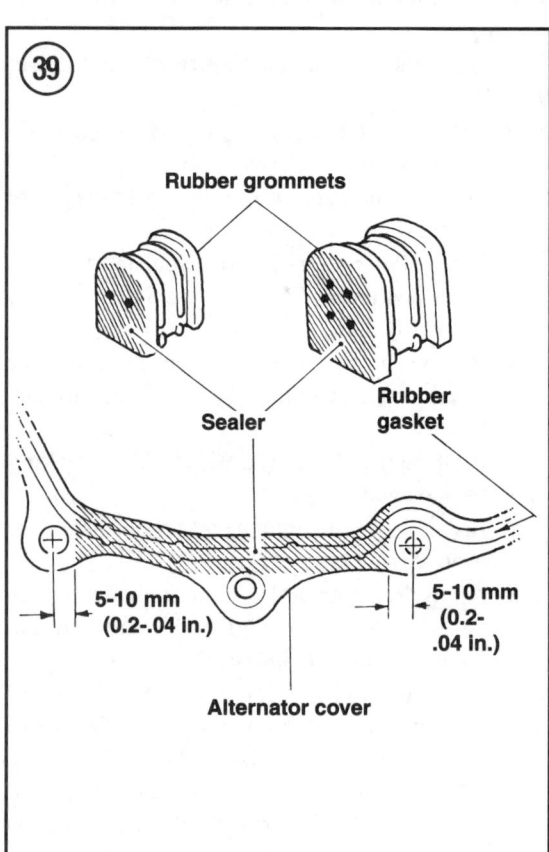

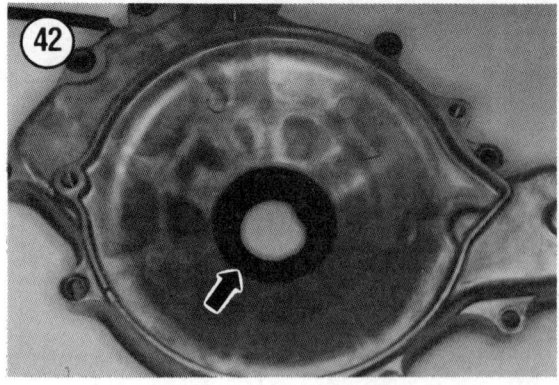

b. Remove the starter bearing with a blind bearing remover (**Figure 44**).

c. Inspect the bearing mounting bore for cracks or other damage. If the bearing is a loose fit in its mounting bore, replace the alternator cover.

d. Press in the new bearing with its manufacturer's marks facing out. Press in the bearing until it bottoms out. Press against the bearing's outer race only.

### Disassembly/Reassembly

Perform these steps to remove the stator coil, ignition pulse generator or neutral/reverse switch assembly.

1. Disconnect the connector from the top of the ignition pulse generator (A, **Figure 45**).

2. Remove the ignition pulse generator (A, **Figure 45**) and stator (B, **Figure 43**) mounting bolts.

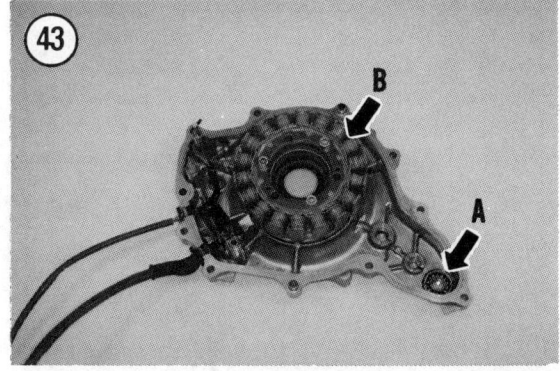

3. Remove the bolt and the neutral/reverse switch assembly (B, **Figure 45**).

4. Install by reversing these removal steps, plus the following:

a. Remove all thread sealer residue from the neutral/reverse switch mounting bolts and bolt threads.

b. Apply a medium strength threadlock onto the neutral/reverse switch mounting bolts (B, **Figure 45**). Install and tighten the bolts as specified in **Table 4**.

c. Tighten the stator (B, **Figure 43**) mounting bolts as specified in **Table 4**.

d. Tighten the ignition pulse generator mounting bolts (A, **Figure 45**) as specified in **Table 4**.

## REAR CRANKCASE COVER

The rear crankcase cover houses the following components:

1. Gearshift spindle and gearshift arm A.
2. Final drive shaft seal.
3. Reverse spindle seal.

### Removal/Installation

The rear crankcase cover can be removed with the flywheel installed on the engine.

1. Remove the alternator cover as described in this chapter.
2. Remove the starter motor (Chapter Nine).

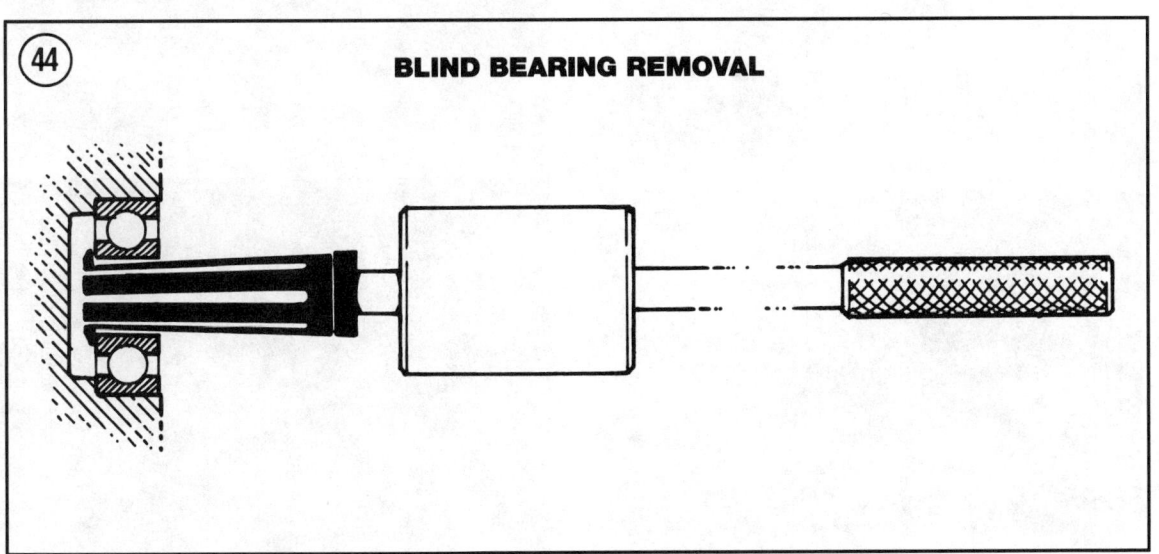

**BLIND BEARING REMOVAL**

3. Remove the reducton gear (A, **Figure 46**) and its shaft (B).

4. Remove the washer (C, **Figure 46**) and reduction gear (D).

> *NOTE*
> *The reduction shaft (**Figure 47**) cannot be removed with the flywheel installed on the engine. To remove the flywheel, refer to **Flywheel and Starter Clutch** in this chapter.*

5. Remove the bolt and the reverse control lever (A, **Figure 48**).

6. Remove the bolts, cable guide (B, **Figure 48**) and the rear crankcase cover (**Figure 49**).

> *NOTE*
> *If the gearshift linkage is removed on the opposite side of the engine, the sub-gearshift spindle (A, **Figure 50**) and its washer (B, **Figure 50**) may come out with the rear crankcase cover.*

7. Remove the washer (**Figure 51**) from the reverse spindle.

8. Remove the 2 dowel pins (**Figure 52**) and gasket.

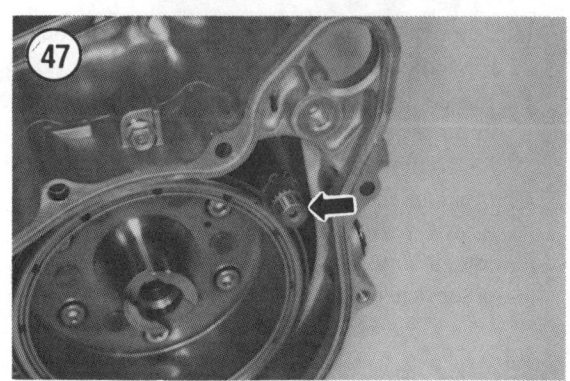

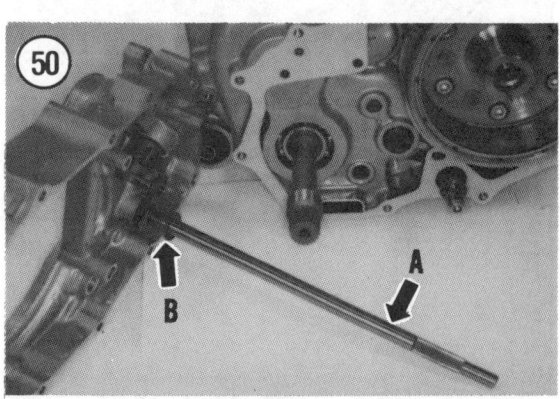

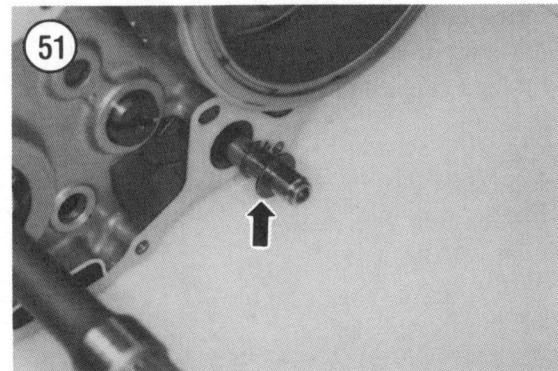

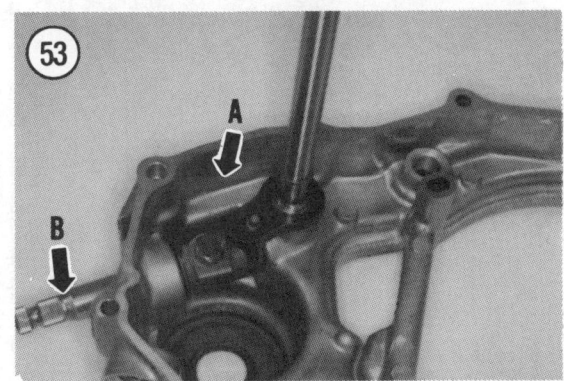

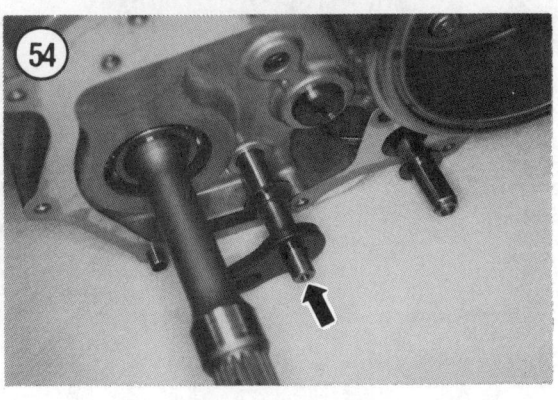

9. Remove all gasket material from the rear crankcase cover and engine mating surfaces.

10. Inspect the rear crankcase cover assembly as described in this section.

11. Install the reverse cover assembly by reversing these removal steps, plus the following:

    a. Pack all of the oil seal lips with grease.

*NOTE*
***Figure 53** shows the sub-gearshift spindle removed from the engine. If the sub-gearshift spindle is installed in the engine (**Figure 54**), align it with the gearshift A arm in the same manner.*

    b. Align the gearshift A arm notch with the sub-gearshift spindle pin (A, **Figure 53**). Install the washer (B, **Figure 50**) onto the sub-gearshift spindle.

    c. Install a new gasket.

    d. Tighten the rear crankcase cover mounting bolts in a crisscross pattern and in two or three steps. Tighten all of the bolts securely.

    e. Install the reverse control lever (A, **Figure 48**) with its OUT mark facing out. Then install and tighten its mounting bolt securely.

**Inspection**

1. Service the starter reduction assembly as described under *Flywheel and Starter Clutch* in this chapter.

2. To service the sub-gearshift spindle assembly (B, **Figure 53**), refer to *Gearshift Linkage* in this chapter.

3. Clean and dry the rear crankcase cover.

4. Inspect the final drive shaft (A, **Figure 55**) and reverse spindle (B) oil seals for leakage or damage. When replacing the oil seals, note the following:

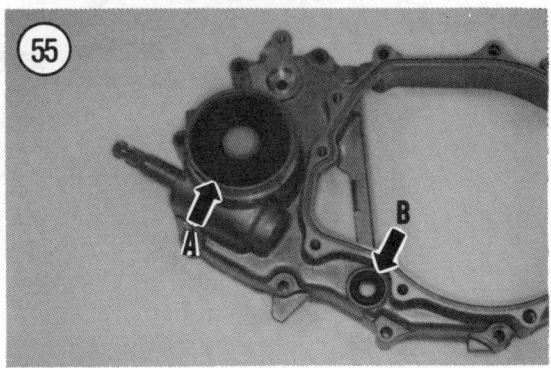

5

a. Remove the clip (**Figure 56**) before removing the final drive shaft oil seal.

b. Remove the oil seal by prying it out of the cover with a wide-blade screwdriver

c. Check the oil seal mounting bore for cracks or other damage.

d. Pack the lip of the new oil seal with grease.

e. Install both oil seals with their flat side facing out (A and B, **Figure 55**).

f. Install the clip (**Figure 56**), making sure it seats in its groove completely.

## FLYWHEEL AND STARTER CLUTCH

This section describes service to the starter reduction gears, flywheel and starter clutch assembly.

The flywheel can be removed with the rear crankcase cover installed on the engine.

Refer to **Figure 57** for this procedure.

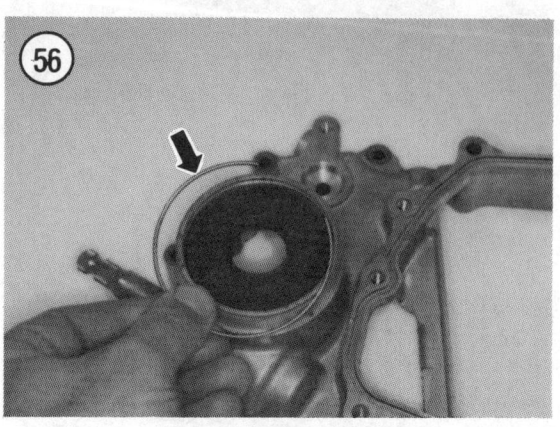

**STARTER CLUTCH ASSEMBLY**

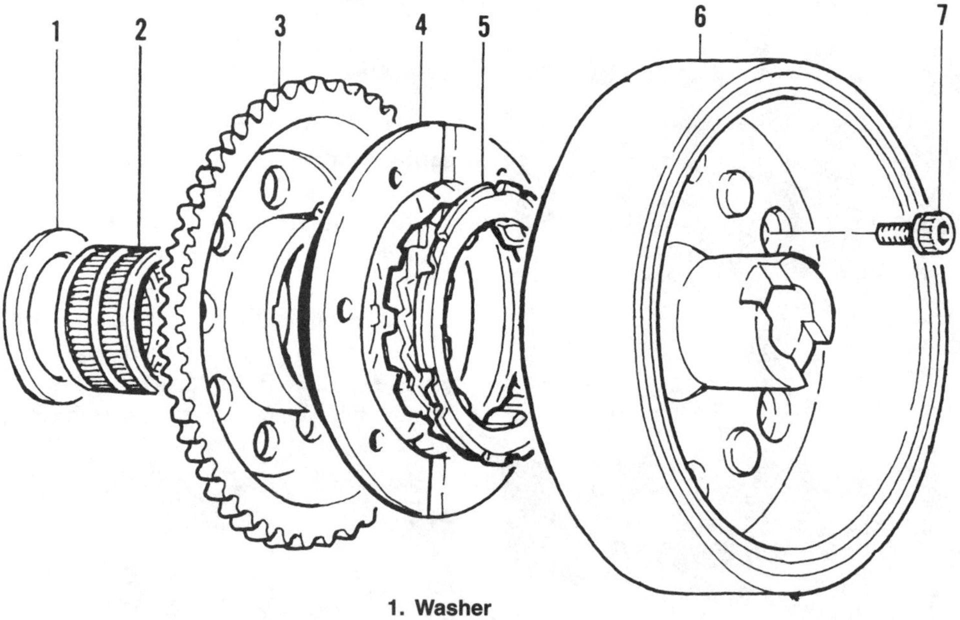

1. Washer
2. Needle bearing
3. Driven gear
4. Clutch outer
5. One-way clutch
6. Flywheel
7. One-way clutch mounting bolts

### Flywheel Puller

A flywheel puller is required to remove the flywheel from the crankshaft. Use one of the following pullers:

    a. Honda flywheel puller (part No. 07933-3950000).

    b. K&L universal rotor puller (part No. 35-9456 [**Figure 58**]).

### Removal

1. Remove the alternator cover as described in this chapter.

2. Remove the starter motor (Chapter Nine).

3. If the rear crankcase cover is installed on the engine, perform the following:

    a. Remove the reducton gear (A, **Figure 46**) and its shaft (B).

    b. Remove the washer (C, **Figure 46**) and reduction gear (D).

4. Screw the flywheel puller (**Figure 59**) into the flywheel.

> *CAUTION*
> *Do not try to remove the flywheel without a puller. Any attempt to do so will ultimately lead to some form of damage to the crankshaft and flywheel.*

> *CAUTION*
> *If normal flywheel removal attempts fail, do not force the puller. Excessive force will strip the flywheel threads, causing expensive damage. Take the engine to a dealership and have them remove the flywheel.*

5. Hold the flywheel and gradually tighten the flywheel puller until the flywheel pops off the crankshaft taper.

6. Remove the puller from the flywheel.

7. Remove the flywheel and the starter clutch assembly (**Figure 60**).

8. Remove the needle bearing (A, **Figure 61**) and washer (B).

9. Remove the reduction shaft (C, **Figure 61**).

10. If necessary, remove the Woodruff key (**Figure 62**) from the crankshaft keyway.

11. Inspect the flywheel, starter clutch and starter reduction gear assembly as described in this section.

## Starter Clutch
## Removal/Inspection/Installation

Refer to **Figure 57** when servicing the starter clutch assembly.

1. Check the one-way clutch operation as follows:
   a. Place the flywheel and starter clutch on the workbench so that the driven gear faces up as shown in **Figure 63**.
   b. Hold the flywheel and try to turn the driven gear clockwise and then counterclockwise. The driven gear should only turn clockwise as viewed in **Figure 63**.
   c. If the driven gear turns counterclockwise, the one-way clutch is damaged and must be replaced as described later in this procedure.
2. Remove the driven gear (**Figure 63**) from the one-way clutch assembly.
3. Inspect the driven gear (3, **Figure 57**) for the following conditions:
   a. Worn or damaged gear teeth.
   b. Worn or damaged bearing shoulder.
4. Inspect the one-way clutch (5, **Figure 57**) for the following conditions:
   a. Severely worn or damaged one-way clutch rollers.
   b. Loose one-way clutch Torx bolts.
5. To replace the one-way clutch (5, **Figure 57**), perform the following:
   a. Secure the flywheel with a strap or band wrench.
   b. Using an impact driver, remove the one-way clutch mounting bolts (7, **Figure 57**).
   c. Note the direction of the sprags in the one-way clutch. You must install the new one-way clutch in the same direction.
   d. Remove the clutch outer (4, **Figure 57**) and the one-way clutch.
   e. Install the one-way clutch and the clutch outer (4, **Figure 57**).
   f. Apply a medium strength threadlock to the threads of each mounting bolt.
   g. Install the one-way clutch mounting bolts finger-tight, then tighten as specified in **Table 4**.
6. Inspect the needle bearing (2, **Figure 57**). The needles should be smooth and polished with no flat spots, cracks or other damage. Inspect the bearing cage for cracks or other damage. Replace the bearing if necessary.
7. Inspect the washer (1, **Figure 57**) for cracks, scoring or other damage.

## Flywheel Inspection

1. Clean and dry the flywheel (**Figure 60**).
2. Check the flywheel for cracks or breaks.

> *WARNING*
> *Replace a cracked or chipped flywheel. A damaged flywheel can fly apart at high rpm, throwing metal fragments into the engine. Do not attempt to repair a damaged flywheel.*

3. Check the flywheel tapered bore and the crankshaft taper for damage.
4. Replace damaged parts as required.

## Starter Reduction Assembly
## Inspection

Replace parts that show damage as described in this section.

1. Clean and dry all parts (**Figure 64**).
2. Inspect the reduction gears for the following conditions:
   a. Excessively worn or damaged gear teeth.

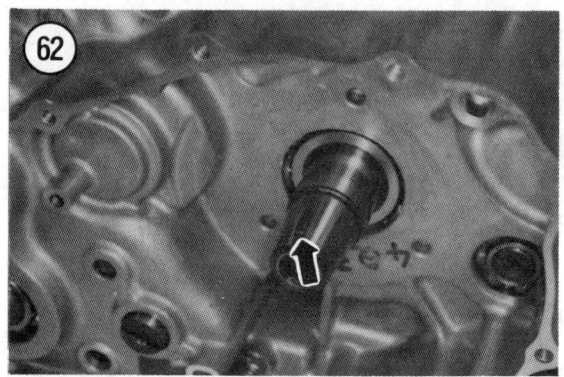

b. Excessively worn or damaged bearing surfaces.

3. Inspect the reduction shaft for the following conditions:

    a. Worn or damaged splines.

    b. Damaged circlip or circlip groove.

    c. Excessively worn pivot ends.

4. If you removed the circlip from the reduction shaft, install a new circlip during installation.

### Installation

1. Apply engine oil to the one-way clutch rollers and the driven gear shoulder.

2. To install the driven gear:

    a. Place the flywheel on the workbench so that the one-way clutch faces up.

    b. Rotate the driven gear *clockwise* and slide it into the one-way clutch (**Figure 63**).

3. Install the Woodruff key (**Figure 62**) into the crankshaft keyway.

4. Apply engine oil onto the washer and needle bearing before installing them onto the crankshaft.

5. Install the washer (B, **Figure 61**) and the needle bearing (A, **Figure 61**) onto the crankshaft.

6. Install the reduction shaft (C, **Figure 61**) into the crankcase.

*NOTE*
*The reduction shaft must be installed before the flywheel.*

7. Align the keyway in the flywheel with the Woodruff key in the crankshaft and install the flywheel (A, **Figure 65**).

8. Secure the flywheel to the crankshaft as follows:

    a. Temporarily install the recoil starter pulley (B, **Figure 65**) and its mounting bolt.

    b. Hold the flywheel and tighten the mounting bolt hand-tight.

*NOTE*
*This step seats the flywheel on its taper. If the flywheel is not secured in this manner, magnetic force will pull the flywheel off the crankshaft when the stator coil (alternator cover assembly) is installed.*

    c. Remove the mounting bolt and the recoil starter pulley (B, **Figure 65**).

9A. If the rear crankcase cover is installed on the engine, perform the following:

    a. Install the reduction gear (D, **Figure 46**) and washer (C).

    b. Install the shaft (B, **Figure 46**) and reduction gear (A).

9B. If removed, install the rear crankcase cover as described in this chapter.

10. Install the alternator cover as described in this chapter.

### GEARSHIFT LINKAGE

The gearshift linkage assembly is mounted on the front side of the engine, behind the clutch cover.

Refer to **Figure 66** when servicing the gearshift linkage assembly in the following sections.

### Removal

1. If the engine is installed in the frame, remove the gearshift pedal.

2. Remove the clutch cover (Chapter Six).

**5**

3. Remove the centrifugal clutch and change clutch assemblies (Chapter Six).

4. Remove the rear crankcase cover as described in this chapter.

5. Remove the sub-gearshift arm (**Figure 67**).

6. Unhook the spring (A, **Figure 68**) from the gearshift plate. Then remove the master arm and return spring (B, **Figure 68**).

7. Remove the guide plate bolt (A, **Figure 69**) and guide plate (B).

8. Remove the gearshift plate (**Figure 70**).

9. Pry the stopper arm away from the drum shifter with a screwdriver, then remove the drum shifter (A, **Figure 71**) and its dowel pin (B).

10. Remove the bolt (A, **Figure 72**), stopper arm (B), washer and return spring (C).

11. Remove the washer (D, **Figure 72**) from the sub-gearshift spindle.

12. Remove the sub-gearshift spindle (A, **Figure 73**) and washer (B) from the rear crankcase.

*NOTE*
*The gearshift spindle (20, **Figure 66**) and gearshift arm (19) are mounted in the rear crankcase cover. To remove these parts, perform Step 13.*

13. Bend the lockwasher tab away from the gearshift arm bolt (A, **Figure 74**). Then remove the bolt, lockwasher, gearshift spindle (B) and gearshift arm (C).

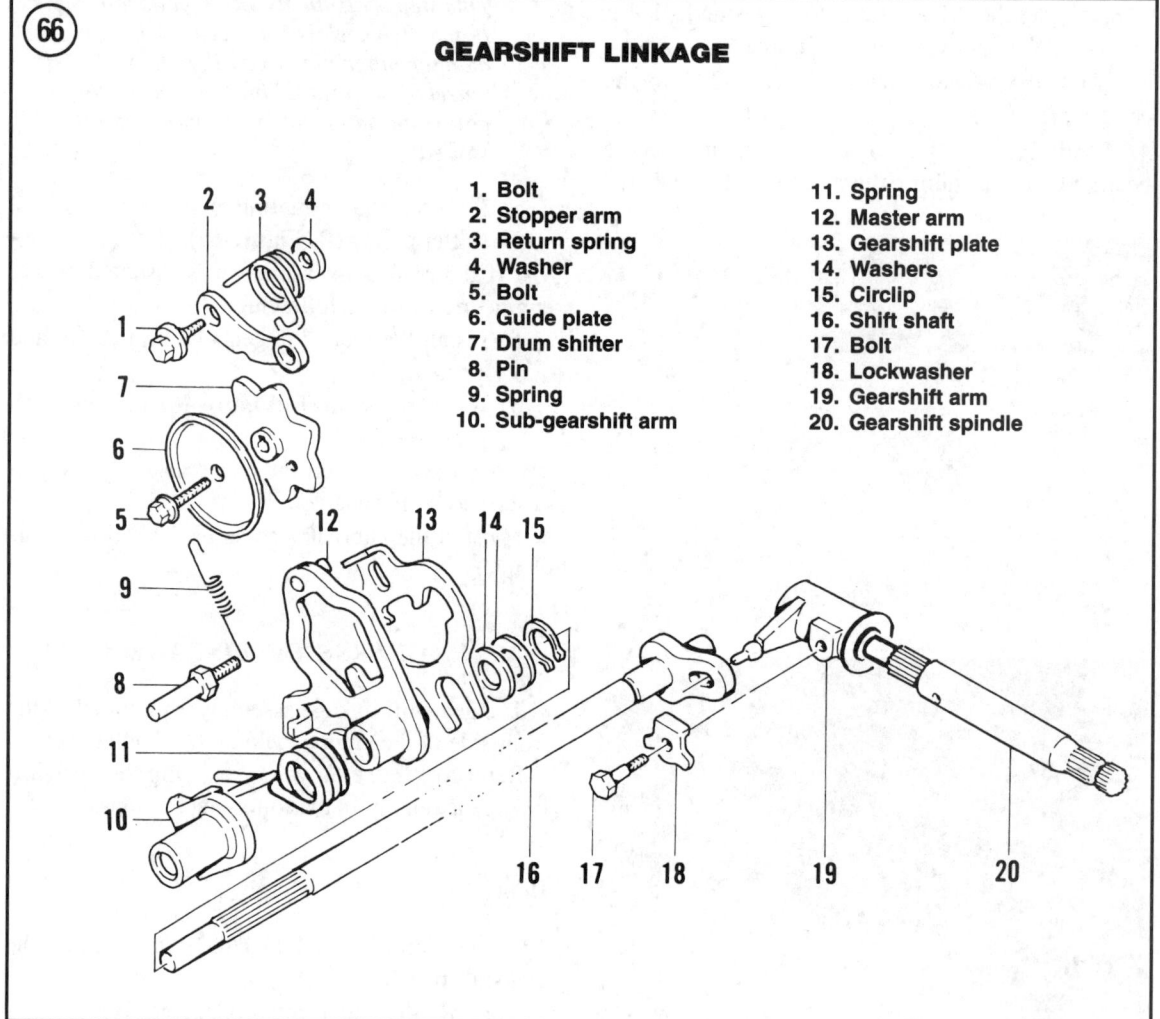

**GEARSHIFT LINKAGE**

66

1. Bolt
2. Stopper arm
3. Return spring
4. Washer
5. Bolt
6. Guide plate
7. Drum shifter
8. Pin
9. Spring
10. Sub-gearshift arm
11. Spring
12. Master arm
13. Gearshift plate
14. Washers
15. Circlip
16. Shift shaft
17. Bolt
18. Lockwasher
19. Gearshift arm
20. Gearshift spindle

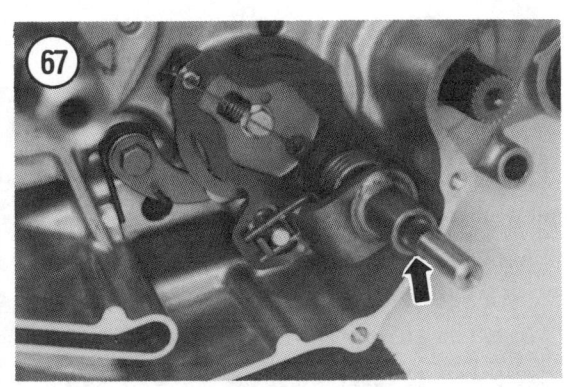

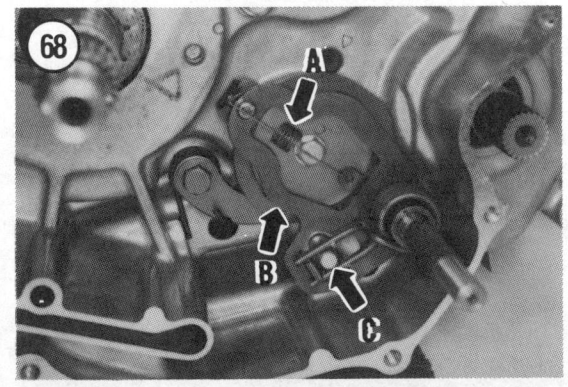

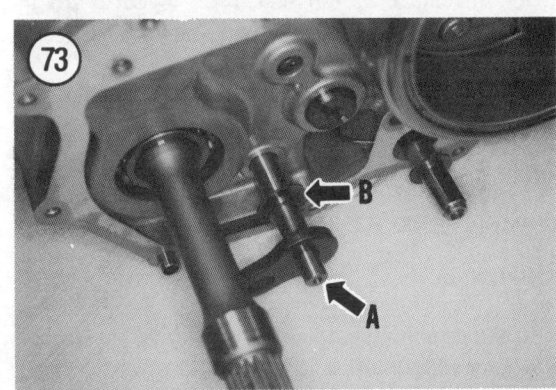

5

## Inspection

Refer to **Figure 66** when inspecting the gearshift linkage assembly. Replace parts that show excessive wear or damage as described in this section.

1. Clean and dry all parts.

2. Check the master arm, sub-gearshift splindle and gear shift spindle for damaged splines.

3. Check the sub-gearshift spindle (A, **Figure 75**) for bending or other damage. Check the circlip groove for cracks or damage. If you removed the circlip (B), install a new one during reassembly.

4. Check the drum shifter for wear, cracks or other damage.

5. Check the stopper arm assembly for:
   a. Damaged stopper arm.
   b. Worn or damaged roller.
   c. Weak or damaged sreturn spring.

6. Check the master arm assembly for:
   a. Damaged master arm.
   b. Weak or damaged return spring.

7. Check the gearshift spindle dust seal and needle bearings (installed in the rear crankcase cover) for damage. Note the following:
   a. To replace the oil seal, refer to *Oil Seals* in Chapter One. Install the oil seal with its closed side facing out.
   b. To replace the needle bearings, first remove the bearing with a blind bearing remover. Then inspect the bearing mounting bores for cracks or other damage. Press in the new bearings.

## Installation

1. If the gearshift spindle (20, **Figure 66**) assembly was removed, install it as follows:
   a. Lubricate the two needle bearings with engine oil.
   b. Pack the dust seal lip with a waterproof grease.
   c. Install the gearshift arm (C, **Figure 74**) and the gearshift spindle (B, **Figure 74**). Align the master splines on both parts to assemble them.
   d. Install a new lockwasher and the gearshift arm bolt (A, **Figure 74**) and tighten as specified in **Table 4**. Bend the lockwasher tab over the bolt to lock it in place.
   e. Pivot the gearshift spindle to make sure it moves smoothly with no binding or roughness.

*NOTE*
*The two washers (14, **Figure 66**) installed on the sub-gearshift spindle are identical.*

2. Install the sub-gearshift spindle (A, **Figure 73**) and washer (B) through the rear crankcase.

3. Install the second washer (D, **Figure 72**) onto the sub-gearshift spindle.

4. Install the stopper arm assembly as follows:
   a. Install the bolt through the stopper arm (roller side), then install the washer onto the bolt (**Figure 76**).
   b. Hook the return spring onto the stopper arm.
   c. Install the stopper arm assembly as shown in **Figure 72**. Make sure that the return spring is hooked onto the stopper arm as shown in **Figure 72**. Tighten the stopper arm bolt (A, **Figure 72**) as specified in **Table 4**.

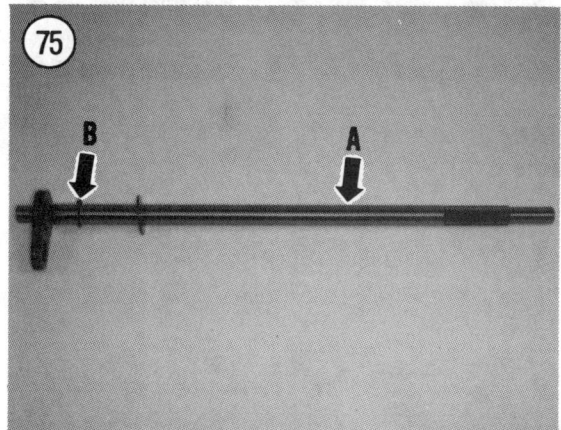

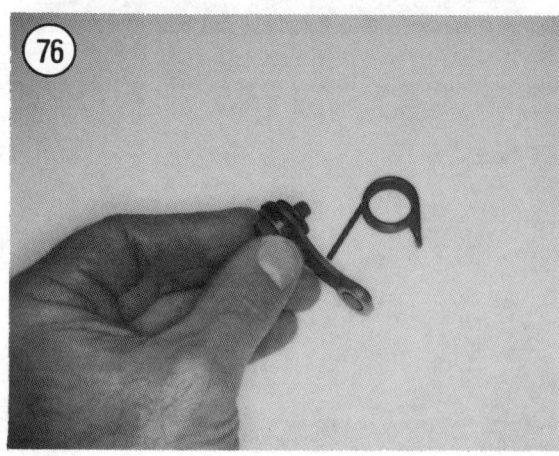

d. Push the stopper arm down and release it. It must move under spring pressure with no binding.

*NOTE*
*If the stopper arm does not move, the bolt is not centered through the stopper arm, washer or spring. Loosen the bolt and reinstall.*

5. Install the dowel pin (B, **Figure 71**) into the shift drum hole.

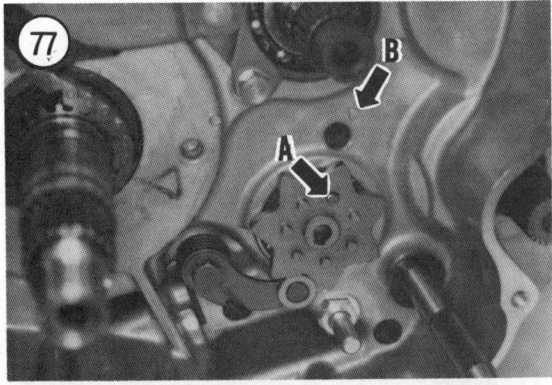

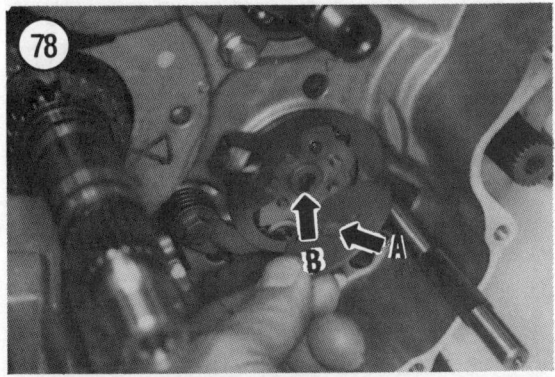

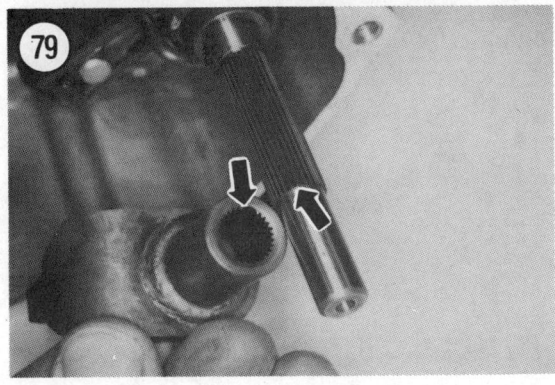

6. Pry the stopper arm away from the shift drum, then install the drum shifter (A, **Figure 71**) over the dowel pin and shift drum. Release the stopper arm.

*NOTE*
*The transmission is in neutral when the dowel pin (A, **Figure 77**) aligns with the crankcase index mark (B).*

7. Install the gearshift plate over the drum shifter and sub-gearshift spindle as shown in **Figure 70**.

8. Install the guide plate by aligning its bent tab (A, **Figure 78**) with the square groove (B) in the drum shifter. See B, **Figure 69**. Then install the guide plate bolt (A, **Figure 69**) and tighten as specified in **Table 4**.

9. Shift the transmission into neutral by aligning the hole in the guide plate (C, **Figure 69**) with the crankcase index mark (D).

10. Install the master arm (B, **Figure 68**) and return spring over the sub-gearshift spindle. Center the return spring over the gearshift stopper pin as shown in C, **Figure 68**.

11. Hook the spring (A, **Figure 68**) between the master arm and gearshift plate.

*NOTE*
*The sub-gearshift arm and sub-gearshift spindle are machined with a master spline (**Figure 79**). Align these splines when installing the sub-gearshift arm in Step 12.*

12. Install the sub-gearshift spindle arm over the sub-gearshift spindle by aligning the master splines (**Figure 79**), then insert the boss on the spindle arm between the return spring (**Figure 67**).

13. Install the rear crankcase as described in this chapter.

14. Install the change clutch and centrifugal clutch assemblies (Chapter Six).

15. Install the clutch cover (Chapter Six).

16. If the engine is installed in the frame, install the gearshift pedal.

## REVERSE SHAFT ASSEMBLY

The reverse shaft assembly consists of the reverse control lever and shaft assembly mounted on the back side of the engine.

**5**

### Removal/Inspection/Installation

1. Remove the engine from the frame as described in this chapter.

2. Remove the reverse control lever (**Figure 80**) and rear crankcase cover as described in this chapter.

3. Remove the washer (**Figure 81**) from the reverse shaft.

4. Hold the reverse arm (A, **Figure 82**) with a screwdriver, then remove the reverse shaft (B) assembly.

5. Inspect the reverse shaft assembly (**Figure 83**) for:

   a. Weak or damaged spring.

   b. Damaged reverse shaft.

   c. Damaged circlip groove.

6. To replace the spring, remove the circlip and spring (**Figure 83**). Install the spring over the reverse shaft as shown in **Figure 83**. Install a new circlip.

7. Install the reverse shaft assembly by reversing these removal steps, plus the following:

   a. When installing the reverse shaft (B, **Figure 82**), insert the end of the reverse arm (A) into the shift drum groove.

   b. Install the reverse control lever (**Figure 80**) with its OUT mark facing out.

## LUBRICATION SYSTEM

The lubrication system consists of the oil pump, relief valve, oil strainer screen, oil filter, oil cooler and engine oil passages. Servicing these items (except the oil filter and oil cooler) is described in this chapter. Service the engine oil and oil filter as described in Chapter Three. Service the oil cooler and cooling fan as described in Chapter Fourteen.

## OIL PUMP

The oil pipe and oil pump assemblies are mounted on the front side of the engine. The oil pump can be removed with the engine mounted in the frame. The following steps are shown with the engine removed for clarity.

Refer to **Figure 84** when servicing the oil pump in this section.

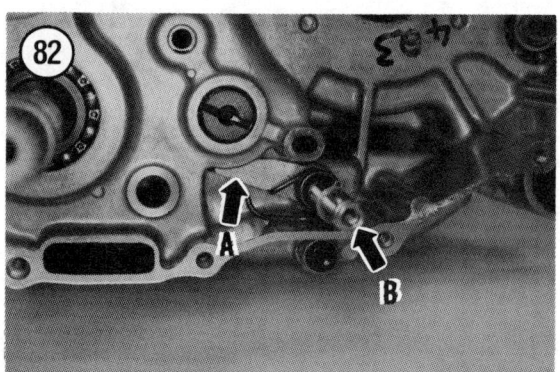

### Removal/Installation

1. Remove the front crankcase cover as described in this chapter.

2. Remove the centrifugal clutch (Chapter Six).

*NOTE*
*The oil pump can be removed and installed with the cam chain mounted on the engine.*

3. Remove the bolts and the oil pump assembly (A, **Figure 85**).

4. If necessary, remove the chain slipper (B, **Figure 85**).

*NOTE*
*If the oil pump is not going to be serviced, store it in a plastic bag.*

5. Service the oil pump as described in this section.

6. Install the oil pump by reversing these removal steps, plus the following:

   a. If removed, install the cam chain slipper onto the crankcase boss as shown in B, **Figure 85**.

   b. Align the shoulder on the end of the pump shaft (A, **Figure 86**) with the groove in the end

**5**

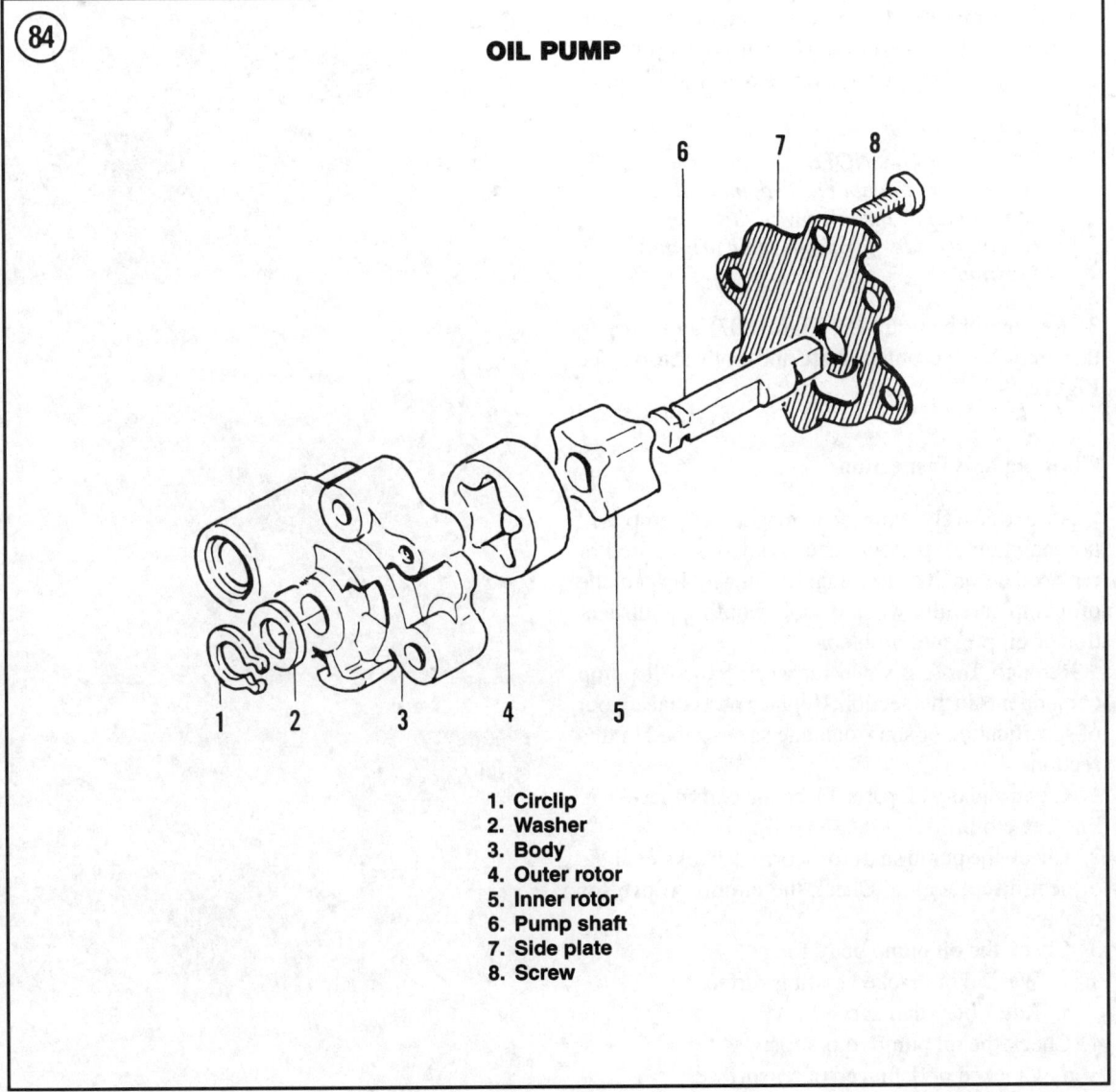

(84) **OIL PUMP**

1. Circlip
2. Washer
3. Body
4. Outer rotor
5. Inner rotor
6. Pump shaft
7. Side plate
8. Screw

of the balancer shaft (B, **Figure 86**) and install the oil pump. At the same, align the side plate tab on the oil pump with the cam chain slipper groove.

   c. Install and tighten the oil pump mounting bolts (**Figure 85**).

   d. Check pump engagement by turning the crankshaft back and forth. When doing so, the pump shaft (visible on the outside of the pump) should turn.

   e. Replace the O-ring (A, **Figure 87**) if damaged.

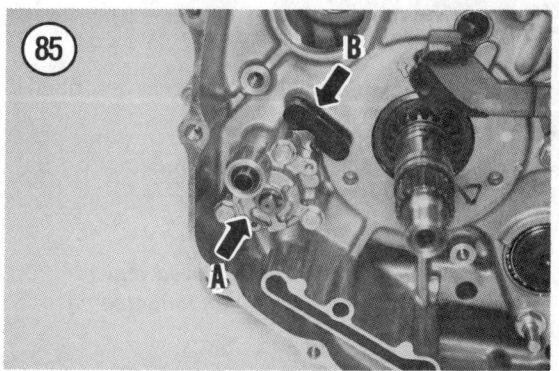

### Oil pump
### Disassembly

Refer to **Figure 84** when servicing the oil pump.

1. Remove the dowel pin and O-ring (A, **Figure 87**).
2. Remove the screw (A, **Figure 88**) and side plate (B).

> *NOTE*
> *If the rotors are not marked, mark them so they can be installed with their upper (exposed) sides facing in their original position.*

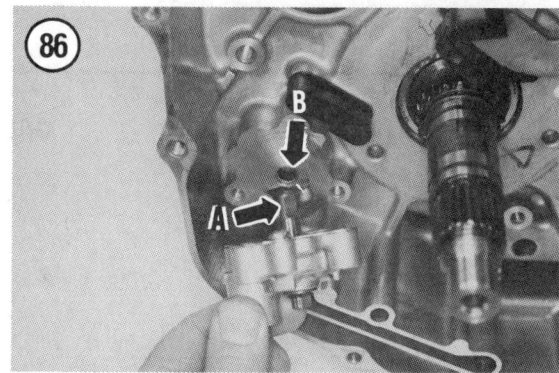

3. Remove the circlip (B, **Figure 87**) and washer, then remove the pump shaft and both rotors. See **Figure 89**.

### Cleaning and Inspection

An excessively worn or damaged oil pump will not maintain oil pressure and should be repaired or replaced before it causes engine damage. Inspect the oil pump carefully when troubleshooting a lubrication or oil pressure problem.

Refer to **Table 2** when measuring the oil pump components in this section. Replace parts that are out of specification or show damage as described in this section.

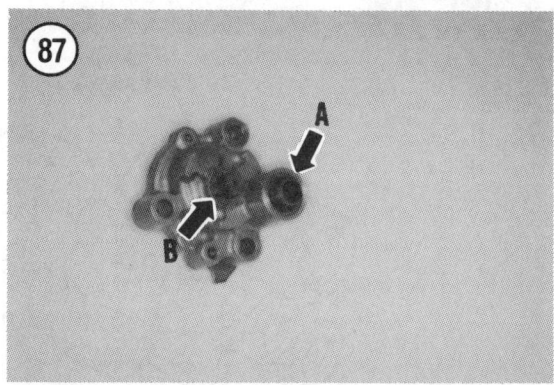

1. Clean and dry all parts. Place the parts on a clean, lint-free cloth.
2. Check the pump shaft for scoring, cracks or signs of heat discoloration. Check the circlip groove for damage.
3. Check the oil pump body for:

   a. Warped or cracked mating surfaces.

   b. Rotor bore damage.

4. Check the oil pump rotors for:

   a. Cracked or damaged outer surface.

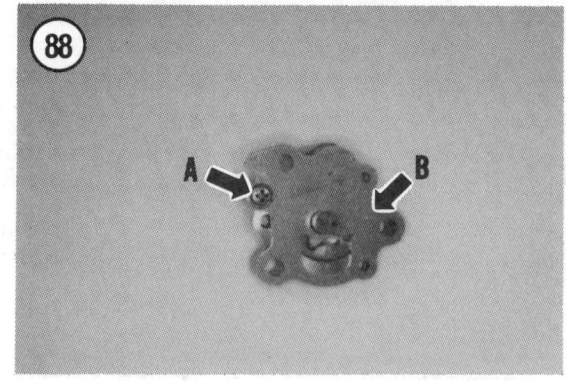

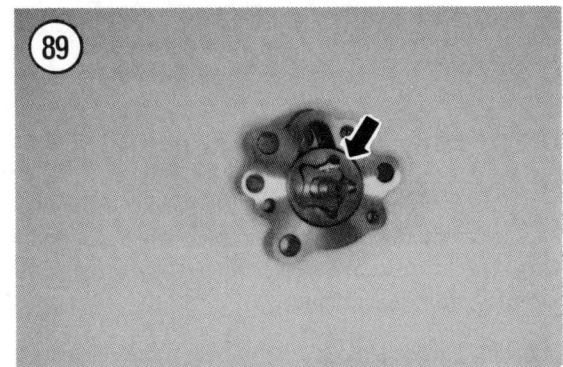

b. Worn or scored inner mating surfaces.

5. If the oil pump side plate, body and both rotors are in good condition, check their operating clearances as described in Steps 6-7.

*NOTE*
*The pump rotors are sold separately. The pump body, pump shaft and side plate are not.*

6. Install the inner and outer rotors and pump shaft into the pump body (**Figure 89**).

7. Using a flat feeler gauge, measure the clearance between the outer rotor and the oil pump body (**Figure 90**) and check against the body clearance in **Table 2**. If out of specification, replace the outer rotor and remeasure. If still out of specification, replace the oil pump assembly.

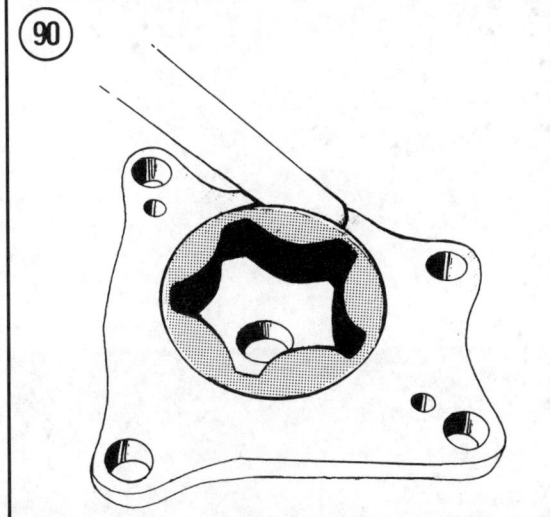

8. Using a flat feeler gauge, measure the clearance between the inner rotor tip and the outer rotor (**Figure 91**) and check against the tip clearance in **Table 2**. If out of specification, replace the inner and outer rotors.

9. Using a flat feeler gauge and straightedge, measure the clearance between the body surface and rotors (**Figure 92**) and check against the end clearance in **Table 2**. If out of specification, replace the oil pump assembly.

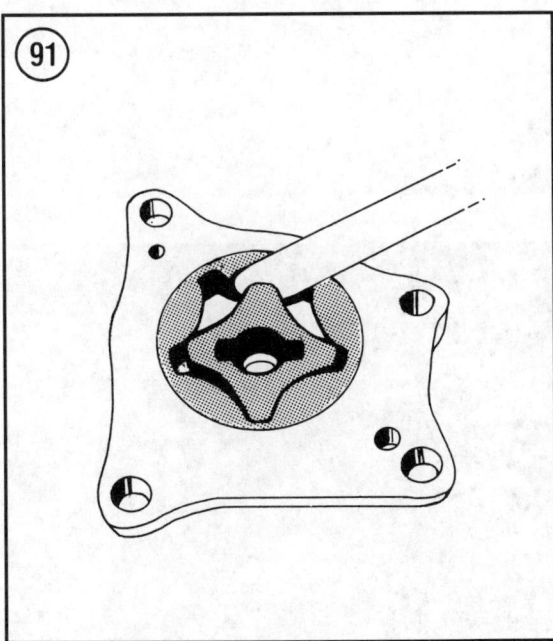

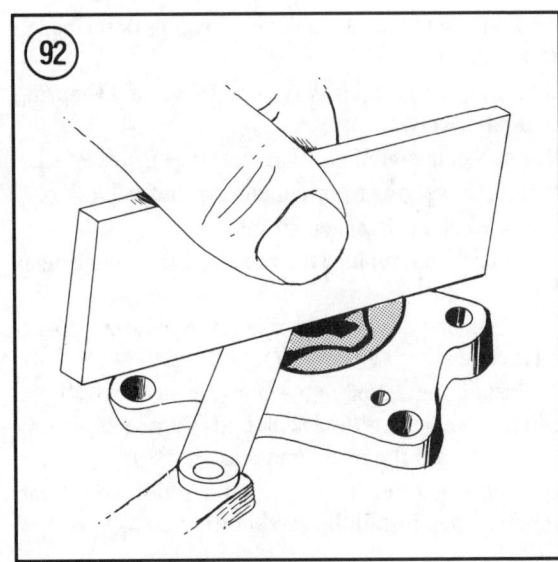

5

## Reassembly

1. If necessary, reclean the parts as described in the previous section. Lubricate the rotors and body rotor bore with engine oil when installing them in the following steps.

2. Install the outer and inner rotors (**Figure 89**). If installing the original rotors, install them with their original side facing up as identified during disassembly.

3. Install the pump shaft (**Figure 89**)

4. Install the washer and a new circlip (Figure B, **Figure 87**). Align the cut-out between the pump shaft and washer. Install the circlip with its chamfered side facing toward the washer.

5. Install the side plate (B, **Figure 88**) and tighten the screw (A, **Figure 88**)) as specified in **Table 4**.

6. Install the dowel pin and a new O-ring (A, **Figure 87**).

7. Turn the pump shaft. If there is any roughness or binding, disassemble the oil pump and check it for damage.

8. Store the oil pump in a plastic bag until installation.

## RELIEF VALVE

The oil relief valve is installed in the front crankcase cover.

### Removal/Inspection/Installation

1. Remove the front crankcase cover as described in this chapter.

2. Remove the relief valve cap (**Figure 93**) spring and relief valve.

3. Inspect the relief valve assembly (**Figure 94**) for:
   a. Severely worn or damaged relief valve.
   b. Weak or damaged spring.

   If necessary, replace the relief valve and spring as a set.

4. Clean and dry the oil passages in the front crankcase cover.

5. Install the relief valve and spring—install the relief valve with its long shaft end (**Figure 95**) facing down (toward the front crankcase cover).

6. Apply a threadlock onto the relief valve cap threads, then install the cap and tighten as specified in **Table 4**.

7. Install the front crankcase cover as described in this chapter.

## OIL STRAINER SCREEN

An oil strainer screen is installed inside the crankcase. Service the oil strainer screen whenever splitting the crankcase. Refer to *Crankcase and Crankshaft* in this chapter.

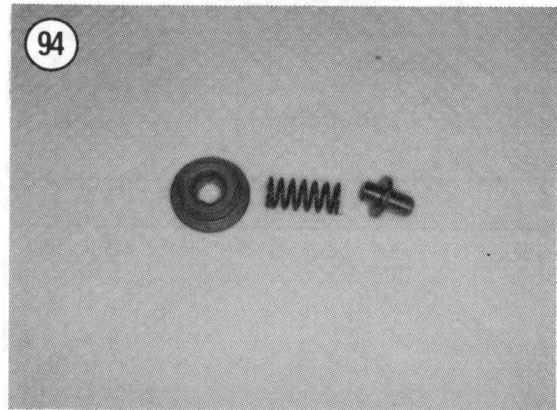

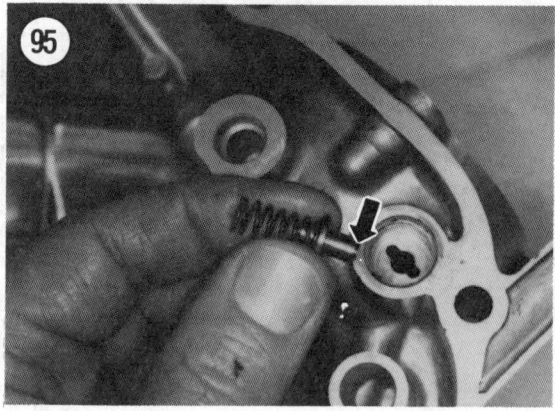

## CRANKCASE AND CRANKSHAFT

The crankcase is made in two halves of thin-wall, precision diecast aluminum alloy. To avoid damage, do not hammer or pry on any of the interior or exterior projected walls. A gasket seals the crankcase halves while dowel pins align the crankcase halves when they are bolted together. The crankcase halves can be replaced separately.

The crankshaft assembly consists of two full-circle flywheels pressed together on a crankpin. Two ball bearings in the crankcase support the crankshaft assembly.

The procedure which follows is presented as a complete, step-by-step major lower end overhaul. If you are only going to service the transmission, you can disassemble and reassemble the crankcase without removing the crankshaft.

References to the front and rear side of the engine, as used in the text, refers to the engine as it sits in the frame, not as it sits on your workbench.

### Special Tools

A press is required to remove the crankshaft from the crankcase.

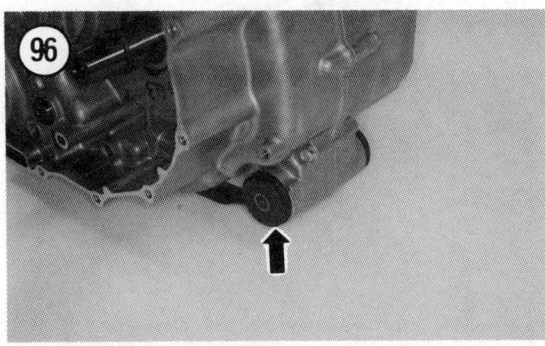

To install the crankshaft into the crankcase, a number of Honda crankshaft installation tools or their equivalents will be required. These tools and part numbers are called out during the crankshaft installation procedure in this chapter.

### Crankcase Disassembly

This procedure describes disassembly of the crankcase halves and removal of the transmission and internal shift mechanism. Crankshaft removal is covered in a separate procedure.

Chapter Seven describes transmission and internal shift mechanism service procedures.

1. Remove all exterior engine assemblies as described in this chapter and other related chapters:
   a. Cylinder head (Chapter Four).
   b. Cylinder and piston (Chapter Four).
   c. Recoil starter (this chapter).
   d. Flywheel and starter clutch (this chapter).
   e. Starter motor (Chapter Nine).
   f. Clutch and primary drive gears (Chapter Six).
   g. Gearshift linkage (this chapter).
   h. Oil pump (this chapter).
2. Remove the engine dampers and bushings (**Figure 96**).
3. Place the engine assembly on a couple of wooden blocks with the front side facing up (**Figure 97**).

> *NOTE*
> *To prevent loss and to ensure proper bolt location during assembly, draw the crankcase outline on cardboard, then punch holes to correspond with bolt locations. Insert the bolts in their appropriate locations after removing them.*

4. Loosen and remove the front crankcase bolts (**Figure 98**) and install them in the cardboard.
5. Turn the engine over so that the rear side faces up.
6. Loosen each rear crankcase mounting bolt (**Figure 98**) one-quarter turn and in a crisscross pattern. Repeat until all of the mounting bolts are loose.
7. Remove all bolts loosened in Step 6 and install them in the cardboard. Be sure to remove all of them.
8. Turn the engine over so that the front side (**Figure 97**) faces up.

> *CAUTION*
> *Perform this operation over and close to the work bench as the crankcase*

5

*halves may easily separate. Do **not** hammer on the crankcase halves as you will damage them.*

*CAUTION*
*Do not pry between the crankcase mating surfaces when separating the crankcase halves. Doing so may cause an oil leak.*

9. Tap on the front crankcase while lifting it off the engine. Tap the transmission shafts if they bind with the crankcase and prevent disassembly.

10. Remove the gasket and dowel pins (**Figure 99**).

11. Remove the oil screen (**Figure 100**).

*NOTE*
*Steps 12-16 describe removal of the transmission assembly.*

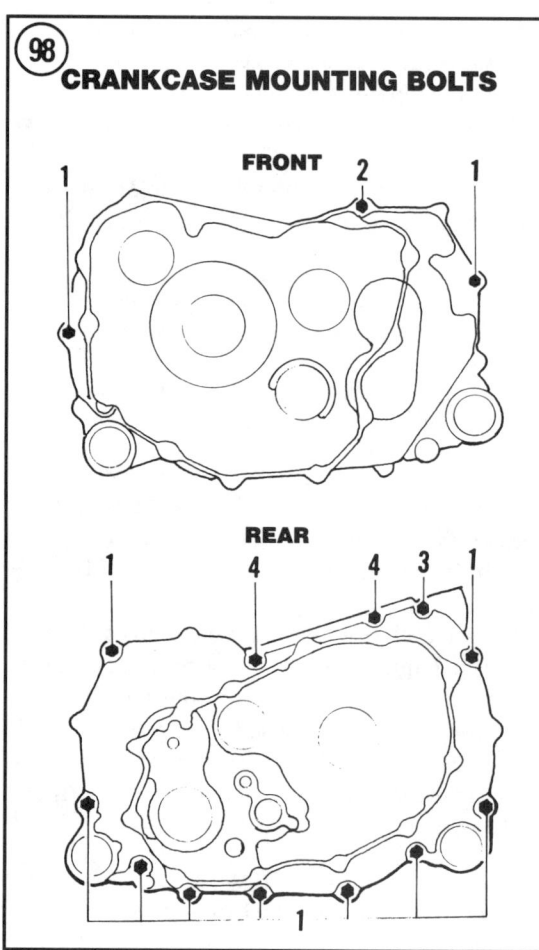

12. Remove the copper washer (A, **Figure 101**) and the countershaft first gear (B) and bushing (**Figure 102**).

13. Remove the thrust washer (A, **Figure 103**) and the reverse idler gear assembly (B).

14. Remove the shift fork assembly as follows:

    a. Remove the shift fork shaft (A, **Figure 104**) and shift drum (B).

    b. Remove the three shift forks (C, **Figure 104**).

15. Remove the mainshaft and countershaft (**Figure 105**) at the same time. See **Figure 106**.

16. Remove the final drive shaft and final drive gear (**Figure 107**).

17. If necessary, remove the crankshaft and balancer shaft as described in the following section.

### Crankshaft/Balancer Shaft Removal

Remove the crankshaft (A, **Figure 108**) and balancer shaft (B, **Figure 108**) as follows.

1. Support the rear crankcase in a press as shown in **Figure 109**.

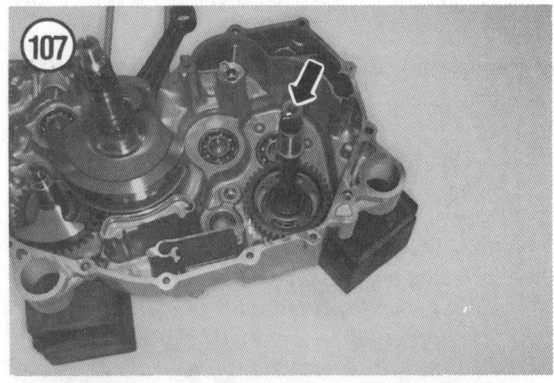

*CAUTION*
*When supporting the rear crankcase in the press, confirm that there is adequate room to press the crankshaft out without the connecting rod hitting against the press bed. If this happens, you may bend the connecting rod. Check your setup carefully before applying pressure to the crankshaft.*

*CAUTION*
*You must catch the crankshaft and balancer shaft once the crankshaft is free of the rear crankcase half. Otherwise, these parts can fall to the floor, causing severe damage to them.*

2. Center the crankshaft under the press ram and press the crankshaft out of the crankcase.

3. Remove the crankshaft and balancer shaft (A and B, **Figure 108**) from the crankcase half.

4. Remove the rear crankcase from the press.

**Crankcase Inspection**

1. Remove the final drive shaft oil seal as described under *Final Drive Shaft Seal Replacement* in this chapter.

2. Remove all sealer and gasket residue from the gasket surfaces.

*CAUTION*
*When drying the crankcase bearings in Step 3, do not allow the inner bearing races to spin. The bearings are not lubricated and damage may result. When drying the bearings with compressed air, do not allow the air jet to spin the bearing. The air jet can rotate the bearings at excessive speeds. This could cause a bearing to fly apart, causing personal injury.*

3. Clean both crankcase halves and all crankcase bearings with solvent. Thoroughly dry with compressed air.

4. Flush all crankcase oil passages with compressed air.

5. Lightly oil all of the crankcase bearings with engine oil before checking the bearings in Step 6.

6. Check the bearings for roughness, pitting, galling and play by rotating them slowly by hand. Replace

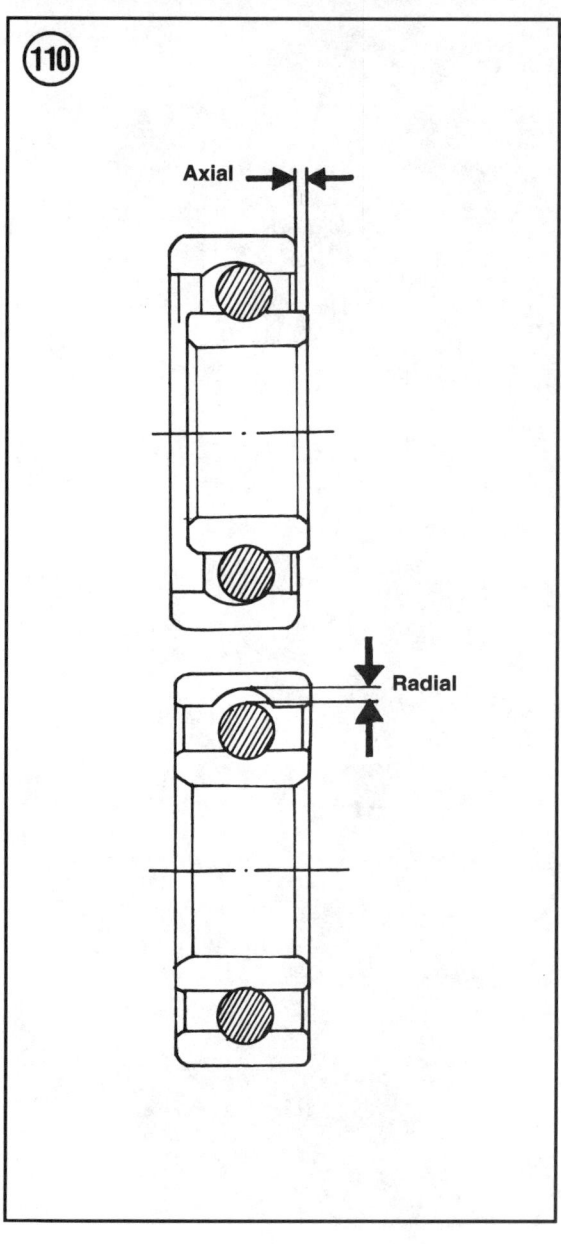

any bearing that turns roughly or has excessive play (**Figure 110**).

7. Replace any worn or damaged bearings as described under *Crankcase Bearing Replacement* in this chapter.

*NOTE*
*Always replace the opposing bearing at the same time.*

8. Carefully inspect the cases for cracks and fractures, especially in the lower areas where they are vulnerable to rock damage.

9. Check the areas around the stiffening ribs, around bearing bosses and threaded holes for damage. Refer crankcase repair to a shop specializing in the repair of precision aluminum castings.

10. Check the threaded holes in both crankcase halves for thread damage, dirt or oil buildup. If necessary, clean or repair the threads with the correct size metric tap. Coat the tap threads with kerosene or an aluminum tap fluid before use.

11. Check the gearshift stopper pin (**Figure 111**) for looseness or damage. During installation, apply a threadlock to the bolt threads and tighten to the torque specification in **Table 4**.

### Crankcase Stud Replacement

The crankcase studs are different lengths. When replacing the studs, measure their length prior to removal.

### Final Drive Shaft Seal Replacement

Replace the final drive shaft seal (**Figure 112**) whenever disassembling the engine or when the oil seal is leaking.

1. Pry the countershaft seal out of the crankcase with a wide-blade screwdriver (**Figure 113**) or a seal removal tool. Place a rag underneath the screwdriver to prevent it from damaging the crankcase.

2. If necessary, replace the final drive shaft bearing before installing the new seal. Refer to *Crankcase Bearing Replacement* in this chapter.

3. Clean the seal bore in the crankcase.

4. Pack the lip of the new seal with a waterproof bearing grease.

5. Position the new seal in the crankcase with its closed side facing out.

6. Press or drive in the new seal until its outer surface is flush with or slightly below the crankcase bore inside surface (**Figure 112**).

### Crankcase Bearing Replacement

When replacing bearings in the following steps, note the following:

1. Because of the number of bearings used in the front and rear crankcase halves, identify the bearings

before removing them. Identify each bearing by referring to its size code marks.

2. Before removing the bearings, note and record the direction in which the bearings size codes face for proper reinstallation.

3. Replace the bearings as described under *Ball Bearing Replacement* in Chapter One. Use a blind bearing remover to remove bearings installed in blind holes (**Figure 114**).

4. Refer to **Figure 115** to identify the bearings installed in the front crankcase half:

   a. Crankshaft (A, **Figure 115**).
   b. Balancer shaft (B, **Figure 115**).
   c. Countershaft (C, **Figure 115**).
   d. Mainshaft (D, **Figure 115**).
   e. Shift drum (E, **Figure 115**).
   f. Final drive shaft (F, **Figure 115**).

5. Refer to **Figure 116** to identify the bearings installed in the rear crankcase half:

   a. Crankshaft (A, **Figure 116**).

   b. Balancer shaft (B, **Figure 116**).
   c. Countershaft (C, **Figure 116**).
   d. Mainshaft (D, **Figure 116**).
   e. Shift drum (E, **Figure 116**).
   f. Final drive shaft (F, **Figure 116**).
   g. Camshaft (G, **Figure 116**).

6. If the rear crankshaft bearing remained on the crankshaft, remove the bearing with a bearing splitter and bearing puller as shown in **Figure 117**. Press a new bearing into the rear crankcase half. Do not install the bearing onto the crankshaft.

### Crankshaft Inspection

Handle the crankshaft carefully when performing the following cleaning and inspection procedures. Individual crankshaft components are not available separately. If the crankshaft is excessively worn or damaged, or if any measurement is out of specification, replace the crankshaft as an assembly.

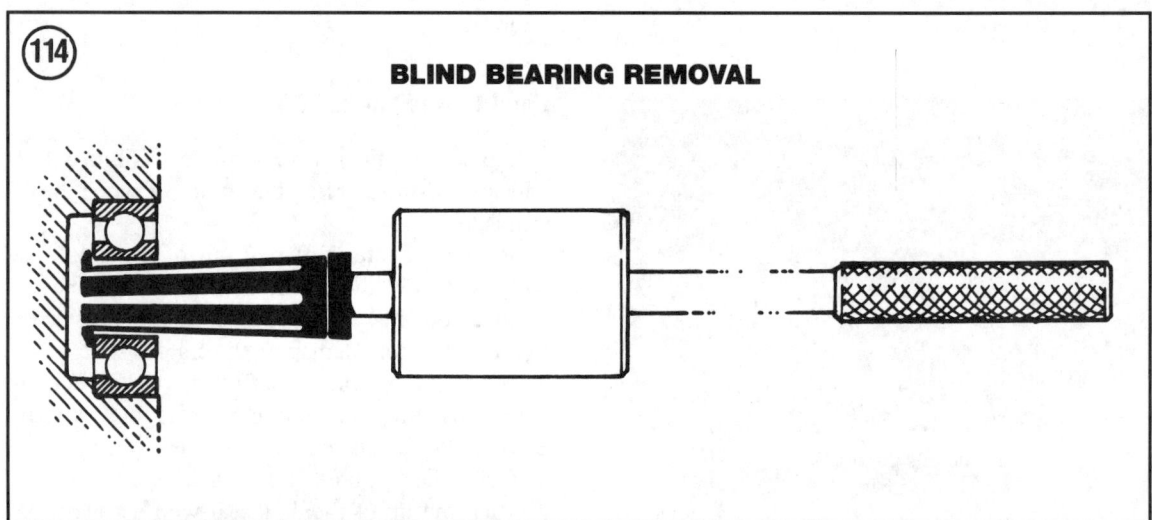

**BLIND BEARING REMOVAL**

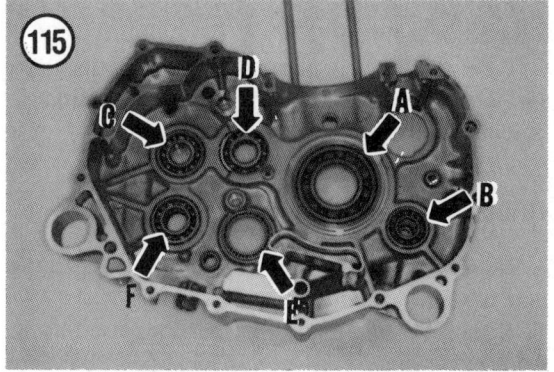

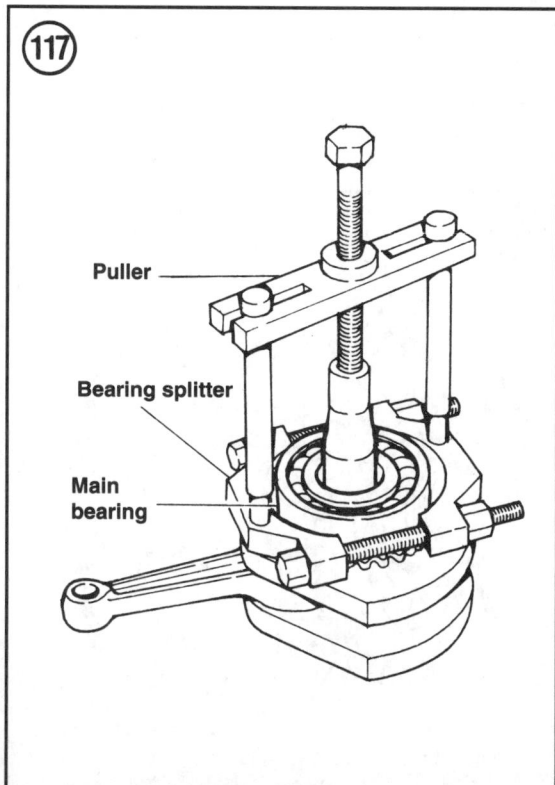

Puller

Bearing splitter

Main
bearing

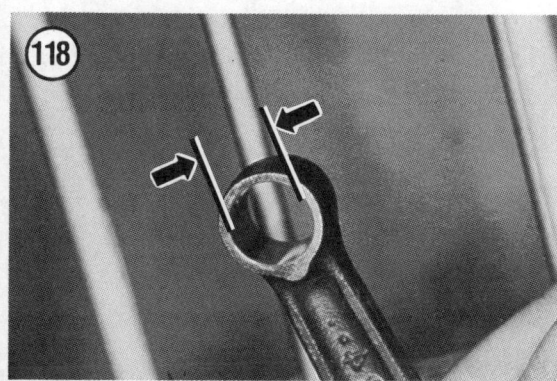

1. Clean the crankshaft thoroughly with solvent. Clean the crankshaft oil passageway with compressed air. Dry the crankshaft with compressed air, then lubricate all bearing surfaces with a light coat of engine oil.

2. Check the crankshaft journals for scratches, heat discoloration or other defects.

3. Check the flywheel taper, threads and keyway for damage.

4. Check the connecting rod big end for signs of damage, as well as bearing or thrust washer damage.

5. Check the connecting rod small end for signs of excessive heat (blue coloration) or other damage.

6. Measure the connecting rod small end inside diameter (**Figure 118**) with a snap gauge or an inside micrometer and check against the dimension in **Table 3**.

7. Slide the connecting rod to one side and check the connecting rod side clearance with a flat feeler gauge (**Figure 119**) and check against the dimension in **Table 3**.

8. Place the crankshaft on a set of V-blocks or between lathe centers and measure runout with a dial indicator at the points listed in **Table 3**. If the runout exceeds the service limit in **Table 3**, take the crankshaft to a Honda dealer for service or replace it.

9. Place the crankshaft on a set of V-blocks and measure the connecting rod big end radial clearance with a dial indicator. Measure in the two directions shown in **Figure 120** and compare to the dimension in **Table 3**.

**Balancer Shaft**
**Inspection**

1. Check the balancer shaft bearing journals (**Figure 121**) for deep scoring, excessive wear, heat discoloration or cracks.

2. Check the keyway in the end of the balancer shaft for cracks or excessive wear.

3. Replace the balancer shaft if necessary.

**Final Drive Shaft and Gear**
**Inspection**

1. Inspect the final drive shaft (**Figure 122**) for:
   a. Worn or damaged splines.
   b. Worn or damaged bearing surfaces.
   c. Bent shaft.

2. Inspect the final drive shaft gear (**Figure 122**) for:

5

a. Missing, broken or chipped teeth.

b. Cracked or scored gear bore.

3. Replace the final drive shaft and gear if necessary.

### Transmission Assembly Inspection

Refer to Chapter Seven for all disassembly, inspection and reassembly procedures.

### Crankshaft and Balancer Shaft Installation

Use the following Honda tools (or equivalent) to install the crankshaft and balancer shaft into the rear crankcase.

a. Threaded adapter (part No. 07931-KF00200): A, **Figure 123**.

b. Shaft puller (part No. 07931-ME4010B USA only or 07965-VM00200): B, **Figure 123**.

c. Threaded adapter (part No. 07931-HB3020A): C, **Figure 123**.

d. Assembly collar (part No. 07965-VM00100): D, **Figure 123**.

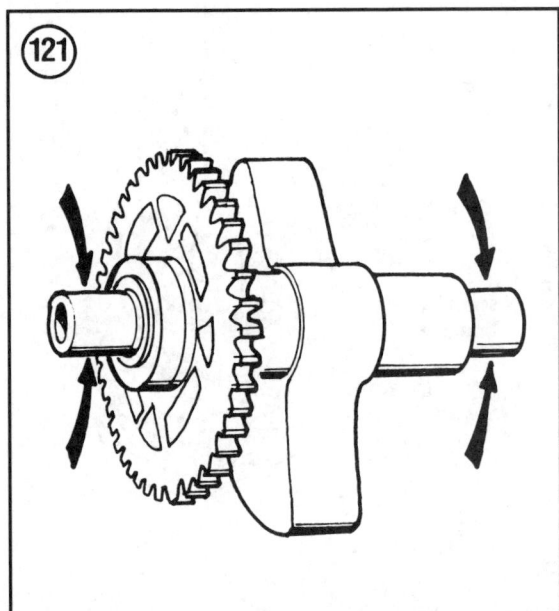

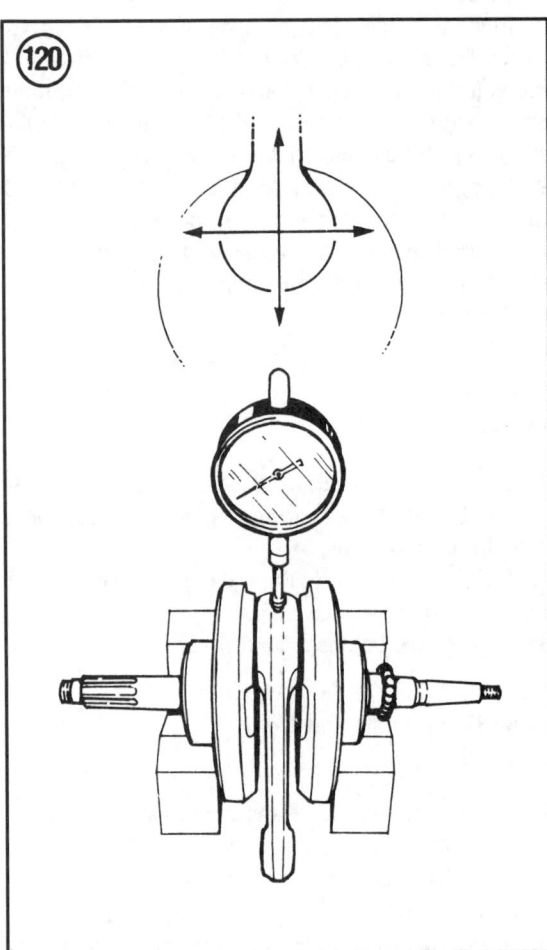

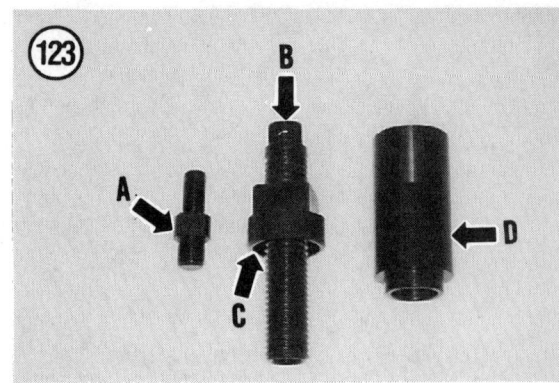

*NOTE*
*Before ordering these tools, confirm the tool part numbers with your Honda dealership.*

1. Place the front crankcase on wooden blocks with its inside surface facing up.

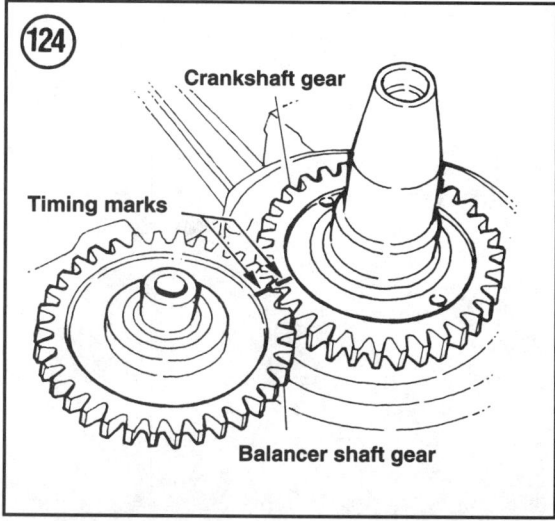

2. Lubricate the crankshaft and balancer shaft bearings with oil.

3. Align the timing marks on the crankshaft and balancer shaft (**Figure 124**) and install both parts into the front crankcase. Recheck the timing mark alignment.

4. Install the rear crankcase over the crankshaft and balancer shaft.

5. Install the threaded adapter into the end of the crankshaft (**Figure 125**).

6. Install the crankshaft puller assembly (**Figure 126**) over the end of the crankshaft and thread it into the threaded adapter. Then center the tool assembly on the main bearing inner race.

*CAUTION*
*When installing the crankshaft in Step 7, position the connecting rod at its TDC or BDC position. Otherwise, the connecting rod may contact the side of the crankcase, causing expensive connecting rod and crankcase damage.*

7. Hold the threaded adapter and turn the shaft puller (**Figure 127**) to pull the crankshaft into the main bearing. When installing the crankshaft, frequently check that it is going straight into the bearing and not binding to one side.

8. Continue to turn the shaft puller until the crankshaft bottoms against the main bearing. Remove the crankshaft tools and turn the crankshaft (**Figure**

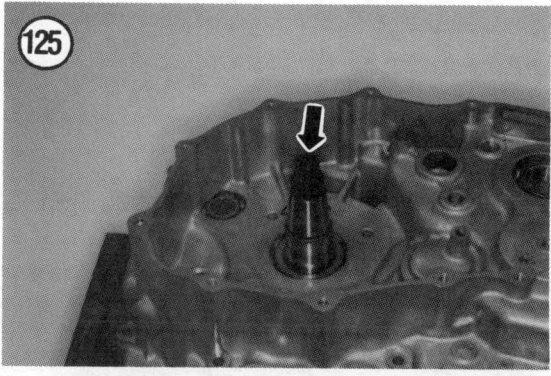

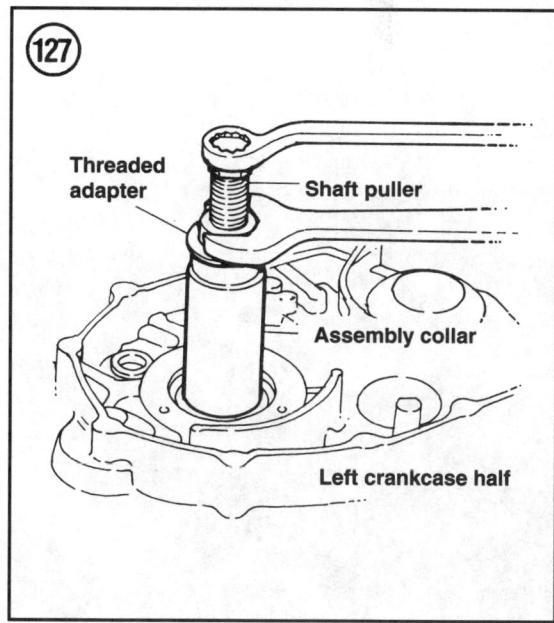

**125**). The crankshaft must turn with no binding or roughness.

9. Turn the crankcase over and rest the rear crankcase on wooden blocks. Remove the front crankcase.

10. Make sure the index marks on the crankshaft and balancer shaft align as shown in **Figure 128**.

> *CAUTION*
> *Severe engine damage will occur if the crankshaft and balancer shaft index marks do not align.*

## Crankcase Assembly

1. Install the crankshaft and balancer shaft into the rear crankcase as described in this chapter.

2. Install a new final drive shaft seal as described in this chapter.

3. Lightly oil all of the crankcase bearings.

4. Check the assembly of the following components as described in Chapter Seven. Check that you installed all washers and circlips in their correct position. Then set each assembly aside until reassembly:

    a. Mainshaft (**Figure 129**).

    b. Countershaft (**Figure 130**).

> *NOTE*
> *Do not install the countershaft first gear bushing, first gear and copper washer at this time. You will install these parts during the following steps.*

    c. Reverse idler gear assembly (**Figure 131**).

5. Place the rear crankcase half on two wooden blocks (**Figure 132**).

6. Check that both crankcase gasket surfaces are clean and dry.

7. Install the final drive gear (A, **Figure 133**) onto the final drive gear shaft (B, **Figure 133**).

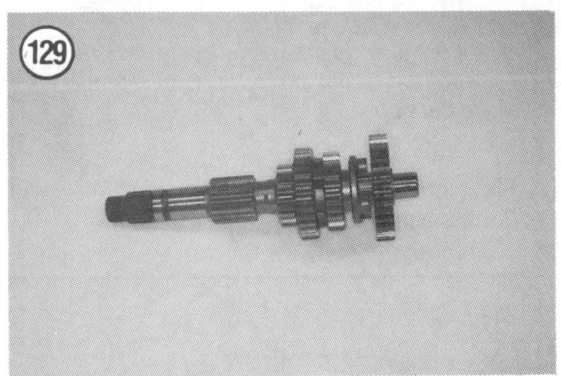

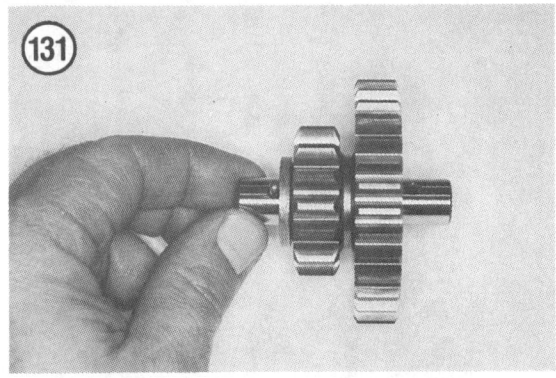

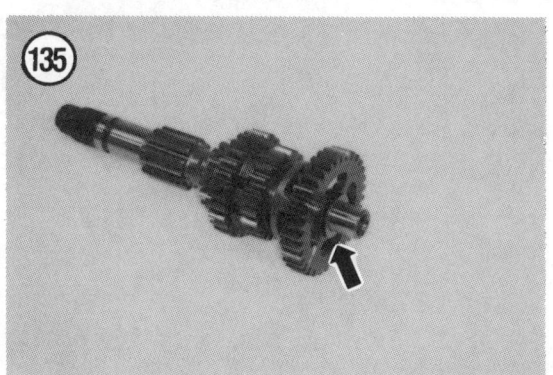

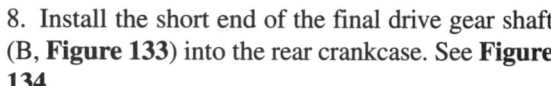

8. Install the short end of the final drive gear shaft (B, **Figure 133**) into the rear crankcase. See **Figure 134**.

9. Install the mainshaft and countershaft as follows:

   a. Check that the washer (**Figure 135**) is installed on the mainshaft.

   b. Check that the washer (**Figure 136**) is installed on the countershaft.

*NOTE*
*The countershaft washer (**Figure 136**) is a press fit and should not fall off.*

   c. Mesh the countershaft and mainshaft together as shown in **Figure 137**.

   d. Install the countershaft (A, **Figure 138**) and mainshaft (B) into the left crankcase half. Check that the outer washer did not fall off the mainshaft.

*NOTE*
*To identify the shift forks when installing them in Step 10, refer to the letter mark(s) on each shift fork: FF (front), C (center) and RR (rear); see **Figure 139**.*

10. Install the shift forks (**Figure 139**) and shift drum assembly as follows:

    a. Install each shift fork with its letter mark facing up.

    b. Install the RR (rear) shift fork into the mainshaft third gear groove (A, **Figure 140**).

    c. Install the C (center) shift fork into the countershaft fourth gear groove (B, **Figure 140**).

    d. Install the shift drum (**Figure 141**) into the crankcase.

    e. Engage the RR shift fork pin into the bottom shift drum groove.

    f. Engage the C shift fork pin into the middle shift drum groove.

    g. Install the FF (front) shift fork into the reverse counter shifter groove (**Figure 142**), then engage the shift fork's pin into the upper shift drum groove.

11. Install the shift fork shaft (**Figure 143**) through the three shift forks. Check that each shift fork is still engaged with its respective gear and that its pin is in the correct shift drum groove.

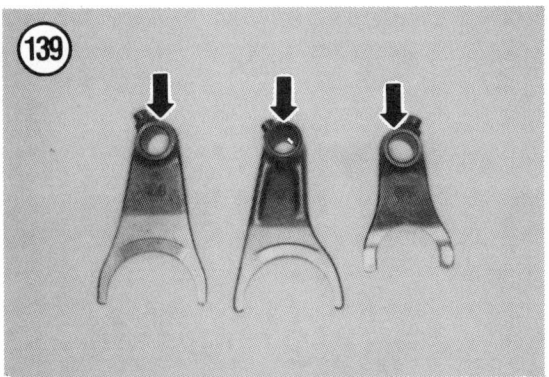

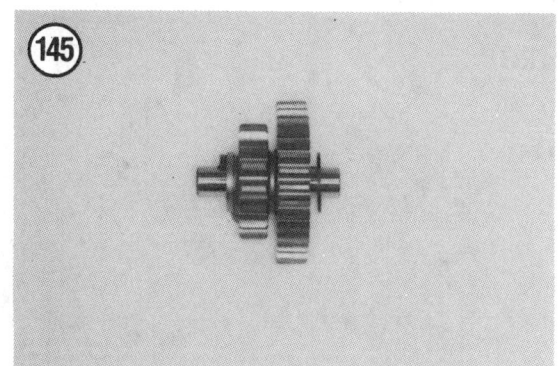

12. Install the reverse idler gear as an assembly (**Figure 144**):

   a. Assemble the reverse idler gear as shown in **Figure 145**.

   b. Install the reverse idler gear by aligning the pin with the groove in the crankcase (**Figure 146**) and meshing the reverse idler gears with the mainshaft gears. See A, **Figure 147**.

   c. Check that the outer washer (B, **Figure 147**) is installed on the reverse idler gear assembly.

13. Install the countershaft first gear assembly as follows:

   a. Align the hole in the bushing with the hole in the countershaft (**Figure 148**) and install the bushing.

   b. Install the countershaft first gear (A, **Figure 149**).

   c. Install the copper washer. See B, **Figure 149**.

14. Spin the transmission shafts and shift through the gears using the shift drum. Make sure it shifts into each gear correctly. Check the shifting into each gear. This is the time to find that you may have installed a part incorrectly—not after you completely assemble the crankcase.

15. After making sure the transmission shifts into all of the gears correctly, shift the transmission assembly into NEUTRAL.

16. Clean the oil screen. Then install the oil screen into the rear crankcase grooves. See **Figure 150**.

17. Install the two dowel pins (**Figure 151**).

18. Install a new crankcase gasket (**Figure 151**).

19. Lubricate all of the shafts and gears with engine oil (**Figure 151**).

20. Align the front crankcase half with the shafts and crankshaft and install it **Figure 152**. Push the crankcase down squarely into place until it engages

**5**

the dowel pins and then seats completely against the opposite crankcase.

*CAUTION*
*When the shafts align  properly, the front crankcase will install without the use of force. If the crankcase halves do not fit together completely, do not pull them together with the crankcase screws. Remove the front crankcase half and investigate the cause of the interfer-*

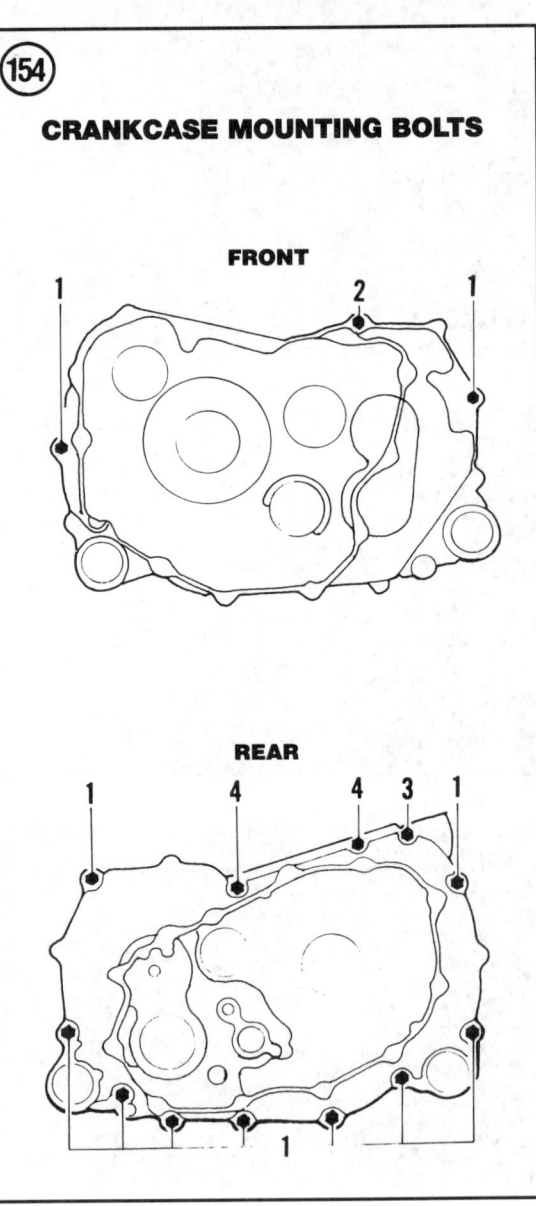

**CRANKCASE MOUNTING BOLTS**

FRONT

REAR

*ence. If you disassembled the transmission or reverse assemblies, check that you did not install a gear incorrectly. If you removed the crankshaft, confirm that it is installed and seated properly in the rear crankcase main bearing.*

21. Turn all of the exposed shafts, crankshaft and shift drum. Each component must turn freely with

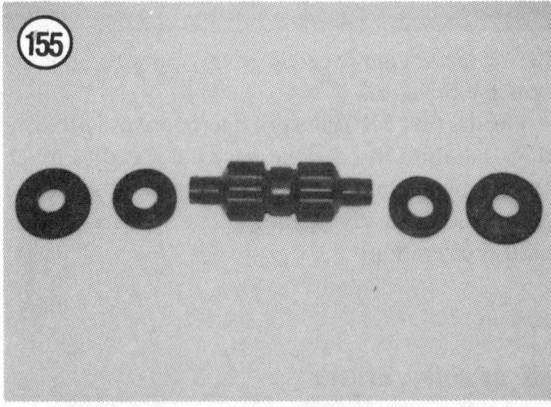

no binding. If everything turns properly, continue with Step 22.

*NOTE*
*Use your cardboard guide (**Figure 153**) and **Figure 154** when installing the crankcase mounting bolts in the following steps.*

22. Install the rear crankcase mounting bolt finger-tight. Then tighten the crankcase mounting bolts securely in 2-3 stages following a crisscross pattern.

23. Turn the engine over and install the front crankcase mounting bolts. Tighten these bolts securely.

24. Rotate the transmission shafts and crankshaft to ensure there is no binding. If there is any binding, remove the crankcase mounting bolts and the right crankcase and correct the problem.

25. Perform the *Transmission Shifting Check* in this chapter.

26. Trim the crankcase gasket before installing the cylinder block.

27. Inspect the engine mounting dust seal and bushing (**Figure 155**) sets for severe wear or damage.

28. Install the bushing sets so that the outer dust seal lips face out as shown in **Figure 156**.

29. Install all exterior engine assemblies as described in this chapter and other related chapters.

## TRANSMISSION SHIFTING CHECK

Transmission shifting can be checked with the engine mounted in the frame or with it mounted on the workbench. Always check transmission shifting after reassembling the engine cases.

1. Install the stopper lever assembly (**Figure 157**) as described under *Gearshift Linkage* in this chapter.

2. Turn the drum shifter so that the dowel pin (A, **Figure 157**) aligns with the crankcase index mark (B, **Figure 157**). The transmission is now in neutral. When the transmission is in NEUTRAL, the countershaft and mainshaft will turn independently of each other (that is, when you turn one shaft, the other shaft will not turn).

3A. To check the forward gears (neutral and first through fifth gears): Turn the mainshaft or countershaft while turning the shifter drum counterclockwise. The transmission is in gear when the stopper arm roller seats into one of the drum shifter segment ramps. When the transmission is in gear, the countershaft and mainshaft are engaged and will turn together.

3B. To check the reverse gear, move the reverse lever (**Figure 158**) down (to disengage it from the shift drum) and then turn the drum shifter (**Figure 157**) clockwise. The transmission should shift into reverse.

4. If the transmission does not shift properly into each gear, disassemble the engine and check the transmission and the internal shift mechanism.

### ENGINE BREAK-IN

If you replaced the piston rings, installed a new piston, honed or rebored the cylinder or performed major lower end work performed, the engine must be broken in as if new. The performance and service life of the engine depends greatly on a careful and sensible break-in.

For the first 5-10 hours of operation, use no more than one-third throttle and vary the speed as much as possible within the one-third throttle limit. Avoid prolonged or steady running at one speed as well as hard acceleration.

#### Table 1 GENERAL ENGINE SPECIFICATIONS

| | |
|---|---|
| Crankshaft type | Two main journals, unit type |
| Engine weight (approximate) | 50.4 kg (111.1 lbs.) |
| Lubrication system | Wet sump, forced pressure |

#### Table 2 OIL PUMP SERVICE SPECIFICATIONS

| | New mm (in.) | Service limit mm (in.) |
|---|---|---|
| Body clearance | 0.15-0.21 (0.006-0.008) | 0.25 (0.010) |
| End clearance | 0.02-0.09 (0.001-0.004) | 0.11 (0.004) |
| Tip clearance | 0.15 (0.006) | 0.20 (0.008) |

#### Table 3 CRANKSHAFT SERVICE SPECIFICATIONS

| | New mm (in.) | Service limit mm (in.) |
|---|---|---|
| Crankshaft runout | — — | 0.05 (0.002) |
| Connecting rod big end radial clearance | 0.006-0.018 (0.0002-0.0007) | 0.05 (0.002) |
| Connecting rod side clearance | 0.05-0.065 (0.002-0.026) | 0.80 (0.031) |
| Connecting rod small end inside diameter | 19.020-19.041 (0.7488-0.7490) | 19.07 (0.751) |

(continued)

**Table 3 CRANKSHAFT SERVICE SPECIFICATIONS (continued)**

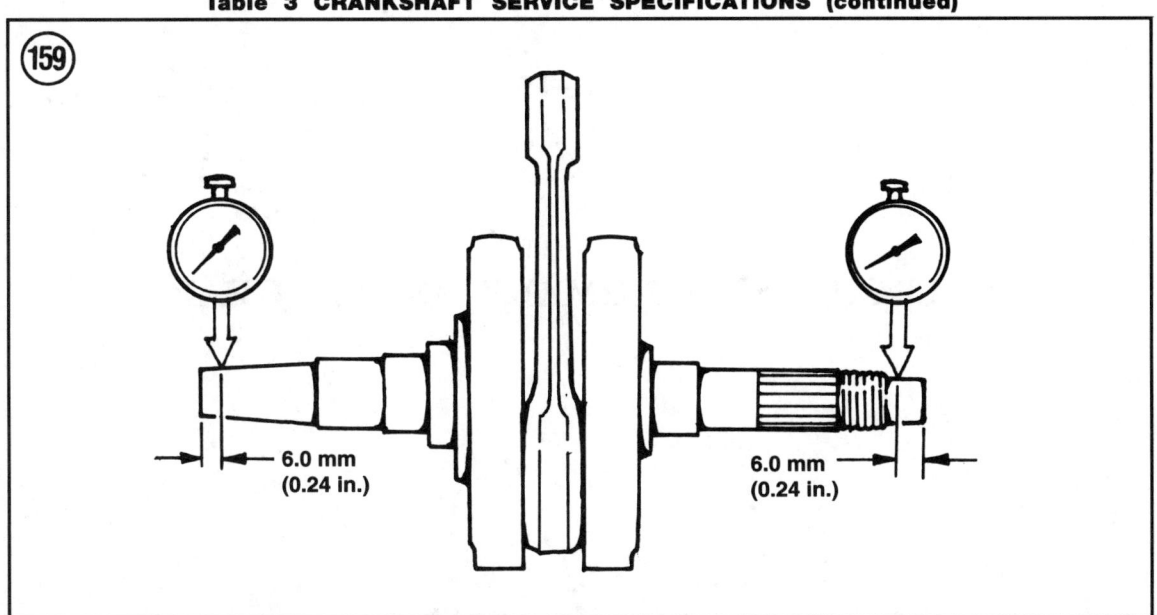

**Table 4 ENGINE LOWER END TIGHTENING TORQUES**

|                                              | N·m | in.-lb. | ft.-lb. |
|----------------------------------------------|-----|---------|---------|
| Cooling fan shroud special bolt              | 18  | —       | 13      |
| Driven pulley mounting bolt                  | 110 | —       | 81      |
| Engine mounting bolts                        |     |         |         |
|   Lower engine hanger bolts/nuts   |     |         |         |
|    Left and right side        | 55  | —       | 41      |
|   Lower engine hanger bracket bolts/nuts | 33  | —       | 24      |
|   Upper engine hanger bolt         | 55  | —       | 41      |
|   Upper engine hanger bracket bolts| 33  | —       | 24      |
| Gearshift arm bolt                           | 25  | —       | 18      |
| Gearshift stopper pin                        | 22  | —       | 16      |
| Guide plate bolt                             | 12  | 106     | —       |
| Ignition pulse generator mounting bolts      | 6   | 53      | —       |
| Oil drain plug                               | 25  | —       | 18      |
| Oil filter cover flange bolt                 | 10  | 88      | —       |
| Oil pump side plate screw                    | 4   | 35      | —       |
| One-way clutch mounting bolts                | 31  | —       | 23      |
| Relief valve cap                             | 19  | —       | 14      |
| Neutral/reverse switch mounting bolts        | 12  | 106     | —       |
| Stopper arm bolt                             | 12  | 106     | —       |
| Skid plate mounting bolts                    | 33  | —       | 24      |
| Starter one-way clutch Allen bolts           | 31  | —       | 23      |
| Stator mounting bolts                        | 10  | 88      | —       |

# CHAPTER SIX

# CLUTCH AND PRIMARY DRIVE GEAR

This chapter describes service procedures for the following subassemblies:

1. Clutch cover.
2. Clutch lever.
3. Centrifugal clutch and primary drive gear.
4. Change clutch.

The clutch cover, clutch and primary drive gear assemblies can be serviced with the engine mounted in the frame. However, because of the engines mounting position in the frame, all of the illustrations described in this chapter depict the engine removed from the frame for clarity.

Service specifications are listed in **Tables 1-3**. **Tables 1-4** are found at the end of the chapter.

## CLUTCH COVER

### Removal/Installation

1. If the engine is mounted in the frame, perform the following steps:
   a. Park the vehicle on level ground and set the parking brake.
   b. Drain the engine oil as described in Chapter Three.
   c. Remove the oil cooler pipes (**Figure 1**) and O-rings from the clutch cover. Plug the hose openings to prevent contamination and leakage.

d. Remove the front drive shaft cover (**Figure 2**).

2. Before removing the clutch cover mounting screws, draw an outline of the cover on a piece of cardboard. Then punch holes along the outline for the placement of each mounting screw.
3. Remove the clutch cover mounting screws and remove the clutch cover (**Figure 3**).
4. Remove the clutch cover gasket and both dowel pins (A, **Figure 4**).
5. Remove the O-ring (B, **Figure 4**) from the oil pump dowel pin.
6. If necessary, remove the clutch lever assembly (C, **Figure 4**) as described in this chapter.
7. Remove all gasket residue from the clutch cover and crankcase gasket surfaces.
8. If the clutch cover is going to be serviced and/or cleaned in solvent, perform the *Clutch Cover Cleaning* procedure in this section. Otherwise, store the clutch cover in a plastic bag until reassembly.
9. Check the crankshaft end bearing (A, **Figure 5**) as described in this section.
10. Install the clutch cover by reversing the preceding steps, while noting the following:
    a. Lubricate the crankshaft end bearing (A, **Figure 5**) with engine oil.
    b. Replace the oil pump O-ring (B, **Figure 4**) if worn or damaged. Lubricate the O-ring with engine oil before installing it onto the dowel pin.

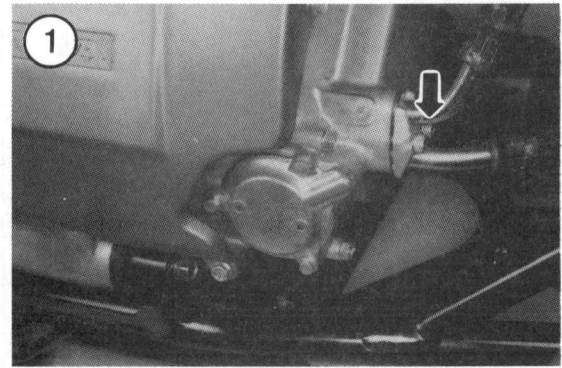

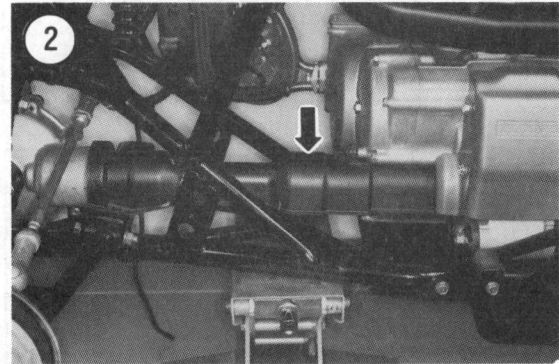

c. Install a new clutch cover gasket.

d. If removed, install the clutch lever assembly (C, **Figure 4**) as described in this chapter.

e. Tighten all of the clutch cover mounting bolts securely.

f. If removed, install the oil filter as described in Chapter Three.

g. Replace the oil hose O-rings if leaking, worn or damaged. Tighten the oil hose bracket Allen bolts (**Figure 1**) securely.

## Clutch Cover Cleaning

The clutch cover houses the crankshaft end bearing, oil filter, oil relief valve and a number of oil passages. Before cleaning or servicing the clutch cover, remove the oil filter and oil relief valve assemblies as follows:

1. Remove the oil filter as described in Chapter Three.

2. Remove the oil relief valve as described in Chapter Five.

3. Clean the clutch cover and its oil passages with solvent. Clean the crankshaft end bearing while it is submerged in solvent. Dry the clutch cover, oil passages and bearing with compressed air.

> *WARNING*
> *Do not spin the bearing with compressed air when drying it. Doing so may cause the bearing to fly apart.*

4. Lubricate the crankshaft end bearing with engine oil.

5. Install the oil relief valve as described in Chapter Five.

6. Install the oil filter after reinstalling the clutch cover onto the engine.

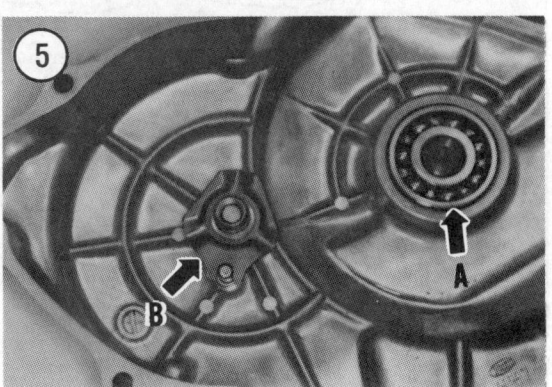

⑥ **BLIND BEARING REMOVAL**

⑦ **CLUTCH LEVER ASSEMBLY**

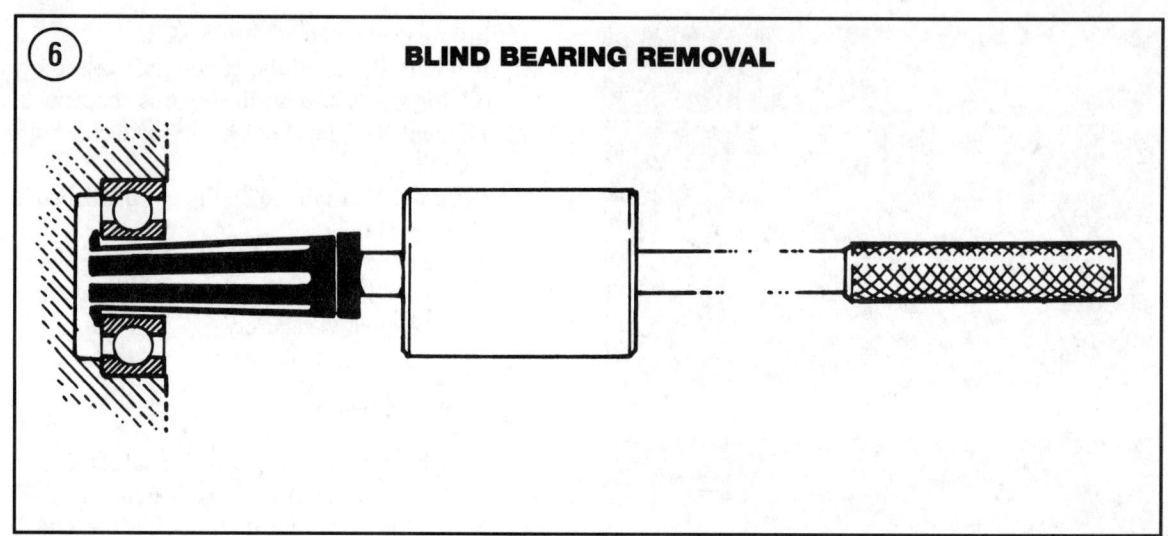

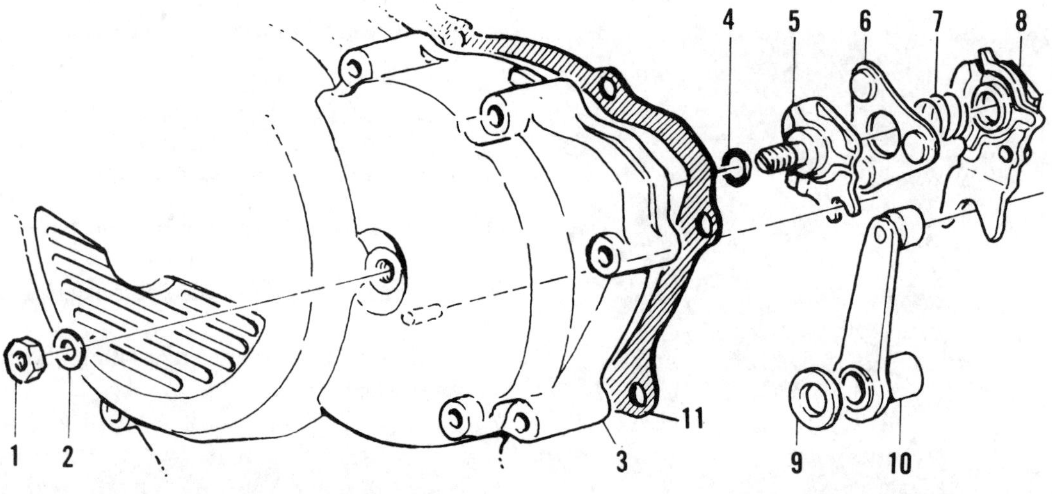

1. Adjust nut
2. Washer
3. Clutch cover
4. O-ring
5. Adjusting plate
6. Ball retainer
7. Spring
8. Clutch cam
   lifter plate assembly
9. Washer
10. Clutch lever
11. Gasket

## Crankshaft End Bearing Inspection and Replacement

The bearing installed in the clutch cover supports the front crankshaft end. This bearing must be in good condition and fit tightly in its mounting bore.

1. Hold the clutch housing and slowly turn the crankshaft end bearing (A, **Figure 5**) inner race. Check for roughness, excessive play or noise. If the bearing feels gritty, clean the bearing as described under *Clutch Cover Cleaning* in this section and then recheck it for wear and damage. If any of these conditions are present, the bearing is probably damaged. Replace the bearing as described in Step 3. If the bearing is good, lubricate it with engine oil.

2. Check that the bearing outer race is a tight fit in its mounting bore. If the bearing is a loose fit, the mounting bore is probably cracked or excessively worn. If the mounting bore is damaged, replace the clutch cover.

3. Replace the bearing as follows:
   a. Remove the oil filter (Chapter Three) and relief valve (Chapter Five) from the clutch cover. Clean the clutch cover in solvent and dry with compressed air.
   b. Support the clutch cover with the bearing facing up.
   c. Heat the area around the bearing with a propane torch, then remove the bearing with a blind bearing remover as shown in **Figure 6**.
   d. Heat the clutch cover again, then press the new bearing into its mounting bore until it bottoms. Install the bearing with its manufacturer's numbers facing out.
   e. After the clutch cover cools to room temperature, install the relief valve as described in Chapter Five.

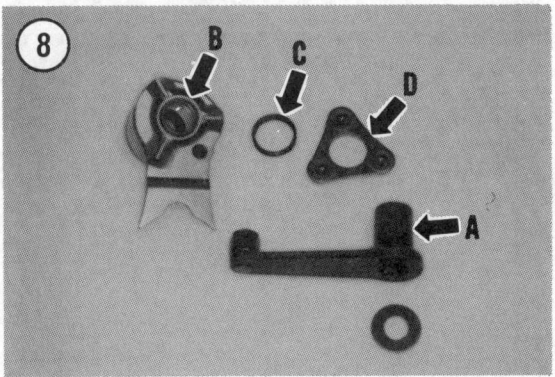

   f. Install the oil filter after installing the clutch cover onto the engine.

## CLUTCH LEVER ASSEMBLY

The clutch lever assembly helps to engage and disengage the change clutch as the gearshift pedal is moved during gear changes.

Refer to **Figure 7** when servicing the clutch lever assembly.

### Removal

1. Remove the clutch cover as described in this chapter.
2. Remove the clutch lever assembly in the following order:
   a. Washer (9, **Figure 7**).
   b. Clutch lever (10).
   c. Ball retainer (6).
   d. Spring (7).
   e. Clutch cam (8).
3. To remove the adjusting plate (5, **Figure 7**), remove the adjust nut and washer and then pull the adjusting plate and its O-ring (4) out of the clutch cover.

### Inspection

Replace parts that show excessive wear or damage as described in this section.

1. Clean and dry all parts.
2. Check the clutch lever (A, **Figure 8**) for damaged splines or a cracked or severely worn lever arm.
3. Check the clutch cam (B, **Figure 8**) for damage where the arm ramps engage the clutch lever arm. Check the lifter cap (attached to the clutch cam with a pivot pin) for excessive wear or damage. Check the pivot pin for excessive wear.
4. Check the spring (C, **Figure 8**) for stretched or damaged coils.
5. Check the ball retainer (D, **Figure 8**) for a cracked ball cage. The balls must turn smoothly in the retainer and not fall out. Check the balls for cracks or flat spots.
6. Check the adjusting plate (5, **Figure 7**) for stripped threads or damaged or severely worn engagement arm tabs. Replace the adjusting plate O-ring (4, **Figure 7**) if cracked or damaged.

## Installation

1. Install the adjusting plate (5, **Figure 7**) assembly as follows:

   a. Lubricate the O-ring (4, **Figure 7**) with engine oil and install it into the adjusting plate bore in the clutch cover.

   b. Install the adjusting plate by aligning its cutout with the clutch cover stopper pin (B, **Figure 5**).

   c. Install the washer (2, **Figure 7**) and adjust nut (1). Tighten the nut finger-tight.

2. Lubricate the lifter cap bore (**Figure 9**) with grease.

3. Install the clutch lever (A, **Figure 10**) as follows:

   a. The clutch lever and shift shaft (B, **Figure 10**) are machined with master splines.

   b. Align the clutch lever and shift shaft master splines and install the clutch lever (A, **Figure 10**). Then check that the clutch lever roller (C, **Figure 10**) points toward the center of the clutch.

   c. Lubricate the clutch lever roller (C, **Figure 10**) with engine oil.

4. Install the clutch cam assembly over the clutch lever and into the lifter plate as shown in **Figure 11**.

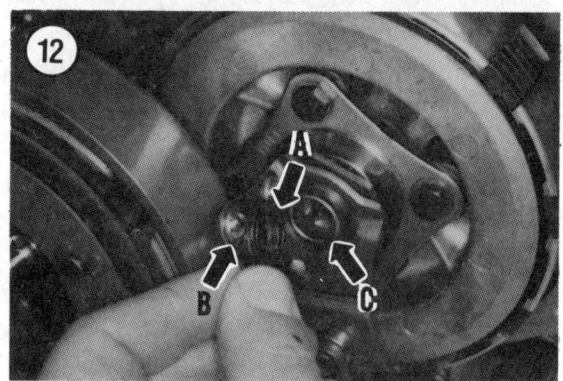

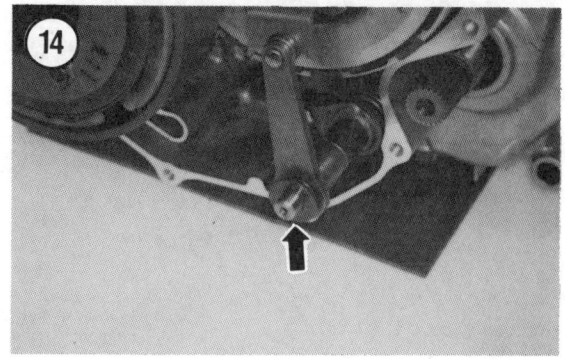

5. Install the spring (A, **Figure 12**) onto the ball retainer (B, **Figure 12**) shoulder.

6. Install the spring and ball retainer onto the lifter plate shoulder (C, **Figure 12**).

7. Check that the clutch lever (A, **Figure 13**) points toward the center of the change clutch (B, **Figure 13**).

8. Install the washer (**Figure 14**) onto the shift shaft.

9. Install the clutch cover as described in this chapter.

## CLUTCH ASSEMBLIES

The TRX400FW uses two clutch assemblies: centrifugal clutch (C, **Figure 13**) and the change clutch (B, **Figure 13**). The centrifugal clutch must be removed first.

## CENTRIFUGAL CLUTCH AND PRIMARY DRIVE GEAR

The centrifugal clutch (C, **Figure 13**) can be removed with the engine installed in the frame.

Refer to **Figure 15** when servicing the centrifugal clutch assembly.

### Special Tools and Replacement Parts

Before removing the clutch locknut, note the following:

1. The clutch drum must be locked in place when loosening and tightening the clutch locknut (1, **Figure 15**). The following list describes two tools that can be used to do this:

   a. Honda clutch holder (part No. 07GMB-HA7010A).

   b. Universal type strap wrench (**Figure 16**).

*NOTE*
*If the engine is mounted in the frame, it may be difficult to hold the clutch drum with a strap wrench.*

2. The Honda clutch puller (part No. 07933-HB3000A [**Figure 17**]) is required to pull the centrifugal clutch off the crankshaft.

6

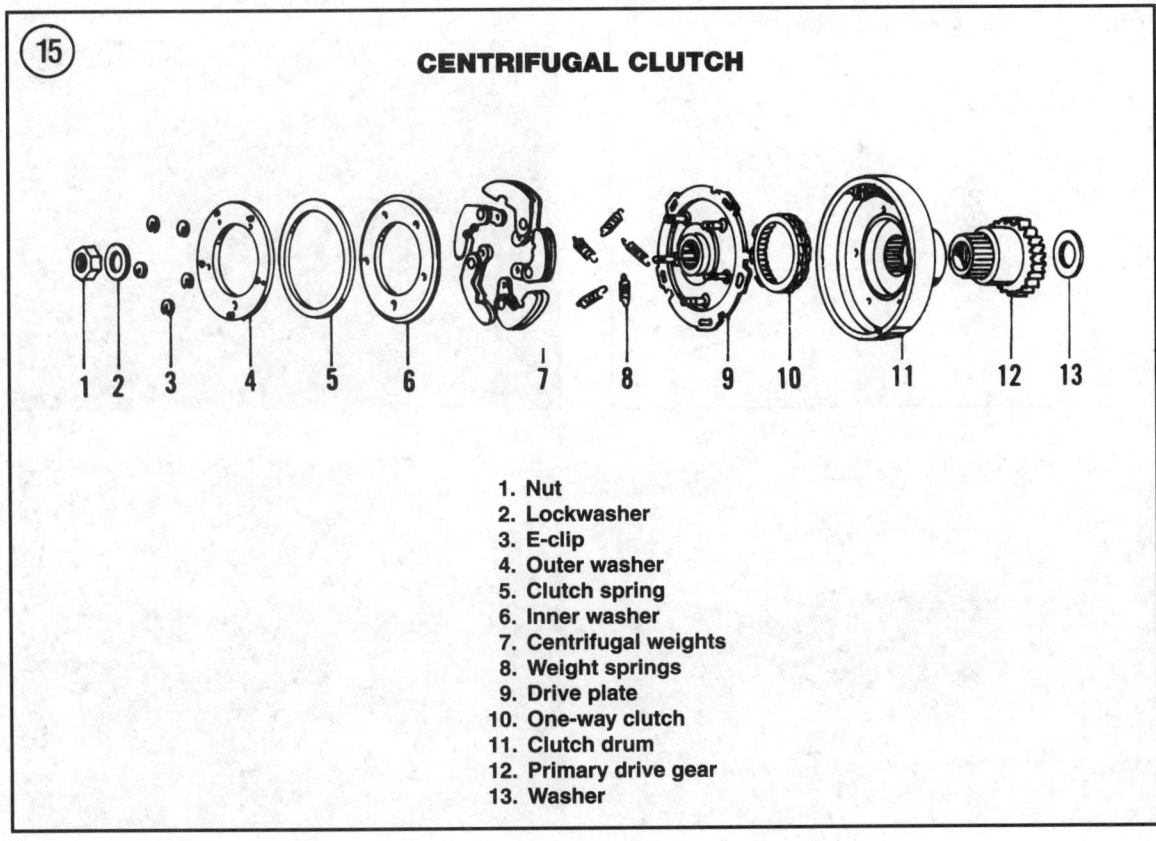

**15**

**CENTRIFUGAL CLUTCH**

1  2  3    4    5    6    7    8    9  10    11    12  13

1. Nut
2. Lockwasher
3. E-clip
4. Outer washer
5. Clutch spring
6. Inner washer
7. Centrifugal weights
8. Weight springs
9. Drive plate
10. One-way clutch
11. Clutch drum
12. Primary drive gear
13. Washer

3. The clutch locknut (**Figure 18**) is staked to a notch in the crankshaft. Purchase a new locknut for reassembly.

### Removal/Installation

1. Remove the clutch cover as described in this chapter.

> *CAUTION*
> *Be sure to unstake the clutch locknut where it contacts the crankshaft. This will prevent the nut from damaging the crankshaft threads as the nut is being removed.*

2. Using a die grinder, unstake the clutch locknut from the groove in the crankshaft (**Figure 19**). Cover the parts (**Figure 19**) so that metal particles do not enter the clutch or engine.

3. Secure the clutch drum with one of the tools listed under *Service Notes and Replacement Parts* in this section. Then loosen and remove the clutch locknut and washer (**Figure 20**). Discard the clutch locknut.

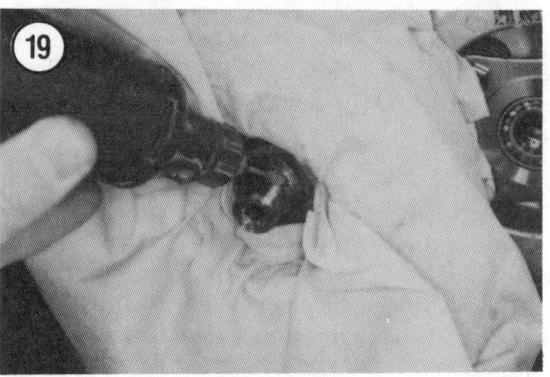

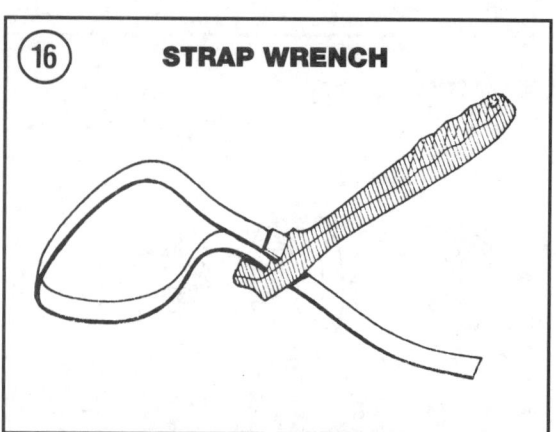

STRAP WRENCH

4. Thread the clutch puller (**Figure 21**) onto the drive plate threads. Hold the clutch puller body with a wrench and then turn its end bolt to pull the centrifugal clutch assembly off the mainshaft. See **Figure 22**.

5. To remove the primary drive gear, perform the following:

    a. Remove the change clutch (B, **Figure 13**) as described in this chapter.

    b. Remove the primary drive gear (A, **Figure 23**) and washer (B, **Figure 23**).

6. Inspect the centrifugal clutch and primary drive gear as described in this section.

7. Install the primary drive gear and centrifugal clutch by reversing these removal steps while noting the following:

    a. Lubricate the mainshaft, primary drive gear bore and washer with engine oil.

    b. Lubricate the clutch weight linings (A, **Figure 24**) with engine oil.

    c. If removed, install the drive plate assembly (A, **Figure 24**) into the clutch drum (B, **Figure 24**).

    d. Install the centrifugal clutch by first aligning the drive plate splines with the crankshaft splines, then rotate the clutch drum and align its splines with the primary drive gear splines. See **Figure 25**.

    e. Center a driver against the drive plate (**Figure 26**) and drive it onto the crankshaft until it bottoms.

    f. Lubricate the washer and the threads of a new clutch locknut (**Figure 20**) with engine oil and install them.

    g. Secure the clutch drum with the same tool used during removal, then tighten the centrifugal clutch locknut as specified in **Table 4**.

**6**

Stake the edge of the clutch locknut to the notch in the crankshaft (**Figure 18**).

## Clutch Drum and One-Way Clutch Inspection

Refer to **Table 1** when measuring the clutch drum components (**Figure 15**) in this section. Replace parts that are out of specification or show damage.

1. Check one-way clutch operation as follows:
   a. Place the assembled clutch assembly on the workbench as shown in **Figure 24**.
   b. Hold the clutch drum (B, **Figure 24**) and turn the drive plate assembly (A, **Figure 24**).
   c. The drive plate assembly should only turn counterclockwise (C, **Figure 24**). If the drive plate turns clockwise, the one-way clutch is faulty and must be replaced as described in this procedure.

2. Remove the drive plate assembly from the clutch drum.

3. Remove the one-way clutch (A, **Figure 27**) from the clutch drum. Inspect the one-way clutch for signs of heat damage, cracks or other damage. Replace the one-way clutch if there is visible damage or if it failed to operate as described in Step 1.

4. Check the drive plate boss (A, **Figure 28**) for scoring, excessive wear or damage. Check for signs of overheating.

5. Check the exterior of the clutch drum (B, **Figure 27**) for cracks or damage. Check the clutch drum inside diameter for excessive wear or damage. Measure the clutch drum inside diameter (B, **Figure 28**) with a caliper and compare to the service limit in **Table 1**.

6. Lubricate the one-way clutch and the clutch drum bore with engine oil. Then install the one-way clutch in the clutch drum with its OUTSIDE mark (**Figure 29**) facing out.

7. Inspect and service the centrifugal weight assembly as described in this section.

8. Inspect the primary drive gear as described in this section.

## Centrifugal Weight Assembly Disassembly/Inspection/Reassembly

Refer to **Table 1** when measuring the centrifugal weight components (**Figure 15**) in this section. Replace parts that are out of specification or damaged.

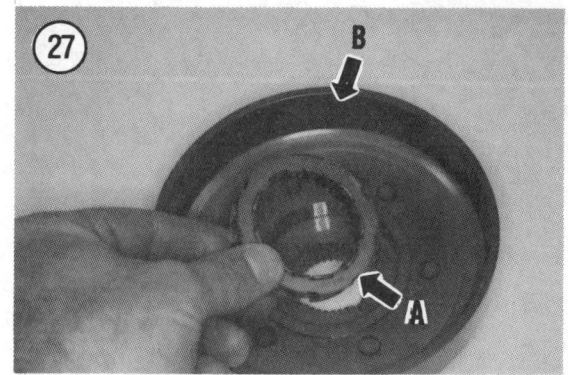

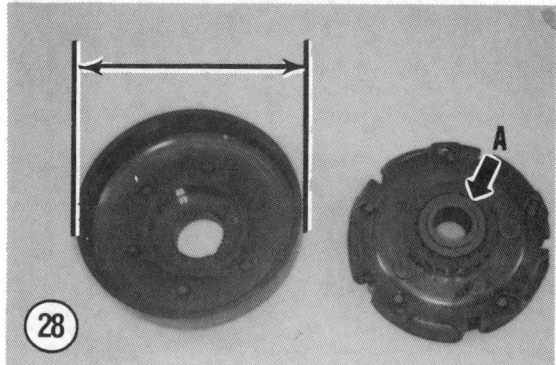

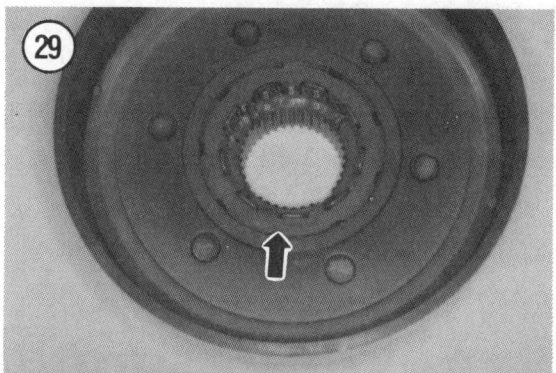

1. Disassemble the centrifugal weight assembly as follows:

   a. Remove the E-clips (**Figure 30**), outer washer, clutch spring and inner washer.

   b. Remove the weight springs (8, **Figure 15**) and clutch weight arms (7, **Figure 15**).

2. Measure the thickness of each weight lining at the points shown in **Figure 31**. If out of specification, replace all of the clutch weight arms as a set.

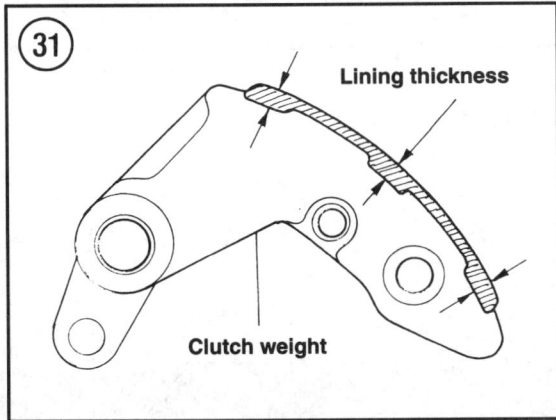

3. Check the clutch spring (5, **Figure 15**) for cracks or signs of heat damage. Then measure the height of the clutch spring with a vernier caliper (**Figure 32**).

4. Check the weight springs (8, **Figure 15**) for cracks or stretched coils. Then measure the free length of each spring with a vernier caliper. If out of specification, replace all of the springs as a set.

5. Check the outer and inner washers and replace if cracked or damaged.

6. Inspect the drive plate for damaged splines, warpage or damaged clutch weight pins. Check the E-clip groove in the end of each pin for damage.

7. Reassemble the clutch weight assembly as follows:

   a. Lubricate the drive plate pins with engine oil.

   b. Install the clutch weights and weight springs. Install the weight springs with their open ends facing down.

   c. Install the inner washer (6, **Figure 15**) with its shoulder facing out.

   d. Install the clutch spring (5, **Figure 15**) with its cupped side facing up.

   e. Install the outer washer (4, **Figure 15**) with its locating pins facing out.

   f. Secure the drive plate in a vise by applying just enough pressure to compress the clutch spring and expose the clip grooves in the end of each drive plate pin. Install the E-clips with the open end of each E-clip against its corresponding locating pin on the outer washer. Check that each E-clip seats in its groove completely.

   g. Remove pressure from the drive plate and check that the outer washer seats evenly against each E-clip.

### Primary Drive Gear Inspection

Refer to **Table 2** when measuring the primary drive gear components in this section. Replace parts that are out of specification or damaged.

1. Clean and dry the primary drive gear and its washer.

2. Check the primary drive gear (**Figure 33**) for:

   a. Worn or damaged gear teeth (A, **Figure 33**) or splines.

   b. Scored or damaged outer bearing surface.

   c. Worn or damaged bushings.

3. Measure the inside diameter of the bushing (B, **Figure 33**) at each end of the gear. Replace the

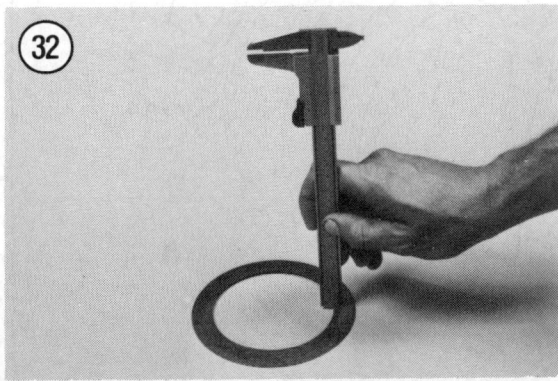

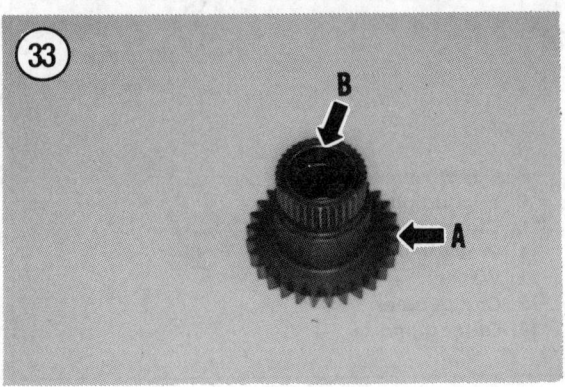

primary drive gear if either bushing diameter is out of specification.

4. Measure the crankshaft outside diameter at the two drive gear bushing operating locations shown in **Figure 34**. Replace the crankshaft if either dimension is out of specification.

## CHANGE CLUTCH

The change clutch (B, **Figure 13**) can be removed with the engine installed in the frame.

**CHANGE CLUTCH**

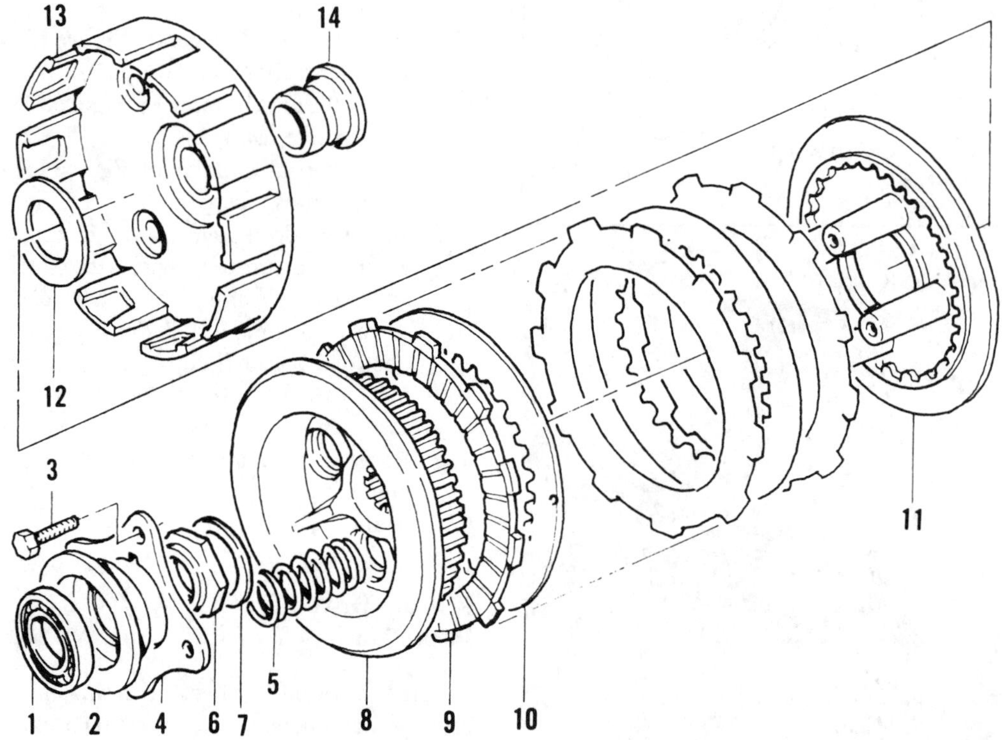

1. Lifter bearing
2. Holder
3. Clutch spring bolts
4. Lifter plate
5. Clutch springs
6. Clutch locknut
7. Washer
8. Clutch center
9. Friction plates
10. Clutch metal plate
11. Pressure plate
12. Washer
13. Clutch outer
14. Outer guide

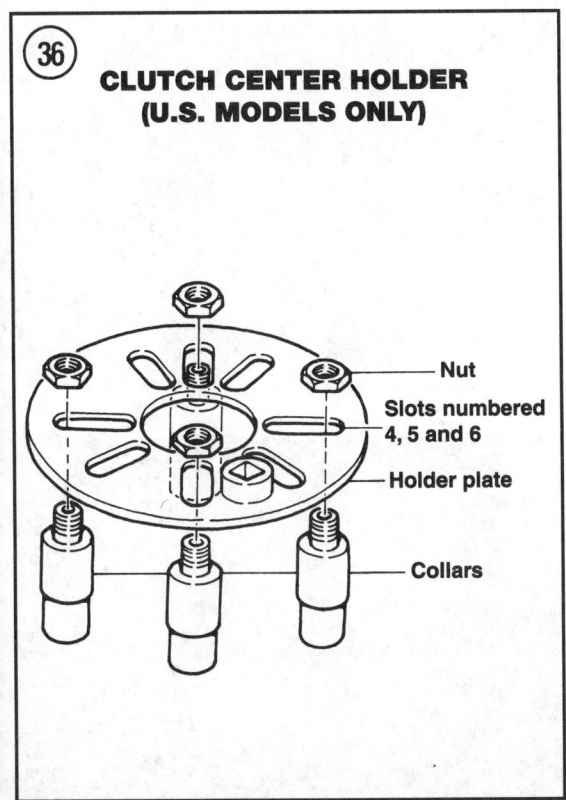

**CLUTCH CENTER HOLDER
(U.S. MODELS ONLY)**

— Nut

— Slots numbered 4, 5 and 6

— Holder plate

— Collars

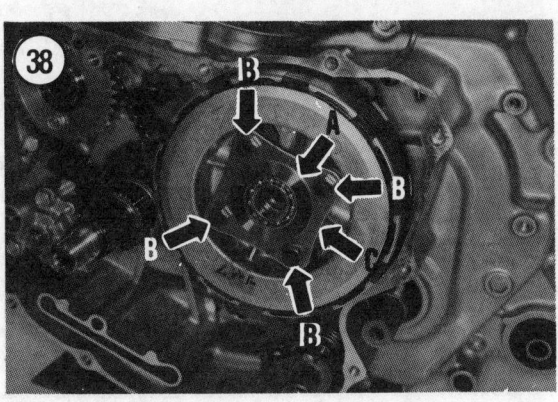

Refer to **Figure 35** when servicing the change clutch assembly.

**Special Tools and Replacement Parts**

Before you remove the clutch locknut, note the following:

1. The clutch locknut (6, **Figure 35**) is staked to a notch in the mainshaft. Purchase a new locknut for reassembly.

2. When loosening and tightening the clutch locknut (6, **Figure 35**), some means of holding the change clutch will be required. The following list suggests methods for the home mechanic:

  a. The Honda clutch center holder (part No. 07JMB-MN50300 [**Figure 36**]) is designed to hold the clutch when loosening and tightening the clutch locknut.

  b. An air impact wrench and air compressor. This tool setup can be used to loosen the clutch locknut. However, when tightening the locknut during clutch assembly, a separate tool setup will be required to hold the clutch so that the clutch locknut can be tightened with a torque wrench. See sub-step c.

  c. A method that works well when tightening the clutch locknut is to use a separate gear to lock the clutch outer gear to the primary drive gear. The text photos show a gear from the Kawasaki gear holder tool set (Kawasaki part No. 57001-1015 [**Figure 37**]). This gear and its use is described under *Clutch Installation* in this section.

**Removal/Disassembly**

1. Remove the clutch lever assembly as described in this chapter.

2. Remove the centrifugal clutch as described in this chapter.

3. Remove the lifter bearing and holder (A, **Figure 38**).

4. Loosen the lifter plate bolts (B, **Figure 38**) 1/4 turn at a time in a crisscross pattern. Then remove the bolts (B), lifter plate (C) and clutch springs.

> *NOTE*
> *If you do not intend to service the clutch plates, keep the clutch assembled with a clutch spring, flat washer and clutch bolt as shown in A, Figure 39.*

*CAUTION*
*Be sure to unstake the clutch locknut where it contacts the mainshaft. This will prevent the nut from damaging the mainshaft threads as the nut is being removed.*

5. Using a die grinder, unstake the clutch locknut from the groove in the mainshaft (B, **Figure 39**). Cover the parts so that metal particles do not enter the clutch or engine.

6. Lock the clutch center using one of the methods listed under *Special tools and Replacement parts* in this section. Then loosen and remove the clutch locknut and washer.

*NOTE*
***Figure 40*** *shows the Honda clutch center tool being used.*

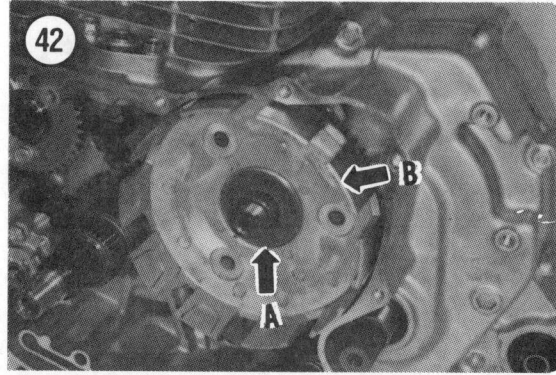

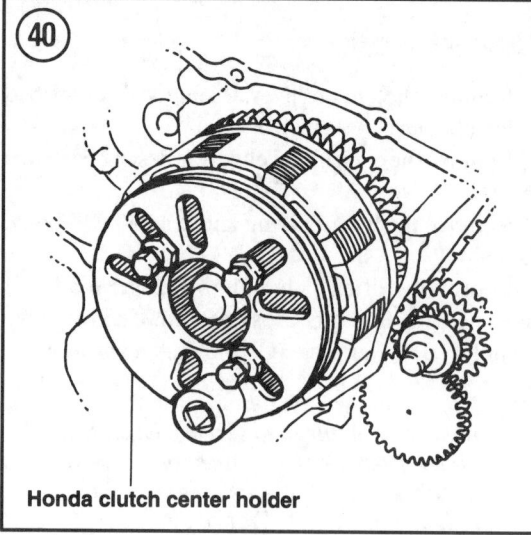

**Honda clutch center holder**

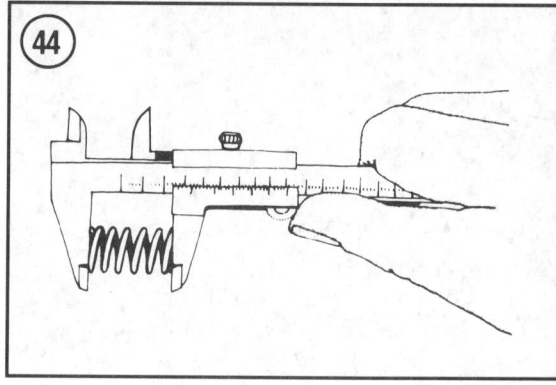

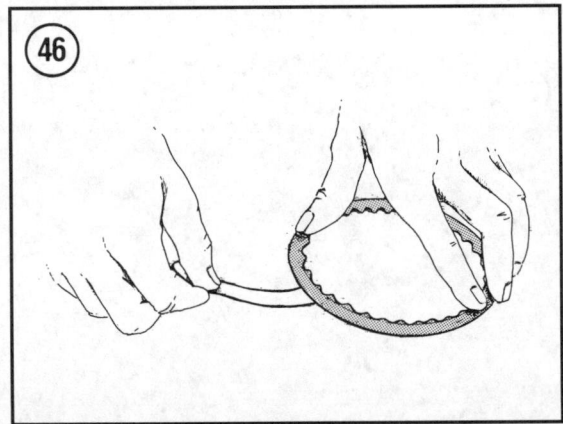

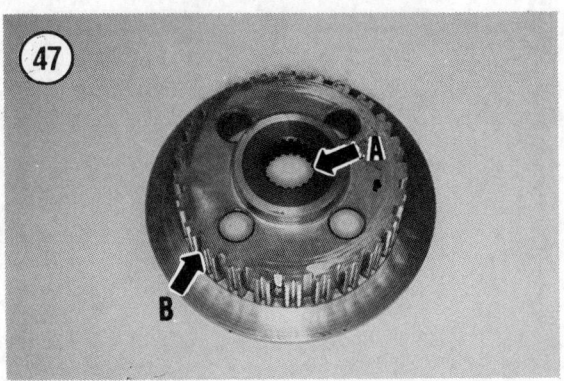

7. Remove the clutch center, clutch plates and pressure plate assembly (**Figure 41**).

8. Remove the flat washer (A, **Figure 42**), clutch outer (B, **Figure 42**) and the outer guide (**Figure 43**).

### Inspection

Refer to **Table 3** when measuring the change clutch components (**Figure 35**) in this section. Replace parts that are out of specification or show damage.

1. Clean all parts in solvent and dry with compressed air.

2. Measure the free length of each clutch spring (**Figure 44**) with a vernier caliper. Replace the springs as a set if any spring is too short.

3. Measure the thickness of each friction plate at several places around the plate (**Figure 45**). Replace all friction plates as a set if any one plate is too thin or damaged. Do not replace only one or two plates.

4. Place each clutch metal plate on a surface plate or a thick piece of glass and measure warpage with a feeler gauge (**Figure 46**). Replace if out of specification.

5. Check the clutch center splines (A, **Figure 47**) and plate grooves (B, **Figure 47**) for cracks or excessive wear.

6. Check the clutch outer slots (A, **Figure 48**) for grooves, steps, cracks or other damage. These slots must be smooth for proper clutch operation. Repair light damage with a fine-cut file or oilstone. Replace the clutch outer if the damage is non-repairable.

7. Check the clutch outer bore (B, **Figure 48**) for excessive wear or damage.

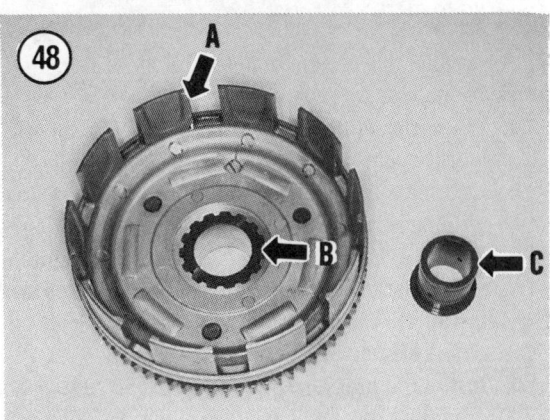

8. Check the clutch outer gear for damaged gear teeth.

9. Check the clutch outer guide (C, **Figure 48**) inside and outside surfaces for cracks, deep scoring or other damage. If there is no visible damage, measure the clutch outer guide (C, **Figure 48**) inside and outside diameters. Replace if either dimension is out of specification.

10. Measure the mainshaft diameter where the clutch outer guide operates (**Figure 49**). Replace the mainshaft if out of specification.

11. Check the pressure plate (**Figure 50**) for thread damage, cracked spring towers or other damage.

12. Check the lifter bearing (**Figure 51**) by turning its inner race. The bearing should turn smoothly with no signs of roughness or damage.

13. Check the holder and lifter plate (**Figure 51**) for damage.

### Assembly /Installation

Refer to **Figure 35** when assembling and installing the change clutch assembly.

1. Lubricate the mainshaft and all clutch parts with engine oil.

> *CAUTION*
> *Never assemble the clutch without lubricating the clutch plates with oil, especially if the clutch was cleaned in solvent or new plates are being installed. Otherwise, these plates may grab and lock up when the engine is first started and cause clutch damage.*

> *NOTE*
> *If you did not separate the clutch plates from the clutch center and clutch outer, go to Step 3.*

2. Assemble the clutch plates, clutch center, and pressure plate as follows:

   a. Place the clutch center (**Figure 47**) on the workbench.

   b. Lubricate the friction and clutch metal plates with engine oil.

   c. Install a friction plate, then install a clutch metal plate. Continue until all of the plates are installed. The last plate installed is a friction plate (**Figure 52**).

   d. Install the pressure plate (**Figure 53**) and seat it against the outer friction plate. Check that

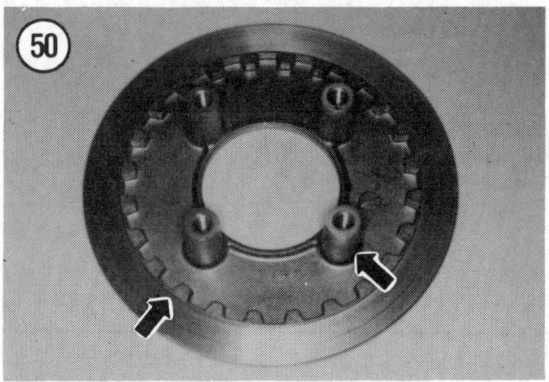

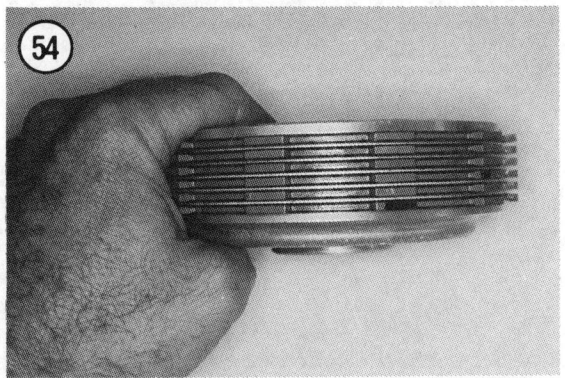

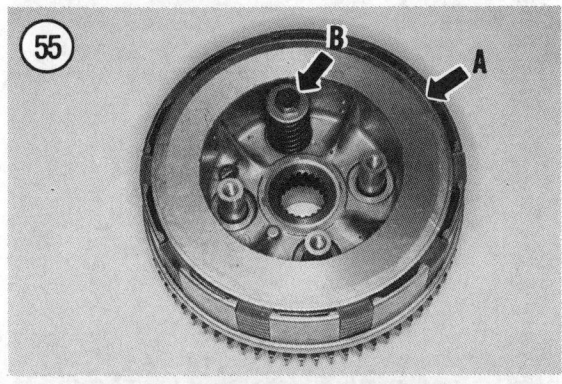

the friction plate tabs engage with the clutch center splines and that the clutch center sits flush against the friction plate as shown in **Figure 54**.

*NOTE*
*Substep e will align the clutch plates with the clutch center. Aligning the clutch plates now will make it easier to install the clutch plate assembly later in this procedure.*

e. Align the friction plates with the clutch outer, then install the clutch plate assembly into the clutch outer (A, **Figure 55**).

f. After you properly align all of the friction plates, install one clutch spring, a flat washer and clutch spring bolt as shown in B, **Figure 55**. Tighten the bolt to hold the clutch plate assembly together, then remove the clutch plate assembly from the clutch outer housing.

g. Check again that you properly aligned all of the friction plates and that the pressure plate seats flush against the outer friction plate (**Figure 54**).

h. Set the clutch plate assembly aside until installation.

3. If removed, install the primary drive gear and its washer as described in this chapter.

4. Slide the clutch outer guide—shoulder side facing in—onto the mainshaft (**Figure 43**).

5. Install the clutch outer (B, **Figure 42**) over the mainshaft and seat it onto the clutch outer guide.

6. Install the large washer (A, **Figure 42**) over the mainshaft and seat it against the clutch outer.

7. Mesh the clutch center (**Figure 41**) with the mainshaft splines and slide the clutch center into the clutch outer. See **Figure 39**.

8. Install the lockwasher (7, **Figure 35**) over the mainshaft and seat it against the clutch center.

9. Using one of the tools described under *Special Tools and Replacement Parts*, lock the clutch center to the clutch outer. Note the following:

a. If you use a gear to lock the clutch outer to the primary drive gear, install two or more clutch springs, flat washers and bolts (5, **Figure 39**) to prevent the clutch center from slipping when you tighten the clutch locknut.

b. **Figure 56** shows the accessory gear used to lock the clutch outer to the primary drive gear.

6

c. When using the Honda clutch center holder tool (**Figure 40**), first remove the clutch bolt, washer and clutch spring set that you installed during Step 2.

10. Tighten the change clutch locknut (B, **Figure 39**) as specified in **Table 4**.

11. Remove the tool setup installed in Step 9.

12. Using a punch (**Figure 57**), stake the locknut shoulder into the mainshaft notch. See **Figure 58**.

13. Remove the clutch spring bolts and flat washers if you have not already done so.

14. Install the clutch springs (**Figure 59**).

15. Install the lifter plate (A, **Figure 60**) with its OUT mark facing out.

16. Install the four clutch spring bolts (B and C, **Figure 60**) and tighten hand-tight in the following order:

    a. First tighten the two bolts (adjacent to the index marks on the lifter plate (B, **Figure 60**) to center the lifter plate.

    b. Tighten the remaining two bolts (C, **Figure 60**) until the lifter plate is flat against all four clutch springs.

c. Finally tighten all four clutch spring bolts as specified in **Table 4**.

17. Install the holder (A, **Figure 61**) and lifter bearing (B, **Figure 61**). Lubricate the lifter bearing with oil.

18. Install the centrifugal clutch as described in this chapter.

19. Install the clutch lever assembly as described in this chapter.

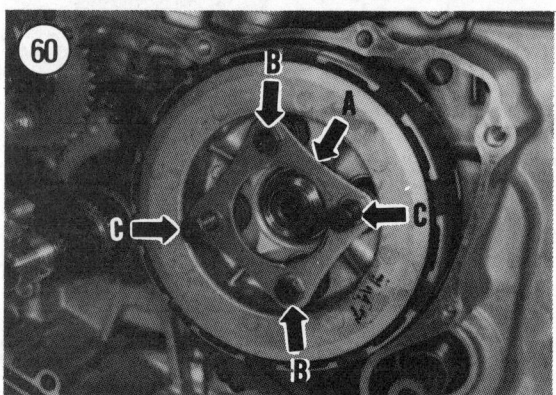

### Table 1 CENTRIFUGAL CLUTCH SERVICE SPECIFICATIONS

| | New mm (in.) | Service limit mm (in.) |
|---|---|---|
| Clutch drum inside diameter | 140.0-140.2 (5.51-5.52) | 140.4 (5.53) |
| Weight lining thickness | 3.0 (01.12) | 2.0 (0.08) |
| Clutch spring height | 3.1 (0.12) | 2.95 (0.116) |
| Clutch weight spring free length | 21.6 (0.85) | 22.5 (0.89) |

### Table 2 PRIMARY DRIVE GEAR SERVICE SPECIFICATIONS

| | New mm (in.) | Service limit mm (in.) |
|---|---|---|
| Crankshaft outside diameter at drive gear | 26.959-26.980 (1.0614-1.0622) | 26.93 (1.060) |
| Primary drive gear bushing inside diameter | 27.000-27.021 (1.0630-1.0638) | 27.05 (1.065) |

### Table 3 CHANGE CLUTCH SERVICE SPECIFICATIONS

| | New mm (in.) | Service limit mm (in.) |
|---|---|---|
| Clutch spring free length | 32.1 (1.26) | 31.0 (1.22) |
| Friction plate thickness | 2.62-2.78 (0.103-0.109) | 2.3 (0.09) |
| Clutch metal plate warpage limit | — | 0.20 (0.008) |
| Clutch outer guide | | |
| Outside diameter | 27.959-27.980 (1.1007-1.1016) | 27.92 (1.099) |
| Inside diameter | 22.000-22.021 (0.8661-0.8670) | 22.05 (0.868) |
| Mainshaft outside diameter at outer guide | 21.972-21.993 (0.8650-0.8659) | 21.93 (0.863) |

### Table 4 CLUTCH TIGHTENING TORQUES

| | N·m | in.-lb. | ft.-lb. |
|---|---|---|---|
| Centrifugal clutch locknut | 120 | — | 89 |
| Change clutch locknut | 110 | — | 81 |
| Clutch spring bolts | 12 | 106 | — |

6

**CHAPTER SEVEN**

# TRANSMISSION AND INTERNAL SHIFT MECHANISM

A 5-speed transmission with reverse is used on all models. You must remove the engine and split the crankcase (Chapter Five) to service the transmission and internal shift mechanism.

**Table 1** lists transmission gear ratios. **Tables 2-5** list transmission and shift fork service specifications. **Tables 1-5** are found at the end of the chapter.

## TRANSMISSION/REVERSE SYSTEM IDENTIFICATION

This chapter describes service to the forward and reverse transmission assemblies identified in **Figure 1**:

a. Mainshaft.

b. Countershaft.

c. Reverse idle gear shaft.

d. Shift fork shaft and shift forks.

e. Shift drum.

## TRANSMISSION TROUBLESHOOTING

Refer to Chapter Two.

## TRANSMISSION OVERHAUL

### Removal/Installation

Remove and install the transmission and internal shift assemblies as described under *Crankcase Disassembly and Crankcase Assembly* in Chapter Five.

### Transmission Service Notes

1. Parts with two different sides (such as gears, circlips and shift forks) can be installed backward. To maintain the correct alignment and position of the parts during disassembly, store each part in order and in a divided container.

2. The mainshaft circlip is a tight fit on the shaft and can bend and twist during removal. Install a new circlip during assembly.

3. To prevent bending and twisting the new circlip when you install it, use the following installation technique: open the new circlip with a pair of circlip pliers while holding the back of the circlip with a pair of pliers (**Figure 2**). Then slide the circlip down the shaft and seat it into its correct transmission groove.

## Mainshaft
## Disassembly/Assembly

Refer to **Figure 3** for this procedure.

1. Clean and dry the assembled mainshaft (**Figure 4**).
2. Remove the flat washer.
3. Remove fifth gear and its bushing.
4. Remove the flat washer.
5. Remove third gear.
6. Remove the circlip and spline washer. Discard the circlip.
7. Remove fourth gear and its bushing.

*NOTE*
*Mainshaft second and first gears are an integral part of the mainshaft.*

8. Inspect the mainshaft assembly as described under *Transmission Inspection* in this chapter.
9. Lubricate all sliding surfaces with engine oil.
10. Install fourth gear (A, **Figure 5**) and its bushing (B, **Figure 5**). The gear dogs on fourth gear (C, **Figure 5**) must face away from first gear (D, **Figure 5**).

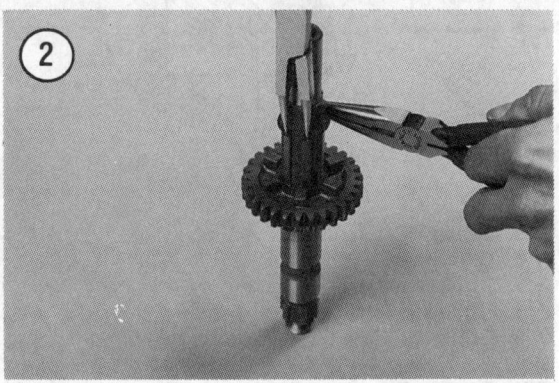

*NOTE*
*In Step 11, install the spline washer and circlip with their flat edge facing away from fourth gear as shown in* **Figure 3**.

11. Install the spline washer (A, **Figure 6**) and a new circlip (B, **Figure 6**). Seat the circlip in the groove next to fourth gear (**Figure 7**). Align the circlip gap with the shaft groove (**Figure 8**).
12. Install third gear with its shift fork groove (**Figure 9**) facing away from fourth gear.

*NOTE*
*The two thrust washers installed in Step 13 are identical (7,* **Figure 3**). *Install both thrust washers with their flat side facing away from fifth gear as shown in* **Figure 3**.

13. Install the first thrust washer (A, **Figure 10**), fifth gear bushing (B), fifth gear (C) and the second thrust washer (D). Install fifth gear with its protruding shoulder facing toward third gear.

## Countershaft
## Disassembly/Assembly

Refer to **Figure 11** for this procedure.

*NOTE*
*The copper washer, first gear and first gear bushing (**Figure 12**) were originally removed during transmission removal (Chapter Five).*

1. Clean and dry the assembled countershaft (**Figure 12**).
2. A number of parts on the countershaft are symmetrical. This means they can be installed with either side facing in either direction. However, on a well-used transmission, a wear pattern will have developed on some of these parts. To prevent excessive wear or transmission noise after reassembling the transmission mark these parts with a grease pencil so that they can be installed facing in their original operating position:
  a. Spline collar (4, **Figure 11**).
  b. Reverse shifter (5).
  c. Spline bushing (7).
  d. Spline collar (9).
  e. Spline bushing (12).
  f. Collar (13).
  g. Fifth gear (14).

7

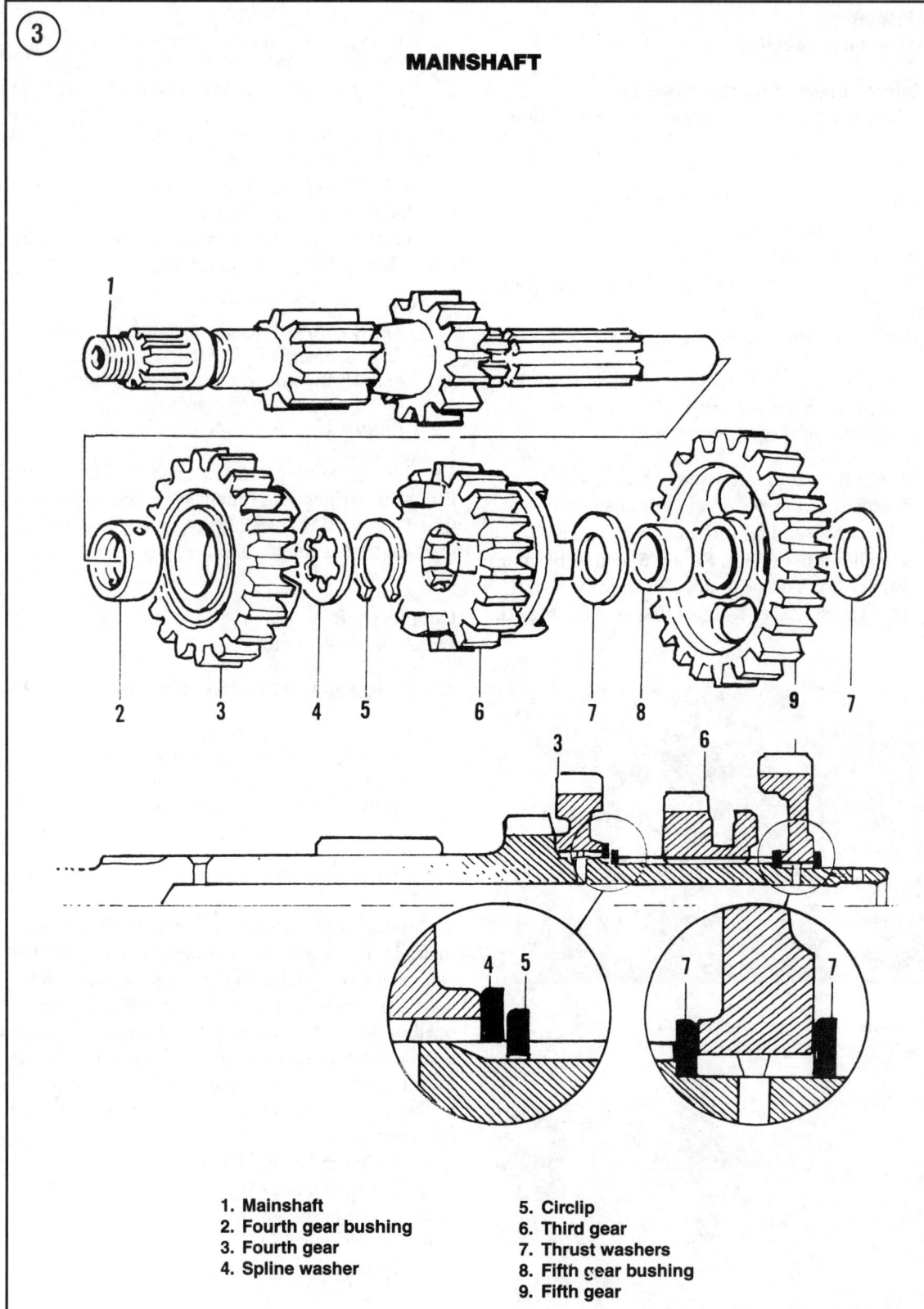

**MAINSHAFT**

1. Mainshaft
2. Fourth gear bushing
3. Fourth gear
4. Spline washer
5. Circlip
6. Third gear
7. Thrust washers
8. Fifth gear bushing
9. Fifth gear

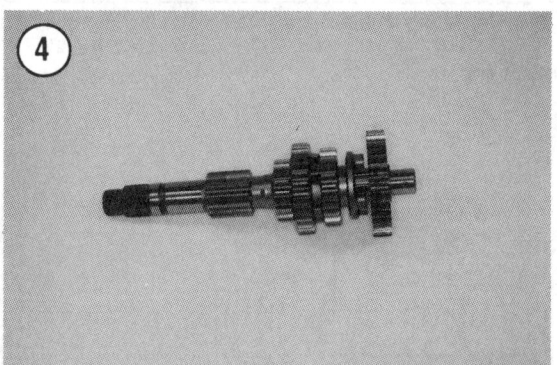

h. Final drive gear (15).

*NOTE*
*The special washer (17, **Figure 11**) is a press fit onto the rear end of the countershaft. This washer holds the gears in place when the countershaft is installed into the crankcase during engine reassembly. If the special washer is removed, install a new one during reassembly.*

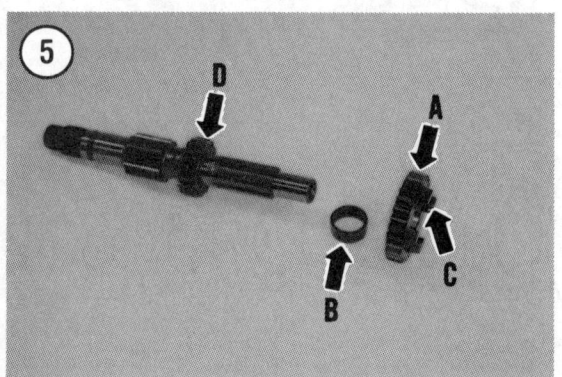

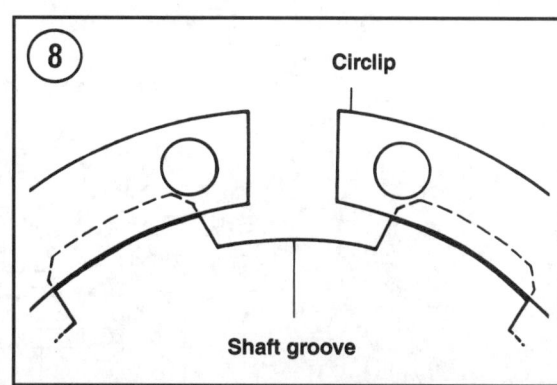

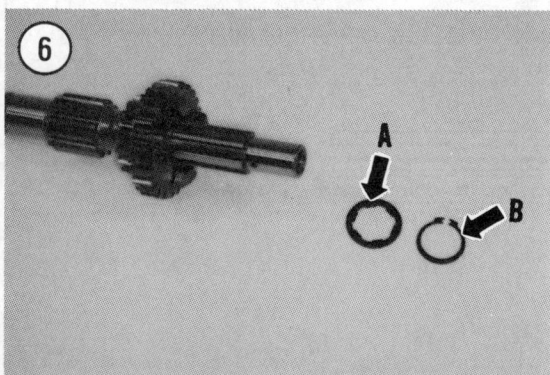

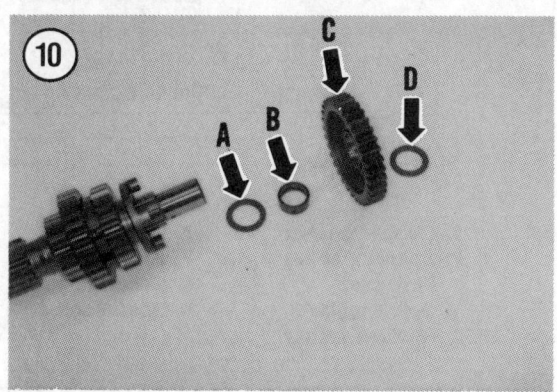

7

⑪

# COUNTERSHAFT

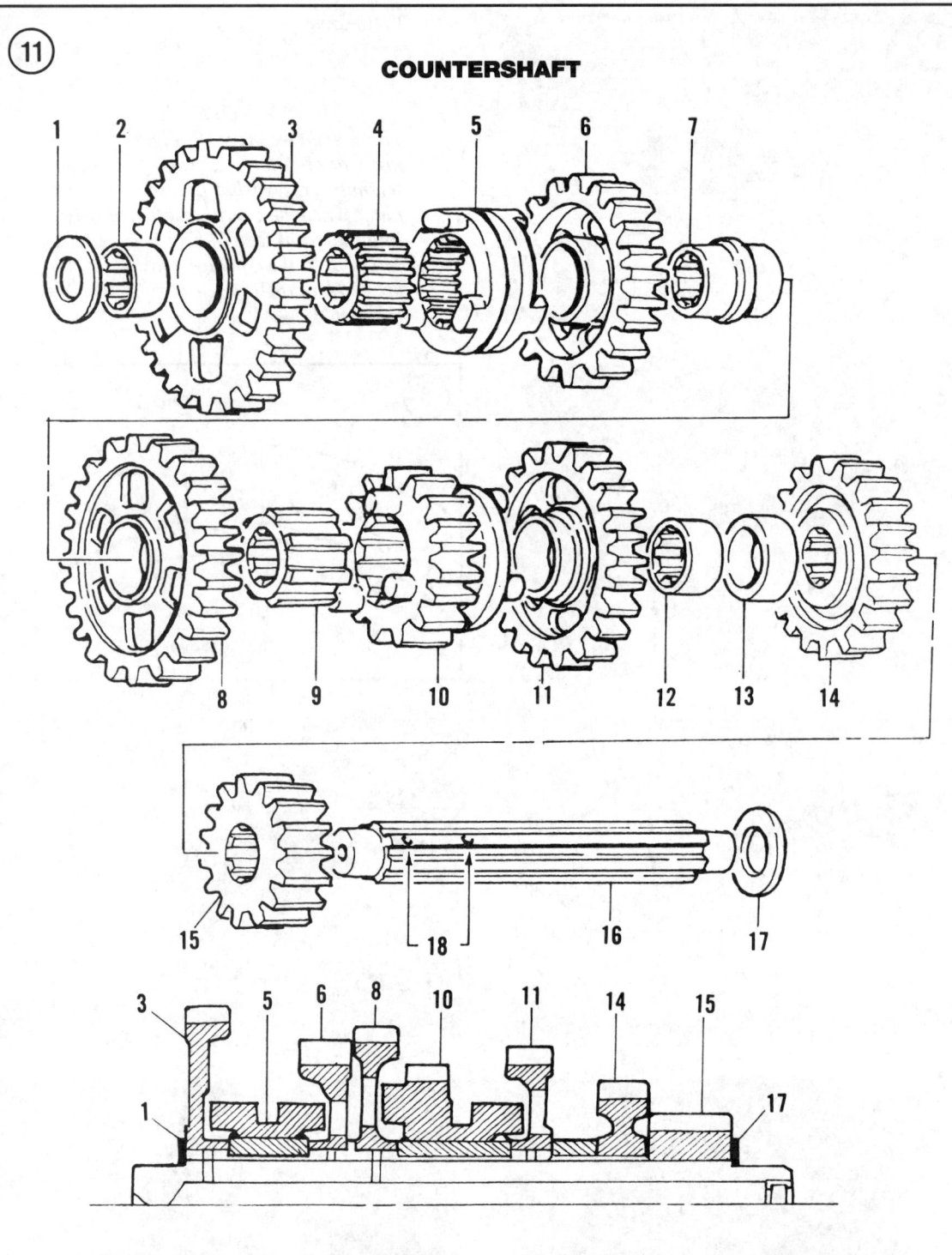

1. Copper washer
2. Spline bushing
3. First gear
4. Spline collar
5. Reverse shifter

6. Reverse gear
7. Spline bushing
8. Second gear
9. Spline collar

10. Fourth gear
11. Third gear
12. Spline bushing
13. Collar
14. Fifth gear

15. Final drive gear
16. Countershaft
17. Special washer
18. Oil holes

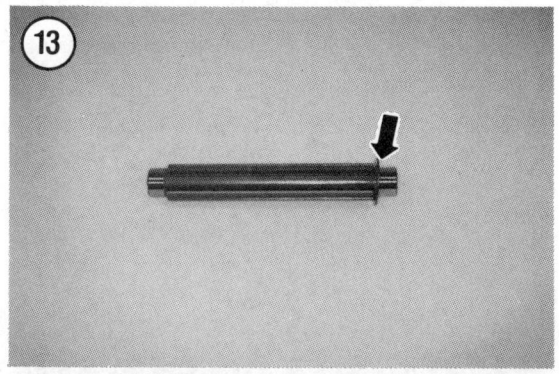

3. Remove the reverse shifter and its spline collar.

4. Remove the reverse gear, spline, bushing and second gear.

5. Remove fourth gear and its spline collar.

6. Remove third gear and its spline bushing.

7. Remove the collar, fifth gear and final drive gear.

8. Service the special washer (**Figure 13**) as follows:

   a. Unless you are going to replace the special washer or countershaft, leave it on the end of the countershaft.

   b. If you are going to replace the special washer or countershaft, carefully remove the special washer (**Figure 13**) from the end of the countershaft. Discard the special washer after removing it.

9. Inspect the countershaft assembly as described under *Transmission Inspection* in this chapter.

10. Lubricate all sliding surfaces with engine oil.

11. When installing the parts listed in Step 2, install them so that they face in their original operating position. Refer to the marks you made on the parts during disassembly.

*NOTE*
*If the special washer (**Figure 13**) was removed from the countershaft, a new washer must be installed on the countershaft's rear shoulder end. Because the countershaft's splines and both shoulder ends are symmetrical, the special washer can be installed incorrectly. The countershaft's rear shoulder end can be identified by the oil feed hole (**Figure 14**) machined in the end of the shaft. The front countershaft end does not have an oil feed hole.*

12. If removed, press a new special washer (**Figure 13**) onto the rear end of the countershaft. Seat the washer against the countershaft shoulder.

13. Install the final drive gear (A, **Figure 15**) and seat it against the special washer.

14. Install fifth gear (B, **Figure 15**) and seat it against the final drive gear.

15. Install the collar (A, **Figure 16**) and seat it against fifth gear.

16. Install the third gear spline bushing (B, **Figure 16**) by aligning its oil hole with the oil hole in the countershaft (C, **Figure 16**).

7

17. Install third gear (A, **Figure 17**) onto its spline bushing with its shoulder facing away from the collar (A, **Figure 16**).

18. Install the fourth gear spline collar (B, **Figure 17**) and fourth gear (C, **Figure 17**). Install fourth gear so that its shift fork groove faces toward third gear.

19. Install second gear (A, **Figure 18**) with its shoulder facing toward fourth gear, then install the combination spline bushing (B, **Figure 18**) and engage it with second gear.

20. Install the reverse gear (**Figure 19**) onto the combination spline bushing with its shoulder facing away from second gear.

21. Install the spline collar (A, **Figure 20**) and the reverse shifter (B, **Figure 20**).

22. Set the countershaft aside until transmission installation (Chapter Five).

> *NOTE*
> *The first gear bushing, first gear and copper washer will be installed during transmission installation (**Chapter Five**).*

## REVERSE IDLE GEAR ASSEMBLY

**Figure 21** shows the reverse idle gear assembly.

### Removal/Installation

Remove and install the reverse idle gear assembly as described under *Crankcase Disassembly and Crankcase Assembly* in Chapter Five.

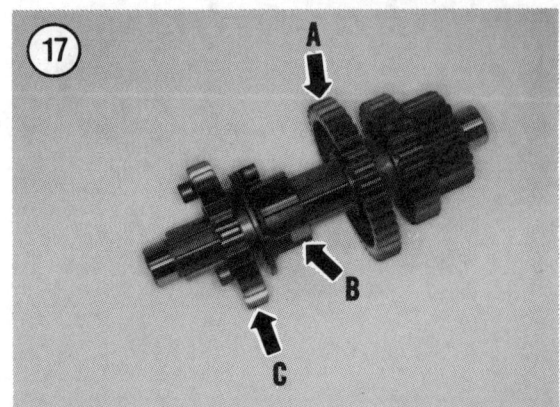

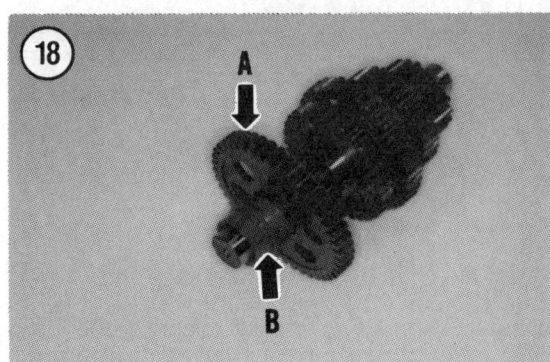

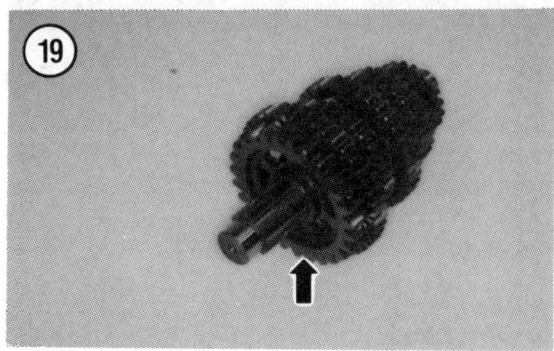

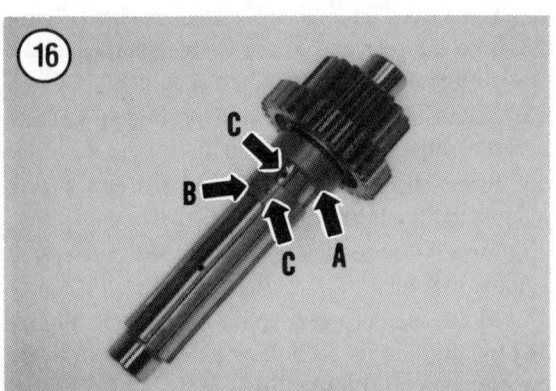

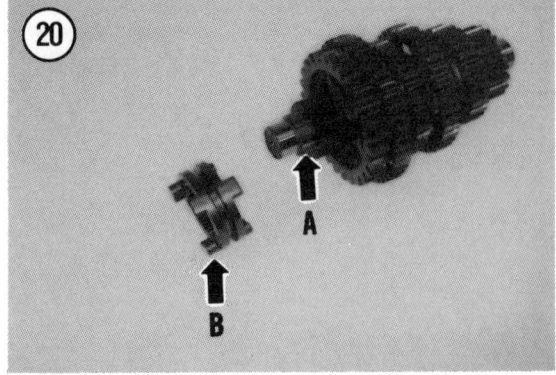

**REVERSE IDLE GEAR ASSEMBLY**

1 2 3 4 5 6

1. Thrust washer
2. Reverse idle gear
3. Bushings
4. Plain washer
5. Shaft
6. Pin

**Reverse Idle Gear Assembly
Disassembly/Reassembly**

1. Clean the assembled reverse idle gear assembly in solvent. Dry with compressed air.

2. Remove the following parts in order:

   a. Thrust washer.

   b. Reverse idle gear.

   c. Both bushings.

   d. Plain washer.

3. Inspect the reverse idle gear assembly as described under *Transmission Inspection* in this chapter.

> *NOTE*
> *Figure 22 identifies the plain (A) and thrust (B) washers. Install both washers with their chamfered side facing in toward the reverse idle gear.*

4. Install the plain washer and both bushings (**Figure 23**) onto the reverse idle gear shaft.

5. Install the reverse idle gear (**Figure 24**) with the small gear facing toward the pin in the end of the shaft.

6. Install the thrust washer (**Figure 25**) and seat it against the gear.

7

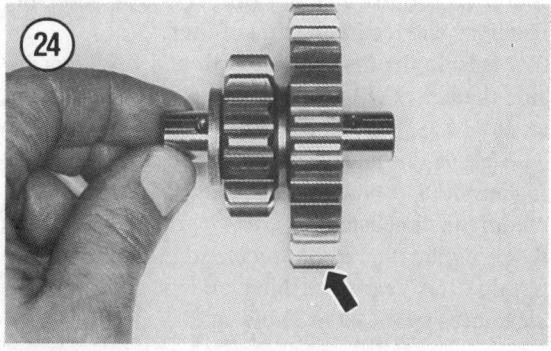

## TRANSMISSION INSPECTION

### Mainshaft
### Cleaning and Inspection

Refer to **Table 2** when measuring the mainshaft components (**Figure 26**) in this section. Replace parts that are out of specification or damaged. When replacing a gear, also replace its mating gear, even though it may not show as much wear or damage.

1. Clean and dry the mainshaft assembly.
2. Inspect the mainshaft (**Figure 27**) for:
   a. Worn or damages splines.
   b. Missing, broken or chipped first (A, **Figure 27**) and second (B) gear teeth.
   c. Excessively worn or damaged bearing surfaces.
   d. Cracked or rounded-off circlip groove.
3. Check each mainshaft gear (**Figure 26**) for:
   a. Missing, broken or chipped teeth.
   b. Worn, damaged or rounded gear lugs.
   c. Worn or damaged splines.
   d. Cracked or scored gear bore.
4. Check each mainshaft bushing for:
   a. Excessively worn or damaged bearing surface.
   b. Worn or damaged splines.
   c. Cracked or scored gear bore.
5. Measure the mainshaft outside diameter at the fourth (C, **Figure 27**) and fifth (D) gear operating positions and record the dimensions.
6. Measure the mainshaft fourth and fifth gear inside diameters (**Figure 28**) and record the dimensions.
7. Measure the mainshaft fourth and fifth gear bushing inside and outside diameters (**Figure 29**) and record the dimensions.
8. Using the dimensions recorded in Steps 5-7, determine the gear-to-bushing and bushing-to-shaft clearances specified in **Table 2**.

### Countershaft
### Cleaning and Inspection

Refer to **Table 3** when measuring the countershaft components (**Figure 30**) in this section. Replace parts that are out of specification or damaged. When replacing a gear, also replace its mating gear, even though it may not show as much wear or damage.

1. Clean and dry the countershaft assembly. Flush the oil holes with compressed air.
2. Inspect the countershaft (**Figure 31**) for:

   a. Worn or damaged splines.
   b. Worn or damaged bearing surfaces.
   c. Plugged oil holes.
3. Check each countershaft gear (**Figure 30**) for:
   a. Missing, broken or chipped teeth.
   b. Worn, damaged, or rounded gear lugs.
   c. Worn or damaged splines.
   d. Cracked or scored gear bore.
4. Check each countershaft bushing for:
   a. Worn or damaged bearing surface.

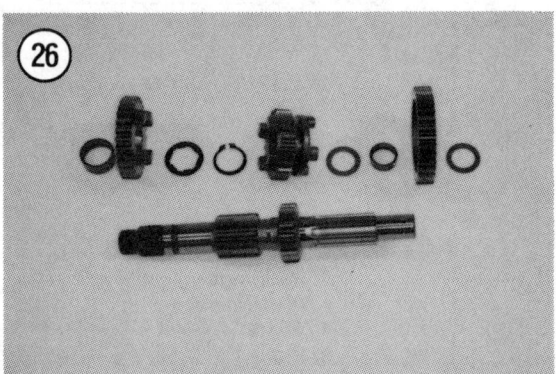

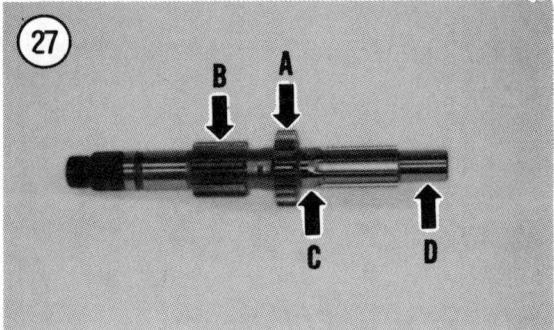

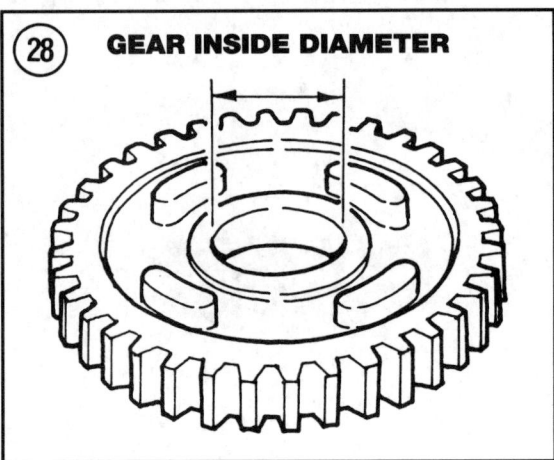

**GEAR INSIDE DIAMETER**

b. Worn or damaged splines.

c. Cracked or scored gear bore.

5. Inspect the reverse shifter for worn, damaged or rounded gear lugs. Check the splines for severe wear or damage.

6. Inspect the shifter collar and collar for excessive wear or damage.

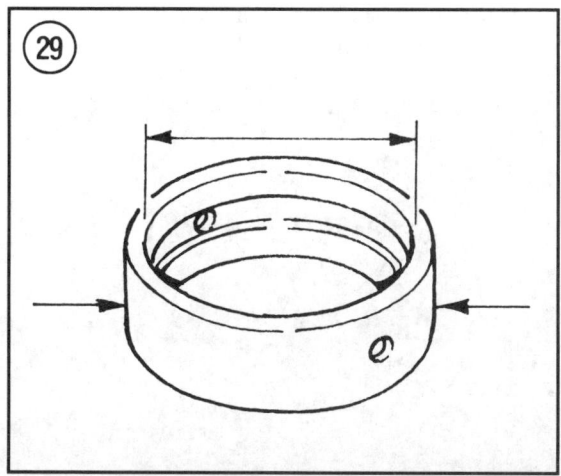

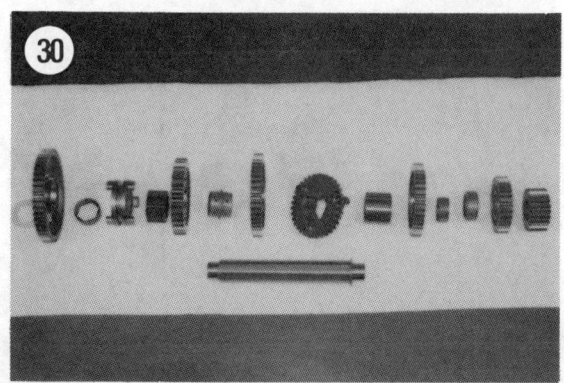

7. Measure the countershaft first, second, third and reverse gear inside diameters (**Figure 28**) and record the dimensions.

8. Measure the countershaft first, second and reverse gear bushing outside diameters (**Figure 29**) and record the dimensions.

9. Using the dimensions recorded in Step 7 and Step 8, determine the gear-to-bushing clearances specified in **Table 3**.

### Reverse Idle Gear
### Cleaning and Inspection

Refer to **Table 4** when measuring the reverse idle gear components (**Figure 21**) in this section. Replace parts that are out of specification or damaged.

1. Clean and dry the reverse idle gear assembly.

2. Check the reverse idle gear shaft (**Figure 32**) for:

a. A loose or damaged pin.

b. Cracked pin hole.

c. Cracked or damaged bearing surfaces.

3. Check the reverse idle gear (**Figure 32**) for:

a. Missing, broken or chipped teeth.

b. Cracked or scored gear bore.

4. Check each reverse idle gear bushing for:

a. Worn or damaged bearing surface.

b. Cracked or scored gear bore.

5. Measure the reverse idle gear shaft outside diameter and record the dimension.

6. Measure the reverse idle gear inside diameter (**Figure 28**) and record the dimension.

7. Measure each reverse idle gear bushing inside and outside diameters (**Figure 29**) and record the dimensions.

8. Using the dimensions recorded in Steps 5-7, determine the gear-to-bushing and bushing-to-shaft clearances specified in **Table 4**.

## INTERNAL SHIFT MECHANISM

### Removal/Installation

Remove and install the transmission assembly as described under *Crankcase Disassembly and Crankcase Assembly* in Chapter Five.

### Shift Drum Inspection

1. Clean and dry the shift drum.
2. Check the shift drum for excessively worn or damaged cam grooves (A, **Figure 33**) or bearing surfaces (B). Replace the shift drum if necessary.

### Shift Fork Inspection

Refer to **Table 5** when measuring the shift fork components (**Figure 34**) in this section. Replace parts that are out of specification or damaged.
1. Inspect each shift fork (**Figure 34**) for signs of wear or damage. Examine the shift forks at the points where they contact the slider gear (A, **Figure 35**). These surfaces must be smooth with no signs of wear, bending, cracks, heat discoloration or other damage.
2. Check each shift fork for arc-shaped wear or burn marks. These marks indicate that the shift fork has contacted the gear.
3. Check the shift fork shaft for bending or other damage. Install each shift fork on the shaft and slide it back and forth. Each shift fork must slide smoothly

with no binding or tight spots. If you notice binding with all three shift forks, check the shaft closely for bending. If you note a binding condition with one shift fork only, check the shift fork closely.
4. Measure each shift fork claw thickness (**Figure 36**).
5. Measure the shift fork inside diameter (B, **Figure 35**) with a snap gauge. Then measure the snap gauge with a micrometer.
6. Measure the shift fork shaft outside diameter at three different points on the shaft.

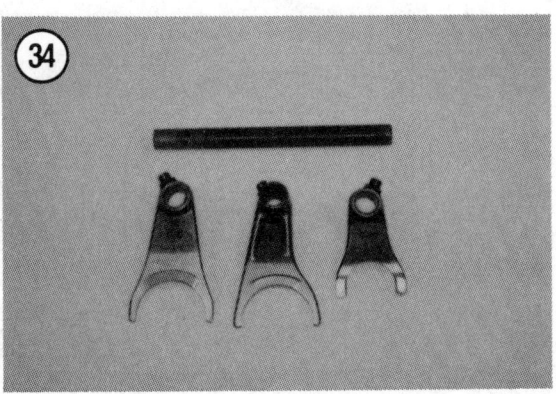

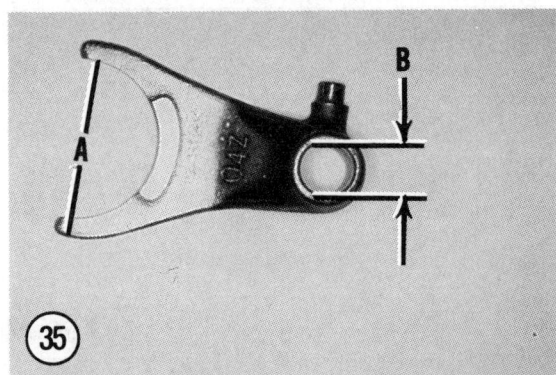

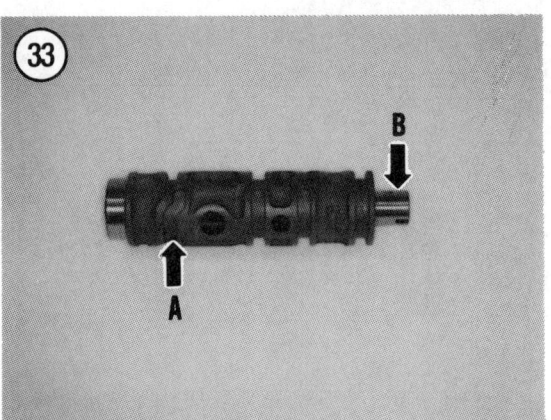

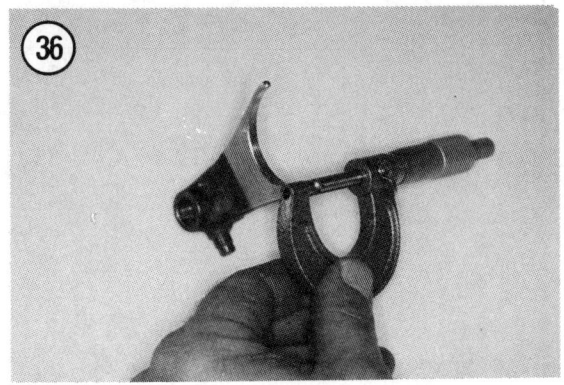

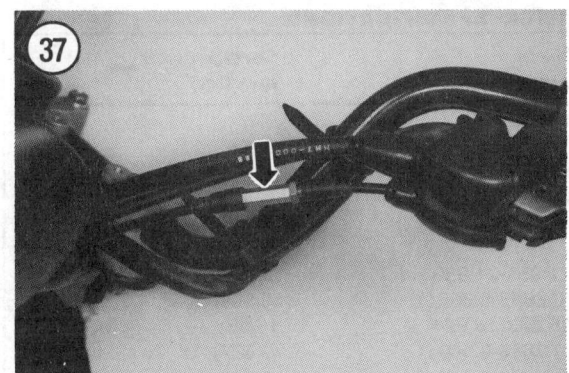

## REVERSE SELECTOR CABLE REPLACEMENT

1. Remove the handlebar cover (Chapter Fifteen).

2. Remove the fuel tank as described in this chapter.

3. Make a diagram of the reverse selector cable routing path from the handlebar to the engine.

4. Remove any cable guides from the reverse selector cable.

5. Loosen the reverse selector cable locknut and loosen the adjuster (**Figure 37**) to obtain as much cable slack as possible.

6. Disconnect the reverse selector cable (**Figure 37**) at the handlebar.

7. Disconnect the reverse selector cable from the engine (**Figure 38**).

8. Remove the reverse selector cable.

9. Reverse these steps to install the reverse selector cable, plus the following:

   a. Lubricate the new cable as described in Chapter Three.

   b. Adjust the reverse selector cable as described in Chapter Three.

**7**

Table 1 TRANSMISSION GENERAL SPECIFICATIONS

| Transmission | Constant mesh, 5-speed and reverse |
|---|---|
| Shift pattern | R-N-1-2-3-4-5 |
| Primary reduction ratio | 2.103 (61/29) |
| Secondary reduction ratio | 2.100 (42/20) |
| Final reduction ratio | |
|   Front | 3.153 (41/13) |
|   Rear | 31.53 (41/13) |
| Gear ratios | |
|   First gear (slow) | 4.083 (49/12) |
|   Second gear | 2.388 (43/18) |
|   Third | 1.608 (37/23) |
|   Fourth | 1.178 (33/28) |
|   Fifth | 0.878 (29/33) |
|   Reverse | 4.781 (34/12 × 27/16) |

Table 2 MAINSHAFT SERVICE SPECIFICATIONS

|  | New mm (in.) | Service limit mm (in.) |
|---|---|---|
| Gear inside diameter | | |
| Fourth gear | 25.000-25.021 | 25.05 |
|  | (0.9843-0.9851) | (0.986) |
| Fifth gear | 20.000-20.021 | — |
|  | (0.7874-0.7882) | |
| Mainshaft outside diameter | | |
| Fourth gear | 21.959-21.980 | 21.93 |
|  | (0.8645-0.8654) | (0.863) |
| Fifth gear | 16.983-16.994 | 16.95 |
|  | (0.6686-0.6691) | (0.667) |
| Gear bushings | | |
| Fourth gear | | |
| Inside diameter | 22.000-22.021 | 22.05 |
|  | (0.8661-0.8670) | (0.868) |
| Outside diameter | 24.959-24.980 | 24.93 |
|  | (0.9826-0.9835) | (0.981) |
| Fifth gear | | |
| Inside diameter | 17.016-17.034 | 17.06 |
|  | (0.6699-0.6706) | (0.672) |
| Outside diameter | 19.966-19.984 | 19.93 |
|  | (0.7861-0.7868) | (0.785) |
| Gear-to-bushing clearance | | |
| Fourth gear | 0.020-0.062 | 0.10 |
|  | (0.0008-0.0024) | (0.004) |
| Fifth gear | 0.016-0.055 | 0.10 |
|  | (0.0006-0.0022) | (0.004) |
| Bushing-to-shaft clearance | | |
| Fourth gear | 0.020-0.062 | 0.10 |
|  | (0.0008-0.0024) | (0.004) |
| Fifth gear | 0.022-0.051 | 0.10 |
|  | (0.0009-0.0020) | (0.004) |

Table 3 COUNTERSHAFT SERVICE SPECIFICATIONS

|  | New mm (in.) | Service limit mm (in.) |
|---|---|---|
| Gear inside diameter | | |
| First, second and third gears | 28.020-28.041 | 28.07 |
|  | (1.1031-1.1040) | (1.105) |
| Reverse gear | 28.021-28.042 | 28.07 |
|  | (1.1032-1.1040) | (1.105) |
| Gear bushing outside diameters | | |
| First gear | 27.984-28.005 | 27.93 |
|  | (1.1017-1.1026) | (1.100) |
| Second gear | 27.979-28.000 | 27.93 |
|  | (1.1015-1.1024) | (1.100) |
| Reverse gear | 27.979-28.000 | 27.93 |
|  | (1.1015-1.1024) | (1.100) |
| Gear-to-bushing clearance | | |
| First gear | 0.015-0.057 | 0.10 |
|  | (0.0006-0.0022) | (0.004) |
| Second gear | 0.020-0.062 | 0.10 |
|  | (0.0008-0.0024) | (0.004) |
| Third gear | 0.015-0.057 | 0.10 |
|  | (0.0006-0.0022) | (0.004) |
| Reverse gear | 0.020-0.062 | 0.10 |
|  | (0.0008-0.0024) | (0.004) |

## Table 4 REVERSE IDLE GEAR SERVICE SPECIFICATIONS

|  | New mm (in.) | Service limit mm (in.) |
|---|---|---|
| Reverse idle gear shaft outside diameter | 13.966-13.984 (0.5498-0.5506) | 13.93 (0.548) |
| Gear inside diameter | 18.000-18.021 (0.7087-0.7095 | 18.05 (0.711) |
| Reverse idle gear bushing | | |
| Inside diameter | 14.000-14.025 (0.5512-0.5522) | 14.05 (0.553) |
| Outside diameter | 17.966-17.984 (0.7073-0.7080) | 17.93 (0.706) |
| Gear-to-bushing clearance | 0.016-0.055 (0.0006-0.0022) | 0.10 (0.004) |
| Bushing-to-shaft clearance | 0.016-0.059 (0.0006-0.0021) | 0.10 (0.004) |

## Table 5 SHIFT FORK SERVICE SPECIFICATIONS

|  | New mm (in.) | Service limit mm (in.) |
|---|---|---|
| Shift fork claw thickness | 4.93-5.00 (0.194-0.197) | 4.50 (0.177) |
| Shift fork inside diameter | 13.000-13.021 (0.5118-0.5126) | 13.04 (0.513) |
| Shift fork shaft outside diameter | 12.966-12.984 (0.5105-0.5112) | 12.96 (0.510) |

7

# FUEL SYSTEM

The fuel system consists of the carburetor, fuel tank, fuel shutoff valve and air filter.

This chapter includes service procedures for all parts of the fuel system. Routine air filter service is covered in Chapter Three.

**Table 1** and **Table 2** lists carburetor specifications. **Tables 1-3** are at the end of the chapter.

## CARBURETOR

### Removal/Installation

1. Park the vehicle on level ground and set the parking brake.

2. Remove the seat and the right lower side cover (Chapter Fifteen).

3. Disconnect the negative battery cable at the battery (Chapter Three).

4. Loosen the front and rear carburetor hose clamps (**Figure 1**).

5. Loosen the intake air duct hose clamp.

6. Remove the air filter housing retaining clips (**Figure 2**).

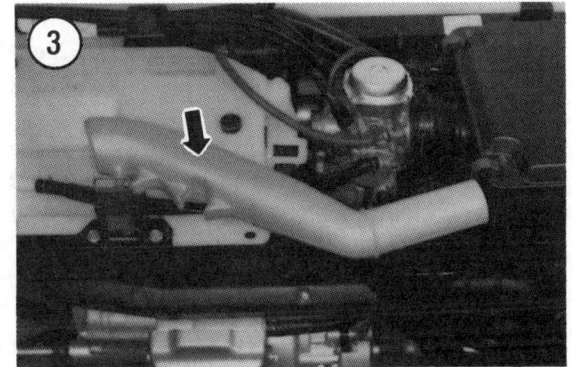

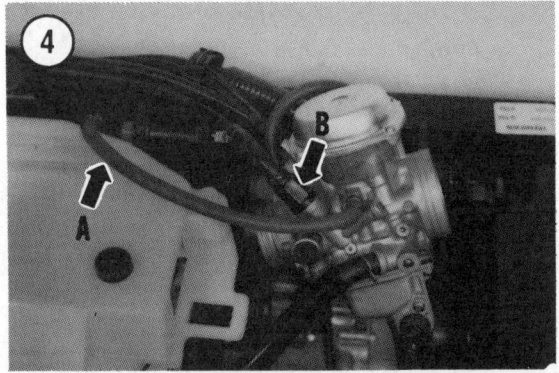

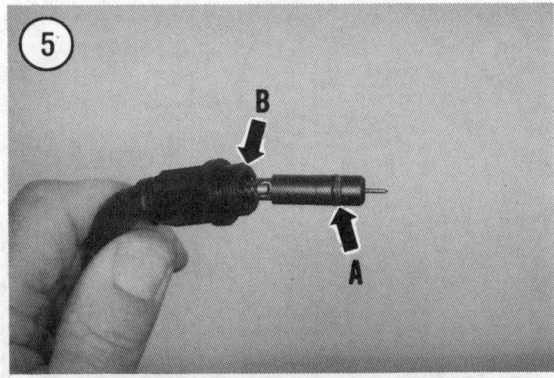

7. Pull the carburetor back to remove it from the intake manifold, then remove the intake air duct (**Figure 3**) from the air box.

8. Remove the carburetor from the air filter housing.

9. Cover the intake manifold and air filter openings.

10. Disconnect the air vent tube (A, **Figure 4**) from the heat guard.

11. Loosen the starting enrichment (SE) valve nut (B, **Figure 4**) and remove the SE valve from the carburetor. Remove the SE valve and spring (A, **Figure 5**) from the end of the choke cable to prevent their loss.

12. Disconnect the throttle cable as follows:

    a. Remove the carburetor cover screw (A, **Figure 6**) and cover (B, **Figure 6**).

    b. Slide the cover (A, **Figure 7**) away from the throttle cable adjuster at the carburetor.

    c. Loosen the throttle cable locknut and unscrew the adjuster from the carburetor.

    d. Disconnect the throttle cable (B, **Figure 7**) from the throttle drum.

13. Remove the carburetor.

14. Install the carburetor by reversing these removal steps, while noting the following:

    a. Apply a dab of grease onto the end of the throttle cable before connecting it onto the throttle drum (**Figure 7**).

    b. When connecting the throttle cable and threading the adjuster (**Figure 7**) into the carburetor, do not twist or kink the cable.

    c. Apply some multi-purpose grease into the SE valve nut at the point shown in B, **Figure 5**. Then install and tighten the SE valve nut securely. Operate the choke cable by hand, making sure the SE valve moves with no binding or roughness.

8

*CAUTION*
*Wipe off any grease that may contact the SE valve. Otherwise, the grease may plug up the choke opening and cause the system to malfunction during engine starting.*

   d. Remove the covers from the intake manifold and air box openings.

   e. Install the carburetor by aligning its intake boss with the intake manifold groove (**Figure 8**) and its locating tab with the intake manifold notch (**Figure 9**).

   f. Connect the air vent tube (A, **Figure 4**) into the hole in the heat guard.

   g. Check and adjust the throttle cable adjustment (Chapter Three).

## Disassembly

Refer to **Figure 10** for this procedure.

1. Remove the screw, air cutoff valve (**Figure 11**), air jet and O-rings.

2. Remove the hoses from the carburetor.

3. Remove the screws and top cover (**Figure 12**).

4. Remove the spring and vacuum cylinder assembly (**Figure 13**).

5. Remove the jet needle (**Figure 14**) as follows:

   a. Turn the jet needle holder (**Figure 15**) counterclockwise to release it from the vacuum cylinder.

   b. Remove the jet needle holder, spring, jet needle and washer.

*NOTE*
*Before removing the jet needle, first record the clip position and compare it to the stock clip position listed in **Table 1**.*

6. Remove the screws, primer valve assembly (**Figure 16**) and spring (**Figure 17**).

7. Remove the float bowl screws (**Figure 18**), float bowl and gasket.

8. Remove the main jet baffle (**Figure 19**).

9. Remove the float pin (**Figure 20**), float and float valve (**Figure 21**).

10. Remove the plug (**Figure 22**).

11. Remove the starter jet (**Figure 23**).

12. Remove the slow jet (**Figure 24**).

13. Remove the main jet (A, **Figure 25**).

14. Remove the needle jet holder (B, **Figure 25**).

15. Turn the carburetor so that its top side faces up and tap the body to remove the needle jet (11, **Figure 10**). If the needle jet does not fall out, gently push it out with a plastic rod.

16. While counting the number of turns, rotate the pilot screw in until lightly seated. Record the number of turns during reassembly. Back the pilot screw out and remove it from the carburetor (A, **Figure 26**).

17. Unscrew and remove the idle speed adjusting screw (A, **Figure 27**) and spring.

18. Remove the drain screw (**Figure 28**) and O-ring from the float bowl.

*NOTE*
*Further disassembly is neither necessary nor recommended. Do not remove the choke shaft or plate as these parts are not available separately.*

19. Clean and inspect all parts as described in this chapter.

## Cleaning and Inspection

1. Clean and dry the carburetor parts.

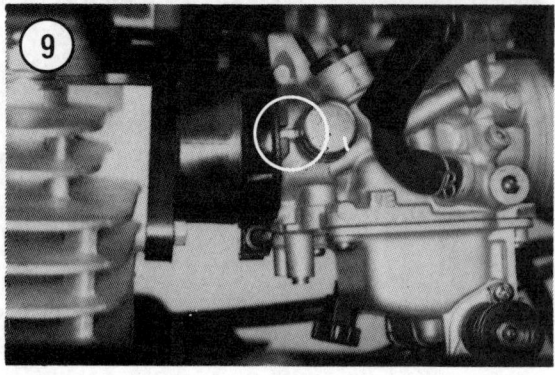

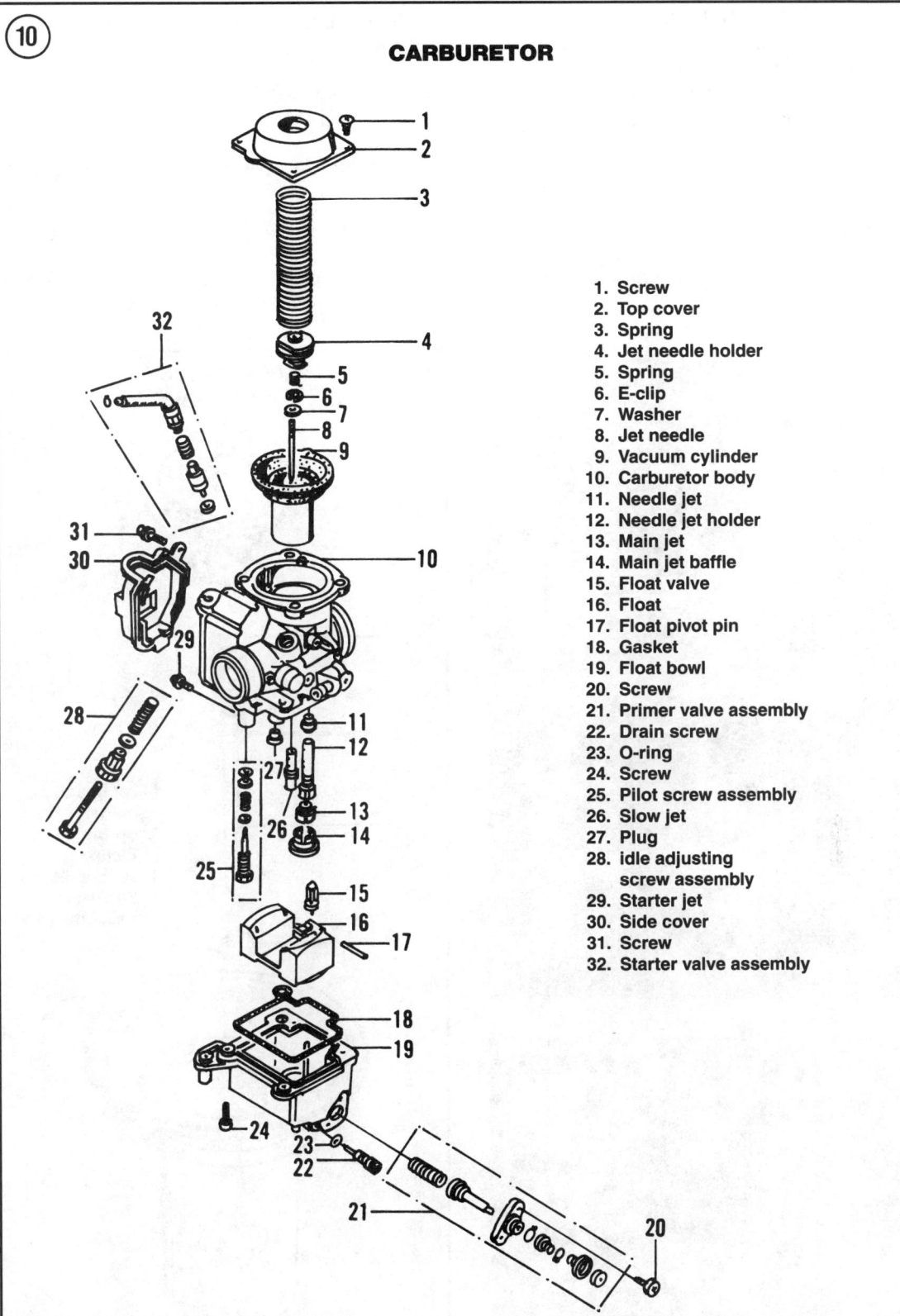

## CARBURETOR

1. Screw
2. Top cover
3. Spring
4. Jet needle holder
5. Spring
6. E-clip
7. Washer
8. Jet needle
9. Vacuum cylinder
10. Carburetor body
11. Needle jet
12. Needle jet holder
13. Main jet
14. Main jet baffle
15. Float valve
16. Float
17. Float pivot pin
18. Gasket
19. Float bowl
20. Screw
21. Primer valve assembly
22. Drain screw
23. O-ring
24. Screw
25. Pilot screw assembly
26. Slow jet
27. Plug
28. idle adjusting
    screw assembly
29. Starter jet
30. Side cover
31. Screw
32. Starter valve assembly

8

*CAUTION*
*Do not dip the carburetor body or any of the O-rings in a carburetor cleaner or other solution that will damage the rubber parts and seals.*

*CAUTION*
*Do **not** use wire or drill bits to clean jets as minor gouges in the jet can alter the flow rate and change the fuel/air mixture.*

2. Clean the float bowl overflow tube with compressed air.

3. Replace the float bowl O-ring if leaking or damaged.

4. Inspect the float valve assembly as follows:

   a. Check the end of the float valve needle (**Figure 29**) for steps, excessive wear or damage.

   b. Check the float valve seat in the carburetor for steps, uneven wear or other damage.

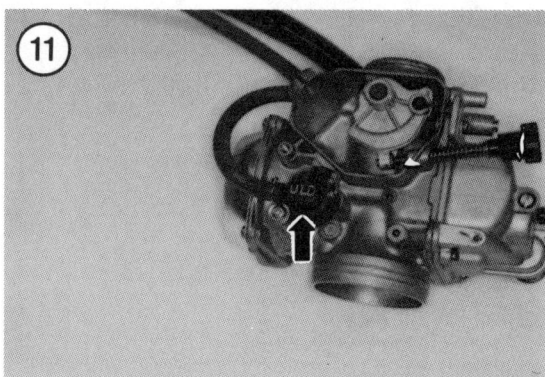

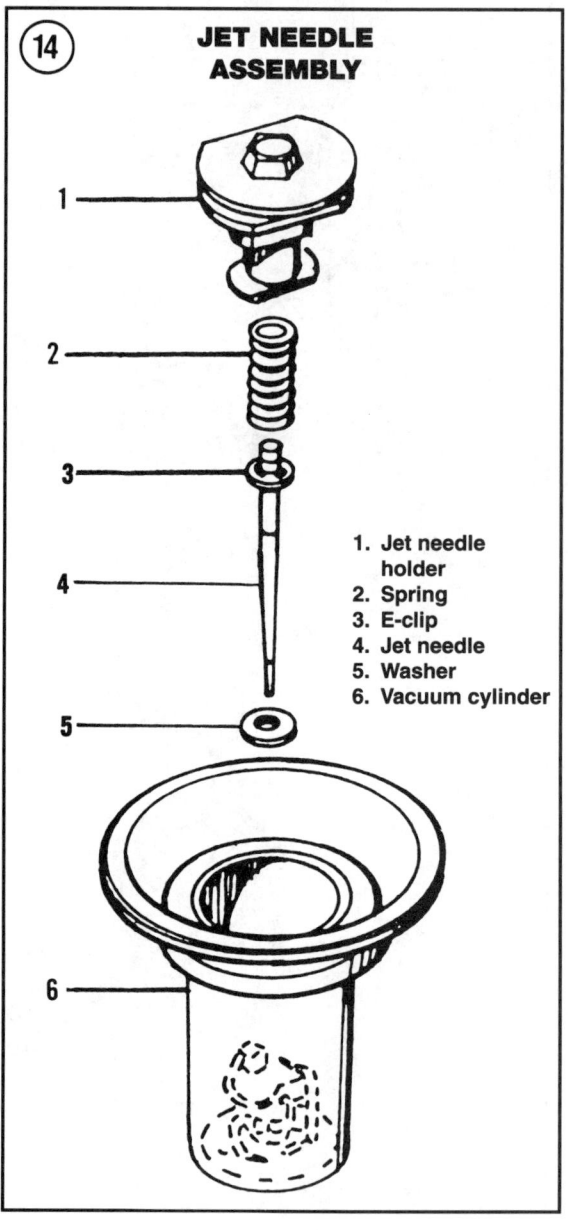

**JET NEEDLE ASSEMBLY**

1. Jet needle holder
2. Spring
3. E-clip
4. Jet needle
5. Washer
6. Vacuum cylinder

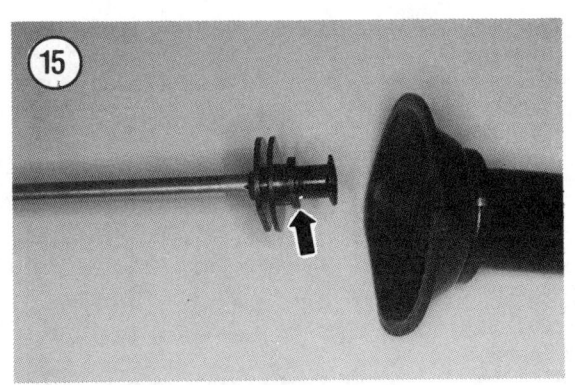

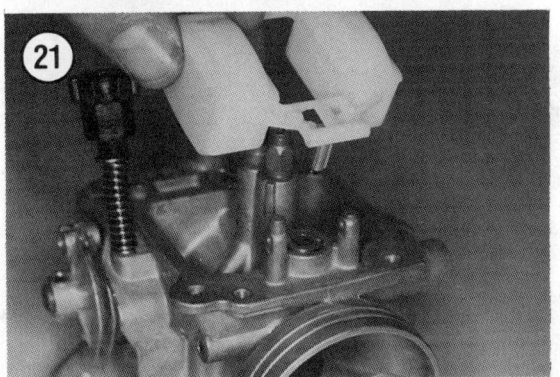

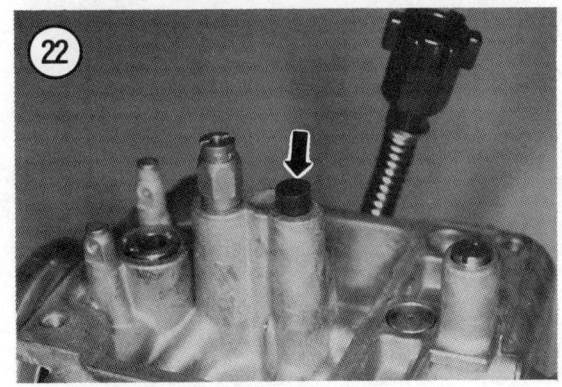

8

5. Inspect the pilot screw (**Figure 30**) and spring for damage. Replace the screw if damaged. Replace both pilot screw O-rings.

6. Inspect the float (**Figure 31**) for deterioration or damage. Check the float by submersing it in a container of water. If water enters the float, replace it.

7. Move the throttle drum from stop-to-stop and check for free movement. If it does not move freely, replace the carburetor body.

8. Make sure all openings in the carburetor body are clear. Clean with compressed air.

9. Check the vacuum cylinder diaphragm (**Figure 32**) for cracks, deterioration or other damage.

10. Check the primer valve assembly (**Figure 33**) for wear, damage or deterioration. Check the rubber diaphragm (**Figure 34**) for cracks or other damage.

11. Make sure all jet openings are clear. Replace any jet that cannot be cleaned.

### Assembly

Refer to **Figure 10** when assembling the carburetor body.

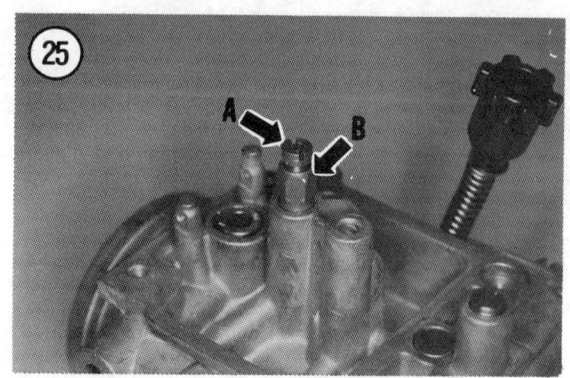

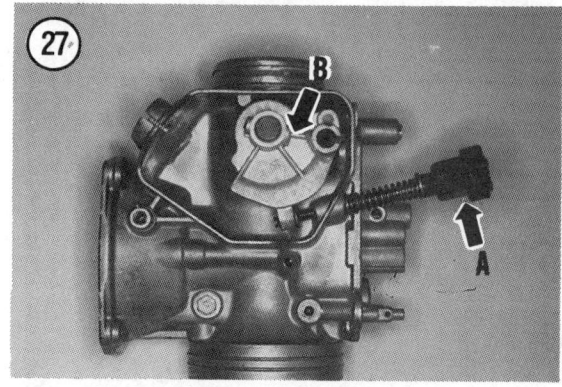

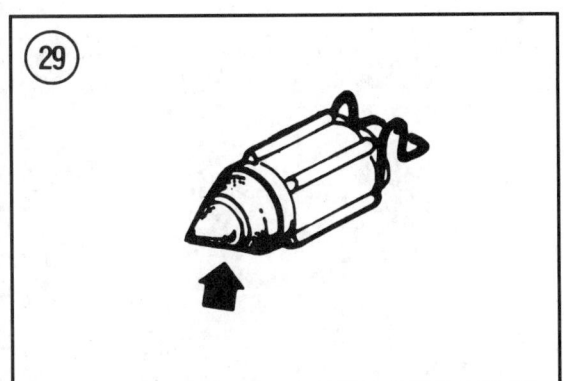

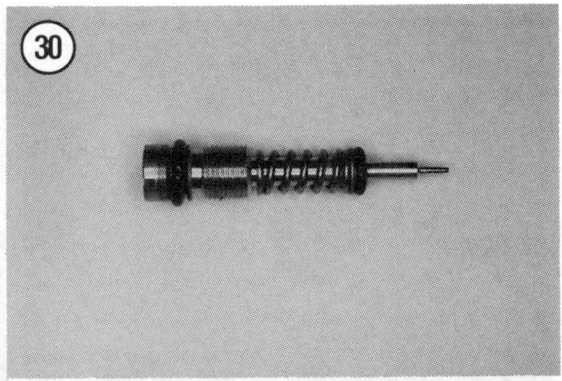

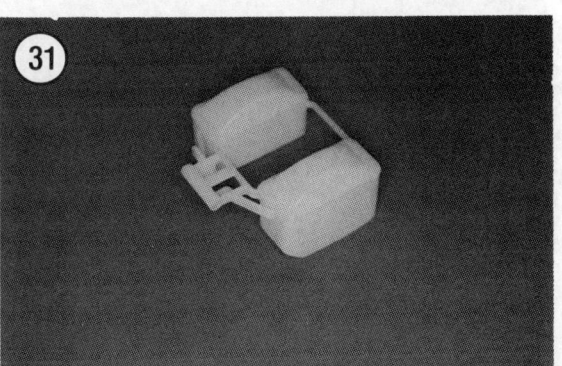

1. Install the drain screw (**Figure 28**) and O-ring into the float bowl. Tighten the drain screw securely.

2. Install the idle speed adjusting screw (A, **Figure 27**) and spring.

3. Install the two O-rings, spring and flat washer onto the pilot screw (**Figure 30**).

4. Install the pilot screw (A, **Figure 26**). Turn it in until it is lightly seated. Back the screw out the number of turns recorded during removal, or set it to the number of turns listed in **Table 1**.

5. Install the needle jet (11, **Figure 10**) with its chamfered end facing toward the needle jet holder, and install the needle jet holder. Tighten the needle jet holder (B, **Figure 25**) securely.

6. Install the main jet (A, **Figure 25**).

7. Install the slow jet (**Figure 24**).

8. Install the starter jet (**Figure 23**).

9. Install the plug (**Figure 22**).

10. Install the float valve onto the float, and then install the float valve into the float valve seat (**Figure 21**). Insert the float pin (**Figure 20**) through the pedestal arms and float.

11. Check the float level as described under *Carburetor Float Level Adjustment* in this chapter.

**8**

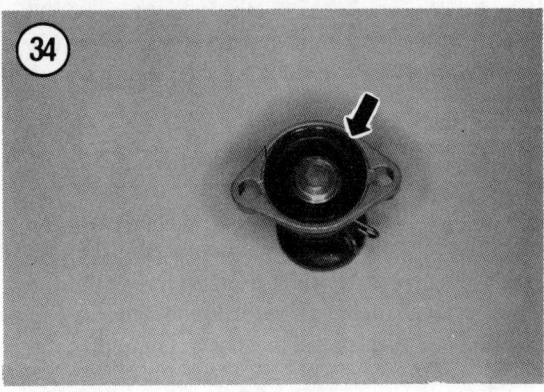

12. Install the main jet baffle (**Figure 19**).

13. Install the O-ring into the float bowl groove (**Figure 35**). Then install the float bowl and secure it with its mounting screws (**Figure 18**).

14. Install the primer valve spring (**Figure 17**) and primer valve (**Figure 16**) into the float bowl. Tighten the screws securely.

15. Assemble the vacuum cylinder and install the jet needle (**Figure 14**) as follows:

    a. If removed, install the E-clip into the jet needle clip groove recorded during disassembly or refer to the stock clip position in **Table 1**.

    b. Install the washer onto the bottom of the jet needle and seat it against the E-clip.

    c. Install the jet needle and washer (**Figure 36**) into the vacuum cylinder.

    d. Insert the spring in the end of the jet needle holder.

    e. Insert the jet needle holder (**Figure 15**) into the vacuum cylinder and turn it 90° clockwise to lock it in place.

16. Install the vacuum cylinder into the carburetor body. Align the tab on the diaphragm (**Figure 32**) with the hole (**Figure 37**) in the carburetor body.

17. Install the spring into the vacuum cylinder (**Figure 13**).

18. Align the hole in the vacuum cylinder (A, **Figure 38**) with the raised boss (B, **Figure 38**) on the top cover. Install the top cover and tighten the screws securely.

19. Connect the hoses at the carburetor. Install the overflow hose so that the one-way valve installed in the hose faces in the direction shown in **Figure 39**.

20. Install the air jet and O-rings, aircut off valve (**Figure 11**) and mounting screw. Tighten the screw securely.

21. Install the carburetor as described in this chapter.

22. Adjust the pilot screw as described under *Carburetor Adjustments* in this chapter.

## CARBURETOR FLOAT LEVEL ADJUSTMENT

The float valve and float maintain a constant fuel level in the carburetor float bowl. Because the float level affects the fuel mixture throughout the engine's operating range, this level must be maintained within factory specifications.

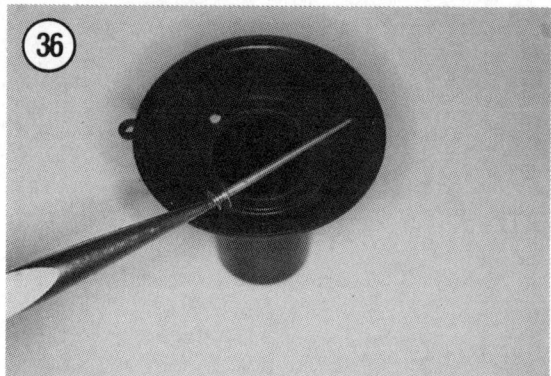

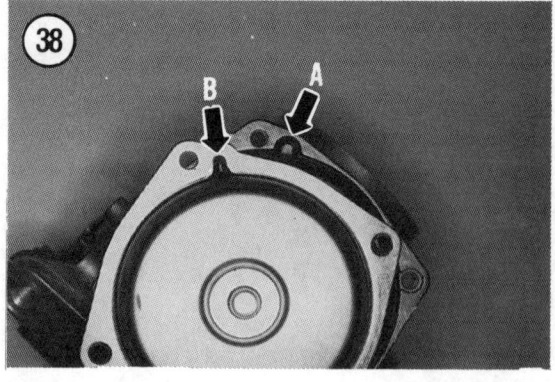

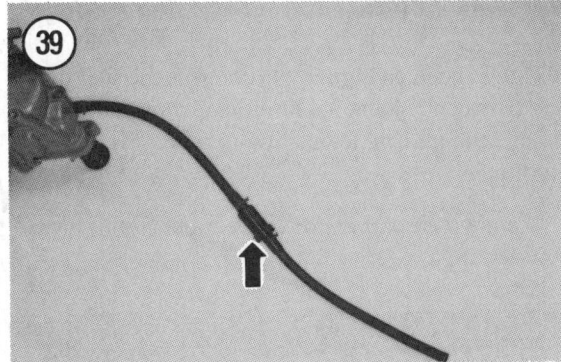

You must remove and partially disassemble the carburetor for this adjustment.

1. Remove the carburetor as described in this chapter.

2. Remove the float bowl mounting screws and float bowl (A, **Figure 40**). Do not remove the O-ring from the float bowl groove.

3. Hold the carburetor so the float valve just touches the float arm without pushing it down. Measure the distance from the carburetor body gasket surface to the float (**Figure 41**) using a float level gauge, ruler or vernier caliper. **Table 2** lists the correct float level dimension.

4. The float is non-adjustable. If the float level is incorrect, check the float pin and float valve for damage. If these parts are in good condition, replace the float and remeasure the float level.

5. Install the float bowl, O-ring and its mounting screws (A, **Figure 40**). Tighten the mounting screws securely.

6. Install the carburetor as described in this chapter.

## CARBURETOR ADJUSTMENTS

### Idle Speed Adjustment

Refer to Chapter Three.

### Pilot Screw Adjustment

The pilot screw (A, **Figure 42**) is preset at the factory. Routine adjustment is not necessary unless the pilot screw was removed or replaced or the carburetor was overhauled.

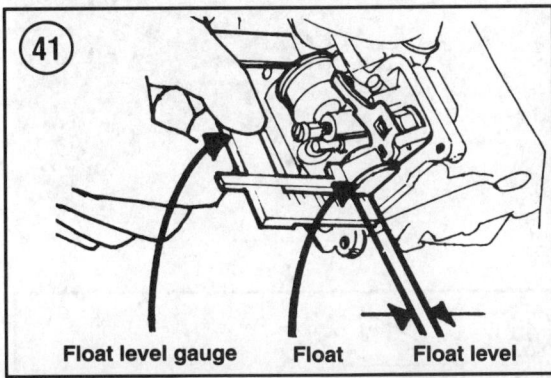

Float level gauge    Float    Float level

> *WARNING*
> *Do not run the engine in an enclosed garage or area when adjusting the pilot screw in this procedure. Doing so will cause carbon monoxide gas to build up in the garage. Dangerous levels of carbon monoxide gas will cause loss of consciousness and death in a short time.*

1. Clean the air filter as described in Chapter Three.

2. Connect a tachometer to the engine following the manufacturer's instructions.

> *NOTE*
> *To accurately detect speed changes during this adjustment, use a tachometer with graduations of 100 rpm or smaller.*

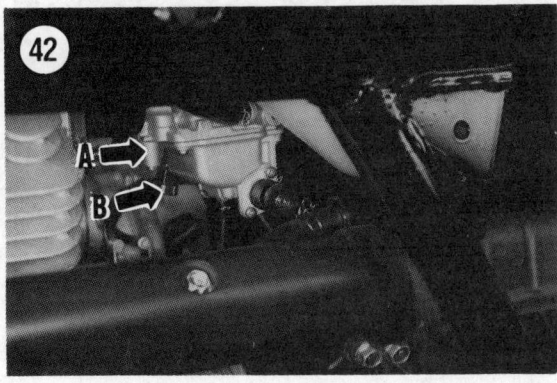

3. Turn the pilot screw (A, **Figure 42**) clockwise until it seats, then back out the number of turns listed in **Table 1** for your model.

4. Start the engine and warm to normal operating temperature.

5. Open and release the throttle lever (**Figure 43**) a few times, making sure that it returns to its closed position. If necessary, turn the engine off and adjust the throttle cable as described in Chapter Three.

6A. On 1995-1997 models, perform the following:

   a. With the engine idling, turn the throttle stop screw (B, **Figure 42**) to set the engine idle speed to the rpm listed in **Table 1**.

   b. Turn the pilot screw (A, **Figure 42**) clockwise until the engine begins to misfire or the engine speed drops, then stop and turn the screw counterclockwise until the engine again begins to misfire or the engine speed drops.

   c. Turn the pilot screw between the two adjustment positions determined in substep b.

   d. If the idle speed changed after adjusting the pilot screw, turn the idle speed screw (B, **Figure 42**) to reset the engine idle speed to the rpm listed in **Table 1**.

   e. Open and close the throttle lever a few times while checking the idle speed reading. The engine must idle within the speed range listed in **Table 1**.

6B. On 1998-on models, perform the following:

   a. With the engine idling, turn the idle speed screw (B, **Figure 42**) to set the engine idle speed to the rpm listed in **Table 1**.

   b. Turn the pilot screw (A, **Figure 42**) in or out to obtain the highest engine idle speed.

   c. Turn the idle speed screw (B, **Figure 42**) to reset the engine idle speed to the rpm listed in **Table 1**.

   d. While reading the tachometer, turn the pilot screw (A, **Figure 42**) in slowly until the engine speed drops 100 rpm.

   e. Open and close the throttle lever a few times while checking the idle speed reading. The engine must idle within the speed range listed in **Table 1**. If necessary, readjust the idle speed with the idle speed screw (B, **Figure 42**).

7. Turn the engine off and remove the tachometer.

## Jet Needle Adjustment

The jet needle (**Figure 44**) controls the fuel mixture between 1/4 and 3/4 throttle openings. You can change the jet needle position to affect the fuel/air mixture.

1. Remove the carburetor as described in this chapter.

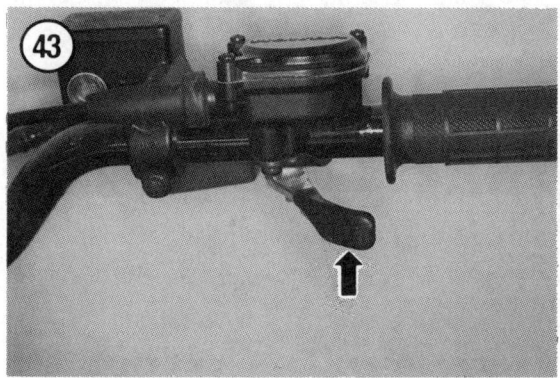

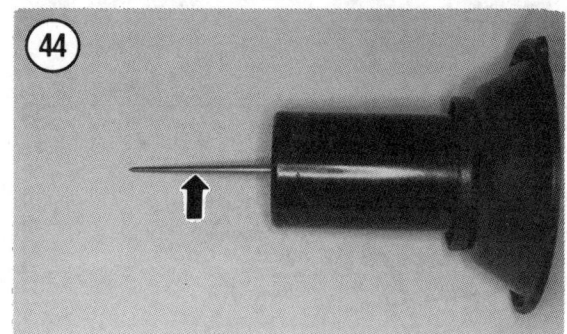

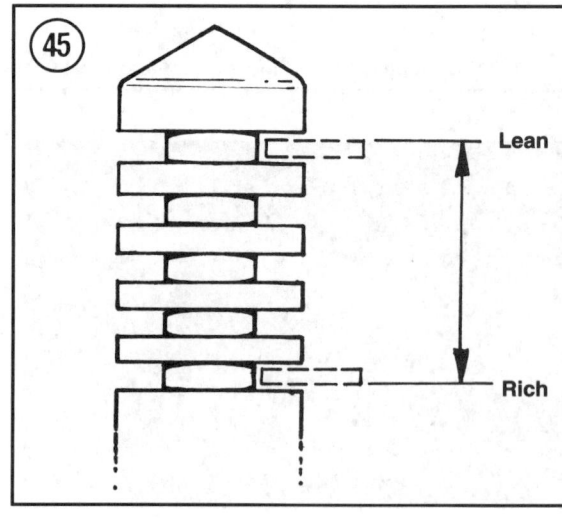

2. Remove the vacuum cylinder and then remove the jet needle (**Figure 36**) as described under *Carburetor Disassembly* in this chapter.

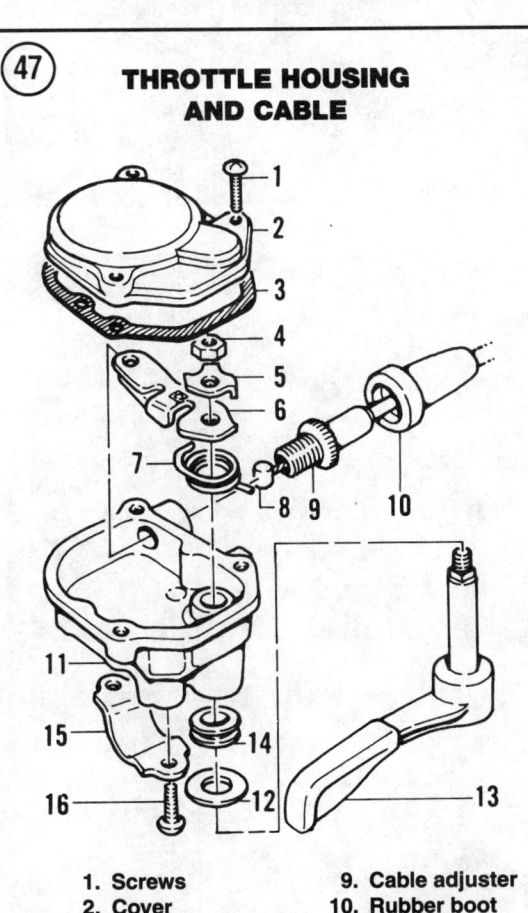

**THROTTLE HOUSING AND CABLE**

1. Screws
2. Cover
3. Gasket
4. Nut
5. Lockwasher
6. Throttle arm
7. Spring
8. Throttle cable
9. Cable adjuster
10. Rubber boot
11. Housing
12. Nylon washer
13. Throttle lever
14. Dust seal
15. Clamp
16. Screws

*NOTE*
*Record the jet needle clip position before removing it. Refer to* **Table 1** *for the standard jet needle clip position.*

3. Raising the needle (lowering the clip) will enrich the mixture between 1/4 and 3/4 throttle openings, while lowering the needle (raising the clip) will lean the mixture. Refer to **Figure 45**.

4. Install the jet needle and vacuum cylinder as described under *Carburetor Assembly* in this chapter.

**High Altitude Adjustment**

Honda specifies two different jetting specifications for TRX400FW models-standard and high altitude. Use the standard jetting when operating the vehicle below 5000 ft. (1500 m). Use the high altitude jetting when operating the vehicle between 3000-8000 ft. (1500-2500 m).

1. Remove the carburetor as described in this chapter.

2. Remove the float bowl mounting screws and float bowl (A, **Figure 40**). Do not remove the gasket from the float bowl groove.

3. Remove the standard main jet (**Figure 46**) and install the correct size main jet for high altitude operation as listed in **Table 1**.

4. Turn the pilot screw (B, **Figure 40**) clockwise 3/4 turn.

5. Reassemble and install the carburetor.

6. Adjust the idle speed as described in Chapter Three. The idle speed is the same for standard and high altitude carburetor settings.

*CAUTION*
*When you operate your vehicle below 3000 ft. (1000 m) with the high altitude jetting, engine overheating may occur. If you are going to ride below this elevation, install the standard main jet and turn the pilot screw out 3/4 turn.*

**THROTTLE HOUSING AND CABLE**

Refer to **Figure 47** when servicing the throttle housing and cable in this section.

8

## Throttle Housing
## Disassembly/Inspection/Reassembly

1. Park the vehicle on level ground and set the parking brake.

2. Remove the handlebar cover (Chapter Fifteen).

3. Slide the rubber boot (A, **Figure 48**) off the cable adjuster.

4. Remove the throttle housing cover screws and cover (B, **Figure 48**). Remove the dowel pins, if used.

5. Loosen the throttle cable adjuster locknut (A, **Figure 49**) and loosen the adjuster.

6. Pry the lockwasher tabs away from the throttle arm pivot nut (B, **Figure 49**).

7. Remove the throttle arm pivot nut (B, **Figure 49**) and lockwasher, and then remove the throttle lever and its plastic washer (**Figure 50**).

8. Disconnect the throttle cable from the throttle arm (A, **Figure 51**), and then remove the throttle arm and spring (B, **Figure 51**).

9. Clean and dry the throttle housing and all its parts.

10. Replace the throttle housing dust seal (14, **Figure 47**) if damaged.

11. Inspect the throttle lever assembly (**Figure 52**) for:

   a. Weak or damaged spring.

   b. Damaged throttle arm.

   c. Corroded or damaged throttle arm.

   d. Worn or damaged plastic washer.

12. Replace the throttle housing cover gasket if damaged.

*NOTE*
*Use a lithium based multipurpose grease (NLGI #2 or equivalent) in Step 13 and Step 17.*

13. Lubricate the dust seal (14, **Figure 47**) with grease.

14. Connect the throttle cable ball into the end of the throttle arm (A, **Figure 51**).

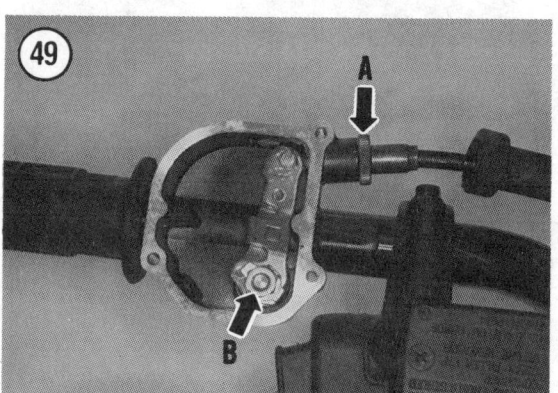

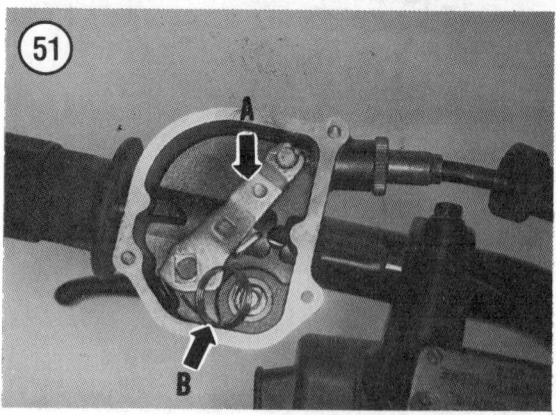

15. Connect the spring to the throttle arm. Then install the spring and throttle arm into the throttle housing. Make sure the spring engages with the throttle arm and against the throttle housing as shown in **Figure 53**.

16. Install the plastic washer (**Figure 50**) onto the throttle lever .

17. Lubricate the throttle lever shaft with grease.

18. Install the throttle lever shaft through the dust seal and throttle arm.

19. Install a new lockwasher as shown in **Figure 54**.

20. Install and tighten the throttle arm nut (B, **Figure 49**). Bend the lockwasher tab against the nut.

21. Install the throttle housing dowel pins, if used.

22. Install the throttle housing cover (B, **Figure 48**) and gasket, and then install and tighten the cover screws.

23. Adjust the throttle cable as described in Chapter Three.

*NOTE*
*After adjusting the throttle cable, make sure to tighten the throttle cable adjuster locknut (A, **Figure 49**) and slide the rubber boot (A, **Figure 48**) over the adjuster.*

**Throttle Cable Replacement**

1. Park the vehicle on level ground and set the parking brake.

2. Remove the handlebar cover (Chapter Fifteen).

3. Remove the fuel tank as described in this chapter.

4. Disconnect the throttle cable at the throttle lever as described under *Throttle Housing Disassembly/Inspection/Reassembly* in this section.

5. Disconnect the throttle cable at the carburetor as described under *Carburetor Removal* in this chapter.

6. Disconnect the throttle cable from any clips holding the cable to the frame.

7. Remove the throttle cable.

8. Install the new throttle cable through the frame, routing it from the handlebar to carburetor. Secure the cable with its frame clips.

9. Connect the throttle cable to the carburetor as described under *Carburetor Installation* in this chapter.

10. Reconnect the throttle cable at the throttle lever as described under *Throttle Housing Disassembly/Inspection/Reassembly* in this section.

11. Operate the throttle lever and make sure the carburetor throttle drum is operating correctly. If throttle operation is sluggish, check that you attached the cable correctly and that there are no tight bends in the cable.

12. Adjust the throttle cable as described in Chapter Three.

13. Test ride the vehicle and make sure the throttle is operating correctly.

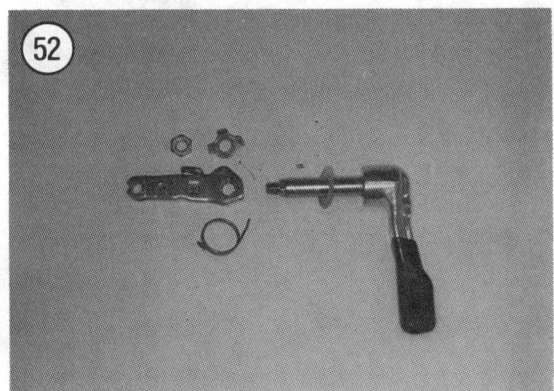

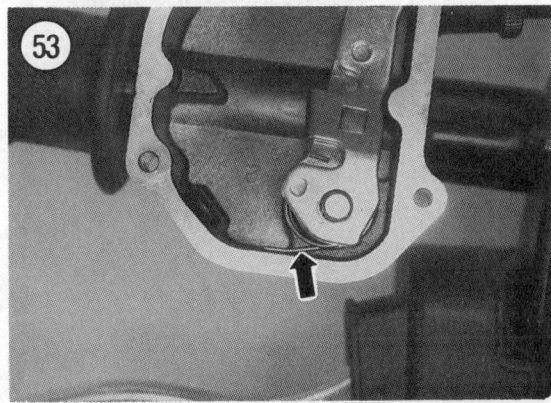

8

## FUEL TANK

**Table 3** lists fuel tank specifications.

### Removal/Installation

1. Park the vehicle on level ground and set the parking brake.
2. Turn the fuel valve off.
3. Remove the seat (Chapter Fifteen).
4. Disconnect the negative battery cable at the battery (Chapter Three).
5. Remove the side and fuel tank cover assembly (Chapter Fifteen).
6. Remove the fuel tank holder bands (**Figure 55**).
7. Remove the front fuel tank mounting bolts (**Figure 56**).
8. Pull the fuel tank up slightly and disconnect the fuel hose from the fuel valve (**Figure 57**).
9. Remove the fuel tank (**Figure 58**).
10. To remove the heat guard, perform the following:
   a. On 1998-on models, remove the rubber snorkel (A, **Figure 59**).
   b. Disconnect the carburetor air vent tube (B, **Figure 59**) from the fuel tank heat guard.
   c. Remove the retaining clips securing the fuel tank heat guard to the frame, then remove the heat guard (C, **Figure 59**).
11. Install the fuel tank by reversing these removal steps, plus the following:
   a. Replace the front fuel tank collars if missing or damaged.
   b. Replace missing or damaged fuel tank dampers or holder bands.
   c. After installing the fuel hose onto the fuel valve, secure the hose with its hose clamp (**Figure 57**).
   d. Tighten the fuel tank mounting bolts (**Figure 56**) securely.
   e. Turn the fuel valve on and check for leaks.

## FUEL VALVE

### Removal/Installation

1. Remove the fuel tank as described in this chapter.
2. Drain the fuel tank of all gas. Store the gas in a can approved for gasoline storage.

3. Remove the screws securing the fuel valve to the bottom of the fuel tank.

4. Remove the O-ring and strainer screen from the fuel valve.

5. Clean the strainer screen in a high-flash point solvent. Replace the strainer screen if damaged.

6. Install a new fuel valve O-ring.

7. Install the fuel valve by reversing the preceding removal steps, plus the following:

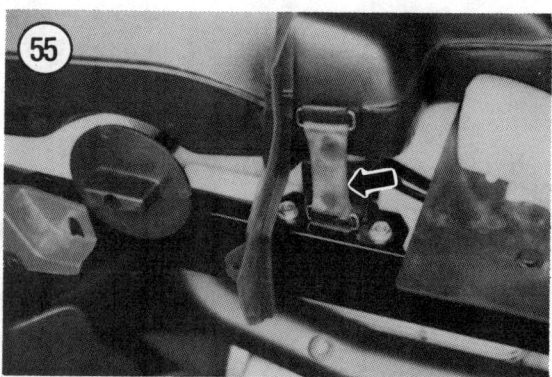

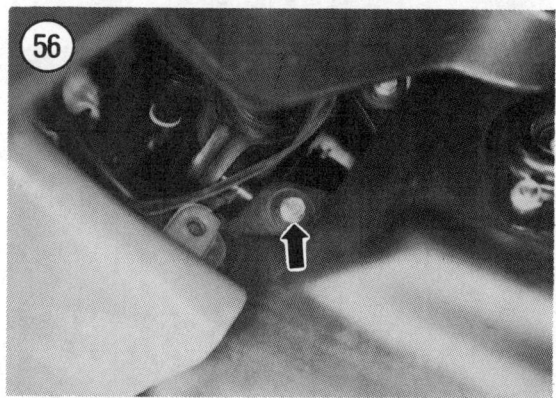

a. Tighten the fuel valve mounting screws to 9 N·m (80 in.-lb.).

b. After turning on the fuel valve, check the fuel valve and hose for leaks.

## AIR BOX

**Figure 60** shows the air box assembly. To service the air filter only, refer to *Air Filter* in Chapter Three.

### Removal/Installation

1. Park the vehicle on level ground and set the parking brake.

2. Remove the seat and side/fuel tank cover (Chapter Fifteen).

3. Remove the rubber snorkel (A, **Figure 59**).

4. Loosen the carburetor hose clamp at the air box (A, **Figure 61**).

5. Remove the air filter housing retaining clips (B, **Figure 61**).

6. Remove the intake air duct (C, **Figure 61**) from the air box.

7. Disconnect the crankcase breather tube from the air box (if so equipped); see **Figure 60**.

8. Remove the air box (D, **Figure 61**) assembly.

9. Cover the carburetor opening.

10. Install by reversing the preceding removal steps, plus the following:

a. Check the air box intake hose for loose parts or other debris before connecting it to the carburetor.

b. Check all of the hoses for proper routing.

## CHOKE CABLE REPLACEMENT

1. Remove the handlebar cover (Chapter Fifteen).

2. Remove the fuel tank as described in this chapter.

3. Make a diagram of the choke cable routing path from the handlebar to the carburetor.

4. Remove any cable guides from the choke cable.

5. Disconnect the choke cable at the left handlebar switch housing as follows:

a. Remove the spring clamp (**Figure 62**).

b. Disconnect and remove the choke cable (**Figure 63**) from the switch housing.

6. Loosen the starting enrichment (SE) valve nut (**Figure 64**) and remove the SE valve from the carburetor. Remove the SE valve (A, **Figure 65**) and spring (B) from the end of the choke cable to prevent their loss.

7. Reverse these steps to install the choke cable, plus the following:

a. **Figure 66** shows the choke cable mounting position with the switch housing removed for clarity. Refer to **Figure 66** when reconnecting the choke cable.

b. Check the choke operation.

8

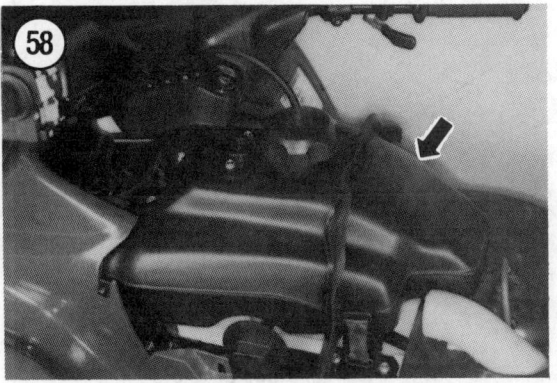

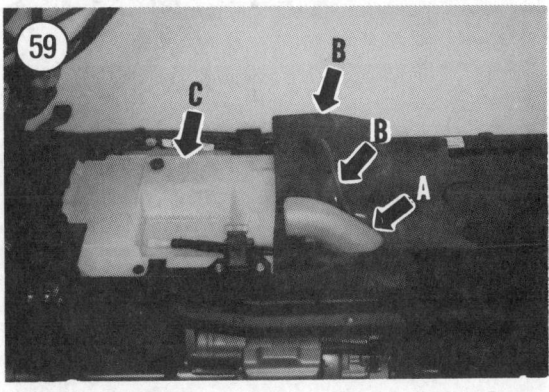

**Figures 60-66 and Tables 1-3 are on the following pages.**

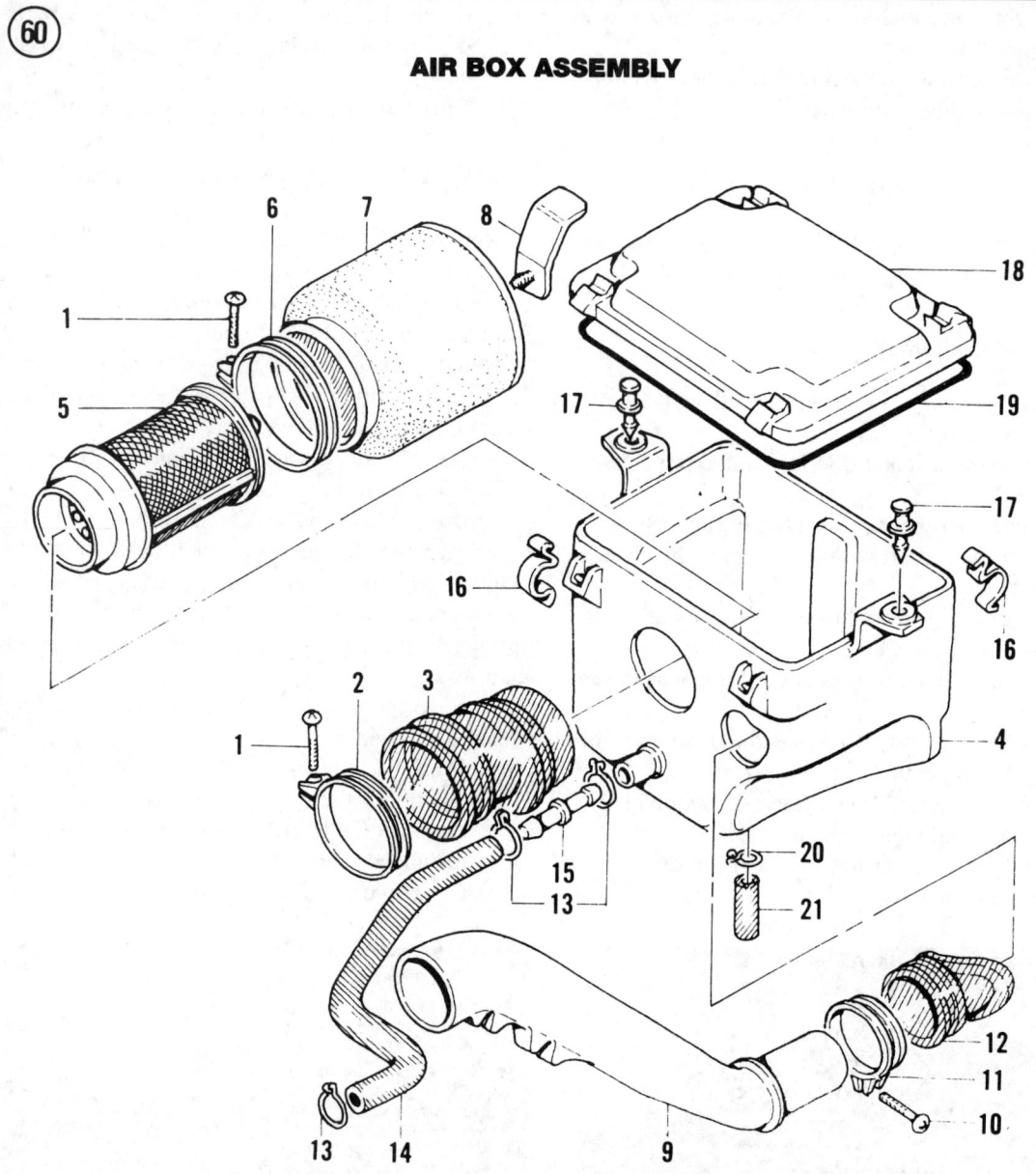

**60**

## AIR BOX ASSEMBLY

1. Screw
2. Hose clamp
3. Intake hose
4. Air box
5. Element core
6. Hose clamp
7. Filter element
8. Holder
9. Intake air duct
10. Screw
11. Hose clamp
12. Hose
13. Clamp
14. Crankcase breather tube
   (1988 California)
   (and all later models)
15. Hose nozzle
16. Retaining clip
17. Retaining pin
18. Cover
19. Seal
20. Clamp
21. Drain tube

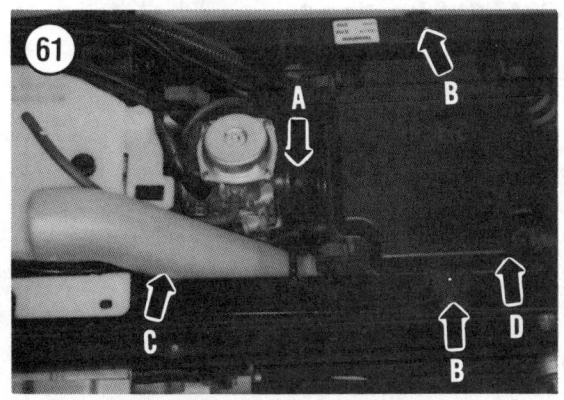

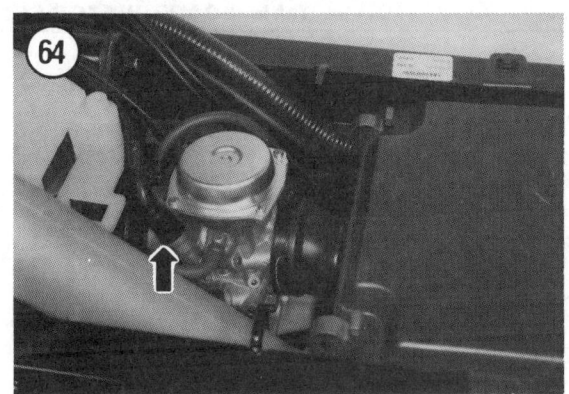

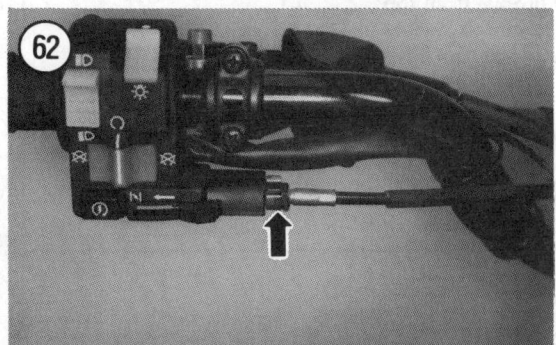

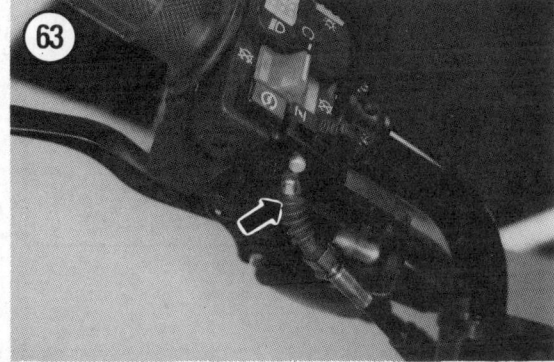

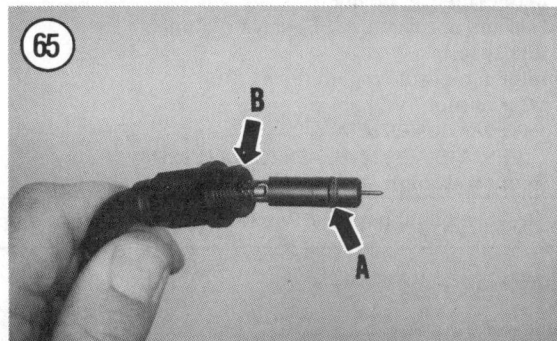

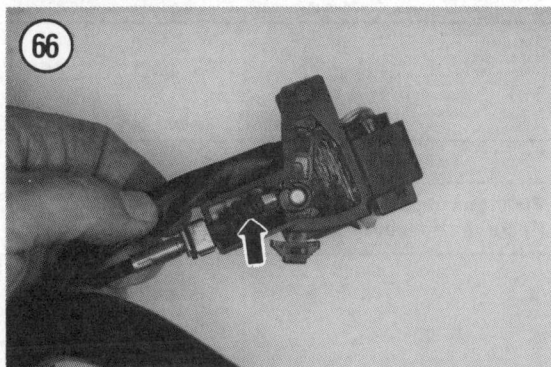

**Table 1 CARBURETOR SPECIFICATIONS**

| Type | Vacuum piston |
|---|---|
| Throttle bore size | 32 mm (1.3 in.) |
| Identification number | |
| 1995 | |
| 49-state models | VE92A-A |
| | VE92A-B |
| California | — |
| (continued) | |

**Table 1 CARBURETOR SPECIFICATIONS (continued)**

| | |
|---|---|
| 1996 | |
| 49-state models | VE92B-A |
| | VE92B-B |
| California | — |
| 1997 | |
| 49-state | VE92B-B |
| California | — |
| 1998 | |
| 49-state | VE92D-A |
| California | VE92C-A |
| 1999-on all models | VE92C-A |
| Main jet | |
| Stock | 130 |
| High altitude setting | 125 |
| Pilot jet | 45 |
| Jet needle clip position | 3rd groove from top |
| Starting enrichment (SE) valve distance | 10-11 mm (0.39-0.43 in.) |
| Idle speed | 1300-1500 rpm |
| Pilot screw adjustment (turns out)* | |
| Carburetor ID number | |
| VE92A-A, VE92B-A | 2 1/4 |
| VE92A-B, VE92B-B, VE92C-A, VE92DA | 3 |
| Pilot screw high altitude adjustment | 3/4 turn in from standard setting |

* Initial adjustment only. See text for procedure and final pilot air screw adjustment (turns out).

**Table 2 CARBURETOR FLOAT LEVEL**

| | |
|---|---|
| Float level | 18.5 mm (0.73 in.) |

**Table 3 FUEL TANK SPECIFICATIONS**

| | Liters | U.S. gal. | Imp. gal. |
|---|---|---|---|
| Fuel tank capacity | 12.0 | 3.18 | 2.64 |
| Reserve capacity | 2.7 | 0.71 | 0.59 |

# ELECTRICAL  SYSTEM

This chapter contains service and test procedures for all electrical and ignition components. Information regarding the battery and spark plug are covered in Chapter Three.

The electrical system includes the following systems:

a. Charging system.
b. Ignition system.
c. Starting system
d. Lighting system.
e. Electrical components.

**Tables 1-6** are at the end of this chapter.

## CHARGING  SYSTEM

The charging system (**Figure 1**) consists of the battery, alternator and a voltage regulator/rectifier. A 30-amp main fuse protects the circuit.

Alternating current generated by the alternator is rectified to direct current. The voltage regulator maintains the voltage to the battery and additional electrical loads at a constant voltage despite variations in engine speed and load.

### Troubleshooting

Refer to Chapter Two.

### Battery Voltage Check

To obtain accurate charging system test results, the battery must be fully charged. Check battery voltage as follows:

Before you test the charging system, measure battery voltage as follows:

1. Remove the seat (Chapter Fifteen).
2. Connect a digital voltmeter across the battery negative and positive terminals and measure the battery voltage (**Figure 2**). A fully charged battery will read between 13.0-13.2 volts. If the voltage reading is less than this amount, recharge the battery as described in Chapter Three.

### Charging System Leakage Test

Perform this test before performing the charging voltage test.

1. Remove the seat (Chapter Fifteen).
2. Turn the ignition switch off.
3. Disconnect the negative battery cable at the battery (**Figure 3**).

> *CAUTION*
> *Before connecting the ammeter into the circuit in Step 4, set the meter to its highest amperage scale. This will prevent a large current flow from damaging*

**9**

*the meter or blowing the meter's fuse, if so equipped.*

4.  Connect an ammeter between the battery ground cable and the negative battery terminal.

5.  Switch an ammeter between its highest and lowest amperage scale while reading the ammeter scale. The ammeter reading should be less than 0.1 mA.

6.  A current leakage rate higher than 0.1 mA suggests a short circuit and a continuous battery discharge. Dirt and/or electrolyte on top of the battery or a crack in the battery case can cause this type of problem by providing a path for battery current to follow. Remove and clean the battery as described in Chapter Three. Then reinstall the battery and retest.

7.  If the current leakage rate is still excessive, consider the following probable causes:

    a.  Damaged battery.

    b.  Short circuit in system.

8.  To find the short circuit, refer to **Figure 1** and the wiring diagram for your model at the end of this book. Measure the current leakage while disconnecting each charging system connector one by one. When the current leakage rate returns to normal, you have found the circuit with the short circuit. Test the circuit further to find the problem.

9.  Disconnect the ammeter from the battery and battery cable.

10.  Reconnect the negative battery cable to the battery.

11.  Install the seat (Chapter Fifteen).

### Charging Voltage Test

This procedure tests charging system operation. It does not measure maximum charging system output. **Table 1** lists charging system specifications.

To obtain accurate test results, the battery must be fully charged; measure battery voltage as described under *Battery Voltage Check* in this chapter.

1.  Start and run the engine until it reaches normal operating temperature, then turn the engine off.

2.  Connect a tachometer to the engine following its manufacturer's instructions.

3.  Connect a 0-20 DC voltmeter to the battery terminals as shown in **Figure 2**.

4.  Start the engine and allow it to run at idle speed.

5.  Gradually increase engine speed from idle to 5000 rpm and read the regulated voltage reading on the voltmeter and compare to the regulated voltage reading in **Table 1**. If the regulated voltage is higher

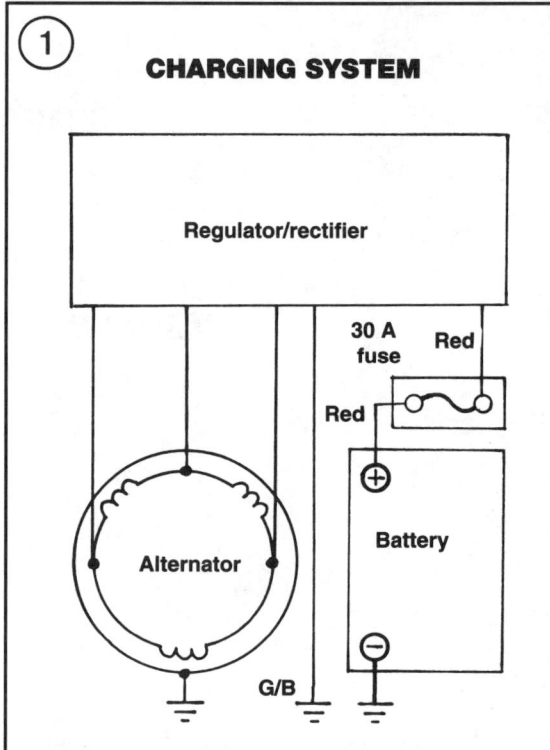

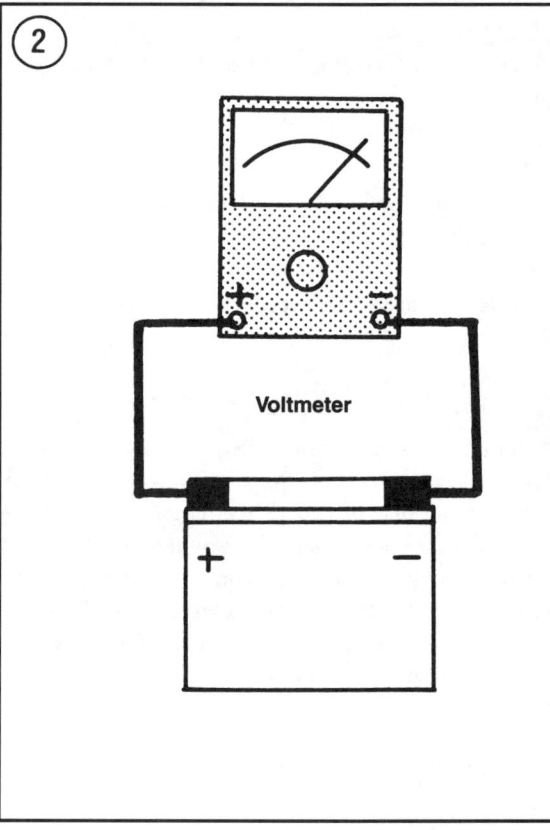

than 15.5 volts, check for a shorted wiring harness, damaged ignition switch or a faulty regulator/rectifier; perform the *Regulator/Rectifier Wiring Test* in this section. If the regulated voltage reading is correct, but there is a problem in the charging system, the battery may be faulty.

6. Disconnect the voltmeter and tachometer.

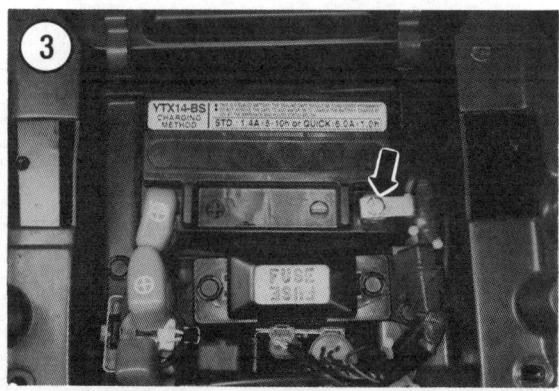

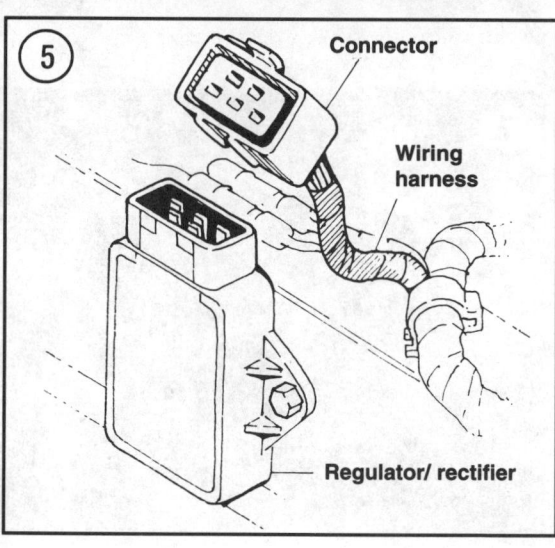

**Connector**

**Wiring harness**

**Regulator/ rectifier**

7. Install the seat (Chapter Fifteen).

### Regulator/Rectifier Wiring Harness Test

1. Disconnect the regulator/rectifier electrical connector. See A, **Figure 4**, typical.

> *NOTE*
> ***Figure 4*** *shows the regulator/rectifier on 1997 and later models. On 1995-1996 models, the regulator rectifier is mounted in the same position, but the connector plugs into the bottom of the unit.*

> *NOTE*
> *Make all of the tests (Steps 2-4) on the wiring harness connector side, not on the regulator/rectifier connector side. See* ***Figure 5***.

2. Check the battery charge lead as follows:
   a. Connect a voltmeter between the red (+) and green (–) connectors.
   b. With the ignition switch off, the voltmeter should read 13.0-13.2 volts (battery voltage).
   c. If the battery voltage is less than specified, check both wires for damage.
   d. Disconnect the voltmeter leads.
3. Check the ground wire as follows:
   a. Switch an ohmmeter to R × 1.
   b. Connect the ohmmeter between the green wire and a good engine ground.
   c. The ohmmeter must read continuity.
   d. If there is no continuity (zero or low resistance resistance), check the green wire for damage.
4. Check the charge coil wires as follows:
   a. Switch an ohmmeter to R × 1.
   b. Measure resistance between each yellow wire.
   c. The ohmmeter must read 0.1-1.0 ohms at 20° C (69° F). An infinity reading indicates an open circuit. Test the stator coil resistance as described in this chapter.
   d. If the resistance reading is excessive, check for dirty or loose-fitting terminals or damaged wires.
5. If any regulator/rectifier measurement is out of specification, replace the regulator/rectifier as described in this chapter.
6. Reconnect the regulator/rectifier electrical connector (A, **Figure 4**, typical).

9

## Regulator/Rectifier
## Removal/Installation

1. Remove the seat.

2. Disconnect the negative battery cable from the battery (**Figure 3**).

3. Disconnect the regulator/rectifier unit electrical connector (A, **Figure 4**, typical).

*NOTE*
*Figure 4 shows the regulator/rectifier on 1997 and later models. On 1995-1996 models, the regulator rectifier is mounted in the same position, but the connector plugs into the bottom of the unit.*

4. Remove the bolts securing the regulator/rectifier (B, **Figure 4**) to the frame and remove it.

5. Install by reversing the preceding removal steps.

## ALTERNATOR

The alternator consists of the flywheel and stator coil assembly. Flywheel and stator removal and installation procedures are covered in Chapter Five.

### Flywheel Testing

The flywheel is permanently magnetized and cannot be tested except by replacing it with a known good one. The rotor can loose magnetism from old age or a sharp hit, such as dropping it onto a concrete floor. Replace the flywheel if defective or damaged.

### Stator Coil Resistance Test

*NOTE*
*The stator coil is also referred to as the charge coil.*

The stator coil (**Figure 6**) is mounted inside the alternator cover. You can test the stator coil with the alternator cover mounted on the engine.

1. Remove the rear fender (Chapter Fifteen).

2. Disconnect the alternator/pulse generator connector (**Figure 7**).

3. Use an ohmmeter set at R × 1 and measure resistance between each yellow wire at the alternator end of the connector (**Figure 7**). **Table 1** lists the specified stator coil resistance.

4. If the resistance is as specified resistance, the stator coil is good. If the resistance is higher than specified, the coil is damaged. Replace the stator assembly.

5. Use an ohmmeter set at R × 1 and check continuity from each yellow wire on the alternator stator side of the connector and to ground. Replace the stator coil if any yellow terminal has continuity to ground. Continuity indicates a short within the stator coil winding.

*NOTE*
*Before replacing the stator assembly, check the electrical wires to and within the electrical connector for any open or poor connections.*

6. If the stator coil (**Figure 6**) fails either of these tests, replace it as described under *Alternator Cover* in Chapter Five.

7. Apply a dielectric grease to the stator coil connector before you reconnect it. This will help seal

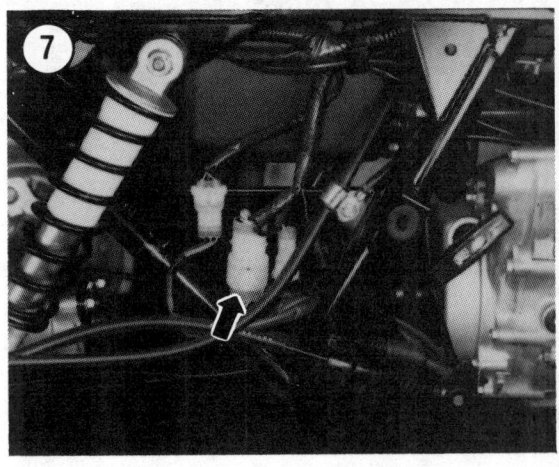

out moisture. Make sure the O-ring is mounted on the stator coil connector.

8. Reconnect the alternator/pulse generator connector (**Figure 7**).

## IGNITION SYSTEM

All vehicle models are equipped with a capacitor discharge ignition system.

**Figure 8** shows a schematic of the ignition system.

## CDI Precautions

You must take certain measures to protect the ignition system when working on it.

1. Never disconnect any of the electrical connections while the engine is running.

2. Apply dielectric grease to all electrical connectors before reconnecting them. This will help seal out moisture.

3. The electrical connectors must be free of corrosion and properly connected.

4. The ignition control module (ICM) unit is mounted in a rubber mount. If you remove the ICM unit, make sure to reinstall it into its rubber mount.

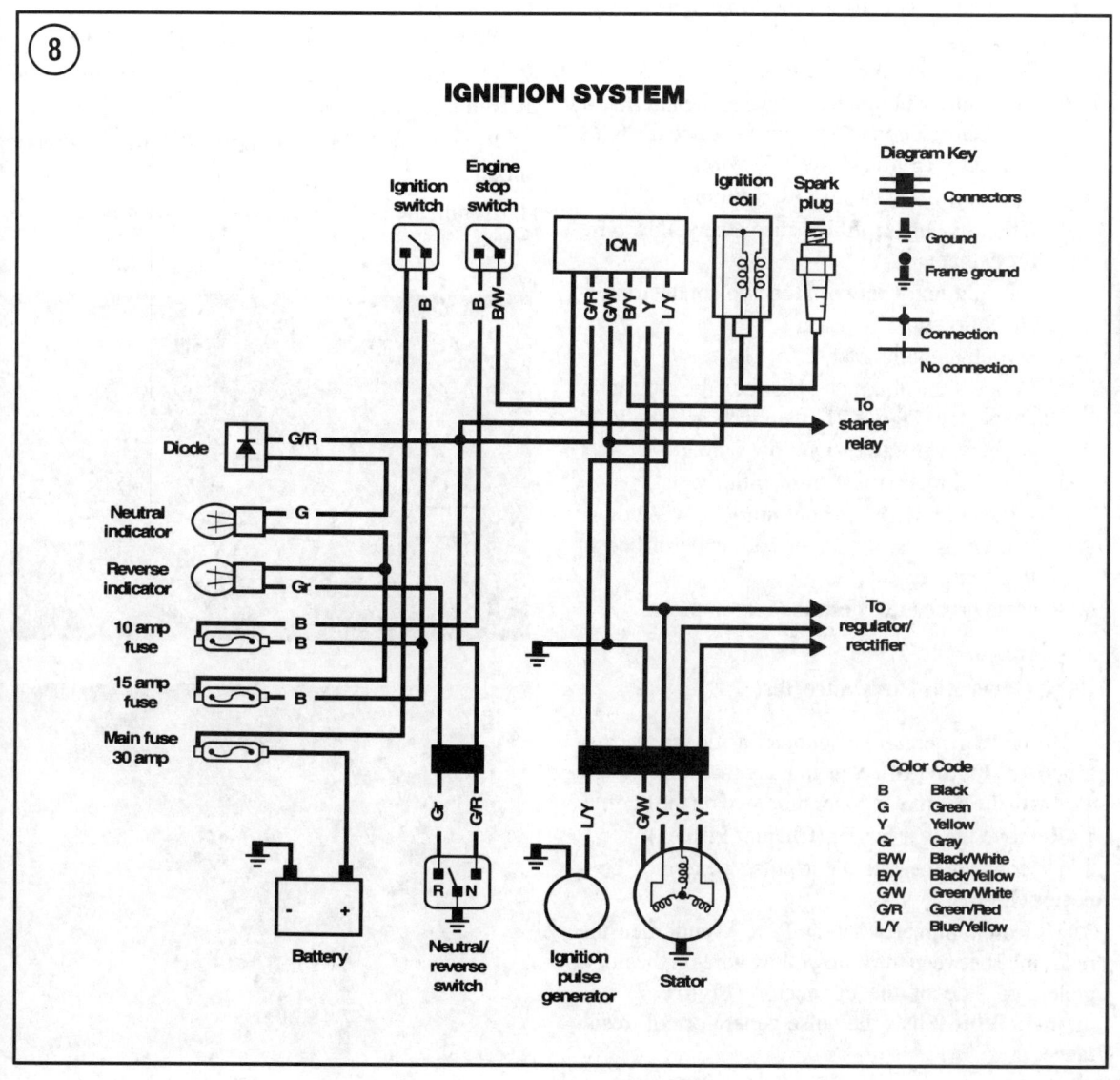

## Troubleshooting

Refer to Chapter Two.

## AC Sensor Line
## Wiring Test

This test checks the wire connecting the ICM unit to the stator coil.

1. Remove the front and rear fenders (Chapter Fifteen).

2. Disconnect the alternator/pulse generator connector (**Figure 7**).

3. Disconnect the ICM four-prong connector (**Figure 9**).

4. Check continuity between the two connector terminals as follows:

   a. Switch an ohmmeter to R × 1.

   b. Connect the ohmmeter between the alternator connector (**Figure 7**) yellow wire and the ICM connector (**Figure 9**) yellow wire.

   c. The ohmmeter must show continuity.

   d. If the reading is infinity, check the yellow wire for damage.

5. Check continuity between the two connector terminals as follows:

   a. Switch an ohmmeter to R × 1.

   b. Connect the ohmmeter between the alternator connector (**Figure 7**) green wire and the ICM connector (**Figure 9**) yellow wire.

   c. The ohmmeter must show infinity.

   d. If the reading shows continuity between these two wires, test the stator coil as described in this chapter.

6. Reverse procedures described in Steps 1-3.

## Pulse Generator Resistance Test

The pulse generator is mounted inside the alternator cover (**Figure 10**). You can test the pulse generator with the alternator cover mounted on the engine.

1. Remove the rear fender (Chapter Fifteen).

2. Disconnect the alternator/pulse generator connector (**Figure 7**).

3. Use an ohmmeter set at R × 1 and measure resistance between the blue/yellow wire on the pulse generator side of the connector (**Figure 7**) and ground. **Table 2** lists the pulse generator coil resistance.

4. If the resistance reading is out of specification, replace the pulse generator as described under *Alternator Cover* in Chapter Five.

5. Apply a dielectric grease to the stator coil connector before you reconnect it. This will help seal out moisture. Make sure the O-ring is mounted on the stator coil connector.

6. Reconnect the alternator/pulse generator connector (**Figure 7**).

## ICM Unit
## Removal/Installation

The ICM (**Figure 11**) unit is mounted on the front of the vehicle.

1. Remove the front fender (Chapter Fifteen).

2. Disconnect the electrical connector from the ICM unit (**Figure 9**).

3. Remove the ICM unit (**Figure 11**) from its rubber mount.

4. Install the ICM unit by reversing the removal steps.

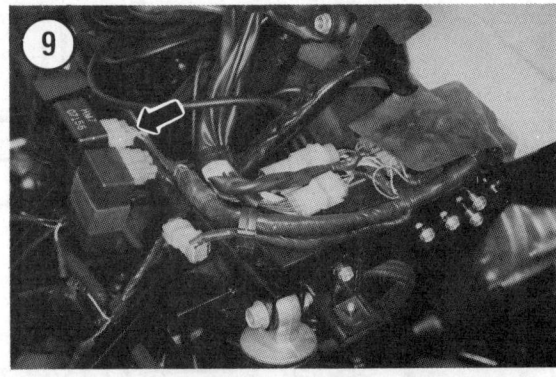

### Ignition Coil Resistance Test
### Testing

The ignition coil (**Figure 12**) is a form of transformer which develops the high voltage required to jump the spark plug gap. The only maintenance required is that of keeping the electrical connections clean and tight and occasionally checking to see that the coil is mounted securely.

If the condition of the coil is doubtful, you can make several checks to test it.

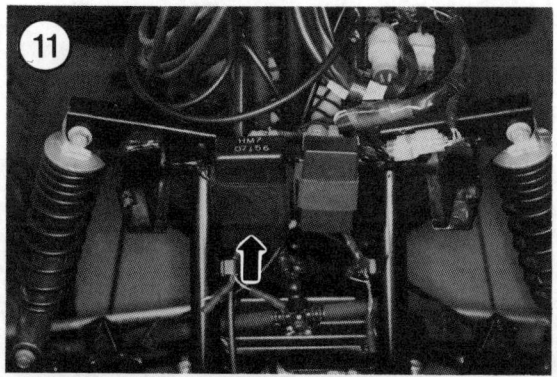

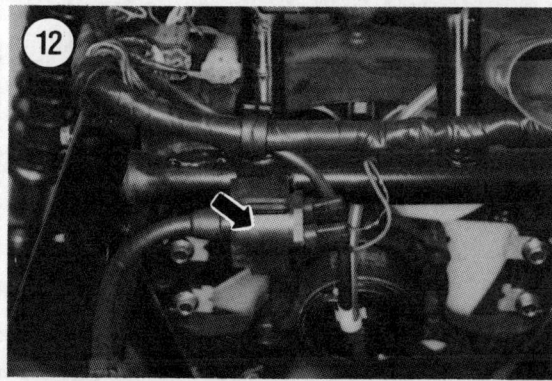

To make a quick check of the coil, disconnect the high voltage lead from the spark plug. Remove the spark plug from the cylinder head. Connect a new spark plug or a spark tester to the high voltage lead and ground the spark plug base or spark tester tool against the cylinder head.

> *WARNING*
> *Do not hold the spark plug cap, except with a pair of insulated pliers. The high voltage generated by the CDI could produce serious or fatal shocks.*

Turn the engine over with the starter. If a fat blue spark occurs, the coil is in good condition. If the spark is weak, or if there is no spark, perform the following tests.

Reinstall the spark plug in the cylinder head.

1. Remove the fuel tank and heat guard (Chapter Eight).

2. Disconnect the two primary wires from the ignition coil (**Figure 12**).

3. Disconnect the spark plug cap (**Figure 13**) from the spark plug.

4. Measure the primary coil resistance as follows:
   a. Switch an ohmmeter to R × 1.
   b. Connect the ohmmeter between the two primary coil terminals (**Figure 14**).
   c. Refer to **Table 2** for the correct primary resistance value.

5. Measure the secondary resistance as follows:
   a. Switch an ohmmeter to R × 1000.
   b. Connect the ohmmeter between the spark plug lead (with the spark plug lead attached) and one of the primary terminals on the ignition coil (**Figure 14**).
   c. Refer to **Table 2** for the correct secondary resistance valve. If the reading is incorrect, perform Step 5.

6. Measure the secondary resistance with the spark plug cap removed. Perform the following:
   a. Remove the spark plug cap (**Figure 13**) from the spark plug cable.
   b. Switch an ohmmeter to R × 1000.
   c. Connect the ohmmeter between the spark plug lead and one of the secondary terminals on the ignition coil (**Figure 14**).
   d. Refer to **Table 2** for the correct resistance value.
   e. Reconnect the spark plug cap.

*NOTE*
*If the resistance reading in Step 6 is correct, but was incorrect in Step 5 the spark plug cap is damaged. Replace the spark plug cap and repeat Step 5.*

7. Replace the ignition coil if any reading is out of specification.

8. Reverse procedures in Steps 1-3 to complete assembly.

### Removal/Installation

1. Remove the fuel tank and heat guard (Chapter Eight).

2. Disconnect the two primary wires from the ignition coil (**Figure 12**).

3. Disconnect the spark plug cap (**Figure 13**) from the spark plug.

4. Remove the ignition coil from the frame mounting bracket.

5. Remove the rubber holder from the old ignition coil and install it onto the new coil.

6. Install the ignition coil by reversing the preceding removal steps. Make sure all electrical connections are tight and free of corrosion.

## ELECTRIC STARTING SYSTEM

The starting system consists of the starter motor, starter gears, solenoid and the starter button.

**Figure 15** shows an electrical diagram of the starting system.

**Table 3** lists starter motor service specifications. The starter gears are covered in Chapter Five.

*CAUTION*
*Do not operate the starter for more than 5 seconds at a time. Let it rest approximately 10 seconds, then use it again.*

### Troubleshooting

Refer to Chapter Two.

### Starter
### Removal/Installation

1. Park the vehicle on level ground and set the parking brake.

2. Remove the seat (Chapter Fifteen).

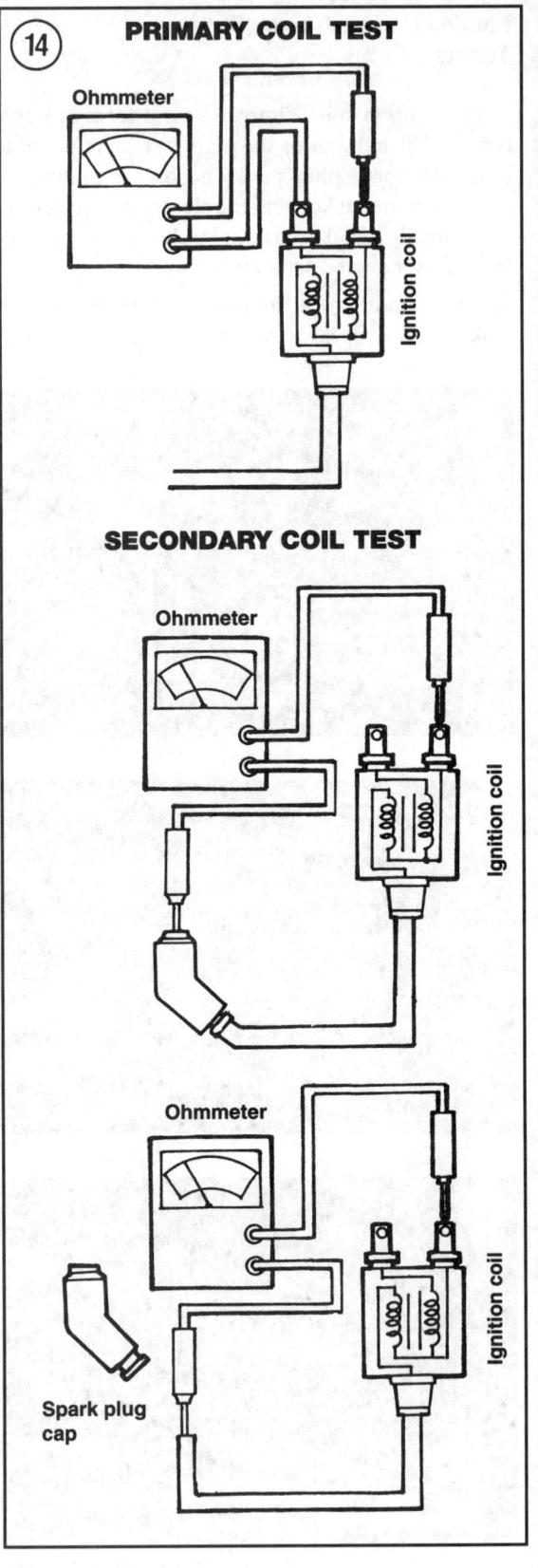

3. Disconnect the negative battery cable from the battery.

4. Remove the bolts, collars and engine right side cover (**Figure 16**).

5. Remove the nut and the starter motor cable (A, **Figure 17**) from the starter motor.

6. Remove the two starter motor mounting bolts (B. **Figure 17**) and the starter motor (C).

7. If necessary, service the starter motor as described in this chapter.

8. Install the starter motor by reversing the preceding removal steps, plus the following:

   a. Lubricate the starter O-ring (**Figure 18**) with grease.

   b. Clean any rust or corrosion from the starter motor cable eyelet.

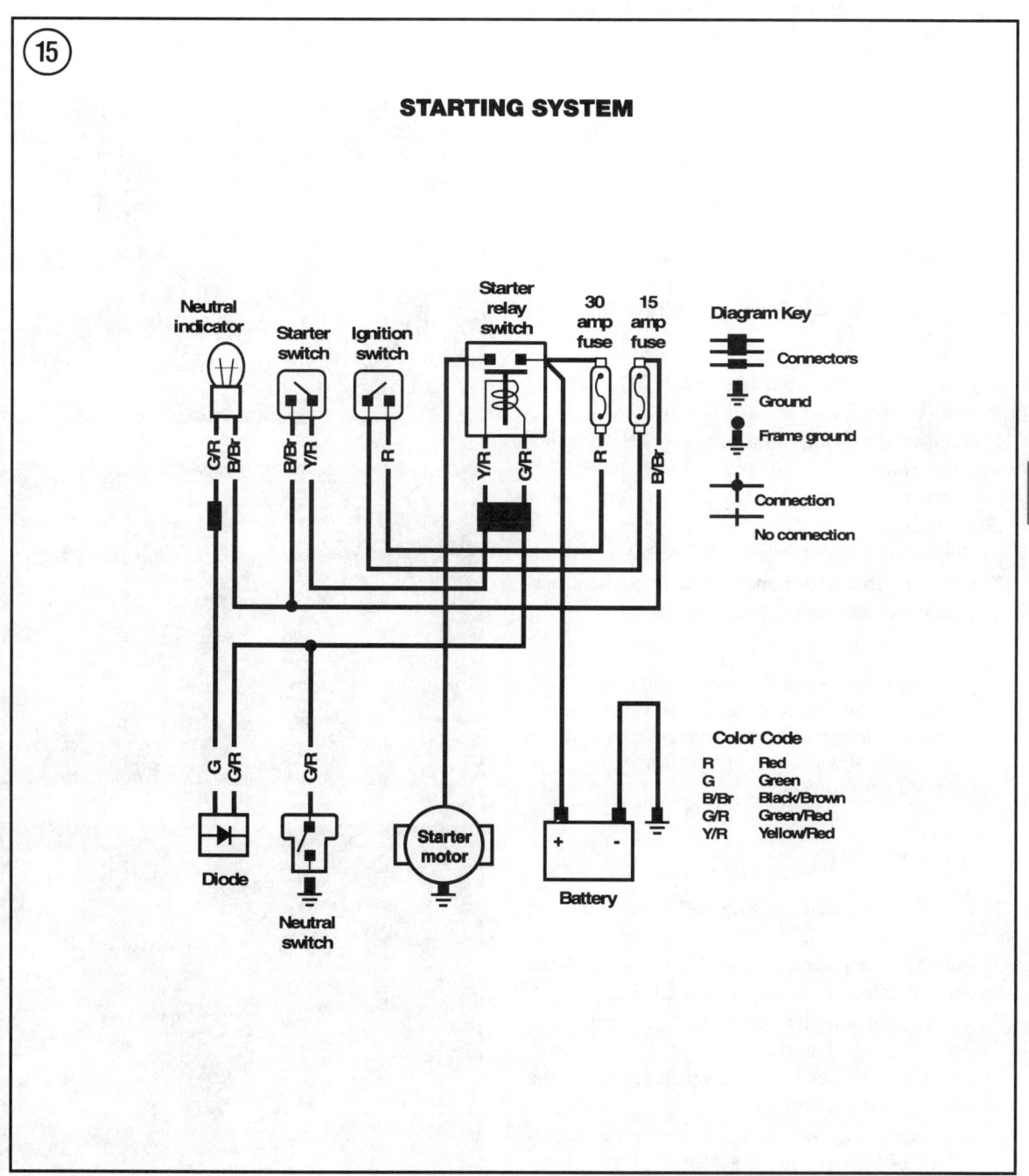

**(15)**

**STARTING SYSTEM**

c. Tighten the starter mounting bolts securely.

## Disassembly

Refer to **Figure 19** for this procedure.

1. Find the alignment marks across the armature housing and both end covers. If necessary, scribe your own marks.

2. Remove the two case bolts, washers, lockwashers and O-rings (**Figure 20**).

> *NOTE*
> *Write down the thickness and alignment of each shim and washer removed during disassembly.*

> *NOTE*
> *The number of shims used in each starter varies. The starter you are working on may use a different number of shims from that shown in the following photographs.*

3. Remove the front cover (A, **Figure 21**) and lock-washer (**Figure 22**).

4. Remove the front shims (**Figure 23**) from the armature shaft.

5. Remove the case (**Figure 24**) and end cover (**Figure 25**).

6. Remove the rear shim set (**Figure 26**).

7. Clean all grease, dirt and carbon from the armature, case and end covers.

> *CAUTION*
> *Do not immerse the wire windings in the case or the armature coil in solvent as the insulation may be damaged. Wipe the windings with a cloth lightly moistened with solvent.*

## Inspection

1. Pull the brush plate (A, **Figure 27**) out of the end cover.

2. Pull the spring away from each brush and pull the brushes (B, **Figure 27**) out of their guides.

3. Measure the length of each brush (**Figure 28**). If the length is less than the service limit in **Table 3**, replace both brushes as a set. When replacing the brushes, note the following:

   a. You do not have to solder the starter motor brushes when replacing them.

b. Replace the terminal bolt and brush (C, **Figure 27**) as an assembly. Remove the terminal bolt (C, **Figure 27**) and brush and replace them. Make sure to install the washer set in the order shown in **Figure 19**.

c. The brush plate and brush (A, **Figure 27**) are replaced as a set. Remove the brush plate and brush and replace them.

4. Inspect the brush springs and replace them if weak or damaged. To replace the brush springs, perform the following:

⑲

## STARTER MOTOR

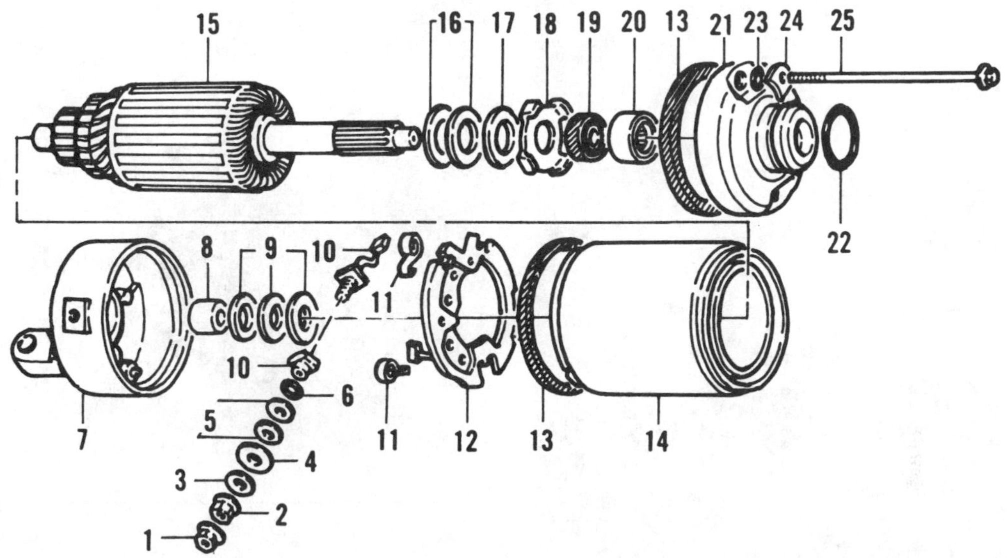

1. Nut
2. Nut
3. Washer
4. Insulated washer (large)
5. Insulated washers (small)
6. O-ring
7. End cover
8. Bushing
9. Shim(s)
10. Terminal bolt and brush
11. Brush spring
12. Brush plate
13. O-rings
14. Case
15. Armature
16. Shims(s)
17. Insulated washer
18. Lockwasher
19. Seal
20. Needle bearing
21. Front cover
22. O-ring
23. O-ring
24. Washer
25. Bolt

9

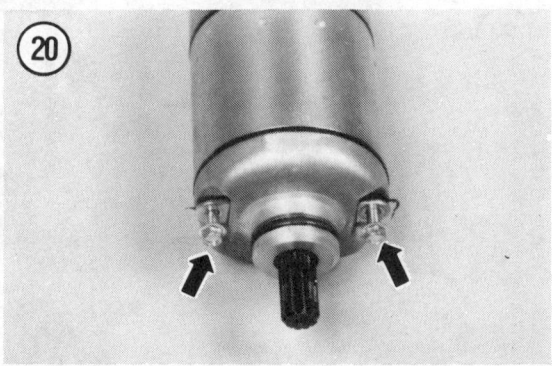

⑳

㉑

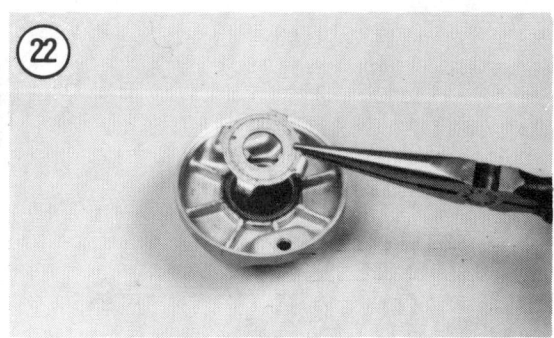

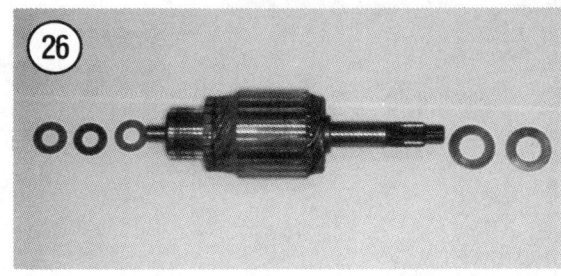

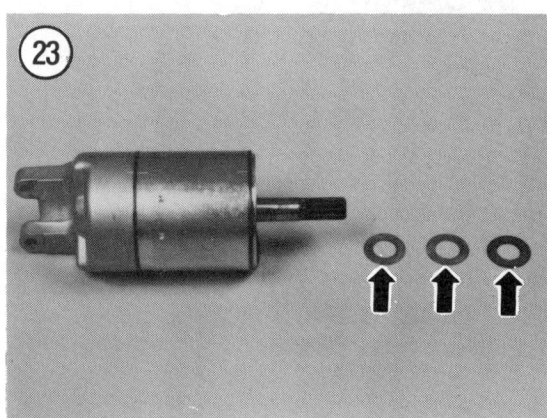

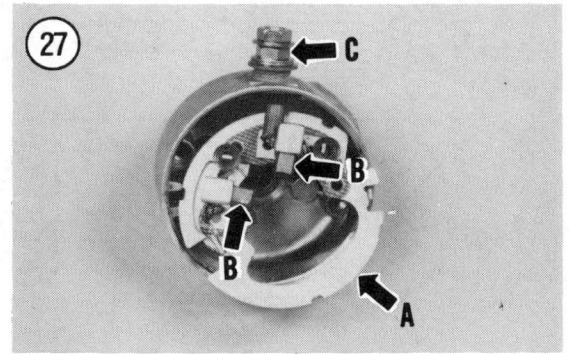

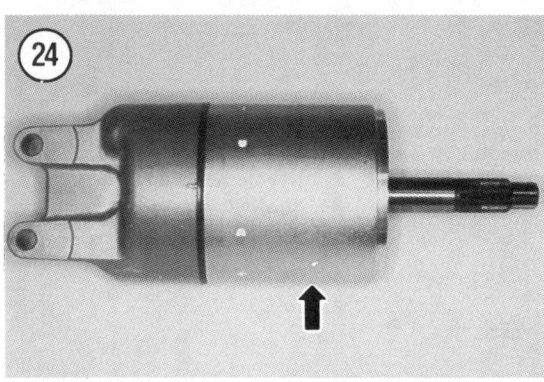

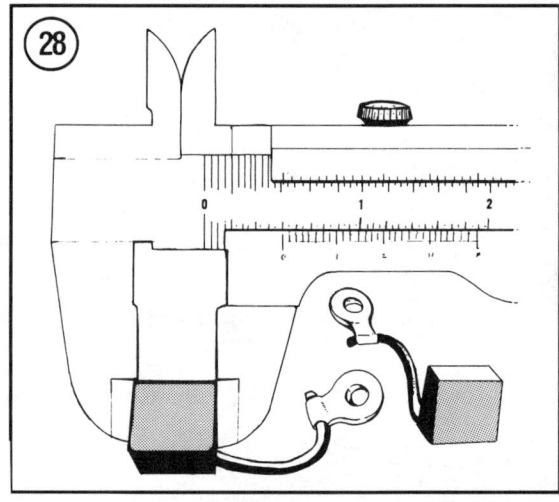

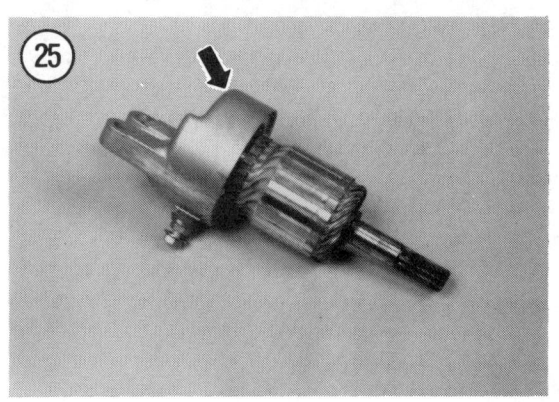

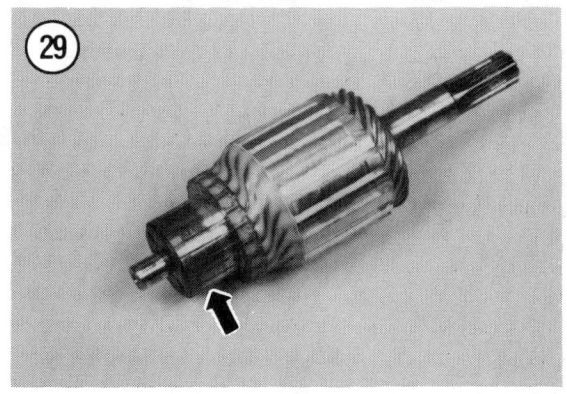

a. Make a drawing that shows the location of the brush springs on the brush holder. Also indicate the direction in which each spring coil turns.

b. Remove and replace both brush springs as a set.

5. Inspect the commutator (**Figure 29**). The mica must be below the surface of the copper bars. On a worn commutator the mica and copper bars may be worn to the same level (**Figure 30**). If necessary, have the commutator serviced by a dealership or electrical repair shop.

6. Inspect the commutator copper bars for discoloration. A discolored pair of bars indicates grounded armature coils.

7. Inspect the armature shaft (**Figure 31**) for excessive wear, scoring or other damage.

8. Use an ohmmeter and perform the following:

a. Check for continuity between the commutator bars (**Figure 32**). There should be continuity (low resistance) between pairs of bars.

b. Check for continuity between the commutator bars and the shaft (**Figure 33**). There should be no continuity (low resistance).

c. If the armature fails either of these tests, replace the starter assembly.

9. Use an ohmmeter and perform the following:

a. Check for continuity between the starter cable terminal and the end case cover (**Figure 34**). There should be no continuity.

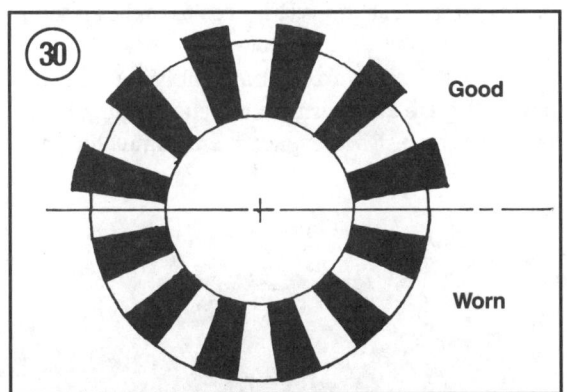

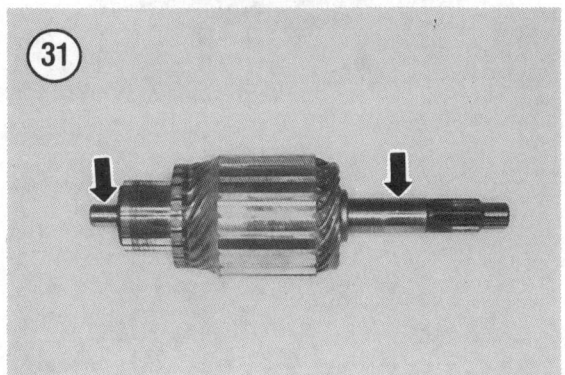

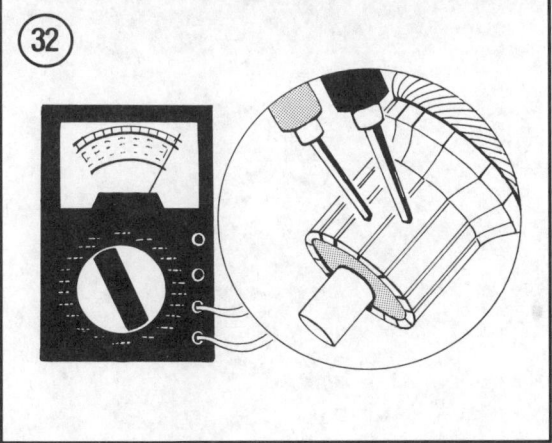

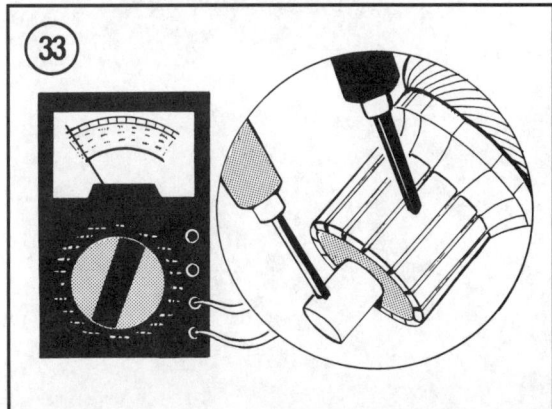

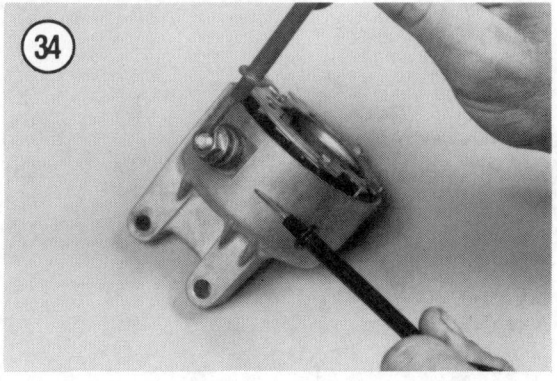

9

b. Check for continuity between the starter cable terminal and the brush black wire terminal (**Figure 35**). There should be continuity.

c. If the unit fails either of these tests, replace the starter assembly.

10. Inspect the front cover seal and needle bearing (**Figure 36**). Replace the front cover if either part is excessively worn or damaged.

11. Inspect the rear cover bushing. Replace the rear cover if the bushing is damaged.

12. Inspect the case (**Figure 37**) for cracks or other damage. Then inspect for loose, chipped or damaged magnets.

13. Inspect the O-rings and replace them if worn or damaged.

**Assembly**

1. If removed, install the brushes into their holders and secure the brushes with the springs.

2. Align the brush plate arm with the notch in the end cover and install the brush plate (**Figure 37**).

3. Install the rear shims (**Figure 26**)on the armature shaft next to the commutator.

4. Insert the armature coil assembly into the rear cover (**Figure 25**). Turn the armature during installation so the brushes engage the commutator prop-

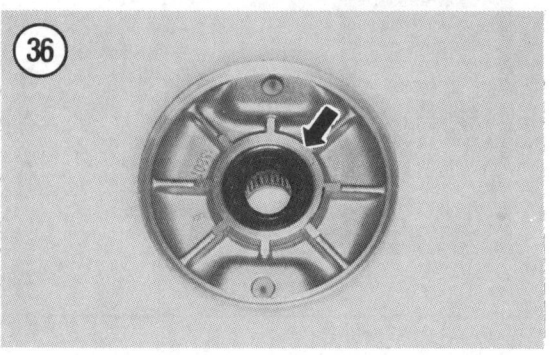

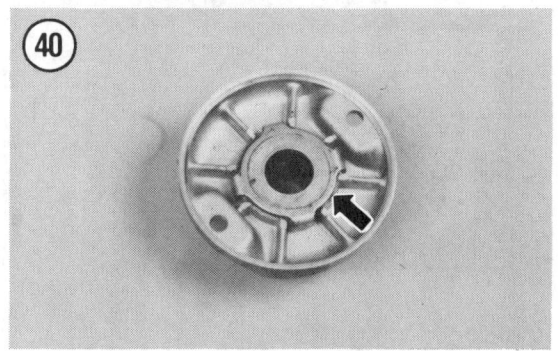

erly. Make sure the armature is not turned upside down or the shims could slide off the end of the shaft. Do not damage the brushes.

5. Install the two O-rings (**Figure 38**) onto the case. Then slide the case over the armature (**Figure 24**). Align the mark on the case and end cover (**Figure 39**).

6. Install the front shims (**Figure 23**) onto the armature shaft.

7. Install the lockwasher (**Figure 22**) onto the front cover so that the lockwasher tabs engage the cover slots (**Figure 40**).

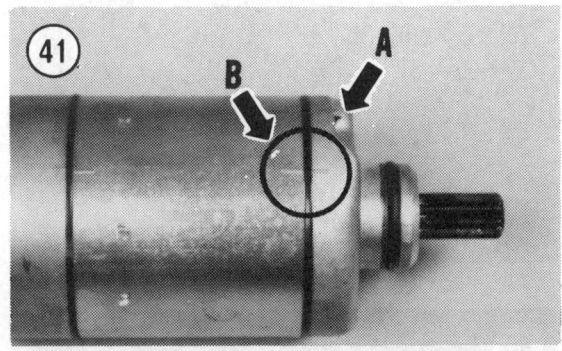

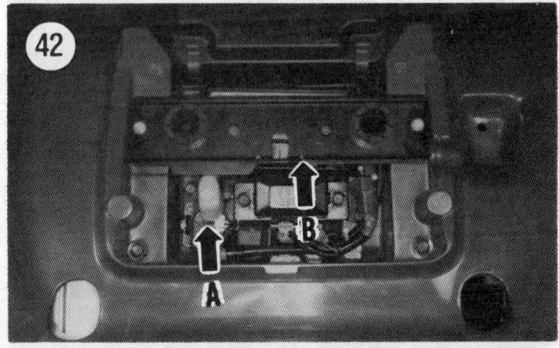

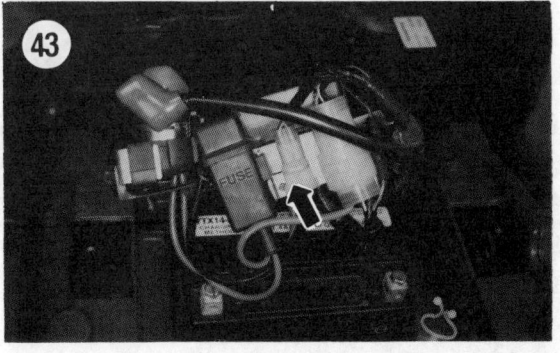

8. Install the front cover (A, **Figure 41**) over the armature shaft. Align the marks on the front cover and the case (B, **Figure 41**).

9. Lubricate the O-rings (23, **Figure 19**) with oil.

10. Install the bolts, washers and O-rings (**Figure 20**) and tighten the bolts securely.

*NOTE*
*If one or both bolts will not pass through the starter motor, the end covers and/or brush plate are installed incorrectly.*

## STARTER RELAY SWITCH

### System Test

System testing of the starter relay switch is described under *Electric Starting System* in Chapter Two.

### Operation Check

1. Remove the seat (Chapter Fifteen).

2. Turn the ignition switch on and depress the starter button. The starter relay (A, **Figure 42**) should click. If the starter relay did not click, perform the *Voltage Test* in this section.

3. Turn the ignition switch off and install the seat (Chapter Fifteen).

### Voltage Test

1. Remove the seat (Chapter Fifteen).

2. Remove the battery holder bracket (B, **Figure 42**).

3. Disconnect the starter relay connector (**Figure 43**).

*NOTE*
*Figure 43 shows the starter relay connector with the relay removed for clarity.*

4. Connect a voltmeter between the starter relay connector yellow/red (+) and green/red (–) wire terminals at the wiring harness end of the connector.

5. Shift the transmission into neutral and turn the ignition switch on, then depress the starter button. The voltmeter should read battery voltage. If the voltmeter reading is incorrect, perform the *Continuity Test* in this section.

6. Turn the ignition switch off.

7. Reverse Steps 1-3 to complete installation.

## Continuity Test

1. Remove the starter relay switch (A, **Figure 42**) as described in this chapter.

2. Connect an ohmmeter to the starter relay switch battery and starter motor terminals (**Figure 44**).

3. Momentarily connect a 12-volt battery to the starter relay switch terminals as shown in **Figure 44** while reading the resistance on the ohmmeter.

4. The ohmmeter must show continuity when battery voltage is applied and no continuity when the battery voltage is removed.

5. If either reading is incorrect, replace the starter relay switch and retest.

## Removal/Installation

1. Remove the seat (Chapter Fifteen).

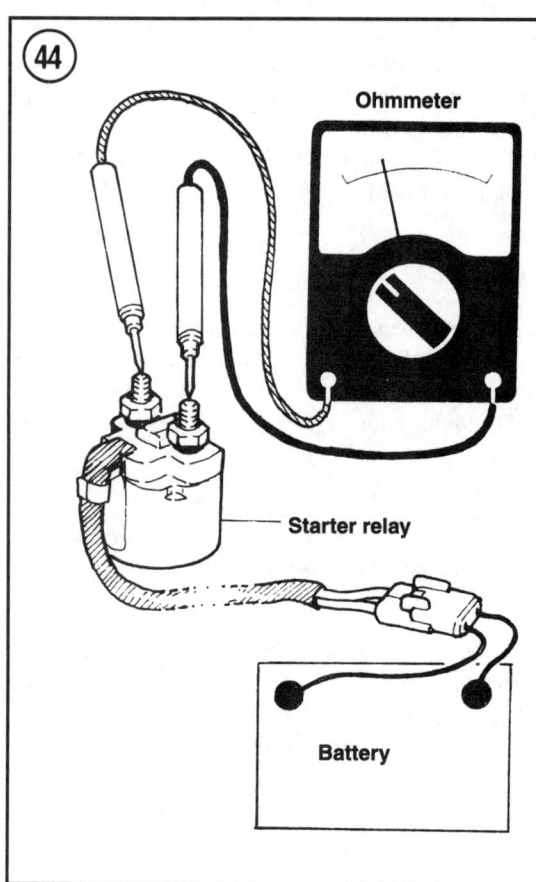

2. Disconnect the negative battery cable from the battery (Chapter Three).

3. Remove the battery holder bracket (B, **Figure 42**).

4. Remove the two pins (**Figure 45**) and lift out the starter relay/fuse box assembly.

5. Disconnect the starter relay connector (**Figure 43**).

6. Slide the two covers away from the terminals on top of the starter relay switch.

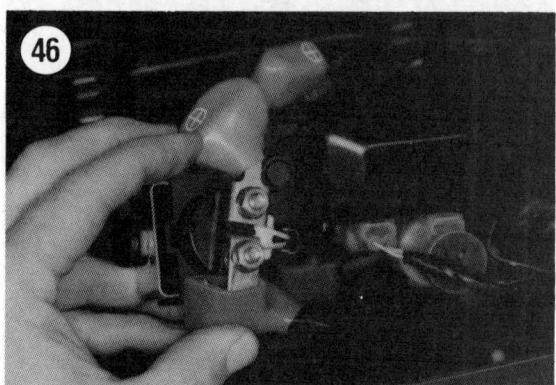

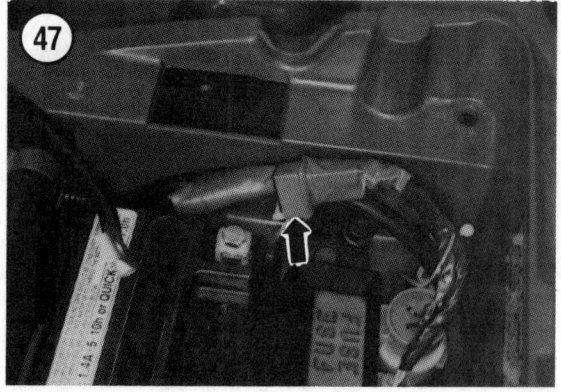

7. Disconnect the battery and starter motor cables from the starter relay switch (**Figure 46**).

8. Remove the starter relay switch and its rubber mount from the frame.

9. Install the starter relay switch by reversing the preceding removal procedures.

## DIODE

A diode is installed in the starting circuit (**Figure 15**). Test the diode when troubleshooting a neutral indicator circuit problem.

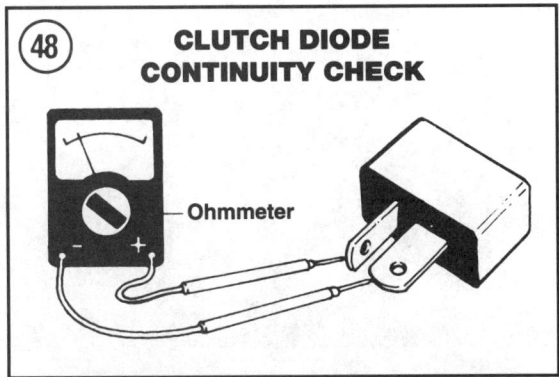

**CLUTCH DIODE CONTINUITY CHECK**

Ohmmeter

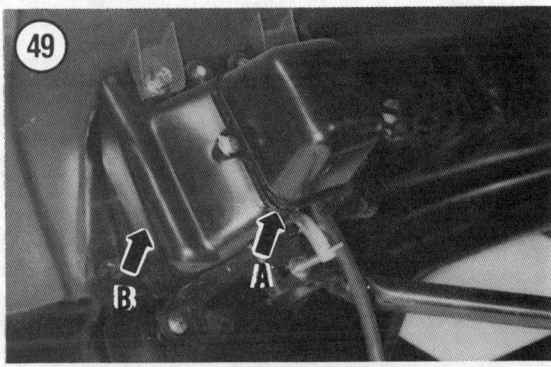

**Removal/Testing/Installation**

1. Remove the seat (Chapter Fifteen).

2. Disconnect the negative battery cable from the battery (Chapter Three).

3. Remove the battery holder bracket (B, **Figure 42**).

4. Remove the tape from around the diode (**Figure 47**) and disconnect the diode from the wiring harness.

5. Test the diode as follows:

   a. Set an ohmmeter to the R × 1 scale.

   b. Check for continuity between the two terminals on the diode (**Figure 48**), then reverse ohmmeter leads and recheck for continuity. The Ohmmeter must read continuity during one test and no continuity (infinite resistance) with the leads reversed.

   c. Replace the diode if it fails the continuity test.

6. Reverse Steps 1-4 to install the diode.

## LIGHTING SYSTEM

The lighting system consists of a headlight, assist headlight, taillight and indicator lights. **Table 5** lists replacement bulbs for these components.

Always use the correct wattage bulb listed in **Table 5**. Using the wrong size bulb will produce a dim light or cause the bulb to burn out prematurely.

**Headlight Bulb Replacement**

*WARNING*
*If the headlight just burned out or you just turned it off, it will be hot! Do not touch the bulb until it cools.*

1. Remove the screw and the headlight bulb cover (A, **Figure 49**).

2. Remove the dust cover (**Figure 50**).

3. Turn and remove the bulb socket (**Figure 51**).

4. Remove the bulb (**Figure 52**).

5. Install the new bulb (**Figure 52**) by aligning the bulb tab with the groove in the bulb housing.

6. Install the bulb socket (**Figure 51**). Turn and lock it in place.

7. Install the dust cover (**Figure 50**) with its TOP mark facing up. Make sure the dust cover seats completely against the headlight housing.

8. Install the headlight bulb cover (A, **Figure 49**) by aligning its tab with the groove in the headlight housing.

9. Check headlight operation.

### Headlight Housing
### Removal/Installation

1. Remove the screw and the headlight bulb cover (A, **Figure 49**).

2. Remove the dust cover (**Figure 50**).

3. Turn and remove the bulb socket (**Figure 51**).

4. Remove the bolts and screws and the headlight housing (B, **Figure 49**).

5. Install the headlight housing by reversing these removal steps. Check headlight operation.

### Assist Headlight
### Bulb Replacement

1. Remove the two bolts (A, **Figure 53**) and the headlight housing (B).

> *NOTE*
> *Metal grommets installed in the headlight housing may fall out after removing the bolts in Step 1.*

2. Disconnect the electrical connector (A, **Figure 54**) from the bulb and remove the headlight assembly.

3. Remove the dust cover (B, **Figure 54**) from around the bulb.

> *CAUTION*
> *All models use a quartz-halogen bulb (**Figure 55**). Because traces of oil on this type of bulb will reduce the life of*

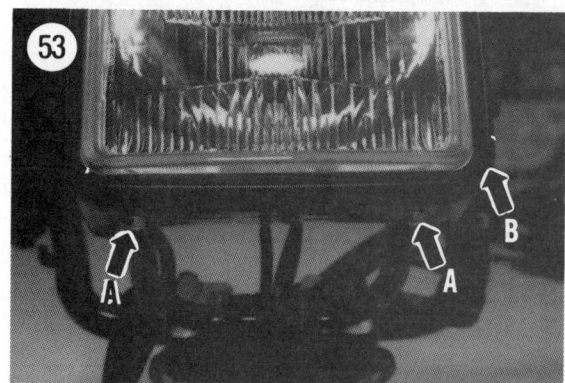

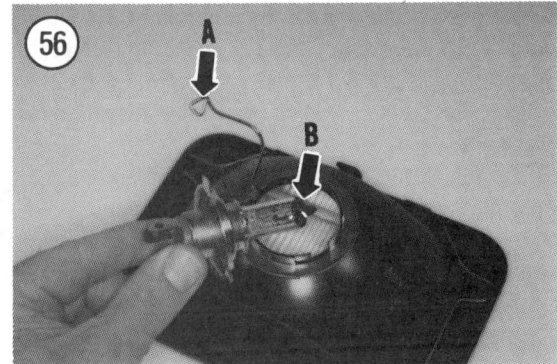

*the bulb, do not touch the bulb glass with your fingers. Clean any traces of oil or other contamination from the bulb with a cloth moistened in alcohol or lacquer thinner.*

4. Unhook the bulb retainer (A, **Figure 56**) and remove the bulb (B, **Figure 56**).

5. Install the bulb by reversing these removal steps, while noting the following.

6. Align the tabs on the bulb with the notches in the bulb holder and install the bulb.

7. Make sure the dust cover fits snugly around the bulb.

8. Start the engine and check the assist headlight operation.

### Taillight Bulb Replacement

1. Turn the bulb holder (**Figure 57**) counterclockwise and remove it from the lens housing.

2. Remove the old bulb (**Figure 58**).

3. Reverse these steps to install a new bulb, while noting the following.

4. Start the engine and check taillight operation.

### Indicator Bulb Replacement

The indicator bulbs are mounted in the handlebar cover. The bulbs can be removed without having to remove the handlebar cover.

1. Remove the lens (**Figure 59**) from the end of the socket.

2. Pull the socket (**Figure 60**) out of the handlebar cover, then remove the bulb (**Figure 61**).

3. Reverse these steps to install the new bulb, while noting the following.

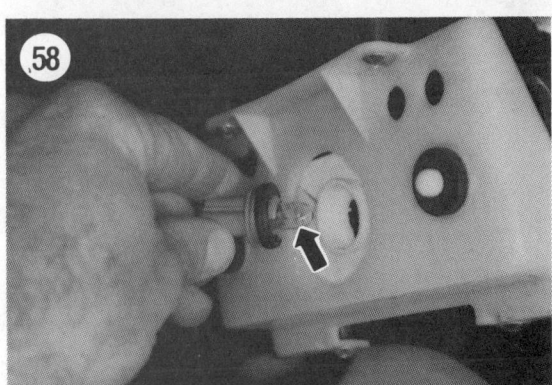

9

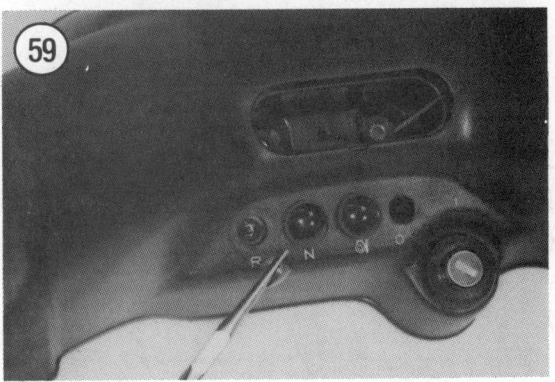

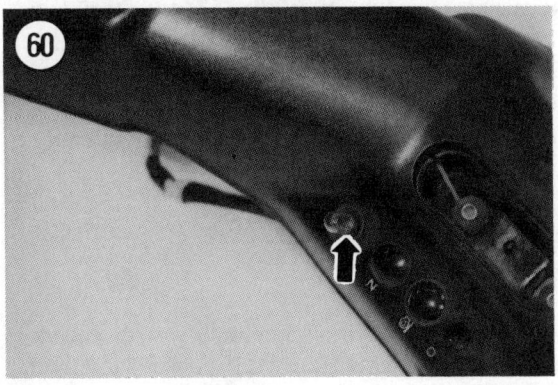

4. When installing the socket, align the tab on the socket with the groove in the handlebar cover.

5. Start the engine and check bulb operation.

## COMBINATION METER

The combination meter (**Figure 62**) consists of an hourmeter, hourmeter indicator, speedometer, odometer and tripmeter. The hourmeter operates whenever the ignition switch is turned on. When the ignition switch is turned on, the hourmeter indicator should blink, indicating that the hourmeter is working properly.

### Troubleshooting

Refer to Chapter Two.

### Bulb Replacement

1. Remove the assist headlight as described under *Assist Headlight Bulb Replacement* in this chapter.
2. Remove the plug and remove the bulb holder. See A, **Figure 63**, typical.
3. Replace the blown bulb with a new one.
4. Install by reversing these steps.

### Removal/Installation

1. Remove the front fender (Chapter Fifteen).
2. Remove the assist headlight as described under *Assist Headlight Bulb Replacement* in this chapter.
3. Disconnect the combination meter electrical connector. Follow the meter's wiring harness from the meter to the connectors mounted on the left side of the vehicle. Then pull the wiring harness past its clamps until it is free from the frame.
4. Remove the nuts (B, **Figure 63**) and the combination meter assembly.
5. Install the combination meter by reversing these removal steps.
6. Start the engine and check the meter's operation.

## SWITCHES

### Testing

You can test switches for continuity with an ohmmeter (see Chapter One) or a self-powered test light.

Test at the switch connector by operating the switch in each of its operating positions and comparing the results with its switch continuity diagram. For example, see the starter switch continuity diagram in **Figure 64**.

When the starter button is depressed, there will be continuity between the black/brown and yellow/red terminals (**Figure 64**). The wire joining the two terminals shows continuity (**Figure 64**). An ohmmeter connected between these two terminals will show no resistance or a test light will light. When the

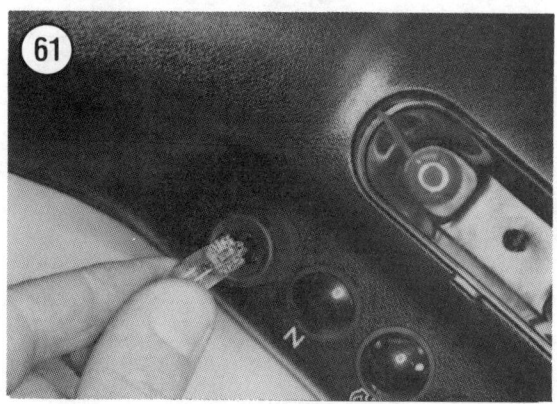

starter button is released (free position), there will be no continuity between the same terminals.

When testing switches, note the following:

a. Check the fuses as described under *Fuses* in this chapter.

b. Check the battery as described under *Battery* in Chapter Three. Charge the battery to the correct state of charge, if required.

c. Before testing the switches, disconnect the negative battery cable from the battery (Chapter Three) and disconnect the switch electrical connector.

*CAUTION*
*Do not attempt to start the engine with the negative battery cable disconnected.*

d. When you separate two connectors, pull on the connector housings and not the wires.

e. After finding a defective circuit, check the connectors to make sure they are clean and properly connected. Check all wires going into a connector housing for loose connections or damage.

f. When joining two connectors, push them until they click or snap into place.

If a switch or button does not perform properly, replace the switch as described in this section. Refer to **Figure 64** for the handlebar switches and **Figure 65** for the ignition switch. The neutral/reverse switch is tested separately in this section.

**Left Handlebar Switch Housing Replacement**

The left handlebar switch housing is equipped with the following switches:

a. Lighting switch (A, **Figure 66**).

b. Dimmer switch (B, **Figure 66**).

c. Engine stop switch (C, **Figure 66**).

d. Starter switch (D, **Figure 66**).

*NOTE*
*The switches mounted in the left handlebar switch housing are not available separately. If one switch is damaged, replace the switch housing assembly.*

1. Remove the handlebar cover (Chapter Fifteen).

2. Remove the front fender (Chapter Fifteen).

3. Disconnect the choke cable at the left handlebar switch housing as follows:

9

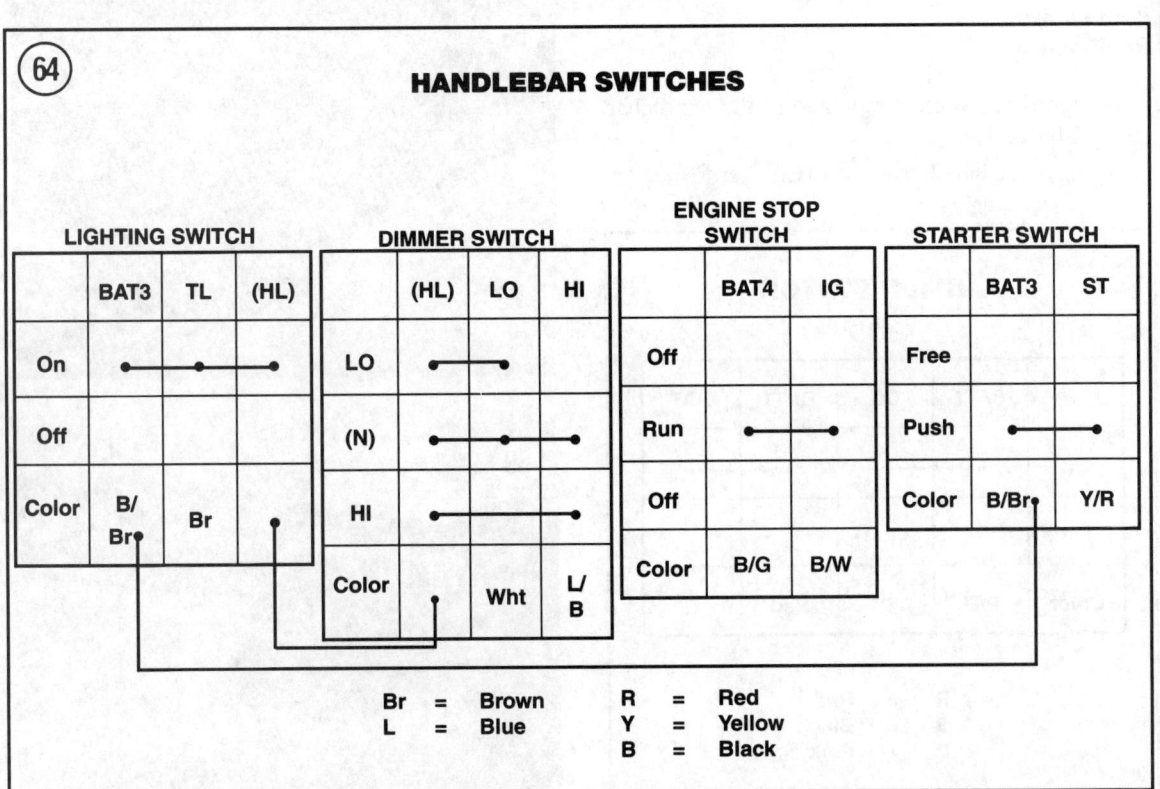

**(64) HANDLEBAR SWITCHES**

**LIGHTING SWITCH**

|  | BAT3 | TL | (HL) |
|---|---|---|---|
| On | •——•——• | | |
| Off | | | |
| Color | B/Br• | Br | • |

**DIMMER SWITCH**

|  | (HL) | LO | HI |
|---|---|---|---|
| LO | •——• | | |
| (N) | •——•——• | | |
| HI | •——•——• | | |
| Color | • | Wht | L/ B |

**ENGINE STOP SWITCH**

|  | BAT4 | IG |
|---|---|---|
| Off | | |
| Run | •——• | |
| Off | | |
| Color | B/G | B/W |

**STARTER SWITCH**

|  | BAT3 | ST |
|---|---|---|
| Free | | |
| Push | •——• | |
| Color | B/Br• | Y/R |

| Br | = | Brown | | R | = | Red |
|---|---|---|---|---|---|---|
| L | = | Blue | | Y | = | Yellow |
| | | | | B | = | Black |

   a. Remove the spring clamp (**Figure 67**).

   b. Disconnect and remove the choke cable (**Figure 68**) from the switch housing.

4. Remove any clamps securing the switch wiring harness to the handlebar.

5. Disconnect the left handlebar switch electrical connectors.

6. Remove the switch housing screws and separate the switch halves. Remove the switch and its wiring harness from the frame.

7. Install the switch housing by reversing these removal steps, while noting the following:

   a. Align the rear switch housing pin with the hole in the handlebar (**Figure 69**), then install the housing.

   b. **Figure 70** shows the choke cable mounting position with the switch housing removed for clarity. Refer to **Figure 70** when reconnecting the choke cable.

   c. Tighten the upper switch housing screw first, then the lower screw.

8. Start the engine and check the switch in each of its operating positions.

## Ignition Switch
## Replacement

The ignition switch is mounted in the handlebar cover (**Figure 71**).

1. Remove the handlebar cover (Chapter Fifteen).

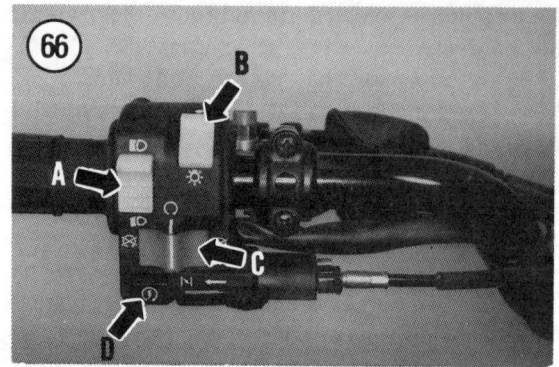

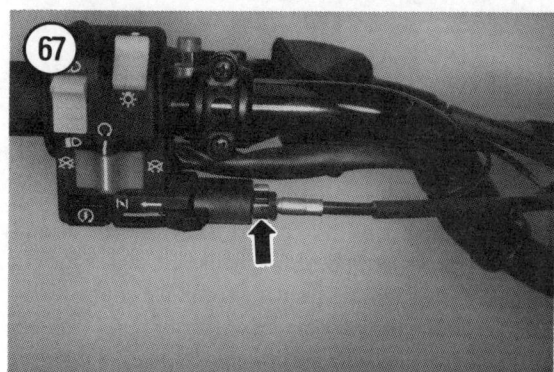

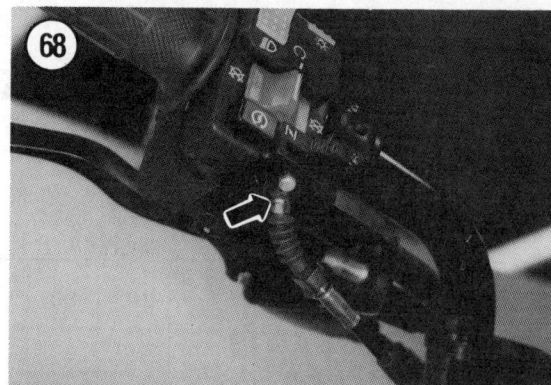

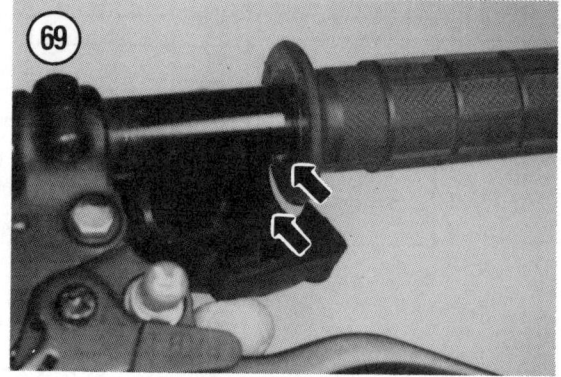

**IGNITION SWITCH**

|        | BAT2 | DC  | BAT1 | BAT |
|--------|------|-----|------|-----|
| On     | ●——— | —● | ●——— | —● |
| Off    |      |     |      |     |
| Color  | R/B  | P   | Red  | B   |

R = Red
B = Black
P = Pink

2. Disconnect the ignition switch wiring harness from the clamp on the bottom of the handlebar cover.

3. Push the ignition switch (**Figure 72**) out from the bottom side and remove it.

4. Install the ignition switch by reversing the preceding steps, plus the following:

  a. Install the new switch by aligning the two plastic guide strips on the switch housing with the notch in the switch mounting hole (**Figure 72**). Then push the switch in place.

  b. Turn the ignition switch on and check its operation.

### Neutral/Reverse Switch Testing/Replacement

The neutral/reverse switch (**Figure 73**) is mounted inside the alternator cover.

1. Disconnect the neutral/reverse switch electrical connector (A, **Figure 74**).

2. Switch an ohmmeter to the R × 1 scale and connect the leads between the light green/red wire terminal and ground. The ohmmeter should show continuity when the transmission is in neutral and infinity when the transmission is in gear.

3. Connect the ohmmeter leads between the gray wire and ground. The ohmmeter should show continuity when the transmission is in reverse and infinity when the transmission is in any other gear or neutral.

4. If one or both readings are incorrect, replace the neutral/reverse switch as follows:

  a. Remove the alternator cover (Chapter Five).

  b. Remove the bolt and the neutral/reverse switch (**Figure 73**).

  c. Remove all threadlock residue from the bolt and bolt threads.

9

d. Apply a threadlock to the neutral/reverse switch bolt threads.

e. Install the new neutral/reverse switch and tighten its bolt securely.

f. Install the alternator cover (Chapter Five).

5. Reconnect the neutral/reverse switch electrical connector (A, **Figure 74**).

6. Start the engine and check the neutral/reverse switch indicator light operation.

## OIL THERMOSENSOR

The oil thermosensor (**Figure 75**) is installed in the rear crankcase .

### Testing

1. Remove the front fender (Chapter Fifteen).

2. Disconnect the cooling fan control unit 2-prong connector (A, **Figure 76**) at the cooling fan control unit. Make sure the wire is connected to the thermosensor at the engine.

3. Switch an ohmmeter to Rx1000. Measure resistance between the blue wire terminal (wiring harness side) and ground. The ohmmeter should read 9500-10,500 ohms. If the reading is out of specification, remove the oil thermosensor (as described in this section) and bench test it as follows.

> *WARNING*
> *Wear safety glasses or goggles and gloves during this test. Keep all flammable materials away from the burner.*

4. Use an ohmmeter with alligator clips on the test lead ends. Attach one of the alligator clips to the electrical connector on the sensor. Attach the other alligator clip to the housing.

5. Suspend the thermosensor in a small pan filled with engine oil.

6. Place a thermometer in the pan of oil. Do not let the sensor or the thermometer touch the pan as it will give false readings.

7. Heat the oil and check the resistance readings at the temperatures listed below:

a. At 150° C (302° F), the ohmmeter should read 306-340 ohms.

b. At 170° C (338° F), the ohmmeter should read 209-231 ohms.

8. If the resistance readings are incorrect, replace the thermosensor.

9. Install the oil thermosensor as described in this section.

10. Reverse Steps 1 and 2 to complete installation.

### Removal/Installation

1. Drain the engine oil (Chapter Three).

2. Disconnect the connector from the thermosensor and remove the thermosensor (**Figure 75**).

3. Reverse Steps 1 and 2 to install the thermosensor, plus the following:

a. Tighten the oil thermosensor as specified in **Table 4**.

b. After starting the engine, check for oil leaks.

## COOLING FAN CONTROL UNIT

The cooling fan control unit (B, **Figure 76**) is mounted at the front of the vehicle, underneath the front fender.

### System Testing

This test does not test the cooling fan control unit; it checks the wires leading to the unit.

1. Remove the front fender (Chapter Fifteen).

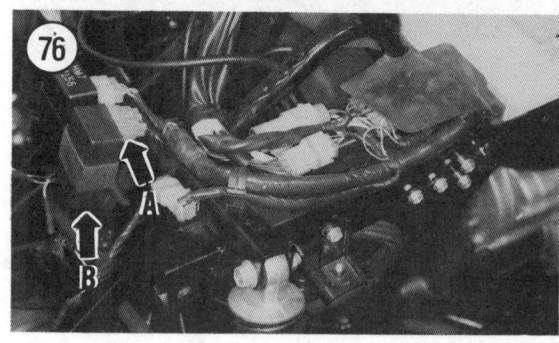

2. Disconnect the two connectors (A, **Figure 76**) from the cooling fan control unit.

3. Check the connectors for loose pins, corrosion or damaged wires.

*NOTE*
*When performing the tests in Steps 4-7, connect the test probes between the connector terminals at the wiring harness end of the connectors, not at the cooling fan control unit end.*

4. *Test 1*—Perform the following:
   a. Switch an ohmmeter to R × 1000.
   b. Connect the ohmmeter between the blue wire and ground.
   c. The ohmmeter should read 9500-10,500 ohms.

5. *Test 2*—Perform the following:
   a. Switch an ohmmeter to R × 1.
   b. Connect the ohmmeter between the sky blue wire and ground.
   c. The ohmmeter should show continuity.

6. *Test 3*—Perform the following:
   a. Switch an ohmmeter to R × 1.
   b. Connect the ohmmeter between the green wire and ground.
   c. The ohmmeter should show continuity.

7. *Test 4*—Perform the following:
   a. Connect a voltmeter between the white/black wire (+) and ground (−).
   b. Turn the ignition switch on and the engine stop switch to run. The voltmeter should read 13.0-13.2 volts (battery voltage).
   c. Repeat this check with the voltmeter connected between the blue/red wire (+) wire and ground (−). Then between the pink wire (+) and ground (−). The voltmeter should read 13.0-13.2 volts each time.
   d. Turn the ignition switch off and disconnect the voltmeter leads.

8. If all of the wires test correctly as described in this section, replace the cooling fan control unit.

9. Reverse Steps 1 and 2 to complete installation.

**Removal/Installation**

1. Remove the front fender (Chapter Fifteen).
2. Disconnect the two connectors (A, **Figure 76**) from the cooling fan control unit.
3. Remove the cooling fan control unit (B, **Figure 76**) from its rubber mount and replace it.
4. Reverse Steps 1 and 2 to complete installation.

## SPEEDOMETER SENSOR UNIT (1997-ON)

The speedometer sensor unit is mounted in the rear crankcase cover (**Figure 77**).

**Testing**

Refer to *Combination Meter* in Chapter Two.

**Removal/Installation**

1. Disconnect the speedometer sensor electrical connector (B, **Figure 74**).
2. Remove the bolts and the speedometer sensor unit (**Figure 78**).
3. Replace the two O-rings (**Figure 79**) if leaking or damaged.
4. Install by reversing the preceding removal steps, plus the following:

a. Lubricate the two O-rings (**Figure 79**) with engine oil.

b. Align the end of the speedometer sensor shaft (**Figure 78**) with the mating hole in the end of the countershaft.

c. Tighten the mounting bolts securely.

## FUSES

Whenever the fuse blows, determine the reason for the failure before replacing the fuse. Usually, the trouble is a short circuit in the wiring, which may be caused by worn-through insulation or a disconnected wire touching ground.

See **Table 6** for fuse ratings.

### Main Fuse

The main fuse (A, **Figure 80**) is mounted in the battery compartment.

1. Remove the seat (Chapter Fifteen).

2. Check that the ignition switch is turned off.

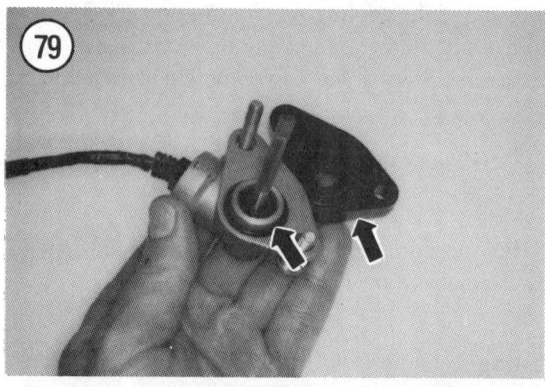

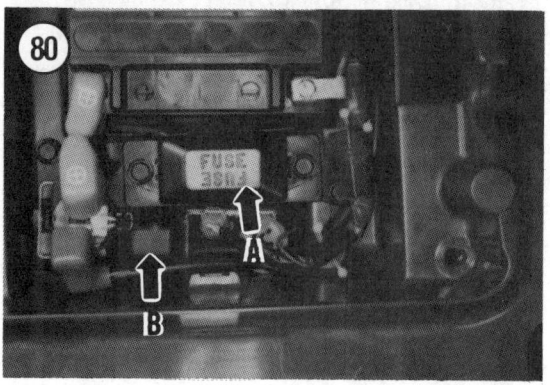

*CAUTION*
*If the main fuse is replaced with the ignition switch turned on, an accidental short circuit could damage the electrical system.*

3. Remove the two pins and lift out the electrical panel, then remove the main fuse box (**Figure 81**).

4. Replace the damaged main fuse (**Figure 82**).

*NOTE*
*Purchase a new replacement main fuse and store it in the fuse box.*

5. Install by reversing the preceding removal steps.

### Sub-Fuses

The sub-fuse box (B, **Figure 80**) is mounted in the battery compartment.

1. Remove the seat (Chapter Fifteen).

2. Check that the ignition switch is turned off.

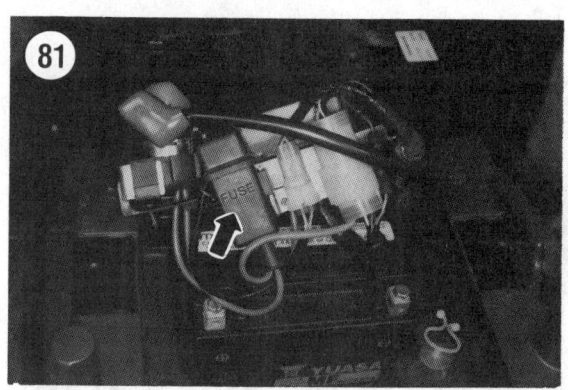

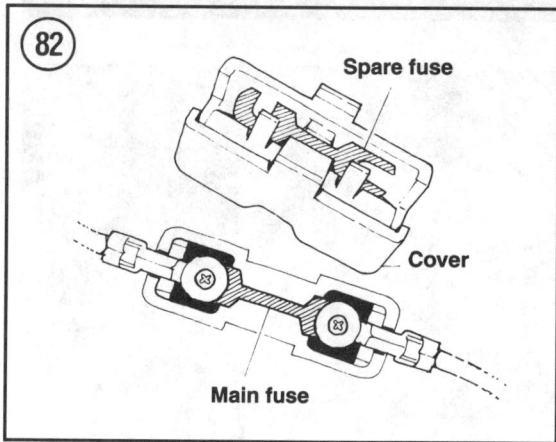

Spare fuse

Cover

Main fuse

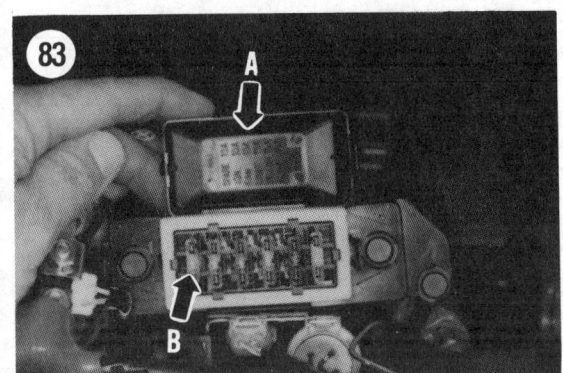

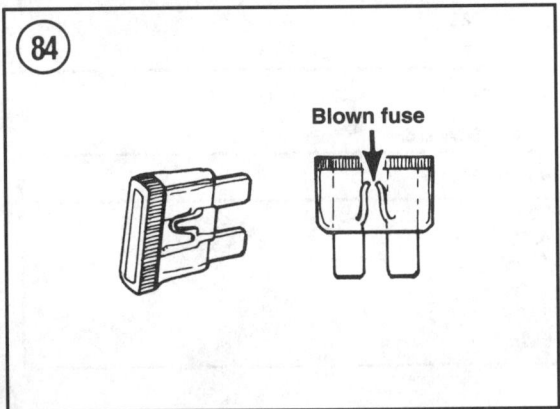

Blown fuse

*CAUTION*
*If the main fuse is replaced with the ignition switch turned on, an accidental short circuit could damage the electrical system.*

3. Remove the fuse box cover (A, **Figure 83**). Remove the fuse (A, **Figure 83**). Replace the fuse if blown (**Figure 84**).

*NOTE*
*The size and function of each fuse is labeled inside the fuse box cover (B, **Figure 83**).*

*NOTE*
*Always carry spare fuses.*

4. Install by reversing the preceding removal steps.

## WIRING DIAGRAMS

Wiring diagrams for all models are located at the end of this book.

**9**

### Table 1 CHARGING SYSTEM SPECIFICATIONS

| | |
|---|---|
| Alternator | |
|   Capacity | 0.310 kW at 5000 rpm |
|   Stator coil resistance* | 0.1-1.0 ohms |
| Regulator/rectifier | |
|   Type | Triple phase/full-wave rectification |
| Regulated voltage | 14.7-15.5 volts at 5000 rpm |

*Tests must be made at 20° C (68° F). Do not test if the engine or component is hot.

### Table 2 IGNITION SYSTEM SPECIFICATIONS

| | |
|---|---|
| Ignition coil peak voltage | 100 volts minimum |
| Ignition pulse generator peak voltage | 0.7 volts minimum |
| Ignition coil resistance* | |
|   Primary | 0.1-0.2 ohm |
|   Secondary | |
|     With spark plug cap | 6500-9800 ohms |
|     Without spark plug cap | 2700-3500 ohms |
| Ignition pulse generator resistance* | 290-360 ohms |

*Tests must be made at 20° C (68° F). Do not test if the engine or component is hot.

## Table 3 STARTER MOTOR SERVICE SPECIFICATIONS

|                            | New<br>mm (in.) | Service limit<br>mm (in.) |
|----------------------------|-----------------|---------------------------|
| Starter motor brush length | 12.5<br>(0.49)  | 9.0<br>(0.35)             |

## Table 4 ELECTRICAL SYSTEM TIGHTENING TORQUES

|                                        | N·m | in.-lb. | ft.-lb. |
|----------------------------------------|-----|---------|---------|
| Starter one-way clutch Allen bolts     | 31  | —       | 23      |
| Stator Allen bolts                     | 10  | 88      | —       |
| Ignition pulse generator Allen bolts   | 6   | 53      | —       |
| Neutral/reverse switch mounting bolt   | 12  | 106     | —       |
| Oil thermosensor                       | 18  | —       | 13      |
| Timing hole cap                        | 10  | 88      | —       |
| Recoil pulley flange bolt (rotor bolt) | 110 | —       | 81      |

## Table 5 REPLACEMENT BULBS

|                    | Voltage-wattage |
|--------------------|-----------------|
| Headlight          | 12V-25W         |
| Assist headlight   | 12V-45W         |
| Neutral indicator  | 12V-1.7W        |
| Oil light indicator| 12V-1.7W        |
| Reverse indicator  | 12V-1.7W        |
| Taillight          | 12V-5W          |

## Table 6 FUSES

|                                | Fuse rating |
|--------------------------------|-------------|
| Main fuse                      | 30 amp      |
| Sub-fuses located in fuse box  |             |
| Fan motor                      | 15 amp      |
| Lights                         | 15 amp      |
| Fan motor control unit         | 10 amp      |
| Ignition                       | 10 amp      |

# FRONT SUSPENSION AND STEERING

This chapter describes repair and maintenance of the front wheels, suspension arms and steering components.

Refer to **Table 1** for general front suspension and steering specifications. **Tables 2-4** list service specifications and torque specifications. **Tables 1-4** are at the end of this chapter.

> *CAUTION*
> *Self-locking nuts are used to secure some of the front suspension components. Honda recommends that all self-locking nuts **must be discarded** once they have been removed. The self-locking portion of the nut is weakened once the nut has been removed and will no longer properly lock onto the mating threads. Always install new self-locking nuts. Never reinstall a used nut once it has been removed.*

## FRONT WHEEL

### Removal/Installation

1. Park the vehicle on level ground and set the parking brake.

> *NOTE*
> *Mark the tires for location and direction before removing them.*

2. Loosen the front wheel lug nuts (**Figure 1**).
3. Support the vehicle with the front wheels off the ground.
4. Place wooden blocks(s) under the frame to support the vehicle securely with the front wheels off the ground.
5. Remove the wheel nuts and front wheel (**Figure 1**).
6. Inspect the nuts and replace them if damaged.
7. Inspect the wheels and replace if damaged. Refer to *Tires and Wheels* in this chapter.
8. Install the front wheel by reversing these removal steps, plus the following:
   a. Install the wheel nuts (**Figure 2**) with their curved side facing toward the wheel. First install the wheel nuts finger-tight and check that the wheel sits squarely against the front hub.
   b. Lower the vehicle so that both front wheels are on the ground.
   c. Tighten the wheel nuts in a crisscross pattern to the torque specification in **Table 4**.

d. Support the vehicle again so that both front wheels are off the ground.

e. Rotate the wheels and then apply the front brake. Repeat this step several times to make sure each wheel rotates freely and that its brake is working properly.

## FRONT HUB

Refer to **Figure 3** when servicing the front hub assembly in the following sections.

### Removal/Installation

1. Remove the front wheel as described in this chapter.

> *WARNING*
> *Do not inhale brake dust. It may contain asbestos, which can cause lung injury and cancer.*

2A. To remove the brake drum only, remove the bolts (A, **Figure 4**) and brake drum.

2B. To remove the brake drum and front hub at the same time, perform the following:

a. Remove and discard the axle nut cotter pin (B, **Figure 4**).

b. Remove the axle nut and front hub assembly (C, **Figure 4**).

3. Inspect the front hub as described in this chapter.

4. Refer to Chapter Thirteen to service the brake drum and brake drum seal (A, **Figure 5**).

5. Install the front hub by reversing these removal steps, plus the following:

a. If the brake drum was removed from the front hub, install the O-ring (B, **Figure 5**) into the brake drum groove.

b. If the brake drum was removed from the front hub, install the brake drum and tighten its mounting bolts (A, **Figure 4**) as specified in **Table 4**.

c. Install and tighten the axle nut (B, **Figure 4**) as specified in **Table 4**.

> *NOTE*
> *If necessary, tighten the axle nut to align it with the cotter pin hole in the axle. Do not loosen the axle nut to align it with the hole.*

> *WARNING*
> *Always install a new cotter pin.*

c. Install a new cotter pin through the nut groove and axle hole, and then spread its ends to lock it in place (**Figure 6**).

### Inspection

1. Inspect the dust seal (C, **Figure 5**) and replace if damaged.

2. Inspect the studs (D, **Figure 5**) and replace if damaged.

3. Clean and dry the hub splines.

4. Check the hub for cracks or other damage.

5. Service the dust seal (A, **Figure 5**) and brake drum as described under *Brake Drum* in Chapter Thirteen.

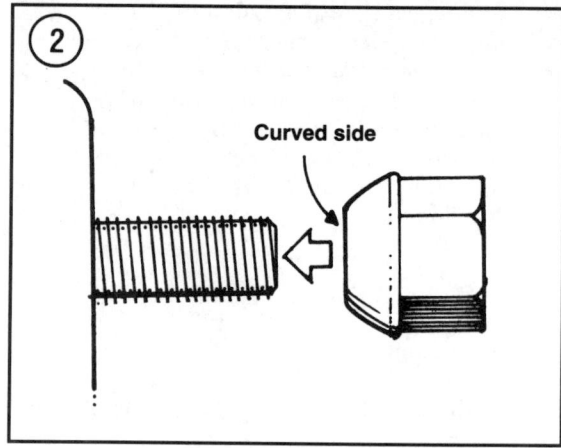

Curved side

③

# FRONT WHEEL AND HUB

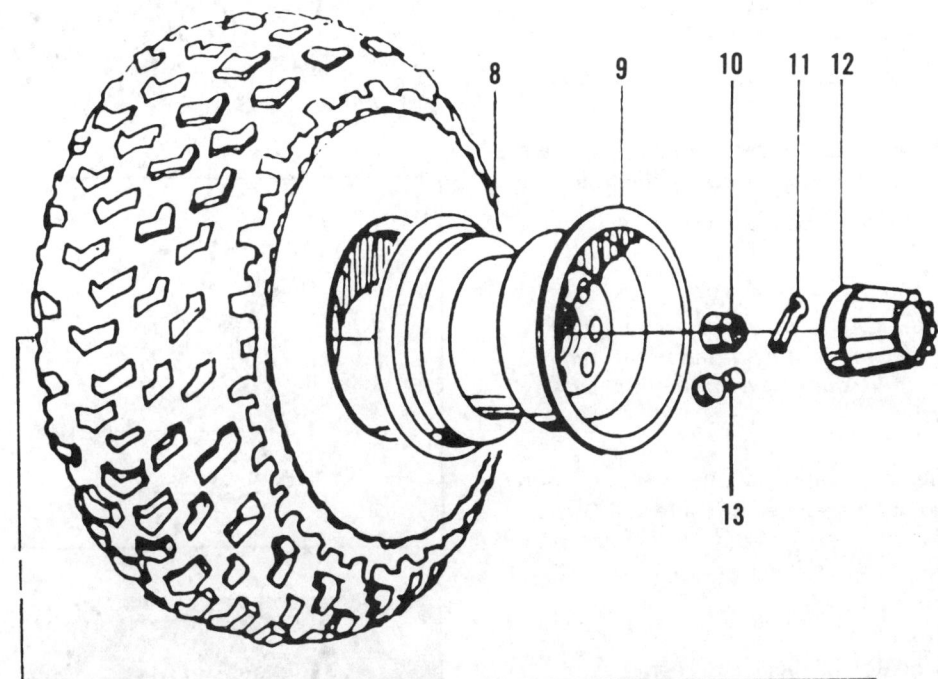

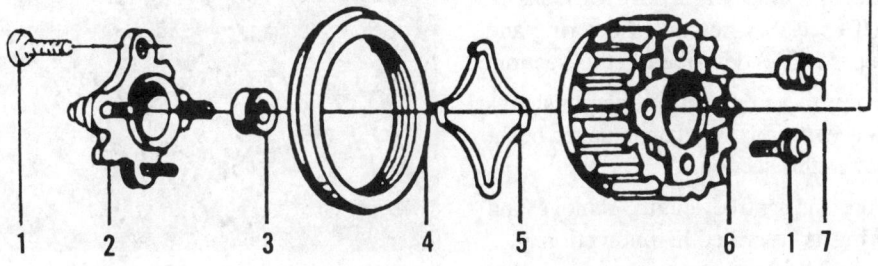

10

1. Bolt
2. Hub
3. Dust seal
4. Waterproof seal
5. O-ring
6. Brake drum
7. Plug
8. Tire
9. Wheel
10. Axle nut
11. Cotter pin
12. Cap
13. Valve stem

## SHOCK ABSORBERS

### Removal/Installation

1. Support the vehicle with the front wheels off the ground.

2. Remove the upper and lower shock absorber locknuts and bolts and remove the shock absorber (**Figure 7**). Discard the locknuts.

3. Inspect the shock absorber as described in this chapter.

4. Install the shock absorber by reversing the preceding removal steps, while noting the following:

    a. Install new shock locknuts.

> *CAUTION*
> *See the CAUTION at the beginning of this chapter relating to the use of self-locking locknuts used on the front suspension.*

    b. Tighten the upper and lower shock absorber locknuts as specified in **Table 4**.

### Inspection

1. Clean and dry the shock absorber.

2. Check the damper unit (**Figure 8**) for leaks or other damage. If necessary, remove the spring and replace the damper unit as described in this section.

3. Inspect the upper and lower rubber bushings (**Figure 9**). Replace severely worn or damaged bushings as described in this section.

4. To inspect the spring free length, remove and measure the spring as described in this section.

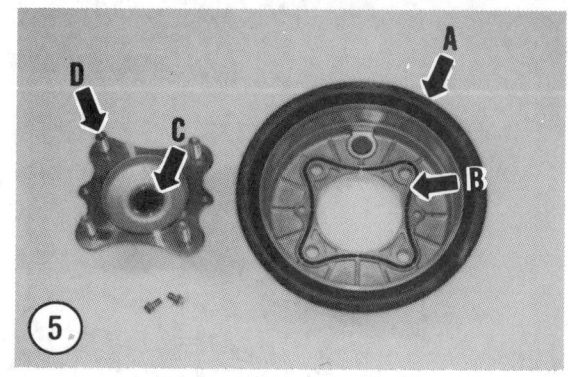

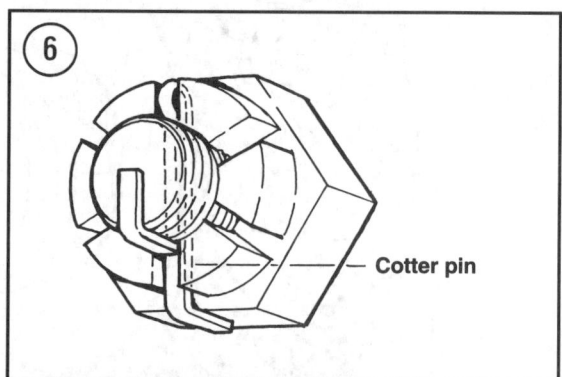

Cotter pin

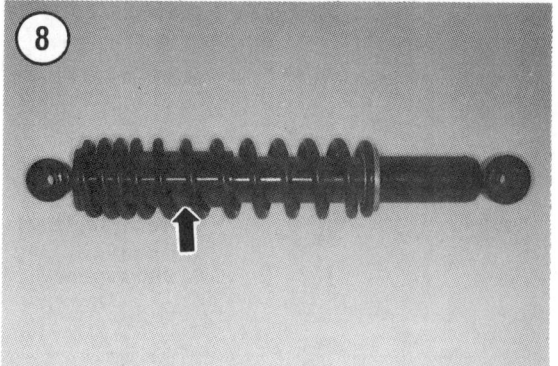

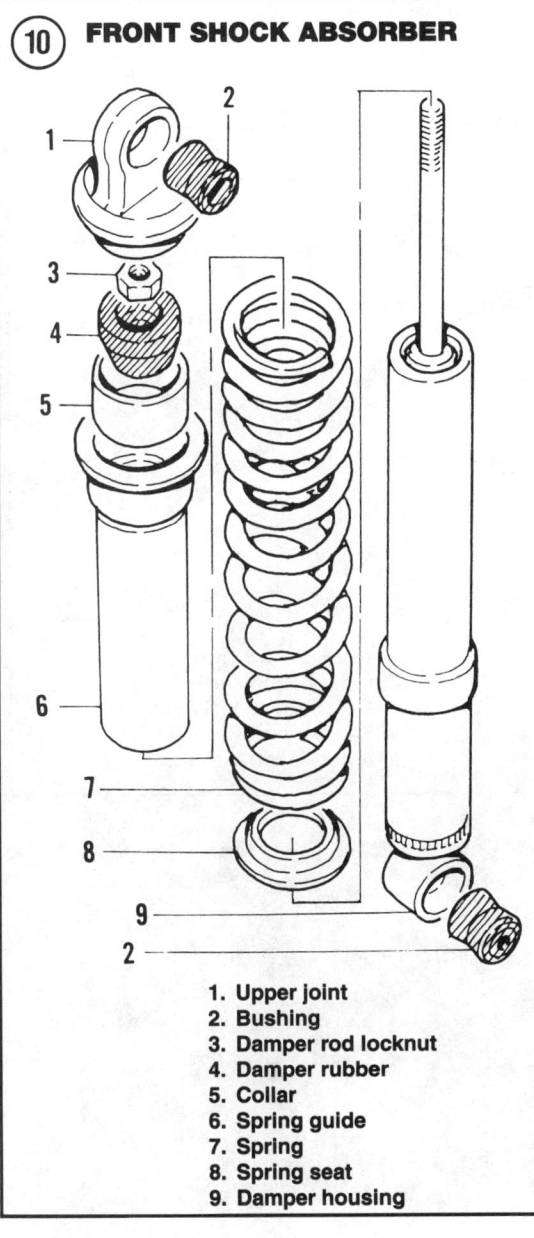

**FRONT SHOCK ABSORBER**

1. Upper joint
2. Bushing
3. Damper rod locknut
4. Damper rubber
5. Collar
6. Spring guide
7. Spring
8. Spring seat
9. Damper housing

## Spring Removal/Installation

The shock is spring-controlled and hydraulically damped. Do not attempt to service the sealed shock damper unit. Service is limited to removal and replacement of the damper unit, spring and shock bushings.

Refer to **Figure 10**.

> *WARNING*
> *Do not unscrew the upper shock joint without a spring compressor. The spring is under considerable pressure and may fly off and cause injury.*

> *NOTE*
> *Always follow the manufacturer's directions when using a spring compressor.*

1. Install the shock absorber into a spring compressor tool. See **Figure 11**, typical.

2. Compress the shock spring just enough to gain access to the locknut. Then loosen the locknut and unscrew the upper joint.

3. Release tension from the spring and remove the shock from the compression tool.

4. Remove the spring guide, collar, damper rubber, spring and spring seat.

5. Measure the spring free length (**Figure 12**). Replace the spring if its length is less than the service limit in **Table 1**.

6. Check the damper unit for leakage and the damper rod for straightness. Replace the damper unit if necessary.

**10**

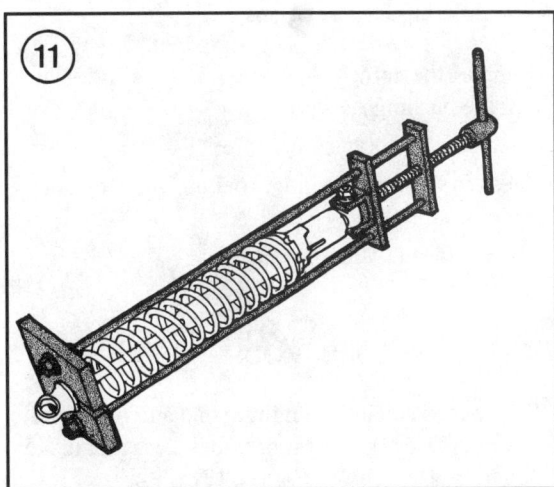

*NOTE*
*The damper unit cannot be rebuilt. If leaking or damaged, it must be replaced as a unit.*

7. Inspect the spring guide and replace if severely worn or damaged.

8. Assemble the shock absorber by reversing the preceding removal steps, plus the following:

*WARNING*
*Do not install the upper spring seat without a spring compressor. The spring is under considerable pressure and may fly off and cause injury.*

a. Install the spring with the closer wound coils (**Figure 8**) toward the top.

b. Apply a threadlock to the threads of the damper rod before installing the locknut. Temporarily screw the locknut all the way down and tighten against the end of the threads.

c. Apply the same threadlock to the upper joint threads. Screw the upper joint on all the way. Then secure the upper joint in a vise with soft jaws and tighten the damper rod locknut against the upper joint to the torque specification in **Table 4**.

d. Release the tension from the spring and remove the shock absorber from the spring compressor.

e. Check that the shock spring seats evenly against the upper joint and spring seat.

**Shock Bushing Replacement**

1. Support the damper unit in a press and press out one of the bushings (**Figure 9**).

2. Clean the shock bushing bore.

3. Press in the new bushing, making sure to center it in the bushing bore.

4. Repeat for the other bushing.

## TIE RODS

The tie rods consist of an inner end and outer end. You can replace all of the individual parts that make up the tie rod assembly (**Figure 13**).

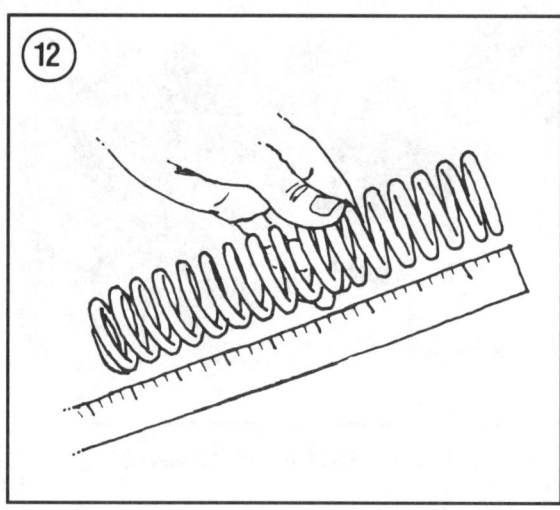

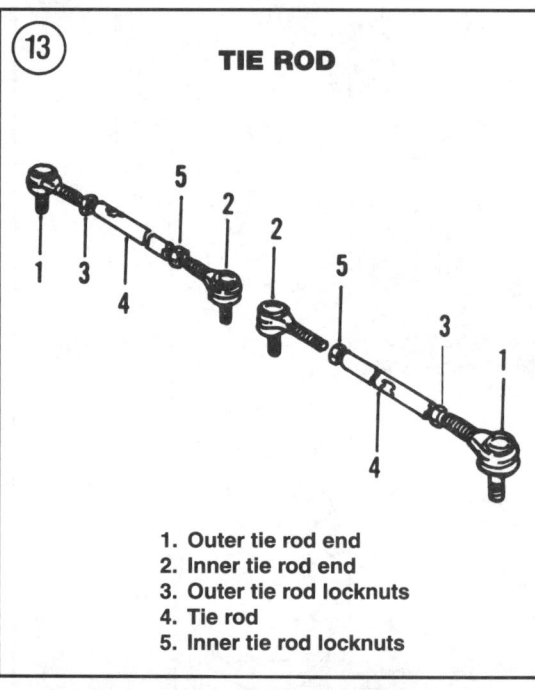

**TIE ROD**

1. Outer tie rod end
2. Inner tie rod end
3. Outer tie rod locknuts
4. Tie rod
5. Inner tie rod locknuts

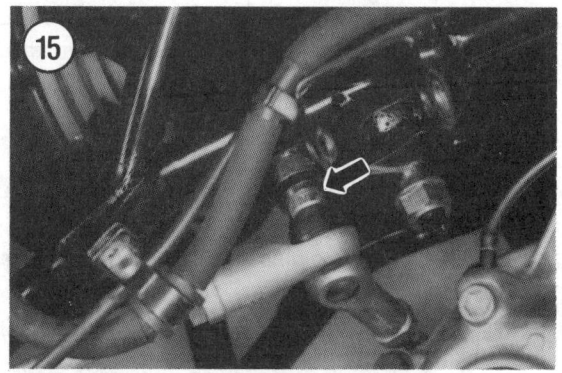

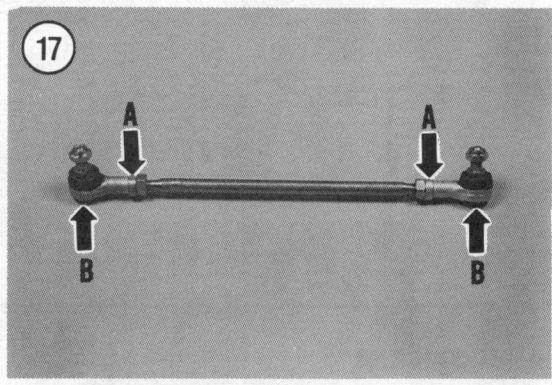

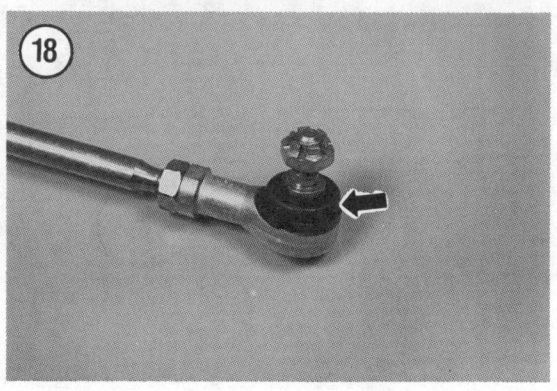

## Removal

1. Support the vehicle with the front wheels off the ground.
2. Remove the cotter pins from both tie rod ends. See **Figure 14** and **Figure 15**.
3. Hold each tie rod flat with a wrench, (**Figure 16**) and remove the tie rod nuts, then remove the tie rod.

## Inspection

*NOTE*
*When cleaning the tie rods, do not immerse the ball joints in any type of chemical that could contaminate the grease and/or damage the rubber boots.*

1. Inspect the tie rod shaft (**Figure 17**) and replace if damaged.
2. Inspect the rubber boot at each end of the tie rod end swivel joint (**Figure 18**). The swivel joints are permanently packed with grease. Replace the ball joint if severely worn or if the rubber boot is damaged. Refer to *Tie Rod Disassembly/Reassembly* in the following procedure.
3. Pivot the tie rod end (**Figure 18**) back and forth by hand. If the tie rod end moves roughly or with excessive play, replace it as described in the following procedure.

## Tie Rod
## Disassembly/Reassembly

If the tie rod ends are to be replaced, refer to **Figure 13** and perform the following.
1. Loosen the locknuts (A, **Figure 17**) securing the tie rod ends. The locknut securing the outside tie rod has left-hand threads.
2. Unscrew the damaged tie rod end(s) (B, **Figure 17**).
3. Clean the mating shaft and tie rod end threads with contact cleaner.
4. The inner tie rod is marked with an L (**Figure 19**). Install this tie rod onto the end of the tie rod without the flat on it. This tie rod has a silver colored nut.
5. The outer tie rod end is not marked, but uses a gold colored nut.
6. Set the distance between the tie rod locknuts and thread ends (**Figure 20**) to 3.5 mm (0.14 in.). Position the tie rod end studs 180° from each other (**Figure 20**). Screw the locknuts up against the tie

**10**

rod end but do not tighten at this time. They will be tightened when checking the wheel alignment in Chapter Three.

### Installation

1. Install the tie rod with its flat end (**Figure 21**) at the steering knuckle.
2. Attach the tie rod assembly to the steering shaft and steering knuckle. See **Figure 14** and **Figure 15**.
3. Thread the castle nut onto each ball joint stud.
4. Hold each tie rod with a wrench (**Figure 16**) and tighten the tie rod nuts as specified in **Table 4**. Tighten the nut(s), if necessary, to align the cotter pin hole with the nut slot. Do not loosen the nut to align the hole and slot.
5. Install new cotter pins through all ball joint studs. Spread the cotter pin arms to lock them in place.
6. Check the toe-in adjustment as described under *Toe-in Adjustment* in Chapter Three. If the tie rod ends were replaced, their locknuts will be tightened during the adjustment procedure.

### STEERING KNUCKLE

Refer to **Figure 22**.

### Removal/Installation

1. Remove the front wheels as described in this chapter.
2. Remove the boot protector (**Figure 23**).
3. Remove the front hub as described in this chapter.

4. Remove the breather tube (A, **Figure 24**) from the guides on the steering knuckle and steering arms.
5. Remove the brake hose guide mounting nut (B, **Figure 24**).
6. Remove the brake panel (Chapter Thirteen).
7. Disconnect the tie rod at the steering knuckle as described in this chapter.
8. Remove the cotter pins and castle nuts (**Figure 25**) from the upper and lower control arm ball joints.
9. Disconnect the upper and lower control arm ball joints using the Honda ball joint remover (part No. 07MAC-SL00200 [**Figure 26**])or equivalent. Perform the following:

> *CAUTION*
> *Do not strike the ball joint or its stud when removing it; otherwise, you will damage the ball joint.*

  a. Mount the ball joint remover between the ball joint upper arm as shown in **Figure 27**.

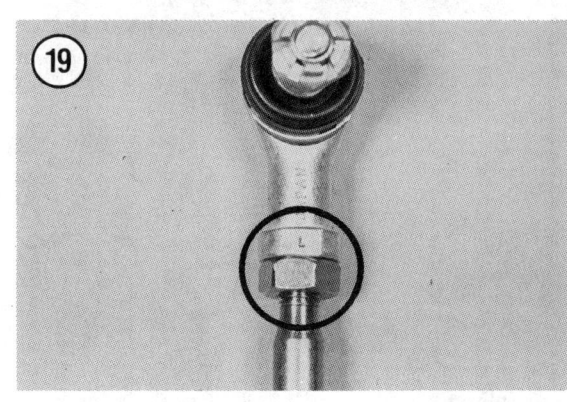

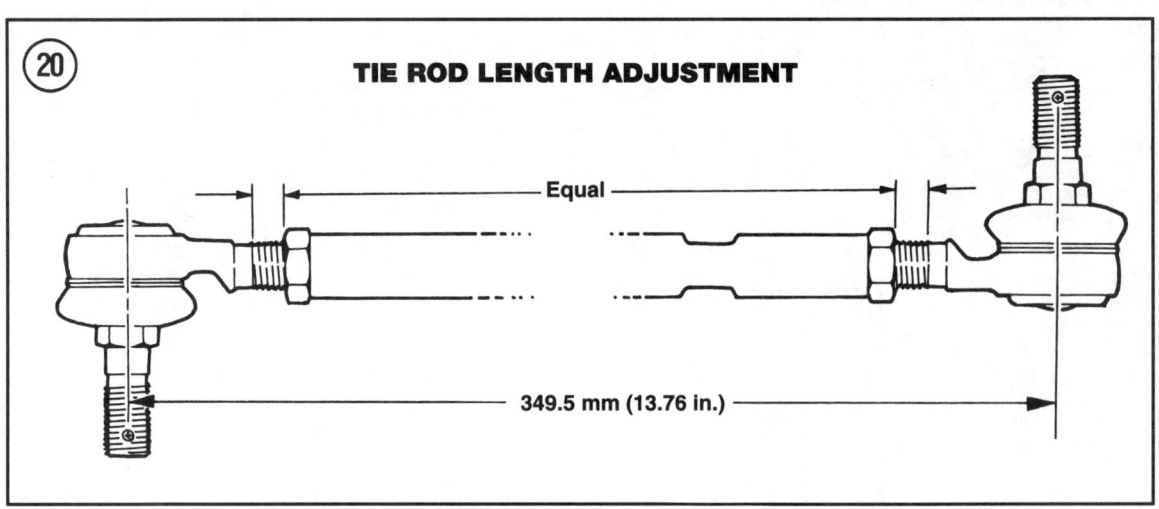

**TIE ROD LENGTH ADJUSTMENT**

Equal

349.5 mm (13.76 in.)

21

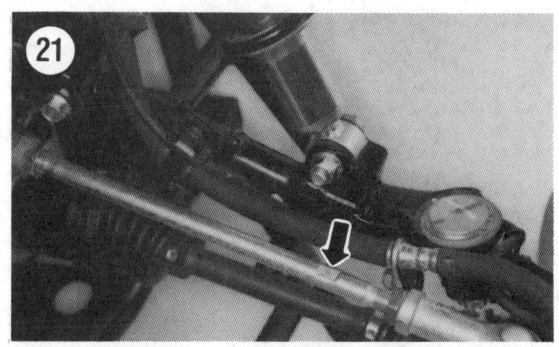

b. Operate the tool and break the upper ball joint loose from the upper arm.

c. Repeat for the lower control arm.

10. Remove the steering knuckle (**Figure 28**), being careful not to damage the drive shaft splines or boots.

11. Inspect the steering knuckle as described in this chapter.

12. Install the steering knuckle by reversing these removal steps, plus the following:

22

**STEERING KNUCKLE**

8
7
1
2
3
5
4
6
2
1
10
9
2
1
1. Cotter pin
2. Nut
3. Steering arm
4. Tie rod
5. Upper arm
6. Lower arm
7. Pivot bolt
8. Locknut
9. Steering knuckle
10. O-ring

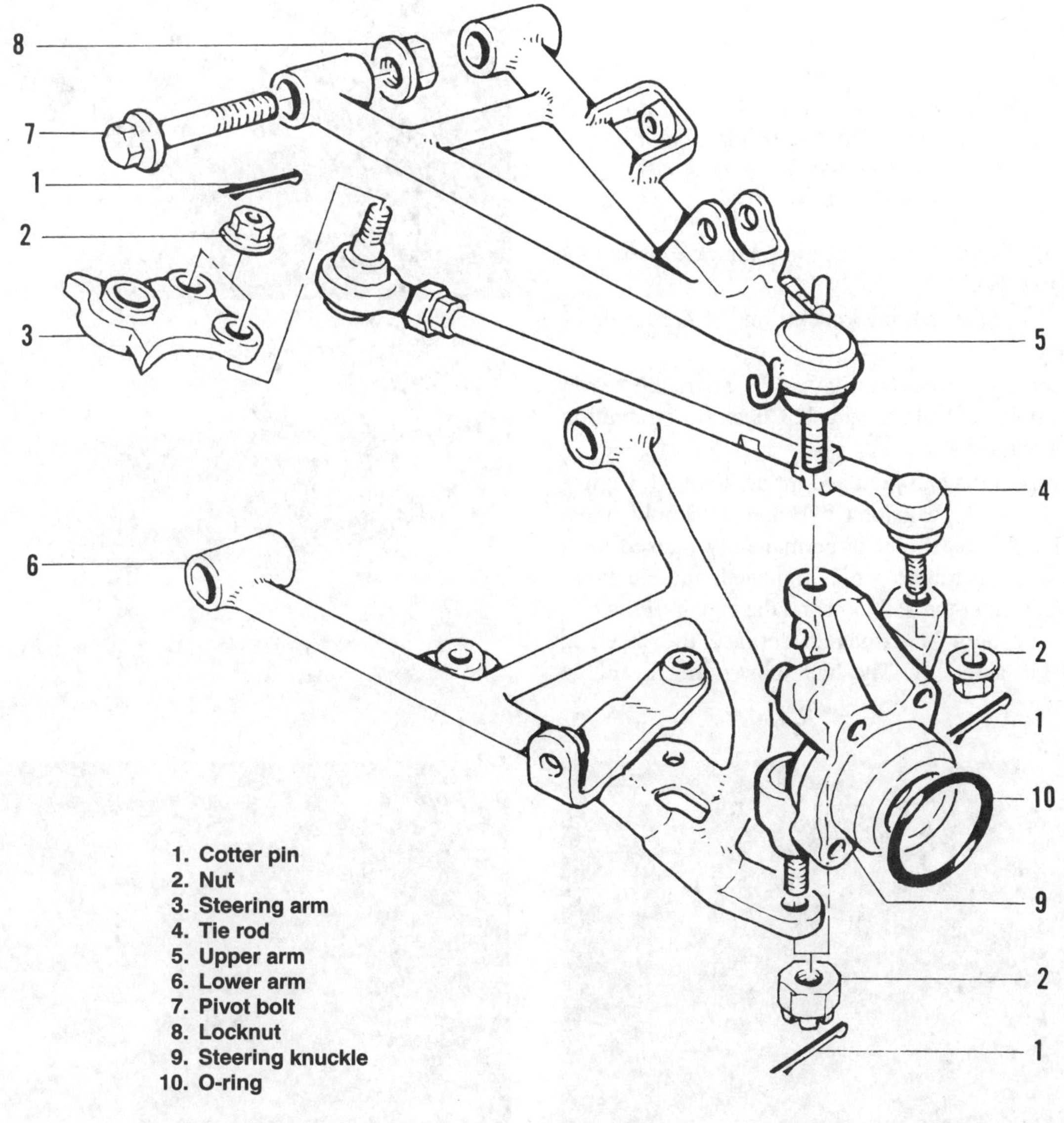

a. Lubricate the steering knuckle seal lips with a waterproof grease.

b. Insert the drive shaft into the steering knuckle (**Figure 28**).

c. Install the steering knuckle onto the upper and lower control arms. Install the castle nuts and tighten as specified in **Table 4**.

d. Install new cotter pins and bend the ends over completely.

e. Check front brake operation before riding the vehicle.

f. Install the brake hose clamps and tighten the nut (B, **Figure 24**) as specified in **Table 4**.

## Inspection

> *CAUTION*
> *When cleaning the steering knuckle, do not wash the ball joint in solvent; otherwise, you may contaminate the grease or damage the ball joint cover.*

1. Clean and dry the steering knuckle assembly (**Figure 29**).

2. Inspect the steering knuckle and replace if damaged.

3. Check the holes (A, **Figure 29**) where the tie rod and upper control arm attach. Check for elongation and fractures.

4. Inspect the ball joint and rubber boot (B, **Figure 29**). Pivot the ball joint by hand. It should move freely. The ball joint is permanently packed with grease. If the rubber boot is damaged, dirt and moisture can enter the ball joint and damage it. If the ball joint or boot is damaged, replace the steering knuckle assembly. The ball joint is not available separately.

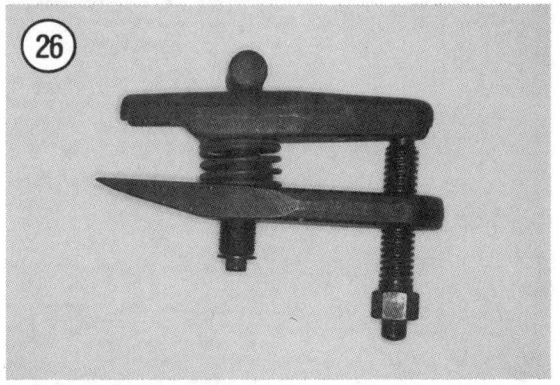

5. Check the hole at the end of the ball joint where the cotter pin fits. Make sure there are no fractures or cracks leading out toward the end of the ball joint. If any are present, replace the steering knuckle.

6. Check the inner (C, **Figure 29**) and outer (A, **Figure 30**) dust seals for severe wear or damage. If necessary, replace the oil seals as described in this section.

7. Turn the inner and outer bearings (B, **Figure 30**) with your finger. Both bearing races should turn freely and without any sign of roughness, catching or excessive noise. Replace the damaged bearings as described in this section.

### Steering Knuckle
### Dust Seal and Bearing Replacement

Refer to **Figure 31** for this procedure.

1. Remove the inner (C, **Figure 29**) and outer (A, **Figure 30**) dust seals. Discard both dust seals.

*NOTE*
*If you are only replacing the dust seals, go to Step 10.*

2. Remove the circlip (4, **Figure 31**).

3. Support the steering knuckle in a press and press out both bearings.

4. If one or both bearings was a loose fit in the steering knuckle, check the bearing bore for cracks or severe wear.

5. Clean the bearing bore.

6. Check the circlip groove for cracks or other damage.

7. Pack the new bearings with grease.

8. Press the new bearings, one at a time, into the steering knuckle. Make sure both bearings are fully seated so the circlip can be installed in its groove. See *Ball Bearings* in Chapter One for bearing installation information.

**10**

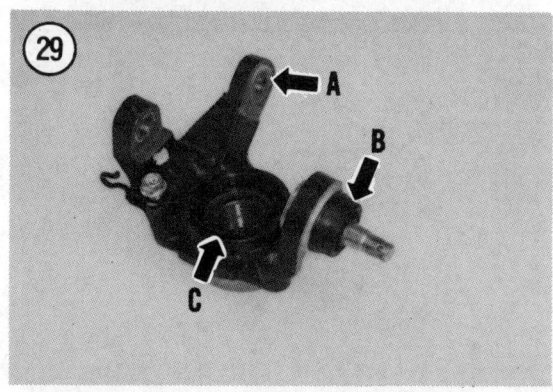

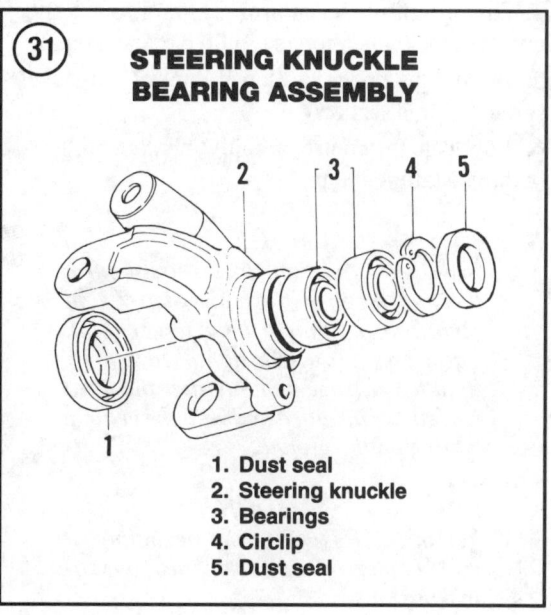

**STEERING KNUCKLE BEARING ASSEMBLY**

1. Dust seal
2. Steering knuckle
3. Bearings
4. Circlip
5. Dust seal

9. Install a new circlip (4, **Figure 31**) into the bearing bore groove. Make sure it seats in its groove completely.

10. Install the dust seals as follows:

 a. Pack the lip of each dust seal with grease.

 b. Install both dust seals with their closed side facing out.

 c. Press both dust seals into the steering knuckle

## CONTROL ARMS

Refer to **Figure 22** when servicing the upper and lower control arms.

### Removal/Installation

1. Remove the steering knuckle as described in this chapter.

2. Remove the upper control arm as follows:

 a. Remove the locknut and bolt (A, **Figure 32**) securing the shock absorber to the upper control arm.

 b. Remove the brake hose and breather tube clamp bolt (B, **Figure 32**) from the upper control arm.

 c. Remove locknuts and bolts and the upper control arm (A, **Figure 33**).

3. Remove the locknuts and bolts and the lower control arm (B, **Figure 33**).

4. Discard all of the control arm and lower shock absorber locknuts removed in Step 2 and Step 3.

5. Inspect the upper and lower control arms as described in this section.

6. Lubricate the control arm pivot bolts with grease before installing them.

*NOTE*
*Install new upper and lower control arm locknuts when performing Step 7 and Step 8 and tighten them finger-tight. These locknuts will be tightened to their final torque specification after the front wheels are installed and with the vehicle resting on the ground.*

*CAUTION*
*See the CAUTION at the beginning of this chapter relating to the use of self-locking nuts.*

7. Install the lower control arm (B, **Figure 33**) onto the frame and secure it with its bolts and new locknuts.

8. Install the upper control arm (A, **Figure 33**) and secure it with its bolts and new locknuts.

9. Install the shock absorber lower mounting bolt and a new locknut (A, **Figure 32**). Tighten the locknut as specified in **Table 4**.

10. Install the brake hose and breather tube clamp bolt (B, **Figure 32**) and tighten as specified in **Table 4**.

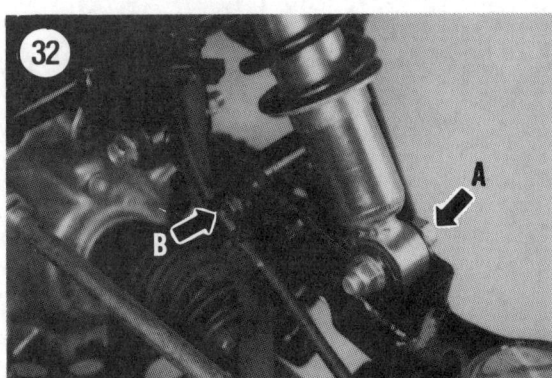

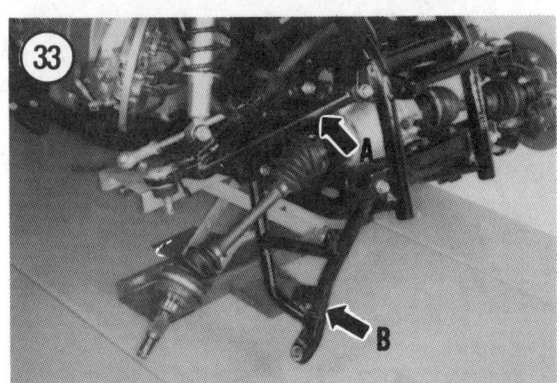

11. Install the steering knuckle as described in this chapter.

12. Install the front wheels as described in this chapter.

13. Lower the vehicle so that all four wheels are on the ground.

14. Tighten the upper control arm locknuts as specified in **Table 4**.

15. Tighten the lower control arm locknuts as specified in **Table 4**.

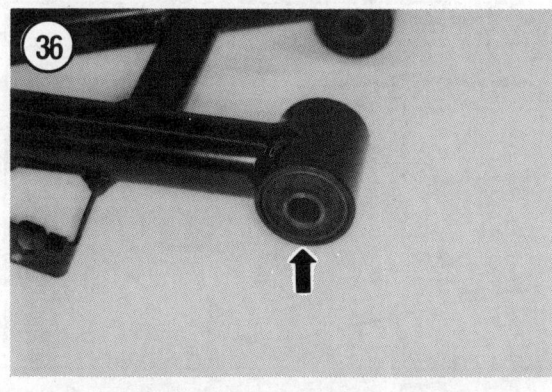

## Control Arm
## Cleaning and Inspection

*CAUTION*
*When cleaning the upper control arm, do not wash the ball joint (**Figure 34**) in solvent; otherwise, you may contaminate the grease or damage the ball joint cover.*

1. Clean and dry the control arms (**Figure 35**).

2. Check both control arms (**Figure 35**) for bending, cracks or other damage. Replace if necessary.

3. Inspect the upper control arm ball joint and rubber boot (**Figure 34**). Pivot the ball joint by hand. It should move freely. The ball joint is permanently packed with grease. If the rubber boot is damaged, dirt and moisture can enter the ball joint and destroy it. If the ball joint or boot is damaged, replace the upper control arm assembly. The ball joint is not available separately.

4. Check the hole at the end of the ball joint where the cotter pin fits. Make sure there are no fractures or cracks leading out toward the end of the ball joint. If any are present, replace the upper control arm.

5. Inspect the pivot bolts and replace them if excessively worn or damaged.

6. Inspect the pivot bushings (**Figure 36**) for excessive wear, separation or other damage. If damaged, replace the control arm as the bushings cannot be replaced separately.

**10**

## HANDLEBAR

### Removal

1. Remove the handlebar cover (Chapter Fifteen).

2. Remove the wiring bands securing the wiring harness to the handlebar.

3. Remove the throttle housing screws, clamp and throttle housing (**Figure 37**).

4. Remove the front master cylinder as described in Chapter Thirteen.

5. Remove the screws and the rear brake lever bracket (A, **Figure 38**).

6. Disconnect the choke cable and remove the switch housing as described under *Left Handlebar Switch Housing Replacement* in Chapter Nine.

7. Remove the upper handlebar holder mounting bolts, holders (**Figure 39**) and handlebar.

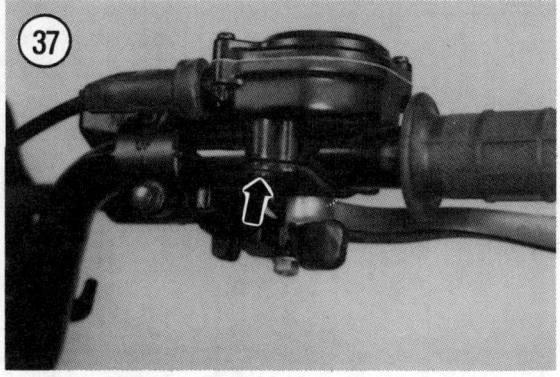

## Installation

1. Position the handlebar on the lower handlebar holders and hold it in place.

2. Install the upper handlebar holders with their cover bosses facing forward as shown in **Figure 39**.

3. Align the punch mark on the handlebar with the top surface of the lower holders (**Figure 40**).

4. Install the handlebar holder bolts. Tighten the forward bolts first and then the rear bolts. Tighten each bolt securely.

5. Install the switch housing and reconnect the choke cable as described under *Left Handlebar Switch Housing Replacement* in Chapter Nine.

6. Install the rear brake lever bracket as follows:
   a. Install the rear brake lever bracket, clamp and mounting screws. Install the clamp (A, **Figure 38**) so that its punch mark faces up.
   b. Align the end of the bracket with the punch mark (B, **Figure 38**) on the handlebar.
   c. Install the clamp screws. Tighten the upper screw first, then the lower screw.

7. Install the master cylinder as described in Chapter Thirteen.

8. Install the throttle housing by aligning the line on the throttle housing (A, **Figure 41**) with the end of the master cylinder (B). Install the clamp and screws (**Figure 37**) and tighten securely.

9. Secure the wiring harness to the handlebars with the wire bands.

10. Check all cable adjustments as described in Chapter Three.

11. Check that the front brake works properly.

12. Check that each handlebar switch works properly.

13. Install the handlebar cover (Chapter Fifteen).

### STEERING SHAFT

Refer to **Figure 42** when servicing the steering shaft assembly.

### Removal

1. Remove the front fender (Chapter Fifteen).

2. Remove both front wheels as described in this chapter.

3. Remove the bolts and the assist headlight assembly (**Figure 43**). Set the headlight aside.

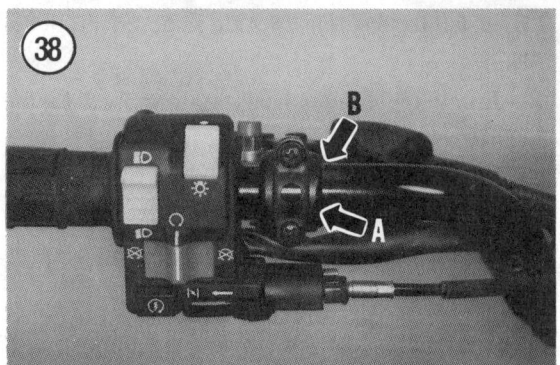

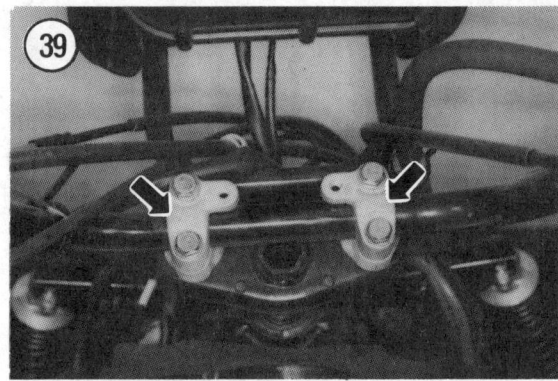

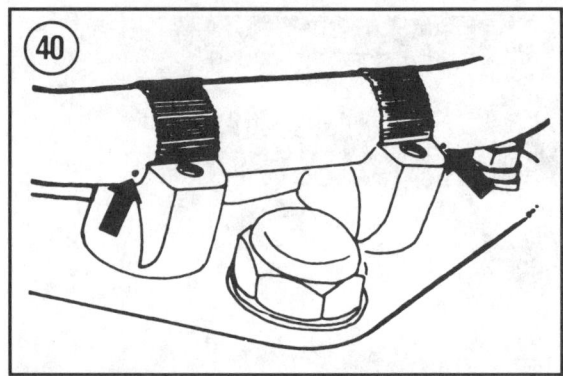

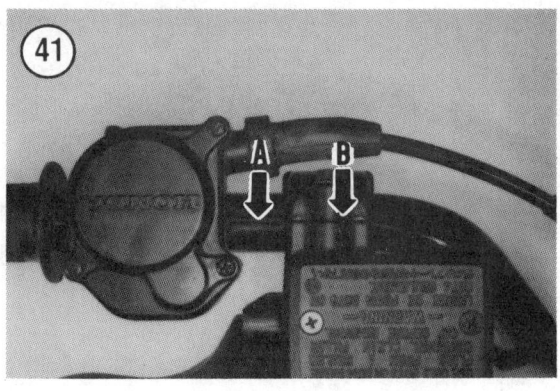

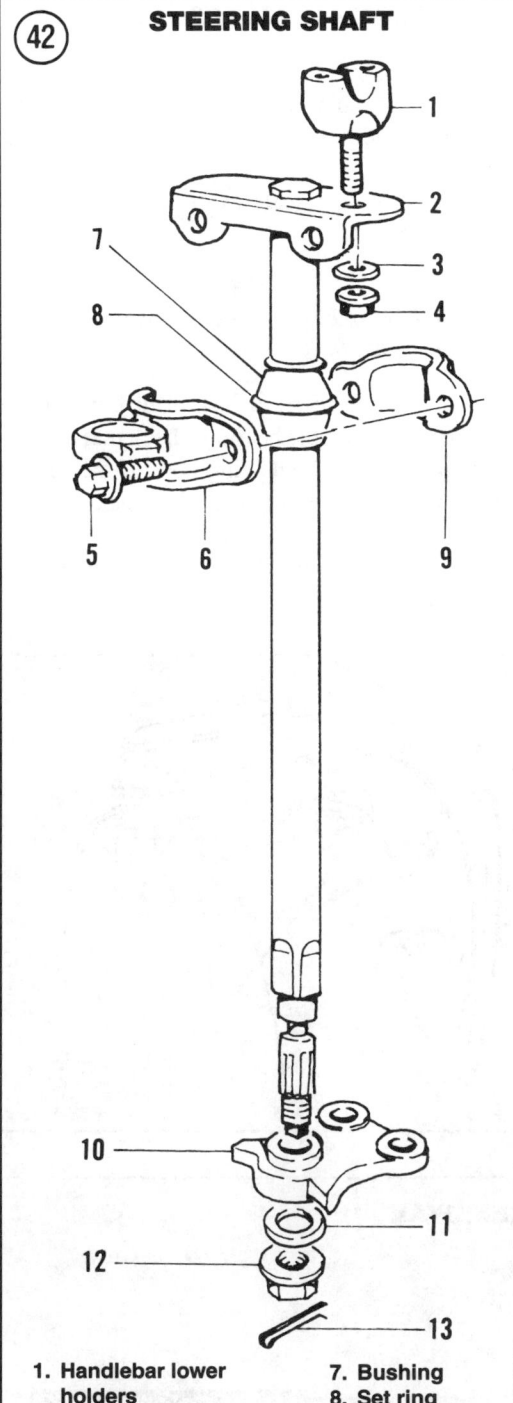

**STEERING SHAFT**

1. **Handlebar lower holders**
2. **Steering shaft**
3. **Lockwashers**
4. **Handlebar lower holder locknuts**
5. **Steering shaft holder mounting bolts**
6. **Steering shaft outer holder**
7. **Bushing**
8. **Set ring**
9. **Steering shaft inner holder**
10. **Steering arm**
11. **Washer**
12. **Steering shaft nut**
13. **Cotter pin**

4. Remove the lower handlebar holder nuts and washers (**Figure 44**), then pull the handlebar assembly back so that you do not damage the brake hose, cables or wiring harness. Discard the lower handlebar holder locknuts as new ones must be installed.

5. Disconnect both tie rods (A, **Figure 45**) from the steering shaft as described under *Tie Rods* in this chapter.

6. Remove the cotter pin and nut at the bottom of the steering shaft (B, **Figure 45**).

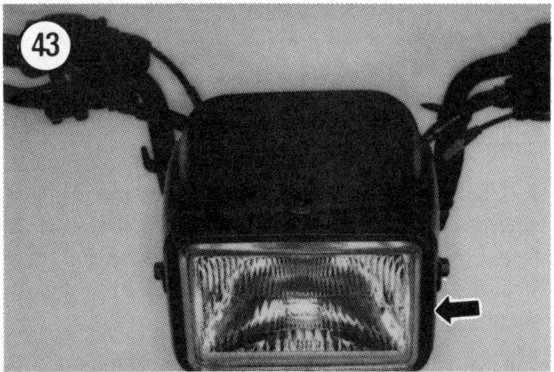

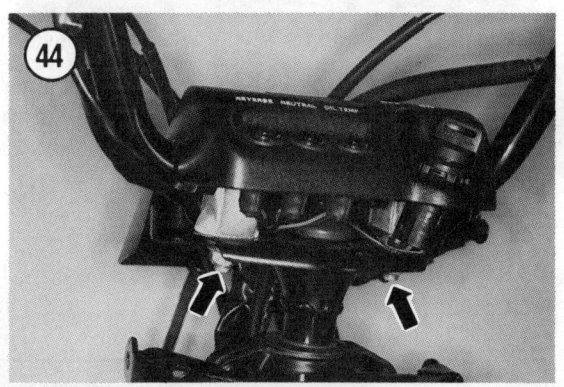

7. Remove the steering shaft holder bolts (A, **Figure 46**) and holder assembly (B).

8. Remove the steering shaft and steering arm assembly from the frame.

### Inspection

Replace parts that are excessively worn or damaged as described in this section.

1. Clean and dry all parts.

2. Remove the set ring and the steering shaft bushing from the steering shaft. Check both parts for excessive wear or damage.

3. Check the steering shaft for bending and spline or thread damage.

4. Check the hole at the end of the steering shaft where the cotter pin fits. Make sure there are no fractures or cracks leading out toward the end of the steering shaft. If any are present, replace the steering shaft.

5. Check the steering arm for cracks, spline or other damage.

6. Check the bushing for severe wear or damage.

7. Inspect the steering bearing by turning its inner race with your finger. Replace the bearing if it turns roughly or has excessive play.

8. Inspect the dust seals for severe wear or other damage.

9. Replace the dust seals and bearing as described in the following procedure.

### Steering Shaft Dust Seal and Bearing Replacement

The steering shaft bearing is pressed into the frame. Do not remove the bearing unless it requires replacement.

1. Remove the dust seals from both sides of the bearing.

*NOTE*
*If you are only replacing the dust seals, go to Step 10.*

2. Remove the circlip from the bearing bore groove.

3. Before removing the bearing, check that its outer race is a tight fit in the bearing bore. If the bearing is loose, check the bearing bore for cracks or other damage.

4. Remove the bearing with a blind bearing remover (**Figure 47**).

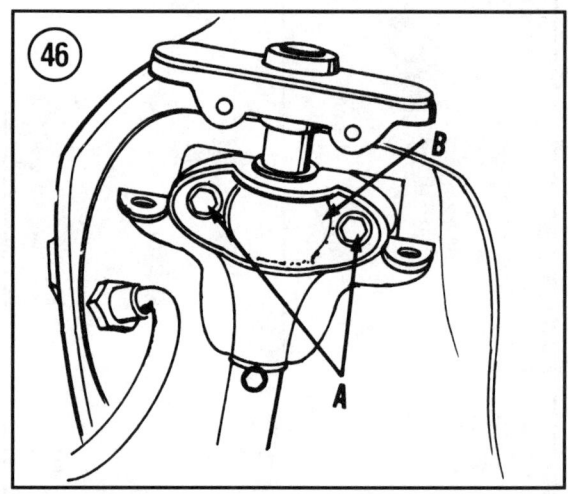

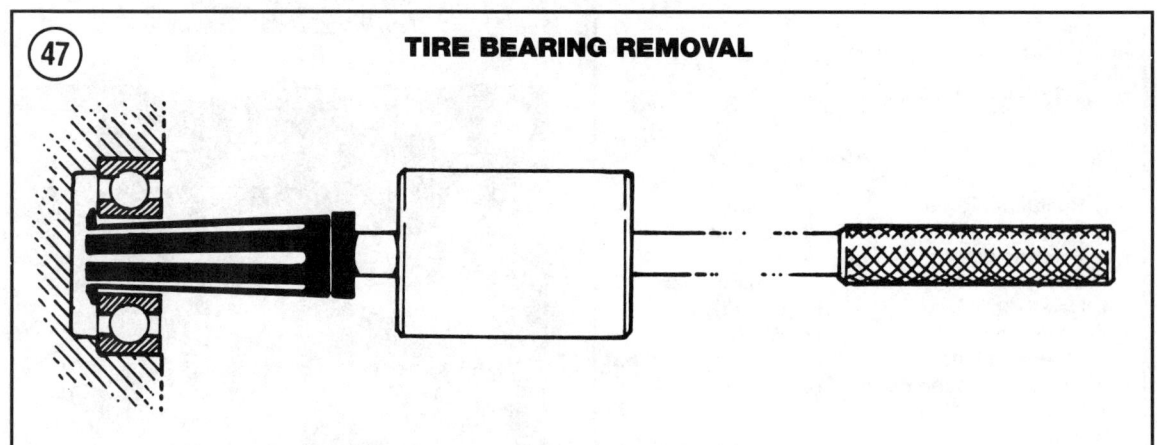

**TIRE BEARING REMOVAL**

5. Clean the bearing bore and check it for cracks or other damage.

6. The OEM replacement bearing is sealed on one side. Pack the open bearing side with grease. Work the grease in between the balls thoroughly. Turn the bearing by hand to make sure the grease is distributed evenly inside the bearing.

7. Install the new bearing with its sealed side facing up.

8. Tap the bearing squarely into place; tap on the outer race only. Use a socket or bearing driver that matches the outer race diameter. Do not tap on the inner race or the bearing might be damaged. Install the bearing so that it is fully seated below the circlip groove in the bearing bore.

9. Install the circlip into the bearing bore groove. Make sure the circlip seats in the groove completely.

10. Pack the lips of the new dust seals with grease, then install each dust seal so that its closed side faces out.

## Installation

1. Lubricate the bushing (7, **Figure 42**) with grease and install it onto the steering shaft so that its UP mark faces toward the handlebar. Install the set ring (8, **Figure 42**) into the bushing groove.

2. Install the steering shaft into the frame

3. Install the inner and outer steering shaft holders (B, **Figure 46**) over the bushing and install the bolts (A). Tighten the steering shaft holder bolts as specified in **Table 4**.

4. Lubricate the steering shaft splines with grease.

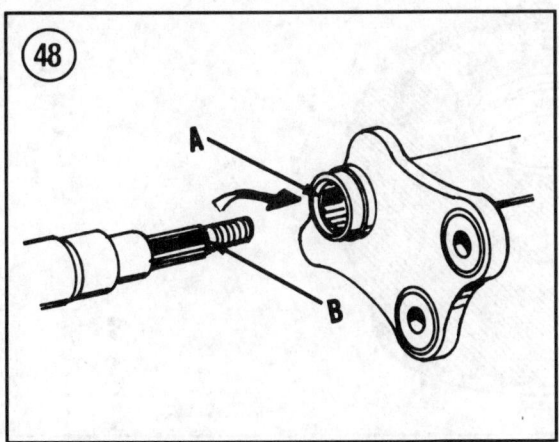

5. Align the wide cutout on the steering shaft splines (A, **Figure 48**) with the wide tooth on the steering arm splines (B).

6. Lubricate the steering shaft nut flange and threads with grease. Install the steering shaft nut (B, **Figure 45**) and washer and tighten as specified in **Table 4**. Secure the nut with a new cotter pin and bend the ends over completely. Do not install a used cotter pin as it may break and fall out.

7. Reconnect both tie rods onto the steering shaft (A, **Figure 45**) as described under *Tie Rods* in this chapter.

8. Install the handlebar assembly onto the steering shaft. Check the routing of the brake hose, cables and wiring harness.

9. Install new handlebar lower holder locknuts (**Figure 44**) and tighten as specified in **Table 4**.

10. Install the assist headlight assembly (**Figure 43**) and tighten its mounting bolts securely.

11. Install both front wheels as described in this chapter.

12. Install the front fender (Chapter Fifteen).

13. Check that the handlebar turns properly and that the throttle returns to its closed position after releasing it.

## TIRES AND WHEELS

Your Honda is equipped with tubeless, low pressure tires designed specifically for off-road use. Rapid tire wear will occur if you ride the vehicle on paved surfaces.

### Tire Changing

You need the following tools to change the tires on your Honda:

   a. Bead breaker tool.

   b. Tire irons.

   c. Rim protectors.

*NOTE*
*If you have the proper tools but find that the tire is difficult to remove or install, do not take a chance on damaging the tire or rim sealing surface. Take the tire and rim to a dealership and have them service the tire for you.*

1. Remove the valve stem cap and core and deflate the tire. Do not reinstall the core at this time.

2. Lubricate the tire bead and rim flanges with a rubber tire lubricant. Press the tire sidewall/bead down to allow the lubricant to run into and around the bead area. Also apply lubricant to the area where the bead breaker arm will contact the tire sidewall.

3. Position the wheel into the bead breaker tool (**Figure 49**).

4. Slowly work the bead breaker tool, making sure the tool arm seats against the inside of the rim, and break the tire bead away from the rim.

5. Using your hands, press the tire on either side of the tool to break the rest of the bead free from the rim.

6. If the rest of the tire bead cannot be broken loose, raise the tool, rotate the tire/rim assembly and repeat Steps 4 and 5 until the entire bead is broken loose from the rim.

7. Turn the wheel over and repeat the preceding steps to break the opposite side loose.

*CAUTION*
*When using tire irons in the following steps, work carefully so that you do not damage the tire or rim sealing surfaces. Damage to these areas may cause an air leak and require replacement of the tire or rim.*

8. Lubricate the tire beads and rim flanges as described in Step 2. Pry the bead over the rim with two tire irons (**Figure 50**). Take small bites with the tire irons. Place rim protectors between the tire irons and the rim.

9. When the upper tire bead is free, lift the second bead up into the center rim well and remove it as described in Step 8.

10. Clean and dry the rim.

11. Inspect the sealing surface on both sides of the rim (**Figure 51**). If the rim is bent, it may leak air.

12. To replace the air valve, perform the following:

   a. Support the rim and pull the valve stem out of the rim. Discard the valve stem.

   b. Lubricate the new valve stem with a tire lubricant.

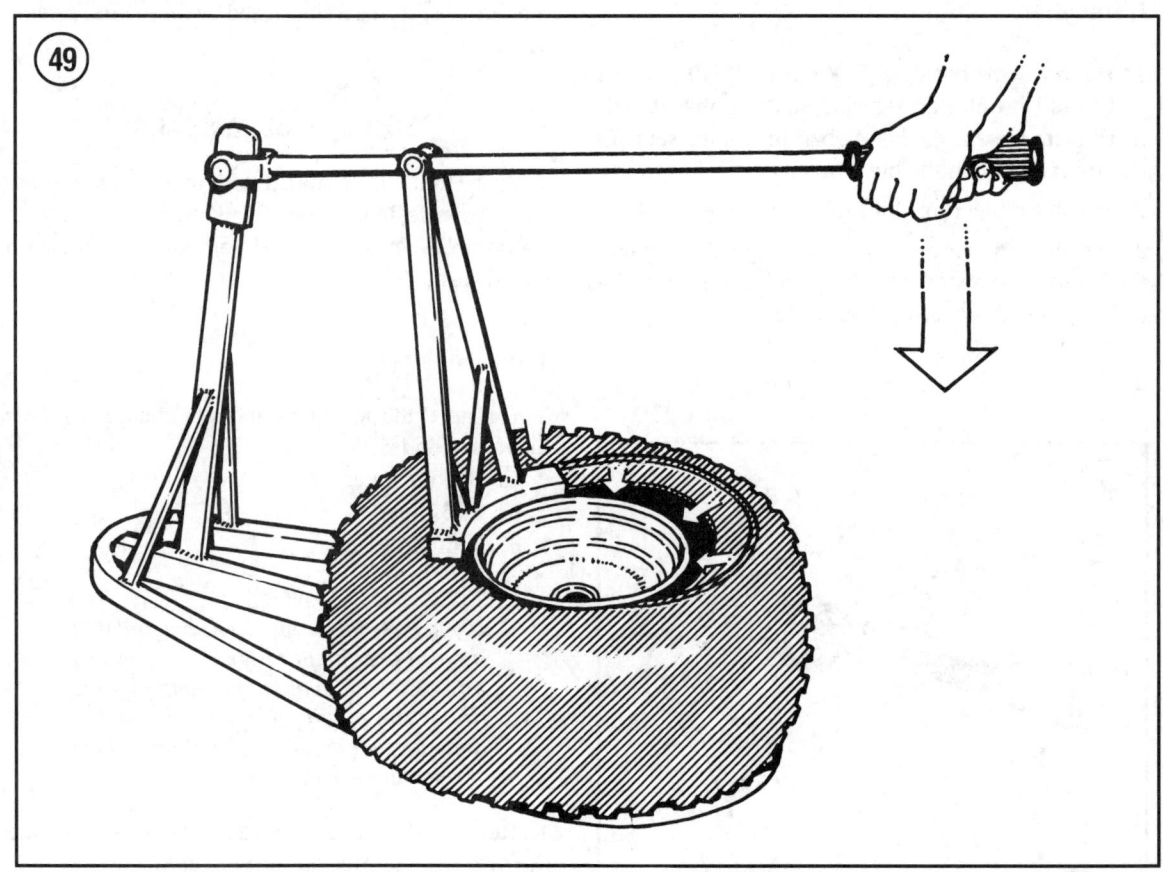

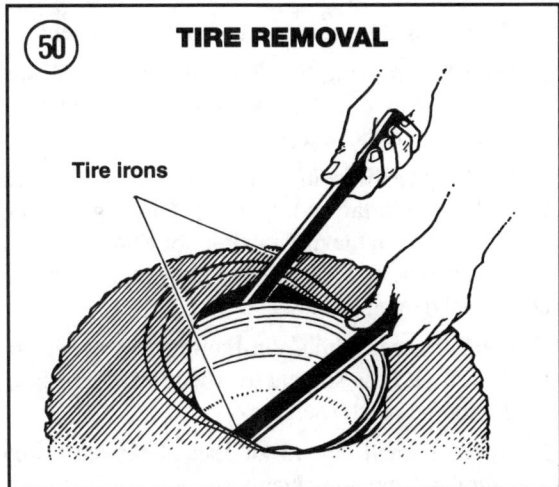

**50** **TIRE REMOVAL**

Tire irons

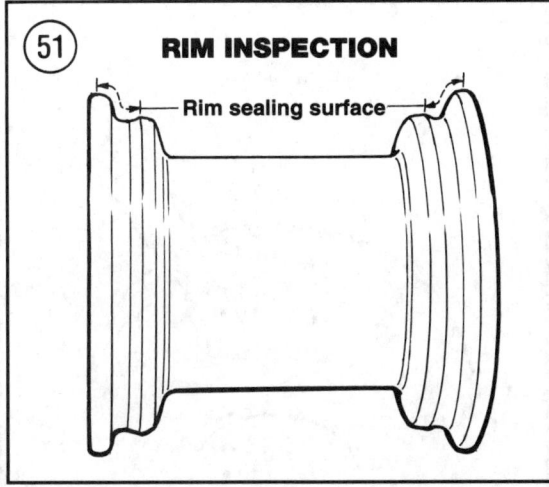

**51** **RIM INSPECTION**

Rim sealing surface

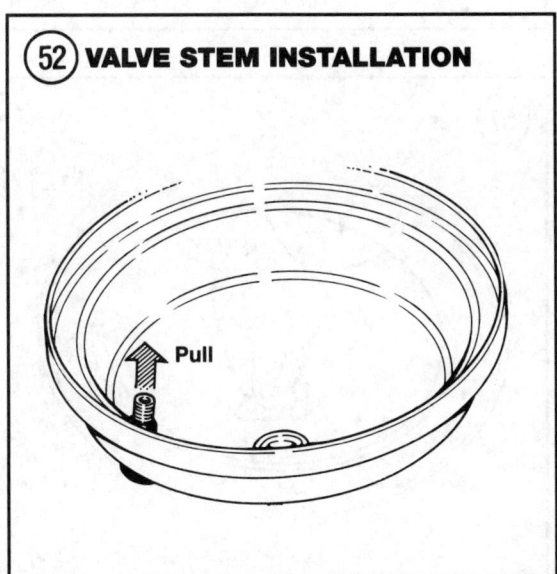

**52** **VALVE STEM INSTALLATION**

Pull

c. Pull a new valve stem into the rim, from the inside out, until it snaps into place (**Figure 52**).

*NOTE*
*Special tools are available for installing this type of valve stem.*

13. Inspect the tire for cuts, tears, abrasions or any other defects.

14. Clean the tire and rim of any lubricant used during removal.

*WARNING*
*When mounting the tire, use only clean water as a tire lubricant. Other lubricants may leave a slippery residue on the tire that would allow the tire to slip on the rim, causing a loss of air pressure.*

*NOTE*
*The tire tread pattern on the factory equipped tires is directional. Position the tire onto the rim so the rotation arrow on the tire's sidewall faces in the correct direction of wheel rotation.*

*NOTE*
*If the tire is difficult to install, place the tire outside in the sun (or in the trunk of a car). The higher temperatures will soften the tire and help with installation.*

15. Install the tire onto the rim starting with the side opposite the valve stem. Push the first bead over the rim flange. Force the bead into the center of the rim to help installation (**Figure 53**).

**10**

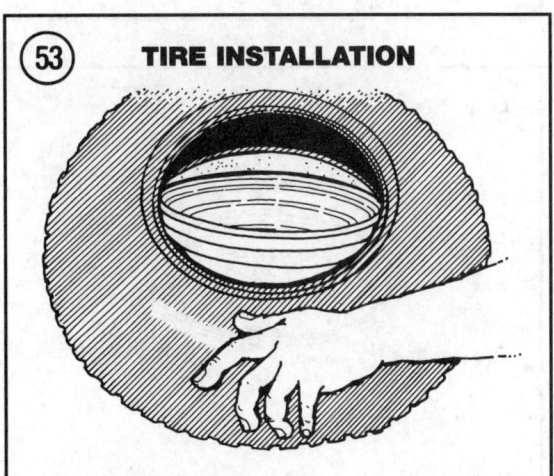

**53** **TIRE INSTALLATION**

16. Install the rest of the bead with tire irons (**Figure 54**).

17. Repeat the preceding steps to install the second bead onto the rim.

18. Install the valve stem core, if necessary.

19. Apply water to the tire bead and inflate the tire to seat the tire onto the rim. Check that the rim lines on both sides of the tire are parallel with the rim flanges as shown in **Figure 55**. If the rim flanges are not parallel, deflate the tire and break the bead. Then lubricate the tire with water again and reinflate the tire.

20. When the tire is properly seated, remove the air valve to deflate the tire and wait 1 hour before putting the tire into service. After 1 hour, inflate the tire to the operating pressure listed in **Table 3**.

21. Check for air leaks and install the valve cap.

### Cold Patch Repair

Use the manufacturer's instructions for the tire repair kit you are going to use. If there are no instructions, use the following procedure.

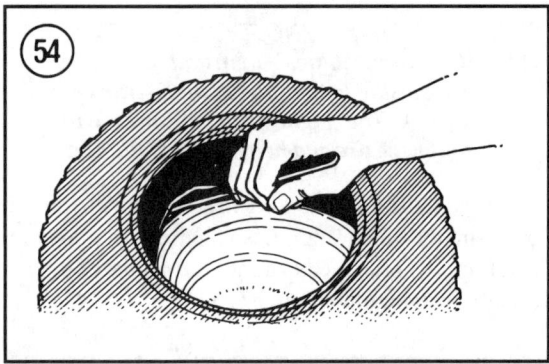

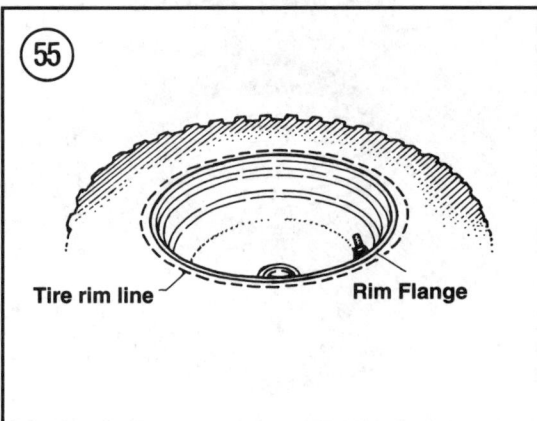

Tire rim line          Rim Flange

1. Remove the tire as described in this chapter.

2. Prior to removing the object that punctured the tire, mark the puncture location with chalk or crayon. Then remove the object (**Figure 56**).

3. Working on the inside of the tire, roughen the area around the hole larger than the patch (**Figure 57**). Use the cap from the tire repair kit or a pocket knife. Do not scrape too vigorously or you may cause additional damage.

4. Clean the area with a non-flammable solvent. Do not use an oil base solvent as it will leave a residue rendering the patch useless.

5. Apply a small amount of special cement to the puncture and spread it evenly.

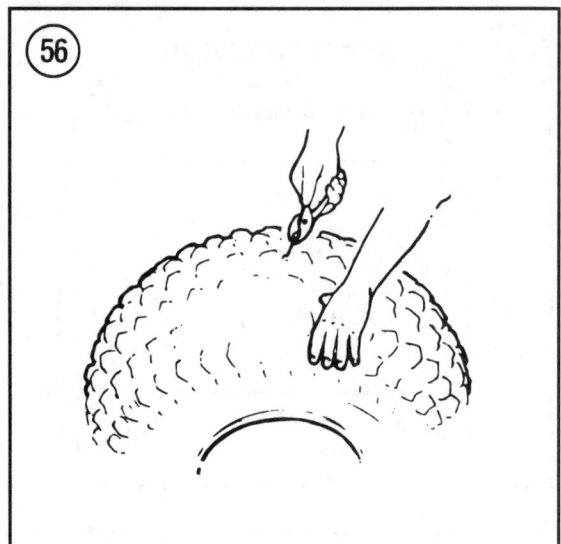

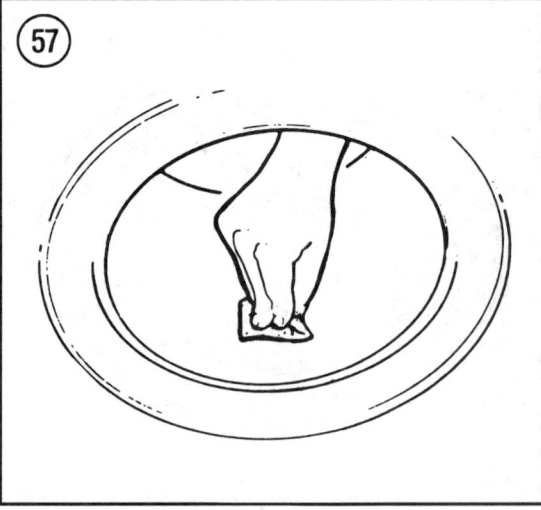

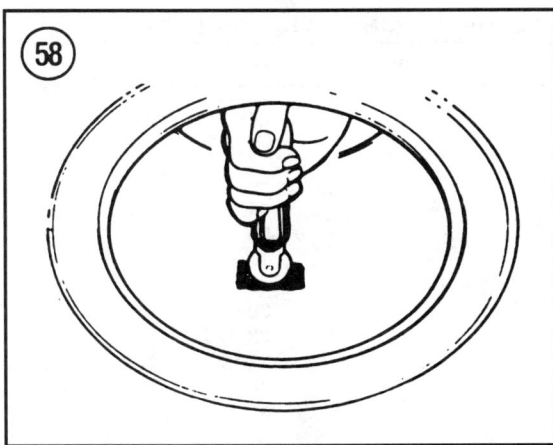

6. Allow the cement to dry until tacky—usually 30 seconds or so is sufficient.

7. Remove the backing from the patch.

*CAUTION*
*Do not touch the newly exposed rubber with your fingers or the patch will not stick firmly.*

8. Center the patch over the hole. Hold the patch firmly in place for about 30 seconds to allow the cement to dry. If you have a roller, use it to press the patch into place (**Figure 58**).

9. Dust the area with talcum powder.

**Table 1 STEERING AND FRONT SUSPENSION SPECIFICATIONS**

| | |
|---|---|
| Front suspension type | Double wish-bone |
| Front wheel travel | 110 mm (4.33 in.) |
| Front damper type | Double tube |
| Toe-in | 16 mm (5/8 in.) |
| Caster angle | 2° |
| Camber angle | 0.1° |
| Trail length | 8 mm (5/16 in.) |
| Shock absorber spring free length | |
|   New | 215.3 mm (8.48 in.) |
|   Service limit | 211.0 mm (8.31 in.) |
| Tie rod distance between ball joints | 349.5 mm (13.76 in.) |

**Table 2 TIRE AND WHEEL SPECIFICATIONS**

| | |
|---|---|
| Tires | |
|   Type | Goodyear Tracker ATT |
|   Size | |
|     Front | AT24 × 8-11 |
|     Rear | AT24 × 10-11 |
| Wheels | |
|   Front rim size | 11 × 6.5AT |
|   Rear rim size | 11 × 7.5AT |

**Table 3 TIRE INFLATION PRESSURE**

| | Front and rear tires psi (kPa) |
|---|---|
| Operating pressure | 3.6 (24.8) |
| Minimum pressure | 3.2 (22) |
| Maximum pressure | 4.0 (27.6) |
| With cargo | 3.6 (24.8) |

10

### Table 4 FRONT SUSPENSION AND STEERING TIGHTENING TORQUES

| | N·m | in.-lb. | ft.-lb. |
|---|---|---|---|
| Axle nut | 80-100 | — | 59-74 |
| Ball joint locknut | 55 | — | 41 |
| Brake drum mounting bolts | 10 | 88 | — |
| Brake hose and breather tube clamp bolt | 12 | 106 | — |
| Brake hose clamp nuts | 15 | — | 11 |
| Damper rod locknut | 38 | — | 28 |
| Front brake hose clamp nut | 15 | — | 11 |
| Front wheel nuts | 65 | — | 48 |
| Handlebar lower holder locknuts | 40 | — | 30 |
| Shock absorber locknut | 45 | — | 33 |
| Steering knuckle castle nut | 30-36 | — | 22-27 |
| Steering shaft holder flange bolt | 33 | — | 24 |
| Steering shaft nut | 110 | — | 81 |
| Throttle case cover screws | 3.5 | 31 | — |
| Tie rod nut | 55 | — | 41 |
| Upper and lower arm locknut | 45 | — | 33 |

# CHAPTER ELEVEN

# FRONT DRIVE MECHANISM

This chapter describes repair and replacement procedures for the front drive mechanism. This includes the front drive axles, propeller shaft and front differential gearcase.

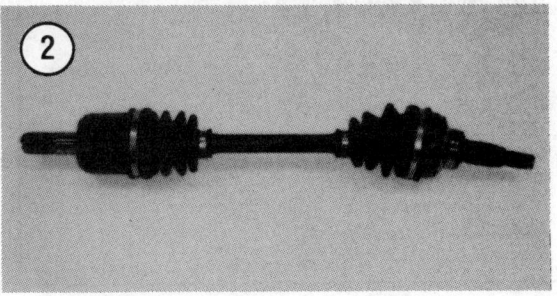

**Table 1** lists torque specifications for the front drive mechanism assembly. **Table 1** is located at the end of the chapter.

## FRONT DRIVE AXLES

### Removal/Installation

1. Remove the steering knuckle (Chapter Ten) for the side you are working on.

> **CAUTION**
> *When removing the front axle, be careful not to damage the rubber boots.*

> **CAUTION**
> *To avoid damage to the front differential oil seal and splines, pull the inboard joint straight out and off the front differential.*

2. Hold the inboard joint and pull the drive shaft (**Figure 1**) out of the differential. See **Figure 2**.
3. Perform the inspection procedures described in this section.
4. Install the front axle by reversing the preceding removal steps, plus the following:

a. Install a new stopper ring (A, **Figure 3**) in the groove in the inboard joint. Make sure it is properly seated in the axle groove.

b. Lubricate the front axle seal (**Figure 4**) and inner splines (B, **Figure 3**) with molybdenum disulfide grease.

c. Carefully guide the front axle into the gearcase (**Figure 1**). Push it in all the way until it bottoms. Then pull the inboard joint a little to

make sure the stopper ring locks into the front differential side gear groove.

d. Install the steering knuckle (Chapter Ten).

**Inspection**

*NOTE*
*The axle boots are subjected to much abuse. Damaged boots allow dirt, mud*

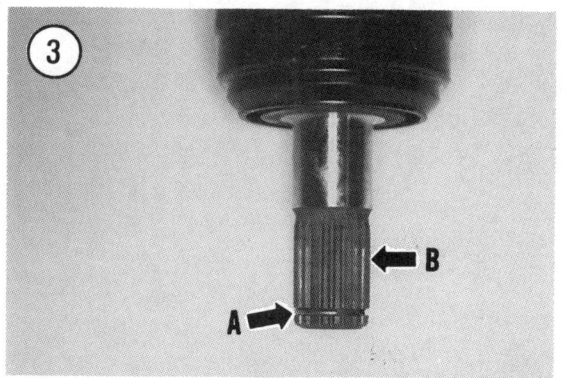

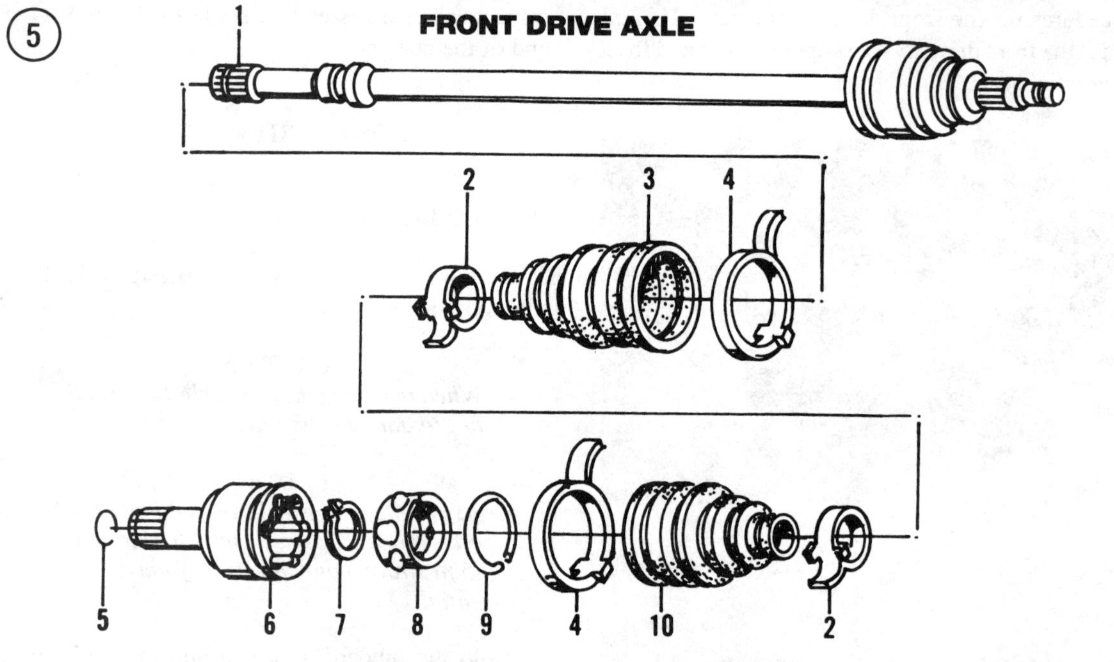

**5** **FRONT DRIVE AXLE**

1. **Drive axle/outer joint assembly**
2. **Clamp**
3. **Outboard boot**
4. **Clamp**
5. **Stopper ring**
6. **Inboard joint**
7. **Circlip**
8. **Bearing**
9. **Stopper ring**
10. **Inboard boot**

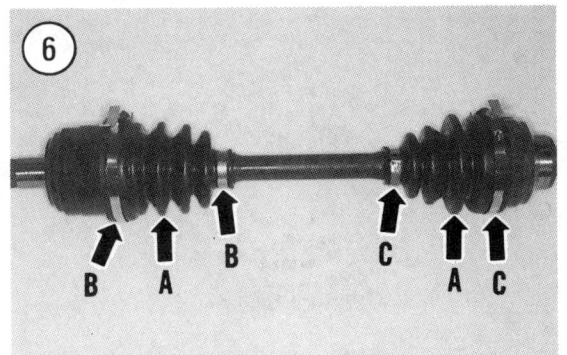

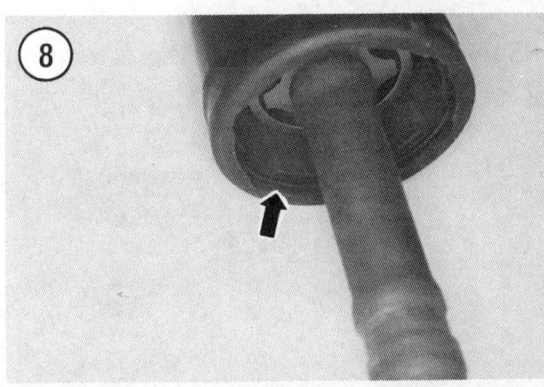

*and moisture to enter the boot, contaminate the grease and damage the bearing.*

1. Inspect the rubber boots (**Figure 2**) for wear, cuts or damage. Replace if necessary as described under the *Disassembly* in this chapter.

2. Move each end of the front axle (**Figure 2**) in a circular motion and check the constant velocity joints for excessive wear or play.

**Disassembly**

Refer to **Figure 5** when servicing the front drive axle in this section.

*NOTE*
*The outboard joint cannot be disassembled or repaired. If damaged or faulty, the drive axle assembly must be replaced.*

1. Open the clamps (B, **Figure 6**) on the inboard joint, then remove clamps. Discard the clamps as they cannot be reused.

2. Carefully slide the boot (A, **Figure 7**) onto the front axle and off the inboard joint.

3. Wipe out all of the grease from the inboard joint cavity (B, **Figure 7**).

4. Remove the stopper ring (**Figure 8**) from the inboard joint.

5. Remove the inboard joint (**Figure 9**).

6. Remove the circlip (**Figure 10**) and slide off the bearing assembly (**Figure 11**). Be careful not to drop any of the steel balls from the bearing cage.

7. Slide the inboard boot off the front axle and discard the clamp. It cannot be reused.

**11**

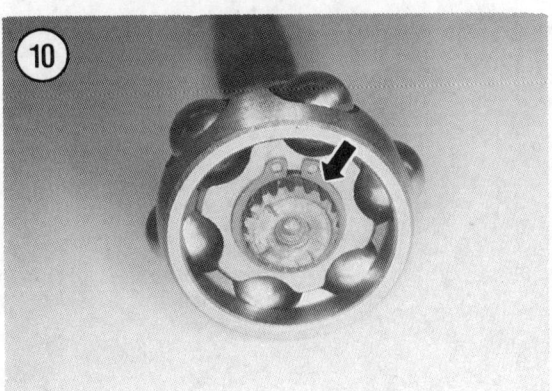

8. If the outboard boot requires replacement, perform the following:

    a. Open the clamps (C, **Figure 6**) on the outboard joint, then remove and discard the clamps.

    b. Slide the outboard boot off the drive axle and discard the clamp.

9. Inspect the drive axle as described in this procedure.

### Inspection

Refer to **Figure 5** for this procedure.

*CAUTION*
*Before cleaning the rubber boots, make sure the cleaning solvent will not damage rubber products.*

1. Clean and dry the bearing assembly.

2. Inspect the steel balls (**Figure 12**), bearing cage (A, **Figure 13**) and bearing race (B, **Figure 13**) for excessive wear or damage.

3. Check the bearing race inner splines (C, **Figure 13**) for wear or damage.

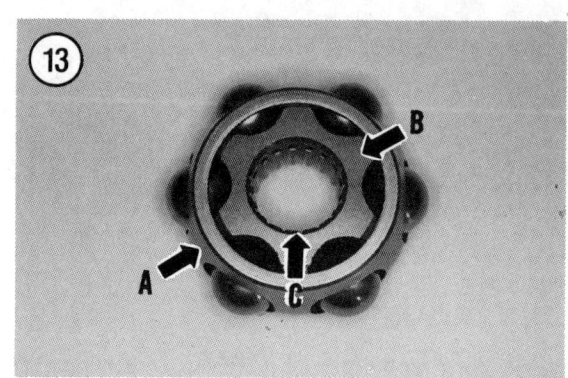

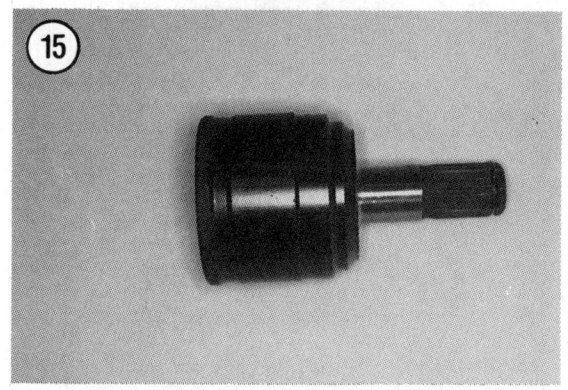

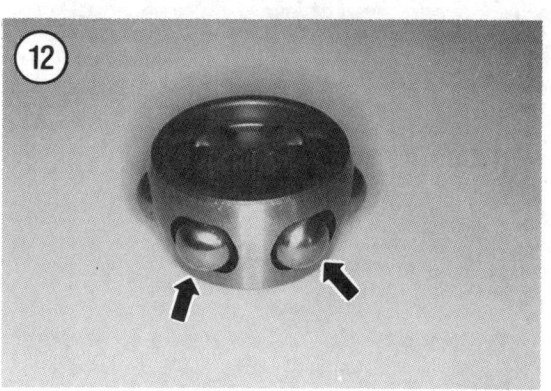

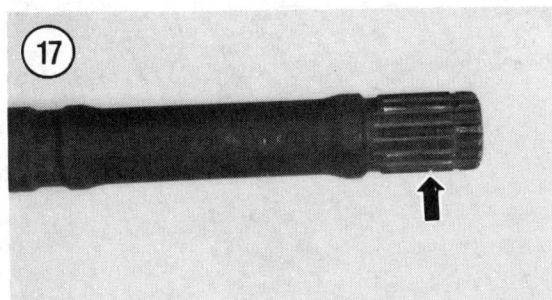

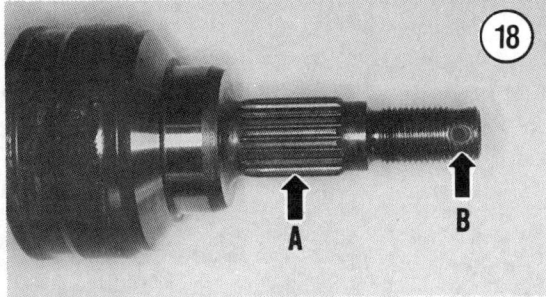

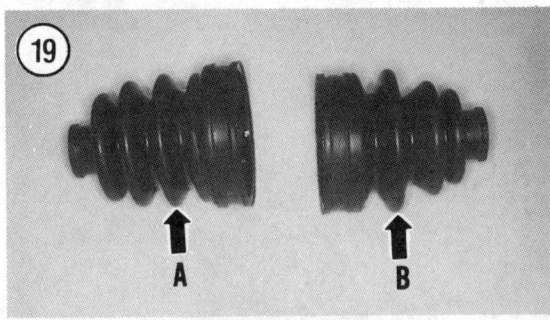

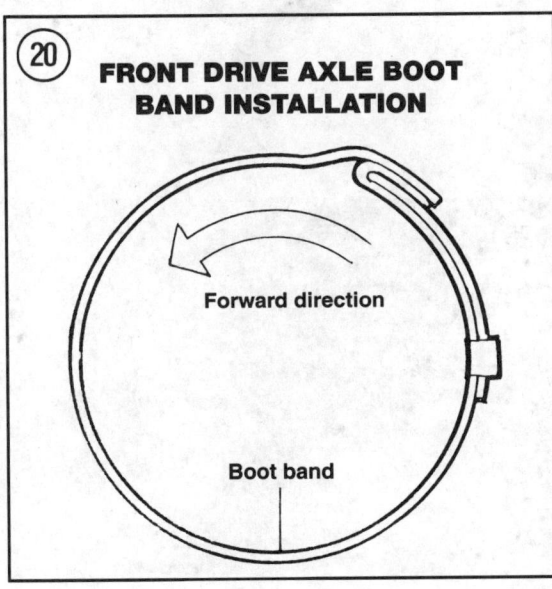

**FRONT DRIVE AXLE BOOT BAND INSTALLATION**

Forward direction

Boot band

4. If necessary, disassemble the bearing assembly for further inspection. Carefully remove the steel balls from the bearing cage then remove the bearing race from the bearing cage.

5. If any of the bearing components are damaged, replace the entire assembly. Individual replacement parts are not available separately.

6. Clean and dry the inboard joint.

7. Inspect the inboard joint ball guides (A, **Figure 14**) for excessive wear or damage.

8. Inspect the inboard joint stopper ring groove (B, **Figure 14**) for wear or damage.

9. Check the stopper ring groove (A, **Figure 3**) in the inboard joint shaft for cracks or other damage.

10. Inspect the axle and inboard joint splines (B, **Figure 3**) for excessive wear or damage.

11. Inspect the inboard joint (**Figure 15**) for cracks or damage.

12. Move the outboard joint axle and check for excessive play or noise (**Figure 16**).

13. Inspect the front drive axle for bending, wear or damage.

14. Inspect the inner end splines (**Figure 17**), the outer end splines (A, **Figure 18**) and the front hub cotter pin hole (B, **Figure 18**) for wear or damage.

15. Inspect the rubber boots for cracks, age deterioration or other damage.

16. Replace the front drive axle assembly if any of the components are excessively worn or damaged. Individual replacement parts for the front drive axle, other than the rubber boots and clamps, are not available.

**11**

## Assembly

Refer to **Figure 5** for this procedure.

1. The rubber boots are not identical and must be installed on the correct joint. Factory replacement boots are marked as follows:

 a. Inboard joint—BJ68 (A, **Figure 19**).

 b. Outboard joint—BJ68L (B, **Figure 19**).

2. If the outboard boot was removed, install a new boot onto the front axle at this time.

*NOTE*
*Install the new boot clamps with their tabs facing in the direction shown in* **Figure 20.**

3. Install two new small boot clamps onto the front axle.

4. Install the inboard boot and move the small boot clamp onto the boot (**Figure 21**). Do not lock the clamp at this time.

5. If the bearing assembly was disassembled, assemble the bearing as follows:

    a. Position the bearing race with the wide inner diameter going on first and install the race (**Figure 22**) into the bearing case. Align the steel ball receptacles in both parts.

    b. Install the steel balls into their receptacles in the bearing case.

    c. Pack the bearing assembly with grease included in the boot replacement kit. Grease will help hold the steel balls in place.

6. Position the bearing assembly with the small end of the bearing going on first and install the bearing onto the drive axle (**Figure 11**).

7. Push the bearing assembly on until it stops, then install a new circlip (**Figure 23**) into the groove in the shaft. Make sure the circlip seats in the groove completely.

8. Apply a liberal amount of grease to the bearing assembly (**Figure 24**). Work the grease between the

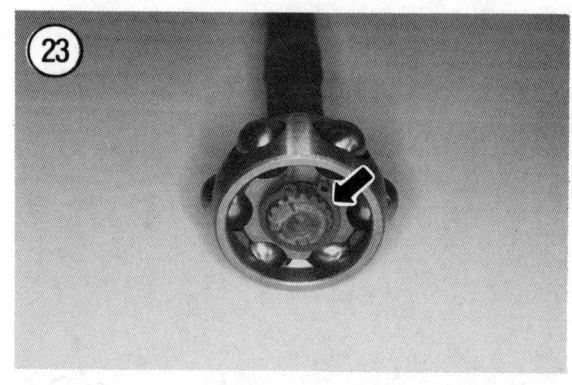

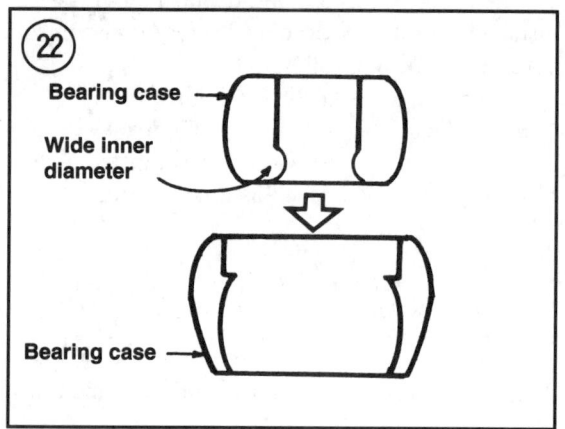

Bearing case

Wide inner diameter

Bearing case

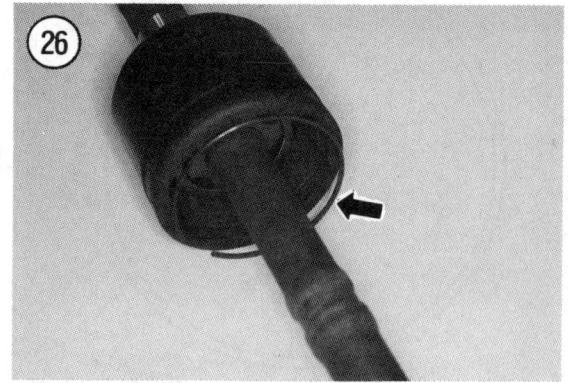

balls, race and case. Check for voids and fill with grease.

9. Lubricate the inboard joint inner surface with grease.

10. Install the inboard joint over the bearing assembly (**Figure 25**) and install the stopper ring (**Figure 26**). Make sure the stopper ring seats in the groove completely.

11. After the stopper ring is in place, fill the inboard joint cavity behind the bearing assembly with grease (B, **Figure 7**).

12. Pack each boot with the following amounts of molybdenum disulfide grease:

    a. Inboard boot—40-60 g (1.4-2.1 oz.).

    b. Outboard boot—30-50 g (1.1-1.8 oz.).

13. Move the inboard boot onto the inboard joint (**Figure 27**).

14. Move the inboard joint on the drive axle until distance between the *ends* of the inboard and outboard joints are as follows (**Figure 28**):

    a. Right drive axle—360-370 mm (14.2-14.6 in.).

    b. Left drive axle—320-330 mm (12.6-13.0 in.).

15. Move the small boot clamp onto each boot (**Figure 29**). Bend down the tab on the boot clamp and secure the tab with the locking clips and tap them with a plastic hammer. Make sure the tab is locked in place (**Figure 30**). Repeat for the opposite boot.

> *NOTE*
> *Install the new boot clamps with their tabs facing in the direction shown in **Figure 20**.*

16. Install the large boot clamps onto each boot. Make sure the boots are not twisted on the axle.

> *CAUTION*
> *Make sure the inboard joint does not move while installing the boot clamps. The dimension achieved in Step 14 must be maintained at all times. This dimension is critical to avoid undue stress on the rubber boots after installation of the front drive axle and while the vehicle runs.*

17. Refer to **Figure 31** and secure all large boot clamps. Bend down the tab (**Figure 32**) on the boot clamp and secure the tab with the locking clips and tap them with a plastic hammer. Make sure they are locked in place (**Figure 33**).

**11**

18. If removed, install a new stopper ring (A, **Figure 3**). Make sure the stopper ring is seated correctly in the drive axle groove.

19. Apply molybdenum disulfide grease to the drive axle splines.

## PROPELLER SHAFT

The propeller shaft can be removed without removing the front differential or front drive axles. For example, before removing the engine from the frame (Chapter Five), the propeller shaft must be removed first. If you are going to remove the front differential also, refer to *Front Differential* in this chapter.

### Removal

1. Support the vehicle with the front wheels off the ground.

2. Remove the bolt, retaining clips and propeller shaft cover (**Figure 34**).

> *NOTE*
> *The propeller shaft can be removed with the front wheels and front axles installed on the vehicle. **Figure 35** shows the differential housing with these parts removed for clarity.*

3. Remove the front mounting bolt and nut (A, **Figure 35**).

4. Remove the two bolts and the front mounting bracket (B, **Figure 35**).

5. Remove the upper mounting bolt (C, **Figure 35**), nut and collar.

6. Remove the rear mounting bolt (D, **Figure 35**).

7. Push the front differential assembly forward in the frame.

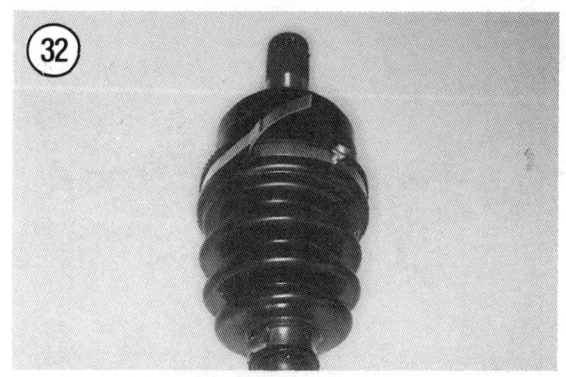

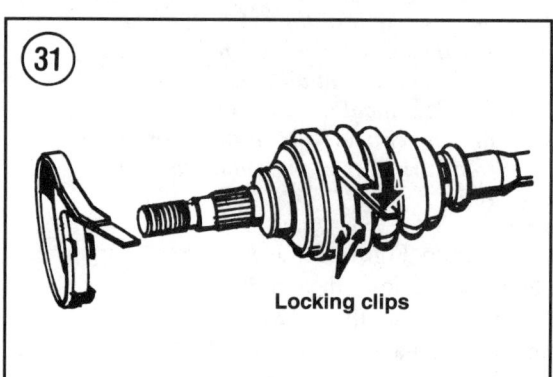

Locking clips

8. Pull the propeller shaft joint (**Figure 36**) forward, then disconnect the propeller shaft from the engine (**Figure 37**) and remove it. See **Figure 38**. Remove the front shaft joint and spring from the propeller shaft.

9. Inspect the propeller shaft as described in this section.

### Inspection

1. Check the propeller shaft (**Figure 39**) for bending or other damage.

2. Check the splines in each end for damage.

3. Check the dust seals (**Figure 39**) for excessive wear or damage. Replace if necessary.

### Installation

1. Lubricate the propeller shaft splines and dust seals with molybdenum disulfide grease.

2. Push the front differential assembly forward in the frame.

3. Apply 5-8 g (0.18-0.28 oz.) of molybdenum disulfide grease onto the pinion joint splines (**Figure 40**).

4. Install the propeller shaft (**Figure 38**) into the pinion joint (**Figure 41**).

5. Insert a piece of wire between the propeller shaft and boot (**Figure 41**) to release air from the pinion joint. Leave the wire in place until Step 17.

6. Install the O-ring (A, **Figure 42**) on the final drive shaft, if removed.

7. Apply 5-8 g (0.18-0.28 oz.) of molybdenum disulfide grease onto the rear propeller shaft splines.

8. Install the spring (B, **Figure 42**) into the front shaft joint (C).

**11**

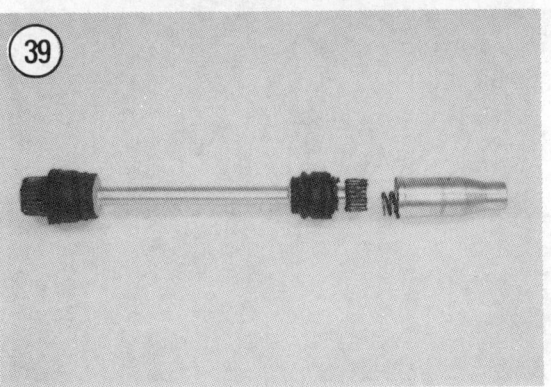

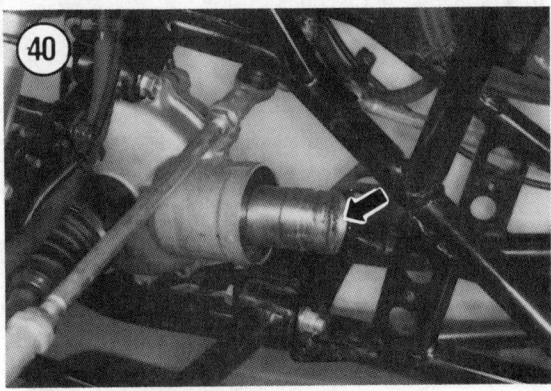

9. Install the spring and front shaft joint onto the propeller shaft and under the boot (**Figure 43**).

10. Push the propeller shaft forward, then connect the propeller shaft to the engine (**Figure 36**). If necessary, rotate the propeller shaft to align the splines.

11. Move the front differential rearward and align its mounting holes with the frame.

> *NOTE*
> *Do not tighten the differential housing mounting bolts until all of the fasteners have been installed.*

12. Install the front mounting bolt and nut (A, **Figure 35**).

13. Install the two bolts and the front mounting bracket (B, **Figure 35**).

14. Install the upper mounting bolt (C, **Figure 35**), nut and collar.

15. Install the rear mounting bolt (D, **Figure 35**).

16. Tighten the gearcase mounting bolts and nuts as specified in **Table 1**.

17. Remove the piece of wire installed in Step 5.

18. Install the propeller shaft cover (**Figure 34**) and secure it with its retaining clips and bolt.

19. Lower the vehicle so that both front wheels are on the ground.

## FRONT DIFFERENTIAL

The front differential gearcase can be removed with one front drive axle still installed. If the gearcase is going to be disassembled, remove both front drive axles before removing the gearcase from the frame. It is easier to remove the front drive axles with the gearcase still installed in the frame. If it is only necessary to remove the propeller shaft, refer to *Propeller Shaft* in this chapter.

### Removal

1. Remove the front fender (Chapter Fifteen).

2. Drain the front differential oil (Chapter Three).

3. Support the vehicle with the front wheels off the ground.

4. Remove the front drive axles as described in this chapter.

5. Disconnect the air vent hose (**Figure 44**) from the differential gearcase.

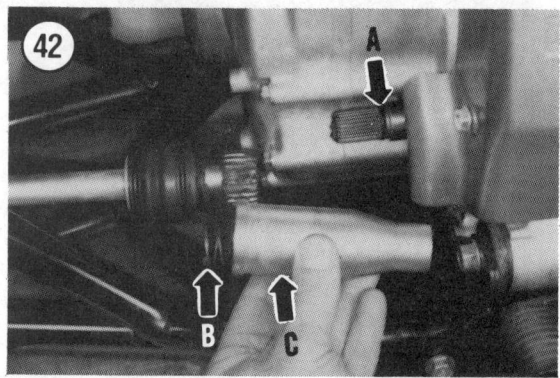

6. Remove the bolt, retaining clips and propeller shaft cover (**Figure 34**).

7. Remove the front mounting bolt and nut (A, **Figure 35**).

8. Remove the two bolts and the front mounting bracket (B, **Figure 35**).

9. Remove the upper mounting bolt (C, **Figure 35**), nut and collar.

10. Remove the rear mounting bolt (D, **Figure 35**).

11. Push the front differential assembly forward in the frame.

12. Pull the propeller joint (**Figure 36**) forward, then disconnect the propeller shaft from the engine (**Figure 37**) and remove it. See **Figure 38**. Remove the front shaft joint and spring from the propeller shaft.

13. Remove the front differential gearcase (**Figure 35**) from the frame.

### Disassembly/Inspection/Assembly

The front differential gearcase requires a number of special tools for disassembly, inspection and reassembly. The price of these tools could be more than the cost of most repairs or for oil seal replacement performed at a dealership. Refer all service to a Honda dealership.

1. Check the gearcase unit for oil leaks, cracks or other damage.

2. Inspect the oil seals for leaks or damage. Replace if necessary.

3. Turn the drive pinion by hand. It should turn smoothly and quietly. If the rotation is rough or noisy, take the gearcase to a Honda dealership for service.

4. Check the gearcase frame mounting brackets for damage. Refer repair to a Honda dealership or welding shop.

### Installation

1. Install the front differential gearcase and position it in front of its frame mounting brackets.

2. Lubricate the propeller shaft splines and dust seals with molybdenum disulfide grease.

3. Apply 5-8 g (0.18-0.28 oz.) of molybdenum disulfide grease onto the pinion joint splines (**Figure 40**).

4. Install the propeller shaft (**Figure 38**) into the pinion joint (**Figure 41**).

5. Insert a piece of wire between the propeller shaft and boot (**Figure 41**) to release air from the pinion joint. Leave the wire in place until Step 17.

6. Install a new O-ring (A, **Figure 42**) on the final drive shaft.

7. Apply 5-8 g (0.18-0.28 oz.) of molybdenum disulfide grease onto the rear propeller shaft splines.

8. Install the spring (B, **Figure 42**) into the front shaft joint (C).

9. Install the spring and front shaft joint onto the propeller shaft and under the boot (**Figure 43**).

10. Push the propeller shaft forward, then connect the propeller shaft to the engine (**Figure 36**). If necessary, rotate the propeller shaft to align the splines.

11. Move the front differential rearward and align its mounting holes with the frame.

*NOTE*
*Do not tighten the differential gearcase mounting bolts until all of the fasteners have been installed.*

12. Install the front mounting bolt and nut (A, **Figure 35**).

13. Install the two bolts and the front mounting bracket (B, **Figure 35**).

14. Install the upper mounting bolt (C, **Figure 35**), nut and collar.

15. Install the rear mounting bolt (D, **Figure 35**).

16. Tighten the gearcase mounting bolts and nuts as specified in **Table 1**.

17. Remove the piece of wire installed in Step 5.

18. Install the propeller shaft cover (**Figure 34**) and secure it with its retaining clips and bolt.

19. Reconnect the air vent hose (**Figure 44**) at the differential gearcase. Secure the hose with its clamp.

20. Install the front drive axles as described in this chapter.

21. Refill the front differential with the correct amount and type of oil (Chapter Three).

22. Install the front fender (Chapter Fifteen).

**11**

Table 1 FRONT DRIVE MECHANISM TIGHTENING TORQUES

|  | N·m | in.-lb. | ft.-lb. |
|---|---|---|---|
| Gearcase mounting bolts and nuts | | | |
| 8 mm | 22 | — | 16 |
| 10 mm | 45 | — | 33 |
| Gearcase drain plug | 12 | 106 | — |

# CHAPTER TWELVE

# REAR AXLE, SUSPENSION AND FINAL DRIVE

This chapter contains repair and replacement procedures for the rear wheels, rear axle, suspension and final drive unit.

Rear suspension specifications are listed in **Table 1** and torque specifications in **Table 2**. Tables 1 and 2 are found at the end of this chapter.

*CAUTION*
*Self-locking nuts are used to secure some of the rear suspension components. Honda recommends discarding all self-locking nuts once they have been removed. The self-locking portion of the nut is weakened once the nut has been removed and will no longer properly lock onto the mating threads. Always install new self-locking nuts. Never re-install a used nut once it has been removed.*

## REAR WHEELS

Refer to **Figure 1**.

### Removal/Installation

*NOTE*
*The tire tread on the factory equipped tires is directional (Figure 2) and must be installed on the correct side of the vehicle. Mark each wheel to identify its operating side before removing it.*

1. Park the vehicle on level ground and set the parking brake. Block the front wheels so the vehicle cannot roll in either direction.
2. Identify the rear tires with an L (left side) or R (right side) mark. Refer to these marks to install the wheels on their correct side.
3. Loosen the wheel nuts (**Figure 3**) securing the wheel to the hub/brake drum.
4. Jack up the rear of the vehicle so that the rear wheel(s) is off the ground. Support the vehicle with safety stands or wooden blocks in the event the jack fails. Make sure they are properly placed before beginning work.
5. Remove the wheel nuts and remove the rear wheel.
6. Clean the wheel nuts in solvent and dry thoroughly.
7. Inspect the wheel for cracks, bending or other damage. If necessary, replace the wheel as described under *Tires and Wheels* in Chapter Ten.
8. Install the wheel onto its original side.
9. Install the wheel nuts with their curved end (**Figure 4**) facing toward the wheel. Tighten the nuts finger-tight to center the wheel squarely against the brake drum or hub.

**12**

10. Tighten the wheel nuts (**Figure 1**) as specified in **Table 2**.

11. After the wheel is installed completely, rotate it and then apply the rear brake several times to make sure that the wheel rotates freely and that the brake is operating correctly.

12. Jack up the rear of the vehicle and remove the safety stands or wooden blocks.

13. Lower the vehicle so that both rear wheels are on the ground and remove the jack.

## TIRE CHANGING AND TIRE REPAIRS

Refer to Chapter Ten for these service procedures.

## REAR AXLE

Refer to **Figure 5** when servicing the rear axle.

① **REAR WHEEL DRIVE HUB**

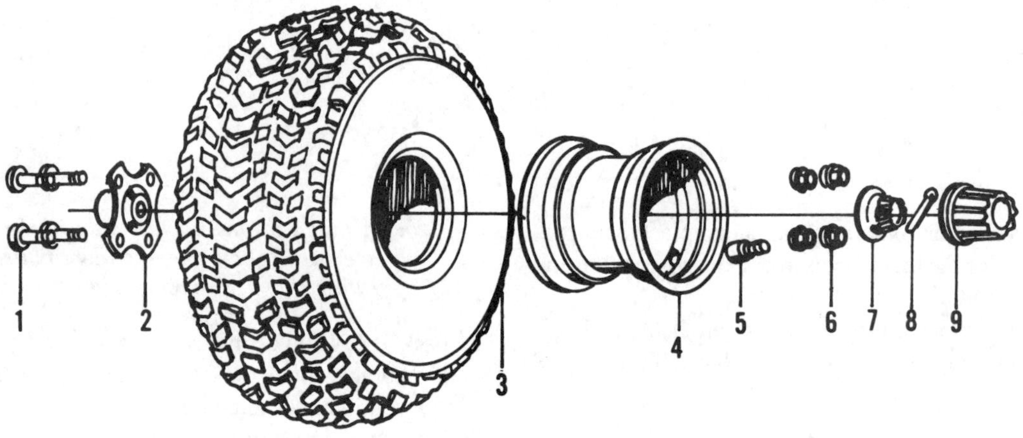

1. Bolt
2. Hub
3. Tire
4. Wheel
5. Valve stem
6. Lug nut
7. Castellated nut
8. Cotter pin
9. Hub cap

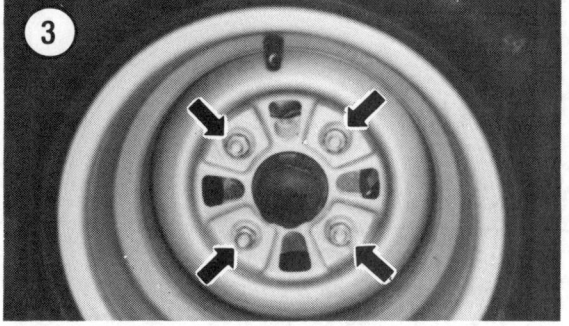

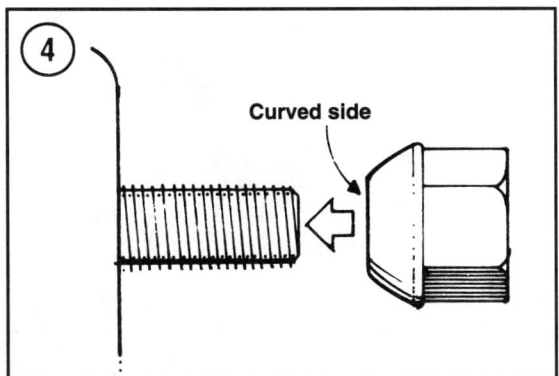

4
Curved side

## Removal

1. Remove both rear wheels as described in this chapter.
2. Remove the left rear axle nut cotter pin and discard it.
3. Remove the left rear axle nut (A, **Figure 6**) and rear hub (B, **Figure 6**).
4. Remove the left shock absorber lower mounting bolt (A, **Figure 7**).
5. Remove the locknuts and the left rear axle housing (B, **Figure 7**). Discard the locknuts.

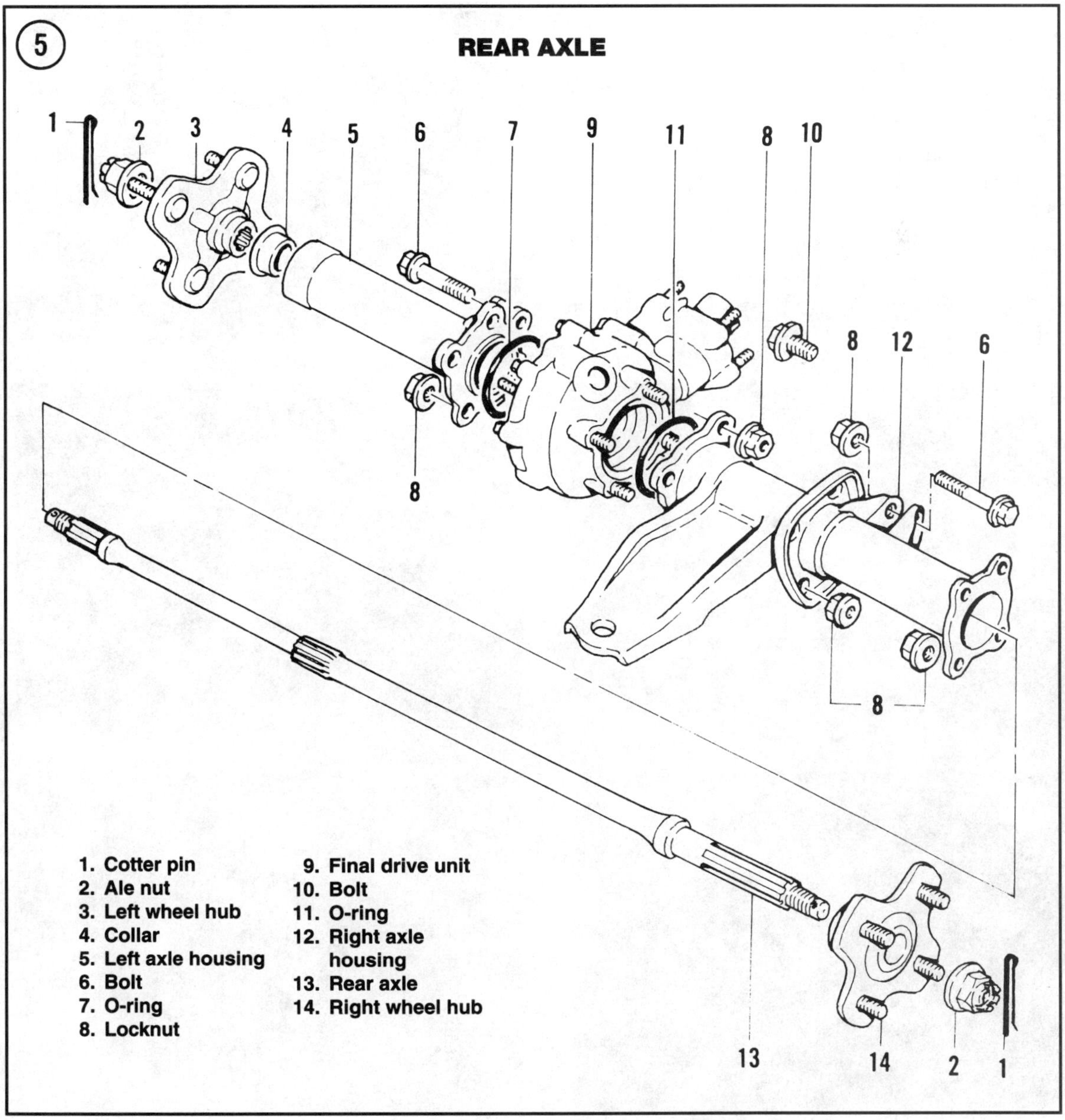

5
REAR AXLE
1
2
3
4
5
6
7
9
11
8
10
8
12
6
8
8
13
14
2
1
1. Cotter pin
2. Ale nut
3. Left wheel hub
4. Collar
5. Left axle housing
6. Bolt
7. O-ring
8. Locknut
9. Final drive unit
10. Bolt
11. O-ring
12. Right axle housing
13. Rear axle
14. Right wheel hub

6. Remove the collar (**Figure 8**).

7. Remove the right rear axle nut cotter pin and discard it.

8. Remove the right rear axle nut (A, **Figure 9**) and rear hub (B, **Figure 9**).

9. Remove the brake drum cover, brake drum and rear brake panel assembly (Chapter Thirteen).

10. Remove the axle (**Figure 10**) from the left side. If necessary, drive out the axle with a rubber hammer.

11. Inspect the rear hubs and axle as described in this chapter.

## Wheel Hubs
## Inspection

1. Inspect the hub inner splines (A, **Figure 11**) for wear or damage. Replace the hub if necessary.

2. Replace the dust seal (A, **Figure 11**) if worn or damaged.

3. Check the studs (B, **Figure 11**) for damaged threads. Replace damaged studs with a press.

4. Inspect the side seal ring (**Figure 12**) and replace if damaged.

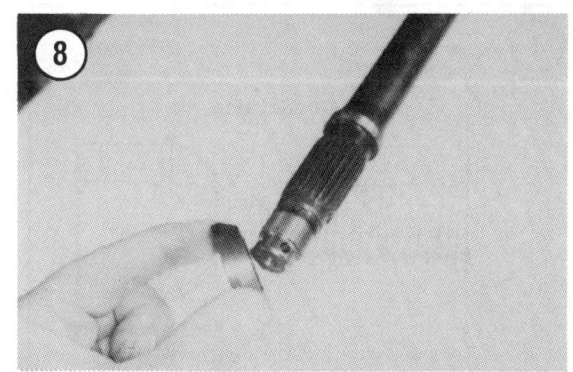

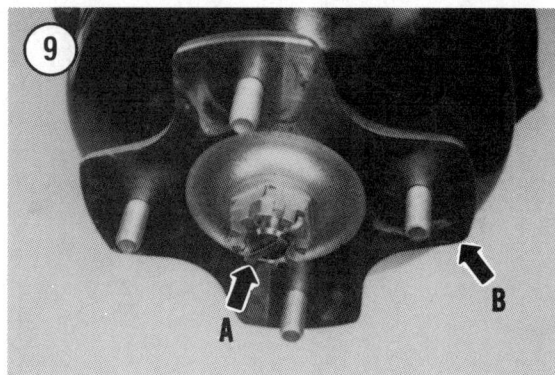

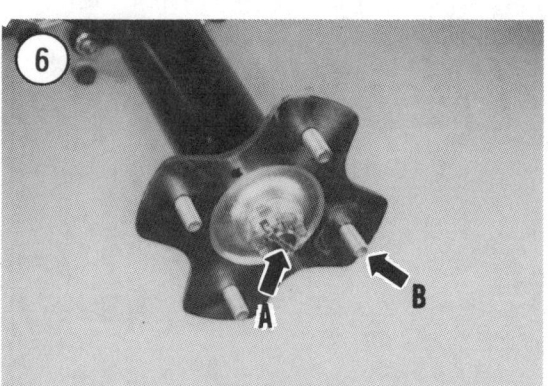

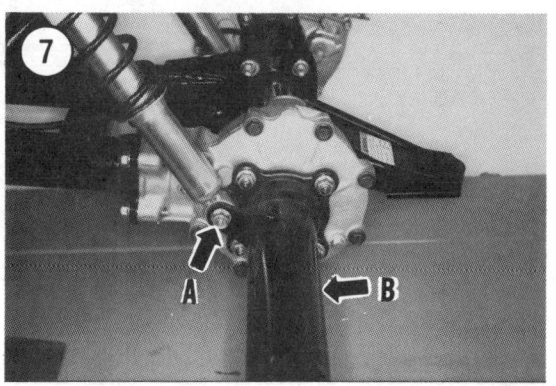

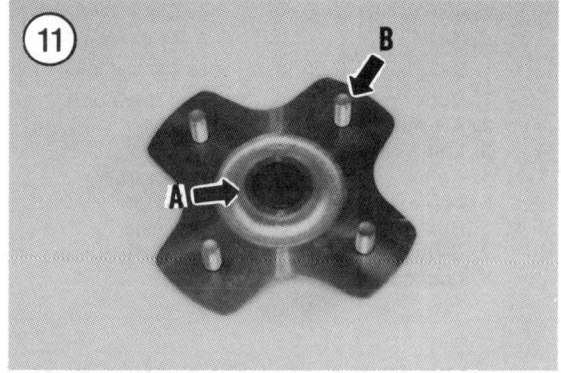

## Rear Axle
## Inspection

1. Clean and dry the rear axle (**Figure 13**).

2. Inspect the axle splines (**Figure 13**) for twisting or other damage.

3. Check the axle cotter pin holes. Replace the axle if either hole is cracked or damaged and cannot hold the cotter pin.

4. Place the rear axle on a set of V-blocks and measure runout with a dial indicator (**Figure 14**). Replace the rear axle if the runout exceeds the service limit in **Table 1**.

## Left Final Drive Housing
## Axle Seal and Bearing
## Inspection and Replacement

1. Inspect the axle seal (A, **Figure 15**) for damage.

2. Check the bearing (B, **Figure 15**) by turning its inner race with your finger. The bearing should turn without roughness, catching, binding or excessive noise. If damaged, replace the bearing as described in this procedure.

3. Support the final drive housing and pry the axle seal out with a seal removal tool.

*NOTE*
*If you are only going to replace the seal, go to Step 8.*

4. Remove the bearing by driving it out of the housing with a long drift or bearing driver.

5. Clean and dry the final drive housing.

6. Check the bearing bore for cracks or other damage.

7. Install the new bearing as follows:

   a. Install the bearing with its closed side facing out.

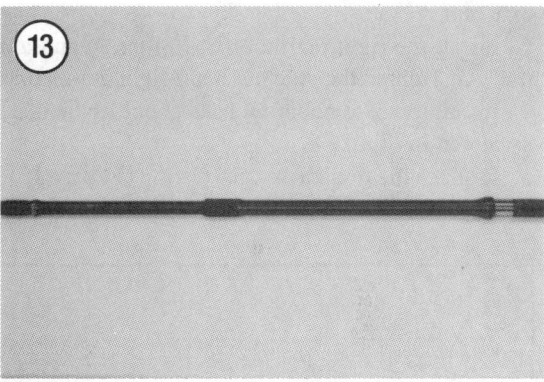

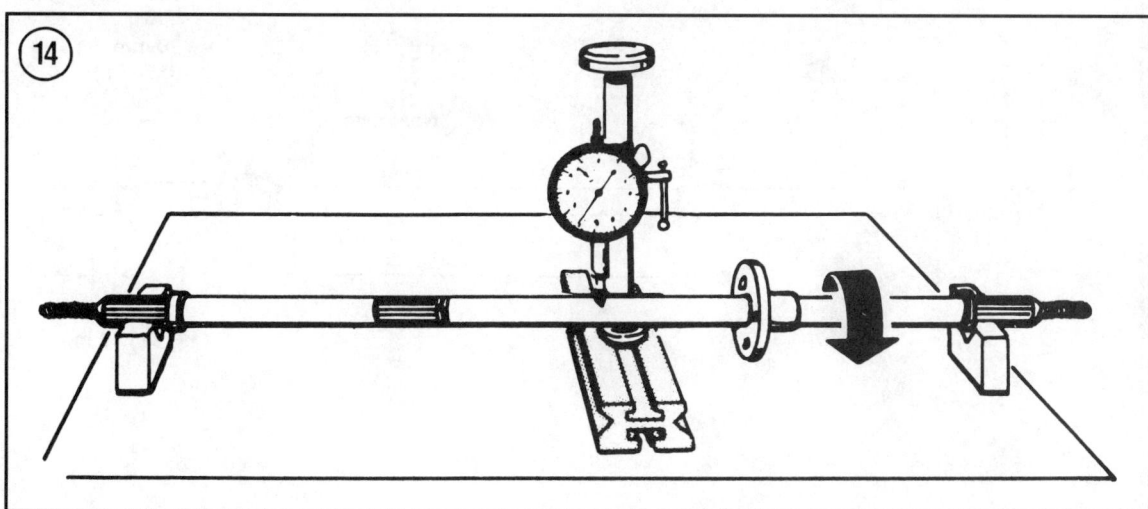

12

   b. Install the bearing into place with a bearing driver to the depth shown in **Figure 16**. Press on the bearing outer race only.
8. Install the new axle seal as follows:
   a. Pack the oil seal lips with a waterproof grease.
   b. Install the new oil seal into the housing in the direction shown in **Figure 16**. Install the new oil seal so that it seats against the bearing.

**Installation**

1. Apply grease to the axle splines as shown in **Figure 17**.
2. Install the rear axle (**Figure 10**) from the right side. At the same time, align the rear axle and final drive housing splines.
3. Install the rear brake panel, brake drum and brake drum cover (Chapter Thirteen).
4. Clean the rear hubs where they contact the brake drum (right side) or bearing (left axle housing).
5. Lubricate the axle shaft splines where the right axle hub operates.
6. Install the right rear hub (B, **Figure 9**) and axle nut (A). Tighten the axle nut hand-tight at this time.
7. Install the axle collar with its shoulder facing in as shown in **Figure 8**.
8. Replace the final drive case O-ring (**Figure 18**) if damaged. Lubricate the O-ring with grease.

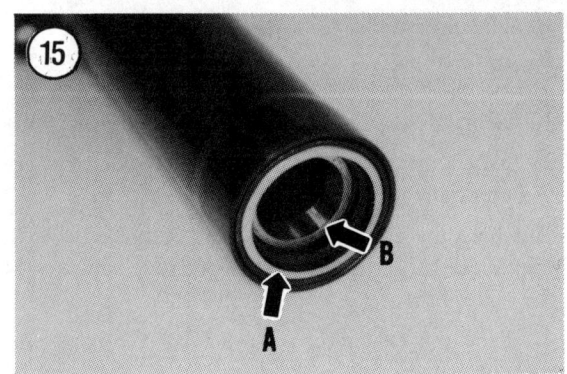

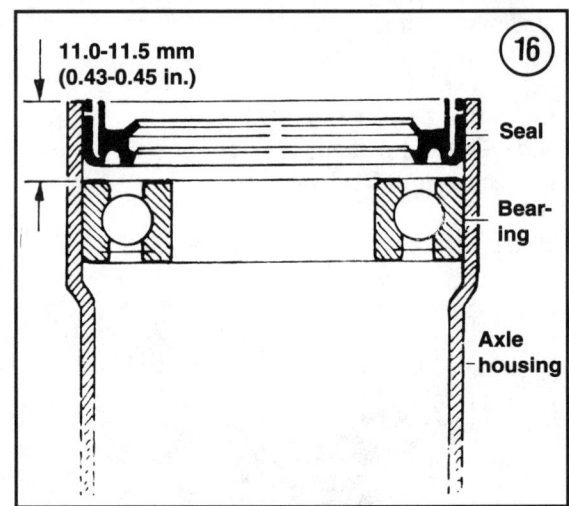

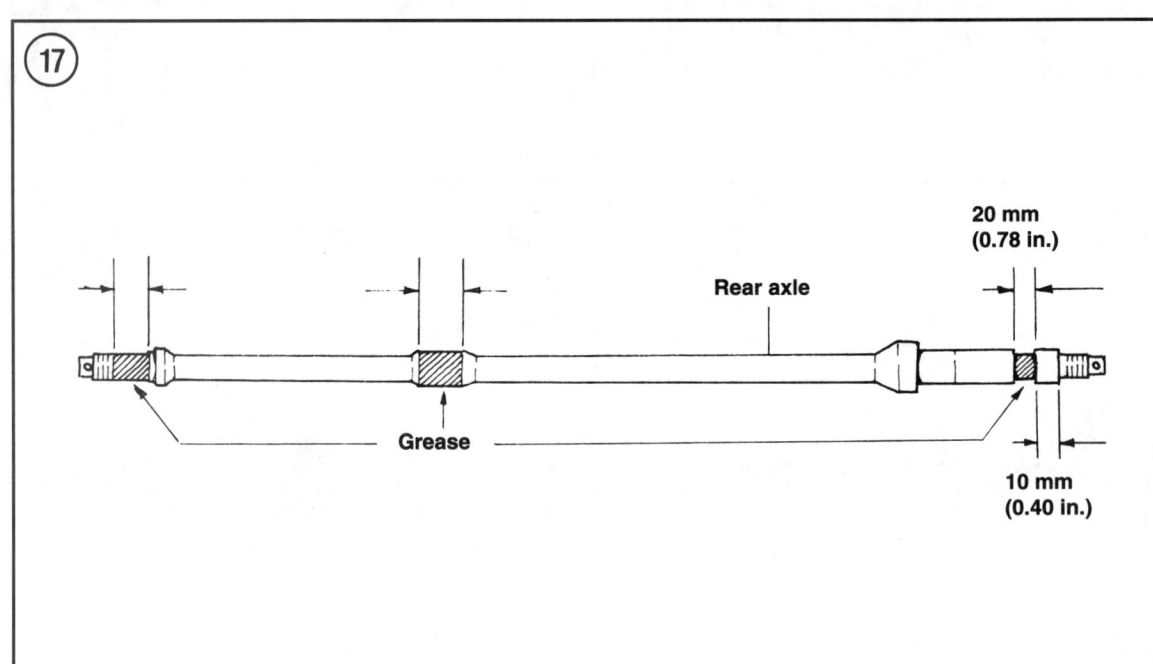

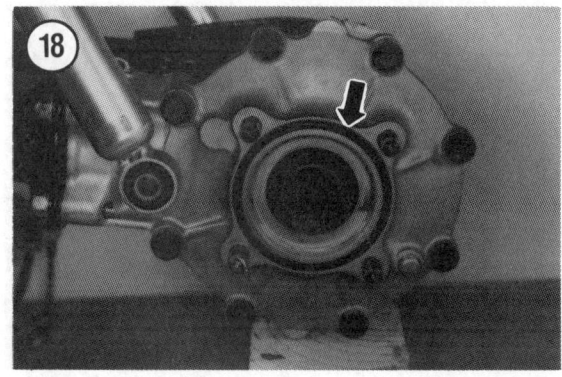

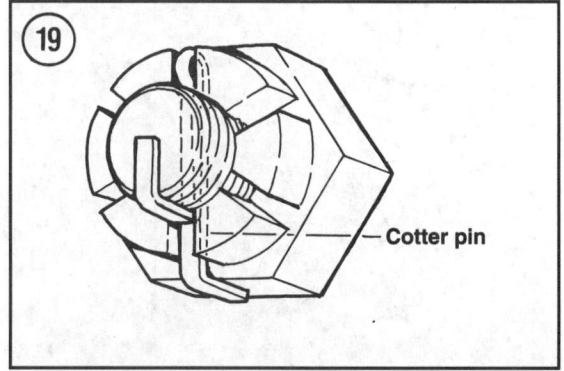

Cotter pin

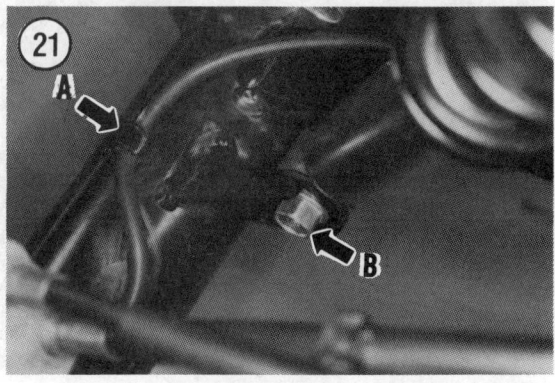

9. Install the left rear axle housing (B, **Figure 7**).

10. Install the left rear hub (B, **Figure 6**) onto the axle and into the axle housing to help center the rear axle. Install the left rear axle nut (A, **Figure 6**) and tighten hand-tight. Install new axle housing locknuts (**Figure 7**) and tighten as specified in **Table 2**.

11. Install the left shock absorber and its mounting bolt (A, **Figure 7**) and tighten as specified in **Table 2**.

12. Tighten the left side axle nut (A, **Figure 6**) as specified in **Table 2**.

13. Tighten the right side axle nut (A, **Figure 9**) as specified in **Table 2**.

14. Secure each axle nut with a new cotter pin. Spread the cotter pin ends to lock it in place. See **Figure 19**.

*NOTE*
*If the cotter pin hole(s) in the axle does not align with the castellations on the nut, tighten the nut further until hole alignment is correct. Never loosen the axle nut to achieve hole alignment.*

15. Install both rear wheels as described in this chapter.

## FINAL DRIVE UNIT

The final drive unit can be removed with or without the rear axle installed. If the final drive unit will be serviced, remove the axle while the final drive unit is mounted in the frame. If you are only going to service the swing arm, the final drive unit and rear axle can be removed as an assembly (**Figure 20**).

**12**

### Removal

1. If necessary, remove the rear axle as described in this chapter.

2. Remove the skid plate from underneath the final drive unit.

3. Drain the final drive oil (Chapter Three).

4. Disconnect the vent hose (A, **Figure 21**) from its clamp on the right axle housing.

5. Support the final drive unit with a jack or wooden blocks.

6. Remove the right shock absorber lower nut and bolt (A, **Figure 22**).

7. Remove the right axle housing locknuts and bolts (B, **Figure 22**).

8. Remove the final drive unit locknuts (C, **Figure 22**) and axle housing (D). See **Figure 23**.

*NOTE*
*Discard the locknuts removed in Steps 6-8.*

9. Disconnect the breather tube (A, **Figure 24**) at the final drive unit.

10. Remove the locknuts (B, **Figure 24**) and the final drive unit (C). Discard the locknuts.

11. Remove the spring (A, **Figure 25**) from the drive shaft.

12. Remove the O-ring (B, **Figure 25**) from the swing arm shoulder.

13. Refer to the *Disassembly/Inspection/Assembly* procedure for further information.

### Disassembly/Inspection/Assembly

The final drive unit requires a considerable number of special tools for disassembly and reassembly. The price of all of these tools could be more than the cost of most repairs or seal replacement by a Honda dealership. This section describes basic inspection procedures that do not require disassembly. If further service is required, take the final drive unit to a Honda dealership.

1. Check the entire unit (**Figure 26**) for oil leakage, cracks or other damage.

2. Inspect the exposed splines for excessive wear or damage.

3. Inspect the threaded studs for damage. Repair minor thread damage with a metric die, or replace the studs as described in Chapter One.

4. Inspect the O-rings (A, **Figure 26**) and oil seals (B) for wear, hardness and deterioration.

5. Check the right axle housing (**Figure 27**) for cracks or other damage.

### Installation

1. Lubricate a new O-ring with grease and install it onto the swing arm shoulder (B, **Figure 25**).

2. Lubricate the spring with grease and install it onto the end of the drive shaft (A, **Figure 25**).

3. Apply 5-8 g (0.18-0.28 oz.) of grease into the pinion joint spline (C, **Figure 26**).

4. Install the final drive unit (C, **Figure 24**) onto the swing arm, making sure you engage it with the drive

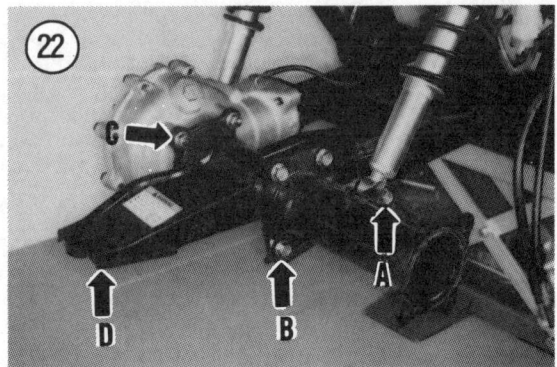

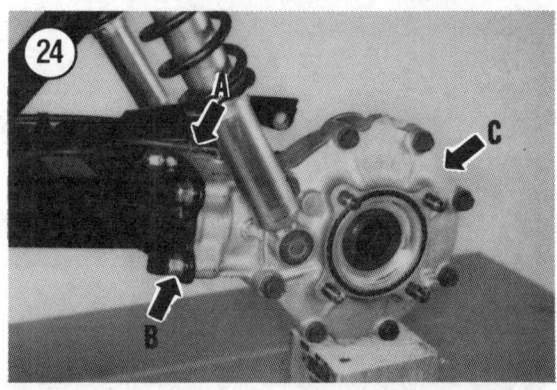

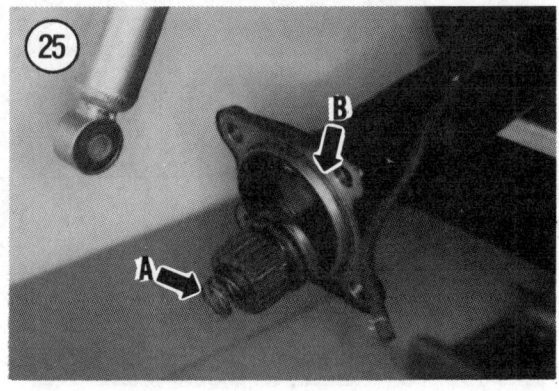

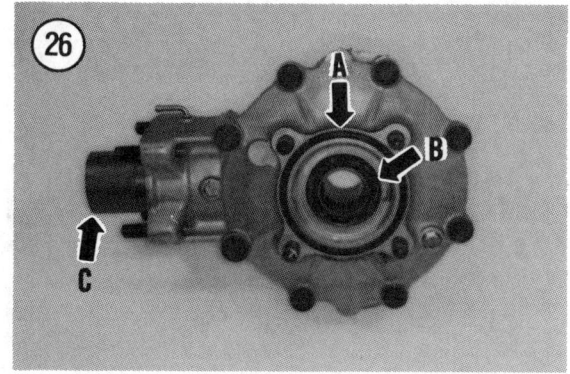

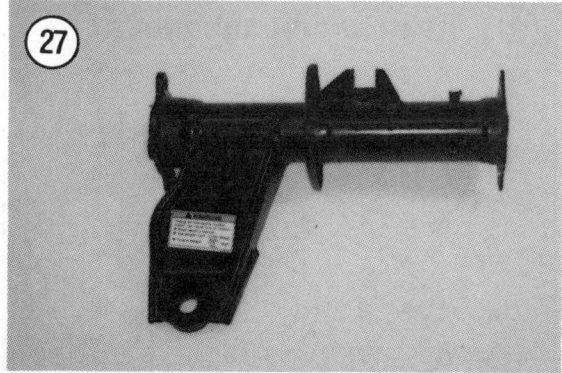

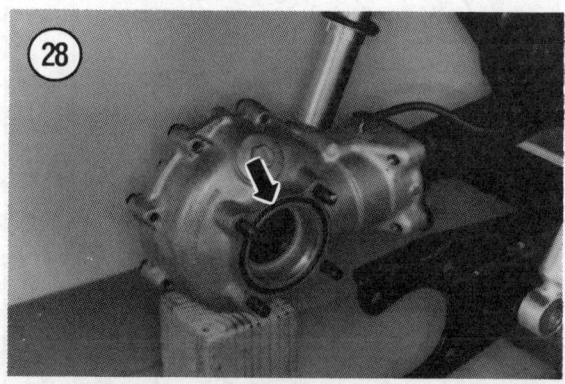

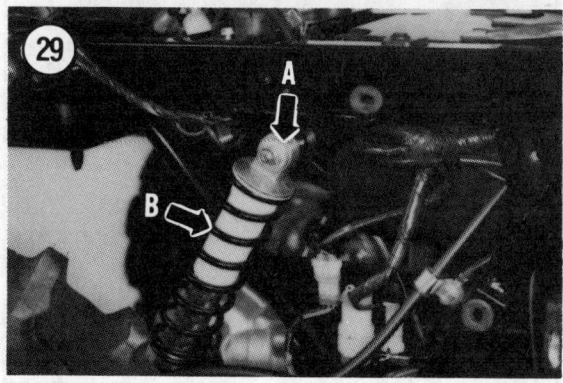

shaft and spring. Install new locknuts (B, **Figure 24**) finger-tight.

5. Reconnect the breather tube (A, **Figure 24**) onto the final drive unit.

6. Install the final drive unit O-ring (**Figure 28**), if removed. Lubricate the O-ring with grease.

*CAUTION*
*See the CAUTION at the beginning of this chapter relating to the use of self-locking locknuts used on the rear suspension.*

7. Install the axle housing (D, **Figure 22**) onto the final drive unit (C) and swing arm (B) using new locknuts. Tighten the locknuts finger-tight.

8. Tighten the right axle locknuts at the final drive unit (C, **Figure 22**) and swing arm (B) as specified in **Table 2**.

9. Install the right shock absorber lower mounting bolt and a new locknut (A, **Figure 22**) and tighten as specified in **Table 2**.

10. Reconnect the vent hose (A, **Figure 21**) onto the right axle housing.

11. Install the skid plate.

12. Install the rear axle as described in this chapter.

13. Refill the final drive unit with the recommended type and quantity of oil as described in Chapter Three.

## SHOCK ABSORBERS

**Removal/Installation**

1. Support the vehicle with the rear wheels off the ground.

2. If the left shock absorber is going to be removed, remove the muffler as described in Chapter Four.

3. Remove the shock absorber upper mounting locknut (A, **Figure 29**) and washer. Discard the locknut.

4. Remove the shock absorber lower mounting bolt (B, **Figure 21**) and locknut. Discard the locknut.

5. Remove the shock absorber (B, **Figure 29**).

6. Inspect the shock absorber as described in this chapter.

7. Install the shock absorber by reversing these removal steps, while noting the following:

    a. Install new locknuts.

**12**

*CAUTION*
*See the CAUTION at the beginning of this chapter relating to the use of self-locking locknuts used on the rear suspension.*

b. Tighten the upper and lower shock absorber locknuts as specified in **Table 2**.

## Inspection

1. Clean and dry the shock absorber.

2. Check the damper unit (**Figure 30**) for leaks or other damage. If necessary, remove the spring and replace the damper unit as described in this section.

3. Inspect the upper and lower (**Figure 31**) shock bushings. Replace excessively worn or damaged bushings as described in this section.

4. To inspect the shock spring free length, remove and measure the spring as described in this section.

## Spring Removal/Installation

The shock absorber is spring-controlled and hydraulically damped. Do not attempt to service the sealed shock damper unit. Service is limited to removal and replacement of the damper unit, spring and mounting bushings.

Refer to **Figure 32**.

*WARNING*
*Do not unscrew the upper shock mount without a spring compressor. The spring is under considerable pressure and may fly off and cause injury.*

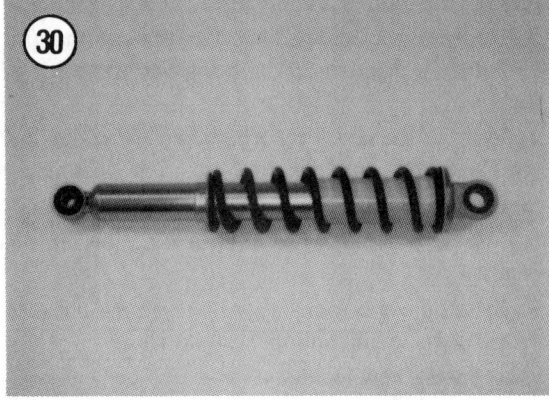

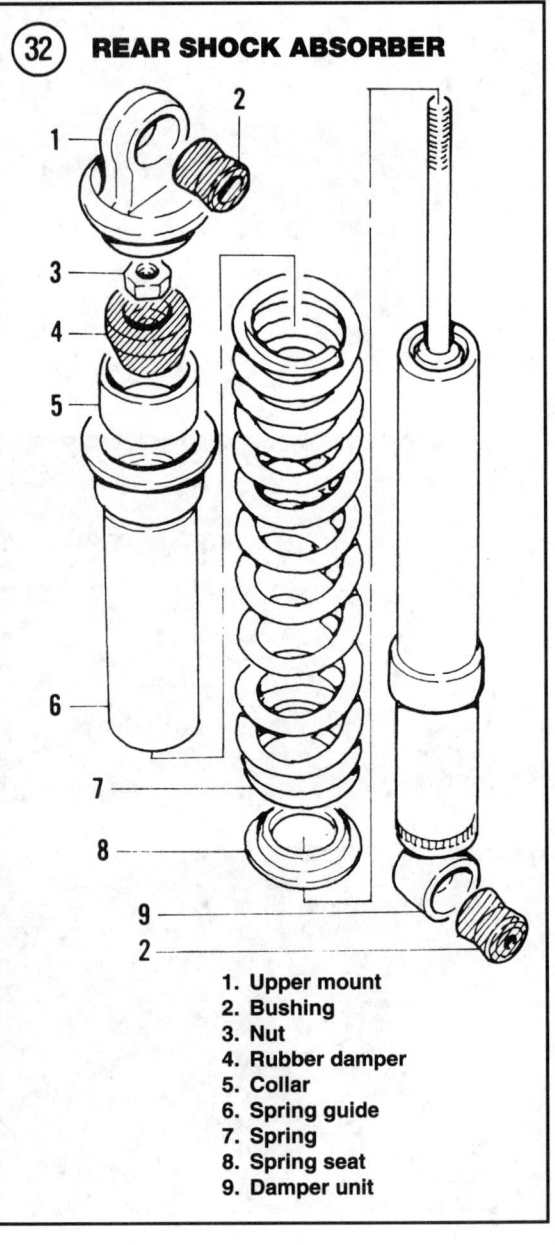

**REAR SHOCK ABSORBER**

1. Upper mount
2. Bushing
3. Nut
4. Rubber damper
5. Collar
6. Spring guide
7. Spring
8. Spring seat
9. Damper unit

*NOTE*
*Always follow the manufacturer's directions when using a spring compressor.*

1. Install the shock absorber into a spring compressor tool. See **Figure 33**, typical.

2. Compress the shock spring just enough to gain access to the locknut. Then loosen the locknut and unscrew the upper joint.

3. Release tension from the spring and remove the shock from the compression tool.

4. Remove the spring guide, collar, damper rubber, spring and spring seat.

5. Measure the spring free length (**Figure 34**). Replace the spring if it has sagged to the service limit in **Table 1**.

6. Check the damper unit for leakage and the damper rod for straightness. Replace the damper unit if necessary.

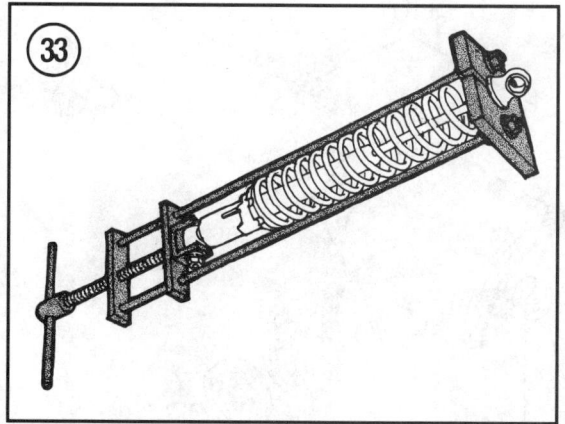

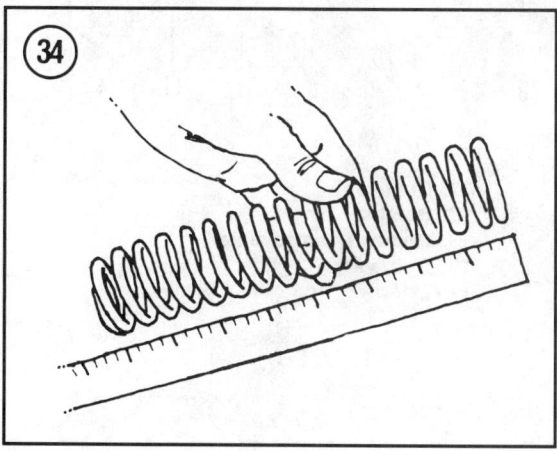

*NOTE*
*The damper unit cannot be rebuilt. If leaking or damaged, it must be replaced as a unit.*

7. Inspect the spring guide and replace if excessively worn or damaged.

8. Assemble the shock absorber by reversing the preceding removal steps, plus the following:

*WARNING*
*Do not install the upper spring seat without a spring compressor. The spring is under considerable pressure and may fly off and cause injury.*

a. Install the spring with the closer wound coils (**Figure 30**) toward the top.

b. Apply a threadlock to the threads of the damper rod before installing the locknut. Temporarily screw the locknut all the way down and tighten against the end of the threads.

c. Apply the same threadlock to the upper joint threads. Screw the upper joint on all the way. Then secure the upper joint in a vise with soft jaws and tighten the damper rod locknut against the upper joint to the torque specification in **Table 2**.

d. Release the tension from the spring and remove the shock absorber from the spring compressor.

e. Check that the shock spring seats evenly against the upper joint and spring seat.

### Shock Bushing Replacement

The upper and lower bushings are different. Identify the bushings before removing them in this procedure.

1. Support the damper unit in a press and press out one of the bushings (**Figure 31**).

2. Clean the shock bushing bore and inspect it for cracks.

3. Press in the new bushing (**Figure 31**), making sure to center it in the bushing bore.

4. Repeat for the other bushing.

## SWING ARM

Bearings are pressed into both sides of the swing arm. Seals are installed on the outside of each bear-

**12**

ing to prevent dirt and moisture from entering the bearings. Refer to **Figure 35** when servicing the swing arm in this section.

### Special Tools

The Honda swing arm locknut wrench (part No. 07908-4690003 [A, **Figure 36**]) and a 17 mm hex socket (B, **Figure 36**) are required to remove and install the swing arm.

### Removal

The swing arm can be removed with or without the final drive unit and rear axle installed in the swing arm. To service the swing arm, first remove the rear axle and the final drive unit as described in this chapter.

1. Remove the rear fender (Chapter Fifteen).

2. Remove the rear axle as described in this chapter.

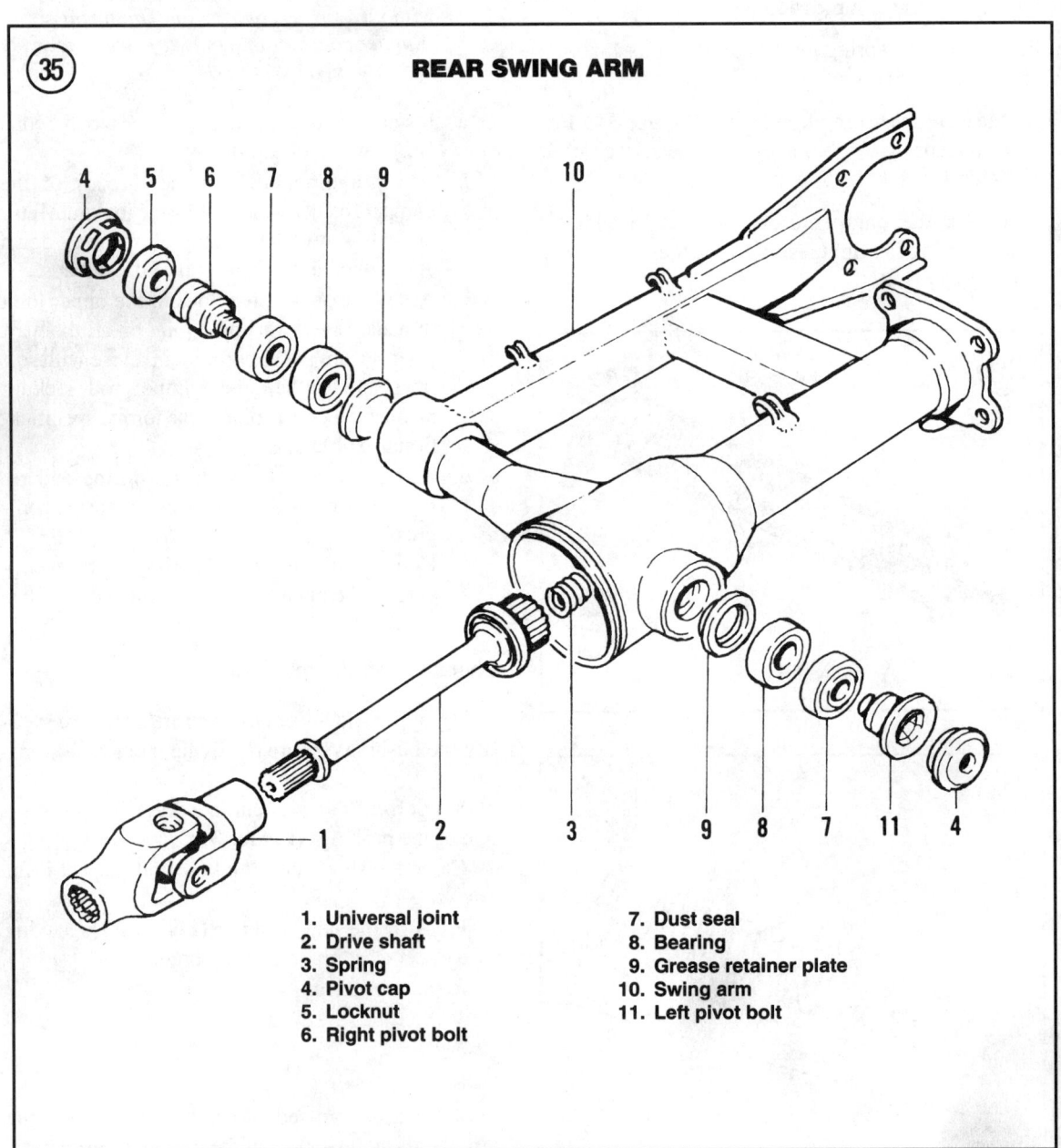

**REAR SWING ARM**

1. Universal joint
2. Drive shaft
3. Spring
4. Pivot cap
5. Locknut
6. Right pivot bolt
7. Dust seal
8. Bearing
9. Grease retainer plate
10. Swing arm
11. Left pivot bolt

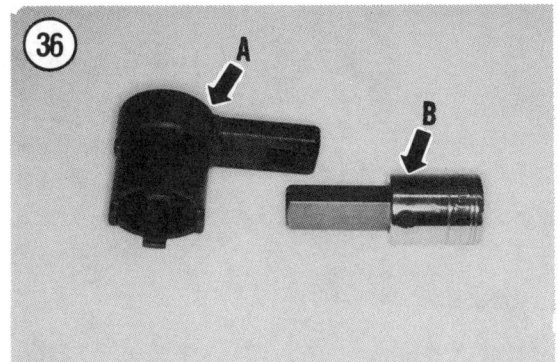

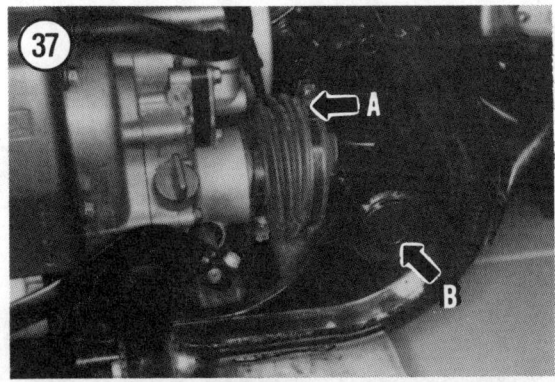

3. Remove the final drive unit as described in this chapter.

4. Remove the rear brake pedal (Chapter Thirteen).

5. Grasp the rear end of the swing arm and try to move it from side to side in a horizontal arc. There should be no noticeable side play. If play is evident and the pivot bolts are tightened correctly, replace the swing arm bearings.

6. Loosen the swing arm boot clamp (A, **Figure 37**).

7. Remove the pivot cap (B, **Figure 37**) from each side of the swing arm.

8. Remove the breather tubes from their clamps on the swing arm.

9. Remove the left pivot bolt using the 17 mm hex socket (**Figure 38**).

10. Loosen and remove the right pivot locknut using the Honda locknut wrench (**Figure 39**). See **Figure 40**.

11. Remove the right pivot bolt (**Figure 41**) and rear swing arm (**Figure 42**).

12. Remove the universal joint (A, **Figure 43**) and drive shaft (B) if they did not come off with the swing arm.

12

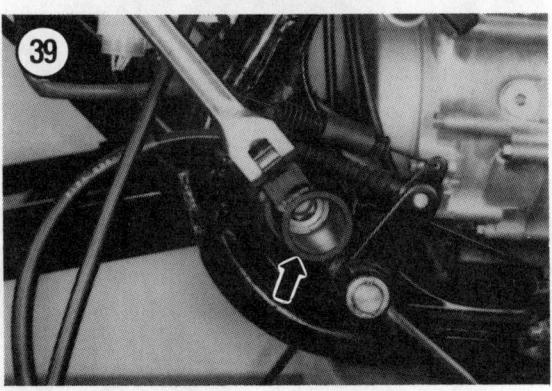

13. If necessary, loosen the remaining clamp and remove the boot (A, **Figure 44**)

## Swing Arm Inspection

1. Clean and dry the swing arm and its components.
2. Inspect the welded sections on the swing arm for cracks or other damage.
3. Remove the dust seals (**Figure 45**) with a seal removal tool or screwdriver.
4. Inspect each bearing (A, **Figure 46**) for severe wear, pitting or other damage. If necessary, replace the bearings as described under *Bearing Replacement* in this section.
5. Check that each grease retainer plate (B, **Figure 46**) fits tightly in its swing arm bore.
6. Inspect the pivot bolts (**Figure 47**) for excessive wear, thread damage or corrosion. Make sure the machined end on each pivot bolt is smooth. Replace if necessary.
7. Check the threaded holes in the frame (B, **Figure 44**) for corrosion or damage.
8. Replace the boot if damaged.

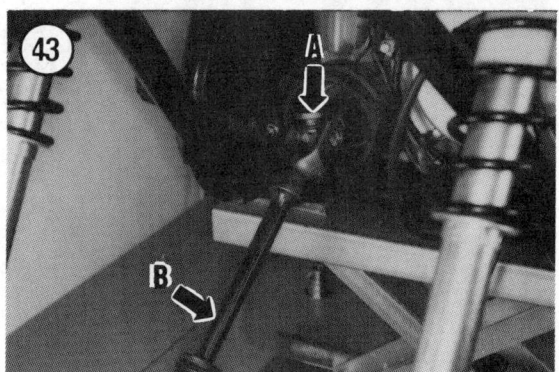

## Drive Shaft and Universal Joint Inspection

1. Check that the universal joint (A, **Figure 48**) pivots smoothly with no binding or roughness.
2. Inspect both universal joint spline ends for damage. If these splines are damaged, inspect the final drive case and engine output shaft splines for damage.
3. Check the drive shaft (B, **Figure 48**) for bending, spline damage or other damage.
4. Replace the dust seal (C, **Figure 48**) if leaking or damaged.

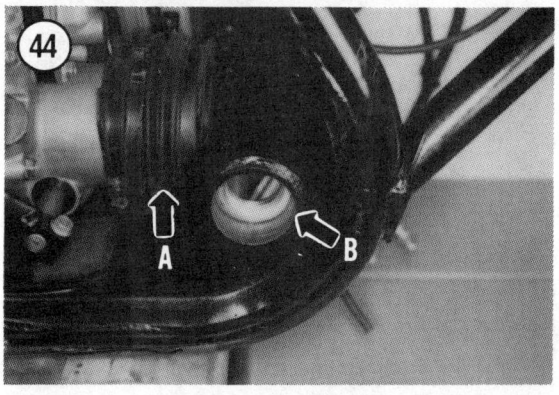

## Bearing Replacement

Replace the left and right side bearings (**Figure 35**) at the same time.
1. Support the swing arm in a vise with soft jaws.
2. Remove the dust seals (**Figure 45**) with a seal removal tool or screwdriver.
3. Remove the bearings with a blind bearing remover (**Figure 49**).
4. Check the grease retainer plates (B, **Figure 46**) for looseness or damage. If necessary, replace the plates as follows:

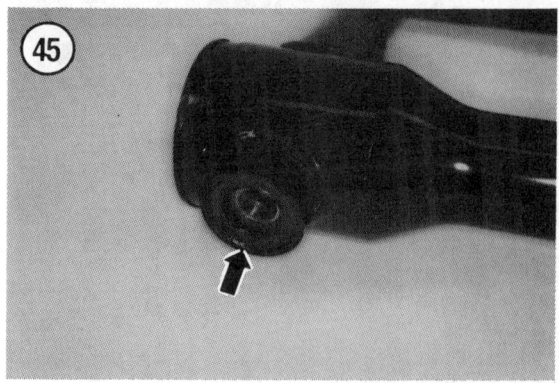

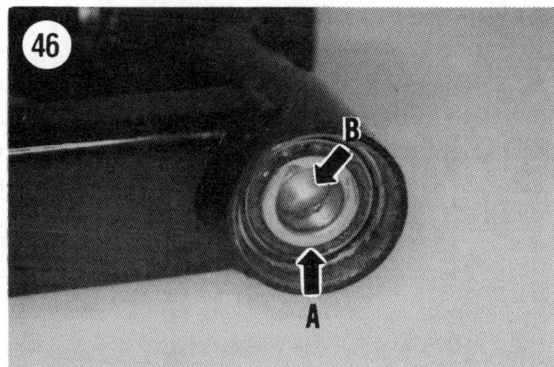

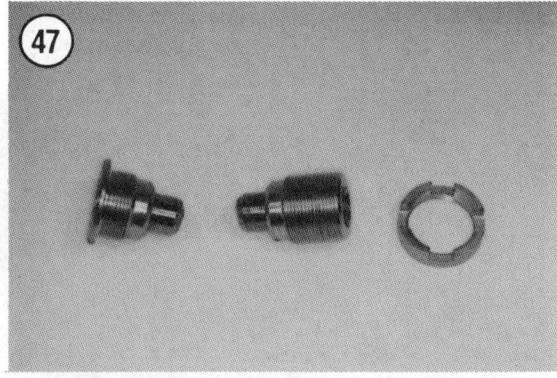

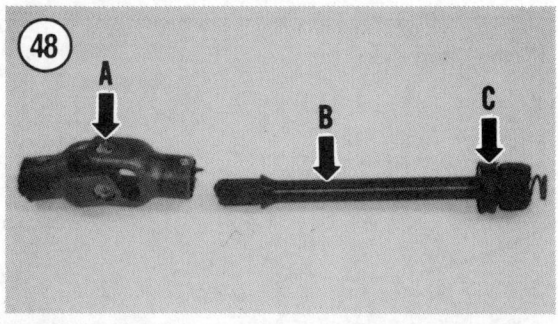

a. Drill a suitable size hole through one of the grease retainer plates (**Figure 50**).

b. Insert a drift through this hole (**Figure 51**) and drive out the opposite grease retainer plate. See **Figure 52**.

c. Repeat Step 2 to remove the opposite grease retainer.

d. Drive a new grease retainer (**Figure 53**) into each side of the swing arm.

5. Lubricate the new bearings with grease.

6. Drive a new bearing (A, **Figure 46**) into each side of the swing arm. Apply pressure on the outer race of each bearing only. Install both bearings with their manufacturer's marks facing out.

7. Lubricate the new dust seal lips with grease and install them into the swing arm with their closed side facing out (**Figure 45**).

## Installation

1. Install the boot (A, **Figure 44**) onto the engine with the tab marked HM7 facing up.

2. Lubricate the universal joint and drive shaft splines with molybdenum disulfide grease.

3. Install the universal joint and drive shaft as shown in **Figure 43**.

*NOTE*
*Refer to **Figure 54** to identify the pivot bolts when installing them in the following steps.*

4. Install the swing arm (**Figure 42**) into the frame, while noting the following:

a. Install the drive shaft through the swing arm.

12

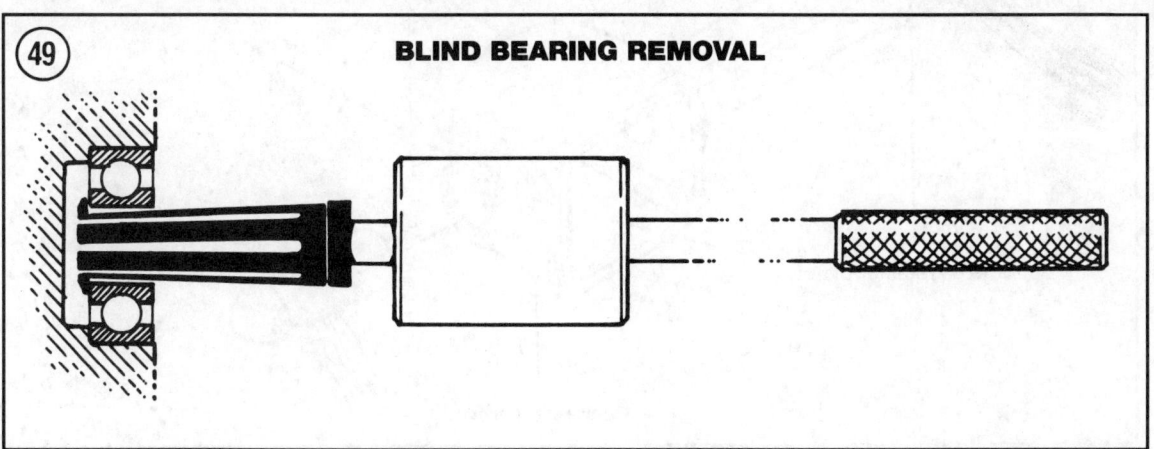

BLIND BEARING REMOVAL

b. Install the right pivot bolt (**Figure 41**) and tighten finger-tight.

c. Install the left pivot bolt (**Figure 55**) and tighten finger-tight.

d. Swing the swing arm up and down, making sure it pivots smoothly with no binding or roughness.

5. Tighten the left pivot bolt (**Figure 55**) as specified in **Table 2**.

6. Tighten the right pivot bolt (**Figure 41**) as specified in **Table 2**.

7. Pivot the swing arm up and down several times to help seat the bearings.

8. Retighten the right pivot bolt (**Figure 41**) as specified in **Table 2**.

9. Install the right pivot bolt locknut (**Figure 40**) and tighten it with the Honda swing arm locknut wrench (**Figure 56**) as follows:

*NOTE*
*Because the Honda swing arm locknut wrench can lengthen the torque wrench, the torque value set on the torque*

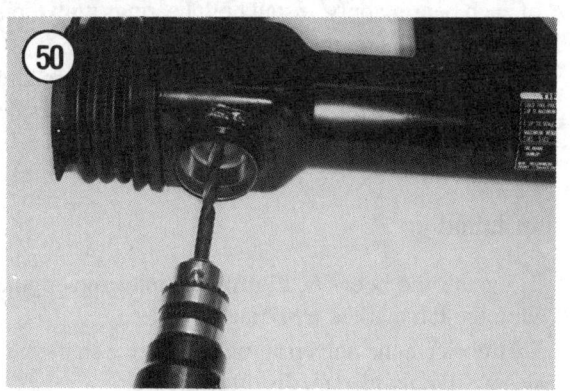

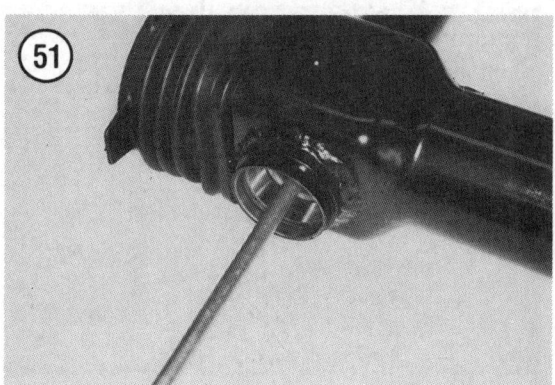

Outer races

Grease retainer plates

Rear swing arm

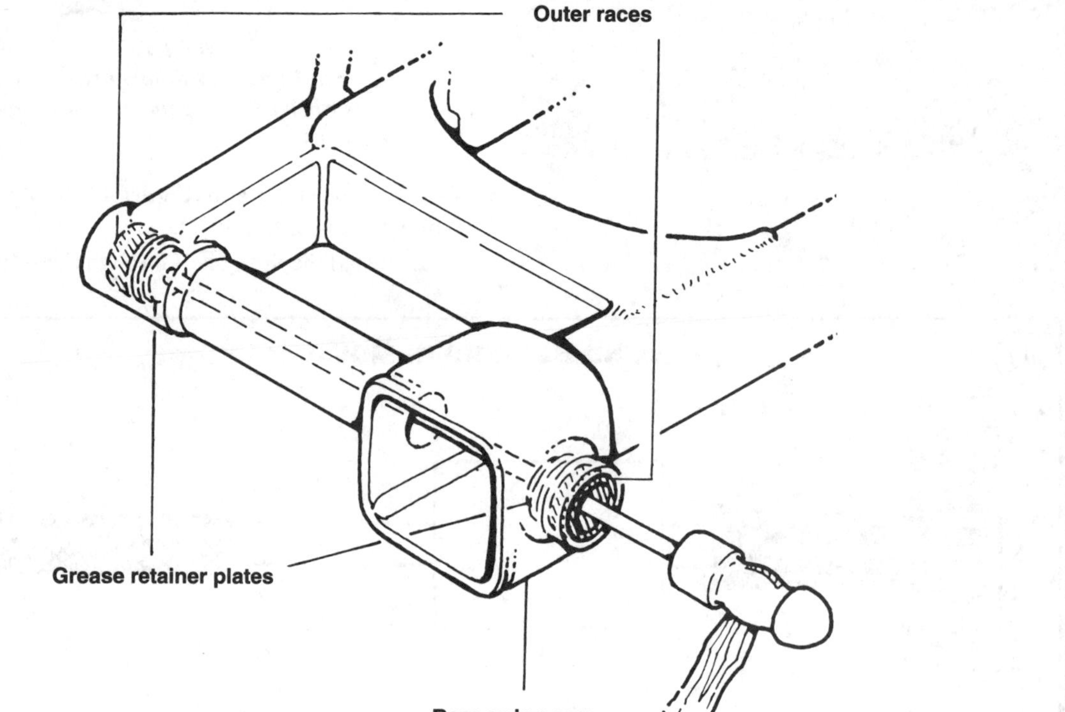

*wrench may not be the same amount of torque applied to the fastener. When using a horizontal adapter that lengthens the torque wrench, you must recalculate the torque reading. To do so, use the information supplied with your torque wrench or refer to the information listed under **Torque Wrench** in Chapter One.*

a. Hold the right pivot bolt with a 17 mm hex socket wrench (**Figure 56**).

b. Tighten the right pivot bolt locknut with the Honda swing arm locknut wrench and a torque wrench (**Figure 56**) to the torque specification in **Table 2**.

10. Install the left and right side swing arm pivot caps (B, **Figure 37**).

11. Secure the breather tubes in the clamps on the swing arm.

12. Tighten the swing arm boot clamps (A, **Figure 37**).

13. Install the rear brake pedal (Chapter Thirteen).

14. Install the final drive unit as described in this chapter.

15. Install the rear axle as described in this chapter.

16. Install the rear fender (Chapter Fifteen).

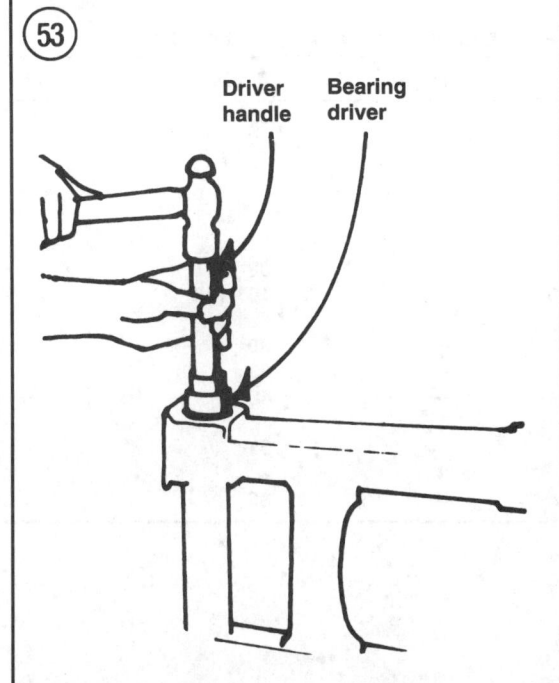

Driver handle  Bearing driver

12

### Table 1 REAR SUSPENSION AND FINAL DRIVE SPECIFICATIONS

| | |
|---|---|
| Rear suspension type | Swing arm |
| Rear wheel travel | 110 mm (4.33 in.) |
| Rear damper | Double tube |
| Rear axle runout service limit | 3.0 mm (0.12 in.) |
| Rear shock absorber spring free length | |
| New | 208.5 mm (8.21 in.) |
| Service limit | 204.3 mm (8.04 in.) |

### Table 2 REAR SUSPENSION AND FINAL DRIVE TIGHTENING TORQUES

| | N·m | in.-lb. | ft.-lb. |
|---|---|---|---|
| Damper rod locknut | 38 | — | 28 |
| Gearcase drain bolt | 12 | 106 | |
| Gearcase cover oil cap | 12 | 106 | |
| Gearcase cover oil check bolt | 12 | 106 | |
| Rear axle housing locknuts | | | |
| At swing arm | 45 | — | 33 |
| At final drive housing | 45 | — | 33 |
| Rear axle nut | 140-160 | — | 103-118 |
| Rear shock absorber locknuts | | | |
| Upper | 40 | — | 30 |
| Lower | 45 | — | 33 |
| Rear wheel nuts | 65 | — | 48 |
| Swing arm | | | |
| Left pivot bolt | 115 | — | 85 |
| Right pivot bolt | 4 | 35 | -- |
| Right pivot bolt locknut | 115 | — | 85 |

# BRAKES

This chapter describes service procedures for the front and rear brake systems.

The front brakes are actuated by the hand lever on the right side of the handlebar. The rear brake is actuated by the brake pedal and left side brake lever. The left side brake lever is also equipped with a lock which allows it to be used as a parking brake.

Brake specifications are listed in **Table 1** and **Table 2**. **Tables 1-3** are at the end of the chapter.

## FRONT BRAKE ASSEMBLY

The front drum brakes are actuated by brake fluid and controlled by a hand lever on the front master cylinder. As the brake shoes wear, the brake fluid level drops in the master cylinder reservoir and automatically adjusts for wear.

When working on hydraulic brake systems, the work area and tools must be clean. Place the parts on clean lint-free cloths and wipe all oil and other chemical residues off of the tools. Tiny particles of foreign matter and grit in the master cylinder or wheel cylinders can damage the components. If there is any doubt about your ability to correctly and safely carry out major service on the brake components, take the job to a Honda dealership.

*NOTE*
*If you recycle your old engine oil, **never** add used brake fluid to the old engine oil. Most oil retailers will not accept the oil if other fluids (fork oil, brake fluid, or any other type of petroleum based fluids) have been combined with it.*

Consider the following when servicing the front drum brake.

1. When adding brake fluid, use only a brake fluid clearly marked DOT 3 or DOT 4 and from a sealed container. Other types may vaporize and cause brake failure. Try to use the same brand name. Before intermixing brake fluid, make sure the two fluids are compatible. Brake fluid will draw moisture which greatly reduces its ability to perform correctly. It is a good idea to purchase brake fluid in small containers and discard any small left-over quantities properly. Do not store a container of brake fluid with less than 1/4 of the fluid remaining as this small amount will draw moisture very rapidly.

13

*CAUTION*
*Do not intermix silicone based (DOT 5) brake fluid as it can cause brake component damage leading to brake system failure.*

*CAUTION*
*Never reuse brake fluid (like fluid ex-
pelled during brake bleeding). Contaminated brake fluid can cause brake
failure. Dispose of used brake fluid according to local or EPA toxic waste
regulations.*

2. Do not allow brake fluid to contact any plastic
parts or painted surfaces as damage will result.

3. Always keep the master cylinder reservoir and
spare cans of brake fluid closed to prevent dust or
moisture from entering. This would result in brake
fluid contamination and brake problems.

4. Use only new DOT 3 or DOT 4 brake fluid to
wash parts. Never clean any internal brake components with solvent or any other petroleum base
cleaners as these cleaners will cause the rubber components to swell resulting in distorted, damaged
parts.

5. Whenever any component has been removed
from the brake system the system is considered
*opened* and must be bled to remove air bubbles.
Also, if the brake feels *spongy* this usually means
there are air bubbles in the system and it must be
bled. For safe brake operation, refer to *Brake Bleeding* in this chapter for complete details.

*CAUTION*
*Never reuse brake fluid. Contaminated
brake fluid can cause brake failure. Dispose of brake fluid according to local
EPA regulations.*

*WARNING*
*When working on the brake system,
never blow off brake components or use
compressed air. Do **not** inhale any airborne brake dust as it may contain asbestos, which can cause lung injury and*

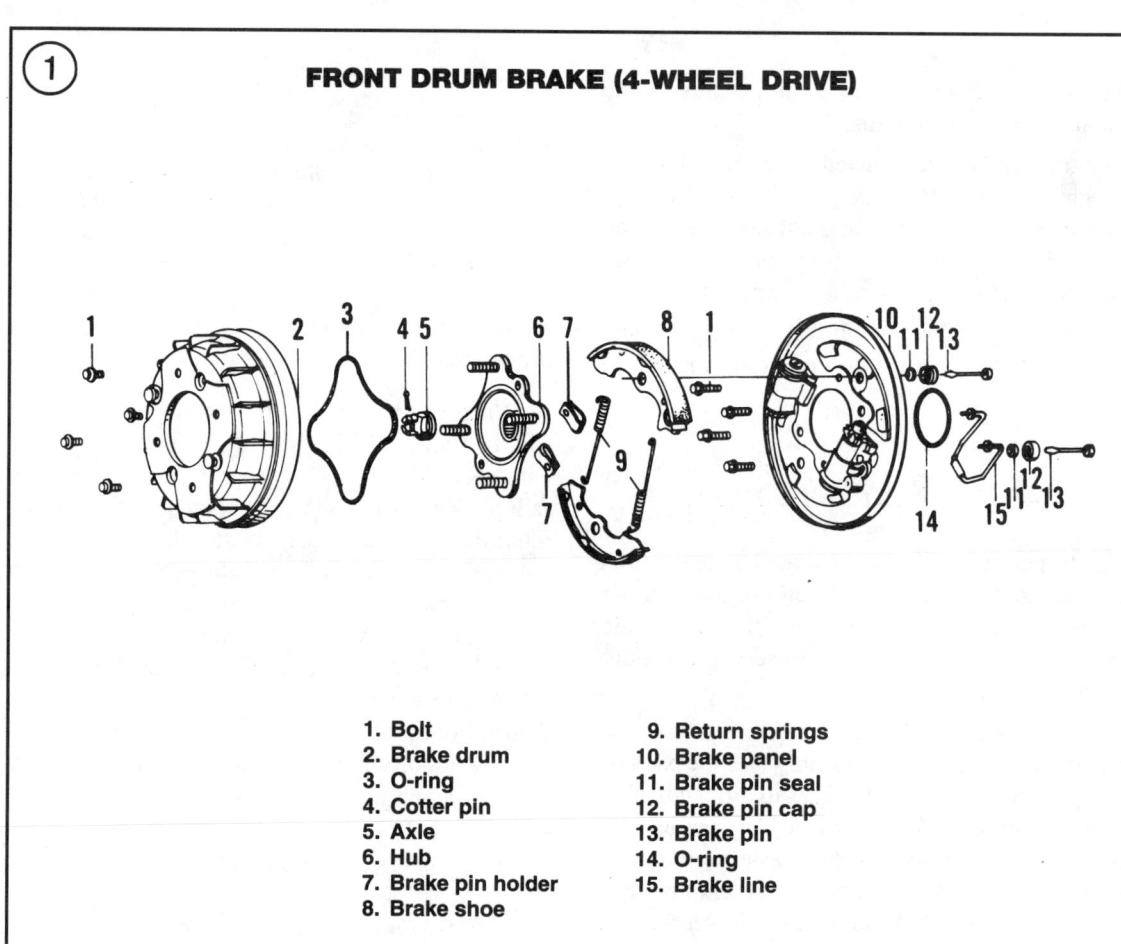

**① FRONT DRUM BRAKE (4-WHEEL DRIVE)**

1. Bolt
2. Brake drum
3. O-ring
4. Cotter pin
5. Axle
6. Hub
7. Brake pin holder
8. Brake shoe
9. Return springs
10. Brake panel
11. Brake pin seal
12. Brake pin cap
13. Brake pin
14. O-ring
15. Brake line

*cancer. As an added precaution, wear an OSHA approved filtering face mask and thoroughly wash your hands and forearms with warm water and soap after completing any brake work.*

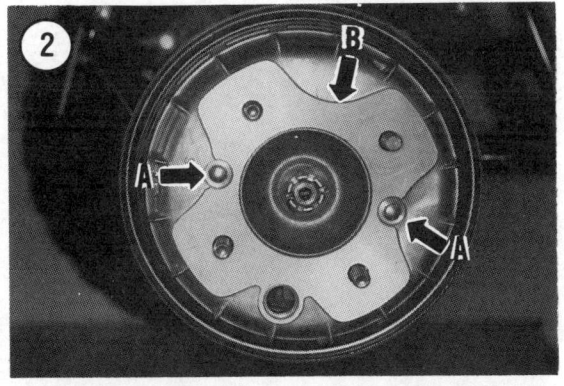

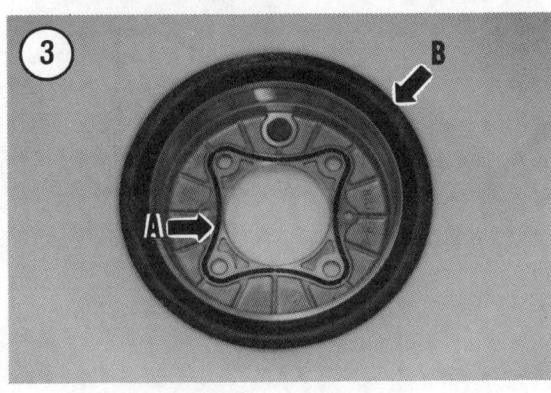

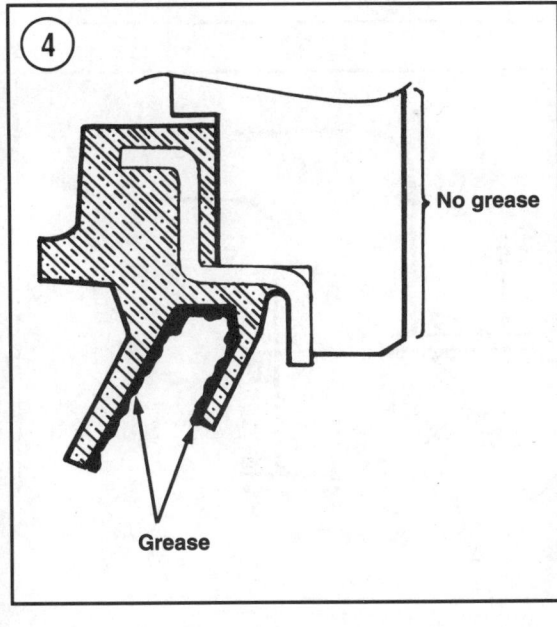

Grease

## FRONT BRAKE DRUM

The front brake drum can be removed without having to remove the front hub.

### WARNING
*When working on the brake system, never blow off brake components or use compressed air. Do **not** inhale any airborne brake dust as it may contain asbestos, which can cause lung injury and cancer. As an added precaution, wear an OSHA approved filtering face mask and thoroughly wash your hands and forearms with warm water and soap after completing any brake work.*

### Removal/Installation

Refer to **Figure 1** for this procedure.

### NOTE
*To remove the brake drum and front hub at the same time, refer to **Front Hub** in Chapter Ten.*

1. Remove the front wheels (Chapter Ten).
2. Remove the bolts (A, **Figure 2**) and the front brake drum (B).
3. Remove the O-ring (A, **Figure 3**), if necessary.
4. Inspect the brake drum and service the waterproof seal as described in this section.
5. Install the O-ring (A, **Figure 3**), if removed.
6. Lubricate the waterproof seal (B, **Figure 3**) with a multipurpose grease (NLGI No. 3) as shown in **Figure 4**. If a new waterproof seal was installed, refer to *Brake Drum Waterproof Seal Inspection and Replacement* for the correct amount of grease to apply to the seal.

### WARNING
*Do not get grease on the inner surface of the brake drum where the brake shoe linings make contact, as this will contaminate the lining surfaces and reduce braking performance. If grease does get onto the brake drum, thoroughly clean off all grease residue with lacquer thinner.*

7. Install the brake drum (B, **Figure 2**) over the wheel hub and brake linings.
8. Install the brake drum mounting bolts (A, **Figure 2**) and tighten as specified in **Table 3**.

13

9. Install the front wheels (Chapter Ten).

## Brake Drum Inspection

1. Inspect the brake drum (**Figure 3**) for cracks, excessive wear or other damage.

2. Replace the O-ring (A, **Figure 3**) if excessively worn or damaged.

3. Inspect and service the waterproof seal (B, **Figure 3**) as described later in this section.

4. Check the brake drum contact surface for grease residue, scoring, cracks or other damage.

> *NOTE*
> *If oil or grease is on the drum surface, clean it off with a clean rag soaked in lacquer thinner—do not use any solvent that may leave an oil residue. Keep the cleaning solution away from the waterproof seal.*

5. Measure the brake drum inside diameter (**Figure 5**) and compare to the service limit in **Table 1**. Measure at several points around the brake drum. Replace the brake drum if out of specification.

## Brake Drum Waterproof Seal Inspection and Replacement

The brake drum waterproof seal keeps water out of the brake drum. Inspect this seal and replace when necessary to prevent excessive brake drum and lining wear from water and other debris.

1. Remove the brake drum as described in this section.

2. Inspect the waterproof seal (B, **Figure 3**) for excessive wear, damage, hardness or deterioration.

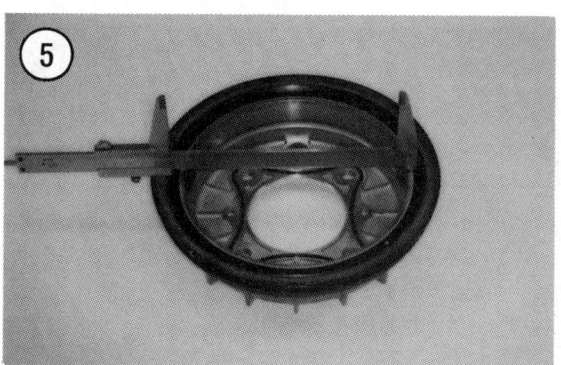

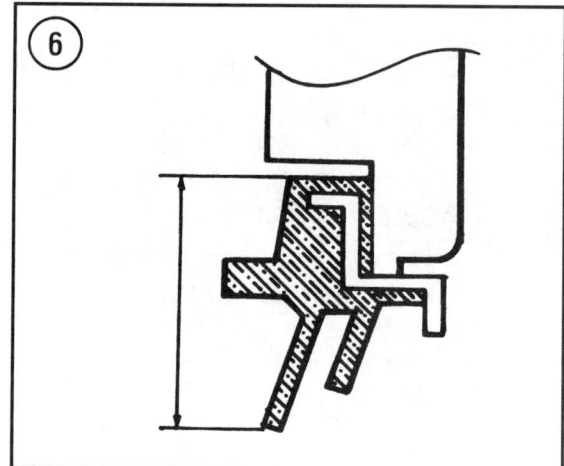

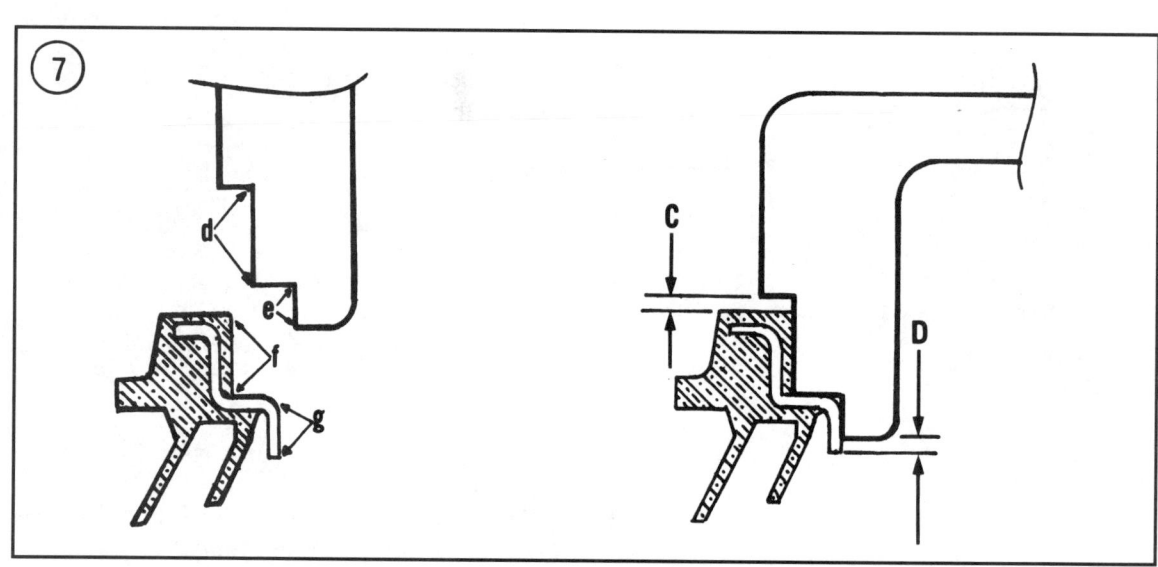

3. Measure the waterproof seal lip length (**Figure 6**). Measure at several different points around the seal. See **Table 1** for service specifications. Replace the seal if out of specification.

*NOTE*
*The following dimensions must be calculated because the inner portion of the waterproof seal cannot be seen when the seal is installed in the brake drum.*

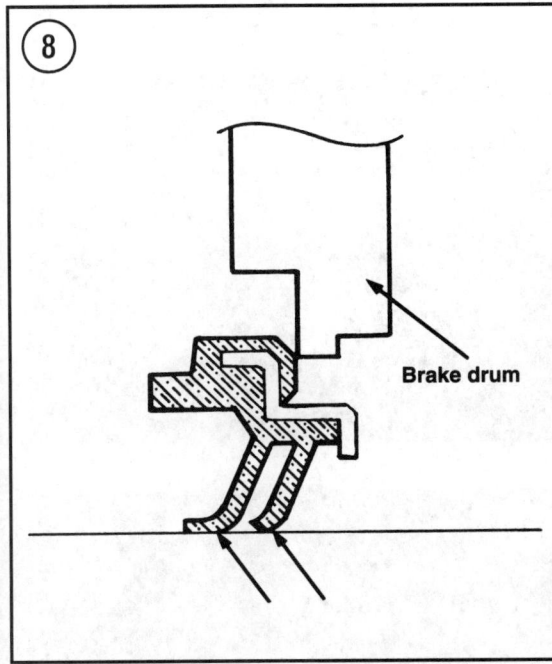

Brake drum

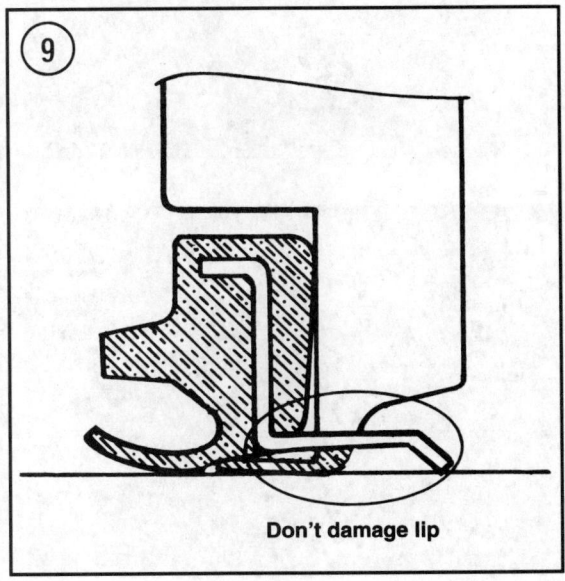

Don't damage lip

4. Perform the following:
   a. Measure the brake drum and seal as shown in **Figure 7**.
   b. Calculate the clearance C and D between the brake drum and the seal. C = d -f and D = g - e.
   c. When the new waterproof seal is installed correctly, dimension C will equal D.
5. Apply clean water to all surfaces of the new waterproof seal (**Figure 8**) and to the surface plate.

*CAUTION*
*The brake drum must be backed up with a round steel plate to prevent it from being warped or damaged. Place a steel plate about 140 mm (5.5 in.) in diameter and more than 10 mm (0.4 in.) thick on the brake drum during Step 6.*

*CAUTION*
*Do not exert too much pressure on the seal during installation, or you may damage the seal lip as shown in **Figure 9**.*

6. Place the new seal on a clean surface plate, then slowly and squarely press the brake drum (and steel backup plate) onto the new seal. Continue to press on the brake drum and frequently check the clearance between the seal and the drum. Refer to the dimensions calculated in Step 4. This dimension must be the same all around the perimeter of the brake drum. If the clearance is not equal, the seal will either not seal properly or wear prematurely.
7. After the seal has been installed correctly with the uniform clearance all around the perimeter, wipe all water from the seal with a lint-free cloth.

*WARNING*
*Do not get grease on the inner surface of the brake drum where the brake shoe linings make contact, as this will contaminate the lining surfaces and reduce braking performance. If grease does get onto the brake drum, thoroughly clean off all grease residue with lacquer thinner.*

8. Uniformly pack the sealing lip cavity (**Figure 10**) with multipurpose grease (NLGI No. 3) as shown in **Figure 4**. Apply 14-16 grams (0.5-0.6 oz.) of grease.
9. Install the brake drum as described in this chapter.

13

## FRONT BRAKE SHOE REPLACEMENT

There is no recommended mileage interval for changing the front brake shoes. Lining wear depends on riding habits and conditions.

> *NOTE*
> *Service one set of brake shoes at a time. Leave the other set intact so you can refer to it for the proper location of the brake components.*

Refer to **Figure 1** for this procedure.

1. Remove the brake drum as described in this chapter.

2. Measure the brake shoe lining thickness with a vernier caliper (**Figure 11**) and compare to the specifications in **Table 1**. Replace the brake shoes if out of specification.

> *NOTE*
> *If brake shoe replacement is necessary, continue with Step 3.*

3. Remove the wheel hub as described in Chapter Ten.

4. Rotate the brake pins 90° (**Figure 12**) and remove the brake pin holders (**Figure 13**).

> *NOTE*
> *If the brake shoes are going to be reused, mark them so that they can be reinstalled in their original position.*

5. Remove the brake shoes and springs (**Figure 14**).

6. If necessary, remove the brake pins (A, **Figure 15**), seals and caps.

7. Inspect the return springs for damaged or stretched coils. Replace both return springs at the same time.

8. Inspect the brake pins and pin holders and replace if excessively worn or damaged.

9. Inspect the wheel cylinders (B, **Figure 15**) for damaged boots or leaking brake fluid. If necessary, service the wheel cylinders as described in this chapter.

> *CAUTION*
> *Silicone brake grease, used in the following steps, is not the same as a silicone sealant (RTV) used on engine gaskets. Make sure the lubricant is specified for brake use. For example, Permatex Ultra Disc Brake Caliper*

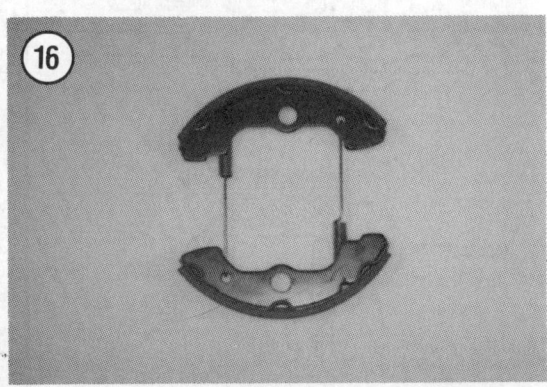

*Lube (part No. 20356) is designed spe-
cifically for use on brake systems.*

*WARNING*
*Do not apply too much grease because
it may fall onto the brake linings and
cause brake slippage.*

10. Apply a light coat of silicone brake grease to the
brake shoe locating notches in the wheel cylinders
and the brake shoe anchor.

11. Apply a light coat of silicone brake grease to the
raised pads on the backside of the brake shoes metal
plates where the brake shoes ride on the brake panel.
Avoid getting any grease on the brake linings.

*NOTE*
*Install the original brake shoes in their
original mounting position.*

12. Install the new brake shoes and attach the
springs as shown in **Figure 16**. Make sure to offset
the spring coils as shown in **Figure 16**. Install the
brake shoes with their flatter edges facing toward the
wheel cylinders.

13. Install the upper brake shoe into the upper wheel
cylinder notches (**Figure 17**).

14. Hold the upper brake shoe in place, then pull on
the lower brake shoe and install it into the lower
wheel cylinder notches (**Figure 17**). If a spring
popped out of its shoe slot, reinstall it with a pair of
locking pliers. Check that both spring ends are
hooked securely into the brake shoe holes and slots
(A, **Figure 15**).

15. Install the brake pins and holders as follows:
   a. Insert the pins, seals and cap into the brake
      panel.
   b. Insert a flat blade screwdriver behind the
      wheel cylinder to hold the pin in place.
   c. Install the holder (**Figure 13**) and secure it
      with a pair of pliers.
   d. While holding the pin in place with a screw-
      driver, compress the holder (**Figure 12**) with
      the pliers, then rotate the pin 90° (**Figure 12**)
      to lock the pin in place.
   e. Remove the pliers and screwdriver and repeat
      for the other retainer and pin assembly.
   f. Make sure both retainers and pins are properly
      locked in place. See **Figure 18**.

16. Repeat the preceding steps to replace the brake
shoes on the opposite side of the vehicle.

**13**

17. Install the front brake drums as described in this chapter.

18. Adjust the brake shoes as described in Chapter Three.

## BRAKE PANEL

Refer to **Figure 2** when servicing the brake panel in this section.

### Warpage Inspection

Before removing the brake panel, check it for warpage as follows. A dial indicator and magnetic stand will be required.

1. Remove the brake drum and brake shoes as described in this chapter.

2. Clean off any grease from the brake panel where the brake drum seal rides.

3. Install a metal plate (A, **Figure 19**) onto the wheel hub and secure it with a wheel nut. This plate provides a mounting location for the magnetic stand.

4. Attach a dial indicator and magnetic stand (B, **Figure 19**) to the metal plate and place the pointer in the area where the brake drum seal rides (**Figure 19**).

5. Slowly rotate the wheel hub and check for warpage. A variation of 0.4 mm (0.02 in.) or more indicates the brake panel is warped and must be replaced.

6. Remove the dial indicator and metal plate.

### Removal/Installation

1. Drain the brake fluid as described under *Brake Fluid Draining* in this chapter.

2. Remove the brake shoes as described in this section.

3. Remove the brake hose banjo bolt and sealing washers (A, **Figure 20**) at the back of the brake panel. Place the loose end of the brake hose in a thick plastic bag or container to prevent the entry of dirt and foreign matter and to prevent brake fluid from leaking out onto the suspension and brake components. Tie the brake hose up out of the way.

> *CAUTION*
> *Wash brake fluid off any painted or plated surfaces immediately as it will destroy the finish. Use soapy water and rinse completely.*

4. Disconnect the vent hose (B, **Figure 20**) from the brake panel.

5. Remove the bolts (**Figure 21**) that hold the brake panel to the steering knuckle and remove the brake panel (**Figure 21**). Discard these bolts.

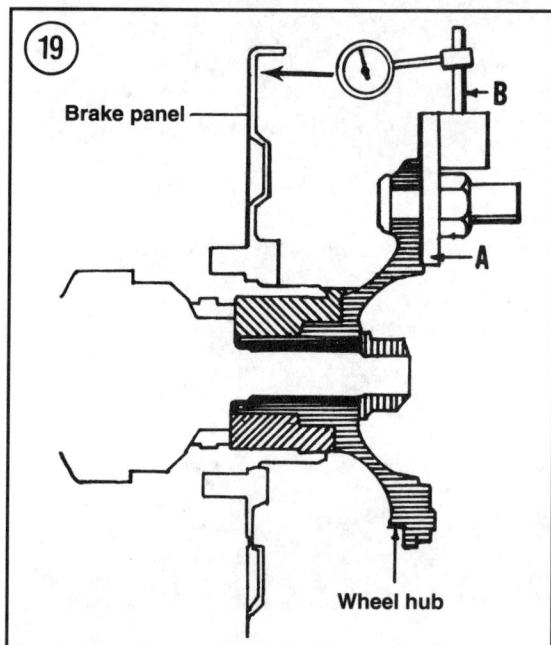

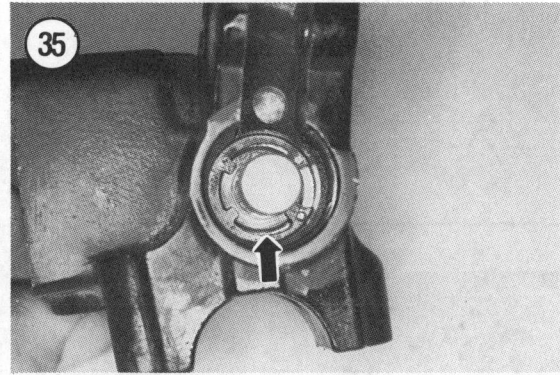

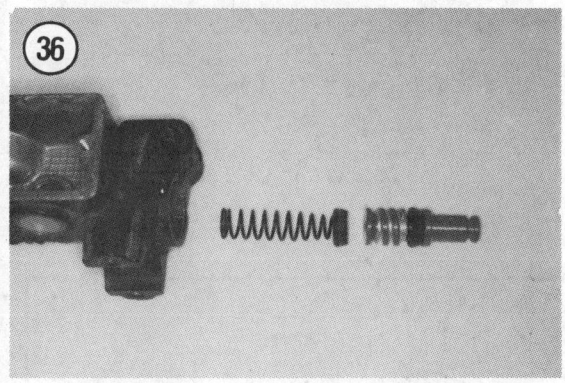

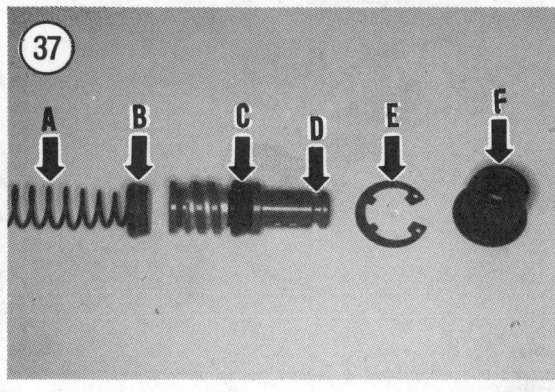

13

*NOTE*
*To hold the master cylinder when re-moving and installing the circlip, thread a bolt with a nut into the master cylinder. Tighten the nut against the master cyl-inder to lock the bolt in place, then clamp the bolt and nut in a vise as shown in* **Figure 34**.

6.  Compress the piston and remove the circlip (**Figure 35**) from the bore groove.

7.  Remove the piston and spring assembly (**Figure 36**).

8.  Remove the oil seal from inside the reservoir.

**Inspection**

Refer to **Table 1** when inspecting and measuring the front master cylinder (**Figure 29**) components in this section. Replace parts that are out of specifica-tion or damaged.

1.  Clean the diaphragm, reservoir housing (inside) and piston assembly with new brake fluid. Place the parts on a clean lint-free cloth.

*NOTE*
*Do not remove the secondary cup (C, Figure 37) from the piston when in-specting it in Step 2. If the secondary cup is damaged, replace the entire pis-ton assembly. Leave the secondary cup in place so you can refer to it when installing the new cup onto the new pis-ton.*

2.  Inspect the piston assembly (**Figure 37**) for:
    a.  Broken, distorted or collapsed piston return spring (A, **Figure 37**).
    b.  Worn, cracked, damaged or swollen primary (B, **Figure 37**) and secondary cup (C, **Figure 37**).
    c.  Scratched, scored or damaged piston (D, **Figure 37**).

If any of these parts are worn or damaged, replace the piston assembly. Individual parts are not avail-able separately from Honda.

3.  Inspect the circlip (E, **Figure 37**) for corrosion, rust, weakness or other damage. Replace if neces-sary.

4.  Inspect the boot (F, **Figure 37**) and replace if damaged.

5. Measure the piston outside diameter (**Figure 38**) and replace if out of specification.

6. Inspect the cylinder bore (**Figure 39**) for scratches, pitting, excessive wear, corrosion or other damage. Do not hone the bore to remove nicks, scratches or other damage.

7. Measure the cylinder bore diameter (**Figure 40**). Replace the master cylinder assembly if the bore diameter is out of specification.

8. Check for plugged supply and relief ports in the master cylinder. Clean with compressed air.

*NOTE*
*A plugged relief port will cause the brake linings to drag on the drum.*

9. Check the entire master cylinder body for wear or damage.

10. Check the cover and diaphragm assembly for damage.

11. Inspect the banjo bolt threads in the master cylinder body bore. Repair minor damage with the correct size metric tap, or replace the master cylinder assembly.

12. Check the hand lever pivot holes and mounting lugs on the master cylinder body for elongation or cracks. If damaged, replace the master cylinder assembly.

13. Inspect the hand lever and pivot bolt and replace if damaged.

**Assembly**

1. Use new DOT 3 or DOT 4 brake fluid when brake fluid is called for in the following steps. Do not use DOT 5 (silicone based) brake fluid.

2A. When installing a new piston assembly, perform the following:

   a. Soak the new secondary cup in new brake fluid for at least 15 minutes to make it pliable.

   b. Lubricate the new piston with brake fluid.

   c. After soaking the secondary cup in brake fluid, install it over the piston as shown in C, **Figure 37**.

   d. Install the new primary cup onto the end of the new spring as shown in B, **Figure 37**.

2B. If reusing the original piston, lubricate the piston assembly with brake fluid.

*CAUTION*
*When installing the piston assembly into the master cylinder bore, do not allow the cups to turn inside out as this damages them and allows brake fluid to leak out of the bore.*

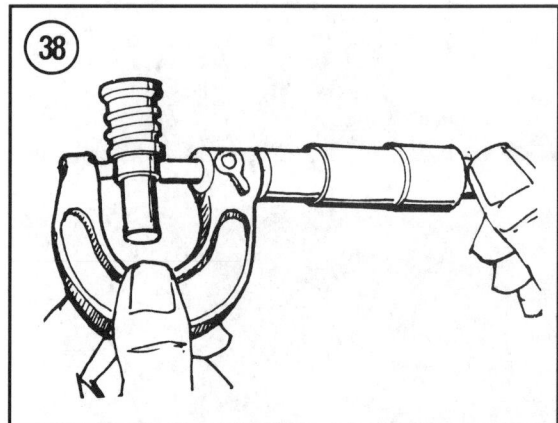

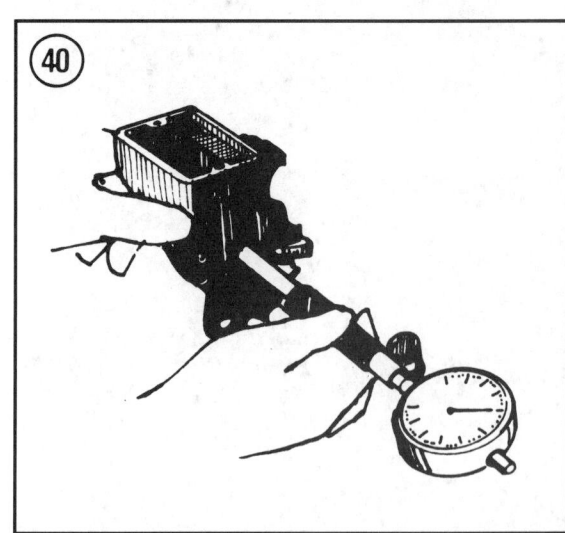

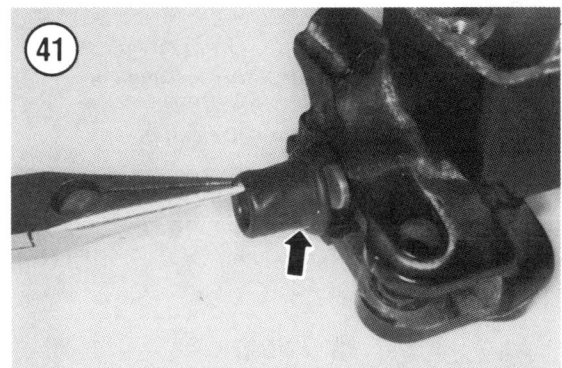

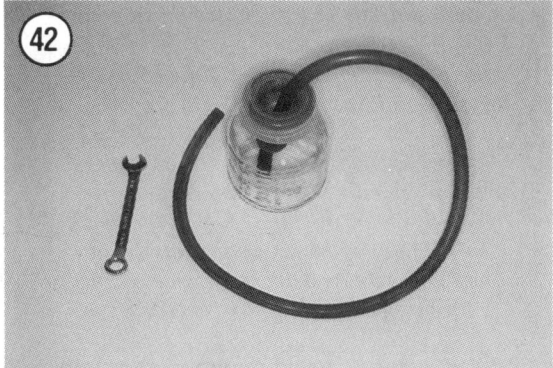

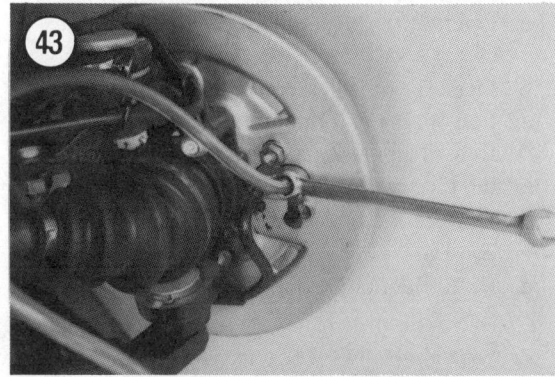

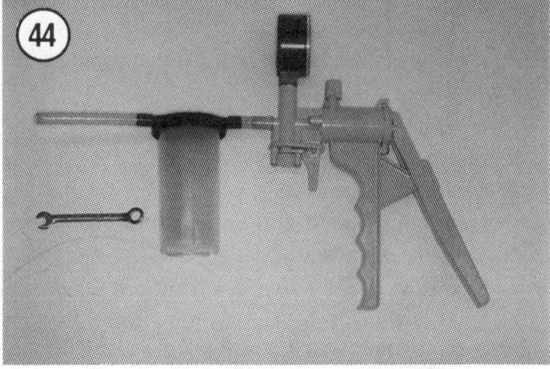

3. Install the spring and piston assembly into the master cylinder bore in the direction shown in **Figure 36**. Check that the cups did not turn inside out.

4. Push the piston in and hold it in place, then install the circlip (**Figure 35**) into the cylinder bore groove. Install the circlip with its flat edge facing out (away from the piston). Check that the circlip is fully seated in the bore groove. Push and release the piston a few times. It should move smoothly and return under spring pressure.

5. Install the dust boot into the end of the cylinder bore. Seat the large boot end against the circlip. Seat the small boot end into the groove in the end of the piston (**Figure 41**). Make sure it is correctly seated in the cylinder bore (**Figure 33**).

6. Install the brake lever as follows:

    a. Install the brake lever and its pivot bolt. Tighten the pivot bolt as specified in **Table 3**. Operate the brake lever, making sure it moves smoothly.

    b. Install the brake lever nut. Then hold the pivot bolt and tighten the nut as specified in **Table 3**. Operate the brake lever again, making sure it moves smoothly with no roughness or binding.

7. Temporarily install the master cylinder cover assembly.

8. Install the master cylinder as described in this chapter.

## BRAKE FLUID DRAINING

The brake fluid should be drained before disconnecting any of the front brake hoses or lines. To drain the front brake system, you need an empty bottle, a length of clear hose that fits tightly onto the wheel cylinder bleed valve and a wrench to open and close the bleed valve (**Figure 42** and **Figure 43**). A vacuum pump (**Figure 44**) can also be used to drain the brake system.

1. Remove the handlebar cover (Chapter Fifteen).

2. Turn the handlebar so that the front master cylinder (**Figure 30**) is level with the ground.

3. Remove the reservoir cover and diaphragm assembly.

4. Connect a hose to one of the wheel cylinder bleed valves. Insert the other end of the hose into a clean bottle. See **Figure 43**.

5. Loosen the bleed valve and pump the brake lever to drain part of the brake system.

6. Close the bleed valve when fluid stops flowing through the valve.

7. Repeat Steps 4-6 for the other side. Because air has entered the brake lines, not all of the brake fluid will drain out.

*NOTE*
*Because some residual brake fluid will remain in the lines, be careful when disconnecting and removing the brake hoses in Step 9.*

8. Reinstall the diaphragm assembly and reservoir cover.

9. Perform the required service to the front brake system as described in this chapter.

10. After servicing the brake system, bleed the front brakes as described in this chapter.

## BRAKE BLEEDING

Bleed the front brakes when they feel spongy, after repairing a leak or replacing parts in the system or when replacing the brake fluid.

This section describes two methods for bleeding the brake system. The first requires a vacuum pump (**Figure 44**), and the second is with a container and a piece of clear tubing (**Figure 42**).

1. Remove the dust cap from the bleed valve on the wheel cylinder.

2A. If using a vacuum pump, assemble the pump by following the manufacturer's instructions. Connect the vacuum pump hose to the wheel cylinder bleed valve.

2B. If a vacuum pump is not being used, perform the following:

   a. Connect a piece of clear tubing onto the bleed valve (**Figure 43**).
   b. Insert the other end of the tube into a container partially filled with new brake fluid. Tie the tube in place so that it cannot slip out of the container.

3. Clean the master cylinder cover of all dirt and foreign matter.

4. Turn the front wheels so that the master cylinder (**Figure 30**) is level with the ground.

5. Cover the area underneath the master cylinder with a heavy cloth to protect the parts from the accidental spilling of brake fluid.

*CAUTION*
*Wash spilled brake fluid from any plastic, painted or plated surface immediately as it will destroy the finish. Clean with soapy water and rinse completely.*

6. Unscrew and remove the master cylinder cover (**Figure 30**) and diaphragm assembly.

7. Fill the master cylinder with DOT 3 or DOT 4 brake fluid.

*WARNING*
*Use DOT 3 or DOT 4 brake fluid from a sealed container. Do not intermix different brands of fluid. Do not use a silicone base DOT 5 brake fluid as it can damage the brake components leading to brake system failure.*

*NOTE*
*When bleeding the front brake, frequently check the fluid level in the master cylinder. If the reservoir runs dry, air will enter the system. If this occurs, the entire procedure must be repeated.*

8A. When using a vacuum pump, perform the following:

   a. Operate the vacuum pump several times to create a vacuum in the attached hose.
   b. Open the bleed valve 1/4 turn to allow extraction of air and fluid through the line. When the flow of air and fluid starts to slow down, close the bleed valve.
   c. Operate the brake lever several times and release it.
   d. Refill the master cylinder reservoir as necessary.
   e. Repeat for the opposite brake line.
   f. Repeat these steps until there is a solid feel when operating the brake lever and there are no bubbles being released from the system.

8B. If a vacuum pump is not being used, perform the following:

   a. Operate the brake lever several times until resistance is felt, then hold it in its applied position. If the system was opened or drained completely, there will be no initial resistance at the brake lever.
   b. Open the bleed valve 1/4 turn and allow the lever to travel to its limit, then close the bleed valve and release the brake lever.

c. Operate the brake lever several times and release it.

d. Refill the master cylinder reservoir as necessary.

e. Repeat for the opposite brake line.

f. Repeat these steps until there is a solid feel when operating the brake lever and there are no bubbles being released from the system.

*NOTE*
*If you are flushing the system, continue with Step 8 until the fluid explelled from the system is clean.*

9. Remove the vacuum pump or container and hose from the system. Snap the bleed valve dust cap onto the bleed valve.

10. If necessary, add fluid to correct the level in the reservoir. It should be to the upper level line inside the master cylinder reservoir.

11. Install the diaphragm and cover. Tighten the screws securely.

12. Recheck the feel of the brake lever. It should be firm and offer the same resistance each time it's operated. If the lever feels spongy, check all of the hoses for leaks and bleed the system again.

### REAR DRUM BRAKE

*WARNING*
*When working on the brake system, never blow off brake components or use compressed air. Do **not** inhale any airborne brake dust as it may contain asbestos, which can cause lung injury and cancer. As an added precaution, wear an OSHA approved filtering face mask and thoroughly wash your hands and forearms with warm water and soap after completing any brake work.*

**Removal**

Refer to **Figure 45** for this procedure.

1. Remove the right side rear wheel (Chapter Twelve).

2. Remove the right rear hub (A, **Figure 46**) as described in Chapter Twelve.

3. Remove the bolts and the brake drum cover (B, **Figure 46**).

4. Remove the brake drum cover O-ring (**Figure 47**), if necessary.

5. Remove the brake drum (A, **Figure 48**). If the brake drum is tight, loosen the brake cable adjusters (B, **Figure 48**) to withdraw the brake shoes away from the brake drum. Then remove the brake drum.

6. Clean and inspect the brake drum cover and brake drum as described in this section.

**Inspection**

When measuring the brake drum in this section, compare the actual measurement to the new and service limit specification in **Table 1**. Replace the brake drum if out of specification or if it shows damage as described in this section.

1. Inspect the brake drum cover for cracks, warpage or other damage.

2. Inspect the brake drum cover dust seal (**Figure 49**) for excessive wear or damage. If necessary, replace the dust seal as follows:

a. Support the brake drum cover and drive the dust seal out of the cover.

b. Clean the dust seal mounting bore.

c. Install a new dust seal by driving or pressing it into the brake drum cover. Apply pressure against the outer dust seal surface with a suitable bearing driver.

d. Pack the dust seal lip with grease.

3. Check the brake drum surface (A, **Figure 50**) for oil or grease and clean with a rag soaked in lacquer thinner. Check the brake shoe linings for contamination.

*NOTE*
*Do not clean the brake drum with any type of solvent that may leave an oil residue.*

4. Clean the brake drum in a detergent solution, then dry thoroughly to prevent rust from forming on the drum surface.

*NOTE*
*Discard the detergent solution and wash your hands.*

5. Check the drum contact surface (A, **Figure 50**) for scoring or other damage.

6. Inspect the brake drum for cracks or damage.

7. Inspect the drum splines (B, **Figure 50**) for twisting or damage.

8. Measure the brake drum inside diameter (**Figure 51**) and compare to the service limit in **Table 2**.

**13**

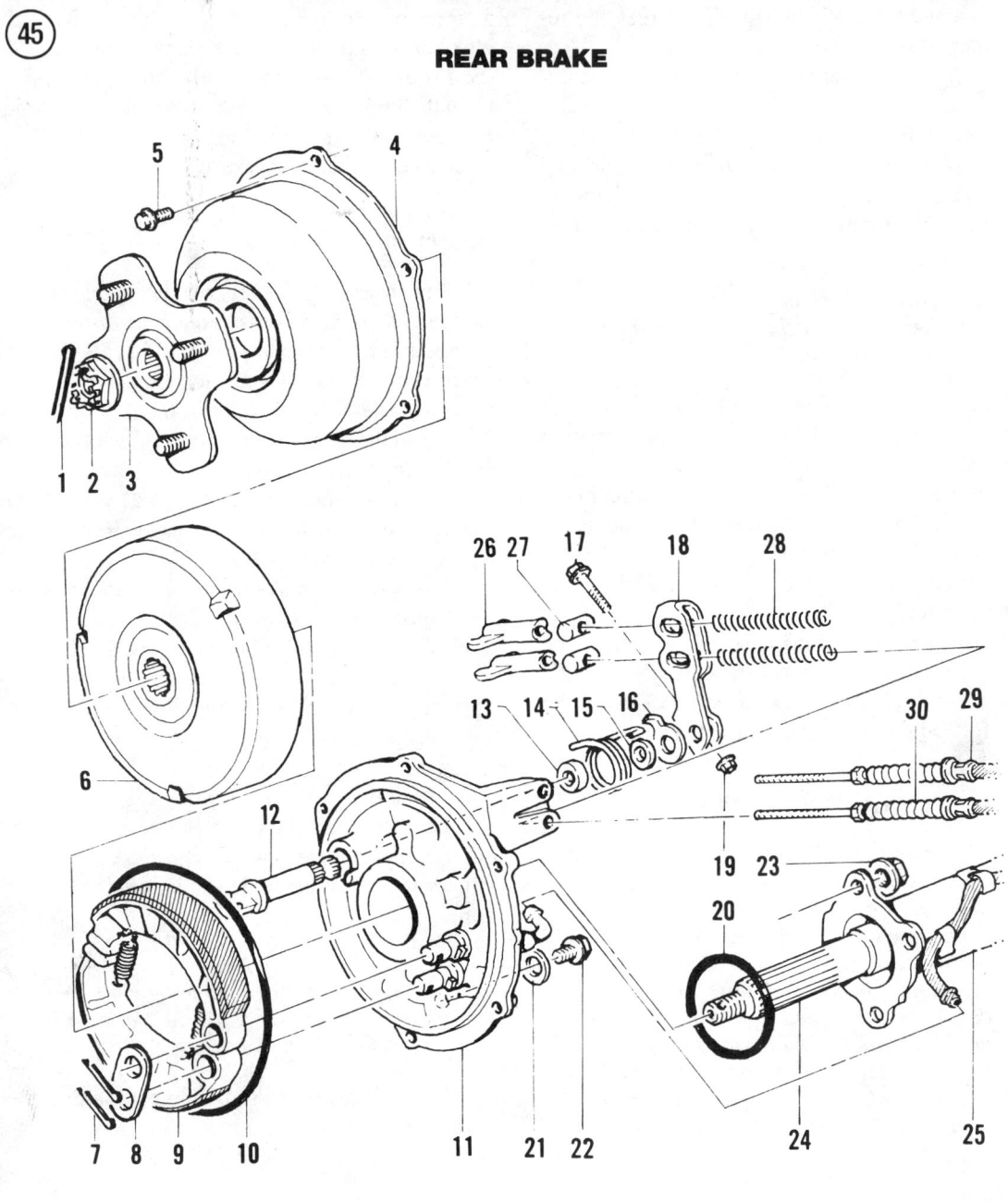

**REAR BRAKE**

| | | | |
|---|---|---|---|
| 1. Cotter pin | 9. Brake shoes | 17. Bolt | 25 Axle housing |
| 2. Axle nut | 10. O-ring | 18. Brake arm | 26. Brake cable adjusters |
| 3. Wheel hub | 11. Brake panel | 19. Nut | 27. Collars |
| 4. Drum cover | 12. Brake cam | 20. O-ring | 28. Springs |
| 5. Bolts | 13. Dust seal | 21. Washer | 29. Rear brake/ |
| 6. Brake drum | 14. Return spring | 22. Drain plug | parking brake cable |
| 7. Cotter pins | 15. Felt washer | 23. Locknuts | 30. Rear brake |
| 8. Washer | 16. Indicator plate | 24. Rear axle | pedal cable |

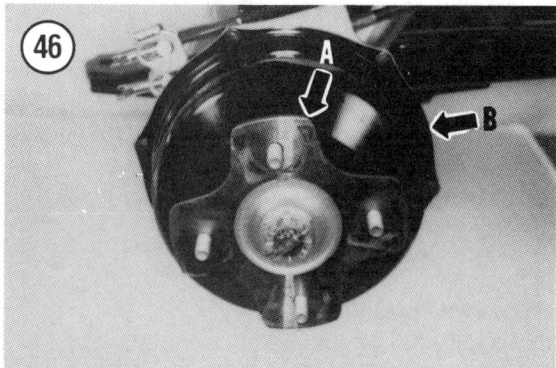

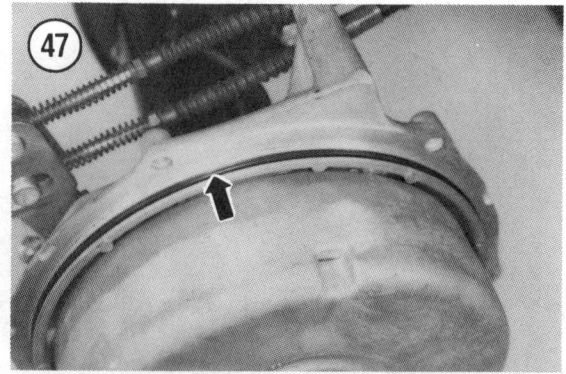

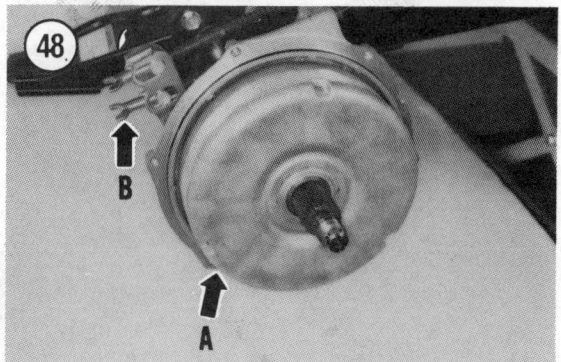

## Installation

1. Apply grease to the brake drum cover dust seal lips (**Figure 49**).

2. Lubricate the brake drum splines (B, **Figure 50**) with grease.

3. Lightly lubricate the brake drum cover O-ring (**Figure 47**) with oil before installing it into the brake panel .

4. Slide the brake drum (A, **Figure 48**) over the rear axle and brake shoes.

5. Install the brake drum cover (B, **Figure 46**) and its mounting bolts. Tighten the brake drum cover mounting bolts securely.

6. Install the right rear hub (A, **Figure 46**) as described in Chapter Twelve.

7. Install the right side rear wheel (Chapter Twelve).

8. Adjust the rear brake as described in Chapter Three.

## REAR BRAKE SHOE REPLACEMENT

Refer to **Figure 45** when replacing the rear brake shoes.

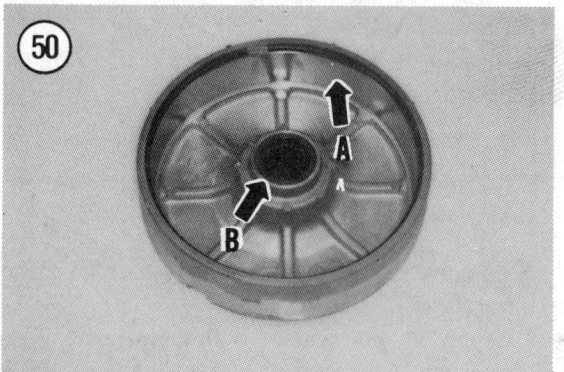

13

There is no recommended mileage interval for changing the rear brake shoes. Lining wear depends on riding habits and conditions.

1. Remove the rear brake drum as described in this chapter.

2. Rear brake shoe lining wear is determined by following the *Rear Brake Lining Check* procedure in Chapter Three. However, always measure the brake lining thickness with a vernier caliper (**Figure 42**) after removing the brake drum to check for nay uneven wear (Table 2). Replace both brake shoes at the same time.

> *NOTE*
> *To protect brake shoes suitable for reinstallation from oil and grease, place a clean shop cloth on the linings during removal.*

> *NOTE*
> *If you are reusing the brake shoes, mark them so that they can be installed in their original mounting position.*

3. Remove the cotter pins and washer (A, **Figure 53**) and brake shoes (B).

4. Disconnect the brake shoe springs and separate the brake shoes.

5. Inspect the springs and replace if there are any bent or unequally spaced coils.

> *NOTE*
> *Always replace both springs at the same time.*

6. Remove old grease from the camshaft and anchor pin surfaces.

7. Apply a light coat of high-temperature brake grease onto the camshaft and anchor pins. Avoid getting any grease on the brake panel where the brake linings can make contact.

8. Install the springs onto the brake shoes.

9. Install the brake shoes onto the brake cam and anchor pins.

10. Install the washer (**Figure 54**) with its chamfered side facing toward the brake shoes.

11. Install two new cotter pins (**Figure 54**) and bend their ends over to lock into place.

12. Install the rear brake drum as described in this chapter.

13. Adjust the rear brake (Chapter Three).

## BRAKE PANEL

The brake panel can be removed with the brake shoes attached. If you are going to service the brake panel, remove the brake shoes before removing the brake panel.

Refer to **Figure 45** when servicing the brake panel in this section.

### Removal/Installation

1. Remove the rear brake drum as described in this chapter.

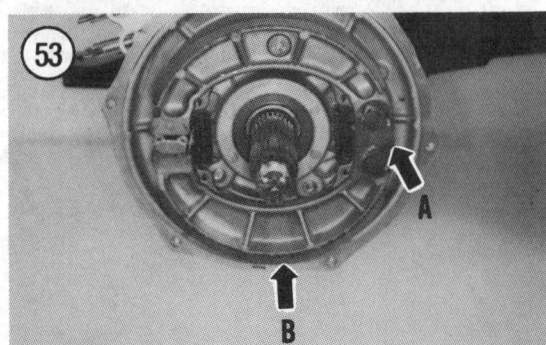

*Brake cables can be left attached to the brake panel if brake panel service is not required.*

2. Unscrew the parking brake (A, **Figure 55**) and rear brake (B) adjusters from the end of the brake cables. Remove the collars and springs. Remove the brake cables from the brake panel.

3. Disconnect the vent hose from the brake panel fitting.

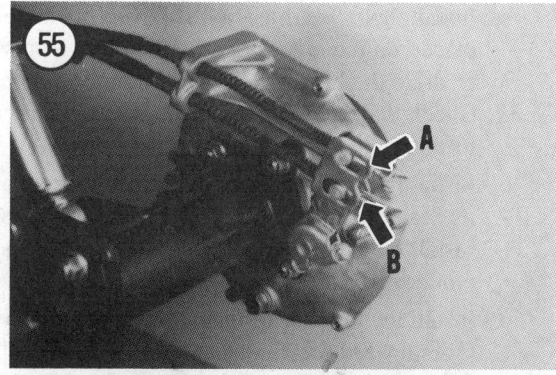

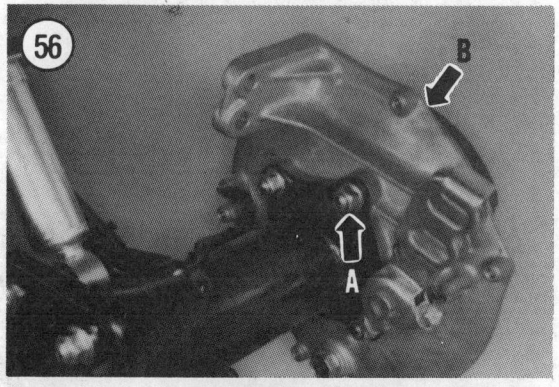

4. Remove the locknuts (A, **Figure 56**) and the brake panel (B). Discard the locknuts.

5. Inspect the brake panel assembly as described in this chapter.

6. Install the brake panel by reversing these removal steps, plus the following:

   a. Lubricate the dust seal lip (A, **Figure 57**) and O-ring (B) with grease.

   b. Secure the brake panel to the rear axle housing using new locknuts (A, **Figure 56**). Tighten the brake panel locknuts as specified in **Table 3**.

   c. Adjust the rear brake as described in Chapter Three.

**Brake Panel Inspection**

1. Service and inspect the brake cam assembly as described in this section.

2. Inspect the dust seal (A, **Figure 57**) for excessive wear or damage. Replace the dust seal as described under *Rear Axle/Brake Panel Bearing Replacement* in this section.

3. Turn the inner race of the rear axle/brake panel bearings (C, **Figure 57**) with your fingers. Both bearings must turn smoothly with no roughness or binding. Also check that the outer race of each bearing fits tightly in the brake panel. Replace both bearings as described under *Rear Axle/Brake Panel Bearing Replacement* in this section.

4. Inspect the O-ring (B, **Figure 57**) for excessive wear or damage. Replace the O-ring if necessary.

5. Check the brake panel for cracks or other damage.

**Brake Cam**
**Removal/Inspection/Installation**

The brake cam can be removed with or without the brake panel mounted on the vehicle. Refer to **Figure 45** for this procedure.

1. If the brake panel is mounted on the vehicle, disconnect the brake cables (**Figure 55**) from the brake arm.

2. Remove the brake shoes as described in this chapter.

3. Remove the brake arm nut and bolt (A, **Figure 58**).

**13**

4. If not already marked, make punch marks on the brake cam and brake arm (**Figure 59**) so they can be installed in the same position.

5. Remove the brake arm (B, **Figure 58**), return spring, indicator plate and brake cam.

6. Remove the felt washer and dust seal from the brake panel.

7. Inspect the brake cam for excessive wear or damage.

8. Replace the felt washer and dust seal if excessively worn or damaged.

9. Inspect the return spring for cracks and other damage.

10. Apply grease to the dust seal before installing it.

11. Apply oil to the felt washer before installing it.

12. Install the dust seal and then the felt washer.

13. Lubricate the brake cam with grease and install it through the brake panel.

14. Install the return spring by hooking its end into the hole in the brake panel.

15. Install the indicator plate by aligning its wide tooth with the wide groove on the brake cam.

16. Install the brake arm (B, **Figure 58**) by aligning its punch mark with the punch mark on the brake cam (**Figure 59**). Hook the return spring onto the brake arm as shown in **Figure 58**.

17. Install the brake arm bolt and nut (A, **Figure 58**) and tighten as specified in **Table 3**. Move the brake arm by hand to make sure it moves smoothly. If there is any binding or roughness, remove and inspect the brake cam assembly.

18. Install the brake shoes as described in this chapter.

19. Reconnect the parking brake (A, **Figure 55**) and rear brake (B, **Figure 55**) cables at the brake arm.

20. Adjust the rear brake as described in Chapter Three.

### Rear Axle/Brake Panel Bearing Replacement

The brake panel is equipped with a dust seal and two bearings (**Figure 60**). The bearings are identical (same part number).

1. Remove the brake shoes and brake panel as described in this chapter.

2. Remove the dust seal (A, **Figure 57**) with a wide blade screwdriver.

*NOTE*
*If you are only replacing the dust seal, go to Step 8.*

3. Remove the circlip.

4. Support the brake panel in a press and press out both bearings. Discard both bearings.

5. Inspect the mounting bore for cracks, galling or other damage. Clean the mounting bore thoroughly.

6. Inspect the circlip groove for cracks or other damage.

7. Install the new bearings as follows:

   a. Install both bearings with a bearing driver placed on the outer bearing race. Use a press or drive the bearings into the mounting bore. Check that each bearing turns smoothly after installing it.

   b. Install the outer bearing (2, **Figure 60**) so that its sealed side faces toward the brake shoes. Install the outer bearing until it bottoms in the mounting bore.

   c. Install the inner bearing so that its sealed side faces toward the circlip and dust seal. Install the inner bearing until it bottoms against the

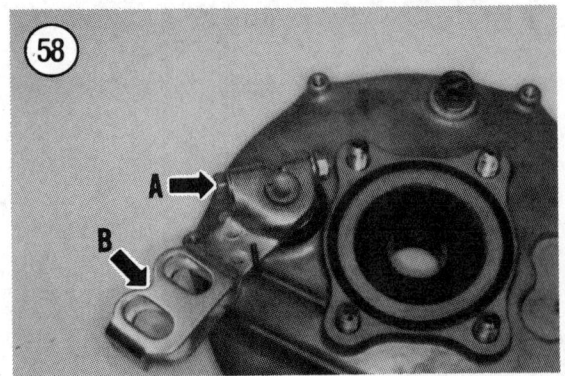

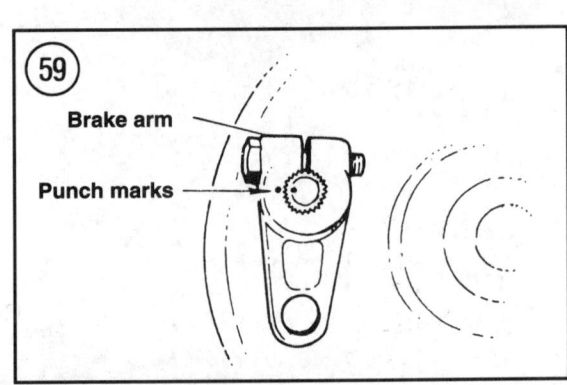

Brake arm

Punch marks

outer bearing and the circlip groove is accessible.

   d. Install the circlip into the mounting bore groove. Make sure the circlip seats in the groove completely.

8. Install the new dust seal (5, **Figure 60**) as follows:

   a. Pack the new dust seal lip with grease.

   b. Align the dust seal with the mounting bore so that its closed side (A, **Figure 57**) faces out.

   c. Tap the dust seal into place until it seats against the circlip.

## FRONT BRAKE HOSE REPLACEMENT

The upper brake hose can be replaced separately from the lower brake hoses. The lower brake hoses must be replaced as an assembly with the 3-way joint (**Figure 61**).

1. Remove the front fender (Chapter Fifteen).

2. Remove both front wheels (Chapter Ten).

3. Draw a diagram of the brake hose routing path from the master cylinder to the 3-way joint and from the 3-way joint to both brake calipers.

4. Drain the front brake fluid as described in this chapter. Because air has entered the brake lines, not all of the brake fluid will drain out.

*NOTE*
*Because some residual brake fluid will remain in the lines, be careful when disconnecting and removing the brake hoses in the following steps.*

5. Remove any bolts and clamps securing the brake hoses to the frame or steering components.

6. Remove the banjo bolt and sealing washers (**Figure 62**) at the back of the wheel cylinder. Hold the open hose end in a container to catch any residual brake fluid. Repeat for the other side.

7. Remove the bolt securing the 3-way fitting to the frame.

8. Remove the banjo bolt and sealing washers (**Figure 63**) from the master cylinder.

9. Note the routing of the brake hose through the frame and the front suspension arms prior to removal of the hose. You must reinstall the hose through the same path to avoid damage to the hose during suspension arm movement when riding.

10. Install new brake hose(s) in the reverse order of removal. Install new sealing washers.

11. Tighten the banjo bolts as specified in **Table 3**.

12. Refill the master cylinder with fresh brake fluid clearly marked DOT 3 or DOT 4. Bleed both front brakes as described in this chapter.

*WARNING*
*Do not ride the vehicle until you are sure that the brakes are operating properly.*

## REAR BRAKE PEDAL AND CABLE

This section describes service to the rear brake pedal and cable (**Figure 64**). To service the rear brake lever/parking brake cable, refer to *Rear Brake Lever/Parking Brake Cable* in this chapter.

1. Loosen and remove the rear brake pedal cable adjusting nut (A, **Figure 65**), collar and spring from the brake arm.

2. Disconnect the brake cable from the bracket on the brake panel.

3. Disconnect the brake return spring (A, **Figure 66**) from the brake pedal assembly.

4. Remove the cotter pin and washer (B, **Figure 66**) and remove the brake pedal assembly (C).

5. Disconnect the brake cable from the brake pedal.

6. When replacing the rear brake pedal cable, perform the following:

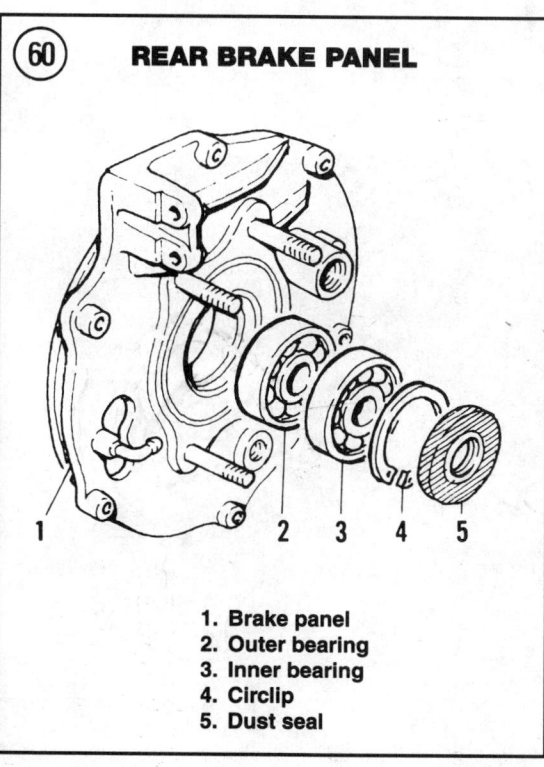

**60** **REAR BRAKE PANEL**

1       2   3   4   5

1. **Brake panel**
2. **Outer bearing**
3. **Inner bearing**
4. **Circlip**
5. **Dust seal**

**13**

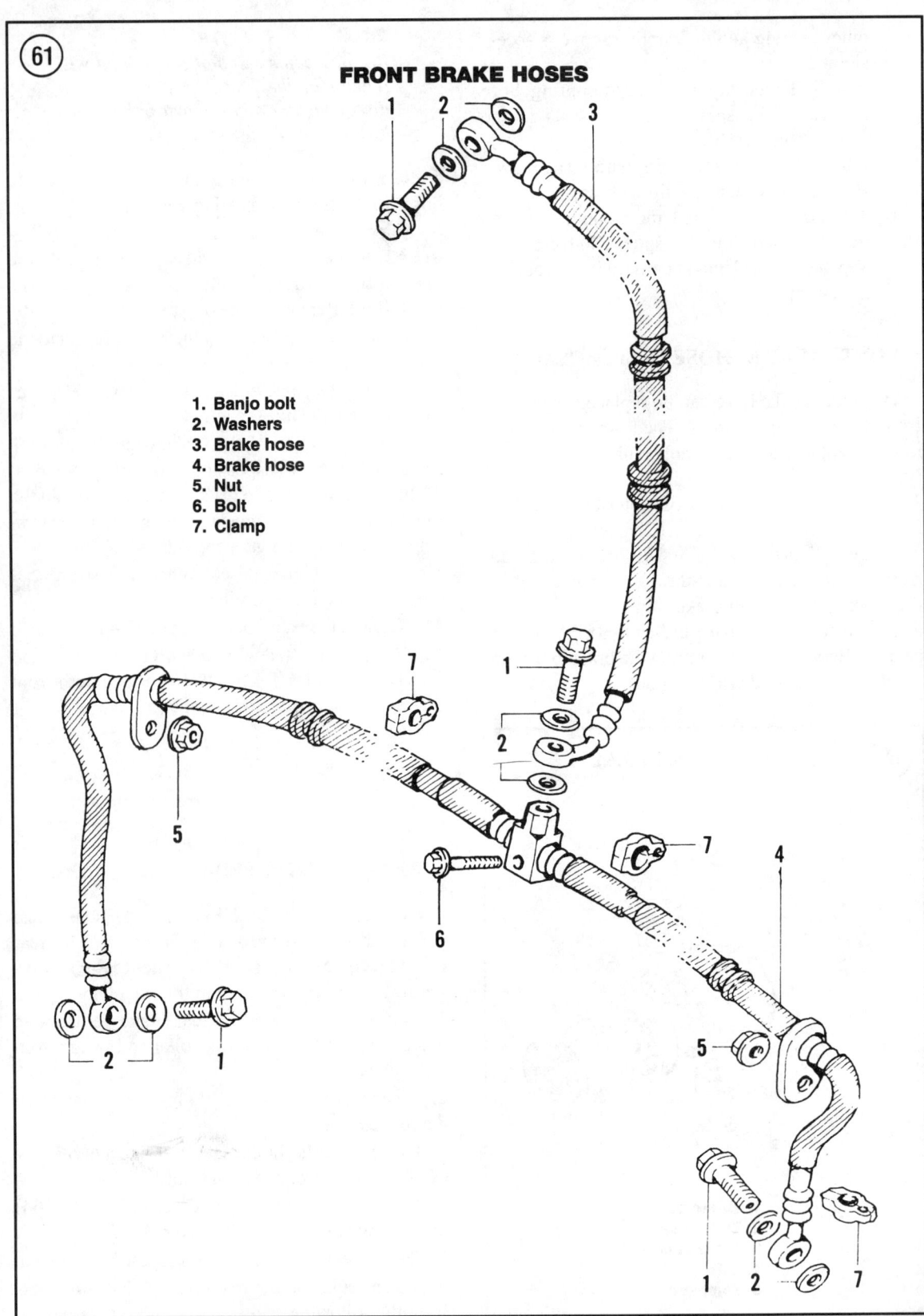

61

**FRONT BRAKE HOSES**

1. Banjo bolt
2. Washers
3. Brake hose
4. Brake hose
5. Nut
6. Bolt
7. Clamp

a. Remove the rear brake cable from the frame, noting any cable guides or brackets.

b. Lubricate the new brake cable as described in Chapter Three.

c. Route the new rear brake pedal cable along the frame and through any cable guides or brackets.

7. Remove all old grease from the brake pedal pivot shaft.

8. Check the brake pedal dust seals and replace if excessively worn or damaged.

9. Pack the dust seal lips with grease.

10. Apply grease to the brake pedal pivot shaft and brake cable end (brake pedal side).

11. Reconnect the brake cable to the brake pedal, then install the brake pedal (C, **Figure 66**) onto its pivot shaft.

12. Install the washer and secure with a new cotter pin (B, **Figure 66**). Bend the cotter pin ends over to lock it in place. Operate the brake pedal by hand, making sure it moves without any binding or roughness.

13. Reconnect the brake return spring (A, **Figure 66**) to the brake pedal.

14. Reconnect the rear brake pedal to the brake panel. Install the spring, collar and adjusting nut (A, **Figure 65**).

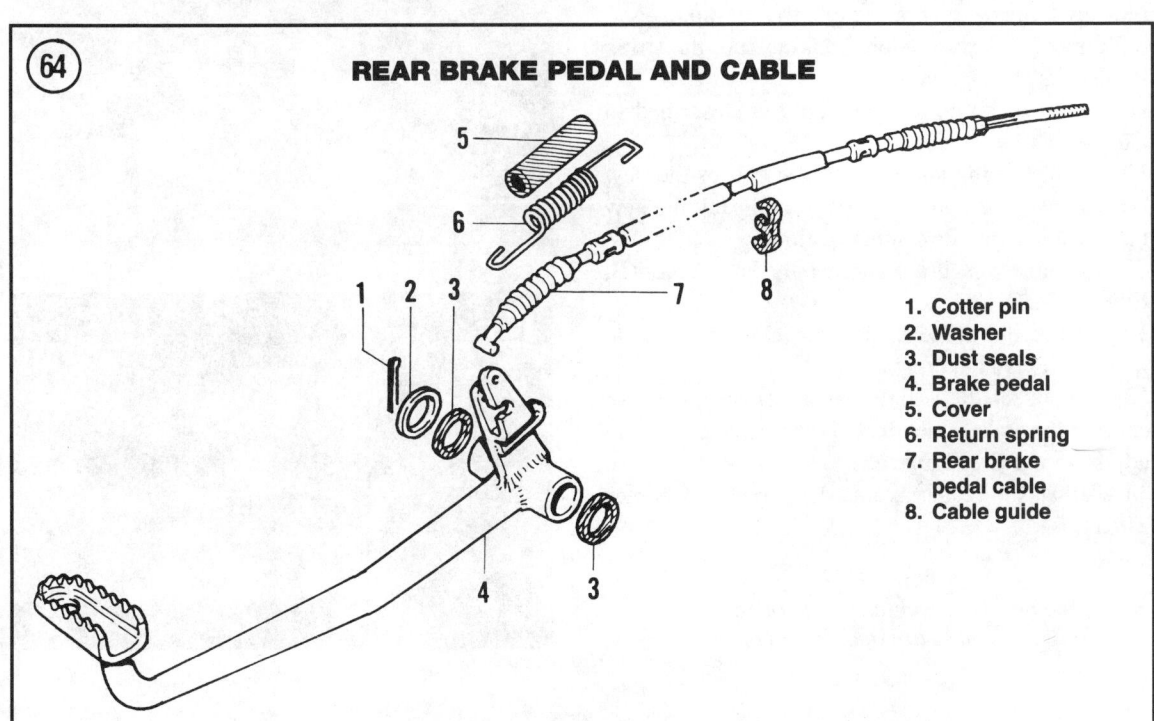

**REAR BRAKE PEDAL AND CABLE**

1. Cotter pin
2. Washer
3. Dust seals
4. Brake pedal
5. Cover
6. Return spring
7. Rear brake pedal cable
8. Cable guide

13

15. Adjust the rear brake as described in Chapter Three.

*WARNING*
*Do not ride the vehicle until you are sure that the brakes are operating properly.*

## REAR BRAKE LEVER/PARKING BRAKE CABLE

The handlebar mounted rear brake lever (A, **Figure 67**) operates the rear brake and is also equipped with a lock which allows it to be used as a parking brake.

1. Remove the handlebar cover (Chapter Fifteen).

2. Remove the front fender (Chapter Fifteen).

3. Loosen and remove the rear brake lever/parking brake cable adjusting nut (B, **Figure 65**), collar and spring at the brake arm.

4. Disconnect the brake cable from the bracket on the brake panel.

5. Disconnect the brake cable (B, **Figure 67**) from the brake lever.

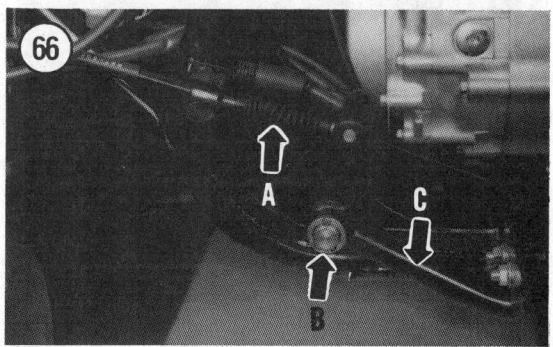

6. Tie a long piece of heavy string to one end of the brake cable. As you remove the brake cable, the string will follow the cable's original path, allowing you to install the new cable correctly.

7. Remove any clamps or cable guides (**Figure 68**, typical) securing the brake cable to the frame.

8. Remove the brake cable, making sure the string follows its original path.

9. Lubricate the new brake cable as described in Chapter Three.

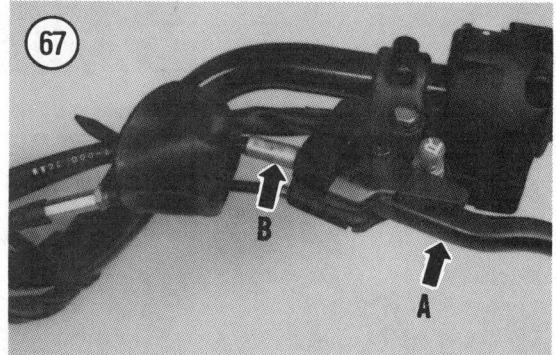

10. Cut the string and tie it to the end of the new brake cable. Then pull the string and install the new brake cable along its original path.

11. Reconnect the brake cable to the brake lever (B, **Figure 67**).

12. Secure the brake cable with clamps or cable guides (**Figure 68**, typical).

13. Reconnect the rear brake lever/parking brake cable to the brake panel. Install the spring, collar and adjusting nut (B, **Figure 65**).

14. Adjust the rear brake as described in Chapter Three.

*WARNING*
*Do not ride the vehicle until you are sure that the brakes are operating correctly.*

## Table 1 FRONT BRAKE SERVICE SPECIFICATIONS

| | New mm (in.) | Service limit mm (in. |
|---|---|---|
| Brake drum inside diameter | 160.0 (6.30) | 161.0 (6.34) |
| Brake shoe lining thickness | 4.0 (0.16) | 2.0 (0.08) |
| Brake panel seal lip wear | — | 0.5 (0.02) |
| Brake panel warpage limit | — | 0.4 (0.02) |
| Master cylinder bore diameter | 14.000-14.043 (0.5512-0.5529) | 14.055 (0.5533) |
| Master cylinder piston outside diameter | 13.957-13.984 (0.5495-0.5506) | 13.945 (0.5490) |
| Wheel cylinder inside diameter | | |
| 1995-1998 | 17.460-17.503 (0.6874-0.6891) | 17.515 (0.6896) |
| 1999-on | 19.050-19.102 (0.750-0.752) | 19.12 (0.753) |
| Wheel cylinder piston outside diameter | | |
| 1995-1998 | 17.417-17.444 (0.6857-0.6868) | 17.405 (0.6852) |
| 1999-on | 18.997-19.030 (0.7479-0.7492) | 18.81 (0.74) |
| Waterproof seal lip length | 22.0 (0.87) | 20.0 (0.79) |

## Table 2 REAR BRAKE SERVICE SPECIFICATIONS

| | New mm (in.) | Service limit mm (in.) |
|---|---|---|
| Brake drum inside diameter | 160.0 (6.30) | 161.0 (6.34) |
| Brake lining thickness | 5.0 (0.20) | see text |

## Table 3 BRAKE TIGHTENING TORQUES

| | N•m | in.-lb. | ft.-lb. |
|---|---|---|---|
| Brake bleeder valve | 6 | 53 | — |
| Brake drum mounting bolts | 10 | 88 | — |
| Brake hose two-way joint | 15 | — | 11 |
| Brake hose clamp flange bolt | 12 | 106 | — |
| Brake lever pivot bolt | 1 | 9 | — |
| Brake lever pivot locknut | 1 | 9 | — |
| Brake hose banjo bolt | 35 | — | 26 |
| Breather tube clamp at steering knuckle | 33 | — | 24 |
| Front brake panel mounting bolts | 30 | — | 22 |
| Master cylinder brake lever | | | |
| Pivot bolt | 1 | 8.8 | — |
| Nut | 6 | 53 | — |
| Master cylinder mounting bolts | 12 | 106 | — |
| Master cylinder reservoir cap screw | 4 | 35 | — |
| Rear brake arm bolt and nut | 20 | — | 15 |
| Rear brake panel drain plug | 35 | — | 26 |
| Rear brake panel locknuts | 45 | — | 33 |
| Wheel cylinder | | | |
| Bolt | 8 | 71 | — |
| Nut | 17 | — | 13 |
| Brake line nuts | 16 | — | 12 |

13

# OIL COOLER AND COOLING FAN

This chapter describes information on servicing the oil cooler and cooling fan assembly. These components can be left in place when servicing the engine and suspension components.

## OIL COOLER

Refer to **Figure 1** when servicing the oil cooler in this section.

### Removal/Installation

1. Drain the engine oil (Chapter Three).
2. Remove the front fender (Chapter Fifteen).
3. Disconnect the oil cooler hoses at the engine as follows:
    a. Remove the Allen bolts and holder (A, **Figure 2**), then disconnect the two oil hoses (B) at the engine. Cover the hose ends to prevent oil leakage and contamination.
    b. Remove the two oil hose O-rings (**Figure 3**).
4. Remove the oil cooler hose clamp (A, **Figure 4**).
5. Remove the bolts and the oil cooler mounting brackets (B, **Figure 4**).
6. Remove the oil cooler (C, **Figure 4**) and hoses from the frame.
7. Install the oil cooler by reversing these removal steps, plus the following:
    a. Replace the O-rings if leaking or damaged.
    b. Lubricate the O-rings with engine oil.
    c. Tighten all of the mounting bolts securely.

### Inspection

1. Inspect the cooler for bent or damaged cooling fins.

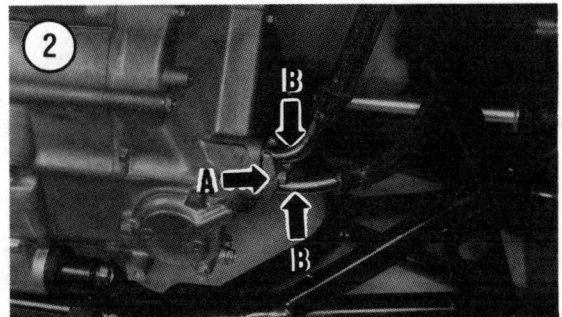

2. Check the hoses for leaks, chafing or other damage. Replace as described in this section.

### Hose Replacement

1. Label the hoses before disconnecting them from the oil cooler.

2. Remove the bolts, hoses and O-rings.

3. Replace the O-rings if leaking or damaged.

**① OIL COOLER**

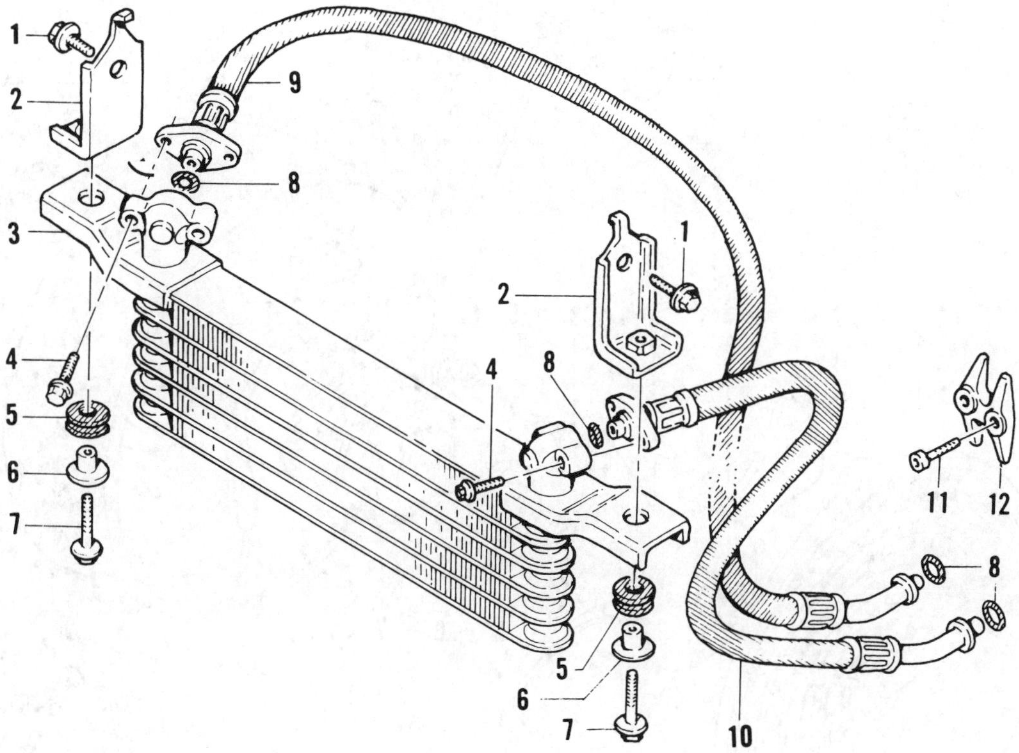

1. Bolt
2. Mounting bracket
3. Oil cooler
4. Bolt
5. Grommet
6. Collar
7. Bolt
8. O-ring
9. Oil hose
10. Oil hose
11. Bolt
12. Holder

14

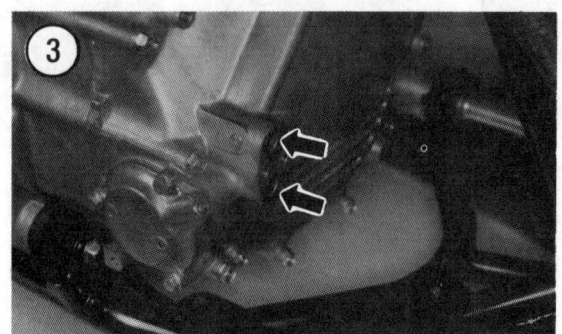

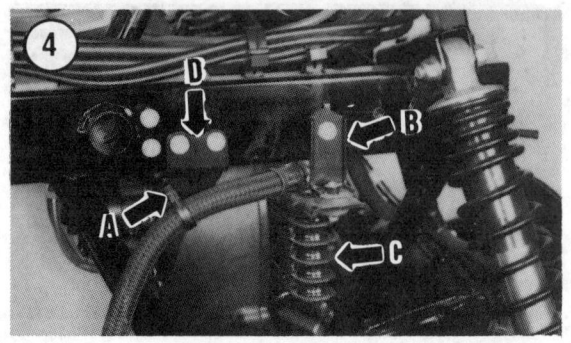

3

4
D
B
A
C

5
COOLING FAN
12
13
14
15
16
18
8
1
2
3
4
9
10
11
5
6
7
17
15
13
1. Screw
2. Fan cover
3. Mounting nut
4. Fan blade
5. Collar
6. Cap
7. Fan motor
8. Breather hose
9. Screw
10. Collar
11. Grommet
12. Hose clamp
13. Bolt
14. Bracket
15. Bolt
16. Shroud
17. Bracket
18. Clamp nut

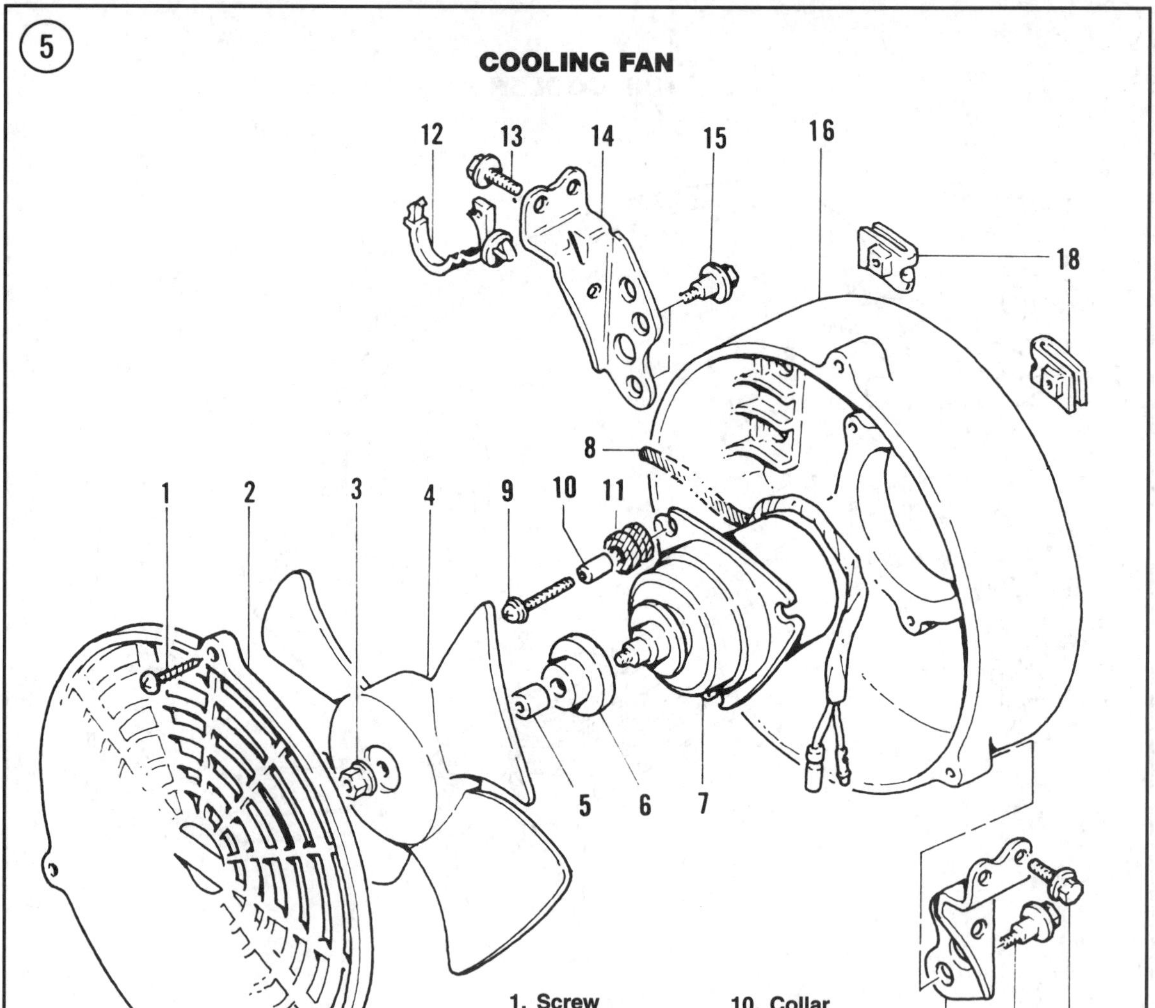

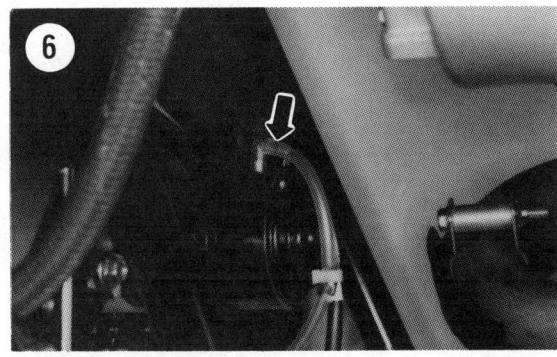

4. Lubricate the O-rings with engine oil.

5. Install the new hoses as shown in **Figure 1**. Tighten the mounting bolts securely.

## COOLING FAN

Refer to **Figure 5** when servicing the cooling fan in this section.

### Removal/Installation

1. Remove the fuel tank (Chapter Eight).

2. Remove the oil cooler (this chapter).

3. Disconnect the cooling fan electrical connectors

4. Disconnect the cooling fan wiring harness clamps from the frame.

5. Disconnect the breather tube clamp and disconnect the breather tube at the cooling fan (**Figure 6**).

6. Remove the cooling fan bracket bolts (D, **Figure 4**) and remove the fan assembly from the left side of the vehicle.

7. Install the cooling fan by reversing these removal steps, plus the following:

   a. Check the wiring harness routing during installation.

   b. Check the breather tube for any obstructions.

   c. Tighten the cooling fan bracket bolts securely.

### Shroud
### Disassembly/Reassembly

Refer to **Figure 5** for this procedure.

1. Remove the cooling fan from the frame.

2. Remove the screws and cooling fan cover.

3. Remove the nut and fan blade.

4. Remove the collar and cap from the fan motor shaft.

5. Mark the fan motor so that its wiring harness and breather tube clamp can be installed in its original position.

6. Remove the screws, fan motor, collars and grommets from the shroud.

7. Inspect all of the parts for excessive wear or damage. Check the fan blade for cracks or other damage.

8. Install the cooling fan motor into the shroud with its wiring harness and breather tube clamp facing up.

9. Secure the cooling fan with the grommets, collars and screws. Tighten the screws securely.

10. Install the cap and collar over the fan motor shaft.

11. Align the fan blade with the fan motor shaft and install the fan blade.

12. Apply threadlocking compound onto the fan motor shaft threads, then install the fan motor nut and tighten securely.

13. Install the cooling fan cover and mounting screws.

**14**

# BODY

This chapter contains removal and installation procedures for the seat, body panels and handlebar cover.

You should reinstall mounting hardware (i.e. small brackets, bolts, nuts, rubber bushings, metal collars, etc.) onto the removed part to prevent loss or misidentification. Honda makes frequent changes during the model year, so the part and the way it is attached to the frame may differ slightly from the one used in the service procedures in this chapter.

## RETAINING CLIPS

The TRX400 uses a plastic retaining clip assembly to secure many body components to the frame or other parts. Refer to **Figure 1** for steps on how to remove and install the retaining clips.

## SEAT

### Removal/Installation

1. Park the vehicle on level ground and set the parking brake.

2. Pull the lever (A, **Figure 2**) to release the seat lock and remove the seat (B).

3. Slide the seat hook underneath the frame brace. Then push the seat down until it locks in place.

4. Check that the seat is firmly locked in place.

> *WARNING*
> *Do not ride the vehicle unless the seat is secured in place.*

## RIGHT LOWER SIDE COVER

### Removal/Installation

1. Park the vehicle on level ground and set the parking brake.

2. Pull the side cover (**Figure 3**) out to release its mounting tabs from the frame grommets and remove the side cover.

3. Install by reversing the preceding removal steps.

## SIDE COVERS AND FUEL TANK COVER

Refer to **Figure 4** for this procedure.

### Removal/Installation

*NOTE*
*Refer to **Retaining Clips** in this chapter when removing the retaining clips in this section.*

1. Park the vehicle on level ground and set the parking brake.
2. Remove the seat as described in this chapter.
3. Remove the right lower side cover as described in this chapter.
4. Remove the retaining clips securing the fuel tank cover and both side covers.
5. Remove the bolts securing the side covers to the frame.

*WARNING*
*Fuel vapor is present when removing the fuel tank cap. Because gasoline is ex-tremely flammable and explosive, per-form this procedure away from all open flames (including pilot lights) and sparks. Do not smoke or allow someone who is smoking in the work area as an explosion and fire may occur. Always work in a well-ventilated area. Wipe up any spills immediately.*

6. Unscrew the fuel tank cap (**Figure 5**) and remove the fuel tank cover and both side covers (**Figure 6**) as an assembly.
7. Reinstall the fuel tank cap (**Figure 5**) and tighten securely.
8. To separate the fuel tank cover and side covers, remove the front mounting screws (5, **Figure 4**).
9. Install by reversing the preceding removal steps. Be sure you tighten the fuel tank cap securely and route the vent hose properly (**Figure 5**).

## FRONT CARRIER AND FRONT BUMPER

Refer to **Figure 7**.

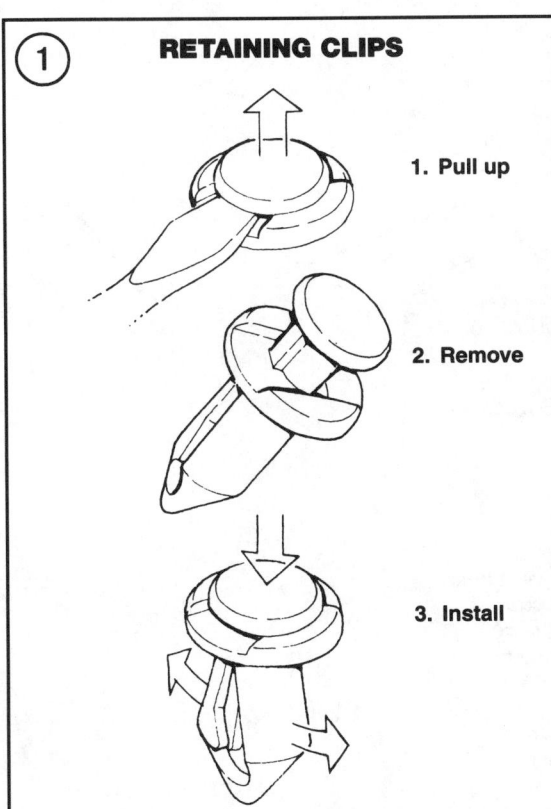

**RETAINING CLIPS**

1. Pull up

2. Remove

3. Install

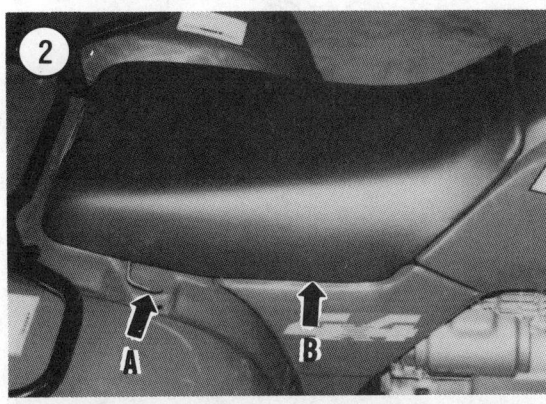

15

④

# SIDE COVERS AND FUEL TANK COVER

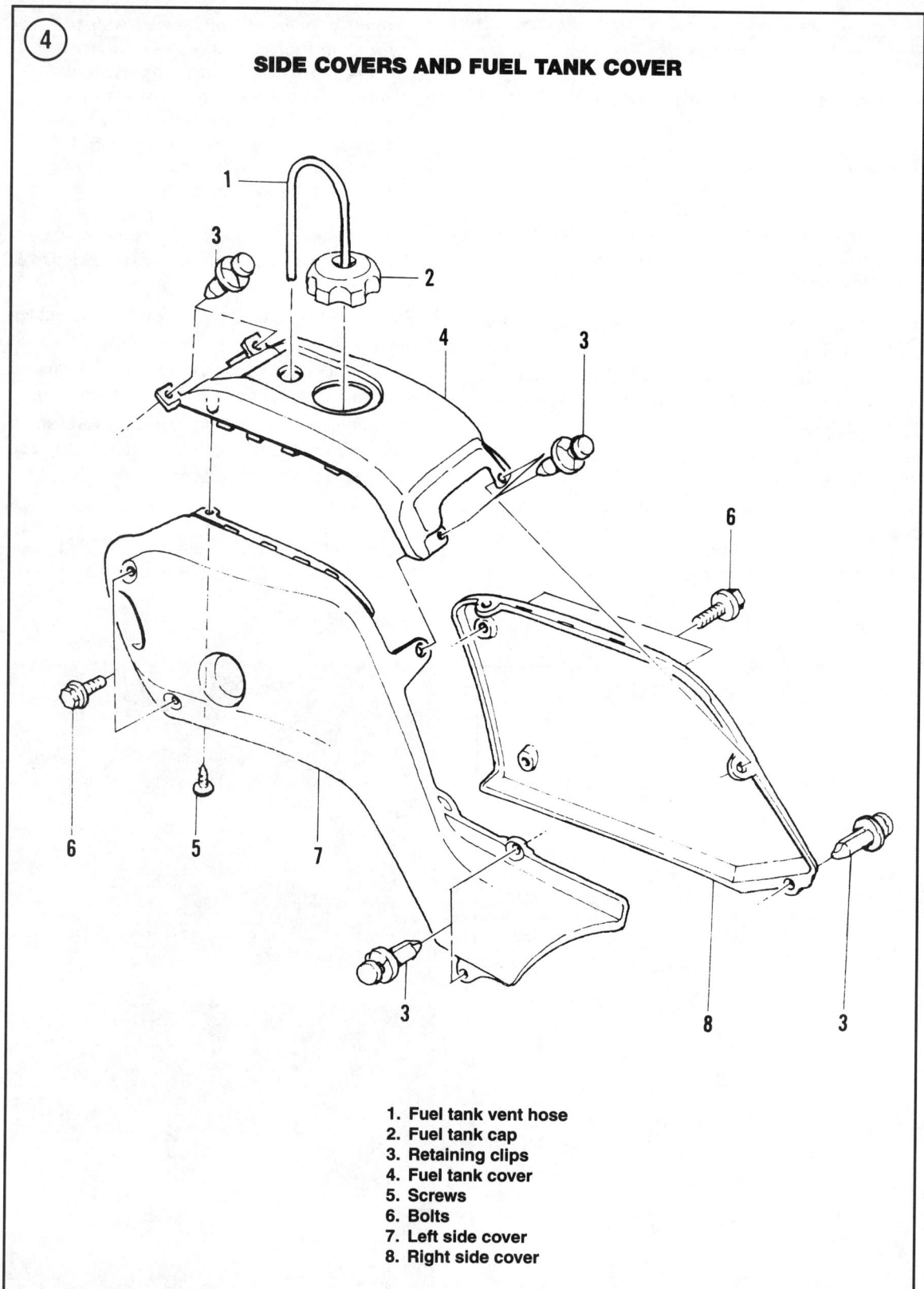

1. Fuel tank vent hose
2. Fuel tank cap
3. Retaining clips
4. Fuel tank cover
5. Screws
6. Bolts
7. Left side cover
8. Right side cover

## Front Carrier
## Removal/Installation

1. Park the vehicle on level ground and set the parking brake.
2. Remove the bolts securing the front carrier to the frame and front bumper.
3. Remove the front carrier (A, **Figure 8**).
4. Install by reversing the preceding removal steps.
5. Tighten the 8 mm mounting bolts to 33 N•m (24 ft.-lb.).

## Front Bumper
## Removal/Installation

1. Park the vehicle on level ground and set the parking brake.
2. Remove the bolts securing the front bumper to the frame.
3. Remove the front bumper (B, **Figure 8**).
4. Install by reversing the preceding removal steps.
5. Tighten the 8 mm mounting bolts to 33 N•m (24 ft.-lb.).

## FRONT FENDER

Refer to **Figure 7** when servicing the front fender in this section.

### Removal

*NOTE*
*Refer to **Retaining Clips** in this chapter when removing the retaining clips in this section.*

1. Park the vehicle on level ground and set the parking brake.
2. Remove the side covers and fuel tank cover assembly as described in this chapter.
3. Remove the front carrier and front bumper as described in this chapter.
4. Disconnect the two front headlight wire clamps underneath the front fender.
5. Disconnect the headlight connectors.
6. Remove the screws (11, **Figure 7**) securing the mud guards to the stay arms.
7. Remove the front fender mounting bolts.
8. Remove the fender joint screws underneath the fender assembly.
9. Spread the front fender (C, **Figure 8**) and remove it.
10. Remove the inner fender mounting bolts and remove the inner fenders. See A, **Figure 9** (left side) and A, **Figure 10** (right side).
11. Remove the mud guard stay mounting bolts and remove the guard stays. See B, **Figure 9** (left side) and B, **Figure 10** (right side).

### Disassembly/Reassembly

Refer to **Figure 7** to service the headlight grill or front fender assembly. Note the position of the washers used on the left and right mud guards.

### Installation

1. Install the mud guard stays and tighten the mounting bolts securely. See B, **Figure 9** (left side) and B, **Figure 10** (right side).
2. Install the inner fenders and tighten the mounting bolts securely. See A, **Figure 9** (left side) and A, **Figure 10** (right side).

**15**

⑦

# FRONT CARRIER, BUMPER
# AND FENDER (TYPICAL)

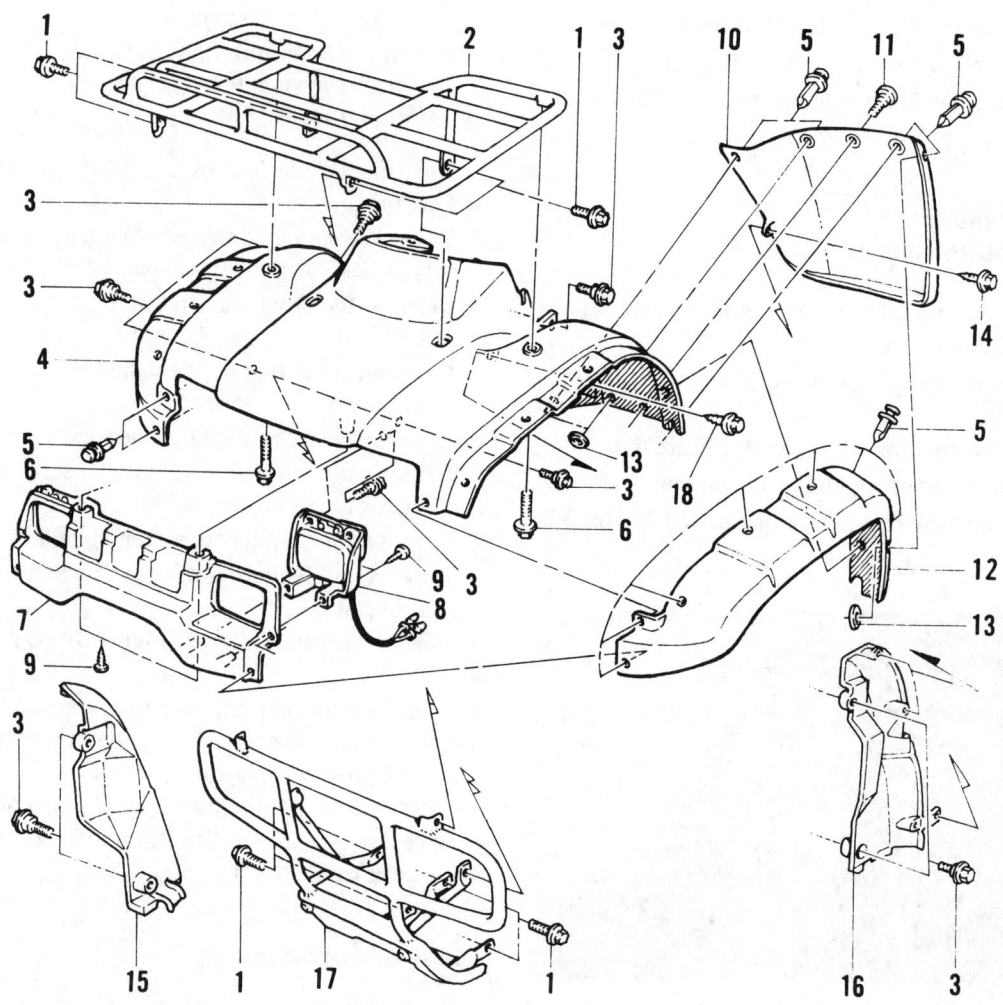

1. Bolt
2. Front carrier
3. Bolt
4. Front fender
5. Retaining clips
6. Bolt
7. Headlight grill
8. Headlight housing
9. Screw
10. Mud guard
11. Screw
12. Over fender
13. Washer
14. Screw
15. Right inner fender
16. Left inner fender
17. Front bumper
18. Screw

3. Install the front bumper (B, **Figure 8**) and its mounting bolts. Tighten the mounting bolts finger-tight.

4. Install the front fender (C, **Figure 8**) assembly.

5. Install the front and rear front fender mounting bolts. Tighten the rear mounting bolts securely. Do not tighten the front mounting bolts.

6. Install the front carrier (A, **Figure 8**) and its mounting bolts.

7. Tighten the front bumper and carrier 8 mm mounting bolts to 33 N•m (24 ft.-lb.).

8. Install and tighten the front carrier 6 mm mounting bolts securely.

9. Tighten the front fender mounting bolts securely.

10. Install and tighten the inner fender joint screws.

11. Install and tighten the mud guard stay screws.

12. Reconnect the headlight connectors.

13. Reconnect the two front headlight wire clamps underneath the front fender.

14. Install the side covers and fuel tank cover assembly as described in this chapter.

15. Start the engine and check the headlight operation.

## REAR CARRIER

### Removal/Installation

Refer to **Figure 11** for this procedure.

1. Park the vehicle on level ground and set the parking brake.

2. Remove the bolts securing the rear carrier to the frame.

3. Remove the rear carrier (A, **Figure 12**).

4. Install by reversing the preceding removal steps.

5. Tighten the 8 mm mounting bolts to 33 N•m (24 ft.-lb.).

## REAR FENDER

### Removal/Installation

Refer to **Figure 11** for this procedure.

*NOTE*
*Refer to **Retaining Clips** in this chapter when removing the retaining clips in this section.*

1. Park the vehicle on level ground and set the parking brake.

2. Remove the seat and right lower side cover as described in this chapter.

3. Remove the rear carrier as described in this chapter.

4. Remove the battery (Chapter Three).

5. Remove the mud guard stay screws (A, **Figure 13**).

6. Remove the retaining clips securing the mud guards to the footpegs (B, **Figure 13**).

7. Disconnect the taillight wiring connectors (**Figure 14**).

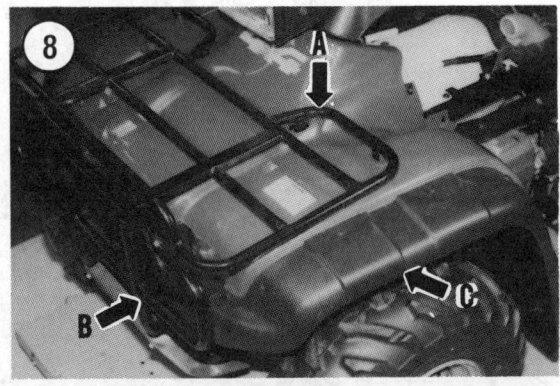

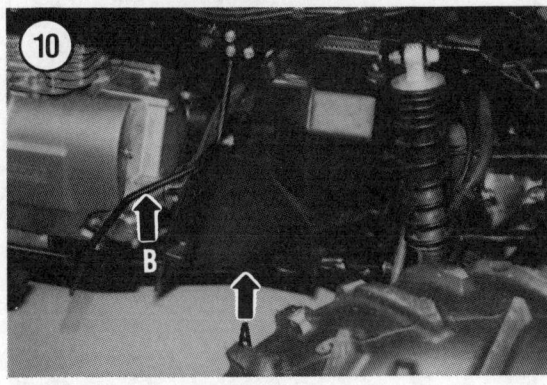

15

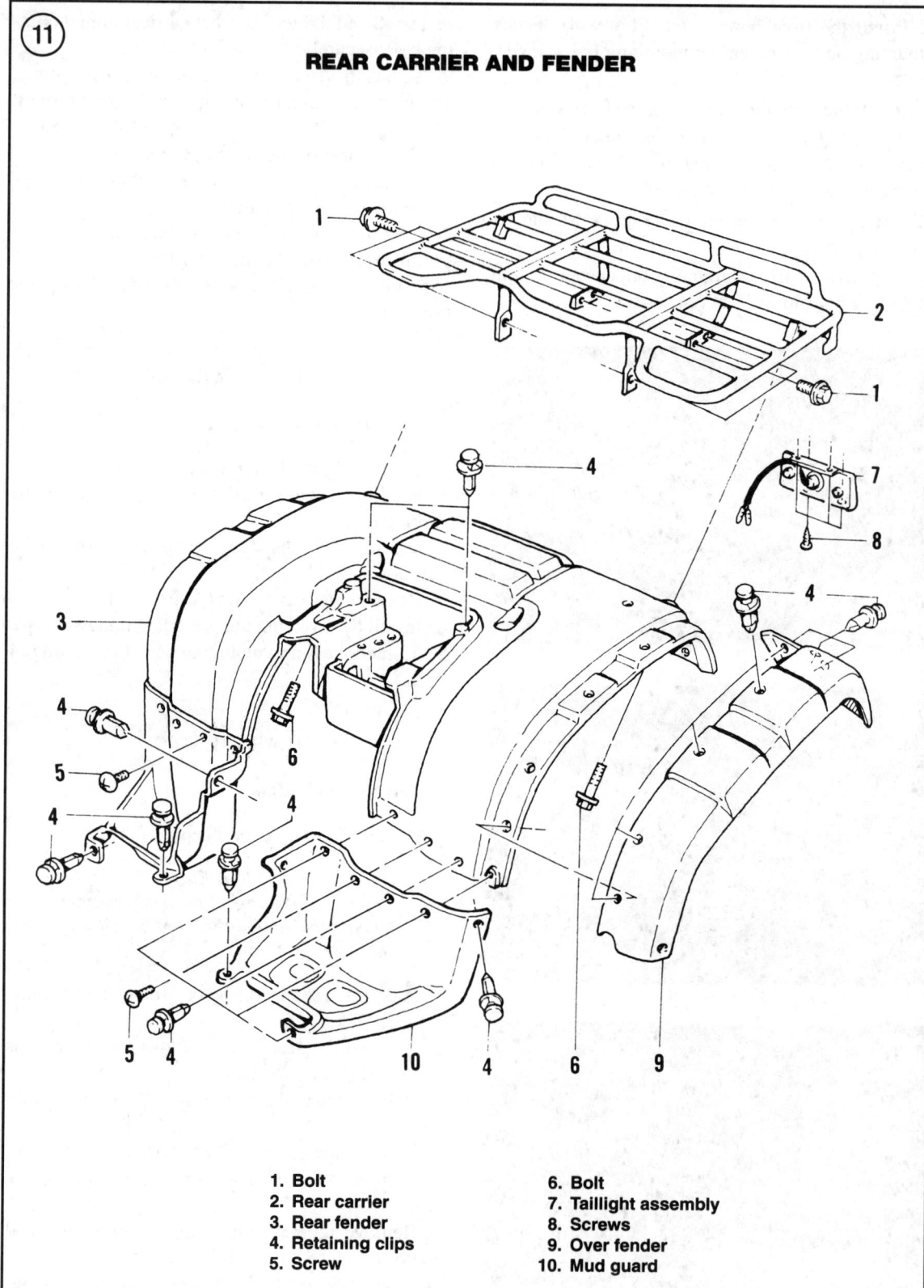

**REAR CARRIER AND FENDER**

1. Bolt
2. Rear carrier
3. Rear fender
4. Retaining clips
5. Screw
6. Bolt
7. Taillight assembly
8. Screws
9. Over fender
10. Mud guard

8. From inside the battery box, perform the following:

    a. Disconnect the wire harness tie clamps.

    b. Remove the two outer retaining clips and the harness bracket assembly (**Figure 15**).

    c. Remove the two rear fender retaining clips.

9. Remove the rear fender assembly (B, **Figure 12**).

10. Install by reversing the preceding removal steps.

## HANDLEBAR COVER

### Removal/Installation

1. Park the vehicle on level ground and set the parking brake.

2. Remove the front fender as described in this chapter.

3. Disconnect the ignition switch (A, **Figure 16**) and indicator light (B, **Figure 16**) electrical connectors.

4. Remove the handlebar cover cap (**Figure 17**).

5. Remove the handlebar cover mounting screws (**Figure 18**).

6. Release both ends of the handlebar cover from the handlebar, then remove the handlebar cover assembly (**Figure 19**).

7. Install by reversing the preceding removal steps, plus the following:

    a. Check the front and brake lever operation after installing the handlebar cover.

    b. Check the indicator light operation after starting the engine.

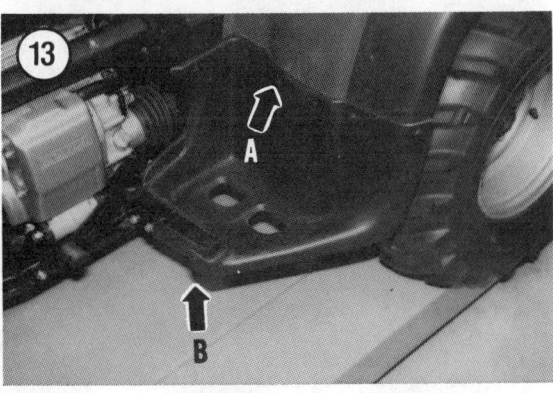

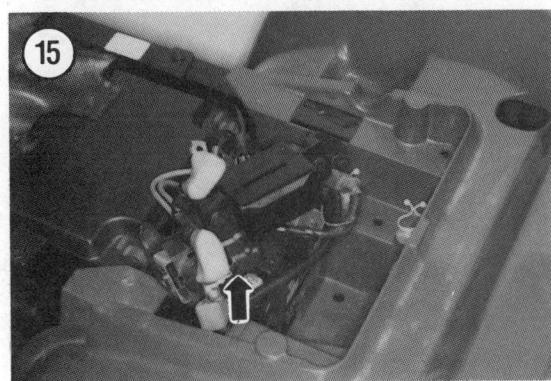

**Figures 16-19 are on the following page.**

15

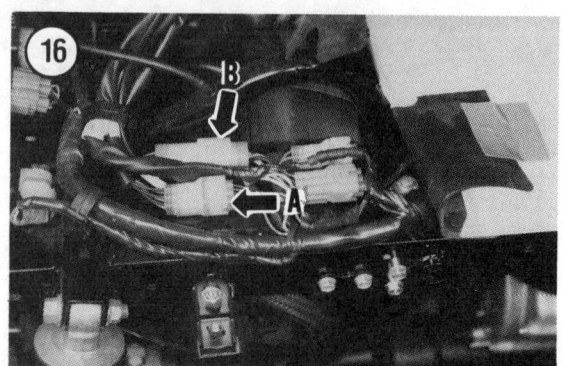

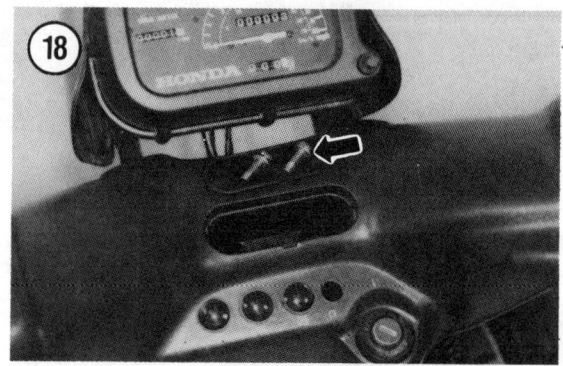

# INDEX

**16**

16

# WIRING DIAGRAMS

# 1995-1996

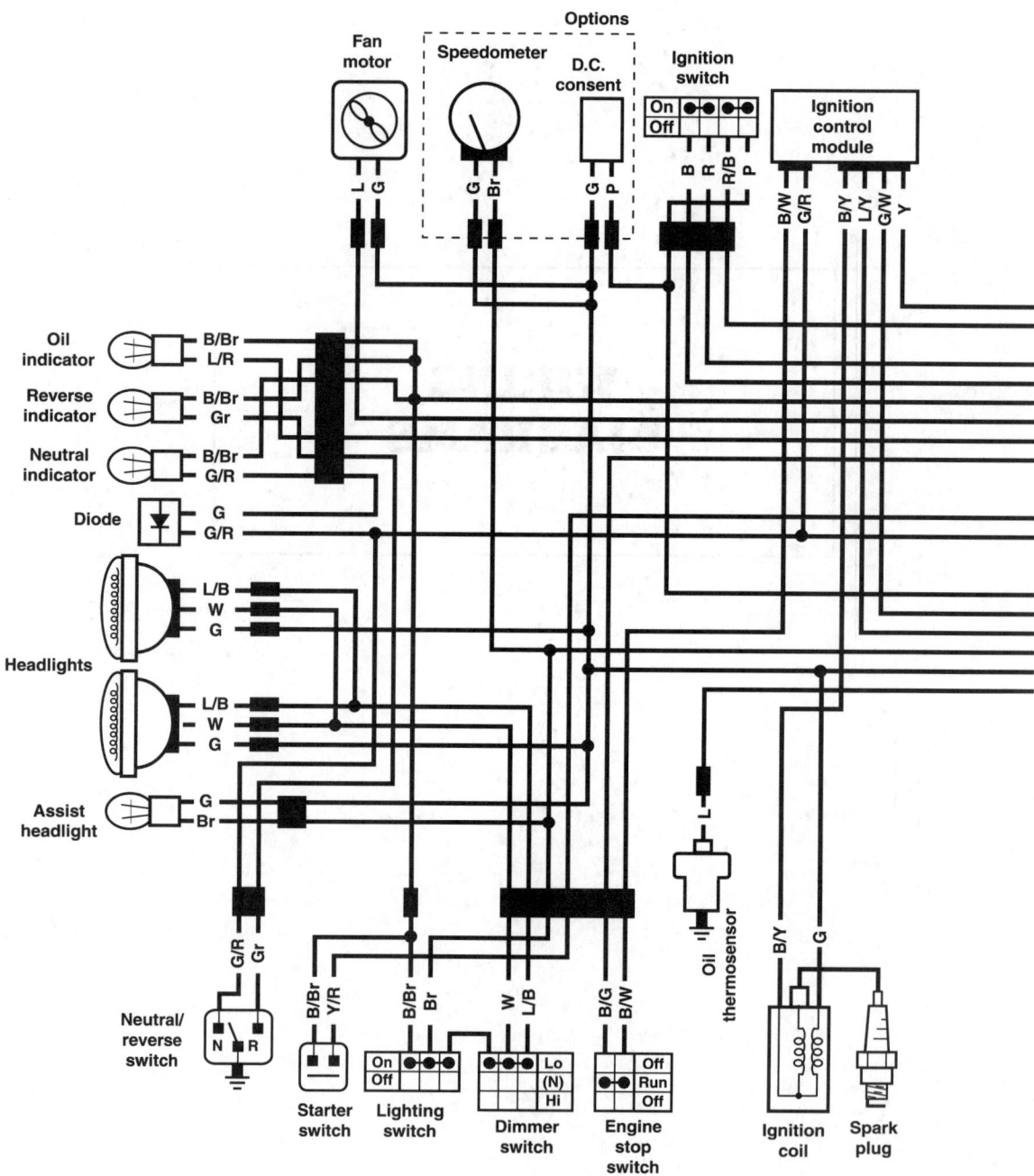

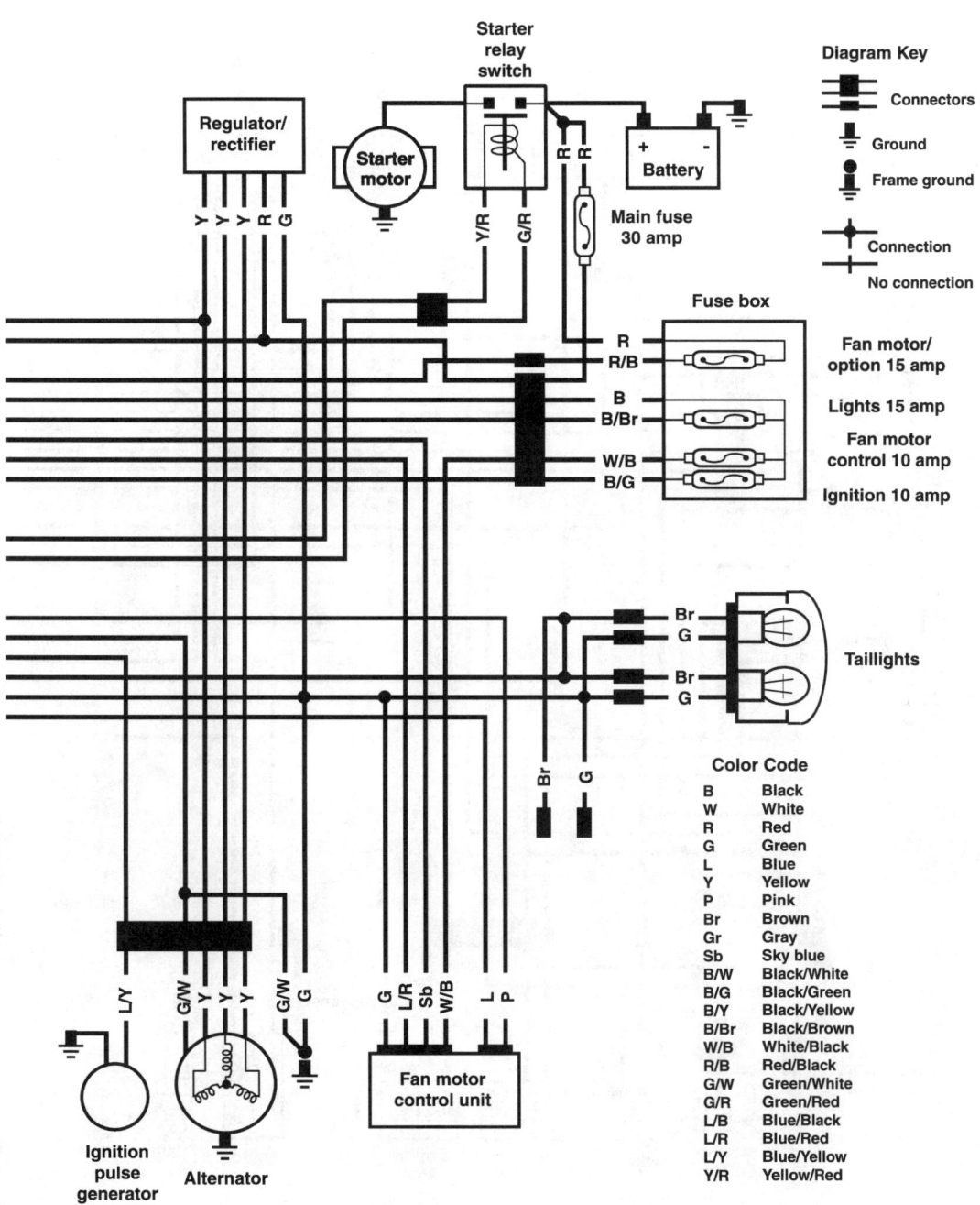

**Diagram Key**

- Connectors
- Ground
- Frame ground
- Connection
- No connection

Starter relay switch

Regulator/rectifier

Starter motor

Battery

Main fuse 30 amp

**Fuse box**

| | |
|---|---|
| R | |
| R/B | Fan motor/option 15 amp |
| B | Lights 15 amp |
| B/Br | |
| W/B | Fan motor control 10 amp |
| B/G | Ignition 10 amp |

Taillights

Ignition pulse generator

Alternator

Fan motor control unit

**Color Code**

| | |
|---|---|
| B | Black |
| W | White |
| R | Red |
| G | Green |
| L | Blue |
| Y | Yellow |
| P | Pink |
| Br | Brown |
| Gr | Gray |
| Sb | Sky blue |
| B/W | Black/White |
| B/G | Black/Green |
| B/Y | Black/Yellow |
| B/Br | Black/Brown |
| W/B | White/Black |
| R/B | Red/Black |
| G/W | Green/White |
| G/R | Green/Red |
| L/B | Blue/Black |
| L/R | Blue/Red |
| L/Y | Blue/Yellow |
| Y/R | Yellow/Red |

17

# 1997-1998

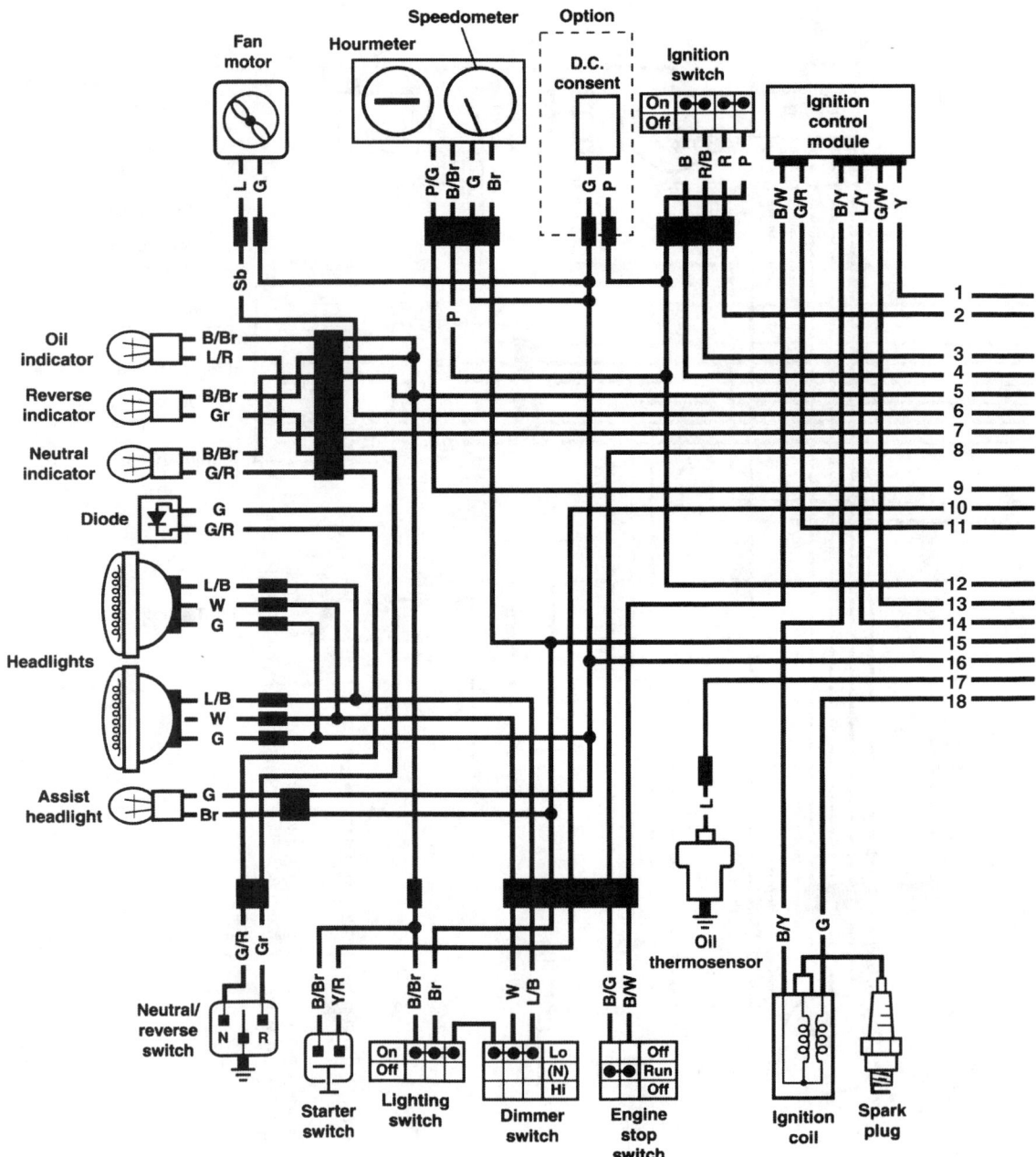

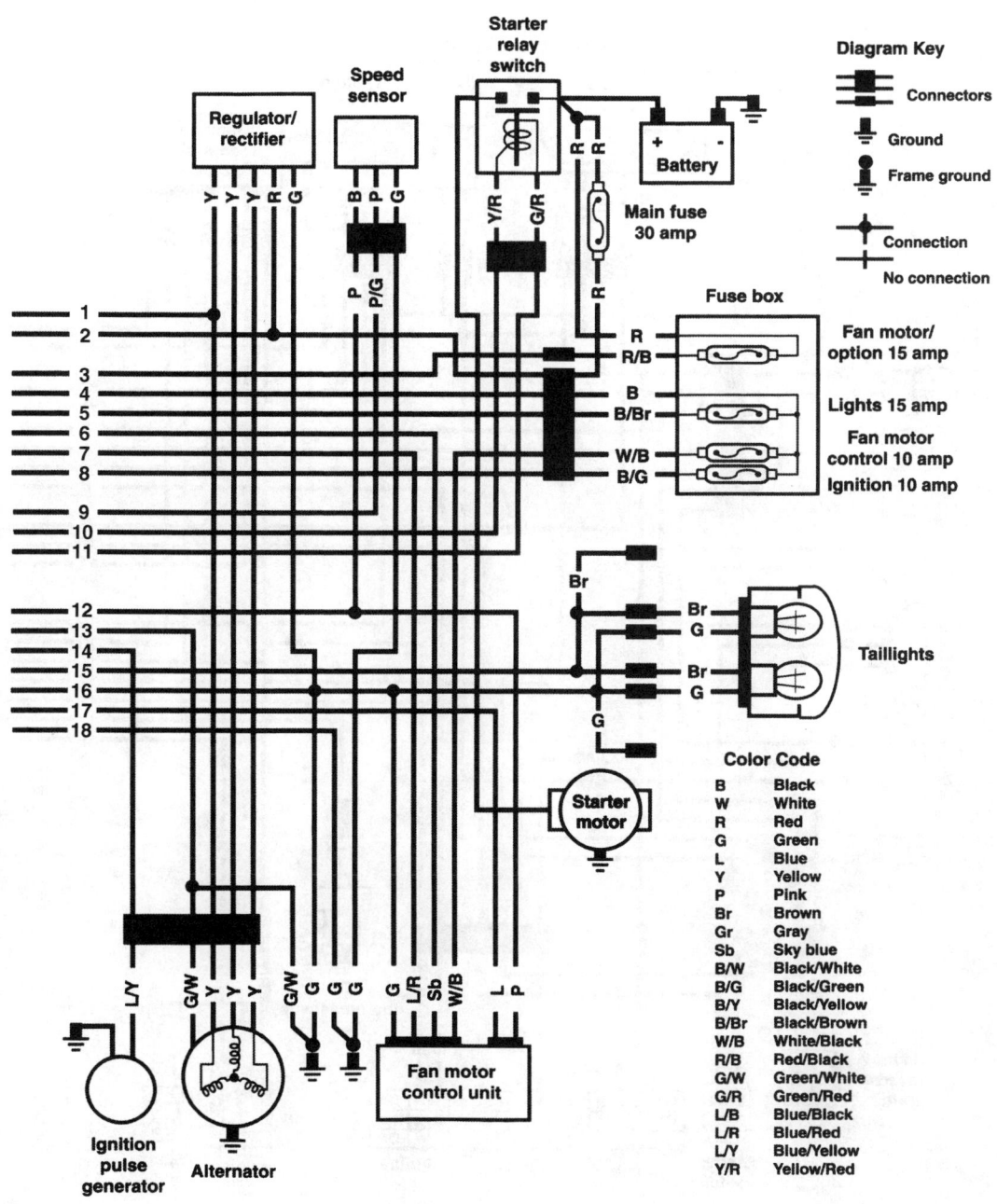

17

# 1999-2001

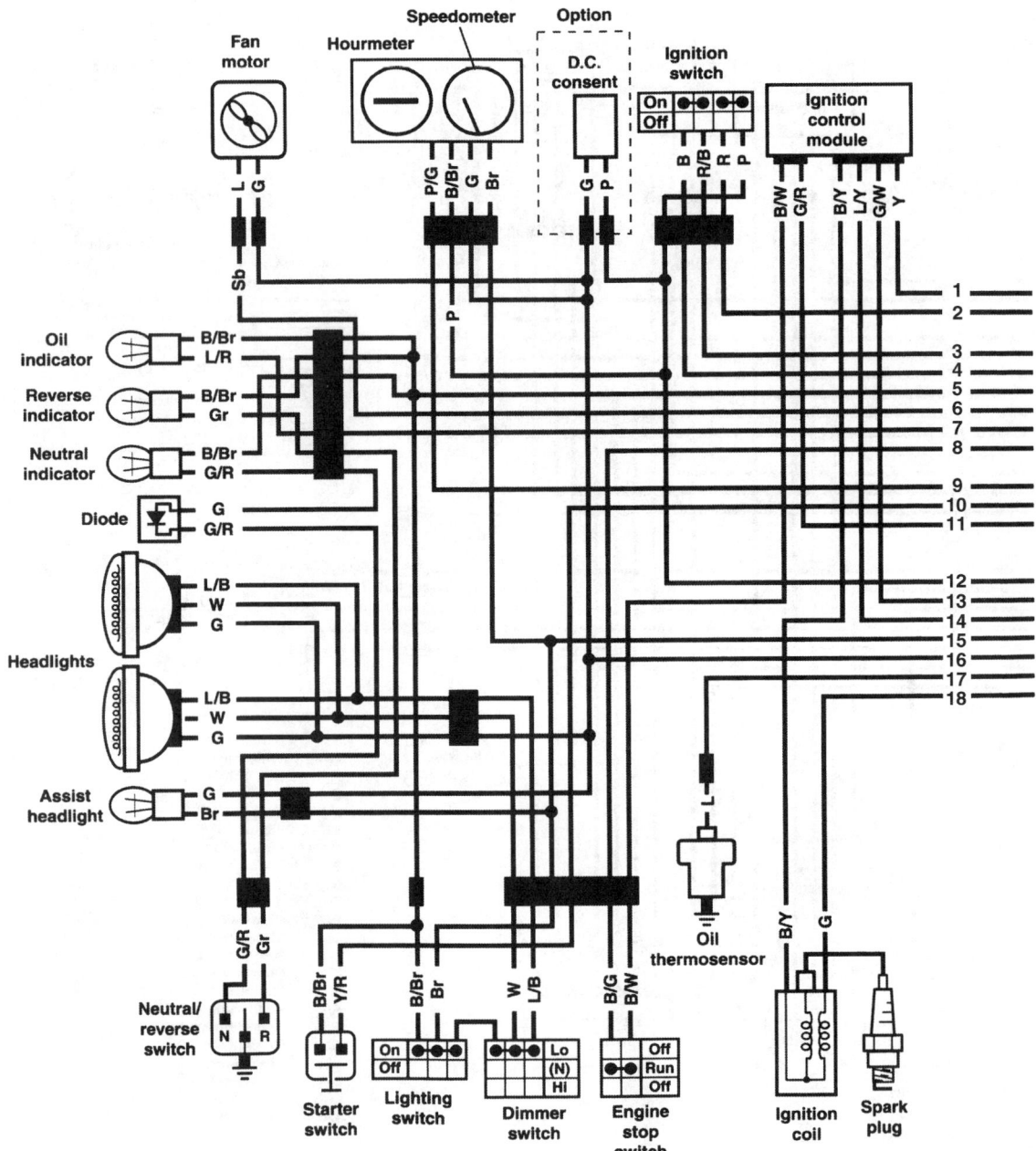

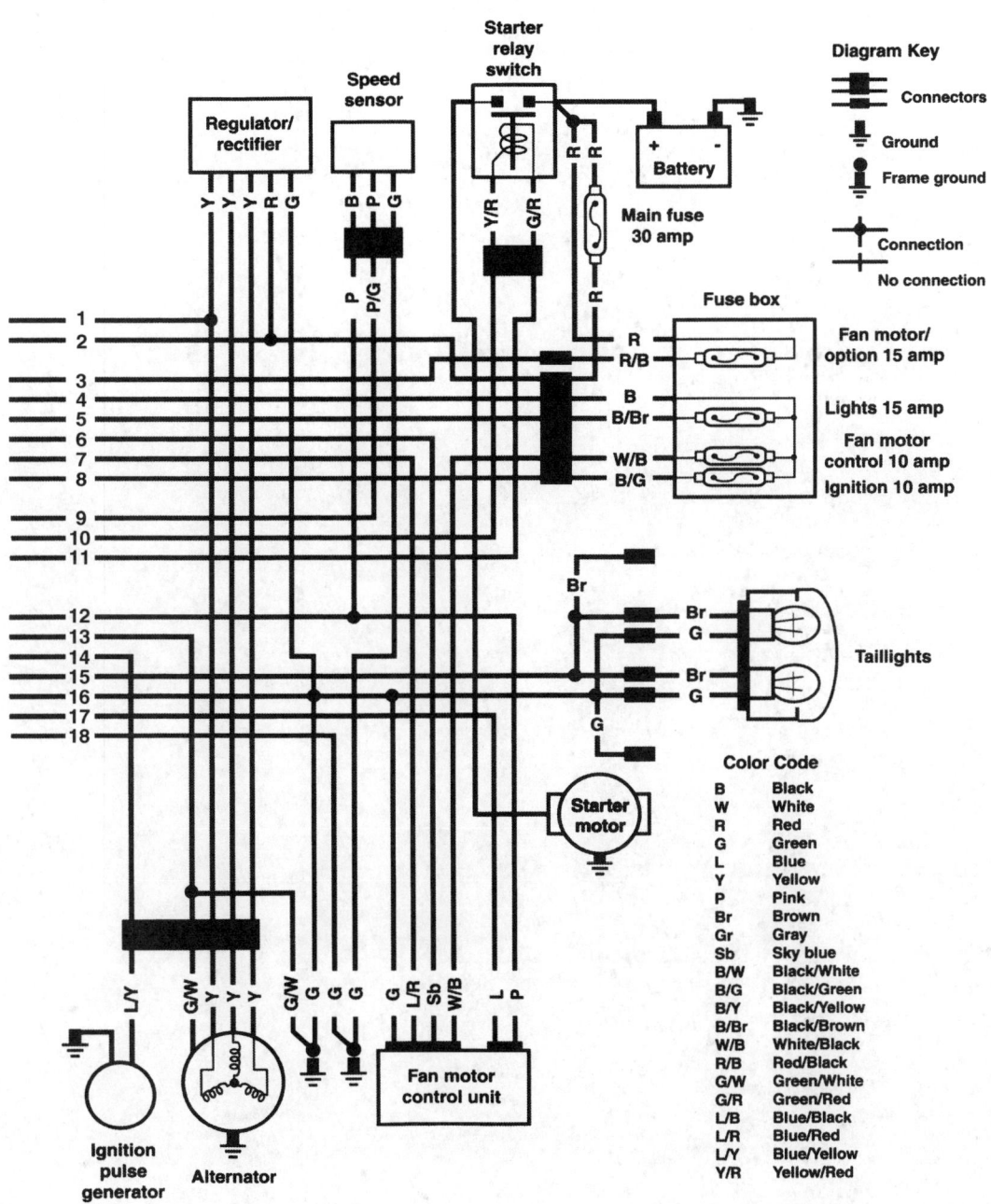

# NOTES

# NOTES

# MAINTENANCE LOG

| Date | Miles | Type of Service |
|------|-------|-----------------|
|      |       |                 |
|      |       |                 |
|      |       |                 |
|      |       |                 |
|      |       |                 |
|      |       |                 |
|      |       |                 |
|      |       |                 |
|      |       |                 |
|      |       |                 |
|      |       |                 |
|      |       |                 |
|      |       |                 |
|      |       |                 |
|      |       |                 |
|      |       |                 |
|      |       |                 |
|      |       |                 |
|      |       |                 |
|      |       |                 |
|      |       |                 |
|      |       |                 |

## BMW

| | |
|---|---|
| M308 | 500 & 600 CC twins, 55-69 |
| M502 | BMW R-Series, 70-94 |
| M500 | BMW K-Series, 85-95 |
| M503 | R-850 & R-1100, 93-98 |

## HARLEY-DAVIDSON

| | |
|---|---|
| M419 | Sportsters, 59-85 |
| M428 | Sportster Evolution, 86-90 |
| M429-3 | Sportster Evolution, 91-02 |
| M418 | Panheads, 48-65 |
| M420 | Shovelheads,66-84 |
| M421 | FX/FL Softail Big-Twin Evolution,84-94 |
| M422 | FLT/FXR Big-Twin Evolution, 84-94 |
| M424 | Dyna Glide, 91-95 |
| M425 | Dyna Glide Twin Cam, 99-01 |
| M430 | FLH/FLT 1999-2002 |

## HONDA

### ATVs

| | |
|---|---|
| M316 | Odyssey FL250, 77-84 |
| M311 | ATC, TRX & Fourtrax 70-125, 70-87 |
| M433 | Fourtrax 90 ATV, 93-00 |
| M326 | ATC185 & 200, 80-86 |
| M347 | ATC200X & Fourtrax 200SX, 86-88 |
| M455 | ATC250 & Fourtrax 200/ 250, 84-87 |
| M342 | ATC250R, 81-84 |
| M348 | TRX250R/Fourtrax 250R & ATC250R, 85-89 |
| M456 | TRX250X 1987-1988, 91-92; TRX300EX 93-96 |
| M446 | TRX250 Recon 1997-02 |
| M346-3 | TRX300/Fourtrax 300 & TRX300FW/Fourtrax 4x4, 88-00 |
| M459 | Fourtrax Foreman 95-98 |
| M454 | TRX400EX 1999-02 |

### Singles

| | |
|---|---|
| M310-13 | 50-110cc OHC Singles, 65-99 |
| M315 | 100-350cc OHC, 69-82 |
| M317 | Elsinore, 125-250cc, 73-80 |
| M442 | CR60-125R Pro-Link, 81-88 |
| M431-2 | CR80R, 89-95, CR125R, 89-91 |
| M435 | CR80, 96-02 |
| M457-2 | CR125R & CR250R, 92-97 |
| M443 | CR250R-500R Pro-Link, 81-87 |
| M432 | CR250R & CR500R, 88-96 |
| M437 | CR250R, 97-01 |
| M312-12 | XL/XR75-100, 75-02 |
| M318 | XL/XR/TLR 125-200, 79-87 |
| M328-2 | XL/XR250, 78-00; XL/XR350R 83-85; XR200R, 84-85; XR250L, 91-96 |
| M320 | XR400R, 96-00 |
| M339-6 | XL/XR 500-650, 79-02 |

## Twins

| | |
|---|---|
| M321 | 125-200cc, 64-77 |
| M322 | 250-350cc, 64-74 |
| M323 | 250-360cc Twins, 74-77 |
| M324-4 | Rebel 250 & Twinstar, 78-87; Nighthawk 250, 91-97; Rebel 250, 96-97 |
| M334 | 400-450cc, 78-87 |
| M333 | 450 & 500cc, 65-76 |
| M335 | CX & GL500/650 Twins, 78-83 |
| M344 | VT500, 83-88 |
| M313 | VT700 & 750, 83-87 |
| M460 | VT1100C2 A.C.E. Shadow, 95-97 |
| M440 | Shadow 1100cc V-Twin, 85-96 |

## Fours

| | |
|---|---|
| M332 | 350-550cc 71-78 |
| M345 | CB550 & 650, 83-85 |
| M336 | CB650,79-82 |
| M341 | CB750 SOHC, 69-78 |
| M337 | CB750 DOHC, 79-82 |
| M436 | CB750 Nighthawk, 91-93 & 95-99 |
| M325 | CB900, 1000 & 1100, 80-83 |
| M439 | Hurricane 600, 87-90 |
| M441-2 | CBR600, 91-98 |
| M434 | CBR900RR Fireblade, 93-98 |
| M329 | 500cc V-Fours, 84-86 |
| M438 | Honda VFR800, 98-00 |
| M349 | 700-1000 Interceptor, 83-85 |
| M458-2 | VFR700F-750F, 86-97 |
| M327 | 700-1100cc V-Fours, 82-88 |
| M340 | GL1000 & 1100, 75-83 |
| M504 | GL1200, 84-87 |

## Sixes

| | |
|---|---|
| M505 | GL1500 Gold Wing, 88-92 |
| M506 | GL1500 Gold Wing, 93-95 |
| M462 | GL1500C Valkyrie, 97-00 |

## KAWASAKI

### ATVs

| | |
|---|---|
| M465 | KLF220 Bayou, 88-95 |
| M466-2 | KLF300 Bayou, 86-98 |
| M467 | KLF400 Bayou, 93-99 |
| M470 | KEF300 Lakota, 95-99 |
| M385 | KSF250 Mojave, 87-00 |

### Singles

| | |
|---|---|
| M350-9 | Rotary Valve 80-350cc, 66-01 |
| M444 | KX60-80, 83-90 |
| M351 | KDX200, 83-88 |
| M447 | KX125 & KX250, 82-91 KX500, 83-93 |
| M472 | KX125, 92-98 |
| M473 | KX250, 92-98 |

### Twins

| | |
|---|---|
| M355 | KZ400, KZ/Z440, EN450 & EN500, 74-95 |
| M360 | EX500/GPZ500S, 87-93 |
| M356-2 | 700-750 Vulcan, 85-01 |
| M354 | VN800 Vulcan 95-98 |
| M357 | VN1500 Vulcan 87-98 |
| M471 | VN1500 Vulcan Classic, 96-98 |

## Fours

| | |
|---|---|
| M449 | KZ500/550 & ZX550, 79-85 |
| M450 | KZ, Z & ZX750, 80-85 |
| M358 | KZ650, 77-83 |
| M359 | 900-1000cc Fours, 73-80 |
| M451 | 1000 &1100cc Fours, 81-85 |
| M452-3 | ZX500 & 600 Ninja, 85-97 |
| M453-3 | Ninja ZX900-1100 84-01 |
| M468 | ZX6 Ninja, 90-97 |
| M469 | ZX7 Ninja, 91-98 |
| M453 | 900-1100 Ninja, 84-93 |

## POLARIS

### ATVs

| | |
|---|---|
| M496 | Polaris ATV, 85-95 |
| M362 | Polaris Magnum ATV, 96-98 |
| M363 | Scrambler 500, 4X4 97-00 |
| M365 | Sportsman/Xplorer, 96-00 |

## SUZUKI

### ATVs

| | |
|---|---|
| M381 | ALT/LT 125 & 185, 83-87 |
| M475 | LT230 & LT250, 85-90 |
| M380 | LT250R Quad Racer, 85-88 |
| M343 | LTF500F Quadrunner, 98-00 |
| M483 | Suzuki King Quad/ Quad Runner 250, 87-95 |

### Singles

| | |
|---|---|
| M371 | RM50-400 Twin Shock, 75-81 |
| M369 | 125-400cc 64-81 |
| M379 | RM125-500 Single Shock, 81-88 |
| M476 | DR250-350, 90-94 |
| M384 | LS650 Savage Single, 86-88 |
| M386 | RM80-250, 89-95 |

### Twins

| | |
|---|---|
| M372 | GS400-450 Twins, 77-87 |
| M481-3 | VS700-800 Intruder, 85-02 |
| M482 | VS1400 Intruder, 87-98 |
| M484-2 | GS500E Twins, 89-00 |

### Triple

| | |
|---|---|
| M368 | 380-750cc, 72-77 |

### Fours

| | |
|---|---|
| M373 | GS550, 77-86 |
| M364 | GS650, 81-83 |
| M370 | GS750 Fours, 77-82 |
| M376 | GS850-1100 Shaft Drive, 79-84 |
| M378 | GS1100 Chain Drive, 80-81 |
| M383-3 | Katana 600, 88-96 GSX-R750-1100, 86-87 |
| M331 | GSX-R600, 97-00 |
| M478-2 | GSX-R750, 88-92 GSX750F Katana, 89-96 |
| M485 | GSX-R750, 96-99 |
| M338 | GSF600 Bandit, 95-00 |

## YAMAHA

### ATVs

| | |
|---|---|
| M394 | YTM/YFM200 & 225, 83-86 |
| M487-3 | YFM350 Warrior, 87-02 |
| M486-3 | YFZ350 Banshee, 87-02 |
| M488-3 | Blaster ATV, 88-01 |
| M489-2 | Timberwolf ATV,89-00 |
| M490-2 | YFM350 Moto-4 & Big Bear, 87-98 |
| M493 | YFM400FW Kodiak, 93-98 |

### Singles

| | |
|---|---|
| M492-2 | PW50 & PW80, BW80 Big Wheel 80, 81-02 |
| M410 | 80-175 Piston Port, 68-76 |
| M415 | 250-400cc Piston Port, 68-7 |
| M412 | DT & MX 100-400, 77-83 |
| M414 | IT125-490, 76-86 |
| M393 | YZ50-80 Monoshock, 78-9 |
| M413 | YZ100-490 Monoshock, 76-8 |
| M390 | YZ125-250, 85-87 YZ490, 85-90 |
| M391 | YZ125-250, 88-93 WR250Z, 91-93 |
| M497 | YZ125, 94-99 |
| M498 | YZ250, 94-98 and WR250Z, 94-97 |
| M491 | YZ400F, YZ426F & WR400F, 98-00 |
| M417 | XT125-250, 80-84 |
| M480-2 | XT/TT 350, 85-96 |
| M405 | XT500 & TT500, 76-81 |
| M416 | XT/TT 600, 83-89 |

### Twins

| | |
|---|---|
| M403 | 650cc, 70-82 |
| M395-9 | XV535-1100 Virago, 81-9 |
| M495 | XVS650 V-Star, 98-00 |

### Triple

| | |
|---|---|
| M404 | XS750 & 850, 77-81 |

### Fours

| | |
|---|---|
| M387 | XJ550, XJ600 & FJ600, 81-8 |
| M494 | XJ600 Seca II, 92-98 |
| M388 | YX600 Radian & FZ600, 86-9 |
| M396 | FZR600, 89-93 |
| M392 | FZ700-750 & Fazer, 85-8 |
| M411 | XS1100 Fours, 78-81 |
| M397 | FJ1100 & 1200, 84-93 |

## VINTAGE MOTORCYCLES

### Clymer® Collection Series

| | |
|---|---|
| M330 | Vintage British Street Bike BSA, 500 & 650cc Unit Twins; Norton, 750 & 850c Commandos; Triumph, 500-750cc Twins |
| M300 | Vintage Dirt Bikes, V. 1 Bulta 125-370cc Singles; Montes 123-360cc Singles; Ossa, 125-250cc Singles |
| M301 | Vintage Dirt Bikes, V. 2 C. 125-400cc Singles; Husqvar 125-450cc Singles; Maic 250-501cc Singles; Hodak 90-125cc Singles |
| M305 | Vintage Japanese Street Bik Honda, 250 & 305cc Twi Kawasaki, 250-750cc Trip Kawasaki, 900 & 1000cc Fo |